CHILDHOOD IN AMERICAN SOCIETY

A READER

Karen Sternheimer

University of Southern California

Allyn & Bacon

Boston   New York   San Francisco
Mexico City   Montreal   Toronto   London   Madrid   Munich   Paris
Hong Kong   Singapore   Tokyo   Cape Town   Sydney

Executive Editor: Jeff Lasser
Editorial Assistant: Lauren Macey
Executive Marketing Manager: Kelly May
Production Manager: Kathleen Sleys
Production Assistant: Maggie Brobeck
Cover Design: Lisbeth Axell
Project Management/Composition: Saraswathi Muralidhar/GGS Higher Education Resources, A Division of
  PreMedia Global, Inc.
Printer/Binder: R.R. Donnelly & Sons
Cover Image: Steve Satushek / Photographers Choice / Getty Images, Inc

Library of Congress Cataloging-in-Publication Data

Childhood in American society: a reader / [edited by] Karen Sternheimer.
   p. cm.
Includes bibliographical references.
ISBN-13: 978-0-205-61713-5
ISBN-10: 0-205-61713-1
1. Childhood—United States—History.   2. Children—United States—History.
I. Sternheimer, Karen.
  HQ792.U6C55 2010
  305.230973—dc22   2009009394

10 9 8 7 6 5 4 3 2 1   13 12 11 10 09

**Allyn & Bacon
is an imprint of**

PEARSON

www.pearsonhighered.com

ISBN-13: 978-0-205-61713-5
ISBN-10:   0-205-61713-1

CONTENTS

INTRODUCTION
Everyone Has a Childhood, Right?

Did you have a "normal" childhood? Instead of wondering whether the answer is yes or no, in this text we will consider how the definitions of "normal" change from time and place, often based on a child's class, race, and gender. As we will see, the "ideal" childhood experience is relative. The selections in this book will help us understand how and why both perceptions and realities of childhood vary and, most centrally, how children themselves make sense of their experiences.

The study of childhood is unique in that childhood is the one social category we all have experienced, albeit differently. It is also one of the few social groups that everyone eventually passes out of and looks back at through the lenses of our personal histories. Childhood is something that most of us have taken for granted as a phase of biological changes that lead to adulthood. But it is much more than that. To understand the way a society makes meaning of the period we call childhood is vital to understanding society. As we will see, childhood is as much a social phase as a biological one; the way that we make meaning of both tells us a great deal about ourselves.

There is not a complete agreement on the meanings of childhood. Many of the most intense social and political debates surround the meanings of childhood. Should children be kept away from information about sex as long as possible? If not, who shall teach them, and what should they learn? Are same-sex couples a threat to children? What about divorce? Single parenthood? Television?

We all probably have opinions about these issues; this collection takes a step back to help us understand why children are often in the middle of these long-standing debates, and to hear the voices of young people themselves through research that places children fully in the center. Within this book, you will find three central themes:

1. *What is the preferred meaning of childhood?*   So back to our initial question: did you have a "normal" childhood? If so, how do you define *normal*? Were your experiences of childhood similar to your parents'? Grandparents'? Just from these questions you can probably see some important changes that have taken place. This doesn't mean that one generation had a "real" childhood and the other did not. The experiences and our perceptions of childhood shift based on economic, political, and social changes. Our ideas of what constitutes an "ideal" childhood change to meet the needs of any culture or society.

Although children are active in constructing the meaning of their experiences and their lives, the construction of the broader meaning of childhood is largely created by and for adults. For instance, when a large proportion of children were needed in the American labor force in the nineteenth century, work was defined as moral, while leisure was suspect. By contrast, most children in the United States are now expected to be in school, as the economy requires a highly educated labor pool. From today's perspective, my grandfather, who left school after the eighth grade to work at his family's business, would be considered a dropout, doomed to a life of poverty and possibly prison. But at the time, most kids left school well before high school graduation to help their families; my grandfather was considered a good son, not a delinquent.

So when we think of the "ideal" childhood, we have to keep in mind that our construction of the meaning of childhood is based on many factors: the economic needs of society, beliefs about gender, one's socioeconomic status, ethnicity, religion, and where we live. Ultimately, childhood is a *social construction*, something to which we ascribe meaning. This does not mean that childhood is merely an illusion; it is a very real experience that we view through the lenses of specific ways of seeing children and childhood itself.

2. *Children are not simply sponges.* While it is important to understand how social forces shape children, too often we ignore how children are active players in their own lives. It is too simple to conclude that children are solely the end product of a socializing machine. If that were the case, parents wouldn't have such a hard time getting their kids to comply with their rules, and in the long run there would be little social change if children were merely carbon copies of the previous generation. Rather than only passive agents of social forces, children also influence the adults around them as well as one another.

Going beyond the traditional socialization approach, we will see that children are co-constructors of their own realities, and understanding how children make sense of their lives takes on greater meaning. As a social group, we have typically studied children to see how they are progressing on the road to adulthood, with childhood being a phase with little other significance. Now, in this text, we will explore childhood from the inside out, as an experience of value not simply for what children will become, but for who they are today.

3. *Children are not always passive, innocent, and vulnerable.* Finally, we tend to make several assumptions about children that are hard to let go of. One is that children are universally "innocent" and that adults are the white knights protecting their virtue. While certainly many adults act as protectors to children, in some cases these acts of protection benefit adults as much, if not more, than children themselves. Often, "protection" is a gentler sounding word than power, which adults sometimes feel slipping away as children grow up and begin to have their own ideas and knowledge about things adults often presume children should not.

Tied to the belief in childhood innocence is the belief that children are in more danger than ever before from the world around them. While many children do face significant threats, particularly those who live in persistently violent environments, have little or no access to health care, or have adults unable to properly care for them, we often overestimate the danger that the outside world poses to kids. Rather, statistically the greatest threats to children are their own parents and other adults closest to them. Understanding the realities of children's lives, rather than our common assumptions, will ultimately help us provide more appropriate policies and services to support their movement into adulthood and independence.

ORGANIZATION OF THIS BOOK

This book is organized in seven parts, each designed to provide rich data to illustrate the three themes mentioned earlier. Part I, *Meanings of Childhood*, contains selections that explore how and why the perceptions and experiences of children have changed over time. Topics such as the shifting perceptions of infancy, work, information, and safety are examined in Part I.

Part II, *Theorizing Childhood*, contains chapters that encourage us to radically rethink our understanding of childhood itself. The four selections challenge the traditional socialization and development approaches to understanding children, and encourage us to broaden our frames for understanding childhood. By changing the way we think about children and childhood, we begin to ask different questions, leading to new kinds of research with kids. Part III,

Studying Children, provides examples and instructions for conducting ethnographic research with children. This method, as the authors illustrate, is best for understanding children on their own terms, in contrast to traditional methods that still locate adult researchers as experts. Through qualitative study, we see the varied nuances of children's perspectives and obtain a deeper understanding of their lives.

The majority of selections in the next four sections are based on ethnographies with children. Part IV, *Relationships*, examines how children actively negotiate relationships with friends and family. Rather than simply look at how children are influenced by their families of origin and by their peers, topics like popularity, navigating the highly sexualized environment of middle school, and how children shape their families' lives help us understand how children are thinking, feeling, social actors.

Likewise, Part V, *Constructing Race, Ethnicity, and Gender*, considers the ways in which children make meaning of race, ethnicity, and gender in their everyday lives. Traditional socialization theory suggests that children merely "acquire" these facets of their identity through the world around them. However, as these ethnographic selections show us, kids—as young as pre-school age—are active in making and *re*-making the meaning of race and gender through interactions with their peers. Instead of just being imitators of the adults around them, kids experience the process of co-creating meaning, which these selections illustrate.

And just as we typically have thought of race and gender as something children merely internalize and reproduce, children are active in making sense of popular culture. Part VI, *Popular Culture, Consumption, and Play*, examines the historical roots of children's rituals and games, in addition to how kids cope with losing teeth, toy shopping, and watching television. While we have tended to view children's leisure as both a birthright and with suspicion, these selections help us understand children's perspectives on "fun."

In stark contrast, childhood is not always a carefree experience. Part VII, *Social Problems and Inequality*, explores some of the significant challenges children face. Children who are chronically ill, sexually abused, or have parents in prison do not get to experience the "ideal" state of childhood, but they are children nonetheless. This part challenges the common assumption that children are prized members of American society, particularly in light of educational disparities that continually place some children last.

As the book's title suggests, this volume predominantly focuses on the varied experiences of childhood in the United States. However, several selections do provide information on children more globally—not just for comparison purposes, but also to understand better the experiences of children internationally. While research on the sociology of childhood flourished outside of the United States before expanding here, the field is growing and offers a rich tapestry of the varied experiences of children within our increasingly diverse society.

ACKNOWLEDGMENTS

I would like to thank the reviewers of the First Edition: Sue Marie Wright, Eastern Washington University; Susan Roxburgh, Kent State University; Laura E. Nathan, Mills College; David M. Hummom, Holy Cross College; Nancy Finley, University of Alabama in Huntsville; and Cheryl Albers, Buffalo State University.

PART ONE

Meanings of Childhood
Why Do Experiences of Childhood Change?

We ascribe meaning to children and childhood before a child is even born. Parents often have highly developed thoughts about the way they would like their children to experience childhood long before their due date. In the age of infertility clinics, surrogates, and other birth-related technologies, children are often intellectually and emotionally conceived long before fertilization even happens.

We might think that infancy is the one stage of life that is mostly immune from social forces. Again, this does not mean infancy is not real or that the physical dependence of infants is only our imagination. Rather, how we make sense of infancy varies over time and place. For instance, controlling a baby's movement has been a long-time concern, but the challenge of monitoring infants has changed considerably over time. During the eighteenth century, many parents used walking stools to prevent babies from injury and to teach them to walk upright. While walking stools certainly had practical aspects, they also reflected a widespread belief that children were born of original sin and that crawling or squirming on the floor reflected the animalistic tendencies of babies that needed to be controlled immediately. By contrast, baby walkers have fallen out of favor today, as they are considered to inhibit the natural growth of a baby's balance, reflecting the more predominant contemporary conception of infancy as a natural period of self-directed growth.

Later in the nineteenth century, both fertility and infant mortality rates began to drop. The Industrial Revolution made large families less necessary for survival, and the period of infancy was more likely to be treasured and sentimentalized. Particularly in middle-class families, the home took on sacred meaning, and children, along with their mothers, were encouraged to become the emotional core, rather than economic units of families, as earlier agrarian life often required for economic and physical survival. By the end of the nineteenth century, a new "science" of child rearing emerged, which encouraged women to focus on children. Infants during this time were thought of as pure and angelic, to be guarded from the taint of the outside world if at all possible.

Elevating child rearing to a science was not simply about providing the best care to infants and children, although that was certainly the overt priority. Embedded in attempts to "perfect" child rearing lay anxieties about issues of ethnicity, class, and gender. The growing ethnic diversity in late-nineteenth-century America led to concerns about "racial purity" and both protecting and preserving the prevailing definitions of whiteness. The "cult of domesticity" served as a means of promoting socioeconomic hierarchies for those who could afford to have the woman of the house devoted full-time to childcare duties.

But many working-class and poor families could not afford this idealized family form. In fact, a large proportion of American families also depended on the economic contributions of their children, either through work on farms or through wages earned in mills or factories. Viviana Zelizer's selection, "From Child Labor to Child Work," discusses the transition from viewing children as economic assets, to *costing* parents money. In her investigation of how "child labor [lost] its nineteenth-century good reputation," she examines how and why children's economic value declined just as their emotional value began to climb.

First, she notes that it was very common for children to work for wages in the first two decades of the twentieth century and earlier. According to U.S. Census Bureau figures, nearly two million American children earned wages in 1910—18 percent of all children. But as the workplace became increasingly automated, machines began to take the place of children in factories and other businesses. Second, household incomes began to rise, making it less necessary for children to bring in money. Children gradually took on more emotional value when middle-class families no longer relied on them as sources of income. At the same time, parents began having fewer children and focused their economic as well as emotional energies on a few rather than many kids.

The notion of children as somehow more pure, more innocent, and in need of protection from the evils of the outside world began after the Industrial Revolution as American cities expanded along with the problems associated with rapid growth. As childhood was increasingly sentimentalized as a time of purity, the dangers of the outside world seemed to grow, and wealthy families sought to keep children separated from adult society, sometimes even from their parents, through extensive use of servants, governesses, and boarding schools. The ability to cordon children off was mostly available only to the wealthy; in that regard, the notion of childhood innocence is a function of prosperity. In reality, most urban children's lives did not reflect this ideal, as they spent much of their time working independently without much adult monitoring. The conflict over maintaining "innocence" has roots in these disparate experiences of childhood and continues today. As Marjorie Heins discusses in "Minors, Censorship, Sex, and History," battles about indecency are frequently waged in the name of protecting childhood "innocence" but often have more to do with controlling information from *adults*. For instance, at the end of the nineteenth century, declines in fertility among native-born white Protestants raised concerns about "the future of the race." Not coincidentally, information about birth control was deemed "obscene" and illegal to disseminate via the U.S. mail—in the name of protecting children's innocence. Heins details how childhood innocence is often used as a political pawn that has little to do with actual kids.

By contrast, a half century later fertility rates rose, and children became more central in defining family life. The emerging suburban lifestyle was largely created around the needs of the growing population of children. The nostalgia we often associate today with the 1950s represents revisionist history, as only a minority of kids experienced the "perfect" childhood. We often focus on the nearly all-white suburbs that emerged mid-century and overlook the large degree of inequality that existed at the time. Critics of mid-century childhood note that the children of the 1950s grew up to be the teens and young adults of the 1960s, viewed by many as self-centered, spoiled, and out of control sexually (and politically). Were the children of the fifties overindulged by permissive parents? Tensions between viewing children as overindulged by parents who give in to their desires too easily as opposed to children in need of more freedom to grow without too much restraint persist to this day. The pendulum between freedom and control shifts based on social, economic, and political contexts.

Yet despite this debate, children are very central in American life. As Paula Fass and Mary Ann Mason detail in "Childhood in America Past and Present," in many instances children have become the single most important emotional connection in adults' lives, particularly as divorce remains widespread. As fertility rates continue to decline, parents increasingly expend more of their financial and emotional resources on a smaller number of children. Peter N. Stearns discusses the tensions between parents and schools during the twentieth century. As children attended schools in greater number and for longer periods of time, many parents were wary of turning over their authority, particularly as schools took over functions previously maintained by families. In "All Are Above Average," Stearns notes how battles over homework—between parents and schools, not parents and their kids—reflect this gradual shift in control of children's time. Yet as higher education grows more important for young people's future economically and college admissions more competitive, parental anxiety over schooling has increased.

So what does childhood mean today? Compared with just a century ago, children have exited the paid labor force in large numbers, mainly because automation has replaced the work children did and an information-based economy requires a highly educated labor force. As this economic shift has taken place, people have fewer kids and at increasingly older ages. And yet despite declines in child mortality rates and violence rates in the last decade, childhood today is marked by feelings of adult anxiety. David Buckingham explores this anxiety in his selection, "In Search of the Child." While children today are mostly free from performing paid work or succumbing to disease, a new concern has taken their place: electronic media. Buckingham considers why fears of electronic media are so widespread, and so misguided. Ultimately he argues that concerns about media serve as a reason to reassert adult authority and control in the name of protecting children. He suggests preparing children for life in an increasingly mediated society, and challenges the idea that childhood is "disappearing."

As Part I details, childhood is constantly mutating and changing form along with other societal changes. But it is not as endangered as we might think. In economic terms, we might say that childhood lasts longer than ever, as young people remain economically dependent on their parents and mostly out of the labor force, in some cases until their mid- to late twenties. Children might have greater access to information, particularly with the advent of the Internet, but does information really mean the end of childhood? And finally, for American children, this is among the safest times to be alive. But yet many people feel like children and childhood itself is in danger.

This Part's final selection, "Kidnapped: Childhood Stolen," looks at fears about child kidnapping and how they reflect broader fears about the demise of childhood. While tragic, abductions and murders by strangers are fortunately rare, particularly when compared with incidences of children harmed by their parents. In addition, by focusing so intensely on a handful of mostly middle-class, white, blonde, blue-eyed girls, the notion of childhood innocence implicitly excludes many children from protection. While nearly one in five American children live in poverty, the general public often looks the other way. This construction of childhood "innocence" requires our scrutiny when it applies only to a select few and has serious policy implications. It becomes easier to slash funding for children in poverty who do not fit into this narrow version of "innocence."

Rather than finding a fixed, stable, or "objective" definition of childhood, the selections in Part I remind us that the meanings of childhood are continually in flux. We will not only see that childhood is something socially constructed, but these chapters will demonstrate *how* and *why* such constructions are formulated at any given time and place.

From Child Labor to Child Work: Redefining the Economic World of Children

VIVIANA A. ZELIZER

INTRODUCTION

It may now seem crass to consider children as holding economic value; as sociologist Viviana A. Zelizer notes in her book, Pricing the Priceless Child, *we now view children as having emotional value rather than economic worth. In her groundbreaking historical study, Zelizer traces the history of how child labor "lost its good reputation" at the end of the nineteenth century and early decades of the twentieth century. In this selection, she considers what work was still considered "good" after this shift took place. Paper routes, some housework, and child acting and modeling remain legal (although restricted) ways that children can earn money.*

Ask a dozen persons "What is child labor?" and you will get a dozen answers, most of them in a rather startled and hesitant manner, and in language that may be violent but is likely also to be vague.

FROM "THE TRUTH ABOUT CHILD LABOR,"
RAYMOND FULLER, 1922

The battle line between proponents and opponents of child labor legislation was confounded by imprecise and ambivalent cultural definitions of child labor. For instance, it was often unclear what specific occupations transformed a child into an exploited laborer, or what determined the legitimacy of some forms of child work. In the early part of the twentieth century this ambiguity frustrated government attempts to reach a precise national accounting of the number of child laborers: "Is a girl at work who merely helps her mother in keeping the house? When a child helps its parents, irregularly, about a little store or a fruit stand, is it working? What of the children who are kept out of school to 'tote dinners'. . . ?"[1]

Opponents of legislation insisted on children's right to work, yet often categorized certain occupations as illegitimate forms of employment. Reformers' passionate advocacy of the useless child was similarly qualified. Accused of giving work a "black eye," they defensively retorted that the anti-child labor movement was also pro-work. Raymond Fuller, at one time Director of Research at the National Child Labor Committee and one of the most vocal spokesmen for child labor reform, protested that "Nothing could be farther from the truth than the . . . widespread notion that child labor reform is predicated on the assumption that children should have no work."[2] As the child labor dispute evolved, the relationship of children to work was increasingly examined and reappraised. Gradually, the nineteenth-century utilitarian criteria of labor and wages appropriate for the useful child, were replaced by a noneconomic, educational concept of child work and child money better suited to the twentieth-century useless child.

ILLEGITIMATE CHILD LABOR OR "GOOD WORK"? THE SEARCH FOR NEW BOUNDARIES

Investigation of why children quit school early suggested that work appealed to them: "The 'call' is one which involves the use of energy in creative work—in accomplishing something useful in the work-a-day world."[3] Yet, where could the useless child find useful outlets? Reformers acknowledged the quandary: "The dilemma for the city child seems to be either painful exhaustion and demoralizing work on the one hand, or futile idleness . . . on the other."[4] One observer only half-jokingly proposed the creation of a Society for the Promotion of Useful Work for Children.[5] Raymond Fuller identified the essential difficulty:

> The category of child labor tends to become . . . too broad or too narrow. Some of us are so sure of the badness of child labor that we call bad nearly every activity that takes the aspect of work; and some of . . . us are so sure that work is a good thing for children that we leave out of the category of child labor much that belongs there.[6]

The solution was to devise criteria that would differentiate more clearly between legitimate and illegitimate economic roles for children. Child labor reform would not simply be an absolutist anti-child labor campaign, but instead a pro "good" child work movement. "To establish children's work," asserted Fuller, "is quite as important as to . . . abolish child labor."[7] . . .

By nineteenth-century standards, the employment of a nine- or ten-year-old had been legitimate and for the most part legal. In fact, age was not considered a very important criterion of legitimacy until after the 1860s. Before then, only four states limited the age of employment of children. Nineteenth-century child labor legislation focused primarily on reducing the hours of work and providing some education for child laborers rather than establishing age limits. In 1899, there were still twenty-four states and the District of Columbia without a minimum age requirement for children employed in manufacturing. Child labor reformers met with formidable resistance as they struggled to institute age as a central boundary distinguishing child work from child labor. Critics objected to a legal requirement keeping children useless until twelve and protested even more forcefully against a fourteen-year age limit. . . . Between 1879 and 1909, the number of states with age limit provisions (for any occupation except dangerous employments and mining) increased from seven to forty-four. The legal age limit was first raised from ten to twelve and then to fourteen. After the 1920s, child labor organizations fought to raise the age limit from fourteen to sixteen.[8]

If it was difficult to establish a proper age boundary, it became even more complex to differentiate between types of jobs. Industrial child labor was the most obvious category of illegitimate employment. As one of the most passionate opponents of early labor explained: "Work is what children need. . . . But the bondage and drudgery of these mill-children and factory children and mine-children are not work, but servitude."[9] Accordingly, the earliest child labor laws were almost exclusively designed to regulate the manufacturing and mining industries. . . .

If defending factory work was unusual, farm labor on the other hand was almost blindly and romantically categorized as "good" work. Even though by 1900, 60 percent of all gainfully employed children (ten to fifteen years old) were agricultural workers, their labor was not defined as a social problem. In his pioneering and dramatic exposé of child labor before Congress in 1906, Senator Beveridge of Indiana deliberately excluded agricultural labor: "I do not for a moment pretend that working children on the farm is bad for them . . . there can be no better training."[10] The legitimacy of farm work was reflected in its legal status. Even as the number of rural child laborers continued to increase, most state laws and the two federal child labor bills focused on industrial child labor, and consistently exempted agriculture from regulation. To be sure, this indemnity was carefully preserved by the powerful farming interests; yet, it was also the result of an equally influential cultural consensus. . . .

The idealization of farm work by child labor reformers wavered as investigations in the 1920s began to uncover some of the hardships experienced by young agricultural laborers. A survey of 845 children in North Dakota, conducted by the U.S. Children's Bureau, found boys and girls under age seventeen engaged in a wide variety of farm work. Seventy-one percent of the children were under fourteen. Aside from field work, herding cattle was their most common task. Boys and girls, often as young as six years old, were "out on the prairie alone on foot or on horseback for long hours in the heat of the summer without shelter or drink . . . in danger of being thrown from horseback . . . or trampled on by the cattle." Others were involved in the construction of barbed-wire fences, digging or drilling holes for posts as well as assisting with butchering jobs, cleaning seed for the spring planting, and even taking care of farm machinery. Out of the 845 children, almost 750 were also responsible for routine chores and housework. One nine-year-old boy, for instance "built the fires in the morning, swept the floors of a two-room house, and brought in fuel and water; in addition, before he made a two-mile trip to school, he helped feed stock (5 horse and 12 cows) and chopped wood; in the evening he did the chores and washed dishes.". . .

But the solution was not a wholesale condemnation of farm labor; instead, reformers sought to differentiate better between "good" farm work and exploitative farm labor. As one writer in the *American Review of Reviews* explained in 1924: "Work on the farm performed by children under parents' direction and without interference with school attendance is not child labor. Work performed by children away from home, for wages, at long hours and under conditions which endanger the child's health, education and morals is child labor."[11] Thus, commercialized agriculture joined the ranks of illegitimate occupations, while the legitimacy of work on the home farm was idyllically preserved.

Between the extremes of industrial child labor and farm work, there was a variety of other occupations for children of a much more uncertain status and with different claims to legitimacy. . . . Working as a Senate page, for instance, was a prestigious occupation for children. Working as a cash-girl or cash-boy in a department store also promised an attractive and legitimate entry into business life.[12]

Street work and particularly newsboys presented child welfare workers with a unique dilemma. As Raymond Fuller explained in his book *Child Labor and the Constitution*: "Many of us . . . are rather strongly prejudiced in favor of it, finding ourselves obliged to overcome serious difficulties in order to recognize it as child labor."[13] Legislatures similarly hesitated to challenge the legitimacy of street work. While other occupations gradually established fourteen as a minimum age limit, children in street work could legally start work at ten or twelve, and many began as young as six or seven. . . .

The legitimacy of newspaper sellers, as well as many child peddlers and bootblacks, was initially determined by nineteenth-century utilitarian values. Unlike factory workers or children in mercantile establishments, street traders were not employees but independent merchants, working for profits and not for wages. It was a glamorous form of entrepreneurship. J. G. Brown, a painter who specialized in nineteenth-century street boys, described them to a reporter: "My boys lived in the open. There wasn't a danger of the streets that they didn't face some time or other during the day. They would take a chance, any time, of being run down by a wagon or a streetcar for the sake of selling a paper or selling a 'shine'. . . they were alert, strong, healthy little chaps."[14] Even twentieth-century reformers were reluctant to put such children out of work. Pioneers in child welfare such as Jacob Riis admiringly referred to the "sturdy independence, love of freedom and absolute self-reliance" of street boys.[15] . . .

As with farm labor, exposés of children working in the streets gradually punctured prevailing myths. A study conducted by the Children's Bureau found children often as young as six and seven selling papers in city streets. As one eleven-year-old newsboy complained, "My little brother sells more . . . because people think he is cute."[16] Newsboys worked late hours, 10 P.M. or sometimes until midnight, especially on Saturday nights, selling the Sunday papers to the theater and restaurant crowds. Street work was found unfit for children, distracting them from school and introducing them into a life of vice and "unnatural desires." . . .

Once again, the boundaries of legitimacy shifted as reformers distinguished more closely between types of street work. Earlier economic criteria (that is, the distinction between wages and profits) were inadequate: "The effect on the child of work is in no wise determined by the form in which his earnings are calculated."[17] While most street occupations, including the sale of newspapers, were declared to be unfit forms of child labor, the neighborhood carrier who delivered newspapers to the homes of subscribers was gradually singled out for legitimacy. The criteria for "good work," however, were dramatically reversed, converting the previously admired independent role of a newsboy into a liability. Why was the delivery of newspapers acceptable? Precisely because "the delivery boy is in no sense an independent merchant or dealer. He neither buys nor sells . . . and he assumes no responsibility except for his own work. He is an employee."[18] Carrying newspapers, concluded the Children's Bureau investigation "puts no temptations in the boy's way to stay out of school, nor does it bring him in contact with such influences as many of the street sellers meet." Unlike the newsboy, the carriers' hours were "unobjectionable"; boys delivering evening papers were finished usually before 6 P.M., "their work did not keep them on the streets after dark . . . nor interfere with their family life." It was a perfect occupation for the domesticated child, not real work but a "schoolboy's job."[19] The day messenger service was another form of legitimate street work for young boys. The night messenger service, on the other hand, was harshly condemned for allegedly employing youngsters to deliver telegrams but in fact using them to carry notes, food, liquor, and drugs to prostitutes, pimps, and gamblers.

Child labor in the home raised even more complex and confusing definitional problems. It also involved a different population; while selling newspapers or bootblacking was a boy's job, home occupations were largely, although not exclusively, a girl's domain. Studies suggest that young girls probably constituted from one half to three fourths of the children involved with homework, while of the 17,669 children ten to fourteen years of age working as newsboys in 1920, only 168 were girls. Unlike a factory, or a street, or a store, the home was sanctioned by reformers as a proper workplace: ". . . every child needs to be taught to work; but he needs to be taught not in the factory but in the home . . ."[20] Officially, domestic activities were not even considered "real" work. Instructions to census enumerators specified that "children who work for their parents at home merely on general household work, on chores, or at odd times on other work, should be reported as having no occupation."[21]

But what about industrial homework, that is factory work done at home mostly by mothers with their young children? It usually involved immigrant families or other unskilled low-paid groups living in the tenement districts of large cities. Industrial homework included a wide range of activities, chiefly finishing men's clothing, embroidering, making artificial flowers, and stringing tags. Children helped with the simpler tasks and often delivered the work from the home to the factory. By the late nineteenth century, homework had become one of the most prevalent forms of child labor. Yet many employers claimed that since the "little helpers" worked with their mothers, they were not really employed.[22] Parents themselves praised an occupation that kept their children busy and safely off the streets. . . . Homework did not necessarily interfere with school work; children usually worked after school hours, Saturdays, and on vacation days.

The industrialized home forced reformers to reassess the meaning of domestic child labor. Tenement homework was condemned as a "peculiarly vicious" form of child labor.[23] After all, it polluted the one traditionally legitimate workplace. . . . Yet what distinguished tenement homework from legitimate housework? At what point did work for a parent become exploitation?. . .

The solution was not to remove all child work from the home, but to discriminate more intelligently among types of domestic employment. Taking factory work out of the home was only the first step. Equally important was to determine appropriate household tasks for children. . . . One progressive Birmingham school even introduced a parents' report card in order "to help the child by recognizing industry and excellence in home occupations."[24] Parents were asked to grade as satisfactory, excellent, fairly good, unsatisfactory, ordinary, or very poor a wide range of domestic activities performed by their children, such as garden work, care of household tools, care of furnace, making fires, care of horse or cow, sweeping and dusting, making beds, and general cooking.

ON THE BOUNDARIES OF LEGITIMACY: THE CASE OF CHILD ACTORS

On January 4, 1910, the Supreme Court of Massachusetts ruled in the landmark case of *Commonwealth v. Griffith* that acting was work. It dismissed the defendant's claims that the word "work" should be given a narrow meaning and limited "to such as is done in a factory, workshop or mercantile establishment." Consequently, the defendant, a theater manager, was found guilty of violating the child labor law by employing a nine-year-old boy and a thirteen-year-old girl for a play at the Majestic Theater in Boston.[25]

Child actors triggered one of the most highly publicized and controversial definitional battles in the child labor controversy. Benjamin B. Lindsey, the noted juvenile court judge and an active supporter of stage work for young children, characterized the issue as, "the only question concerning child labor that has threatened any division of opinion among the best known of those in this country who have been foremost in the fight against child labor."[26] Indeed, in a bizarre turnabout, prominent child labor reformers were suddenly the leading advocates of child labor on the stage. . . .

It was a dispute that lasted from the 1870s through the 1920s. It began in 1876 when Elbridge T. Gerry, president of the New York Society for the Prevention of Cruelty to Children, sponsored one of the first laws designed to regulate the employment of children in public exhibitions. Aimed primarily against street performances and dangerous acrobatic acts, the law became controversial when Gerry attempted to enforce it against the then very popular juvenile operettas. Theater managers accused him of a "monstrous discrimination against singing by children."[27] In 1881, when the well-known ten-year-old singer Corinne was stopped from appearing at New York's Metropolitan Casino, the *Nation* condemned the decision, reminding its readers that "as long as the theater continues to exist, some children will be fitted for theatrical life."[28]

In 1887, eight-year-old Elsie Leslie "took playgoers by storm," in "Editha's Burglar," at the Lyceum Theater.[29] Her next success, in "Little Lord Fauntleroy," triggered a national "public craze" with child stars: "Little Lord Fauntleroys sprang up on every side, and every new play produced had its child interest. Some of the old plays were revised, and juvenile parts were written in."[30] Consequently, annoyance with existing restrictions of child actors intensified. An 1892 amendment to the New York law, which made the mayor responsible for licensing stage children, thus indirectly reducing Gerry's discretionary power, was hailed by the *New York Times* as "one of the few things for which the present Legislature may fairly claim some credit."[31] Support for child actors was formalized by the incorporation in 1893 of the Association for the Protection of Stage Children. Child actors themselves organized an "Anti-Gerry Society," which actively lobbied their cause. As one commentator observed some years later: "To infantile applicants the Gerry Society is a great ogre, lurking in wait to pounce upon and devour them. . . . If any one told them that this society was meant to do them good, they would think he was a lunatic."[32]. . .

The main legislative battles were waged in Massachusetts, Illinois, and Louisiana, the three most restrictive states for child labor on the stage. Theater advocates won their case in Louisiana, when the 1911 session of the legislature approved an amendment to the child labor law, authorizing children of all ages to work in the theater. . . . The Massachusetts and Illinois legislatures were less accommodating. Despite extensive lobbying, the almost universal support of the press, and the endorsement of prominent figures such as Merritt Pinckney, the noted Chicago juvenile court judge, and even an overseas telegram from Sarah Bernhardt, exemptions for child actors were rejected by both states. Yet, the theater interests were not easily discouraged. . . . By 1932, only seventeen out of forty-eight states, and the District of Columbia required a minimum age limit of fourteen or sixteen for the appearance of children in theatrical performances. In its report on stage children, the *White House Conference* of 1932 remarked that, "diverse as are the child labor laws of the various states, regulations applying to the appearance of children in public exhibitions are even more unstandardized."[33]

The intensity of the controversy surprised and dismayed many contemporary observers. After all, numerically, child actors were an insignificant sideline of the child labor problem. Reformers were criticized for this apparently unwarranted diversion from "child laborers who are really oppressed."[34] Yet, if the intensity of the efforts against child acting seemed misguided, the enthusiasm of theater sympathizers was no less mystifying. What explained the increasing appeal and legitimacy of child actors precisely at a time when other children were being put out of work? Why, as one theater expert remarked, "In no country has the child of tender years been permitted to hold so important a place on the stage as in the United States"?[35] The persecution of child actors by some as well as their absolution by others, reflected more than any other facet of child labor, the changing interaction between the economic and sentimental value of children in twentieth-century America.

CHILD ACTING AS ILLEGITIMATE CHILD LABOR

For its opponents, a child actor was no different from any other child worker. When the press accused Elbridge T. Gerry of preventing children from "earning an honest living," he responded that "no parent has any right to profit pecuniarily by the exhibition of a child . . . . It was to protect children . . . that the law was passed, just as it forbids their use in begging, peddling, or in factories." In fact, theater work compounded the evil of economic exploitation with the risk of moral perversion: ". . . the associations are bad for the children . . . they are constantly brought into contact with persons about whose morality . . . the less said the better. . . the girls soon lose all modesty and become bold . . . they . . . usually end in low dance-houses, concert-saloons, and the early grave. . . . The boys. . . end by becoming thieves or tramps."

Children, contended Gerry, were put on the stage for the same mercenary reasons that they were sent to work in a factory or a department store, "to put money in the pockets of somebody," generally their parents.[36] As early as 1868, it was the "shrewd and business like" stage mother who took the brunt of the criticism.

In the 1910 Massachussetts legislative debates, opponents of child labor on the stage . . . raised the specter of profiteer mothers, "hawking their children as commercial assets at stage doors." Opponents of child acting also had to contend with religious and moral prejudice against the theater generally and not just against children on stage. . . .

The necessity of an early apprenticeship was particularly controversial. While supporters of stage work produced long lists of ex-child actors . . . who later became prominent adult stars, opponents of child acting claimed that only a few successful adult actors had begun their career as children. Everett W. Lord, secretary for New England of the National Child Labor Committee, noted that, according to the *Who's Who on the Stage in America*, only eighty-eight of almost 500 prominent actors and actresses of the time began their stage career under fourteen years of age. Ethel Barrymore, Sarah Bernhardt, and Eleanor Robeson were among those who began working after fifteen while . . . many others made their first professional appearance after they were eighteen. . . .

During a public debate about child actors in 1911, Owen R. Lovejoy, secretary of the National Child Labor Committee, rejected claims that "the American public has demanded the army of babies that are clamoring . . . for [theater] permits."[37] Instead, he attributed the success of child actors in the first decade of the twentieth century simply to the business skills of theater managers who exploited a cheap and vulnerable labor force. Allowing this "industry for children on the stage," concluded a speaker at the seventh annual conference on child labor that same year, was a "social abomination."[38]

CHILD ACTING AS LEGITIMATE CHILD WORK

Supporters of stage work refused to categorize the child actor as a child worker. . . . Unlike ordinary child laborers, the child actor or actress loved to work. But opponents responded this was a misguided and dangerous infatuation. As Gerry had explained in 1890, "Of course they cry when not permitted to perform. Children proverbially cry when deprived of what is hurtful to them. They enjoy the performance on account of the excitement . . . their brilliant tinsel costumes, and the applause of the audience, which flatters their vanity."[39]

The theater interests carefully delineated their boundary of legitimacy, for support of theater work did not extend to other forms of child labor. Accused by Bishop William Lawrence of Massachusetts of undermining factory laws by requesting exemptions for child actors, Francis Wilson responded: ". . . not a man or woman who stood up in defense of the stage child but is as firmly opposed to child labor in the mill, the sweatshop and the factory as the good bishop himself."[40] In a letter to the *New York Times*, the chairman of the Sweatshop Committee conveyed a similar distinction: "As a strong opponent of child labor of any kind, I yet feel dramatic work is quite different . . . I have never been able to see why children, (even little ones) . . . should not be allowed to develop the theatrical instinct."[41]

An 1868 report described the typical career sequence of a stage child: "From his wages of $1 as a 'squalling babe,' in a few years the toddling boy will earn $3 a week, and so he goes on, filling the successive roles of 'street urchin,' 'Babe of the Wood,' . . . for sums that enable his family to keep him in clothes and food, at least."[42] In its early stages, the defense of child acting relied heavily on such economic arguments; acting was not ordinary labor but lucrative work for children. A *New York Herald* journalist observed in 1892, that "very many children in this big city . . . work much harder and get much less for their pains than the children on the stage." The reporter contrasted the "rosy cheeked, happy" child actresses, who "work at play," for five dollars a week to cash girls or a shop girl: "Without overcoat or rubbers she hurried on. The little face was pinched and thin, and her bony fingers clutched the $1.75 she had just drawn after the hardest week's work in a year."[43]

Economic claims to legitimacy were still periodically invoked between the 1910 and 1912 stages of the controversy. In a newspaper interview, actress Ellen Terry explained that "stage children were cared for and looked after because they are wage-earners for the family and their health and well-being determine their value."[44] Yet, the defense of acting gradually shifted grounds; it was more often justified as education than as elite work: "The stage, with its lessons of history, costume, and custom . . . is a liberal education . . . in going to the stage [the child] is going to school."[45] As playwright Auguste Thomas put it, acting was "as valuable for a child as a scholarship for Oxford is for a young man."[46] Inflexible laws, warned Francis Wilson, arbitrarily deprived children of their singular "medium of expression": "Who would advocate a law prohibiting children with musical gifts from playing the piano? . . . Who . . . would deny the Chicago child scientist, or the Harvard child student?"[47] Even the alleged mercenary qualities of stage mothers disappeared in the sympathetic portrayals of theater supporters: ". . . They are more tender and painstaking with their stage children than the average mother."[48]

Opponents of stage work distinguished between commercial acting and educational drama. Jane Addams, for instance, encouraged an amateur children's theater in her own Hull House, explaining "The children of course are not paid for their services. . . . Any money that they make is spent for their summer outings."[49] The 1876 New York law sponsored by Gerry to regulate the employment of children in public exhibitions had similarly exempted children's vocational or philanthropical participation as singers or musicians in a church, school, or academy. Thus, acting was legitimate work as long as it did not become "real" wage labor. Theater advocates, however, insisted that even commercial stage work provided an artistic education. Payment was beside the point. . . . Thus, while admitting that child gymnasts, dancers, and singers were unfortunate laborers, theater enthusiasts upheld the stage child as a privileged exception.

The conflict over child acting could be characterized as another economic struggle: one between theater managers eager to increase box-office returns and reformers committed to prevent child labor. Yet, the evidence shows that allegiances did not follow these predictable patterns; interest in child welfare did not necessarily mean opposition to child labor on the stage. Both the enthusiasm and the consternation over child actors were tied to the cultural redefinition of the economic and sentimental roles of children. Children on the stage created a curious paradox; they were child laborers paid to represent the new, sentimentalized view of children. They worked to portray the useless child. The Little Lord Fauntleroys captivated by provoking "emotional havoc" in theater audiences largely composed of women. Already in the mid-nineteenth century, the cult of child mourning reached the stage; popular plays often dwelt on the sorrows of a young child's untimely death. . . . In the early twentieth century, theater enthusiasts raved about the "child-value" in plays, "the emanation of the spirit of childhood; an emanation that only a little child can convincingly give forth . . ."[50] . . . In this celebration of the sentimental value of children, the work role of child actors was ironically camouflaged by their fictional roles. They succeeded as popular symbols of the new "sacred" child. Recognizing that "the charm of the child on the stage is its childishness," theater managers took every precaution to guard and publicize the ingenuous qualities of their young employees. Reporters certified that "a moment's talk with these little folk of the theater assures you that they belong as much to the land of dolls and tin soldiers as to the realm of limelight and rouge. . . ."[51] The specific appeal of childhood also meant that, unlike other forms of labor, child acting did not replace adult work. Significantly, while most labor unions opposed child labor, the Theatrical Stage Employees supported child acting.

The very sentimentalization of childhood on stage that seduced theater advocates infuriated its opponents. Ridiculing "the comfortable belief that these little inhabitants of Stage-land know only the silks and laces of existence," they refused to confuse fiction with reality, the stage role with the child laborer, "who lives in a disagreeable quarter of the city, with a father or mother whom she supports and who is only interested in the money she can bring home."[52] Critics spent so much time and energy against this apparently benign form of child labor precisely because acting transformed the essence of childhood into a commercial asset:

> [T]here are some gifts of which no man has a right to make a capital. It would ill
> become one to whom a talent of friendship has been given to trade upon his powers
> of sympathy or a saint upon his devotional capacities; and in like manner the idea
> of a professional child—a child in whose case simple childhood is the sole stock
> in trade . . . is touched with sacrilege.[53]

In other forms of child labor, monetary value was assigned to the performance of specific tasks, but in acting, the "appeal of childhood is the commodity actually offered for sale to a sentimental and unthinking public."[54]

The dispute over child labor on the stage was fueled by the cultural redefinition of a child's worth. Acting was condemned as illegitimate labor by those who defined it as a profane capitalization of the new "sacred" child. Yet, ironically, at a time when most other children lost their jobs, the economic value of child actors rose precisely because they symbolized on stage the new economically worthless, but emotionally priceless child.

HOUSE CHORES AND A WEEKLY ALLOWANCE: THE ECONOMIC WORLD OF THE USELESS CHILD

By 1930, most children under fourteen were out of the labor market and into schools. Yet, significantly, federal regulation of child labor contained some exceptions. The most influential statute in the field of child labor, the Fair Labor Standards Act of 1938, allowed children under fourteen to work in newspaper distribution and in motion pictures and the theater. Except for manufacturing and mining, a child also remained legally entitled to work for her or his parents. Agricultural labor, which still employed the largest number of children, was only semiregulated as children were permitted to work outside of school hours. . . . The defeat of the Child Labor Amendment in the 1920s and again in the 1930s was partly the result of its failure to recognize any differentiation between children's occupations. By empowering Congress to "limit, regulate, and prohibit the labor of persons under eighteen years of age," the amendment presumably left no room even for legitimate child work.[55]

To be sure, the cultural and legal immunity of certain occupations was partly dictated by the market, in particular, the powerful farming, newspaper, and entertainment industries that had much to lose by a child work prohibition. But it was also based on a radically revised concept of child work. As twentieth-century American children became defined by their sentimental, noneconomic value, child work could no longer remain "real" work; it was only justifiable as a form of education or as a sort of game. The useful labor of the nineteenth-century child was replaced by educational work for the useless child. While child labor had served the household economy, child work would benefit primarily the child. . . . The legal and cultural differentiation between legitimate an illegitimate occupations for children was thus guided by an entirely new set of criteria suitable for the unemployed "sacred" child. Labor on the home farm, for instance, was condoned "for the unselfishness and the sense of family solidarity it develops." Newspaper work was a legitimate "character-building" occupation. The Children's Bureau investigation in the 1920s found that parents of carriers were "emphatic in their approval of the work . . . because they believed that it provides training in the formation of good habits. . . . It was not the financial reason that stood out in their expressions of approval.". . . Acting, claimed its advocates, was not work at all but a liberal education and above all, a joyful child's game. "Work?" queried the *New York Dramatic Mirror,* "most child actors consider it play, and so it is practically that, except that their little minds are being unconsciously developed in a way which would be impossible elsewhere."[56]

As child work shifted from instrumental to instructional, special consideration was given to domestic chores. When an article appearing in *Home Progress* advised parents, "Let your children work," the work referred to "some little household task," not too difficult of course, "for their tender bodies."[57] Already in 1894, popular magazines alerted their middle- and upper-class readers about their children's "eagerness to seize opportunities for sharing the work as well as the play of the home. . . . Shelling peas on Monday because the cook is washing is to him as enchanting as counting pearls on a string. . . ."[58] As working-class children left the labor force for the classroom, their mothers were likewise instructed to keep them busy at home. "It is pitiful . . . for a woman to believe that she is 'bettering' her children by . . . allowing them to think that it is degrading for them to help in the housework. . . ."[59]

Yet, the point was not to assist the mother, but to educate the child. In 1931, the Subcommittee on Housing and Home Management of the White House Conference on Child Health and Protection strongly recommended that "less emphasis . . . be placed on the amount of assistance rendered and more on the educational values [to the child] of the responsibilities involved in the performance of household tasks."[60] . . .

House chores were therefore not intended to be "real" work, but lessons in helpfulness, order, and unselfishness. Parents were warned to "take great care not to overburden the child with responsibility . . . lest the weight of it should crush him instead of develop a greater strength."[61] . . . A survey of junior high school students by the 1930 White House Conference noted that urban children performed about three-fourths as many household tasks as did the rural child.[62] The "servant-keeping" class was particularly limited in this respect. One well-meaning parent reported the *Journal of Home Economics*, had tried to teach her young child the "dignity of labor," but the only available job was flower arrangement. In another family, the son simply tipped the butler to do the boy's chores. . . . The new rules and problems of child work cut across classes, equally applicable to all unemployed children. . . . The expanding school system attempted to incorporate "good" work into their curricula. As Edward T. Devine explained, "work which we deny . . . in the factory, for profit, may be demanded in school . . . for education and training."[63]

As children's involvement with work changed, so did their relationship to money. The wages of a working child had been considered legitimate family property. Thomas Dublin's analysis of the mid-nineteenth-century records of the Hamilton Manufacturing Company, a major textile mill in Lowell, Massachusetts, suggests that fathers signed for, and probably picked up their children's pay envelopes. . . . This financial collaboration survived into the twentieth century. In the Amoskeag Mills in Manchester, New Hampshire, Tamara Hareven found that "the custom for working children to contribute most of their wages to their families was an unwritten law."[64] . . .

Yet, children often regained a small portion of their wages in the form of a spending allowance. For instance, a 1909 survey of 622 working children from several cities found that over half of them received a regular weekly allowance (usually between twenty-five and fifty cents), while others had more irregular arrangements. The 1914 studies of New York's West Side remarked that "some allowance from [the working child's] earnings is his by right." It was also noted that children's contributions were usually "standardized. How much they keep for themselves, how much they give in, is made a matter of rule and custom."[65] Yet, the rules for children's money depended more on parental attitudes than any economic logic. For instance, the 1909 Senate report discovered that some of the children earning the highest wages received no allowance while some children earning small amounts, received allowances of fifty cents or more. Immigrant parents were less apt than the native-born to give their children spending money. Girls were more likely to contribute all their wages to the family, less likely to receive an allowance or, if they did, their stipends were smaller than boys'.[66] Tips were apparently considered a child's property. The 1914 West Side study noted that it was "a mark of high virtue to surrender them. A woman will tell with pride, 'He knew I was hard up and he gave me his tips.'"[67]

Even after being shut off from factories and stores, young working-class children sought alternative ways of raising some spending money. When an investigator asked a sample of over one thousand Chicago children between the third and eighth grades: "How do you get the money you have to spend?" 70 percent of the boys and almost 60 percent of the girls responded: "I earn it." The girls ran errands or did housework and babysitting for their parents and neighbors, while the boys, in addition to working for their parents, ran errands for strangers ("going to the store for a lady" meant from 1 cent to a nickel profit), sold papers or ice, caddied, and bootblacked. The working-class child, concluded the investigator, "sees a very close relation between money and service, and makes the receipt of one dependent on the performance of the other." As one young boy explained, "We must work to earn money."[68]

If a working child earned money through labor, what was to be the source of income once children stopped working? As the American economy turned out thousands of new consumer items, many of them directed at a juvenile audience, children's money became increasingly problematic. . . . Working-class parents were not only relinquishing the income of their children, but also assumed significant new expenses of clothing and school supplies. Indeed, a 1903 investigation found few social class differences in children's spending habits. All children spent their money in school shops, purchasing supplies, but they also spent money on candy, toys, ice cream, theater tickets, and often tobacco and gambling. Regardless of class, boys spent more than girls. Concerned with children's "fever for spending," surveys investigated the "financiering of the child who is not a regular wage-earner.". . .

To be sure, middle- and upper-class children were already veteran paupers. As the *Outlook* remarked in 1903: "Servants, bootblacks, and the poorest class are rich in comparison with many young people who are dependent for their pennies . . ." Children, observed the article, "are often at their wits' ends to know how to get a dollar together."[69] When children from affluent families were asked how they obtained spending money, most responded: "It's given me," but not without first having to tease and cajole their parents or else beg "sympathetic relatives or friends, expecting a donation."[70] "Tipping" other people's children seems to have caused some controversy in the early twentieth century. When *Home Progress* asked its readers "What should parents do when guests in the house offer the children small sums of money?" responses ranged from warm approval to harsh condemnation. "My children," wrote a mother from Calmet, Michigan, "always explain to people that they are not permitted to receive money from callers, visitors, or people they meet in the street."[71]

The proposed solution to the economic insolvency of young children was an allowance to be provided by parents on a regular weekly basis. As early as 1893, the allowance was endorsed as "the best method . . . for giving children an income."[72] . . . While the concept of the allowance was a middle-class invention, it was advocated by childcare experts and others as a solution for all children, regardless of class. For instance, Justice Mayer of the New York City Court, assured that an allowance would even serve as a crime deterrent for lower-class children. Lack of access to legitimate spending money, argued the judge, often turned decent, studious youngsters into thieves. . . . Ironically while money given to children by their parents was upheld as "safe" money, money earned by children was stigmatized by reformers as "dangerous" money, allowing the child an anomalous economic independence from its parents. The White House Conference found a relationship between delinquency and the source of spending money; adolescent nondelinquent boys were more likely to receive an allowance, while predelinquent boys were more likely to earn their money.[73]

But how could poor parents afford this additional gift of money? Although the evidence is limited, it suggests that the allowance became an expectation and sometimes a reality even among working-class families. As children lost their economic value, the nineteenth-century economic contract between parents and children had to be revised. Thus, parents were not only expected to forgo their children's wages, but they were expected to subsidize children's expanding spending habits. . . . Even prospective foster parents (recruited largely from the working class) were expected to provide their charges with a regular weekly allowance.[74]

It was difficult, however, to develop proper guidelines for the allowance money of a nonworking child. If wages were contingent on work, what did an allowance depend on?

Could money be divorced from labor, and should it? From the start, the allowance was justi-fied as educational money. . . . In the new consumer society of the twentieth century, the old lessons of thrift and saving were no longer sufficient. By teaching how to spend wisely, the allowance would train children as efficient shoppers. . . . The new American ideal was a child "who spends wisely, saves wisely and gives wisely."[75]

A regular allowance served more than the child's best interest. For parents, it was an expedient arrangement to regulate their children's stepped-up requests for money. . . . In order to be effective, the allowance had to be a fixed "unearned" salary. Parental regulation of the expen-sive, nonworking child was further assured by closely supervising children's use of money. . . .

Ironically, once children were removed from the market, their home became a place of employment. After all, if parents were one of the few remaining legitimate employers, where else could the child earn money? Parents were warned against the dangers of commercializing the home and urged to distinguish between the "principles of the home . . . and [those] of the shop."[76] . . .

The preferred solution, however, was to firmly establish the allowance as "free" educa-tional money just as domestic chores were expected to remain "free" unpaid instructional child work. . . . By the 1930s, the differentiation of allowance from wages was unequivocally endorsed. . . . Allowances and wages were consequently two distinct categories of money; the former was a "right . . . earned by personality," the other, "specified sums that [the child] earns by specific acts."[77] The allowance, affirmed Sidonie Gruenberg, Director of the Child Study Association of America, "is as 'free' as food and clothing, for the child must spend before he can earn."[78] . . .

In the first three decades of the twentieth century, children's money was thus invested with new educational, moral, and social functions. In addition, as all children became primarily consumers, some former economic distinctions between working-class and middle-class children were blurred. While the spending money of the useful child had been derived from his or her wages, the allowance for economically useless children, regardless of class, came primarily from their parents' pocket-book. Defined as "the child's own portion of the family income," children's money, even when earned, also became progres-sively differentiated from adult money. For instance, older children who remained in the labor market were increasingly less likely to hand over their entire paychecks to the family.[79] . . . When newsboys were allowed to keep part of their wages, it was often spent in "useful" purchases, such as clothing or other necessities. For instance, the thirteen-year-old son of an Italian street-car motorman who earned three dollars a week selling and carrying papers, "gave his money to his mother for groceries, keeping twenty-five cents for spending money. He had also saved ten dollars with which he had bought a suit of clothes." Another ten-year-old earned two dollars and forty cents a week, "bought his clothes, put 10 cents in the school bank, spent 10 cents 'for a show,' and gave the rest to his family." Newspaper carriers, on the other hand, who were more likely to come from middle-class families, usually spent their earnings on themselves. A publisher's eleven-year-old son, for instance, earned two dollars and fifteen cents a week on his route, "out of which he paid $1 a week for violin lessons, paid his carfare to work, kept 10 cents a week for spending money, and in four years had saved $95."[80] In his study *Children of the Great Depression*, Glen H. Elder, Jr., found that the economic function of children's money became newly significant in the 1930s. Severely deprived households depended on a portion of their children's earnings for basic expenses.

Yet, despite some exceptions, the new rules were increasingly accepted; children were entitled to unearned spending money, and when they earned some pocket money, it was theirs to keep. . . .

In this new cultural and economic context, parents of successful child actors, particularly during the mid-1920s and 1930s Hollywood child star craze, were caught in a curious predicament. Their children not only worked, but made fortunes, often claiming their parents as dependents for income tax purposes. For instance, Jackie Coogan, at age eight, commanded a million dollars plus a percentage of profits for a four-picture contract with Metro. Shirley Temple's mother was paid $500 a week for managing her daughter, while Mr. Temple received a 10 percent commission as Shirley's agent. In her autobiography, Baby Peggy, another child star from the 1920s, recalls reporters' intense curiosity as to "how many dollars we were putting into our parents' pockets."[81] Hollywood "mammas" received even harsher press treatment than their predecessors, stage mothers.

In 1938, Jackie Coogan, then twenty three years old, sued his mother and step-father to recover the four million dollars he had earned as a child actor. But the defendants contended that under common law, Coogan's earnings as a minor child were their legitimate property, not his. The widely publicized lawsuit resulted in the 1939 passage by the California legislature of a Child Actor's Bill, better known as the "Coogan Act." The bill established that half of a child's earnings had to be set aside for the child in a trust fund or another type of savings. The Coogan lawsuit thus successfully challenged the historical rule of law that the earnings of minor children belonged to their parents.[82] The verdict reaffirmed the new cultural and economic contract between parent and child.

Parents of other child stars felt compelled to publicly justify their children's income by demonstrating it legitimate uses. For example, the Temples were "proud of the way they have arranged Shirley's finances. Her father says they have really taken very little money from her income for expenses."[83] The public was reassured that Shirley's money was safely invested. But the ultimate confirmation of good parenting was that even Shirley Temple received an allowance of four dollars and twenty-five cents a week. She was not the only one. Jane Withers, among many others, received a five dollar weekly allowance, and also "makes her own bed, does housework, and even runs errands."[84] In 1937, Louis B. Mayer offered thirteen-year-old screen star Freddie Bartholomew a $98,000 a year contract. A clause provided for a one dollar weekly spending allowance for Freddy. A Los Angeles judge involved with the arrangements commented "That probably is the best contract of them all."[85] The real earnings of these often millionaire children were thus neutralized with a legitimate educational income. The allowance permitted the comfortable fiction that the "deviant" useful child was not so different from its useless unemployed counterpart.

The transformation of children's economic roles during the first half of the twentieth century illustrates the interaction between economic and noneconomic factors in advanced industrial societies. Children were removed from the market between 1870 and 1930 in large part because it had become more economical and efficient to educate them than to hire them. But cultural guidelines profoundly shaped and directed the process of social change by differentiating legitimate from illegitimate occupations for children and distinguishing licit from illicit forms of child money. As children became increasingly defined as exclusively emotional and moral assets, their economic roles were not eliminated but transformed; child labor was replaced by child work and child wages with a weekly allowance. A child's new job and income were validated more by educational than economic criteria.

Discussion Questions

1. How did reformers distinguish between "good" and "bad" work for children?

2. According to the author, why did child actors become more popular just as child labor was challenged as immoral?

3. What does it mean to say that children's work shifted from "instrumental" to "instructional"?

4. Do you think there is a moral conflict over child labor today? If so, how and why?

Notes

1. *Report on Condition of Woman and Child Wage-Earners in the United States* 7(Washington, D.C., 1910):15.

2. Raymond G. Fuller, "Child Labor Versus Children's Work," *The American Child* 3(Feb. 1922):281.

3. Theresa Wolfson, "Why, When, And How Children Leave School," *The American Child* 1(May 1919):61.

4. William Noyes, "Overwork, Idleness or Industrial Education," *Annals of the American Academy of Political and Social Sciences* 27(Mar. 1906):87. There was also a nostalgic recollection of apprenticeship as a lost form of "good" work.

5. Arthur D. Dean, "Child-Labor or Work for Children." *The Craftsman* 25(Mar. 1914):515.

6. Raymond G. Fuller, *Child Labor and the Constitution* (New York: Thomas Y. Crowell, 1923), p. 32.

7. Fuller, "Child Labor Versus Children's Work." p. 281.

8. See William F. Ogburn, "Progress and Uniformity in Child Labor Legislation," Ph.D. diss. New York: Columbia University Press, 1912, pp. 90, 103. "Child Labor," *White House Conference on Child Health and Protection* (New York: Century Co., 1932), pp. 27–30; Elizabeth Sands Johnson, "Child Labor Legislation," in John R. Commons, *History of Labor in the United States*, 1896–1932 (New York: Macmillan, 1935), pp. 413, 428–30.

9. Edwin Markham, "The Smoke of Sacrifice," *Cosmopolitan* 42(Feb. 1907):393.

10. Reprinted in Grace Abbott, *The Child and the State* (Chicago: University of Chicago Press, 1938), p. 474.

11. E. C. Lindeman, "Child Labor Amendment and the Farmers," reprinted in "The Child Labor Amendment," *University of Texas Bulletin* No. 2529(Aug. 1, 1925):87. For an overview of the studies of children employed in agriculture, see *White House Conference*, pp. 222–61.

12. Franklin N. Brewer, "Child Labor in the Department Store," *Annals of the American Academy* 20(1902):167–77.

13. Fuller, *Child Labor and the Constitution*, p. 76.

14. *Survey* 30(June 14, 1913):380.

15. Jacob A. Riis. *How the Other Half Lives* (New York: Dover Publications, 1971, 1st ed. 1890), p. 153.

16. Nettie P. McGill, "Child Workers on City Streets," U.S. Children's Bureau Publication, No.188 (Washington, D.C., 1928):4.

17. Quoted in Clopper, *Child Labor in City Streets*, p. 15.

18. "Children in Gainful Occupations," Fourteenth Census (Washington, D.C., 1924):53.

19. McGill, "Child Workers in City Streets," pp. 6–7, 36–7.

20. Charles W. Dabney, "Child Labor and the Public Schools," *Annals of the American Academy* 29 (Jan. 1907), p. 112. See *White House Conference*, pp. 128–9; "Children in Gainful Occupations," pp. 52, 59. Most street regulations also fixed a higher minimum age for girls than for boys. Domestic and personal service were other predominantly female occupations.

21. "Children in Gainful Occupations," p. 16.

22. Hall, *Forty Years*, p. 89. No precise figures of the number of child home workers exist.

23. Fuller, *Child Labor and the Constitution*, p. 87.

24. *Journal of Education* 78(Oct. 2, 1913):325.

25. 204 Mass. 18, 90 N.E. 394.

26. "Children on the Colorado Stage," *Survey* 27 (Oct. 14, 1912):996. There is surprisingly little information on child acting. As the White House Conference on Child Health and Protection discovered in 1932: "There is no type of employment for children about which so little is known as about their employment in theatrical exhibitions and other public entertainments," p. 51.

27. Letter to the Editor, *New York Times*, Dec. 25, 1882, p. 2. See *Manual of the New York Society for the Prevention of Cruelty to Children* (New York: published by the Society, 1913), pp. 64–69.

28. "The Protection of Child Performers," *The Nation* 33(Dec. 29, 1881):508.

29. "Children of the Stage," *New York Times* June 16, 1889, p. 16.

30. Arthur Hornblow, "The Children of the Stage," *Mumsey's Magazine* 12(Oct. 1894):33.

31. "Children of the Stage," Editorial *New York Times* Apr. 19, 1892, p. 4.

32. "Where Children Are Chosen for Positions on the Stage," *New York Times* Apr. 17, 1904, p. 22.

33. *White House Conference*, p. 196; F. Zeta Youmans, *Stage Children and the Law* (Chicago: Juvenile

Protective Association, 1923), p. 5. See also Benjamin B. Blydenburgh, "The Child and the Theatre," 18 *Case and Comment* (Mar. 1912):584–86. The confusion and conflict over the regulation of child acting was not uniquely American. For some comparative information, see George K. Behlmer, *Child Abuse and Moral Reform in England, 1870–1908* (Stanford, CA: Stanford University Press, 1982), p. 104, and "The Age of Admission of Children to Employment in Non-Industrial Occupations," *International Labour Conference* (Geneva: International Labour Office, 1931), pp. 19–28.

34. *New York Times*, Dec. 7, 1911, p. 12. No adequate sources exist on the exact number of children employed in theatrical productions. The 1920 census listing of 400 children between the ages of ten and fifteen under the category of "Actors and Showmen" is clearly an underestimate.

35. Hornblow, "The Children of the Stage," p. 33.

36. Elbridge T. Gerry, "Children of the Stage," *North American Review* 151 (July 1890):18–19.

37. Owen R. Lovejoy, "Employment of Children on the Stage," *Child Labor Bulletin* 1(Nov. 1912):78.

38. Henry Baird Favill, "Child Labor As Related To The Stage," National Child Labor Committee publication No. 165, 1911, p. 15.

39. Gerry, "Children of the Stage," p. 17.

40. Letter to the Editor, *Survey* 24(June 18, 1910):496. While supporters of child acting opposed the prohibition of stage work, they recognized the need for proper regulation. See "Stage Children of America," p. 1.

41. Letter to the Editor, *New York Times*, June 26, 1910, p. 8.

42. "Children on the Stage," *New York Times* Apr. 12, 1868, p. 11.

43. "Lillian Russell's Juvenile Pets," *New York Herald* Jan. 10, 1892, p. 9.

44. Quoted in "Defending the Child Actors," *Literary Digest* 41(Nov. 12, 1910):861.

45. "Stage Children of America," pp. 7–8.

46. Quoted in *New York Times*, Dec. 7, 1911, p. 12. In 1914, the Professional Children's School was opened in New York City, providing flexible schedules for child actors, which made it possible to formally combine stage work with an education.

47. Wilson, "The Child on the Stage."

48. "Children of the Stage," *Bellman* 10(Mar. 25, 1911):359.

49. Letter to Harry Powers, manager of the Power's theater of Chicago, on file at the Performing Arts Research Center.

50. "Stage Children of America," p. 16.

51. Eleanor Robson, "Happy Experiences of the Child Who Acts, and His Beneficent Influence on Grown-Up Actors Upsets Old-Fashioned Theories," *New York Times* Dec. 15, 1907, VI, p. 1.

52. Ibid. There is little information on the gender of children on the stage. It appears that at the turn of the century young girls were more likely to appear on stage than boys, often taking male parts.

53. "The Show-Child: A Protest," *Longman's Magazine*. Reprinted in *Living Age* 208 (Jan. 11, 1896):113.

54. F. Zeta Youmans, "Childhood, Inc.," *Survey* 52 (July 25, 1924):462.

55. See Jeremy Felt, "The Child Labor Provisions of the Fair Labor Standards Act," *Labor History* 11 (Fall 1970):467–81; "Second Thought On the Child Labor Amendment," 9 *Massachusetts Law Quarterly* 15–21 (July 1924); "Comments," 7 *Fordham Law Review* 223–25 (May 1938); Anne Kruesi Brown, "Opposition to the Child Labor Amendment," Ph.D. diss., Chicago, 1937, pp. 46–49.

56. John Mason, "The Education of the Stage Child," *New York Dramatic Mirror* (Mar. 8, 1911):5.

57. Lillian Davidson, "Idle Children," *Home Progress* 6(June 1917):474.

58. Helen C. Candee, "In the Beginning," *Outlook* 49(May 5, 1894):787.

59. Henriette E. Delamare, "Teaching Children to be Helpful at Home," *Home Progress* 3(Nov. 1913):115.

60. "The Home and the Child," *White House Conference on Child Health and Protection*, 1931 (New York: Arno Press & The *New York Times*, 1972), p. 90.

61. Miriam Finn Scott, "The Perfect Child," *Ladies' Home Journal* 39(June 1922):30.

62. "The Adolescent in the Family," *White House Conference on Child Health and Protection*, 1934 (New York: Arno Press & The *New York Times*, 1972), p. 37.

63. Edward T. Devine, "The New View of the Child," *Annals of the American Academy* 32 (July 1908):9. See Editorial, *Journal of Home Economics* 7(Aug. 1915):372. On the development of industrial education in the early decades of the twentieth century, see Marvin Lazerson and W. Norton Grubb, *American Education and Vocationalism* (New York: Teachers College Press, 1974).

64. Tamara K. Hareven, *Family Time and Industrial Time* (New York: Cambridge University Press, 1982), p. 189; Thomas Dublin, *Women at Work* (New York: Columbia University Press, 1979), pp. 174–5.

65. *Report on Condition of Woman and Child Wage-Earners in the United States* 7(Washington, D.C., 1910):94–97. *Boyhood and Lawlessness*, p. 69; Katharine Anthony, *Mothers Who Must Earn* (New York: Survey Associates, 1914), p. 136.

66. See Hareven, *Family Time and Industrial Time*, p. 189; Louise C. Odencrantz, *Italian Women in Industry* (New York: Russell Sage, 1919), pp. 175–77; Leslie W. Tentler, *Wage-Earning Women* (New York: Oxford University Press, 1979), pp. 89–90; *Report on Condition* 7:95–96. In *Children of the Great Depression* (Chicago: University of Chicago Press, 1974), Glen H. Elder, Jr. found that girls were more likely than boys to be given money when needed rather than receiving a regular allowance, thus increasing their financial dependence on parents. (pp. 72–73).

67. *Boyhood and Lawlessness*, p. 69.

68. Gertrude E. Palmer, "Earnings, Spendings and Savings of School Children," *The Commons* 8(June 1903):3–6.

69. Helen B. Seymour, "Money Matters with Young People," *Outlook* 48 (Sept. 23, 1893):553.

70. Ibid., Palmer, "Earnings, Spendings and Savings," p. 3.

71. *Home Progress* 6(Nov. 1916):141.

72. Seymour, "Money Matters," p. 553.

73. See *New York Times*, Nov. 7, 1903, p. 2, and "The Adolescent in the Family," p. 229.

74. *Boyhood and Lawlessness*, p. 68. On foster children, see chapter 6, and for contemporary data on allowances and social class, see Conclusions.

75. *New York Times*, July 4, 1931, p. 11; "Have You a Little Miser in Your Home?," *The Literary Digest* 110(July 18, 1931):44.

76. Burrell, "The Child and Money," p. 1721.

77. Elliot, "Money and the Child's Own Standards of Living," p. 4.

78. Sidonie M. Gruenberg, "The Dollar Sign in Family Life," *Parents Magazine* 9(Dec. 1934):85–86.

79. Sidonie M. Gruenberg, quoted in *New York Times*, Feb. 10, 1932, p. 25. See also Tentler, *Wage-Earning Women* p. 92.

80. Nettie P. McGill, "Child Workers on City Streets," U.S. Children's Bureau Publication No. 188 (Washington, D.C., 1928), pp. 29–30, 39. See also Howard G. Burdge, *Our Boys*, Ph.D. diss., Columbia University, 1921, p. 215.

81. Diana Serra Cary, *Hollywood's Children* (Boston: Houghton Mifflin, 1979), p. 91. See also Norman J. Zierold, *The Child Stars* (New York: Coward-McCann, 1965) and "Child Movie Stars Make Millions—For Others!" *Chicago Sunday Tribune*, July 18, 1937.

82. Harry Hibschman, "The Jackie Coogan Case," 72 *United States Law Review* 214(Apr. 1938). Coogan's victory was mostly symbolic; he was only awarded $126,000. For two earlier cases that also challenged the parental right to a working child's wages, see Rounds Brothers v. McDaniel 133 Ky. 669, 118 S.W. 956 (1909) and Jacobs v. Jacobs, 130 Iowa 10, 104 N.W. 489 (1906).

83. "Whose Is The Money A Child Film Star Earns?" *Sunday News*, Apr. 24. 1938, p. 55. On file at The Performing Arts Research Center. A study conducted by the National Child Labor Committee in 1941 discovered that the earnings of most child actors were used for their own expenses and training, in dancing, music, or dramatic lessons. Anne Hood Harren and Gertrude Folks Zimand, *Children in the Theater* (National Child Labor Committee, 1941). pp. 52–54.

84. "Guarding Their Pots of Money," *Silver Screen* (1938). On file at The Performing Arts Research Center. Jackie Coogan himself had received an allowance of six dollars and twenty-five cents a week.

85. *New York Times*, Oct. 24, 1937, IV, p. 2.

Minors, Censorship, Sex, and History

MARJORIE HEINS

INTRODUCTION

In this provocative excerpt, author Marjorie Heins explores the assumption that children need to be shielded from certain ideas or information, particularly about sex. By examining fears of youth corruption dating back to ancient Greece, she puts our contemporary concerns about youth and media in perspective. Protecting kids from "indecency" has been used over the centuries to regulate, censor, and control information to people of all ages, not just children.

The notion that young people need special protection from improper ideas was not a moral tenet of the ancient world. . . . The ancient Greeks associated children with grossness and lewdness, not innocence.[1] Youngsters had to be tamed and educated, but not kept ignorant of sexual realities. On the contrary, the most highly prized sexual relationship in ancient Athens was between an adult man and an adolescent boy; it was viewed as critical to male socialization.[2] Ethicists may have pondered the intricacies and agonized over the pleasures of "Greek love," but Plato's preference for nonsexual affections was largely a protest against things as they were.[3] The same is true of his desire to ban literary descriptions of the gods' erotic activities because they would "engender laxity of morals among the young."[4]

The puritanical Plato, fundamentally suspicious of creative art, rejected the humanism and democracy of Athens and "embraced the barbarism of Sparta," Athens's militaristic rival.[5] That the Spartan program resulted in "a narrow and brittle personality is appalling," according to one historian, but "certainly these virtuous prehistoric people had nothing to learn from us about the possibilities of molding the child."[6]

Plato's pupil Aristotle took a more nuanced view of the imitative effects of art and entertainment. Spectators at tragic dramas, Aristotle said in his *Poetics*, do not imitate the dreadful acts depicted onstage but instead, through the phenomenon of *katharsis*, are purged of violent and unruly emotions.[7] Artists, critics, and philosophers have debated, expanded upon, and modified Aristotle's catharsis theory ever since.[8] But although Aristotle's aesthetics were a break from Plato's more simplistically didactic approach, the younger philosopher was also not exactly a libertarian when it came to minors. In his *Politics*, Aristotle urged that "all unseemly talk" be "kept away from youth," for "the unseemly remark lightly dropped results in conduct of a like kind." Thus, "younger persons" should not be permitted "at comedies or recitals of iambics" (a poetic meter "often used for scurrilous purposes").[9] . . .

Plato and even Aristotle may have disagreed with such exposure of minors to erotic art or ideas, but it was Christianity that radically changed attitudes about sexual knowledge. With the ascendancy of the peculiarly Christian notion that sexual desire is sinful,[10] children's virginity now assumed interior, spiritual value. Simultaneously and paradoxically, Christianity viewed children as untamed vessels of depravity and Original Sin.[11] Up to this point, as historian John Sommerville says, "even the few authors who reflected on the child's needs had considered children to be only potentially human"—infanticide, abandonment, and sales into brothers being among their frequent fates. The precepts of Jesus "exactly reversed the expectations of his hearers" by elevating the helplessness of children, and their ignorance of social convention, to a state of grace.[12] . . .

Christian sexual proscriptions clashed with economic and practical realities. In medieval and early modern Europe, adults and children often slept together around a common fire. A child "learned about intercourse by being in the same bed with parents when they did it."[13] This youthful familiarity with the "primal scene," later thought by Freud to be a source of neurosis, persisted into the 17th century.[14] . . .

THE INVENTION OF CHILDHOOD?

Philippe Ariès argued in his 1960 book, *Centuries of Childhood*, that the modern concept of childhood as a period of prelapsarian innocence was an invention of the 17th century. In the 1500s, "[e]verything was permitted in their presence: coarse language, scabrous actions and situations." "The idea did not yet exist that references to sexual matters . . . could soil childish innocence," because "nobody thought that this innocence really existed." It was only toward the end of the 16th century that "certain pedagogues . . . refused to allow children to be given indecent books any longer." Until then, "nobody had hesitated to give children Terence [the bawdy Roman playwright] to read, for he was a classic. The Jesuits removed him from their curriculum."[15]

Ariès concluded that the idea of a separate and uniquely innocent childhood produced anxieties and neuroses that are still with us. Children had to be taught to conceal their bodies from each other. The new moral climate produced "a whole pedagogic literature for children." As a result, the modern world "is obsessed by the physical, moral, and sexual problems of childhood" in a way that did not occur to ancient or medieval minds. An "increasingly severe disciplinary system" in boarding schools deprived youngsters of the freedom they had previously enjoyed among adults.[16]

Centuries of Childhood has had tremendous influence, and many critics. Historian Natalie Zemon Davis, describing adolescent rituals and escapades in the Renaissance and Middle Ages, concludes that a separate preadult period of maturation was recognized before the 17th century.[17] Lawrence Stone is even more dismissive of theories that adolescence, "and the nuisance it causes to society," were not recognized as problems at least by the Renaissance.[18] John Sommerville points out that not all Christian pedagogues advocated censorship. Martin Luther, for example, "objected that children could not be protected from ribaldry but must conquer it instead."[19] Psychohistorian Lloyd de Mause faults Ariès for minimizing the brutality of beatings, rapes, and other forms of child abuse that existed from earliest times.[20]

Much of the criticism of Ariès is well taken, but does not really undermine his basic insight. All historical periods embody tensions between conflicting social trends. In 19th-century England, Victorian sexual repression coexisted with—even stimulated—a brisk trade in erotica, while simultaneously in the United States rigidly antisexual "Comstockery" thrived, while contending against a vocal movement promoting free love. Thus, Linda Pollock's evidence (to take a nonsexual example) that many 16th-to-18th-century parents doted on their offspring does not negate the fact that other children and adolescents in the same period were starved, beaten, and psychologically abused.[21] Stone's account of English apprentices' precocious social life from the 16th century on suggests that youthful sexuality flourished even while, as Ariès documents, pedagogues were inventing new rationales to control it.[22] As historian David Archard argues, Ariès's claim was not so much that the separate nature of childhood was not recognized in the Middle Ages but that our modern sense of what that nature is—uncorrupted, asexual, and psychologically vulnerable—evolved later.[23] And with the modern perception came heavier, more institutionalized censorship and control.

Michel Foucault took Ariès a step further. It has only been in recent centuries, Foucault said, that childhood sexuality began to be isolated, examined, and viewed as sinful precisely so that authority could be exerted to control it. One has only to "glance over the architectural layout," the "rules of discipline," and the "whole internal organization" of secondary schools in 18th-century Europe to see that "the question of sex was a constant preoccupation." "The space for classes, the shape of the tables, the planning of the recreation lessons, the distribution of the dormitories (with or without partitions, with or without curtains), the rules for monitoring bedtime and sleep periods—all this referred, in the most prolix manner, to the sexuality of children." Eventually, "a whole literature of precepts, opinions, observations, medical advice, clinical cases, outlines for reform, and plans for ideal institutions" developed to control the sexuality of the young.[24]

Certainly, the 17th and 18th centuries brought the West closer to contemporary ideas about childhood and sexual expression. Historians note a stronger sense of parental involvement in 17th-century England and America, "new methods of child-rearing, based on the small, nuclear family," a reduction in the number of children being sent from home to become apprentices, and a proliferation of medical interventions and parental-advice manuals.[25] Seventeenth-century Puritanism viewed children as carriers of Original Sin, who must be controlled and indoctrinated into right behavior, but it also led to John Locke's 1693 *Thoughts Concerning Education*, which dramatically influenced pedagogy and child rearing for the next several centuries.

Locke argued for a reasoned, humane, and noncoercive style of teaching and socializing youth. His theory of learning was based on "sensationalist epistemology"—the idea that the human mind is a tabula rasa and that parents and educators are therefore responsible for children's development. Implicitly denying Original Sin, Locke set the stage for increasing state interference in children's upbringing to correct any failings by the formerly autonomous patriarchal father.[26] Some of the effects were salutary—swaddling and wet-nursing declined; revulsion against flogging and other brutalities increased.[27] But new, institutionalized concern for youngsters had its ominous side. If the authoritarian child rearing of Puritan days was justified in the interest of saving youth from sin and damnation, so the more nurturing philosophies that succeeded it rationalized repressive practices as necessary to protect youth from frailty, disease, or corruption. Censorship became a concern because "sensationalist epistemology" assumed that amoral literature could create "impressions as real to the mind as those made by other experience."[28] The most repressive and brutalizing manifestation of the new protectionism was the collection of myths and practices directed toward suppressing youthful masturbation. . . .

It is not easy to understand why adults began in the 18th century so severely to punish their children for responding to a natural impulse. One is even tempted to consider Lloyd de Mause's theory (not credited by most historians) that parents, doctors, educators, and government officials had reached a "psychohistorical" stage at which children became the unfortunate scrims on which adults projected their own sexual anxieties.[29] But whatever the cause of the obsession, for the next 150 years, as Peter Gay recounts, preventive measures ranged from the relatively mild "avoidance of tight lacing, licentious novels, featherbeds, and similar luxuries" to horrifying practices like "cauterization of the sexual organs, infibulation, castration, and clitoridectomy," and elaborate mechanical restraints: "modern chastity belts for girls and ingenious penile rings for boys or straitjackets for both, all designed to keep growing or adolescent sinners from getting at themselves."[30] . . .

Emile, or On Education, Jean-Jacques Rousseau's fictionalized 1762 treatise on child rearing, insisted on the natural innocence of youth, urged withdrawal of adolescents from the libertine and "scandalous morals" of 18th-century French life, and imposed detailed prescriptions for an ideal education. Although Rousseau acknowledged that sexual potency comes with puberty, he wanted to postpone initiation and even instruction until the age of 20. In the meantime, he urged, adults must avoid arousing youngsters' erotic curiosity. "Put their nascent imaginations off the track with objects which, far from inflaming, repress the activity of their senses."[31] Although Rousseau has been credited with at least "calling attention to the needs of children,"[32] his pedagogical theories had an authoritarian edge; and despite his sentimentalizing of childhood, he left his own five illegitimate children at foundling homes.[33] . . .

"PROTECTING THE YOUNG AND IMMATURE"

Heresy and sedition were the primary targets of censorship before the 19th century. Censors simply "did not think it worth their while to concern themselves with chap-books and similar light literature, some of which was very coarse."[34] Although there were a few prosecutions in the 18th century, resulting in a new "common law" crime of obscene libel, enforcement was sporadic, and such Enlightenment classics as John Cleland's *Memoirs of a Woman of Pleasure* (*Fanny Hill*) and Benjamin Franklin's *Advice to a Young Man on the Choice of a Mistress* circulated freely. The "few shots fired" were "mostly blanks."[35] . . .

The United States, like England, had only a smattering of obscenity prosecutions in the 18th century.[36] Massachusetts did pass a law in 1711 that banned "any filthy, obscene, or profane song, pamphlet, libel, or mock sermon," but the essence of the offense was in the "mimicking of preaching, or any other part of divine worship."[37] It was not until 1835 that the law was modified to criminalize "obscene or indecent" speech divorced from religious impiety— if it "manifestly" tended "to the corruption of the morals of youth."[38] In the interim, Massachusetts used the "common law" of obscenity, borrowed from England: in 1821, it charged a publisher with contriving "to debauch and corrupt" the morals of youth as well as "other good citizens," and to "create in their minds inordinate and lustful desires," by "wickedly, maliciously and scandalously" publishing a "lewd, wicked, scandalous, infamous and obscene" book. The object of the prosecutors' ire was *Fanny Hill*.[39]

Pennsylvania was also a trendsetter. As early as 1815, it prosecuted the exhibition of a painting from the Naples Museum that was said to depict "a man in an obscene, impudent and indecent posture with a woman, to the manifest corruption and subversion of youth, and other citizens of this commonwealth." The defendant, relying on the British distinction between ecclesiastical and secular courts, argued that the alleged offense was not a punishable crime; but the presiding judge insisted that "actions of *public indecency* were always indictable [in England], as tending to corrupt the public morals."[40]

These early state cases suggested that "obscene" expression could be censored to protect the morals of youth and other impressionable folk, but prosecutions were rare.[41] It was not until 1842 that Congress enacted the first federal ban, authorizing the U.S. Customs Service to confiscate "obscene or immoral" pictures or prints and bring judicial proceedings for their destruction.[42] Legal historians James Paul and Murray Schwartz comment on the swiftness and lack of debate that marked this radical legal change. "In hindsight it was a novel measure, a type of censorship statute and the first of its kind in this country. Yet it slipped into the law unnoticed." Its significance "as a technique to control reading and press freedom was not appreciated."[43]

This first federal sex-censorship law reflected a confluence of new social pressures. Industrialization and urbanization in Europe and the United States were breaking down traditional demographic patterns and making urban poverty, crowding, prostitution, drinking, gambling, and other "vices" increasingly visible. The 18th century's relatively relaxed sexual standards, partly a reaction against Puritanism, gave way to new evangelical strands of Christianity, which in turn spawned moral-purity crusades. YMCAs, and "sex hygiene" campaigns that encouraged celibacy by detailing the ravages of venereal disease. Immigration to the United States heightened nativist fears that foreigners with "low morals" would not only gain political power but "outbreed" Americans whose ancestors had arrived a few generations (or, in some cases, centuries) before. The spread of literacy and consequent availability of sex education tracts and cheap novels to workers and adolescents (including females) only heightened middle- and upper-class anxieties. "Licentious" books and prints were visible and symbolically important targets.[44]

Children and adolescents were not the only objects of the purity crusaders, but they were increasingly important ones. The culture's growing attention to children's separate status culminated in Romantic- and Victorian-era celebrations of youthful sexual innocence. The loosening of patriarchy meanwhile led to increased reliance on law to police youthful morality. The social-purity movement, with support from government and professional groups, now justified censorship by denying the existence of, or else maintaining the need to repress, the sexual interests of youth. Institutionalization and medicalization of public health, welfare, and education created new opportunities for control. By the close of the century, the new "science" of psychology was turning adolescence into a conceptually separate and vulnerable stage of life, worthy of scholarly study as well as institutional concern. Responding to pressures for purity and campaigns against prostitution, particularly among working-class girls with limited economic alternatives, legislators increased statutory ages of sexual consent— from medians of 10 or 12 to 14, 16, 18, or (in the case of U.S. federal territories) 21.[45] Historian Alison Parker summarizes: by the late 19th century, "focus on the morality of youth was central to the public's support of all censorship campaigns."[46]

A paradoxical aspect of the new repression, as Michel Foucault notes, was the increasing *centrality* of sex—especially of youthful interest in sex—as a public concern. Even "the refusal to talk about it," as one Foucaultian explains, "marks it as the secret and puts it at the heart of discourse."[47] It was thus Victorian prudery that fed pornography, which "flourished as never before" alongside the new obscenity bans.[48] At the economic level, there was a brutal irony in the simultaneous myth of childhood innocence and the exploitation of actual children in the Industrial Revolution's mines and factories.[49] By the late 19th century, adolescents in Massachusetts were on average providing one-third of their family's income; in the United States overall, only about 7 percent were in high school, with most of the remainder presumably at work,[50] but social purists were busy trying to shield them from corrupting literature.

In 1865, Congress expanded the federal obscenity ban from controls on importation to restrictions on domestic use of the mails. Salacious literature was being sent to Union soldiers, and the Postmaster General had been confiscating these packages without statutory authority. The 1865 law was largely intended to legitimize the seizures. Some congressmen did raise questions about both the invasions of privacy and the unrestrained censorship likely to result from a legislative grant to administrative officials of broad, discretionary authority to seize art and literature of which they disapproved.[51] But this first obscenity mail ban passed without significant controversy. It provided that no "obscene, lewd, or lascivious book, pamphlet, picture, print, or other publication of vulgar and indecent character shall be admitted into the mails,"[52] on pain of criminal penalties, and became the basis for a broad-ranging bureaucratic censorship of the mails that went unchallenged for most of the next century.

Like the United States, Britain passed its first obscenity statute in the mid-19th century. (The earlier prosecutions had been under the common law of obscene libel.) The Obscene Publications Act of 1857 was the handiwork of Lord Chief Justice John Campbell, who had started the legislative ball rolling by asking his fellow aristocrats in the House of Lords whether something should not be done about the free circulation of "a poison more deadly than prussic acid, strychnine or arsenic—the sale of obscene publications and indecent books," which were now so modestly priced that they were "sold to any person who asked for them."[53] Campbell's brethren were not swept away by his charged rhetoric; indeed, they put up a much greater struggle than Congress did in 1865, or would do in 1873 when it expanded the U.S. government's censorship powers. Lord Brougham, for example, with more than a hint of irony, said "he was sure that no one was more competent to judge of the extent of the evil" of pornography than "the noble and learned" Lord Campbell, but asked "how did he propose to define what was an *obscene publication*?" Brougham reminded his "noble and learned Friend, that, in the works of some of their most eminent poets there were some objectionable passages."[54] Lord Lyndhurst chimed in with two examples from visual art: Correggio's "Jupiter and Antiope," showing "a woman stark naked, lying down, and a satyr standing by her with an expression on his face which shows most distinctly what his feelings are": and "Danaë" showing "a naked woman lifting her eyes to heaven, but standing in a very strange attitude, the shower of gold descending upon her, a little Cupid peeping over her shoulder pointing with his dart, and other circumstances which I will not describe." Lyndhurst mentioned also the bawdy plays of the English Restoration: there was "not a page in any one of them," he said, "which might not be seized under this Bill." One of Congreve's characters is "Lady Wishfor't," he said, and Dryden "is as bad as any of them," having translated Ovid's *The Art of Love*.[55]

Campbell replied that his proposed law was "intended to apply exclusively to works written with the single purpose of corrupting the morals of youth, and of a nature calculated to shock the common feelings of decency in any well-regulated mind."[56] With support from the clergy and the Society for the Suppression of Vice, he continued to insist that the young must be shielded from the licentious and "abominable" works available at any railway station.[57] Lord Campbell's Act passed despite the protest, giving police (with a warrant) the power to seize books or pictures they believed to be obscene and to destroy them unless the owner appeared before two justices and disproved the government's accusation. Eleven years later, in the landmark case of *Regina v. Hicklin,* the new law received an expansive, youth-oriented judicial interpretation that would dominate English and American law for most of the next century.

The literature at issue in *Hicklin* was an anticlerical pamphlet, *The Confessional Unmasked,* distributed by the Protestant Electoral Union and designed to oppose the election of Catholics to Parliament by "showing the depravity of the Romish priesthood, the iniquity of the Confessional, and the questions put to females in confession."[58] One Henry Scott, from whom a collection of the pamphlets had been seized, claimed the work was not obscene because it was written and distributed for legitimate political purposes. A lower court agreed, and quashed the order of seizure (Benjamin Hicklin was one of the judges). But Chief Justice Alexander Cockburn, writing for the Court of Queen's Bench on appeal, held that legitimate intentions were no excuse for publishing or disseminating obscenity. The standard for judging the work, said Cockburn, was whether the tendency of the matter charged as obscenity is to deprave and corrupt those whose minds are open to such immoral influences and into whose hands a publication of this sort may fall.[59]

How was one to identify those whose minds might be "depraved and corrupted" by "immoral influences"? As Chief Justice Alexander Cockburn explained, a medical treatise "with illustrations necessary for the information of those for whose education or information the work is intended, may, in a certain sense, be obscene, and yet not the subject for indictment; but it can never be that these prints may be exhibited for any one, boys and girls, to see as they pass." *The Confessional Unmasked,* like this hypothetical medical text, was obscene because it "would suggest to the minds of the young of either sex, and even to persons of more advanced years, thoughts of a most impure and libidinous character."[60] The purpose of obscenity law was thus to prevent immoral literature from falling into the wrong hands, whether they be those of servants, the mentally deficient, women, or minors. That women and mental defectives were included among the classes to be "protected" was consistent with the ideology of an era when, as Peter Gay recounts, women were also classed with "criminals, idiots, and minors" for purposes of property and inheritance law.[61] By the early 20th century, as egalitarian sentiments began to replace sexual and class hierarchies, shielding the young became ever more pivotal as the justification for obscenity laws.

Contrary to Lord Campbell's assurances, the Obscene Publications Act was soon used to suppress not merely pornography or even racy anticlerical pamphlets but also works of high literary art. The prosecution and imprisonment of the publisher Henry Vizetelly in 1888 for making the works of Zola, Flaubert, Daudet, and Maupassant available to the British public was one dramatic early consequence of the *Hicklin* test, Vizetelly, elderly and ailing, was jailed for three months in 1889 and died five years later "a ruined man."[62] The first volume in Havelock Ellis's massive *Studies in the Psychology of Sex* was suppressed in 1898; the author, incensed, refused to publish the other volumes in England until the 1930s.[63] The condemnation of Ellis's *Studies,* says sociologist Bill Thompson, "put British sexology into hibernation for over 60 years."[64] England exported its Victorian culture, including its obscenity standard, and censorship tests almost identical to *Hicklin* soon appeared in India, Australia, and of course the United States. . . .

FREUD, THE FIRST AMENDMENT, AND
A FIRST ROUND WITH ULYSSES

The same year judge Learned Hand wrote in *United States v. Kennerley* that "the understanding and morality of the present time" rejected Victorian-era sexual repression, Dr. Sigmund Freud published an article describing the influence of his psychoanalytic theories of dream interpretation, childhood sexuality, and neurosis on virtually every facet of modern culture. Eight years earlier, Freud's soon to be famous *Three Essays on the Theory of Sexuality* had detailed "the universality and normality of infantile and childhood sexuality." Another essay, "The Sexual Enlightenment of Children," had labeled society's usual reasons for keeping youngsters sexually ignorant "absurd."[65] Freud's "unblinking candor about sex"[66] distinguished him from earlier critics of Victorianism, and his historic 1909 lectures at Clark University in Massachusetts brought the issue squarely into American cultural life.

No intellectual revolution arrives without antecedents, of course, and despite its well-earned reputation for prudery, the late 19th century was obsessed with the question of sex. Its elaborate mechanisms of repression and campaigns for social purity were ways of talking and writing incessantly about the subject Michel Foucault explains: "From the bad habits of children to the phthises of adults, the apoplexies of old people, nervous maladies, and the degenerations of the race, the medicine of that era wove an entire network of sexual causality to explain them."[67] The plentiful anti-vice tracts and guides to "sex hygiene," as other historians have observed, had "all the trappings of soft-core pornography and undoubtedly titillated quite a number of readers."[68]

Havelock Ellis was as sexually explicit as Freud, but more empirically grounded and tolerant of sexual variety. Ellis's six-volume *Studies in the Psychology of Sex*, published in the early decades of the 20th century, challenged the orthodoxy of such Victorian pundits as Lord William Acton, who denied the existence of female sexual response (except among immoral women) and urged stern repression of youthful masturbation. Ellis surveyed the universality of "auto-eroticism" among youth, and although not entirely discounting the possibility of "harmful consequences," noted its "primarily sedative effect."[69] Although Ellis was initially condemned as a pornographer, his fact-based approach eventually came to dominate 20th-century thinking about sex.[70]

Freud and Ellis created a new openness in public discourse that the "party of reticence" noted with ambivalence, if not trepidation. In 1914, the vice president of the U.S. Social Hygiene Association wrote ominously to *The Nation*: "The silence is now broken and whatever may be the wisdom or folly of this change of attitude, it is a fact, and it constitutes a social emergency."[71] Adding to the ferment were anthropologists like Bromislaw Malinowski, who reported on societies where childhood and adolescent sexuality were encouraged and adults shared sexual talk with the young.[72] . . .

G. Stanley Hall inspired what historian Joseph Kett calls a "massive reclassification of young people as adolescents and the creation of institutions to segregate them from casual contacts with adults." The newly created public high school, for example, with its busy extracurricular schedule, was a means of channeling teenagers into approved activities and away from "sleazy dance halls in the neighborhood." Compared with college administrators of the 1890s, "who did not object to occasional skylarking by the undergraduates, high school officials in the early 1900s were virtually obsessed with instilling conformity and obedience in students."[73] Pundits like Hall thus generated not so much youthful liberation from Victorian repression as newer, more institutionalized styles of control. Historian Constance Nathanson adds that by creating an ideology of adolescent irresponsibility, psychologists paved the way for reform schools and homes for unwed mothers, repressive institutions whose purposes were to shame and control young women if their behavior departed from "age- and gender-based norms of sexual propriety."[74] . . .

MINORS AND OBSCENITY IN THE '30S AND '40S

By the 1930s, the effects of Freudianism, feminism, artistic innovation, and post–World War I cultural upheavals could be perceived in the courts. The first jurisprudential dent in the *Hicklin* harm-to-minors standard came with a modest sex education pamphlet by Mary Ware Dennett, a birth control and women's suffrage leader. Dennett had written *The Sex Side of Life* in 1915 because her 11- and 14-year-old sons were asking questions. She found the available sex education literature "very misleading and harmful"; many points were avoided, "partly from embarrassment, but more, apparently, because those who have undertaken to instruct the children are not really clear in their own minds as to the proper status" of sex education.[75] *The Sex Side of Life* was hardly a raunchy thriller, as evidenced by its popularity among YMCAs and other social service organizations. But in 1929 John Suinuer arranged a mail-order decoy. Dennell responded and after fourteen years of relatively unmolested existence, *The Sex Side of Life* became a target of the Comstock Act.

In addition to its relative explicitness, *The Sex Side of Life* may have offended Post Office authorities because of what today would be called its sex-positive approach. Dennett waxed lyrical about "the climax of sex emotion" as "an unsurpassed joy, something which rightly belongs to every normal human being."[76] She also tried to allay fears about masturbation: there is "no occasion for worry unless the habit is carried to excess." (Here, she repeated the still-common myth that "the sex secretions are specially needed within your body, and if you use them wastefully before you are grown, you are depriving your body of what it needs.")[77] Her advice may not have been as accepting of self-pleasure as William Butler Yeats's contemporaneous poetic reference to "boys and girls, pale from the imagined love of solitary beds,"[78] but it was certainly an advance from Victorian hysteria. Given that *The Sex Side of Life* was written for minors, the prosecution of Dennett directly posed the question whether they are harmed by straightforward, guilt-free sexual information.

Dennett argued that her benevolent educational motive in writing *The Sex Side of Life* demonstrated its lack of capacity to deprave and corrupt. The trial judge was not convinced; he instructed the jury to apply the *Hicklin* test (that is, to decide whether the pamphlet would harm the most vulnerable readers). Dennett was duly convicted; but in 1930 the Second Circuit Court of Appeals reversed in an opinion by Augustus Hand, Learned's cousin (Learned by this time was also on the federal appeals court). The appellate ruling did not disagree that, under the Comstock law, it was the content of a work and not its author's motive that counted; but A. Hand rejected the notion that every publication that "*might* stimulate sex impulses" was therefore obscene. If that were true, he said, then "much chaste poetry and fiction, as well as many useful medical works" would be unlawful. As for minors, Hand said he "assumed that any article dealing with the sex side of life and explaining the functions of the sex organs is capable in some circumstances of arousing lust. The sex impulses are present in every one . . . and without doubt cause much of the weal and woe of human kind."

> But it can hardly be said that, because of the risk of arousing sex impulses, there should be no instruction of the young in sex matters, and that the risk of imparting

instruction outweighs the disadvantages of leaving them to grope about in mystery and morbid curiosity and of requiring them to secure such information, as they may be able to obtain, from ill-informed and often foul-mouthed companions, rather than from intelligent and high-minded sources.[79]

Hand's *Dennett* decision thus did not reject *Hicklin*, but narrowed it. His reasoning rested on a stylistic distinction: explicit speech even to minors is acceptable, as long as it is not conveyed in "clearly indecent" terms.[80] This was an advance from the rigors of *Hicklin*, in that it recognized a legitimate social interest in satisfying the "sexual curiosity of youth," but it left open the large question of when language becomes "clearly indecent," and who is to decide. . . .

The fate of *Hicklin* in the U.S. courts now converged with the literary fortunes of the century's most scandalous novel. Parts of *Ulysses* had already been adjudicated obscene under New York law in the 1920 *Little Review* case. Although the complete novel was published by Shakespeare & Company in France in 1922, and seven book-length studies of its literary intricacies had also appeared by the early 1930s, it was still not available in the United States or England except clandestinely.[81] Four hundred copies had been burned by U.S. Customs in 1922; the British government destroyed five hundred the following year, while its Director of Public Prosecutions, Sir Archibald Bodkin, tried to prevent F. R. Leavis, then a young Cambridge don, from teaching the novel to "boy and girl undergraduates."[82] (Bodkin also distinguished himself by calling Freud's work "filth and threatening its publishers with prosecution unless they restricted its circulation to those doctors and professors who were prepared to give their names and addresses."[83])

In 1933, Bennett Cerf of Random House, having secured a contract with Joyce for a U.S. edition of *Ulysses,* attempted to bring a copy into the country. The Customs Bureau seized the book and filed a forfeiture application in federal court, Judge John Woolsey, who had previously relied on the *Dennett* precedent to rule an English sex education book—Dr. Marie Stopes's *Married Love*—not obscene or "immoral,"[84] was assigned the *Ulysses* case.

Woolsey studied the massive novel over many weeks. . . . Because Woolsey found nowhere in *Ulysses* "the leer of the sensualist," he concluded that the book did not tend to "stir the sex impulses or to lead to sexually impure and lustful thoughts," and was thus not obscene within the meaning of recent decisions like *Dennett*. . . .

Woolsey wound up by opining that while the effect of *Ulysses* was "undoubtedly . . . somewhat emetic, nowhere does it tend to be aphrodisiac."[85]

Judge Woolsey's rightly famous *Ulysses* opinion was more literary review than legal analysis, but the Second Circuit remedied the oversight in its 1934 decision affirming that the bulky tome was not obscene. Hand's opinion for himself and cousin Learned now repudiated the *Hicklin* harm-to-minors test and in its place enunciated an obscenity standard that considered the "dominant effect" of a work, "taken as a whole," on the average person, rather than the possibly libidinous impact of selected passages on the most vulnerable child. . . .

Like Woolsey, Hand did not mention youthful readers; the obscenity standard was now keyed to the libidinous inclinations of average adults. And that standard, in turn, was applied in a way that sanitized *Ulysses,* denuding the novel of its sexual import in the interest of avoiding the underlying conflict between literary freedom and legally enforced disapproval of lascivious thoughts. Judge Martin Manton, in dissent, at least did not purify Joyce's at once heroic and scabrous work; he would have censored *Ulysses* on the basis of the presumed governmental power to protect those most vulnerable to lewd ideas.[86]

The new *Ulysses* obscenity test, turning not on "the young and immature" but on the average adult, was adopted by many but far from all U.S. judges. Massachusetts, most notably, clung to *Hicklin* through the 1940s and '50s, condemning Erskine Caldwell's *God's Little Acre* (the high court rejected evidence of literary merit as irrelevant) and Lillian Smith's *Strange Fruit*, a nonexplicit novel about an interracial love affair (ruled obscene because likely to corrupt "the morals of youth").[87] Federal courts in Ohio also stuck with *Hicklin*: in one case, although the judge did order police to stop a campaign of threats against booksellers, he noted the importance of preventing "the distribution of all forms of lewd and indecent literature, with its demoralizing effect upon the young."[88] Even using the *Ulysses* "taken as a whole" standard, a New York judge in 1946 found the memoir *Call House Madam* obscene because, "in the hands of the adolescent and easily suggestible of both sexes," it "may do considerable harm."[89] The Post Office retained on its unmailable list works by Margaret Mead, Simone de Beauvoir, and that fabulist who caused so much difficulty in the first place, Sigmund Freud.[90]

Even in the Second Circuit, as Learned Hand said in a 1936 case, there might be circumstances where obscenity should be judged by the capacity to deprave adolescents. The case involved two pseudo-anthropological works, *Secret Museum of Anthropology* and *Crowdys of Sex,* and a novel, *Black Lust*; the buyer of one of the books may have been a youth. In future cases, Hand said, the court might consider "the possible injury to such a youthful reader."[91] Hand did not specify the nature of the "possible injury," but presumably it was the same inspiration to bad behavior or libidinous thoughts that had worried courts and legislators since Anthony Comstock's day.

It was probably inevitable that as the new academic fields of psychology and sociology gained respectability, scholars would try to quantify these presumably bad effects. Thus, in the 1930s, the Motion Picture Research Council, with a grant from the Payne Foundation, sponsored a series of studies of cinema's impact on impressionable youth. Although the "most conclusive" of the Payne studies "showed that the movies did not have any significant effect in producing delinquency," it also found that "boys and young men, when suitably predisposed, sometimes have used gangster films to stimulate susceptible ones toward crime," or "have idealized themselves imaginatively" to engage in the same "romantic activities as gangster screen heroes."[92] Another study in the Payne series argued that although only 11 percent of inmates interviewed at a juvenile correction facility felt movies had "some definite influence on their criminal careers," there was a wide range of indirect harms, including demonstration of crime methods, glamorization of "the fast life," and "emotional possession of a sexual character."[93] The technology may have changed— cinema rather than 19th-century dime novels or bodice rippers—but the perceived danger to youth was much the same. . . .

By the late 1940s, the suppression of a word by as celebrated a literary figure as Wilson caused embarrassment among the middlebrow as well as the intellectual elite. It fell to a judge in the Second Circuit to articulate that concern. . . . The case involved Samuel Roth, who had already been sued for publishing pirated sections of *Ulysses back* in 1927. Now, in *Roth v. Goldman*, he was challenging the Post Office's seizure of several of his publications without any prior determination that they were obscene.[94]

The Second Circuit upheld the confiscations, primarily on grounds of misleading advertising. But the judges did tackle the obscenity question for one book *Waggish Tales from the Czechs* which they said was "obscene or offensive enough by any refined standards." Then they muddied the issue by opining that in any event the judgment of the Post Office should not be second-guessed.[95] Judge Frank was horrified by this judicial deference to bureaucrats untrained in the niceties of First Amendment rights.

Frank reviewed the literary censorship problem. "In the light of the First Amendment," he said, "it is not, I think, frivolous to ask a question about the constitutional power of Congress to authorize an official to bar from the mails, and probably thus largely to suppress, any book or writing he finds obscene." He questioned obscenity law's traditional justification, the suppression of sexual excitement:

> I think that no sane man thinks socially dangerous the arousing of normal sexual
> desires. Consequently, if reading obscene books has merely that consequence,
> Congress, it would seem, can constitutionally no more suppress such books than
> it can prevent the mailing of many other objects, such as perfumes, for example,
> which notoriously produce that result.

No proof existed that reading arousing books actually "conduces to socially harmful sexual conduct," Frank added; indeed, the recently published report by Alfred Kinsey and his colleagues, *Sexual Behavior in the American Male,* suggested the opposite.[96] . . .

Dismissing . . . obscenity charges, [Philadelphia] Judge [Curtis] Bok produced a detailed, scholarly history of censorship from ancient times. His critique of *Hicklin* was unrestrained: "strictly applied," he said, the test "renders any book unsafe, since a moron could pervert to some sexual fantasy to which his mind is open the listings in a seed catalogue." Bok argued that the First Amendment test of "clear and present" danger ought to apply here just as in other contents where speech is censored. As for minors, including his own "young daughter," he opined that "by the time she is old enough to wish to read" these books, "she will have learned the biologic facts of life and the words that go with them"; there is "something seriously wrong at home if those facts have not been met and faced and sorted by then."[97]

Judge Bok's proposal that government should have to show a clear and present danger in order to justify literary censorship never attracted significant support from scholars or other judges, but he had at least raised the issue of precisely what harm sexually explicit speech causes to anyone, including the young. A New Jersey court added to the chorus of questioners four years later, in a decision enjoining a state prosecutor from suppressing "objectionable" publications by circulating a list compiled by a local "citizens committee," then sending police to visit stores and newsstands to check compliance. After reviewing the history of harm-to-minors censorship, the state judge asked "just what the effect of a book on a young person may be," and responded by citing surveys of youngsters who rarely mentioned "dirty books" among their sources of sex information. He concluded: "The influences which operate on a child in the swift movement of our society are as infinite as they are varied. One may not single out the printed page as the one source of moral infection."[98]

JUVENILE DELINQUENCY, SOCIAL SCIENCE, COMIC BOOKS, AND PROFESSOR KINSEY

The time was approaching when the Supreme Court could no longer avoid the urgent questions raised by obscenity law. Jerome Frank and Curtis Bok had challenged the Court to bring some coherence, and constitutional protection, to sexual speech. Their protests had inspired debate among practitioners and scholars.[99] What, if any, definition of obscenity should apply? Should the standard be different for minors and adults? More fundamentally, how did obscenity law square with the constitutional guarantee of free speech and access to ideas?

Early 1950s America was not the most hospitable environment for asking such questions. Arguments against censorship of any sort had rough sledding in a political atmosphere dominated by investigations of seditious speech, loyalty tests for employment, and blacklists of suspected Communists attacked sympathizers.[100] Sexual unorthodoxy was associated with left-wing politics: homosexuals particularly were attacked as a "corrosive influence" on fellow employees and corrupters of "young and impressionable people."[101] At Senate hearings in 1950, Undersecretary of State John Peurifoy testified that most of the ninety-one employees recently fired by the department for "moral turpitude" were homosexuals; and Republicans eager to brand the Truman administration as subversive "pounced upon Peurifoy's remarks," warning that "sexual perverts," who were "perhaps as dangerous as actual communists," had "infiltrated our government."[102]

Artists who painted nudes or—worse—abstractions that might be filled with "mysterious but surely dirty symbols were also suspect."[103] The radical psychoanalyst Wilhelm Reich, theorist of the origins of authoritarianism in sexual repression, was pursued by the Food and Drug Administration throughout the 1950s; in 1957, six tons of his writings including *The Mass Psychology of Fascism* were burned by court order, and he died in prison while serving a sentence for contempt of court.[104] Congressional hearings in 1955 and again in 1959 built an ideological connection between left-wing politics and exposure of minors to "obscene materials." One legislative report concluded that the "loose portrayal of sex" in literature "serves to weaken the moral fiber of the future leaders of our country."[105]

It was in this unpromising atmosphere that Professor Alfred Kinsey's Institute for Sex Research at Indiana University published *Sexual Behavior in the American Male* (1948), followed by *Sexual Behavior in the American Female* (1953). These hefty tomes applied the painstaking classification techniques of Kinsey's academic specialty, zoological taxonomy, to human sexual behavior. Based on sexual history interviews with about 12,000 volunteers, Kinsey's research revealed, among other things, that oral sex and other perceived deviations from conventional missionary-position heterosexuality were widespread in the United States; that masturbation was the most frequent and, in orgasmic terms, efficient of sexual activities; that the experience of premarital, including adolescent, sexual activity was common and, particularly among females, correlated with more satisfying sex during marriage; and perhaps most disturbing given the prevailing homophobia, that 37 percent of American males had had at least one homosexual experience leading to orgasm.[106] Even accepting the probable overrepresentation of homosexuals and men in prison (Kinsey interviewed where he could, and random sampling was not possible), these figures were striking. Thanks in part to Kinsey's public relation skills, his messianic sense of purpose, and his support from the Rockefeller Foundation–funded National Research Council, his graph and statistic-laden reports were extensively publicized, popularized, and debated. *Sexual Behavior in the American Male* sold over 200,000 copies in the first two months of 1948.[107]

Of course, many reviews and comments resorted to euphemisms, and others simply refused to publicize Kinsey's findings lest they contribute to the destruction of sexual morality or insult "American womanhood."[108] But Kinsey's arguments against the soul- and body-distorting harms of sexual repression, and in favor of sexual diversity and the needs of youth, carried legitimacy because of his scientific approach and the imprimatur of the National Research Council. Historian Paul Robinson, hardly an uncritical fan, calls Kinsey's advocacy of the sexual rights of youngsters a major contribution to less guilt-ridden views about sex.[109]

The backlash to Kinsey was intense. In a widely circulated article in *Christianity and Crisis,* Union Theological Seminary's Reinhold Niebuhr criticized the Indiana professor's "absurd hedonism" and "moral anarchism." Critic Lionel Trilling faulted Kinsey for his sometimes extreme subjectivity and failure to make "any connection between the sexual life and the psychic structure." Indianapolis's Catholic bishop, Paul Schulte, complained of the "great harm" caused by making information in the reports available to "the young, the unlearned, the mentally deficient." One letter writer accused Kinsey of "aiding the Communist's aim to weaken and destroy the youth of your country," views echoed by J. Edgar Hoover, who wrote in a 1948 *Reader's Digest* symposium that Kinsey's work was a threat to "our civilization" and "our way of life," and ordered the FBI to compile a dossier on the Institute for Sex Research and its founder.[110] (The controversy over Kinsey's accuracy, and his own sexual proclivities, continues to this day.[111])

Politicians who saw opportunities to link sex and Communism joined the fray. Shortly after *Sexual Behavior in the American Female* appeared, a congressional committee chaired by B. Carroll Reece of Tennessee began to investigate the funding of "Communists and Socialists" by tax-exempt foundations.[112] Although the Reece Committee's report blasting Kinsey's research and by inference the Rockefeller Foundation did not have a major impact, the investigation had its effect in helping persuade the foundation's new president, Dean Rusk, to cancel further funding.[113] But the revolution wrought by Kinsey in opening up discourse about sex turned out to be more lasting than either the antisubversion purges of the 1950s or the equation of Communism and sexual unorthodoxy. . . .

In the 1950s, New York psychiatrist Fredric Wertham invoked science to bolster his campaign against comic books. Wertham's methods—asking young offenders about their reading habits without testing his hypothesis through comparison with a control group—were flatly unreliable; had he bothered to ask, he would have found that many nondelinquents also read comics. But as one student of the era writes, Wertham achieved credibility because he was a professional and "couched his findings in scientific terms."[114] His luridly illustrated 1953 book, *Seduction of the Innocent,* was widely praised despite its overwrought style and its attribution of juvenile ills, from nightmares to murder, to the influence of crime and adventure comics.[115]

Wertham claimed in *Seduction* that his research showed "a significant correlation between crime-comics reading and the more serious forms of juvenile delinquency." In one case of arson, a judge found that the young perpetrators "favored a particular comic book which has on its cover a burning human being." Western, sci-fi, jungle, and superhero adventures were all corrupting—*Batman* especially so because of the "subtle atmosphere of homoeroticism which pervades the adventures of the mature 'Batman' and his young friend 'Robin.' "[116] Wertham had no patience with defenders of comics who called them "the modern version of fairy tales," riposting that there are no "heroin addicts in Grimm, marihuana smokers in Andersen, or dope peddlers in Mother Goose." He attacked those who posited multiple causes for criminal behavior—"unconscious factors, infantile experiences," and so forth—these were "pseudoerudite and utterly false."[117]

Wertham's scientific bona fides did not escape criticism. Education professor Frederic Thrasher said Wertham's studies lacked "the most essential element of scientific validity, a control group," and illustrated a dangerous habit of projecting our social frustrations upon some specific trait of our culture, which becomes a sort of 'whipping boy' . . . or scapegoat for parental and community failures to educated and socialize children.[118] A *New Republic* reviewer likened Wertham to other psychiatrists who "have deluded themselves" with fallacies about the impact of fiction; while the author of a child-rearing advice book argued that violent media were "not the *cause* of aggression in our youngsters. The aggression, as we know by now, is already there," and the child "gets a vicarious thrill" from watching fantasy characters act it out.[119]

This author reflected the more permissive attitudes heralded by a popularized Freudianism and articulated most prominently in the 1950s by Dr. Benjamin Spock. The supposedly repressed 1950s also saw new interest in anthropologist Margaret Mead's descriptions of cultures where "casual nudity, social masturbation, and sex play (both heterosexual and homosexual)" were common.[120] But neither the popularity of Mead and Spock not measured critiques of Wertham had significant impact on the politics of child protection. By 1955, two states had legislated against comic books, while Los Angeles County passed an ordinance criminalizing the sale to anyone under 18 of comics depicting the commission of a crime. (The state high court struck it down.)[121] Congress meanwhile held hearings on the media's effects on juvenile behavior three times between 1950 and 1954; in the last of these, Senator Estes Kefauver displayed a cover from EC Comics' *Crime SuspenStories* depicting a man holding a bloody ax and a severed head while other popular title such as *Tales from the Crypt* and *Vault of Horror* were excoriated, and Wertham testified against *Superman* because it created in children "phantasies of sadistic joy in seeing other people punished . . . while you yourself remain immune."[122]

Given the luridness of the hearings, the Senate Judiciary Committee's 1955 report, *Comic Books and Juvenile Delinquency*, was comparatively measured. By this point, though, the industry had responded to the brouhaha by creating two good-conduct codes, one in 1948 (which the Senate committee said was ineffective) and a second in 1954—an extensive list of dos and don'ts complete with a Comics Code Authority that would review stories, art, and advertising to assure compliance with such values as "honorable behavior" and "respect for parents." Participating publishers displayed a Code seal of approval, and distributors refused to handle comic books without the seal. In short order, twenty-four of the twenty-nine publishers of crime and violence comics had gone out of business.[123] The Senate report applauded this industry self-censorship, even while expressing skepticism about Wertham's more extreme statements. As the report noted, some experts believed that reading about zombies, vampires, and other staples of comic book literature had a cathartic effect.[124]

The comic book industry had modeled its self-censorship on the by then entrenched Hollywood Production Code, or Hays Code, established in the early days of talkies in an unsuccessful attempt to forestall governmental licensing for movies. Until the 1960s, a multitude of city and state licensing boards practiced film censorship alongside the industry-imposed strictures of the Hays Code. These boards granted or denied permission for film exhibition based on varying local standards—pictures with racial themes, for example, often being denied permits in southern states—but the suppression of sexual subjects was almost universal. In New York, licensing was handled by the education department, which, as one critic commented, tended to fix its standards "at the intellectual level of school children."[125]

It was shortly before the comic book campaign, in 1948, that the Supreme Court first addressed the harm-to-minors issue. New York courts had found the magazine *Headquarters Detective—True Cases from the Police Blotter* to violate a state law banning publications "principally made up of" criminal news or police reports or "pictures or stories of deeds of bloodshed, just or crime." (The ban had originally been aimed at minors but was "later broadened to include all the population.") In *Winters v. New York*, the Supreme Court invalidated the law because terms like "bloodshed" and "lust" were too vague to put publishers on notice of what was illegal: but it acknowledged "the importance of the exercise of a state's police power to minimize all incentives to crime, particularly in the field of sanguinary or salacious publications with their stimulation of juvenile delinquency."[126] The justices thus seemed to assume that youngsters would imitate the "sanguinary and salacious" deeds about which they read—an assumption on which Justice Felix Frankfurter focused in his *Winters* dissent. Frankfurter did not claim there was any proof that certain kinds of literature incited youthful crime, but the argued that psychological judgments should be left to legislatures and not second-guessed by courts. New York's lawmakers had a right to believe that crime publications "cater to morbid and immature minds," with the consequence that "deeply embedded, unconscious impulses may be discharged into destructive and often fatal action," especially given "the destructive and adventurous potentialities of boys and adolescents."[127]

The *Winters* case is best known for rejecting the argument that a publication's trashy style robs it of First Amendment protection. As Justice Stanley Reed wrote in the majority opinion: "We do not accede to appellee's suggestion that the constitutional protection for a free press applies only to the exposition of ideas. The line between the informing and the entertaining is too elusive for the protection of that basic right."[128]

INTELLECTUAL RUMBLINGS

Despite *Winters's* invalidation of New York's ban on "bloodshed, lust or crime" stories, by the mid-1950s the Supreme Court still had not addressed the constitutional implications of obscenity law. A 1942 decision had suggested in passing that the "lewd and obscene," along with "the profane" and "the libelous," are "no essential part of any exposition of ideas and are of such slight social value as a step to truth that any benefit that may be derived from them is clearly outweighed by the social interest in order and morality."[129] This "step to truth" limitation on the First Amendment had originated not with the Supreme Court but with a Harvard professor. Zechariah Chafee, Jr., who wrote in a 1941 book that "profanity and indecent talk and pictures, which do not form an essential part of any exposition of ideas, have a very slight social value as a step toward truth, which is clearly outweighed by the social interests in order, morality, the training of the young, and the peace of mind of those who hear and see."[130] Some twenty years before, Chafee's writings had persuaded Justice Oliver Wendell Holmes, Jr., that proof of clear and present danger should be required before government can ban political protest,[131] but Chafee's solicitude for speech did not extend to "indecent talk and pictures." The Supreme Court borrowed from Chafee, and the "exposition of ideas" limitation became an established tenet of constitutional law . . .

In the mid-1950s, legal scholars were busy trying to figure out, in the words of one article, "a rational resolution" to the obscenity problem. It fell to judge Jerome Frank to propose such a "rational resolution" in 1956.

. . . The occasion was *United States v. Roth*, another case involving the indefatigable Samuel Roth, who had now been prosecuted under the Comstock Act for mailing a variety of publications, including *American Aphrodite*, an erotically oriented quarterly with literary pretensions. The issue included the artist Aubrey Beardsley's prose rendition of the myth of Venus and Tannhäuser, complete with a titillating description of the love goddess's performance of oral sex on her pet unicorn.

The Second Circuit affirmed Roth's *American Aphrodite* conviction, Frank concurred in the judgment, as he had in *Roth v. Goldman* seven years before, but his opinion read more like a dissent.

. . . Frank . . . questioned the historical basis for obscenity law. The literature available in the library of "a colonial planter in Virginia or a colonial intellectual in New England" was likely to have included "Tom Jones, Tristram Shandy, Ovid's Art of Love, and Rabelais." In view of the liberality of those times, "it seems doubtful that the constitutional guaranty of free speech and free press could have been intended to allow Congress validly to enact the 'obscenity' act." Indeed, the social attitude "towards writings dealing with sex" that gave rise to obscenity legislation "arose decades later, in the mid-19th century." Courts should adhere to the Framers' 18th-century expectations, not "the later 'Victorian' Code."[132]

Finally, Frank detailed and unusual correspondence with Dr. Marie Jahoda, whose report on psychological assumptions in the censorship debate had been cited by [Judge Charles] Clark in his majority opinion. Frank had asked Jahoda for a summary of the report in order to "avoid any possible bias in my interpretation." She responded that in the "vast research literature on the causes of juvenile delinquency,"

> there is no evidence to justify the assumption that reading about sexual matters or about violence leads to delinquent acts. Experts on juvenile delinquency agree that it has no single cause. Most of them regard early childhood events, which precede the reading age, as a necessary condition for later delinquency.

Jahoda did not discount the possibility of imitation from literature, at least where "childhood experiences and subsequent events" have predisposed youngsters to delinquency; but, she said, it was equally likely that reading "could provide for a substitute outlet of aggression in fantasy, dispensing with the need for criminal action. There is no empirical evidence in either direction."[133]

Frank ended his concurrence in *United States v. Roth* on a less scholarly note. "Youngsters get a vast deal of education in sexual smut from companions of their own age," he opined. "A verbatim report of conversations among young teen-age boys (from average respectable homes) will disclose their amazing proficiency in obscene language."[134] Frank's view would not prevail when *Roth* made its way to the Supreme Court the next year, but the questions he raised about youthful innocence and psychological harm would continue to simmer just beneath the surface of obscenity, harm-to-minors, and "indecency" law.

Discussion Questions

1. How were concerns about indecency in past centuries different than today? Similar to today?
2. In what way was the idea of indecency linked with the "invention" of childhood?
3. How are obscenity laws passed in the nineteenth century different from our conceptualization of obscenity today? Similar to today?
4. How do you think future generations might respond to our definitions of obscenity and indecency today?

Notes

1. Mark Golden, *Children and Childhood in Classical Athens* (Baltimore & London: Johns Hopkins U. Press, 1990), pp. 5, 7; see also James Redfield, "From Sex to Politics: The Rites of Artemis Triklaria and Dionysos Aisymnêtês at Patras," in *Before Sexuality: The Construction of Erotic Experience in the Ancient Greek World* (Davis Halperin *et al.*, eds.) (Princeton, NJ: Princeton U. Press, 1990), pp. 116–28.

2. John Gagnon, *Human Sexualities* (Glenview, IL.: Scott, Foresman, 1977), p. 14; see also Michel Foucault, *The History of Sexuality*, Vol. 2: *The Use of Pleasure* (New York: Random House, 1985); Vol. 3: *The Care of the Self* (New York: Random House, 1986); Nicole Loaux, "Herakles: The Super-Male and the Feminine," in *Before Sexuality, supra* n. 2; François Lissarrague, "The Sexual Life of Satyrs," *id.*, p. 64 ("in Greek

practice, there is always a difference of age between male lover and beloved").

3. See Plato, *Symposium*, in *Five Great Dialogues* (Benjamin Jowett, trans.) (New York: Walter J. Black, 1942); Plato, *The Laws* (Trevor Saunders, trans.) (London: Penguin, 1970), pp. 332–41 (condemning sexual acts for purposes other than procreation, and advocating chaste [i.e., "platonic"] relationships); Warner Fite, *The Platonic Legend* (New York: Scribner's, 1934); Roger Cox, *Shaping Childhood: Themes of Uncertainty in the History of Adult-Child Relationships* (London: Routledge, 1996), pp. 3–4.

4. Plato, *The Republic and Other Works* (Benjamin Jowett, trans.) (New York: Doubleday, 1973), p. 79; see also *The Laws, supra* n. 4, pp. 282–92, 300–4.

5. Fite, *supra* n. 4, p. 152; see also *The Laws, supra* n. 4, p. 91 (nothing that "virtually all states" except Egypt do not censor music, but allow youngsters to be taught *anything* by way of rhythm, tune and words," without considering the effect "as regards virtue and vice"). On Plato's puritanism and distrust for any art "outside the full control of the rational mind," see Iris Murdoch, *The Fire and the Sun: Why Plato Banished the Artists* (Oxford: Clarendon, 1977), pp. 12–13; Karl Popper, *The Open Society and Its Enemies,* Vol. 1: *The Spell of Plato* (Princeton, NJ: Princeton U. Press, 1962).

6. John Sommerville, *The Rise and Fall of Childhood* (Beverly Hills: Sage, 1982), p. 27. Judge Jerome Frank made a similar point when he noted that the correct translation for Plato's "guardians" is "guards," a term that more accurately reflects their totalitarian character. *Roth v. Goldman,* 172 F. 2d 788, 796 & n. 33 (2d Cir. 1949) (Frank, J., concurring), citing Fite, *supra* n. 4, p. 14.

7. Aristotle, *The Poetics, in Aristotle's Theory of Poetry and Fine Art* (S. M. Butcher, trans.) (New York: Dover, 1951), p. 7.

8. See Elizabeth Belfiore, "Aristotle: Survey of Thought," Richard Janko, "Reception of Aristotle in Antiquity," and Leon Golden, "Reception of Aristotle in Modernity," in *Encyclopedia of Aesthetics,* Vol. 1 (Michael Kelly, ed.) (New York: Oxford U. Press, 1998), pp. 98–99, 104–6, 106–8; John Gassner, "Introduction," in *Aristotle's Theory, supra* n. 8.

9. Aristotle, *The Politics* (T. A. Sinclair, trans.; Trevor Saunders, rev.) (London; Penguin, 1962), pp. 446–47. The reference to "scurrilous purposes" is in the reviser's footnotes. Aristotle was apparently thinking of younger children, for he added that censorship is not needed for those who "have reached the age at which they come to recline at banquets with others and share in their drinking; by this time their education will have rendered them completely immune to any harm that might come from such spectacles." *Id.*; see also Gerald Silk, "Censorship and Controversy in the Career of Edward Kienholz," in *Suspended License: Censorship and the Visual Arts* (Elizabeth Childs, ed.) (Seattle: U. of Wash, Press, 1997), p. 283 (noting that age restrictions on viewing "objectionable" works go back to Aristotle's *Politics*).

10. See Elaine Pagels, *Adam, Eve, and the Serpent* (New York: Vintage, 1988), p. xix; Lawrence Stone, *The Family, Sex and Marriage in England, 1500–1800* (one-volume ed.) (Harmondsworth: Penguin, 1977). p. 125.

11. See Foucault, Vol. 2, *supra* n. 3, pp. 63, 125; Richard Lyman, Jr., "Barbarism and Religion: Late Roman and Early Medieval Childhood," in *The History of Childhood, supra* n. 12, pp. 76–87; Stone, *supra* n. 14, pp. 109, 116, 124–25, 145, 254; Sommerville, *supra* n. 7, pp. 52–53; David Archard, *Children: Rights and Childhood* (London: Routledge, 1993), p. 37.

12. Sommerville, *supra* n. 7, pp. 47–49.

13. Gagnon, *supra* n. 3, p. 8.

14. See John D'Emilo & Estelle Freedman, *Intimate Matters: A History of Sexuality in America* (New York: Harper & Row, 1988), p. 17; Joseph Illick, "Child-Rearing in Seventeenth-Century England and America," in *The History of Childhood,* p. 330.

15. Ariès, *supra* n. 23. pp. 103, 109, quoting in part Père de Dainville, *La Naissance de l'humanisme moderne* (Paris: Beauchesne et Ses Fils, 1940), p. 261.

16. *Id.,* pp. 116, 119, 411, 413.

17. Davis, *supra* n. 26.

18. Stone, p. 241. Linda Pollock in turn critiques Stone for overstating the pervasiveness of birchings, whippings, and other forms of brutality visited on children, and for simplistically overgeneralizing about changes in social attitudes toward youth. Pollock, *supra* n. 23; see also pp. 1–25 for Pollock's summary of the widely varying views on the history of childhood.

19. Sommerville, p. 94.

20. De Mause, *supra* n. 12, p. 5; see also Elizabeth Marvick, "Nature Versus Nurture: Patterns and Trends in Seventeenth Century French Child-Rearing," in *The History of Childhood, supra* n. 12.

21. Stone, pp. 115–17, 120–22; see also Sommerville, p. 64.

22. Stone, pp. 84, 241–42, 318, 426. As Stone has written, cultural history is less a linear progression than "an unending dialectic of competing interests and ideas." *Id.,* p. 435.

23. Archard, *supra* n. 15, pp. 15–19, 26; see also Henry Jenkins, "Introduction," in *The Children's Culture Reader* (Henry Jenkins, ed.) (New York: NYU Press, 1998), p. 16 (whether or not Ariès "is correct on every particular, his book opened a space for examining the social construction of childhood as an ongoing historical process and for questioning dominant constructions of childhood innocence"); Karin Calvert, "Children in the House: The Material Culture of Early Childhood," *id.,* pp. 72–75; James Kincaid, *Erotic Innocence: The Culture of Child Molesting* (Chapel Hill: Duke U. Press, 1998), p. 53 ("if we think of it as illuminating modern ways of seeing rather than as offering a confident description of the past, the idea of the invented child can be useful"); Anne Higonnet, *Pictures of Innocence: The History and Crisis of Ideal Childhood* (London: Thames & Hudson, 1998), p. 120 (tracing the sentimentalized ideal of sexually innocent, vulnerable childhood in 18th-century Western art and culture; the

"Romantic child belongs to the modern affluent west. To anyone outside our culture or not influenced by it, the ideal meanings we have attached to the child's body would be odd if not incomprehensible"); Margaret Talbot, "Against Innocence," *New Republic,* Mar. 15, 1999, p. 27 (discussing "re-Victorianized hypervigilance" about minors' sexuality in the late-20th century United States); Cox, *supra* n. 4, p. 1, quoting Ariès, *supra* n. 23, p. 129 (Ariès has often been misunderstood: he did not claim that "childhood did not exist" or that children were "neglected, forsaken or despised"; only that in premodern times "awareness of the particular nature of childhood" was lacking; For a simplified view of "the invention of childhood," and complaints about its imminent demise, see Postman, *supra* n. 1.

24. Michel Foucault, *The History of Sexuality,* Vol. 1: *An Introduction* (New York; Random House, 1978), pp. 28, 30.

25. Illick, *supra* n. 21, pp. 303, *passim,* quoting Keith Thomas, *Religion and the Decline of Magic* (New York: Scribner, 1971), p. 111. Stone has expanded on this theme at length, identifying 1500–1800 in England as the period in which "affective bonding" in families developed, and with it a decline in communal life, and increasing sense of personal autonomy, and a lessening association of sex with guilt; see also Jay Fliegelman, *Prodigals and Pilgrims: The American Revolution Against Patriarchal Authority, 1750–1800* (Cambridge: Cambridge U. Press, 1982).

26. John Locke, *Some Thoughts Concerning Education,* in *The Educational Writings of John Locke* (John W. Adamson, ed.) (Cambridge: Cambridge U. Press, 1922); Fliegelman, *supra* n. 42, pp. 1–12 (noting the "enormous political implications" of Locke's *Essay Concerning Human Understanding,* which rejected Descartes's doctrine of innate ideas); Michael Grossberg, *Governing the Hearth; Law and Family in Nineteenth Century America* (Chapel Hill: U. North Carolina Press, 1985), pp. 5–11; see also Stone, pp. 177, 254; Archard, pp. 1–12; Sommerville, pp. 109–24 (Puritans published the "great bulk of child-rearing advice," which generally discouraged parental indulgence, and emphasized "natural love and wise correction"); Pollock, pp. 98–127 (17th- and 18th-century diaries suggest parents believed children were not depraved but pliable and that it was the duty of parents to bend the child's will).

27. Stone, pp. 267–79.

28. Fliegelman, *supra* n. 42, p. 26.

29. De Mause, p. 43.

30. *Education of the Senses, supra* n. 47, pp. 301, 303, 304; see also MacDonald, *supra* n. 48 (describing "contraption patented in the United States in 1908 of 'Sexual Armor,'" that "consisted of a jacket encased in steel armor with perforations, a hinged trapdoor with bolts and a padlock and optional handcuffs"); Kathryn Kelley, "Adolescent Sexuality: The First Lessons," in *Adolescents, Sex and Contraception* (Donn Byrne & William A. Fisher, eds.) (Hillsdale, NJ: Lawrence Erlbaum, 1983.), p. 129. "By the nineteenth century," writes de Mause, the campaign against masturbation "reached an unbelievable frenzy.

Doctors and parents sometimes appeared before the child armed with knives and scissors, threatening to cut off the child's genitals; circumcision, clitoridectomy, and infibulation were sometimes used as punishment; and all sorts of restraint devices, including plastic casts and cages with spikes, were prescribed." Graphs assembled by one scholar showed "a peak in surgical intervention in 1850–79, and in restraint devices in 1880–1904. By 1925, these methods had almost completely died out, after two centuries of brutal and totally unnecessary assault on children's genitals." De Mause, pp. 48–49.

31. Jean-Jacques Rousseau, *Emile, or On Education* (Allan Bloom, trans.) (New York: Basic Books, 1979), pp. 220, 231, *passim.*

32. Priscilla Robertson, "Home as a Nest: Middle-Class Childhood in Nineteenth Century Europe," in *The History of Childhood,* p. 407.

33. Sommerville, p. 131; see also, on Rousseau, Plato, and totalitarian philosophy, Popper, *supra* n. 6, pp. 246, 257; Michael Ignatieff, *Isaiah Berlin* (New York: Henry Holt, 1998), pp. 202–3.

34. Craig, p. 21; see also *Regina v. Read* (1708), II Mod. 205 (Q.B); *Rex v. Curl* (1727), 2 Str. 789, 93 E.R. 849 (K.B.); Margaret Blanchard, "The American Urge to Censor: Freedom of Expression Versus the Desire to Sanitize Society," 33 *Wm. & Mary L. Rev.* 741, 773 (1992); Frank Fowell & Frank Palmer, *Censorship in England* (New York: Burt Franklin, 1913, 1970); Geoffrey Robertson, *Obscenity* (London: Weidenfeld & Nicolson, 1979). pp. 17–21.

35. Leo M. Alpert, "Judicial Censorship of Obscene Literature," 52 *Harv. L. Rev.* 40, 47 (1938); see also Craig, p. 34; Robertson, *supra* n. 62, p. 23; Stone, p. 335 (describing, *Fanny Hill's* "long and prosperous history").

36. See William Lockhart and Robert McClure, "Literature, the Law of Obscenity, and the Constitution," 38 *Minn. L. Rev.* 295, 325 (1954).

37. Prov. St. 1711–12, c. 6, §19, 1 Prov. Laws, 682; see Sidney Grant & S. E. Angoff, "Massachusetts and Censorship," 10 *BU L. Rev.* 36, 147, 152 (1930); Alpert, at 56; *Roth v. United States,* 354 U.S. 476, 483 (1957).

38. Grant & Angoff, *supra* n. 71, at 147–48; see *Commonwealth v. Isenstadt,* 318 Mass. 543, n. 1 (1945), characterizing the 1711 blasphemy law as "the germ" of Massachusetts's modern obscenity statute, M.G.L. c. 272, §28.

39. The state's high court affirmed the conviction. *Commonwealth v. Holmes,* 17 Mass. 336 (1821). Its view remained unchanged 144 years later when it again found John Cleland's fable obscene; this time, the Supreme Court reversed; see ch. 3.

40. *Commonwealth v. Sharpless,* 2 Serg. & Raw. 91, 101 (Pa. 1815).

41. D'Emilio & Freedman, p. 157.

42. Tariff Act of 1842, c. 270, 5 Stat. 563–66, 27th Cong. (1842): see James Paul & Murray Schwartz, *Federal Censorship; Obscenity in the Mail* (New York: Free Press of Glencoe, 1961), pp. 249–50,

tracing the sparse legislative history of the 1842 law and its successors.

43. *Id.*, p. 12.

44. See Hunt, *supra* n. 69, p. 12; James Jones, *Alfred C. Kinsey: A Public/Private Life* (New York: Norton, 1997), p. 67; Alison Parker, *Purifying American Women, Cultural Reform, and Pro-Censorship Activism, 1873–1933* Urbana U. of Ill. Press, 1997); Paul Boyer, *Purity in Print: The Vice-Society Movement and Book Censorship in America* (New York: Scribner, 1968), pp. 1–52; D'Emilio & Freedman, pp. 130–70; William Leach, *True Love and Perfect Union: The Feminist Reform of Sex and Society* (Middletown, CT: Wesleyan U. Press, 1989), pp. 62–63; Kett, *supra* n. 58, pp. 164–72.

45. See D'Emilio & Freedman, p. 153; Jeffrey Weeks, *Sex, Politics and Society: The Regulation of Sexuality Since* 1800 (London: Longman, 1981), pp. 87–88; Constance Nathanson, *Dangerous Passage: The Social Control of Sexuality in Women's Adolescence* (Philadelphia: Temple U. Press, 1991), pp. 75, 199; Viviana Zelizer, *Pricing the Priceless Child* (New York: Basic Books, 1985) (detailing change in the United States from the 1870s "useful child" to the emotionally "priceless" child of the 20th century); Grossberg, *supra* n. 43, pp. 105–44, 278, 301 (describing unsuccessful efforts early in the 19th century to raise the age of consent; and change in attitude after 1850).

46. Parker, *supra* n. 78, p. 19.

47. Weeks, *supra* n. 79, p. 19; see Foucault, Vol. 1.

48. John Chandos, "Unicorns at Play," in *"To Deprave and Corrupt": Original Studies in the Nature and Definition of "Obscenity"* (London: Souvenir Press, 1962), p. 179; see also Craig, pp. 40–43 (noting the popularity, especially among youth, of titillating works by the French novelist Paul de Kock, or the flagellation poetry of Swinburne); Marcus, *supra* n. 49 (describing the pornographic culture of Victorian England).

49. See Sommerville, p. 160 ("[o]ne of the puzzles of our history is the fact that the greatest exploitation of children coincided with the greatest glorification of childhood").

50. Jerome Kagan, *The Nature of the Child* (New York: Basic Books, 1984), p. 267; Postman, *supra* n. 1, p. xii.

51. See Paul & Schwartz, *supra* n. 76, pp. 251, 254–55; Blanchard, *supra* n. 62, at 747.

52. Post Office Act, c. 89, §16, 13 Stat. 504, 507 (1865).

53. *Hansard's Parliamentary Debates,* 3rd Series, Commencing with the Accession of William IV, 1857, Vol. 145 (London: Cornelius Buck, 1857), p. 103; see also J. E. Hall Williams, "Obscenity in Modern English Law," 22 *Law & Contemp. Probs.* 630, 632 (1955); Craig, p. 40. Campbell opined that higher prices were "a sort of check," preventing lascivious publications from getting into the wrong hands. *Hansard's, supra.*

54. Brougham's fears were hardly fantastic: in France, writings by Gustave Flaubert, Charles Baudelaire, and Eugène Sue were prosecuted for offending public morals in the same year that Lord Campbell's Act was passed; see *Education of the Senses,* p. 359.

55. *Hansard's,* Vol. 146, pp. 330–32. Lyndhurst said the paintings "come within the description in this Bill as much as any work you can conceive," yet both are celebrated; the Correggio "hangs in the large square room of the Louvre, right opposite an ottoman, on which are seated daily ladies of the first rank from all countries of Europe, who resort there for the purpose of studying the works of art in that great gallery"; *id.*; see also pp. 336–37 (Lord Wensleydale opining that "there was not a library in which books could not be found containing passages which a strict dealing magistrate might consider to bring them within the operation of this Bill," including the classics of Lucian, Lucullus, and Juvenal).

56. *Hansard's* Vol. 146 (June 25, 1857), p. 329.

57. *Id.*, pp. 1152–53, 1355–63.

58. *Regina v. Hicklin,* 3 Q.B. at 362; see Lockhart & McClure, *supra* n. 70, at 325.

59. *Hicklin,* 3 Q.B. at 371.

60. *Id.* at 367, 371–72.

61. *Education of the Senses,* pp. 175–77.

62. Craig, pp. 40–115; see also Edward de Grazia, *Girls Lean Back Everywhere: The Law of Obscenity and the Assault on Genius* (New York: Random House 1992), pp. 40–53; Felice F. Lewis, *Literature, Obscenity, and Law* (Carbondale: So. Ill. U. Press, 1976), p. 24; Robertson, pp. 31–32. Eleanor Marx Aveling (daughter of Karl) was the translator of Vizetelly's edition of *Madame Bovary;* Vizetelly also, at the instance of Havelock Ellis, initiated the celebrated Mermaid Series of English dramatists; see Publisher's Note, *Marlowe* (Havelock Ellis, ed.) (New York: Mermaid Drama Book, Hill & Wang, 1956), p. 345.

63. Weeks, pp. 84–92, 142, 181; see also Craig, pp. 52–65; and Ellis's Foreword to *Studies in the Psychology of Sex, supra* n. 47, pp. ix–xxiii, describing the tortured publication history of the *Studies* following the prosecution of the secretary of the Legitimation League, which had published the original first volume, *Sexual Inversion.*

64. Bill Thompson, *Soft Core: Moral Crusades Against Pornography in Britain and America* (London: Cassell, 1994), p. 17; see also Chandos, "Introduction," in *"To Deprave and Corrupt," supra* n. 82, pp. 27–28 ("for the next ninety-one years" after *Hicklin,* "literature in England and for almost as long in America was subject to a control designed to preserve the innocence or ignorance of a hypothetical adolescent girl, and at times it would seem, a feeble-minded one").

65. "The Claims of Psycho-Analysis to Scientific Interest," in *The Standard Edition of the Complete Psychological Works of Sigmund Freud,* Vol. 13 (London: Hogarth Press, 1953), pp. 165, 184; Steven Marcus, "Introduction," in Sigmund Freud, *Three Essays on the Theory of Sexuality* (James Strachey, trans.) (New York: Basic Books, 1962), pp. xx–xxi;

"The Sexual Enlightenment of Children," in *Standard Edition*, Vol. 9 (London: Hogarth Press, 1959), p. 152; see generally Peter Gay, "Introduction," in *The Freud Reader* (New York: Norton, 1989), pp. xxii, xi (characterizing Freud as one of a "small handful of supreme makers of the twentieth-century mind"). Another article, in 1908, indicted the sexual ideology of abstinence until marriage: "Civilized Sexual Morality and Modern Nervousness," in *Standard Edition*, Vol. 9, pp. 181, 193; on the impact of "Civilized Sexual Morality," see Rochelle Gurstein, *The Repeal of Reticence* (New York: Hill & Wang, 1996), p. 98; John D'Emilio & Estelle Freedman, *Intimate Matters: A History of Sexuality in America* (New York: Harper & Row, 1988), pp. 171–75.

66. The phrase is Rochelle Gurstein's *supra* n. 1, p. 99.

67. Michel Foucault, *The History of Sexuality*, Vol. 1: *An Introduction* (New York: Random House, 1978), pp. 104–5, 65; see also Vol. 2, *The Use of Pleasure* (New York: Random House, 1985); Vol. 3, *The Care of the Self* (New York: Random House, 1986); Joseph E. Kett, *Rites of Passage: Adolescence in America, 1790 to the Present* (New York: Basic Books, 1977); Steven Marcus, *The Other Victorians* (New York: Bantam, 1967). Foucault identifies four primary areas in which professional medicine and emerging social science in the 19th century asserted control over sexuality: hysteria among women, youthful masturbation, "socialization of procreative behavior" through prohibitions on contraception, and "psychiatrization of perverse pleasure"—that is, categorizing nonconformist sexuality as pathological. *History of Sexuality*, Vol. 1, *supra*.

68. D'Emilio & Freedman, *supra* n. 1, pp. 277–78.

69. D'Emilio & Freedman, p. 224; see Havelock Ellis, *Studies in the Psychology of Sex*, Vol. 1 (1st ed.) (Philadelphia: F. A. Davis Co., 1901), pp. 248–81; *Of Life and Sex* (New York: New American Library, 1957); Paul Robinson, *The Modernization of Sex* (Ithaca, NY: Cornell U. Press, 1989); Ellen Chesler, *Woman of Valor: Margaret Sanger and the Birth Control Movement in America* (New York: Simon & Schuster, 1992), pp. 110–25, describing Ellis's influence on and affair with Margaret Sanger.

70. See Robinson, *supra* n. 5.

71. Quoted in Gurstein, pp. 92–93. Gurstein's title derives from Agnes Repplier's essay, "The Repeal of Reticence," *Atlantic Monthly*, Mar. 1914, p. 297; Repplier's complaint was "not so much the nature of the information showered opon us," but "the fact that a great deal of it is given in the wrong way by the wrong people"; sex information, for example, was finding its way "into the hands of young women whose enthusiasm for the cause lets down their natural barriers of defenes." *Id.*, p. 298; see also Pual Boyer, *Purity in Print. The Vice Society Movement and Book Censorship in America* (New York: Scribner, 1968), p. 41 (describing anticensorship sentiment before World War 1).

72. Bronislaw Malinowski, *Sex and Repression in Savage Society* (New York: Meridian, 1955) (first published 1927); see also Bronislaw Malinowski, *The Sexual Life of Savages* (Boston: Beacon Press, 1987) (first published 1929); Margaret Mead, *The Coming of Age in Samoa* (New York: Morrow, 1928); Boyer, *supra* n. 7, p.149. Malinowski rejected the "exorbitant claims of psychoanalysis," as well as "its chaotic arguments and tangled terminology"; but nevertheless acknowledged "a deep sense of indebtedness" to Freud "for stimulation as well as for valuable instruction in some aspects of human psychology." *Sex and Repression*, p. 5.

73. Kett, *supra* n. 3, pp. 216, 183, 186; see also Thomas Hine, *The Rise and Fall of the American Teenager* (New York: Avon, 1999), pp. 4–9 (tracing the ideas of adolescent immaturity and angst and the development of an insular, segregated teen culture in the 20th century to Hall's influence).

74. Constance Nathanson, *Dangerous Passage: The Social Control of Sexuality in Women's Adolescence* (Philadelphia: Temple U. Press, 1991), pp. 3–4; see also Henry Jenkins, "The Sensuous Child," in *The Children's Culture Reader* (Henry Jenkins, ed.) (New York: NYU Press, 1998), pp. 212–15 (describing the mid-20th-century influence of behaviorist psychology on child care advice; according to John Watson, the leading behaviorist, the body required "constant discipline," and sensual pleasures from thumb sucking to masturbation were to be discouraged). Behaviorism, in sharp contrast to Freudianism, "bracketed off questions of interior mental life as ultimately not open to scientific examination, focusing instead on understanding external behaviors." *Id.*, p. 212; see also Erich Fromm, *The Anatomy of Human Destructiveness* (New York: Henry Holt, 1973), p. 24 (behaviorism "does not interest itself in the subjective forces which drive man to behave in a certain way," but only in "the social conditioning that shapes his behavior").

75. *United States v. Dennett*, 39 F.2d 564, 565 (2nd Cir. 1930); see also Constance Chen, *"The Sex Side of Life": Mary Ware Dennett's Pioneering Battle for Birth Control and Sex Education* (New York: The New Press, 1996), pp. 171–77.

76. Chen, *supra* n. 30, Appendix B (a reproduction of the original pamphlet).

77. *Id.*, Appendix B, p. 11.

78. "The Statues" (1938), in *The Collected Poems of William Butler Yeats* (New York: Macmillan, 1956), p. 322.

79. *United States v. Dennett*, 39 F. 2d at 568.

80. *Id.*, at 569.

81. See Vanderham, pp. 85–86.

82. Geoffrey Robertson, "Foreword," in *The Trail of Lady Chatterley: Regina v. Penguin Books, Ltd.* (G. H. Rolph, ed.) (London: Penguin, 1961), p. xvi; see also de Grazia, *supra* n. 21, p. 54; Alee Craig, *The Banned Books of England* (London: George Allen & Unwin, 1937), p. 26; Alan Travis, "Secret Files Expose Joyce Fiasco," *The Guardian*, May 15, 1998, Friday Review, p. 1. In 1936, three years after Judge Woolsey exonerated *Ulysses* in the United States, the Bodley Head published a British edition; in response, the government finally acknowledged that *Ulysses* was not obscene. *Id.*

83. Robertson, "Foreword," *supra* n. 40, p. xvi.

84. *United States v. One Obscene Book Entitled "Married Love,"* 48 F.2d 821, 824 (S.D.N.Y. 1931).

85. *United States v. One Book Called "Ulysses,"* 5 F. Supp. 182, 183–85 (S.D.N.Y. 1993).

86. *Id.* at 709–11 (Manton, J., dissenting). Manton resigned five years later after evidence surfaced that he had been taking bribes; he was convicted and sentenced to two years in prison. See Joseph Borkin, *The Corrupt Judge* (New York: Clarkson N. Potter, 1962); Gunther, *supra* n. 10, pp. 504–6.

87. *Attorney General v. A Book Named "God's Little Acre,"* 326 Mass, 281, 283 (1950); *Commonwealth v. Isenstadt,* 318 Mass. 543, 549–50 (1945).

88. *New American Library v. Allen,* 114 F.Supp. 823, 834 (N.D. Ohio 1953). The same year, the Ninth Circuit Court of Appeals condemned as obscene Henry Miller's *Tropic of Cancer* and *Tropic of Capricorn; Besig v. United States,* 208 F.2d 142 (9th Cir. 1953).

89. *People v. London,* 63 N.Y.S.2d 227, 230 (City Mag. Ct., Mid-Manhattan 1946); see, by contrast, *Parmelee v. United States,* 113 F.2d 729 (D.C. Cir. 1940), finding *Nudism in Modern Life* not obscene; *People v. Gotham Book Mart,* 158 Misc. 240 (City Mag. Ct. 7th Dist. 1936), exonerating the Gotham Book Mart, a New York literary shrine, for selling André Gide's *If It Die.*

90. See de Grazia, pp. 278–79; Paul & Schwartz, pp. 63–137; Boyer, pp. 207–74.

91. *United States v. Levine,* 83 F.2d 156, 156–58 (2d Cir. 1936).

92. Frederic Thrasher, "The Comics and Delinquency: Cause or Scapegoat," 23 *J. Educ. Sociology* 195, 199 (1949), citing Paul Cressey, *The Role of the Motion Picture in an Interstitial Area* (unpublished manuscript on deposit at NYU library); Paul Cressey, "The Motion Picture Experience as Modified by Social Background and Personality," 3 *Am. Sociol. Rev.* 516 (1938); see Willard Rowland, Jr., *The Politics of TV Violence* (Beverly Hills: Sage, 1983), pp. 92–95.

93. Herbert Blumer & Philip Hauser, *Movies, Delinquency, and Crime* (New York: Arno Press & The New York Times, 1970 reprint ed.) (original, New York: Macmillan, 1933), pp. 15, 73.

94. See de Grazia, pp. 273–326, describing Roth's career; William Lockhart & Robert McClure, "Censorship of Obscenity: The Developing Constitutional Standards," 45 *Minn. L. Rev.* 5, 22–23 n. 88 (1960) ("Lockhart & McClure, II"); *Roth v. Goldman,* 172 F.2d 788, 796 (2d Cir.) (Frank, J., concurring), cert. denied, 337 U.S. 938 (1949); Jerome Frank, *Law and the Modern Mind* (New York: Brentano's, 1930) (criticizing "legal fundamentalism" as a remnant of childish wishes for an omnipotent father figure).

95. *Roth v. Goldman,* 172 F.2d at 789.

96. *Id.* at 792; see note 72.

97. *Commonwealth v. Gordon,* 66 Pa. D & C 101, 125, 154 (1949), aff'd *sub nom. Commonwealth v. Feigenbaum,* 166 Pa. Super. 120 (1950). Bok added: "I should prefer that my own three daughters meet the facts of life and the literature of the world in my library than behind a neighbor's barn, for I can face the adversary there directly." *Id.* at 110.

98. *Bantam Books, Inc. v. Melko,* 25 N.J. Super. 292, 318 (1953).

99. See Lockhart & McClure, 38 *Minn. L. Rev. at* 357, nothing that "[o]nly in few reported trial court opinions" before *Hecate County* "was thoughtful consideration given to the constitutional issue," and in only one of these, Judge Bok's opinion in *Commonwealth v. Gordon,* "was the constitutional issue given careful and detailed analysis."

100. There is a large literature on the red-hunting and blacklisting decade after World War II; see, for example, David Caute, *The Great Fear* (New York: Simon & Schuster, 1978); Ellen Schrecker, *Many Are the Crimes: McCarthyism in America* (Princeton, NJ: Princeton U. Press, 1998).

101. U.S. Senate, 81st Cong. 2d Sess., Comm. on Expenditures in the Executive Departments, *Employment of Homosexuals and Other Sexual Perverts in Government* (Washington, DC: Gov't Printing Office, 1950), p. 4; see also John D'Emilio, *Sexual Politics, Sexual Communities: The Making of the Homosexual Minority in the United States, 1940–1970* (Chicago: U. of Chicago Press, 1983), p. 42; Gayle Rubin, "Thinking Sex: Notes for a Radical Theory of the Politics of Sexuality," in *Pleasure and Danger* (Carole Vance, ed.) (London: Routledge & Kegan Pual, 1984), p. 270; Jonathan Katz, *Gay American History: Lesbians and Gay Men in the USA: A Documentary Anthology* (New York; Thomas Crowell, 1976). Replicating the federal government's fixations, the Communist Party-USA also expelled homosexuals in the late 1950s, "on the grounds that their vulnerability to blackmail in the repressive sexual climate of the period would endanger their comrades." Schrecker, *supra* n. 66, 19–20.

102. D'Emilio, *supra* n. 67, p. 41; D'Emilio & Freedman, pp. 292–93.

103. Beanvais Lyons, "Artistic Freedom and the University," 50 *Art Journal* 78 (College Art Ass'n) (1991).

104. See Myron Sharaf, *Fury on Earth: A Biography of Wilhelm Reich* (New York: St. Martin's, 1983), pp. 460–61; de Grazia, pp. 347, 394.

105. U.S. House of Representatives, 86th Cong., 1st Sess., Comm. on Post Office & Civil Service, Subcomm. on Postal Operations, *Obscene Matter Sent Through the Mail* (Washington, DC: Gov't Printing Office, 1959), pp. 1, 14.

106. Alfred Kinsey *et al., Sexual Behavior in the Human Male* (Philadelphia: W.B. Saunders, 1948); Alfred Kinsey *et al., Sexual Behavior in the Human Female* (Philadelphia: W. B. Saunders, 1953); see also Robinson, *supra* n. 5, pp. 42–119; Jones, *supra* n. 13.

107. Jones, p. 563; see also Jonathan Gathorne-Hardy, *Sex, the Measure of All Things: A Life of Alfred C. Kinsey* (Bloomington: Indiana U. Press, 2000); Jeffrey Moran, *Teaching Sex: The Shaping of Adolescence in the 20th Century* (Cambridge, MA: Harvard U. Press, 2000), pp. 135–36 ("So fascinated

were Americans with Kinsey's work that word of *Sexual Behavior in the Human Female's* publication in 1953 pushed off the front pages news of verification of the Soviet hydrogen bomb and Mohammed Mossadegh's surrender in Iran").

108. Jones, pp. 707–11, 712, quoting *New York Post,* Aug. 30, 1953.

109. Robinson, *supra* n. 5, pp. 90–91, 117.

110. Jones, pp. 720–21, 713, 632, quoting Reinhold Niebuhr, "Sex and Religion in the Kinsey Report," *Christianity and Crisis,* Nov. 2, 1953, p. 138; Bishop Schulte's remarks in *Indianapolis News,* Aug. 20, 28, 1953; J. Edgar Hoover, "Must We Change Our Sex Standards?" *Reader's Digest,* June 1948, p. 6; see also Lionel Trilling, "The Kinsey Report," in *The Liberal Imagination* (New York: Anchor, 1953), pp. 223, 225 (originally published in *Partisan Review,* Apr. 1948).

111. See Martin Duberman, "Kinsey's Urethra," *The Nation,* Nov. 3, 1997, p. 40 (faulting Jones for "crude psychologizing [which is really moralizing]" about Kinsey's sexuality); Gathorne-Hardy, *supra* n. 73 (arguing that Kinsey's bisexuality diminished neither his accuracy nor his scientific contribution, and characterizing Jones's as "the Kenneth Starr school of biography," *id.,* p. viii).

112. Jones, pp. 632, 712–23; see also James Jones, "Dr. Yes," *The New Yorker,* Aug. 25 & Sept. 1, 1997, pp. 99, 100.

113. Jones, pp. 715–37; Gathorne-Hardy, p. 408 (the Reece Committee's findings were "demolished" by journalists); Rubin, *supra* n. 67, p. 273; see also Paul Gebhard, "The Institute," in *Sex Research: Studies from the Kinsey Institute* (Martin Weinberg, ed.) (New York: Oxford U. Press, 1976), pp. 10–22.

114. Margaret Blanchard, "The American Urge to Censor: Freedom of Expression Versus the Desire to Sanitize Society," 33 *Wm. & Mary L. Rev.* 741, 789 (1992).

115. See Publisher's Note, in Fredric Wertham, *Seduction of the Innocent* (New York: Rinehart & Co., 1953), p. v (noting Wertham's scientific bona fides); Blanchard, *supra* n. 80, at 788–95; John E. Twomey, "The Citizens' Committee and Comic Book Control: A Study of Extragovernmental Restraint," 20 *Law & Contemp. Probs.* 621, 622, 624 (1955).

116. *Seduction of the Innocent, supra* n. 81, pp. 164, 167, 189–90.

117. *Id.,* pp. 84, 115, 239–41; see also *Ron Goulart's Great History of Comic Books* (Chicago: Contemporary Books, 1986), pp. 263–72 (describing Wertham's influence, and comic book bonfires in several cities); Fred von Bernewitz & Grant Geisman, *Tales of Terror!* (Timonium, MD: Gemstone, 2000), pp. 26–27.

118. Thrasher, *supra* n. 51, at 197, 200; see also Twomey, *supra* n. 81, at 623 n. 11; Blanchard, *supra* n. 80, at 791.

119. Reuel Denney, "The Dark Fantastic" (Book Review), *New Republic,* May 3, 1954, p. 18; see also Dorothy Walter Baruch, "Radio Rackets, Movie Murders and Killer Cartoons," in *New Ways to Discipline: You and Your Child Today* (New York: McGraw-Hill, 1949), excerpted in *The Children's Culture Reader, supra* n. 18, p. 493 (suggesting that more active play outlets for youthful aggression were needed); Reuel Denney, *The Astonished Muse: Popular Culture in America* (New York: Grosset & Dunlap, 1964), p. 164 (Wertham's assertions were "without evidence of any weight").

120. Henry Jenkins, "The Sensuous Child," in *The Children's Culture Reader,* p. 220.

121. *Katzev v. County of Los Angeles,* 52 Cal.2d 360 (1959); see Gail Johnston, "Crime Comics and the Constitution," 7 *Stan, L. Rev.* 237, 238 (1955). The LA ordinance had an exemption for "actual historical events" and "occurrences actually set forth in the sacred scriptures of any religion." Maryland's and Washington's anti-comics laws were invalidated in *Police Comm'r of Baltimore v. Siegel Enterprises,* 223 Md. 110 (1960) and *Adams v. Hinkle,* 51 Wn. 2d 763 (1958).

122. *Juvenile Delinquency (Comic Books),* 1954: Hearings on S. 190 Before the Subcomm. to Investigate Juvenile Delinquency of the Senate Comm. on the Judiciary, 83d Cong., 2d Sess. (1954), pp. 86, 103; see also *Comic Books and Juvenile Delinquency,* Interim Report of the Senate Comm. on the Judiciary, 84th Cong., 1st Sess.; Blanchard, at 790; Lynn Spigel, "Seducing the Innocent: Childhood and Television in Postwar America," in *The Children's Culture Reader,* p. 117; Rowland, *supra* n. 51, pp. 99–105 (describing Kefauver Committee's examination of violence on television—then in its infancy—as well); *Tales of Terror, supra* n. 83, pp. 26–27 (reprinting Senate testimony of EC Comics publisher William Gaines).

123. Blanchard, at 793; Fredric Wertham, *A Sign for Cain: An Exploration of Human Violence* (London: Lowe & Brydone, 1966), p. 197.

124. *Comic Books and Juvenile Delinquency, supra* n. 88, p. 14. As for Dr. Wertham, he moved on to other media in the 1960s and '70s, defending "fanzines" as healthy fantasy, while condemning *The Three Stooges* television show as "an ideal primer" for violence. *A Sign for Cain, supra* n. 89, p. 194; Fredric Wertham, *The World of Fanzines* (Carbondale: So. Ill. U. Press, 1973), p. 126.

125. Nat'l Council on Freedom from Censorship (organized by the ACLU), *What Shocked the Censors: A Complete Record of Cuts in Motion Picture Films Ordered by the New York State Censors from January, 1932 to March, 1933* (Sept. 1933), p. 2. On the Hays Code, see Leonard Leff & Jerold Simmons, *The Dame in the Kimono: Hollywood, Censorship, and the Production Code from the 1920s to the 1960s* (New York: Doubleday, 1990); Lea Jacobs, *The Wages of Sin: Censorship and the Fallen Woman Film, 1928–1942* (Berkeley: U. of Cal. Press, 1995). The system of film licensing was held in place by a 1915 Supreme Court ruling that movies were just a business, not a form of expression; the Court did not change its mind on this point until 1948. *Mutual Film*

Corp. v. Industrial Comm'n, 236 U.S. 230 (1915), contradicted by *United States v. Paramount Pictures,* 334 U.S. 131, 166 (1948). Four years later, it invalidated New York's denial of a license to Roberto Rossellini's *The Miracle,* a film about a simple-minded woman who believes she is the Virgin Mary. (Under pressure from Francis Cardinal Spellman, New York had revoked *The Miracle's* exhibition license on grounds of sacrilege.) *Burstyn v. Wilson,* 343 U.S. 495 (1952).

126. *Winters v. New York,* 333 U.S. 507, 508, 511 (1948).
127. *Id.* at 523, 530–31 (Frankfurter, J., dissenting).
128. *Id.* at 510.
129. *Chaplinsky v. New Hampshire,* 315 U.S. 568, 572 (1942). *Chaplinsky* held that so-called "fighting words"—words more likely to provoke a fight than invite a conversation—were not protected by the First Amendment. The decision upheld the criminal conviction of a Jehovah's Witness for calling a city marshal a "God damned racketeer" and "a damned Fascist."
130. Zechariah Chafee, Jr., *Free Speech in the United States* (Cambridge, MA: Harvard U. Press, 1941), p. 150.
131. See Rabban, *supra* n. 19; Chafee, *supra* n. 96. Although Chafee believed sexual speech hardly merited the same protection as political speech, he acknowledged that literary censorship had sometimes been excessive. *Id.,* p. 151.
132. *Id.* at 806–7, 809.
133. *Id.* at 815, quoting Jahoda letter. Jahoda's report was *The Impact of Literature: A Psychological Discussion of Some Assumptions in the Censorship Debate* (Research Center for Human Relations, New York University, 1954).
134. *U.S. v. Roth,* 237 F.2d at 816–17.

Childhood in America Past and Present

PAULA S. FASS AND MARY ANN MASON

INTRODUCTION

In this brief essay, historians Paula S. Fass and Mary Ann Mason detail the changing importance of children in American society. Children link adults to one another in the context of schools and neighborhoods; their social networks often shape parents' social networks. The authors also note that in an age of high divorce rates, children are often the most central emotional connection that adults maintain. Their brief historical overview points to the fact that children are continually defined and redefined by adults in ways that best suit the needs of a culture and society at any given time.

VALUING CHILDREN

Children are constantly on our minds. They are convenient symbols for our better selves, and we use them to make points, make laws, win elections. But children have also become a necessity in new ways. For many adults . . . , the parent-child relationship . . . replaced marriage as their primary social and emotional connection. Adults can no longer count on husbands and wives for lifelong emotional support and affection as statistics prove the unreliability of marriage. Only with children, many adults are coming to believe, can one hope to find long-term emotional ties. Without children, one often has difficulty finding comfort even in the secondary web of human connections: neighborhoods and civic institutions. Children provide the links to neighbors and school activities that tie the adult to the community. Indeed, the . . . boom in medically assisted reproduction reflects this need. The urgent desire to parent has created a rich industry based in new technological interventions that allow infertile or gay or lesbian couples to circumvent each stage of the usual procedure of insemination, conception, pregnancy, and childbirth. . . . These interventions raise basic questions about the biological essence of motherhood and fatherhood. More important, they attest to the pressing centrality of children in the lives of adults. When children are not born naturally, adults must invent them in new ways.

Children have always been critically important for parents as well as communities, but not always for the same reasons. For most of our history, until the twentieth century, the social worth of children was understood primarily in terms of economic rather than emotional value. From early settlement in the first half of the seventeenth century until well into the nineteenth, the family was an interdependent unit in which children played an integral part. From the earliest age when a child could hold a spinning card, she was likely engaged in household industry. By the age of twelve or so most children were treated as adult producers. . . . For most Americans, childhood as we have come to know it in modern times did not exist.

Beginning in the eighteenth century, children's personalities became an important philosophical matter and the subject of artistic representation, but the value of children was still measured in terms of the services they performed. Even in the nineteenth century, when sentimental images of children and childhood innocence were treasured in public language and culture, most children were firmly part of a family economy and their contribution was viewed in those terms. Individual children may have been loved and even spoiled, but most parents depended on their labor for family survival.

Children worked from an early age, and learned as they worked to become adults, under the supervision of their fathers if they were boys, of their mothers if they were girls. The father, as head of the household, held almost complete power of custody and control over children; the mother was a distant second in command. Orphans, defined as children who had no fathers, and children born out of wedlock were apprenticed at an early age (by means of a legal contract) to masters who included them in the household with their own children, teaching them a trade in return for their services. . . . Still another class of children—children born into slavery—came under the control of the masters of the household. When the War for Independence began in 1776, about one in five American children were slaves. These children were not only early put to hard physical labor, but they were legally considered chattel who could be freely bought and sold by their masters.

In the middle of the nineteenth century the family, one might say, was stood on its head. In middle-class households, at least, mothers replaced fathers in supervising their children. With industrialization and the growth of cities, the economic production that had been central to the household moved out, leaving behind a largely domestic space. As a result of these dramatic changes in nineteenth-century social life, mothers took over most aspects of child nurture. Where earlier the father had controlled the everyday activities of children beyond infancy, the mother now became preeminent. Mothers supervised even boys beyond early childhood at home in the father's absence and at school, where women rather than men began to dominate as teachers. In law and in social attitudes mothers were elevated as the nurturers and caretakers of children. Children in turn were viewed as tender innocents in need of gentle moral nurture. The Victorian mother and child came to dominate sentimental representations of family life.

By the second half of the nineteenth century, the first wave of feminism also enlarged women's legal rights to their children as women struggled for more public roles. For the first time, a mother could be granted custody in the event of separation or divorce and a father could not bequeath his children to a guardian other than the mother in the event of the father's death.

Despite the new child consciousness and sentimentalization of children and mothers in nineteenth-century culture, it was not until the end of the nineteenth century and the beginning of the twentieth that children began to be widely valued primarily in emotional rather than economic terms. As a result of new laws prohibiting child labor and enforcing extended periods of schooling, children were transformed into emotional rather than economic assets. Parents had fewer children and were directed to put more effort into raising them rather than receiving the services of many children, as had earlier generations. Society invested in institutions designed to extend the period of leisured growth and development, especially schools and institutions that emphasized play. It was in this context that what we have come to know as modern childhood began.

It is important to remember that even in this new environment in which children were cherished and their development sheltered, not all children were given the freedom to play and to learn. With the reduced role of children as economic producers children who had no parents, or whose parents were too poor to raise them, were increasingly placed in institutions, mostly orphanages, which held them to a strict work routine. Some children, usually the homeless children found begging on city streets, were "placed out" to farms where child labor was still needed. Poor parents were rarely given help to raise children in their own homes. Poverty, for the most part, was considered a defect of character from which children should be protected by removal. And while slave children were freed as a consequence of the Civil War, most of them shared in the hard toil their parents came to know as southern sharecroppers. Some serious efforts were initially made toward schooling this newly freed class of children, but little of the life of modern childhood with its focus on play and learning was allotted them.

The early part of the twentieth century ushered in a new social awareness of the welfare of children that attempted to bring the lives of the poorest children into line with the developing perspectives of childhood, but the results were often ambiguous as child labor laws and mandatory school attendance interfered with the rights of parents to raise their children as they saw fit. Immigrant parents, in particular, had depended on their children's labor in Europe, Latin America, and Asia and resisted what they perceived as an oppressive and unfair usurpation of their authority. Some of the newer interventions, however, helped families stay together. For the first time, the state worked with private charities to create mothers' pensions and private stipends to keep poor children with their families. Adoption and foster care were promoted as family-centered alternatives to orphanages for children without parents.

During the early twentieth century children's lives were increasingly routinized around school, not work, and augmented with more varied forms of play and entertainment. . . . Then as now, children were valued almost exclusively in emotional terms, or as investments in a brighter future, not as the working constituents of the economy. By then too, psychologists were deluging mothers with advice on how to rear their children according to the latest and best scientific theories, while doctors had taken over the delivery process and were helping the young to weather the most dangerous periods of infancy and childhood. Science and technology were transforming childhood into the object of new specialized attention that required that children become ever more the precious focus of parental solicitude. A scientifically raised child would become, it was believed, a predictably successful (and later, a happy, well-adjusted) adult. On the other hand if parents, mothers especially, failed to apply proper child-raising techniques, the adult would fail and the mother would be to blame.

Today the emotional value of children has soared despite, and perhaps because of, the breakdown of marriage. For many, parenthood now serves as a replacement for marriage bonds. But most children are no longer part of a traditional family structure. Among the surest signs of this change is the erosion of the centrality of Victorian motherhood as an anchor of child life. Today more than half of all mothers return to work outside the home during the first year following their child's birth. Children increasingly spend their days outside the home, in day care and other institutions. At the same time, divorce and the sharp increase in out-of-wedlock births are transforming family relationships. The household, too, has been reconfigured as natural parents are replaced by stepparents, and half-siblings and stepchildren are added to the roster of household members. Fewer than half of all children will be raised in a family with their two natural parents.

Amidst this vast institutional transformation, we no longer imagine that our children will help to support the family with their labor, and as the conventional family is transformed we are losing confidence in scientific parenthood. We look instead to children for the bonds and personal ties they provide over a lifetime. Not all children are well cared for or treasured, but our expectation of children has changed radically, along with our own feelings about our right to expect love. We now need children more than ever before.

REINVENTING CHILDREN

Just as each generation writes its own history, each writes a prescription for a new perception of children to meet its changing needs. Children who were valued for their services were perceived very differently than they are today, when they are looked to for a complex range of emotional supports and human ties. A child who was expected to perform serious farming tasks at age ten must early on be shaped to adult patterns of responsibility. The notion of an emotionally stormy adolescence, a nearly universal expectation in the twentieth-century West, could not be entertained in a work-oriented environment. . . . Puritan parents may have loved their children, as the poet Anne Bradstreet attests, but their culture ultimately defined all unredeemed children in terms of sin and animalistic corruption, and work (often in the households of others) provided the discipline to keep children in line and parents from overindulging them. When the Enlightenment invented the new child of the eighteenth century, he brought with him a rational and malleable nature that could be brought up systematically to adulthood, while schooling trained him for work, citizenship, and responsibility. The more romantic notions of the early nineteenth century became the basis for the sentimentalization of childhood, in which sweetly innocent children were made newly lovable and vulnerable, and opened up play as a whole new arena for child life. Starting with the views of John Locke, the great English philosopher of the Enlightenment, all of these images left some residue in our understanding of childhood, but it was ultimately the view of the child as a separate being whose nature was not pre-adult, but non-adult, and for whom play rather than work was the defining environment, that was most indelibly inscribed in modern views of childhood.

Despite these intellectual and conceptual antecedents, the modern child, whose importance to parents and others is defined by her emotional value, was a creation of the late nineteenth century, a social creation strongly supported by a newly visible and potent state. It was the innocent child the state stepped in to protect at the turn of the century. The concept behind the formation of the juvenile court was to remove children from abusive parents and to save still malleable children who were leaning toward a life of crime. The state would offer comfort and rehabilitation, not punishment. And increasingly, children were to be raised by families, not institutions, as foster homes and adoption substituted for orphanages and as mothers' pensions provided support to the unfortunate. . . .

In recent times the state has started to focus on children in a new way, no longer perceiving them as tender innocents, but rather as young adults ready to take on responsibilities and punishment. Partly because families are less stable and parental authority less clear, the state has begun to give children rights independent of their parents. . . . These newly gained rights allow children limited civil liberties, the right to some reproductive choices, and greater due process rights for juvenile offenders in the courtroom. But this also means that playful irresponsibility is cut off for many children. Ironically, but not altogether coincidentally, as children are being given the rights of adults they are also being newly held to adult standards. Children as young as thirteen can now be tried as adults for some crimes. The fate of the juvenile court, which emerged at the turn of the twentieth century to protect the separateness of childhood, is in doubt—one indication among others of the profound changes now under way.

While childhood experience changed slowly in the past, the vast acceleration of social change in the last century and especially the last twenty-five years has led to major reevaluations of many of the essential components of our earlier vision of childhood. We may well be in the midst of a new invention of childhood to meet our radically changing social lives and circumstances. The changes in the family are surely one of these. But so are many broader social changes, whose effects we are only now beginning to evaluate. Among the most prominent of these has been the enormous expansion of that domain that our nineteenth-century ancestors called play and we today define as entertainment. New commercial toys and especially electronic media like television, video games, and computers have profoundly altered the world of childhood. . . . So have the accelerated demands for skills in today's world that have placed schools so often at the top of our list of complaints and so fundamentally at the center of all discussions of the reforms required for a more adequate modern childhood. . . . But the new demands that schools adequately prepare children for adult skills can often ignore the childhood spaces they occupy. Where schools were initially expanded in order to substitute a longer childhood for the rush to work, they are today being increasingly tied to the work world. . . .

In considering children we must always keep in mind that in every era there are wide social variations within the population. For most of our history, for example, a high percentage of children lived as slaves. Throughout the twentieth century, race and immigrant status as well as economic standing and membership in an ethnic community have had a marked effect on how children were viewed and treated and the kinds of lives they could be expected to lead. We have tried to maintain this awareness of difference without losing sight of a common thread.

Childhood is like a many-faceted prism, whose light is both reflected and distorted in the eyes of the beholder. We look at the many facets of childhood through the eyes of many witnesses, turning the prism from childbirth through adolescence, from the angles of sexuality, learning, and gender, and from the perspective of the growing supervision provided by the state. . . . Our aim is to capture how children in the modern world have penerated into every aspect of culture and how our understanding of them has changed over time. It is also . . . to capture the multiple realities that coexist today and in the past in the lived experience of children themselves. This is, of course, the most daunting challenge, since children are the most elusive witnesses. They are rarely asked to reflect on their experiences in writing (even when they can write), and when they are, what they have to say is all too often not saved. . . .

In the twentieth century definitions of childhood's end have been progressively extended first into the once "new" realm of adolescence . . . and then beyond, as schooling has expanded into college and graduate training. . . . We are today at a loss to say when we are grown-up, or we prefer not to admit it. In the other direction, some of what had previously been constituted as the essence of childhood, sexual innocence, for one example, has been attenuated, and younger children know much more than they did in the past. We may well be at a point when the life cycle and its parts are being radically reconfigured and with them the scope, meaning, and value of childhood. What all this means to our conceptions of children, their emotional value to adults, and the quality of their lives it seems too soon to know, though not too soon to ask about. This, then, is an especially good time to learn where we've been in order to better understand where we might be going, not because it is all completely clear, but because it is germinating. . . .

Discussion Questions

1. Why do the authors argue that childhood as we know it today did not exist for most Americans?
2. When did childhood, as we define it today, emerge? What factors helped "create" childhood?

3. How have children been valued differently across historical periods? What caused shifts in how children are perceived and valued?
4. What are the ironies associated with children's rights today?

All Are Above Average

Peter N. Stearns

INTRODUCTION

Today we take for granted that education is vitally important for children. But this wasn't always the case—schooling in the United States has a history. Until the 1930s, most Americans did not attend high school, let alone graduate. Historian Peter N. Stearns explores how and why major changes in the American educational system happened. From widespread suspicion of schools to concerns about too much homework and misbehaving students, Stearns considers how both philosophy and practices have changed in American schools.

CHILDREN AT SCHOOL

. . . The early 20th century brought not only new but also fundamental shocks in parental perceptions of children and schools in the United States. This may not seem surprising. Many readers will legitimately feel that, given the distance of a hundred years, we should expect to see some fundamental problems of adjustment between past and present. . . .

To a historian, who tries to live partly in the past, the anguish provoked by early 20th-century schools, particularly for middle-class parents, was initially an unexpected finding. That immigrant parents felt anxious, encountering formal education for the first time and in a foreign, partly hostile culture, was predictable, and this did form part of the early 20th-century climate. But there was more.

Widespread education was not new. American kids, particularly middle-class kids, had been going to school regularly since the 1830s, except in the South. So why the early 20th century as a special point of tension, as if parents were seriously reconsidering what schools were doing to their children?

The answer is partly the host of innovations at that time, all in the context of the new ideas that promoted a sense of children's frailty. In addition to the tides of immigrant children in the schools, widespread coeducation added a new ingredient, provoking real concern about protecting boys' masculinity in view of the surge in the number of female schoolteachers in the primary grades. More important still, regular grading began to be imposed for the first time. Most 19th-century schools had operated on a loose pass-fail basis, which sometimes included considerable commingling of age groups. This now changed. Report cards emerged as standard practices, directed as much at parents as at children, from the 1920s on. This was a huge change, particularly increasing parental anxieties. School discipline also became more formal, even though random physical punishments declined. There were more rules, including enforcement of attendance and punctuality. All this occurred, further, as big city school bureaucracies increased, along with centralized direction of teachers and curricula. Children might more easily fall victim to impersonal decisions made by unseen authorities.

Schooling also expanded. Some high school education now embraced the majority of the working class for the first time, which meant that middle-class commitment to high school had to increase, as well. College attendance began to climb, but at the same time admission procedures in the best schools became more rigorous and uniform, based more clearly, if still imperfectly, on academic achievement. These were the years of the first College Board efforts, right around 1900, with the SATs (Scholastic Aptitude Tests) introduced later, in 1926.

And schooling was altered, finally, by changes in subject matter and increased expectations. Education was now not just the three Rs, but also modern history, some science, maybe even a modern language. Colleges shifted from emphasis on moral instruction to increased reliance on research-based science and social science, and the results could filter down to the better high schools.

Thus, while the early 20th century did not bring the birth of mass education in the United States (except in the South, which now began to climb on board), it did bring the birth of a modern educational experience. The resultant tensions, combined with the redefinition of childhood, become understandable.

Two other aspects of the American educational scene deserve notice as part of the general context, before we turn to the evidence of new anxieties. First, while all modern societies grapple with tensions between elite and mass education, the tensions in the United States had and still have some distinctive qualities. On the whole, before the college level at least, Americans have done better with the mass part than with distinguishing elite tracks. To be sure, early in the 20th century, new testing began to occur that was designed to assign students in secondary schools to different paths depending on presumed ability. And residential and racial segregation limited school democracy, as well. But the United States never plumped for complete separation of professionally bound and blue-collar-bound students before college, as routinely occurred in Europe and Japan. The result had many admirable features, but it also could impose anxieties on middle-class parents, worried that their kids were not appropriately challenged or recognized, just as other children, and their parents, might wonder about the relevance of their educational fare to their probable future lives. Some confusions of expectations were possible in American schools, in other words, that differed from some of the characteristic drawbacks (mainly hothouse testing and unduly rigid social divides) of other systems.

More generally still, Americans had already developed a love-hate relationship with education that was unusual, and that persists today. On the one hand, as children of the Enlightenment, Americans placed tremendous value on education. They were willing to spend a great deal of money on schools (though never enough, at least for my university). They viewed education as the great social obligation: if children had access to decent education, society had provided them with the components of success, so that, if they later failed, it was their own fault. Europeans, more convinced that certain social barriers were hard to transcend, never assumed quite so much (which is also why they supported welfare systems more readily, to compensate for social injustice). And Americans expected schools to do all sorts of things, providing lessons in driving and safety, hygiene, and temperance and sports experience that went beyond conventional education itself. Have a social problem? Install a class in the schools to teach children what to do. Training in chastity is but a recent example of a long-standing trend.

Yet Americans were also very suspicious of schools, easily believing that they were not doing their job (in part, of course, because expectations were so high). American teachers had relatively low prestige, compared to their counterparts elsewhere. Recurrent experiments tried to probe teachers' competence, but the results were not readily accepted. Laments about school quality dot the 20th century, and not just the most recent decades. Every twenty or thirty years since the 1890s, for example, Americans have learned that lots of students don't know much American history. From 1917: "Surely, a grade of 33 in 100 on the simplest and most obvious facts of American history is not a record in which any high school can take pride." From 1942: high school students are "all too ignorant of American history." From 1987: student test scores indicate that they are "at risk of being gravely handicapped upon entry into adulthood." Each probe resolutely refused to cite its predecessors, creating a sense of novel failure every generation. Reports on a new set of American history test results in 2002 again tried to create a sense that only contemporary American kids would not know that Bryan had attacked the gold standard. But this was part of the yin to the yang that was American enthusiasm for education.[1] . . .

What developed was in fact a twofold response. First, and most obviously in the initial reactions, was a concern that schools threatened to overburden youngsters, exposing them to unnatural stress. Second, not entirely consistently, came a sense that parents had a responsibility for the intelligence and achievement of their offspring, that they ought to be able to ensure successful schooling. Both of these strands continued to affect parental response throughout the 20th century. But they also came together, by the 1960s, in a third current, particularly vivid in the self-esteem movement. Schools should be sufficiently gentle on students that they could do well; schools should ease up on a number of traditional practices; and they should amplify rewards so that fragile childish psyches and parental obligation would both be honored.

SCHOOL AS THREAT

The early 20th century saw the full installation of schooling as childhood's chief responsibility. Children were not consulted as this transformation was completed, which was no big surprise, and adults proved quite wary of it, which was less predictable. A number of experts, led by G. Stanley Hall, contended that children were unprepared for schooling until age eight; Hall conceded that, at most, schooling might begin earlier so long as it had no academic content. Otherwise, children's physical and mental growth might be permanently retarded because their frail constitutions would be overly burdened.

Posture concerns were the focus of one protective reaction. Beginning in the 1880s, doctors began to claim that school desks and the amount of time spent in the classroom posed an unnatural risk for students, with severe implications for posture. One physician, with the hyperbole typical of posture anxieties for several decades, claimed that school desks were causing 92 percent of all students to suffer spinal cord deviations. Another expert attacked education more generally. "For if the State compels the child to go to school, and to undergo the constant risk of developing curvature of the spine . . . universal education must be considered as at least a doubtful blessing." And it was not just the time in school: homework also compelled children to hunch over, again in unnatural activities, with disastrous effects on their vulnerable bodies.[2] . . .

A more serious and longer-lasting attack on schools focused on homework, providing a surprising counterpart to the American enthusiasm for education in the early 20th century. . . .

Homework had not been a standard part of the 19th-century school experience, in part because so many children dropped out after fifth grade and so missed the exposure. High schools did set two to three hours of reading a night, which required some real adjustments in domestic chores, but again, most children were not affected. Like students with other difficulties that affected their schooling, like hyperactivity, kids who did not choose to handle the situation would just drop away, at a time when entering high school, much less completing it, was not a middle-class essential.

A full-bore encounter with homework, then, was part of the expansion and intensification of schooling around 1900, which is why reactions, though unexpected in contemporary terms, were not really surprising. With school requirements going up, children who disliked homework no longer had the easy option of dropping out. Parents quickly felt the brunt. A former Civil War hero, the father of two, lamented in the 1890s that homework tasks easily outstripped any educational value and became "the means of nervous exhaustion and agitation, highly prejudicial to body and to mind."

This combined argument—that homework did no educational good and that it sapped children's mental and physical health (an obvious corollary, perhaps indeed partly a cause, of the image of the vulnerable child)—persisted for many decades. . . .

From this point on, particularly through the 1950s but even beyond, experts began to debate the merits of homework, reaching no systematic conclusion. Some contended that the evidence definitely indicated that homework benefited children academically. Other studies, seemingly equally exhaustive, demonstrated that homework had no merit. The debates mirrored the more general adult uncertainties and also contributed to them. In this area, parents had no solid bank of expertise through which to resolve their own anxieties.

Buffeted by conflicting signals, from 1900 on a host of cities pondered and often regulated homework. Mother's clubs in Los Angeles, for example, worked hard to persuade schools to shape requirements to the ideas of the child study movement. Academic content in the primary years was diluted—with more attention to coloring, pasting, play skills, and naps, in a curriculum that survived into the 1930s. Early reading was downplayed, as we will see. Arithmetic was largely delayed until grade 3, and grammar instruction was abolished, making the primary grades, as one critic put it, "kindergartenized." And homework was banned entirely until the fourth grade, then doled out in fifteen- or thirty-minute intervals for in-school assignments for the rest of primary school. "The object specially in view in these changes," said the president of the school board, "has been to remove the obvious pressure which has been burdening the children." By 1901, two-thirds of American urban school districts had restricted homework; California, always in the vanguard of child protection, banned obligatory homework even in the first years of high school. . . .

By the 1920s, eye strain and what we would today call stress were being singled out. Children needed play, and an opportunity to be outside; schooling should nurture the whole child, not just the academic side, and it should be fun. The attacks on homework broadened into wider doubts about the link between childhood and academic endeavor, picking up larger American uncertainties not just about childhood but about intellectual life itself. . . .

And homework was attacked as a burden on parents, who had their own lives to lead, unencumbered by the need to supervise their children's schooling. Even some teachers worried that parents were too ignorant to give their children guidance and that homework would become the source of more confusion than anything else. An obvious compromise was the study hall, in which children did homework but in professionally supervised surroundings, and without the demands on afterschool hours that provoked attacks from so many different directions. Legal bans on homework endured and even expanded during the 1920s and 1930s; some regulations persisted into the 1960s.

By the 1940s, to be sure, while doubts lingered, advocates of homework began to gain the upper hand. Concerns about children's educational performance, heightened during the cold war, undercut most systematic anti-homework arguments, though individual parents continued to worry about overburdening the vulnerable child—and themselves. The Sputnik scare in 1957 gave an important boost to the homework argument, and so did the international competitiveness scare of the 1980s. In that decade, the 1983 report *A Nation at Risk* contended that two of the reasons America was falling behind academically were the reduction in homework and a short school year. . . .

For their part, parents, while largely accepting homework as inevitable, continued to have a battle to fight: how much should they themselves get involved? . . . In 2000, 58 percent of all American parents helped their children considerably. Some claimed that their children would not work otherwise: "He won't have it any other way. It's like 'If you don't sit down with me, I'm not going to do it'." Others phrased the issue in terms of obligation: "I know I should work with my children a lot more than I do. . . . They could have made straight As with a little effort—not only on their part, but on my part." . . .

More revealing was the installation of guidance systems and their transformation, a distinctive American twist on the mass education process between the world wars. Guidance programs in the schools initially aimed at providing vocational advice to lower-end, often immigrant children, early in the century, beginning with an effort in Michigan in 1907 and one in Boston in 1908. . . .

Parents still stood ready to protest aspects of schooling on the grounds that they overburdened children. The revival of testing and the increased emphasis on homework during the 1990s produced an interesting backlash. By 2001, some cities, like Alexandria, Virginia, passed laws limiting the amount of homework teachers could assign (in Alexandria, an hour and a half each night). Groups of parents, for example in suburban New York, attacked standardized testing that they believed placed too much pressure on their offspring. While the dominant approach shifted, children were still seen as needing protection from school demands.

HYPERACTIVE CHILDREN

The rise of modern schooling inevitably pinpointed children who had particular difficulty in fitting in. But the modes of identification and treatment could change. The story of hyperactive children in the 20th century shows both change and continuity in parents' efforts to deal with a sneaking sense that, given children's vulnerabilities, schooling was an unnatural act.

The pinpointing of hyperactivity in children illustrates a fascinating link between medical research and popular attitudes about, and settings for, children. Until the 20th century, the issue was subsumed in the larger question of discipline and was not specifically targeted. In colonial America, Protestant clergymen often resorted to physical discipline with children who could not sit still for long church services, but, since this was seen as an expression of children's original sin and natural unruliness, it did not come in for specific comment. School situations produced similar reactions, again with use of physical discipline and shaming well into the 19th century. We have no systematic indications of how what we would now call hyperactivity affected children's work performance.

The first signs of a new concern emerged in Europe. A German children's book in the 1850s featured a character, Fidgety Phil, who was the characteristic hyperactive child, unable to sit still. By this point, the demand for better manners in children included explicit injunctions about body control, which singled out children who had difficulties in this area; more regular schooling pointed in the same direction. A truly troubled child could still be pulled out of school and either sent directly to work or (in wealthy families) given private tutoring. . . .

But all of this background had little impact on most American parents and children. Already, in 1904, one researcher, Sanford Bell, had argued that childhood is nothing but motor activity, which made behavior problems in school inevitable: "one never sees a child of five devoting himself to mental things." Bell extended his argument that schooling constricted children and that restlessness was the natural result. "If anything should change in this equation, it should be school, not the child." A number of popular articles in the 1920s picked up the same theme. "It is rather that our treatment of these children is not calculated to develop the best type of adjustment of which they are capable." A number of studies did make claims about the large percentage of children who could not pay attention in school, but the implications were buried in the continued insistence on children's natural unfittedness for modern demands. A 1935 article in *Parents Magazine* noted: "At the very time when growing bodies demand movement and action, children enter school. . . . They want to run, to jump, to shout. They need such activity."[3] . . .

For more than half of the 20th century, then, American schools and parents were encouraged to recognize behavior problems associated with hyperactivity but not to apply any systematic remedies. The assumption that children were naturally troublesome in artificial settings like schools, combined with the urgent appeals for parental involvement in shaping natural emotions, seemed to cover the territory. American suspicions of schooling helped mask the problem. Assumptions about parental responsibility and the inevitability of anxiety generated the response to whatever problem was perceived.

But this situation began to change dramatically from the late 1950s on. A key innovation was the introduction of new psychostimulant medication, particularly the drug Ritalin. Now it was possible to be more candid about special problems of otherwise intelligent children and to identify them at a young age. As a *Scientific American* article put it, in 1970, "the hyperactive children's troubles had generally started at a very early age. About half of the mothers had begun to notice that their child was unusual before he was two years old." The formula did not change entirely: parents were still left with anxiety about their children. And there still could be a suspicion of schools themselves ("Parents . . . may want to consider the proposition that it is the schoolroom atmosphere and not the child's behavior which is pathological."). But, now, changes in attitudes, combined with the possibility of pharmaceutical redress, led to drastic changes in approach.[4]

Other factors entered the picture by the 1960s. Fewer children were being encouraged to drop out of school before completing high school. With more mothers working, parental availability to help with hyperactive children declined, and interest in finding other assistance intensified. With more children in day care facilities, opportunities to identify or investigate problems of hyperactivity at a younger age expanded. Increasing school integration in the United States exposed teachers to categories of children they might more readily define as behavior problems, and there was considerable evidence that minority boys were being singled out as unruly on the basis of teacher discomfort and stereotyping. Finally, teacher discipline was increasingly constrained by new rules: even minor physical punishments were outlawed. Children who had once been brought to attention by a slap on the hand were now described as hyperactive and given a pill, instead. And, summing up and extending the new approach, the problem gained a dramatic disease label by the 1970s: Attention Deficit Disorder (ADD).

The idea that something was wrong with one's child played on parents' old concerns once the buffering assumption that children in general found school restrictive was removed. Some parents resisted the label, insisting that their children simply had spunk that teachers should learn to accommodate. In general, however, the pressure increased to force parents to look for a special set of behavior problems in their children, as both advice literature and the general news media advertised the pervasiveness of ADD. "His mother found Jeremy hard to handle even as a baby. His teacher complained that he was hyperkinetic (overactive) and had an extremely short attention span . . . Jeremy was a 'classic case of minimal brain dysfunction'." "Very mild brain injuries are a much more common cause of excitability than people generally realize," an expert was noting as early as 1960.[5]

Acceptance of hyperactivity as a disease category gained ground steadily, and some schools refused to let certain children attend unless they were medicated. Estimates in 1980 that 3 percent of all children suffered from ADD grew to 5 percent a decade later. Production of Ritalin soared 500 percent between 1990 and 1996. Initial requirements that a full year of behavior problems formed the basis of diagnosis were soon cut back to six months. . . .

The 20th-century history of hyperactivity shows the pervasiveness of the sense that school and children, or at least some children, did not mix well—the constant during the entire century. Experts pressed for identification of particular children as dysfunctional. But it took a more sweeping set of factors, including available medication but also changes in schools and parental activities, to bring acceptance of the idea of disease. Particularly interesting, in this change, was the increased acceptance of limitations on traditional discipline, in school as well as at home, which made the search for other remedies truly urgent. But there was more to the change: after decades of combat, more parents had come to accept schooling as given and were now willing to change their children accordingly. Efforts to limit the rules attached to schooling had given way to anxiety-ridden diagnosis of one's own young children, to see whether yet another disease was present. By 1990, *Redbook* was even offering a new parental quiz: "Was your child unusually active in the womb?" Even with the promise of subsequent medication, the furrow of worry about children's adaptation to school still ran deep.[6] . . .

By the 1930s, most parents had experienced at least some high school. Generation gaps persisted, as each new generation faced educational requirements and opportunities greater than those that had faced its parents, but the degree of unfamiliarity with schooling declined. An increasingly service-based economy made education seem more meaningful (particularly for girls, who began by the 1920s to go to school longer on average than boys). While placement in high positions still depended less on educational level in the United States than in Europe, the educational requirements for success rose steadily. The turn to mass college attendance after World War II was decisive in this transition. Even by 2001, only a minority (25 percent) of all Americans had graduated from college, but the association of middle-class identity and some college attendance became increasingly close, and this in turn put a new premium on the educational attainments that would get one into college and at least partway through. National pressures could enter in, particularly the recurrent fears after World War II that American educational lags jeopardized competition in the cold war—the Sputnik crisis of

1957—or, later, in juxtaposition with the rise of Japan, that such lags threatened our global economic standing. It became harder to emphasize the need to protect children from schools instead of working toward maximizing their opportunity to do well.

PREPARING THE SUCCESSFUL CHILD

Assimilation of schooling goals, beyond sheer attendance, encouraged parental attention to the relevant aptitudes in their children. Here, too, by the early 20th century, experts were ready to step in with claims of capacity to test the kinds of intelligence that would lead to success in school and life. Ironically, while middle-class Americans favored aptitude tests, they did not sit still out of respect for their logic. For kids might not only be tested for aptitude, they could be coached to display greater aptitude (and it turned out, as College Board critics would later point out, that "aptitude" could indeed be improved by training). So American parents played a game of anxious inquiry into their children's academic potential combined with assiduous efforts to improve that potential through a variety of adult-guided activities. Here was a crucial twist on the vulnerable child motif: children might not, without parental assistance, have the natural aptitude to meet parental expectations for school success.

Schools used aptitude tests widely in the 1920s to sort populations, often heavily immigrant, into educational tracks. Once critic noted the enthusiasm as an "orgy of tabulation."[7] Middle-class parents largely accepted the tests, assuming their own children would naturally do well, but the result put pressure on these same parents to anticipate and promote good results.

Concern about possible deficiencies in young children was hardly a 20th-century invention. Many cultures urge parents to check their infants for deformities or for more subjective marks of inadequacy. Earlier in Western history, children born with a caul were viewed as possibly possessed by the devil. But the idea of explicitly evaluating intelligence, at a young age, was a product of the growing acceptance of schooling and schools [sic] goals. This gave new shape to what otherwise might seem a traditional anxiety, and it also promoted a host of parental efforts to remedy or prevent inadequacy.

The testing pressure gained ground in the 1920s, with experts like Lewis Terman claiming great precision in identifying school aptitude. As the decade wore on, testing claims were challenged, but, ironically, the claims were enhanced by other expert studies that showed that aptitude not only could be identified but could be improved. . . .

More generally, however, the idea of helping children prepare for school success followed from the growing internalization of educational goals as part of childhood, combined with some suspicion that schools themselves might not be up to the task or might not acknowledge the special qualities of one's own child. The American propensity for testing, including the growing frequency of school tests and the heavy relevance on aptitude, have drawn legitimate attention in terms of their impact on lower-class and minority groups. They also deserve attention for their role in shaping middle-class concerns about their own kids.

Two kinds of parental anxieties reflected the growing commitment to the educational process: a desire to stimulate younger children before the age of formal schooling and, by the 1960s, the growing competitive frenzy over college admissions as a badge of parental fulfillment.

Interest in stimulating cognitive development in young children began to take new forms in the 1920s and 1930s. It built on Enlightenment beliefs that children were open to improvement through education, on earlier parental commitments to buying toys and books that could awaken a child's intellectual interests, and on kindergarten programs designed in part to promote later school success. But the 20th century added new particulars to this broader current.

By the 1920s, child-rearing books and articles began to add cognitive concerns to their predominant emphasis on health, hygiene, and character. . . .

For it was increasingly argued, as in other aspects of child rearing, that the child's early years were crucial in preparing for school success. Schooling, in this sense, could not be left to schools alone, for the years of greatest parental responsibility were decisive in facilitating later results. Hence the anxious interest in early indications of intelligence and the growing array of school-related stimulation offered to infants and toddlers.

These currents were amplified in the 1960s and 1970s, when the commitment to schooling escalated nationwide. Books like Joan Beck's *How to Raise a Brighter Child* (1975) or Glenn Doman's *How to Multiply your Baby's Intelligence* summed up the growing interest and sold hundreds of thousands of copies. Nationally, this interest generated programs such as Head Start, aimed at poorer families. In the middle class, the interest stimulated a growing commitment to buying things that would advance the child's intelligence from infancy on. Outfits like the Princeton-based Creative Playthings seized on parents' desire to acquire toys that would directly instill the process of self-improvement. Cribs began to be filled not just with emotionally comforting teddy bears but with eye-catching mobiles that, the experts argued, would push Jane or Johnny a bracket higher in later intelligence. Color began to factor in, as pundits urged that painting the infant's room orange had stimulating effects.

There were also lessons, and competitive nursery schools from the toddler years on. Some lessons, like dance for girls or soccer, recalled older middle-class traditions of equipping children with appropriate social graces, leisure skills, and gender identities; some embraced related goals of character building and the fostering of team skills. But the new goal of stimulation, of giving one's offspring a leg up on later studies, gained growing momentum. Music lessons began to be sold, for example, not just for their intrinsic merits but on the basis of research that suggested their role in developing intelligence. . . .

The second big middle-class school commitment, building on the concern about school aptitude and its testing and enhancement, involved the post-World War II assumption that college attendance and middle-class status went hand in hand. . . . Post-World War II programs for veterans provided unprecedentedly wide college access. . . . The conversion of many elite schools to coeducation, beginning in the 1960s, added to this thrust. By the 1960s, about half of all Americans of standard college age were entering college, and while this was admittedly a smaller percentage than the 85 percent of the population that claimed to be middle class, it marked a huge surge in the commitment to college attendance. Parents and children both participated in these new assumptions. And the trend continued; between 1974 and 1988, enrollment among white Americans of the relevant age shot up from 47 percent to 60 percent.

A decisive step in this process, and the one that converted a new pattern to a new level of anxiety, occurred in the 1960s, when the baby boom generation began competing for college access. Already, of course, the surge in attendance had strained facilities. Now, it became increasingly clear that many students could not expect to get into the level of college they had anticipated, for the top schools simply did not expand as rapidly as the demand. The blow was particularly acute for groups, like middle-class Anglo-Saxon males, that suffered not only from the results of overall crowding but from the increasingly successful incursions by second- and third-generation immigrants, women, African Americans, and, soon, Asian Americans.

The situation converted a well-established pecking order among institutions of higher learning to a competitive frenzy in which parents were, if anything, more involved than their offspring. It became a test of parental adequacy to do everything possible not just to make sure the child got into college but to ensure that he or she got into a good one. Multiple applications to colleges soared as parents tried to encourage children to maximize their chance to attend a top school, while maintaining a safety school application in case the best hopes were dashed. The competitive game could be played at multiple levels, for the pecking order extended from top to bottom. Some parents and children aimed desperately at the Ivies; others, no less eager but operating in a different financial or academic context, pinned their hopes on the state's top public university. Needless to say, discussions among parents of college-age children routinely included carefully worded reminders about the status factors involved, as parents gleefully noted their children's success or tried to avoid condescension when friends admitted that a second-tier state college was the best they could muster.

What was particularly interesting about this anxiety about college was that it outlasted the baby boom. Anxiety about getting into the appropriate college persisted in the 1970s and 1980s, when in fact admission into a very good college became easier and admission to a good college was widely attainable. It remained so important to aim high that the competitive worries did not ebb. Colleges, of course, played this situation to the hilt, assuring parents that their admission standards were indeed quite high and that their children's future might well depend on this particular opportunity. . . .

In this context, the proliferation of college rating publications, launched in the 1980s, fed on and in turn nourished the competitive anxiety. The idea of ranking colleges played off parental status commitments on their children's behalf and made the markers involved more concrete and public than ever before. *U.S. News and World Report,* which particularly profited from the frenzy, steadfastly refused to ease the pressure, and no major college was bold enough to refuse to participate in the ranking program.

Predictably, the college competitive anxiety deepened by the late 1990s and early 2000s when the growth of the college-age cohort—the result of the baby boom echo—really did make it harder once again to get into top colleges. Parents were described as "frantic" in the college application year. They desperately monitored children's grades, the playing time they got on the soccer field—all the components of a successful college push. Some claimed even to despair that their children would get into college at all, which was frankly ridiculous, given the number of slots available. Horror stories circulated, and expanded in the process, about National Merit Scholar kids who did not get into even less desirable but still top-tier schools. Amid the undeniably increasing competition (which . . . lessened in 2008), the anxiety threatened to spin out of control.

Parental anxiety mounted for yet another, perhaps more tangible reason: the burden of college costs. The United States was unique in assuming that parents were the primary source of support for college training—an assumption with which most parents agreed. To be sure, other sources were important, including government payments.

ABOVE-AVERAGE AVERAGES

So far this chapter has dealt with anxieties about schooling and about children's potential for achievement. . . . Rapid suburbanization after World War II represented in part a quest for good schools, defined in terms not only of safety and considerable homogeneity but also of solid academic standards.

Yet this is not the entire story. As achievement concerns intensified, particularly from the 1960s on, parents and other adults groped for a fuller reconciliation between an acceptance of academic goals and a concern that children might be overburdened. Without disputing the importance of academic goals directly, there was a new search for innovations that would reduce the load. Two related movements particularly captured this flavor, and both led to significant changes in the presentation of school: the self-esteem campaign and the persistent tendency toward grade inflation. Both trends sought to make it easier for schools to ensure success without forcing frontal attacks like the earlier assault on homework. These trends developed at about the same time as the formal recognition of Attention Deficit Disorder, which offered medical treatment for another set of students who could, with assistance, hope to measure up.

SELF-ESTEEM

It is not easy to explain why the self-esteem movement kicked off in the post–World War II decades. Of course, it was prepared by earlier expertise and then enhanced by a new generation of studies; in part, we're back in the chicken-and-egg causation problem that 20th-century expertise routinely evokes. But if one assumes, as in previous discussions, that more is involved in explaining why the public picked up on the issue—that parents and school authorities were not merely being shepherded by the gurus—three concurrent factors come into play.

First, the American economy was shifting rapidly toward service-sector functions—sales work and middle-management coordination—in which social skills played a growing role. There is no question that middle-class parents were becoming increasingly sensitive to this transition by the 1950s. The transition meant, in turn, a growing concern with sociability—good social skills, the ability to get along with others. And the experts made a convincing case that self-esteem was in turn a crucial variable in this social equation. As one put it, "Success . . . is measured by the concern, attention, and love expressed by others. These expression of appreciation and interest are subsumed under the general terms of acceptance and popularity, while their polar opposites are termed rejected and isolation."[8] School performance and sociability became increasingly linked: both were essential for adult success, and both should be enhanced by appropriate attention to self-esteem. The self-esteem movement was directly associated with growing sensitivity to social criteria and the opinions of others, as Americans moved from a manufacturing to a service-sector economy, from entrepreneurship to organizational skills. David Riesman captured this sea change as the rise of "other-directedness," and attention to self-esteem was a vital attribute.

Second, the self-esteem emphasis played on growing uneasiness felt by many middle-class parents about the quality of family life they were offering to their children. Divorce rates were soaring by the 1950s. Women were going back to work. Surely developments of this sort must take a toll. Measuring and bolstering children's self-esteem became something of a barometer in an anxious period in American family history. Schools might be called upon to pick up the slack, and many school authorities, worried about family conditions even in suburbia, ratcheted up their commitment to protecting children's psyches. Whether wittingly or not, expert formulations about self-esteem directly played on uncertainties about the quality of family life, even in middle-class households.

Finally, the focus on self-esteem captured developments that more directly involved children. There was an obvious link, chronologically and substantively, to the more permissive disciplinary approach, after the behaviorist fling of the interwar decades and to the ongoing worries about the corrosive effects of guilt. While studies suggested that strict standards, equitably applied, might actually bolster self-esteem, a more popular conclusion was that children needed help and latitude in living up to standards, less chance to feel guilty about failure, and more opportunity to express the self in the process. The height of the baby boom also raised explicit concerns, within families and in crowded classrooms, about whether individual children were now receiving the attention they deserved; some special compensatory actions, in the form of attention to self-esteem, might be essential.

The self-esteem movement, as an adjustment between school commitments and worries about overburdening children, arose, then, at a time of significant rethinking about the preconditions of adult success, amid some lessening of confidence in the middle-class home environment, and in the presence of some very practical problems in dealing with the baby boom surge. Prepared by earlier psychological inquiry, the movement sought a new intermediation between school and child, while bolstering parental interests in providing a supportive disciplinary approach outside of school. . . .

GRADE INFLATION

A 1983 study noted that 60 percent of high school grades were As and Bs, compared to less than 50 percent in 1968. By 1979, again in the high schools, among college-bound students, there were twenty-one A averages for every twenty C averages, as the number of A averages increased by about two-thirds. Between 1969 and 1981, all students, whether college-bound or not, saw the rates of largely—A performances shoot up by 15 percent. And the trend continued. Between 1987 and 1994, as SAT scores declined by about ten points, the total number of high school students receiving As jumped another 12 percent, to a total of 32 percent. Colleges followed suit. By the 1990s, prestigious colleges like the Ivies and Stanford were giving more than 60 percent of all students honors upon graduation. A notorious Yale case, in which a California junior college failure faked his credentials to gain entry, only to find he made As and Bs with ease, drove the point home.[9] . . .

The real explanation lies, as many critics have recognized, in changes in attitudes, among teachers and parents, toward their own, middle-class kinds of kids. It relates closely to the assumption of the self-esteem movement that education must make students feel capable and empowered. Grade inflation builds on a growing adult desire to be friends with kids—the dad-as-pal approach—as well as a desire to minimize confrontation with anxious parents. Traditional grading encourages stress and competition, and a newer approach was required to create a greater sense of harmony. . . .

Approaches to children and schooling, as they developed in the 20th century, obviously permitted many variations on the part of individual parents or larger social and cultural groups. The huge range, from the idea of natural aversion to school to the embrace of hothouse promotion of academic success, permitted a host of gradations. While some parents felt perfectly comfortable intervening for a child with a hard-grading teacher, others held back, embarrassed or convinced that children might benefit from a few hard knocks. Mothers and fathers debated what approach to take; studies from the 1920s on, feeding off gender stereotypes, portrayed mothers as more eager to protect children's fragile psyches. And there were generational differences, as well, with adults' moods shifting somewhat over time. Overall, some 20th-century parents pushed their children hard toward school success, eschewing the protections of self-esteem ideas or grade inflation, while others were more indulgent.

And there were always exceptions to the general patterns. Sports and music provide two fascinating examples. For devoted children and their parents, both offered clear goals that overrode adult concerns about childhood vulnerability in a way that academic schooling never quite managed to do. The implied priorities were intriguing.

I watched two of my children commit to a serious interest in musical productions in high school. I would pick them up after rehearsals (which always ran late) and watch as the music director berated the whole cast, telling them how lazy and incompetent they were, driving them frequently to tears. And I wondered why the students put up with this kind of treatment, which they never would have tolerated from a classroom teacher. My children told me to mind my own business, that the show was the important thing and they needed to be driven.

The same thing happened with my stepson's basketball: his coaches could shout, curse, even physically intimidate, and the players found the behavior perfectly natural. Coaches could seem to be throw-backs to the era of the sturdy child, when passionate commitments could lead to what, in other settings, 20th-century parents would have regarded as abusive goading, with anger and shame were seen as valid motivators. Even a coach like Bobby Knight, long of Indiana University, could survive repeated reports of verbal harassment and physical violence against his players, because of a larger commitment to winning and because many parents harbored a sneaking suspicion that this approach was best for character growth. The oddity was that the same tolerance rarely extended to the tough, abrasive teacher. . . .

Another adjustment area was fascinating. Claims for special needs for children accelerated steadily by the later 20th century. By 2002, a quarter of all children in the Fairfax (VA) County public schools were designated special needs. This ran the gamut from Attention Deficit Disorder to particular nutritional requirements, but the percentage was nevertheless staggering, in one of the most affluent regions of the nation. The claims reflected a rich school district's sincere attempt to accommodate students; it reflected middle-class parental alertness in claiming every possible advantage for one's own children. It also reflected, on the part of parents and authorities alike, an assumption that frailty was likely, and that it legitimately commanded compensation lest schooling prove overwhelming.

CONCLUSION

Is school too hard for my kid? Did my kid do well enough? Both questions are reasonable, as parents consider contemporary schooling. Each, however, points in somewhat different directions. It's the combination that promotes parental anxiety and prompts many of the reactions that developed during the past century in the United States.

During the course of the 20th century, with many specific twists and turns, adults tried to accommodate their worries about children—their own precious cargo particularly—and schooling. It would be easy, especially in noting the eventual move toward self-esteem movements and grade inflation, to go on to the standard lament about academic decline. . . .

Most claims of academic deterioration use some (often illusory) earlier 20th-century benchmark against post-1960s degeneration. But, in fact, parents have worried about schooling, while embracing aspects of it, for a full century. Specific accommodations to schooling have changed, but not the fundamental tension. This is one reason that studies of student achievement do not reveal the deterioration so often claimed: laments about performance gaps pervade the early 20th century as well as our own decade, and the sum total, measured over time, is complex.

Furthermore, we have been talking about an embrace of tensions, not a renunciation of standards. Parents who attacked homework may have been nervous about other aspects of schooling, but they did not request that their children not be educated. Implicit proponents of grade inflation do not usually argue that there should be no norms or differentiations. Many of the same parents who press their children's teacher for As also put their kids through rigorous sets of lessons. And they expect some strictly academic challenges, in the form, for example, of the College Board SATs, which they cannot directly finesse with the lures of grade inflation. It is a mixture of rigor and protections for self-esteem, not the latter alone, that predominate. . . .

The formula, since the 1960s, has been fairly clear, if rarely fully articulated. Teach the children, but not too hard and with some attention to childhood frailties, accommodated through sympathetic grades or a bit of medication. In return, we parents accept, on behalf of our children, the almost unavoidable challenge of getting into college and in the process facing some tests that cannot be entirely cushioned. These are the exercises, separate from grade inflation, that can be prepared for but not ultimately controlled—whether the hurdle is the SATs or their slightly across-the-tracks cousins, the ACTs. We'll accept the results, consoling our kids (but sending them off to the best school possible) as necessary. This bargain established more strident voices, like the loudest critics of the SATs who urge really different measurements and standards that, for example, tap into less familiar kinds of creative talents, win an indulgent smile but little more. For a large group of Americans, a difficult encounter with contemporary education has been managed, within the parameters shaped by assumptions of childhood vulnerability and with no small amount of anxiety about what level of achievement to prepare for, what weaknesses to cater to. . . .

Discussion Questions

1. Why do you think concerns about children being overloaded by school work have recurred throughout the decades?

2. Consider the growth in prescribing children drugs for Attention Deficit Disorder. Why do you think that behavior problems like ADD are often first brought up by teachers?

3. According to the author, what is behind the tremendous anxiety about college admissions?

4. What do you think the self-esteem movement described in this chapter tells us about the social construction of childhood?

Notes

1. Sam Wineburg, "Making Historical Sense," in Peter N. Stearns, Peter Seixas, and Sam Wineburg, eds., *Knowing, Teaching, and Learning History* (New York, 2001), p. 306.
2. Tait Mackenzie, "The Influence of School Life on Curvature of the Spine," *American Physical Education Review* 3 (1893), pp. 274–80; Walter Truslow, *Body Poise* (Baltimore, 1943), p. 130.
3. Sanford Bell, "The Significance of Activity in Child Life," *Independent* 55 (1903), pp. 9, 11; Adeline Dartt, "What Can I Do with Johnny?" *Mental Hygiene* 10 (1926), p. 54.
4. Gertrude Driscool, "What's behind Naughtiness?" *Parents Magazine* 10 (June 1935), p. 26.
5. Martin Stewart, "Hyperactive Children," *Scientific American* (April 1970), p. 96; Lucy Kavaler, "If You Have a High-Strung Child," *Parents Magazine* 36 (Mar. 1961), p. 120.
6. Stephanie Garber, M. D. Garber, and Robyn Spizman, "Is Your Child Hyperactive?" *Redbook* (Oct. 1990), p. 32.
7. Gregory Cizek, "Pockets of Resistance in the Assessment Revolution," *Educational Measurement: Issues and Practice* (summer 2000), pp. 16–23; Julia Wrigley, "Do Young Children Need Intellectual Stimulation? Experts' Advice to Parents, 1900–1985," *History of Education Quarterly* 29 (1989), pp. 41–75.
8. Sidonie Gruenberg, *The Parent's Guide to Everyday Problems of Boys and Girls* (New York, 1958), p. 192.
9. Wayne Lanning and Peggy Perkins, "Grade Inflation," *Journal of Instructional Psychology* 22 (1990), pp. 163–68.

In Search of the Child

DAVID BUCKINGHAM

INTRODUCTION

Many people believe that children are growing up "too fast." This notion presumes that there is a "natural" pace at which children "should" grow up. However, as author David Buckingham points out in this selection, children's lives take place in social, cultural, and economic realities that not only shape their experiences, but adults' understandings of the meaning of childhood itself. Rather than lamenting its demise, Buckingham encourages us to think critically about how—and why—we construct the meaning of childhood the way that we do.

The claim that childhood has been lost has been one of the most popular laments of the closing years of the twentieth century. It is a lament that has echoed across a whole range of social domains—in the family, in the school, in politics, and perhaps above all in the media. Of course, the figure of the child has always been the focus of adult fears, desires and fantasies. Yet in recent years, debates about childhood have become invested with a growing sense of anxiety and panic. Traditional certainties about the meaning and status of childhood have been steadily eroded and undermined. We no longer seem to know where childhood can be found.

The place of the child in these debates is profoundly ambiguous, however. On the one hand, children are increasingly seen as threatened and endangered. Thus, we have seen a succession of high-profile investigations into child abuse, both in families and in schools and children's homes. There are frequent press reports about child murders and the scandal of neglected 'home alone kids'; and public hysteria about the risk of random abduction by pedophiles has steadily intensified. Meanwhile, our newspapers and television screens show scenes of the very different childhoods of children in developing countries: the street children of Latin America, the child soldiers in Africa and the victims of sex tourism in Asia.

On the other hand, children are also increasingly perceived as a threat to the rest of us—as violent, anti-social and sexually precocious. There has been growing concern about the apparent collapse of discipline in schools, and the rise in child crime, drug-taking and teenage pregnancy. As in the 1970s, the threat of an uncontrollable underclass of young people, caught in the liminal space between school and work, has begun to loom large—although this time around, the delinquents are even younger. The sacred garden of childhood has increasingly been violated; and yet children themselves seem ever more reluctant to remain confined within it.

The media are implicated here in contradictory ways. On the one hand, they serve as the primary vehicle for these ongoing debates about the changing nature of childhood—and in the process, they undoubtedly contribute to the growing sense of fear and panic. Yet on the other hand, the media are frequently blamed for *causing* those problems in the first place—for provoking indiscipline and aggressive behavior, for inflaming precocious sexuality, and for destroying the healthy social bonds which might prevent them from arising in the first place. Journalists, media pundits, self-appointed guardians of public morality—and increasingly academics and politicians—are incessantly called on to pronounce on the dangers of the media for children: the influence of violent video [games], the 'dumbing down' of children's television, the explicit sexuality of teenage magazines and the easy availability of pornography via the internet. And the media are now routinely condemned for 'commercializing' childhood—for transforming children into rapacious consumers, seduced by the deceptive wiles of advertisers into wanting what they do not need.

Meanwhile, the media themselves display an ambivalent fascination with the very *idea* of childhood. Hollywood movies have become preoccupied with the figure of the child-like adult (*Forest Gump, Toys, Dumb and Dumber*) and the adult-like child (*Jack, Little Man Tate, Big*). Advertising images display a similar ambivalence, from the notorious black devil/white angel of the campaign for Benetton clothing to the waif-like supermodels of the Calvin Klein ads. Meanwhile, the resurgence of the Disney Corporation points to the global marketability of conventional 'children's culture' to both adults and children—although, ironically, *Kids*, Larry Clark's controversial documentary-style film of casual sex and drugs among younger teenagers in New York, is also owned by a Disney subsidiary.

And then there is the figure of Michael Jackson—in the words of his biographer, 'the man who was never a child and the child who never grew up'.[1] From the children's crusade represented in his 'Heal the World' video, through his obsession with the imagery of Disney and Peter Pan, to the scandals surrounding allegations about his sexual abuse of children, Jackson epitomizes the intense uncertainty and discomfort that has come to surround the notion of childhood in the late modern era.

The responses of politicians and policy-makers to this sense of crisis have been largely authoritarian and punitive. To be sure, there has been a renewed emphasis on children's rights in recent years, in the wake of the United Nations Convention on the Rights of the Child; although in practice, this has often been interpreted as simply a matter of children's right to protection by adults. In most other respects, there has been increasing enthusiasm for more disciplinary social policies. Thus, we have seen the introduction of curfews and the building of new children's prisons. . . . Such policies appear to be designed not so much to protect children from adults as to protect adults from children.

In relation to the media, the official response has also been predominantly a disciplinary one. In the wake of growing moral panics about the influence of sex and violence in the media, governments in many countries have introduced tighter censorship legislation; and in North America we have seen the introduction of the V-chip, a technical device fitted to all new television sets that will apparently filter out 'violent' material. Meanwhile, there is growing interest in the potential of blocking software, programs with symptomatically anthropomorphic titles like 'Net Nanny' and 'Cyber Sitter' that promise to restrict children's access to proscribed sites on the internet. Yet despite this search for a 'technological fix', national governments appear ever more incapable of regulating the commercial corporations that now control the global circulation of media commodities—not least those aimed at the children's market.

Nevertheless, interpretations of these changes in childhood—and of the role of the media in reflecting or producing them—have been sharply polarized. On the one hand, there are those who argue that childhood as we know it is disappearing or dying, and that the media— particularly television—are primarily to blame. From this perspective, the media are seen to have erased the boundaries between childhood and adulthood, and hence to have undermined the authority of adults. On the other hand, there are those who argue that there is a growing generation gap in media use—that young people's experience of new media technologies (and particularly of computers) is driving a wedge between their culture and that of their parents' generation. Far from erasing the boundaries, the media are seen here to have reinforced them—although now it is adults who are believed to have most to lose, as children's expertise with technology gives them access to new forms of culture and communication that largely escape parental control.

To some extent, these arguments can be seen as part of a more general anxiety about social change which has accompanied the advent of a new millennium. The metaphor of 'death' is everywhere around us—not least on bookshelves, where books about the death of child- hood sit alongside those about the death of the self, of society, of ideology, and of history. Such debates often seem to permit only a narrow choice between grandiose despair and breathless optimism.

In the first part of this (chapter), I review these contrasting arguments in more detail, and seek to challenge the totalizing rhetoric that characterizes them. As I shall indicate, both positions are based on essentialist views of childhood and of communications media—and indeed of the relationships between them. Yet for all their limitations, these arguments point to two significant assumptions which form the basis of my analysis here. Both implicitly and ex- plicitly, they suggest that the notion of childhood is itself a social, historical construction; and that culture and representation—not least in the form of electronic media—are one of the main arenas in which that construction is developed and sustained.

CONSTRUCTING CHILDHOOD

The idea that childhood is a social construction is now commonplace in discussions of the history and sociology of childhood; and it is even being increasingly accepted by some psy- chologists.[2] The central premise here is that 'the child' is not a natural or universal category, which is simply determined by biology. Nor is it something which has a fixed meaning, in whose name appeals can unproblematically be made. On the contrary, childhood is historically, culturally and socially variable. Children have been regarded—and have regarded themselves—in very different ways in different historical periods, in different cultures and in different social groups. Furthermore, even these definitions are not fixed. The meaning of 'childhood' is subject to a constant process of struggle and negotiation, both in public discourse (for example, in the media, in the academy or in social policy) and in interpersonal relation- ships, among peers and in the family.

This is not to imply that the biological individuals whom we might collectively agree to call 'children' somehow do not exist, or that we cannot describe them. Rather, it is to say that these collective definitions are the outcome of social and discursive processes. There is a kind of circularity here. Children are defined as a particular category, with particular characteristics and limitations, both by themselves and by others—by parents, teachers, researchers, politi- cians, policymakers, welfare agencies, and (of course) by the media. These definitions are codified in laws and policies; and they are embodied within particular forms of institutional and social practice, which in turn help to *produce* the forms of behavior which are seen as typically 'child-like'—and simultaneously to generate forms of resistance to them.[3]

Schooling, for example, is a social institution that effectively constructs and defines what it means to be a child—and indeed a child of a particular age. The separation of children by biological age rather than 'ability', the highly regulated nature of teacher/student relationships, the organization of the curriculum and the daily timetable, the practice of grading—all in various ways serve to reinforce and to naturalize particular assumptions about what children are and should be. And yet these definitions are, for the most part, only made explicit in specialized forms of institutional and professional discourse from which children themselves are largely excluded.

Of course, these various definitions and discourses are not necessarily consistent or coherent. On the contrary, we should expect them to be characterized by resistance and contradiction. The school and the family, for instance, appear to lay out clear definitions of the rights and responsibilities of both adults and children. Yet as teachers and parents know only too well, children routinely challenge and renegotiate these definitions, not always directly but often through what amounts to a form of guerrilla warfare. Furthermore, the expectations of these institutions are often themselves contradictory. On the one hand, for example, parents and teachers will routinely exhort children to 'grow up', and to behave in what they perceive as a mature and responsible way; while on the other, they will deny children privileges on the grounds that they are not yet old enough to deserve or appreciate them. And at the same time, becoming—and being perceived to be—an adult necessarily involves suppressing elements of one's behavior which others might deem to be inappropriately 'childish'.

'Childhood' is thus a shifting, relational term, whose meaning is defined primarily through its opposition to another shifting term, 'adulthood'. Yet even where the respective roles of children and adults are defined in law, there is considerable uncertainty and inconsistency. Thus, the age at which childhood legally ends is defined primarily (and crucially) in terms of children's *exclusion* from practices which are defined as properly 'adult', most obviously, paid employment, sex, drinking alcohol and voting. Yet in each case, children are seen to attain majority at a different age. . . .

REPRESENTING CHILDHOOD

Broadly speaking, the definition and maintenance of the category 'childhood' depends on the production of two main kinds of discourses. First, there are discourses *about* childhood, produced by adults primarily *for adults*—not only in the form of academic or professional discourse, but also in the form of novels, television [programs] and popular advice literature. Indeed, 'scientific' or 'factual' discourses about childhood (for example, those of psychology, physiology or medicine) are often intimately connected with 'cultural' or 'fictional' ones (such as philosophy, imaginative literature, or painting). Second, there are discourses produced by adults *for children*, in the form of children's literature, television and other media—which, despite the label, are rarely produced by children themselves.

Thus, the period in which our characteristic modern definition of childhood emerged—the second half of the nineteenth century—was characterized by an explosion of such discourses. During this period, children were gradually and systematically segregated from the world of adults, for example through the raising of the age of consent, the introduction of compulsory education, and attempts to eradicate child labor. Children were gradually moved out of the factories, off the streets and into the schools; and a whole range of new social institutions and agencies sought to oversee their welfare in line with a broadly middle-class domestic ideal, and thereby to ensure the 'health of the nation'.[4]

This demarcation of childhood as a distinct stage of life—and the removal of children from what Harry Hendrick has termed socially significant activity[5]—was both justified by and reflected in discourses of both kinds. The work of the Romantic poets and Victorian novelists, for example, placed a central emphasis on the innate purity and natural goodness of children. For writers as diverse as Dickens and Wordsworth, the figure of the child became a powerful symbol in their critique of industrialism and social inequality. Childhood became, according to the historian Hugh Cunningham, 'a substitute for religion'.[6] It was also at this time that the scientific study of children—most notably in the form of pediatrics and developmental psychology—began to be established,[7] and such work quickly found its way into popular advice literature directed at parents.

Meanwhile, this period is also often seen as the Golden Age of children's literature: the work of writers such as Lewis Carroll, Edward Lear and J. M. Barrie reflected the widespread fascination and longing for childhood—not to mention the unresolved tensions around children's sexuality—which were characteristic of the time.[8] At the same time, the origins of more 'vulgar' (and indeed 'violent') forms of popular literature aimed at children—and particularly at working-class boys—can also be traced to this period; as can the first wide-scale marketing of toys and educational materials designed for use in the home.[9]

Of course, this is not to say that 'children' were somehow conjured into existence by these means, or indeed that such discourses and representations had not previously existed. It is merely to note that broader historical shifts in the social status of children are often accompanied by this kind of proliferation in discourse. . . . Similar developments occurred in the sixteenth and seventeenth centuries, and are also taking place at the present time.

Inevitably, the audiences for these two types of discourse are bound to overlap. Children are often extremely interested in certain forms of discourse *about* childhood, particularly where this touches on the most obviously forbidden forms of adult behavior. And adults play a significant part in mediating texts *to* children, for example by buying and reading books for them, or by accompanying them to the cinema. Certain kinds of texts—the contemporary 'family' films of Walt Disney or Steven Spielberg, for example—could be seen precisely to unite these two audiences: they tell both adults and children very powerful and seductive stories about the relative meanings of childhood and adulthood. As in a good deal of nineteenth-century literature, the figure of the child here is at once a symbol of hope and a means of exposing adult guilt and hypocrisy. Such films often define the meaning of childhood by projecting its future loss: both for adults and for children, they mobilize anxieties about the pain of mutual separation, while offering reassuring fantasies about how it can be overcome.[10]

These cultural representations of childhood are thus often contradictory. They frequently say much more about adults' and children's fantasy investments in the *idea* of childhood than they do about the realities of children's lives; and they are often imbued with nostalgia for a past Golden Age of freedom and play. However, these representations cannot be dismissed as merely illusory. Their power depends on the fact that they also convey a certain truth: they must speak in intelligible ways, both to children's lived experiences and to adult memories, which may be painful as well as pleasurable.

As Patricia Holland argues, these representations of childhood are part of a continuous effort on the part of adults to gain control over childhood and its implications—not only over actual children, but also over our own childhoods, which we are constantly mourning and constantly reinventing. Such imagery, she argues,

> displays the social and psychic effort that goes into negotiating the difficult distinction between adult and child, to keep childhood separate from an adulthood that can never be fully achieved. Attempts are made to establish dual and opposing categories and hold them firm in a dichotomy set against the actual continuity of growth and development. There is an active struggle to maintain childhood—if not actual children—as pure and uncontaminated.[11]

As Holland emphasizes, these cultural constructions of childhood serve functions not merely for children, but also for adults. The idea of childhood serves as a depository for qualities which adults regard both as precious and as problematic—qualities which they cannot tolerate as part of themselves; yet it can also serve as a dream world into which we can retreat from the pressures and responsibilities of maturity.[12] Such representations, Holland argues, reflect 'the desire to use childhood to secure the status of adulthood—often at the expense of children themselves'.[13]

CHILDHOOD, POWER AND IDEOLOGY

This view of childhood as a social and cultural construction is thus to some extent a relativist one. It reminds us that our contemporary notion of childhood—of what children are and should be—is comparatively recent in origin, and that it is largely confined to Western industrialized societies. The majority of the world's children today do not live according to 'our' conception of childhood.[14] To judge these alternative constructions of childhood—and the children whose lives are lived within them—as merely 'primitive' is to display a dangerously narrow ethnocentrism. Likewise, this perspective causes us to question the notion that the modern age was one in which the innate 'needs' of children were truly recognized for the first time. On the contrary, such definitions of children's unique characteristics and needs are themselves culturally and historically produced; and they necessarily imply particular forms of political and social organization.

Furthermore, this view of childhood reminds us that any description of children—and hence any invocation of the idea of childhood—cannot be neutral. On the contrary, any such discussion is inevitably informed by an *ideology* of childhood—that is, a set of meanings which serve to rationalize, to sustain or to challenge existing relationships of power between adults and children, and indeed between adults themselves.[15]

This is most apparent when one considers how the figure of the child is invoked by social movements, ranging from the broadly progressive to the distinctly reactionary. In his analysis of the moral panics that have characterized British social life over the past two decades, Philip Jenkins identifies a 'politics of substitution' which has been practiced by moral entrepreneurs of both left and right.[16] In a climate of growing uncertainty, invoking fears about children provides a powerful means of commanding public attention and support: campaigns against homosexuality are redefined as campaigns against pedophiles; campaigns against pornography become campaigns against child pornography; and campaigns against immorality and Satanism become campaigns against ritualistic child abuse. Those who have the temerity to doubt claims about the epidemic proportions of such phenomena can therefore easily be stigmatized as hostile to children.

However, this is not to imply that such concerns are necessarily illegitimate or false. On the contrary, they would not be so widely felt if they did not in some way build on pre-existing anxieties—which, as Jenkins indicates, are themselves a response to fundamental social changes, for example in the nature of the family. Nevertheless, invoking the figure of the threatened child clearly serves particular functions, both for campaigning groups and for government. The wave of concern around child abuse in the 1980s, for example, furthered the political ambitions both of Christian evangelical groups and of feminists, whose influence came to dominate social work and welfare agencies. Yet it also enabled the government to distract attention from the more intractable economic and social problems of the time; and as a result, the extent to which children themselves can be seen to have benefited from such campaigns is certainly debatable.

Of course, moral panics of this kind are not the only arena in which the notion of childhood is invoked in this way. The discourse of environmentalism, for example, is often implicitly addressed to children, on the grounds that they represent 'the future' and are somehow 'closer to nature'. . . . The child is often seen as the most helpless victim of social policies that are primarily directed against women, or against the working classes; and here again, the call to protect children acts as a powerful means of mobilizing support.[17] For those with a wide range of motivations, adult politics are often carried out in the name of childhood.

Likewise, the production of texts *for* children—both in the modern electronic media, and in more traditional forms like children's literature—can also be seen to sustain particular ideologies of childhood. Such activity has traditionally been characterized by a complex balance between 'negative' and 'positive' motivations. On the one hand, producers have been strongly informed by the need to protect children from 'undesirable' aspects of the adult world. Indeed, in some respects, texts for children could be characterized primarily in terms of what they are *not*—that is, in terms of the *absence* of representations that are seen to constitute a negative moral influence, most obviously in the form of sex and violence.[18] On the other hand, there are also strong pedagogical motivations: such texts are frequently characterized by the attempt to educate, to provide moral lessons or 'positive images', and thereby to model forms of behavior that are seen to be socially desirable. Cultural producers, policy-makers and regulators in this field are thus concerned not only to protect children from harm, but also to 'do them good'.

In both domains, adult definitions of childhood are thus simultaneously repressive *and* productive. They are designed both to protect and control children—that is, to keep them confined to social arenas and forms of behavior which will not prove threatening to adults, or in which adults will (it is imagined) be unable to threaten *them*. Yet they are seeking not just to prevent certain kinds of behavior, but also to teach and encourage others. They actively produce particular forms of subjectivity in children, just as they attempt to repress others. And, as I have suggested, they serve similar functions for adults themselves.

Yet, perhaps inevitably, adults have always monopolized the power to define childhood. They have laid down the criteria by which children are to be compared and judged. They have defined the kinds of behavior which are appropriate or suitable for children at different ages. Even where they have purported merely to describe children, or to speak on their behalf, adults have unavoidably established normative definitions of what *counts* as child-like. To be sure, children can and do 'speak for themselves', although they are rarely given the opportunity to do so in the public domain, even on matters which directly concern them. The contexts in which they can speak, and the responses they can invoke, are still largely controlled by adults; and their ability to articulate alternative public constructions of 'childhood' remain severely circumscribed. Even arguments for 'children's rights' are predominantly made by adults, and in adult terms.

Of course, children may resist, or refuse to recognize themselves in, adult definitions—and in this respect, adult power is very far from absolute or uncontested. Nevertheless, their space for resistance is largely that of interpersonal relationships, amid the 'micropolitics' of the family or the classroom. Furthermore, children may be actively complicit in sustaining these definitions of what is 'adult' or 'child-like', if only by default: age differences, and the meanings that are attached to them, are a primary means through which power relationships are enacted, not only between adults and children, but also between children themselves. Children will routinely put other children 'in their place' by mocking or condemning them for their 'babyish' tastes or behavior; and they will often strenuously attempt to distance themselves from such accusations. Such distinctions between 'adult' and 'child' are mutually policed on both sides. As we shall see, this has significant implications for research into children's relationships with the media—an arena which they sometimes perceive as uniquely their own.

CHILDHOOD AS EXCLUSION

This analysis points towards a rather less benign view of the construction of childhood than that which is typically invoked in debates about the 'death of childhood'. To be sure, definitions of childhood are diverse and often contradictory. At any given historical moment, or within any given social or cultural group, it is possible to trace many conflicting definitions—some of which may be residues of older conceptions, while others are perhaps newly emergent. Nevertheless, in the recent history of industrialized countries, childhood has essentially been defined as a matter of *exclusion*. For all the post-Romantic emphasis on children's innate wisdom and understanding, children are defined principally in terms of what they are *not* and in terms of what they *cannot* do. Children are not adults; and hence they cannot be allowed access to the things which adults define as 'theirs', and which adults believe they are uniquely able to comprehend and to control. By and large, children are denied the right to self-determination: they must rely on adults to represent their interests, and to argue on their behalf. 'Childhood', as it is predominantly conceived, is in this respect actively disempowering for children.

This is largely a consequence of the way in which children are defined as in some way not social—or, more accurately, as *pre*-social. Thus, the academic discipline which has until recently enjoyed exclusive claim to the study of children is that of psychology. It is a discipline which (at least in its most influential and dominant forms) interprets the study of human interaction in terms of the individual psyche or personality; and it defines the ways in which children change over time as a teleological process of development towards a preordained goal. Children are constructed here as isolated individuals, whose cognitive development proceeds through a logical sequence of 'ages and stages' towards the achievement of adult maturity and rationality. If childhood is thus defined as a process of becoming, adulthood is implicitly seen as a finished state, in which development has effectively ceased. Those who do not attain this state are judged in terms of individual pathology, and hence identified as suitable cases for treatment.[19]

While this approach has been increasingly questioned (not least within psychology itself), the dominant psychological construction of children clearly sanctions a view of them as essentially lacking or incomplete. Children's behavior is assessed in terms of the extent to which it is or is not 'appropriate' to their biological age. The index of 'maturity' and 'immaturity' becomes the standard against which they are measured, and come to measure themselves. And these differences are themselves defined in terms of what are seen to be specifically adult qualities: rationality, morality, self-control and 'good manners'.

This is not, of course, to imply that adulthood is necessarily always privileged above childhood in these discourses—at least overtly. Children may be defined in terms of their lack of rationality, social understanding or self-control; yet, by the same token, they can also be extolled (in however patronizing a way) for their lack of artifice, self-consciousness and inhibition. There is, of course, a whole self-help industry which is premised on the claim that adults need to get in touch with their 'inner child'—claims that implicitly reinforce romantic notions of childhood as a site of truth and purity.[20]

Nevertheless, what remains disturbing for so many adults are the consequences of children 'crossing the line'. Manifestations of 'precocious' behavior threaten the separation between adults and children, and hence represent a challenge to adult power. It is at this point that liberal discourses of child development, with their emphasis on nurturance and natural growth, begin to crack. Children's psychological health, it seems, positively requires us to police the line between adults and children, in the home, in the school and in the wider arena of public culture. This process is thus not just a matter of the *separation* between children and adults: it also entails an active *exclusion* of children from what is seen to be the adult world.

This attempt to exclude children applies most obviously to the domains of violence and sexuality, of the economy and of politics. And the significance of the electronic media in this context is, of course, that they provide one of the primary sources of knowledge about these things. Both in relation to the media, and in these other social domains, this leads to a situation in which the fundamental dilemmas are seen to be those of *access* and *control*. As I shall indicate, such dilemmas are becoming ever more acute as a result of new technology, and of the global proliferation of electronic media. Renewed calls for control are emerging precisely because the possibility of control is steadily passing away.

However, my position here is not a liberationist one. In principle, I would not deny children's prolonged biological dependency on adults; nor would I contest the idea that individuals do indeed develop and change as they grow older. 'Maturity' is certainly a relative term, but it is not entirely unconnected with biological age. Furthermore, the exclusion I have identified is not simply about the imposition of some monolithic form of 'adult power'. On the contrary, it is achieved with the active complicity of children themselves; and it functions equally to exclude *adults* from what are seen to be the appropriate domains of children. Furthermore, while I have emphasized the changing social constructions of childhood, I am not thereby implying that these constructions are a falsification of the essence of childhood, or a kind of artificial imposition on the 'natural' child. Nor am I suggesting that this natural essence would somehow be released if the sources of power were to be magically removed. In these respects, the call for 'children's liberation' seems to be characterized by a kind of Romanticism which is very similar to that of the protectionist arguments it has sought to oppose.

Nevertheless, I would argue that the dominant construction of children as pre-social individuals effectively prevents any consideration of them as social beings, or indeed as citizens. Defining children in terms of their exclusion from adult society, and in terms of their inability or unwillingness to display what we define as 'adult' characteristics, actively *produces* the kinds of consciousness and behavior which some adults find so problematic. The differences which are observed to exist between adults and children justify the segregation of children; but this segregation then gives rise to the behavior that justifies the perception of differences in the first place.

As I have implied, culture and representation are crucial aspects of this process, both for children and for adults. For a whole variety of reasons, the electronic media play an increasingly significant role in defining the cultural experiences of contemporary childhood. Children can no longer be excluded from these media and the things they represent; nor can they be confined to material that adults perceive to be good for them. The attempt to *protect* children by restricting their access to media is doomed to fail. On the contrary, we now need to pay much closer attention to how we *prepare* children to deal with these experiences; and in doing so, we need to stop defining them simply in terms of what they lack. . . .

Discussion Questions

1. What evidence does the author introduce to counter the idea that children are growing up "too fast"?

2. What does the author mean when he notes that childhood is often defined by "exclusion"?

3. What do adults gain by defining children by what they supposedly lack?

4. Thinking back to your experiences as a child, were there things that adults presumed about you because you were a child that were not correct? How did you feel about these kinds of assumptions?

Notes

1. Andersen (1995), p. 10.
2. For representative instances of this argument, see James, Jenks and Prout (1998), James and Prout (1990), Jenks (1996), Jordanova (1989) and Stainton Rogers and Stainton Rogers (1992).
3. The theoretical underpinnings of this approach are of course derived from the works of Michel Foucault: see, for example, Foucault (1980, 1981).
4. Useful accounts of these developments can be found in Cunningham (1991), Davin (1996), Hendrick (1997) and Steedman (1990).
5. Hendrick (1990).
6. Cunningham (1991), p. 152.
7. See Archard (1993), pp. 32–6.
8. See Rose (1984); and for a more celebratory account, Wullschlager (1995).
9. See Kline (1993), Fleming (1996).
10. See Forgacs (1992).
11. Holland (1992), pp. 12–13.
12. Archard (1993), p. 39.
13. Holland (1992), p. 14.
14. For useful cross-cultural studies of childhood, see Amit-Talai and Wulff (1995) and Stephens (1995).
15. This formulation is derived from Thompson (1990).
16. Jenkins (1992).
17. This is particularly apparent in Steedman's (1990) analysis of the work of the socialist reformer Margaret Macmillan.
18. Our research suggests that this is one way in which children themselves perceive and define 'children's television': see Kelley, Buckingham and Davies (1999).
19. For critiques of psychological theories of child development along these lines, see Burman (1994), Henriques et al. (1984), Rose (1985) and Stainton Rogers and Stainton Rogers (1992).
20. For a discussion, see Ivy (1995).

References

Amit-Talai, V. and Wulff, H. (eds) 1995: *Youth Cultures: A Cross-Cultural Perspective*. London: Routledge.

Andersen, C. 1995: *Michael Jackson Unauthorized*. New York: Pocket Books.

Archard, D. 1993: *Children: Rights and Childhood*. London: Routledge.

Burman, E. 1994: *Deconstructing Developmental Psychology*. London: Routledge.

Cunningham, H. 1991: *The Children of the Poor: Representations of Childhood since the Seventeenth Century*. Oxford: Blackwell.

Davin, A. 1996: *Growing Up Poor*. London: Rivers Oram.

Fleming, D. 1996: *Powerplay: Toys as Popular Culture*. Manchester: Manchester University Press.

Forgacs, D. 1992: Disney animation and the business of childhood. *Screen* 33(4), 361–74.

Foucault, M. 1980: *Power/Knowledge*, ed. C. Gordon. Brighton: Harvester.

Foucault, M. 1981: *The History of Sexuality*, vol. 1. Harmondsworth: Penguin.

Hendrick, H. 1990: Constructions and reconstructions of British childhood: an interpretive survey, 1800 to the present. In A. James and A. Prout (eds), *Constructing and Reconstructing Childhood: Contemporary Issues in the Sociological Study of Childhood*, London: Falmer.

Hendrick, H. 1997: *Children, Childhood and English Society, 1880–1990*. Cambridge: Cambridge University Press.

Henriques, J., Hollway, W., Urwin, C., Venn, C. and Walkerdine, V. 1984: *Changing the Subject: Psychology, Social Regulation and Subjectivity*. London: Methuen.

Holland, P. 1992: *What is a Child? Popular Images of Childhood*. London, Virago.

Ivy, M. 1995: Have you seen me? Recovering the inner child in late twentieth century America. In S. Stephens (ed.), *Children and the Politics of Culture*, Princeton: Princeton University Press.

James, A. and Prout, A. (eds) 1990: *Constructing and Reconstructing Childhood Contemporary Issues in the Sociological Study of Childhood*. London: Falmer.

James, A., Jenks, C. and Prout, A. 1998: *Theorizing Childhood*. Cambridge Polity.

Jenkins, P. 1992: *Intimate Enemies: Moral Panics in Contemporary Great Britain*. New York: Aldine de Gruyter.

Jenks, C. 1996: *Childhood*. London: Routledge.

Jordanova, L. 1989: Children in history; concepts of nature and society. In G. Scarre (ed.), *Children, Parents and Politics*, Cambridge: Cambridge University Press.

Kelley, P., Buckingham, D. and Davies, H. 1999: Talking dirty: children, sexual knowledge and television. *Childhood* 6(2), 221–42.

Kline, S. 1993: *Out of the Garden: Toys and Children's Culture in the Age of TV Marketing*. London: Verso.

Rose, J. 1984: *The Case of Peter Pan: On the Impossibility of Children's Fiction*. London: Macmillan.

Rose, N. 1985: *The Psychological Complex*. London: Routledge.

Stainton Rogers, R. and Stainton Rogers, W. 1992: *Stories of Childhood*: *Shifting Agendas of Child Concern*. Toronto: University of Toronto Press.

Steedman, C. 1990: *Childhood, Culture and Class in Britain: Margaret Macmillan 1860–1931*. London: Virago.

Stephens, S. (ed.) 1995: *Children and the Politics of Culture*. Princeton, NJ: Princeton University Press.

Thompson, J. B. 1990: *Ideology and Modern Culture*. Cambridge: Polity.

Wullschlager, J. 1995: *Inventing Wonderland*. London: Methuen.

Kidnapped: Childhood Stolen?

KAREN STERNHEIMER

INTRODUCTION

Fears about children's safety seem normal today. But many of the things we fear most—like child abductions—are extremely rare events. In fact, the way in which we deal with this fear ironically often places children in more danger. Beyond the statistical unlikelihood of kidnapping, we can understand fears of child abduction as symbolic. During a time when people fear that childhood is disappearing or even "taken away" by popular culture, stories of actual abductions strike a nerve.

O n February 1, 2002, a seven-year-old girl was taken from her bedroom in an affluent San Diego community. Within days, a video of spunky and cherubic Danielle Van Dam was broadcast nationwide, as were the pleas of her panicked parents. Danielle became America's child for a few weeks, drawing us in with her broad smile, shiny blonde hair, and signature rope necklace. Shots of her upscale Sabre Springs home also became ubiquitous on the news coverage. The neighborhood seemed to represent the American dream, on the surface at least. A jury later found a middle-aged neighbor in this suburban Shangri-la guilty of Danielle's abduction and murder.

Months later on June 5, a fourteen-year-old girl was taken from her upscale home in the Salt Lake City area. Elizabeth Smart was also blonde, also angelic-looking in the home-video footage that aired across the stunned country. As time passed we heard about more little girls taken, and about attempts to take other children against their will. Parents were warned that this could happen to any child at any time. From the heightened coverage it seemed as though a rash of kidnappings was taking place across the country, and that the world was no longer a safe place for children.

So why have we come to believe that the outside world has become increasingly dangerous for children? The fear was fueled in 2002 because the kidnappings of a few photogenic kids dominated the news. Timothy W. Maier wrote in *Insight on the News* that we lacked a "juicy summer sex scandal" in 2002, and kidnappings invoke a preexisting sense "of childhood lost."[1] While there was no real kidnapping epidemic, what *had* exploded in 2002 was news coverage of kidnapping. Newspaper coverage of child abductions was 60 percent higher in 2002 than in 2001 and 31 percent higher than in 2003.[2] News of high-profile abductions and attempted abductions seemed to confirm what we had already suspected, that the world had become a very dangerous place, and that even children tucked away in upscale bedrooms were in danger. In this chapter, I examine how and why news coverage of child abductions both creates and reaffirms our fears that children, and childhood itself, are in danger from the outside world.

HAS CHILDHOOD BEEN STOLEN?

The 2002 kidnapping panic was about much more than the handful of tragedies that happened that year. It represented our mistrust of one another, our feeling that paradise had been lost, and our sense that it had been stolen from children. Kidnapping challenges our perception that the experience of childhood is primarily carefree. According to historian Paula S. Fass, our obsessive fear about child abduction began in the mid- to late-nineteenth century.[3] Certainly kidnappings occurred before, but during the Victorian era the image of childhood shifted from that of an economic one, when their labor was necessary for family survival, to a sentimental and emotional one. No longer valued mostly for their labor on family farms or later in factories, children became emotionally prized, and childhood itself became viewed as a time symbolizing innocence.

Fass describes how before this, young people were traditionally taken from their families for economic reasons, to work off family debts or when a family could no longer afford to feed a child. African-American slave children were routinely sold off as the property of slaveholders. In the twentieth century our economy became less dependent on children's labor, however, and communities also became less interdependent. Goods and services were no longer traded only within small rural communities as city populations grew; thus families gradually became more independent of one another. By century's end, the outside world was largely viewed as a threat to families and the children within them.

The shift toward individualism, and away from a more collective orientation to social life, can be seen in our recent treatment of children overall. We are very afraid of what might happen to our own children, but mostly indifferent to the plight of other people's. This societal indifference is reflected in our reluctance to fund social programs for families in poverty or to provide sufficient funding for schools that serve the poorest children. We maintain the illusion of collective concern when a child, one that could be ours, goes missing, however. As Fass notes, a search for a missing child is often a way to renew and strengthen community bonds.[4] The abduction of middle-class and affluent children hits a nerve that the victimization of other children does not. We are able to project our anxieties for children in general onto these missing kids in a way that we don't when hearing about abused or poor children. We reinforce the idea of childhood innocence by selectively focusing on those children who best represent this image, as we all but ignore those who do not.

In a broader sense, we often fear that something more than individual children will be taken away, that childhood itself is gone. Books like Neil Postman's *The Disappearance of Childhood* and David Elkind's *All Grown Up and No Place to Go* decry the apparent loss of childhood as we once knew it. Children symbolize our past and our future, what we were and what we might become. The loss of that idyllic stage of childhood is something we mourn not only for our children's sake, but for our own.

Childhood is a loaded concept. Idealizing it allows us to reminisce about what our lives were like and bemoan changes that we have experienced. During the last century, we have witnessed drastic changes economically, socially, politically, and technologically, so in some ways the past bears little resemblance to the present. Perhaps more relevant, with many two-parent families working in the labor force, child care has been increasingly relegated to outsiders, whom we may not completely trust. Our concern that the world is no longer safe for children emerges when we take a look around and aren't sure how we got here, and wonder if things weren't better in the past. The fear that our children will be taken away from us is symbolic of the anxiety that childhood itself has been taken away.

The truth is, it hasn't. The experience of childhood has changed in many notable ways, and children in some instances may be less isolated from the adult world than perhaps some of us would prefer. What hasn't changed . . . is the concern that children themselves are somehow uniformly different from those who came before them. Kidnapping fears recast all kids as potential victims. Whereas most concerns about kids today consider adults as challenged by the failures of youth, our kidnapping fear is unique in that it casts all unknown adults as potential thieves of childhood innocence.

Of course, this is not to deny that even a statistical rarity can be a major tragedy to a family and community. But our fear that children are at heightened risk of being victims of the world's evil tells us as much about our disconnection from each other and our rapidly changing society as the tragedies that made news in 2002. When we are confronted with frightening accounts of incidents in neighborhoods nearby and across the country, it is only natural that we would then believe that the problem is getting worse. Journalists and news producers are subject to the same social currents as the rest of us in the United States; they sense when we are anxious, and they know that when we are scared we crave more information, which in turn boosts their ratings. News producers bank on our fear to draw us in when we could easily change the channel. Kidnapping scares don't just happen; they are created, and are more likely to be created at some times than others.

ANATOMY OF A KIDNAPPING SCARE

The 2002 kidnapping scare began early, when Danielle Van Dam was taken from her home in February. By the summer, the fear of kidnapping had spread across the country, leading many people to believe that children were being taken and killed more than ever. In the expanded news coverage about kidnapping, we heard about cases we normally wouldn't otherwise; abduction attempts, flashers near schools, and custody disputes that turned ugly became top news stories.

The way these stories were told also heightened our fears and seemed to support the idea that kidnapping was a looming threat to all children. To assess the heightened nature of kidnapping coverage during that year, I examined newspaper reports from around the country from February to the end of September 2002, when Danielle Van Dam's kidnapper was tried and convicted. News tends to be concentrated in cycles, and this case heightened awareness during the spring and summer, which then declined in the fall. Thus, my analysis focuses on the time period when child abductions were at the center of public attention. Although television images are arguably the most powerful in communicating emotion, they are ephemeral and more difficult to analyze on a national scope because of their ubiquity.

I conducted a Lexis-Nexis newspaper search on the terms *child* and *kidnap*, which yielded 608 hits during this time frame, compared with just 391 in 2001, 437 in 2000, and 323 in 1999.[5] Note that these are not reports of 608 kidnappings, but instead 608 articles discussing the subject. In fact, in all 608 stories, only five children were taken and not returned soon after.[6] During these months of heightened attention, stories of child abductions increased by 63 percent compared with the average number of similar news reports during the same time frame over the past three years.

KIDNAPPING EPIDEMIC?

While national statistics on child abductions are murky due to different reporting practices, there was no evidence that child abductions were on the rise in 2002. If anything, FBI data suggested that stranger abductions had slightly declined from the preceding years. Kidnapping is very rare when placed in a context of violent acts against children. Abduction represents less than 2 percent of all crimes against juveniles reported to the police.[7] A 2002 U.S. Department of Justice report, "National Estimates of Missing Children," concluded that 84 percent of all minors reported missing were either runaways or the subject of a report based on miscommunication or a misunderstanding between the child and guardian.[8] Department of Justice estimates suggest that each year about one hundred children are abducted by strangers and are in serious danger because the abductor detains the child overnight, transports the child at least fifty miles, holds the child for ransom, or intends to keep or kill the child.[9] According to the 2002 report, more than half of these kids are returned alive, as Elizabeth Smart eventually was, but a small proportion are never found, and about 40 percent of those abducted under these rare circumstances are killed, as was Danielle Van Dam.

In spite of the fear that these cases inspired, Department of Justice data indicate that a minor's odds of being kidnapped by a stranger and of being in serious danger is less than two in a million.[10] The chance of any American child being killed in this scenario is less than seven in ten million.[11] Children under fifteen are seven and one-half times more likely to die from flu or pneumonia, forty-three times more likely to die of cancer, and sixty-five times more likely to die in a motor vehicle accident than die in a stranger abduction.[12]

Additionally, for the previous ten years crime rates have generally fallen, especially violent crime rates.[13] But despite a 42 percent decline in homicides nationally during the 1990s, the public tends to believe that crime has only gotten worse with time.[14] Children under fifteen have been and continue to be the group least likely to be victims of homicides of any type; young adults eighteen to thirty-four are the group most likely to be murdered.[15] Of all minors reported missing, teens make up the majority—74 percent of all cases and 58 percent of the most serious described earlier. But stories of young children's abductions elicit the greatest sense of anxiety.

In spite of the fact that the actual number of children kidnapped by strangers apparently declined in 2002, news reports intimated otherwise. We heard television news anchors dourly state that "there's been yet another kidnapping," and newspapers across the country also told us that things were getting worse than ever. The press did this in several ways: by providing more prominent coverage for both abductions and attempted abductions than in the past; by linking a local kidnapping or kidnapping attempt to a national, high-profile case; and most centrally, by stating that we were in the midst of a new epidemic. Of the 608 news hits mentioned above, I analyzed 58 that were about specific kidnappings or kidnapping attempts and found that fully 40 percent of those stories implied that child abductions were rising at an alarming rate. For example:

> After a summer rocked by a string of child abductions and homicides across the country, three attempted kidnappings have been reported in Cobb County since school began. (*Atlanta Journal–Constitution*)[16]
>
> The attempted child abduction is the latest in a spate across the Bay State. (*Boston Herald*)[17]

A *Boston Globe* headline warned that "Crimes Against Children [Are] Common," leading readers to believe that we had indeed entered into a scary, new phase.[18] Other stories used words or phrases like "a string" (*Daily News* [New York]), "latest victim" (*Plain Dealer* [Cleveland]), and "a rash of kidnappings" (*Denver Post*).[19] The *Washington Post* described "a recent wave" of abductions, and the *Daily News* claimed that an attempted abduction they reported on was the "latest in a series of little girls who have been kidnapped in recent weeks."[20]

Stories quoted nervous parents in city after city who seemed to concur that they couldn't let their kids out of their sight, even in their own backyards. Letter writers to the *San Diego Union–Tribune*, Danielle Van Dam's hometown paper, wrote that "this year, children have been kidnapped at an alarming rate . . . even our homes might not be as safe as they were ten years ago," and that neighborhoods, even affluent ones, were unsafe for children, unlike "when we were young."[21] "Places aren't as safe as they used to be," a woman told Minneapolis's *Star Tribune*.[22]

In addition to quotes from scared parents and alarming language, mentions of custodial cases made the headlines in greater numbers. Family members are responsible for the vast majority of child abductions, but these abductions generate very few dramatic news stories. Hearing that a noncustodial parent ran away with a child is certainly not as scary for the general public as when a stranger takes a child. Still, stranger kidnapping attempts and abduction stories during the period I surveyed greatly outnumbered the more common form of noncustodial kidnapping by a margin of about six to one, making it appear that strangers are a bigger threat to a child than the adults the child knows. *The Tampa Tribune* wrote of "lowlifes stealing our children," thus framing the problem as one caused by outsiders entering and violating the sacred space of the family.[23] The fear of kidnapping seemed worse than ever, and the danger seemed to compel parents to restrict children from playing outside their own homes.

In short, it felt like kidnappings were on the rise in 2002 because news reports throughout the country told us that they were. Of course they also told us the truth from time to time, that stranger abductions are rare and are responsible for a tiny proportion of all missing children cases. But we were understandably drawn to the alarming and heart-wrenching stories that told us what we had long suspected, that the world is not safe for children anymore.

THE DANGER OF STRANGER DANGER

With all the attention on *stranger danger*, we run the risk of overlooking the more mundane but even more serious risks children face within their own families. Amid our collective sense of shock and outrage at predators that have taken kids from their families, the much larger problem of family and acquaintance danger gets pushed into the background.

Statistically speaking, the biggest threat children will ever face comes from inside their own homes. U.S. Department of Justice records indicate that when children are kidnapped, it is a parent or other family member that usually takes them.[24] Even when children are murdered, the culprit is still most likely one of the parents. Children are far more likely to be physically or sexually abused by family or family friends than a stranger. According to the U.S. Department of Health and Human Services, of all reported child-abuse cases in 2002, 87 percent of the perpetrators were the parents or other relatives of the child.[25] Family members or acquaintances were also responsible for about three-quarters of all reported cases of sexual abuse.

The younger the child, the more likely he or she is to be killed by his or her parents than by strangers. In 2002, 1,400 minors died as the result of abuse or neglect, and in 80 percent of the cases, the perpetrator was one or both of the parents.[26] Children under four years old accounted for 76 percent of the victims, and 88 percent were under eight. Based on these reports, one might expect about forty kids to die at the hands of strangers in the United States each year (out of over 70 million minors under eighteen), and over 1,100 kids—twenty-seven times as many—to die at the hands of a parent.

But when strangers do hurt children, we are far more likely to hear about it. On some level, we still see children as the property of their parents, so the rare yet highly publicized stranger abduction is perceived as a crime against both the child and the rights and responsibilities of the parent. According to the Department of Justice, of children abducted, nearly half (49 percent) were taken by a family member and nearly a third (27 percent) were taken by an acquaintance.[27] Less than a quarter (24 percent) were taken by strangers.

Children aren't always as safe at home as they ought to be. Nor is media attention typically focused on the consistent danger that many children face at home. Nearly a third of news accounts that I analyzed focused on stranger danger, including specific instructions and safety tips on how to avoid strangers. Kids do need to learn to protect themselves; there is no doubt about that. But focusing attention *only* on strangers as children's central threat presents a skewed version of reality and does nothing to help young people who are victimized by adults they already know.

"Make sure the kids know to stay away from strangers . . ." a *Boston Herald* article began.[28] "Strangers abduct 5,000 children every year in the United States," noted the *Houston Chronicle*, without reference to the fact that the vast majority of these kids are returned unharmed within 24 hours, and that nonstrangers are most likely to be the abductors.[29] A mother told the *San Diego Union–Tribune* that her daughter "doesn't have to be polite to strangers," while a *San Francisco Chronicle* article offered the age-old advice, "Don't talk to strangers,"[30] The *Atlanta Journal–Constitution* warned parents to "teach your child about strangers," and a *Denver Post* story suggested that children should yell "fire if a stranger tries to talk to you."[31]

Yell fire? Do we really want a society where we grow up universally distrusting each other and are encouraged to be afraid of people we don't know? Not only will this make us more disconnected (and even more likely to be fearful of one another), it may not keep kids safe from the strangers who really are a threat. Gavin de Becker, security expert and author of *The Gift of Fear*, cautions that remaining in a constant state of fear blocks out real messages of danger that our intuition sends us. If every stranger contact is scary, then we never know when we are truly in danger. In fact, strangers often intervene when an actual threat arises, and children need to learn to sense when someone can come to their aid if they are lost or in trouble. "Don't talk to strangers" is a cliché that often does more harm than good.

Aside from the fact that strangers only represent a small threat to children's safety overall, it's not realistic to expect that children won't interact with strangers. As adults, we do so on a daily basis and model these interactions for children. But news accounts continually tell us that strangers are dangerous, and so we close ranks and shut each other out, often to our own peril. By discouraging kids from trusting, we close down a possible safety net for kids victimized by those closest to them.

We are encouraged to teach kids how to fight off a stranger's attack, but not how to cope when the danger comes from inside the family. The fear of child abduction impacts children in other ways too: parents are afraid to let kids out of their sight and are hesitant to allow them to play in their neighborhoods. Ironically, the fear of outsiders may keep some kids in their places of abuse and away from potential sources of aid.

Fear of the outside world encourages us to retreat from our neighbors and communities, to stay home and watch more scary news on television. In a classic study, communications scholar George Gerbner found that the most fearful individuals also watched more television, perhaps creating a vicious cycle of fear. Gerbner called this phenomena the "mean world syndrome," which we could rephrase to the "mean world for children syndrome," one that encourages us to believe that the only really safe place for children is in their own homes, under their parents' watchful eyes.

The problem with the mean world for children syndrome is that it encourages us to ignore the most common threats to children in favor of the most dramatic but least common ones. By focusing on stranger danger, parents are encouraged to control children's environments even more, and to trust outsiders less. In worst-case scenarios, children are therefore placed in greater danger, and are further isolated from other adults that could help in situations of abuse. Whereas in households free of family violence, the danger consists of leaving young people ill-prepared to safely negotiate their interactions with strangers. . . .

The truth is, parents can never fully protect or control their children. By insisting that they can and should, we deprive kids of an important opportunity for learning to navigate the outside world and learning to make appropriate decisions. We also create a burden of shame and guilt for parents whose children have been victimized by strangers. Most perilously, increased parental control in some instances means increasing the power of abusers.

REALITY CHECK?

While two in five news stories in 2002 implied that child kidnappings were a growing trend, about a quarter of the stories I analyzed reminded readers that the threat of stranger kidnappings is quite rare. Interestingly, reality checks often followed sentences that implied an epidemic by using descriptors such as *spate, trend,* or *spurt.* Reality checks promoted the appearance of balance, while still maintaining the drama of fear. But fear often prevails; dry statistics, regardless of how impressive an expert's credentials, tend to make less of an impact than the emotional accounts of parents or community members. These parents appear to feel as many of us do, so we connect with their words much more than with the experts'.

In spite of providing the voice of reason, these caveats tended to be canceled out by the overwhelming influence of dramatic quotes or anecdotes elsewhere in the story. So even though we were occasionally told that there really was no new kidnapping epidemic, we were encouraged to *feel* as though one existed. Emotion is often more powerful than logic when we are dealing with our fears about children's safety.

The *Seattle Times* provides a good example of juxtaposing emotion with reality. A September 10 article noted that parents' fear was "out of proportion to reality," yet for every dose of reality, the story presented the fears of parents, which were much more vivid when compared to the more staid voices of experts.[32] The article contrasted information about the statistical rarity of kidnapping and the greater likelihood of car accidents and drowning. But quotes like "They can tell me as many times as they want that it's not going to happen," from the scared mother of a five-year-old, resonate with a frightened public not interested in probability but instead in protecting their kids at any cost.[33]

A *Tampa Tribune* story acknowledged that stranger abductions are uncommon, but then devoted a large portion of its discussion to suggesting how children avoid strangers, with no information given about how children might cope with threats from adults whom they know.[34] The *Boston Herald* noted that stranger kidnappings represent less than 1 percent of all abductions, but immediately backtracked, stating that "however rare . . . the scenario . . . is a danger that parents should take seriously.[35] The story went on to offer safety tips focused exclusively on guarding against strangers, with no mention of how the other 99 percent of kids might safeguard themselves against threats from people they know. An *Atlanta Journal–Constitution* story titled "Reported Kidnap Tries Leave Parents Fearful" paused after seven paragraphs to remind readers that the number of reported missing children was on the decline, but immediately returned in the next paragraph to discuss "the latest Cobb [County] incidents."[36] The story then encouraged parents "to be on heightened alert" and offered safety tips for kids about how to avoid strangers.

An *Omaha World–Herald* editorial used a "yes-but" approach to the reality issue by stating that stranger abductions are rare, "but Samantha [Runnion]'s story was just days old when a Philadelphia girl was snatched . . . [and] a little girl was grabbed and killed in Missouri. Then, the double California abduction."[37] The list of headline grabbers offset the reality check by invoking an emotional response simply by mentioning the name or locale of a tragedy. A *Washington Post* story used a similar tactic, contrasting a reality check with tearful quotes. A mother interviewed for the article described trying to calm her frightened daughter, who feared being taken from her bedroom as Danielle Van Dam and Elizabeth Smart had been.[38] Neither the mother nor the article offered answers to allay these fears. In a sense we feel we have no answers in the face of extreme fear. Even statistical realities provide little comfort when we hear over and over of the shocking stories of brutalized children.

THE FORGOTTEN CHILDREN

Our media-fed obsession with stranger danger may frighten us so much that we ignore the more common perils that children face in the United States. Compared to other industrialized nations, the United States isn't taking such great care of its children. In our country, an estimated 16 percent of children live in poverty, 896,000 are victims of abuse or neglect, and approximately 14 percent have no healthcare coverage.[39]

While high-profile child abductions can yield massive round-the-clock coverage and public concern, across the country more than 500,000 children's lives are seriously disrupted each year when they are placed in foster care.[40] More than 91,000, or almost 1 in 5, stay in the system for five years or more. These kids are likely to grow up in a series of homes, some caring, and some not so caring. In fact, according to the most recent data, 528 kids died while in foster care in 2001.[41] Sometimes their stories make headlines, but rarely does the wave of fear rival that of stranger abduction cases.

Why is it that we are so attached to the lives of a few but pay little attention to the thousands of young people whose lives are far from an idealized, carefree state of childhood? For one, we tend to focus on and fear the rare event more than the common event. The thousands who grow up without families are so numerous that they are rarely deemed newsworthy unless brutally killed. Awareness of this problem calls for complex institutional solutions, rather than prosecution and punishment of individual offenders. According to a 2004 U.S. Department of Health and Human Services report, all fifty states' child-welfare programs were found to be seriously deficient.[42] Sixteen states, including California, which bears the country's largest caseload, met none of the federal government's basic standards for safety and well-being.

In fact, states have occasionally lost kids in their custody. According to the *Washington Times*, at one point Iowa lost track of about five hundred kids.[43] Florida also received a great deal of criticism for at one time losing track of 393 of its wards.[44] If these young people can fall off the radar of the agencies that are supposed to protect them, it's not surprising that the rest of us don't know about them either.

Perhaps the biggest reason that these kids don't get much attention is the fact that they're not "poster" children—they don't represent the fantasy of childhood innocence as well as girls like Danielle Van Dam and Elizabeth Smart. Many likely live in poverty. Most of these kids, 73 percent, are not white. The blonde, affluent child certainly does not describe the majority of American children, but she represents the height of our fantasy of childhood innocence. The abduction and injury of children like this tend to strike a nerve in a way that the thousands of children in the foster-care system, or other kidnapping victims, do not. For instance, within two months of Danielle Van Dam's kidnapping, a two-year-old African-American boy named Jahi Turner disappeared from a San Diego park. In the first thirty days after Danielle disappeared, her name was mentioned in 183 news stories, while Jahi Turner's disappearance yielded 55 mentions in the first thirty days, less than a third of the attention Danielle's abduction received.[45] As of this writing, Jahi has not been found.

A similar disparity was evident in Cleveland during the fall of 2003. An eleven-year-old African-American girl, Shakira Johnson, disappeared after leaving a block party. No Amber Alert (immediate notification of the public) was issued. Two weeks later, a fourteen-year-old white teen, Amanda Mullikin-White, disappeared from suburban Cleveland Heights, and an Amber Alert was quickly issued. A few hours later, she was seen walking down a street in the community—Amanda had apparently stayed out too late and was afraid of coming home and getting in trouble.[46] Shakira's body was found about a month after she disappeared.

The Cleveland Police Department was soon criticized for not issuing an Amber Alert for Shakira. The department responded that an Amber Alert would have been inappropriate, since there was no concrete evidence that Shakira was abducted, nor was there a suspect or vehicle description.[47] A review board later concluded that neither case qualified for Amber Alert designation because there was no evidence of abduction in either case, but the two cases sparked controversy and concern that children of color are dealt with differently when they disappear.

BEHIND THE 2002 KIDNAPPING PANIC

Kidnapping serves as a powerful metaphor for our time, as we frequently mourn the loss of what appears to be a simpler, safer past. Children, particularly white, fair-haired girls, are held up as symbols of purity, and their violation triggers major concerns about public safety. But if stranger kidnappings are exceedingly rare, are no match for the threat posed by parents, and were on the decline in 2002, where did the panic come from?

Danielle Van Dam's kidnapping took place when we were still reeling from the September 11 attacks less than five months earlier. For many of us, we had never before felt so vulnerable at home, where we had once felt relatively safe from attack. Just as two oceans no longer protected us from foreign attack, the affluent suburbs appeared to provide little protection for these girls. The crimes committed against them seemed to be crimes against innocence: the innocence of sleeping children, and the innocence that should protect us all from the world's evil. As blonde, affluent girls, they became unwitting symbols of innocence violated, much as we felt that America's innocence had been violated on September 11. Just as Wall Street brokers are supposed to return safely to their families in the suburbs after a day at the office, children in these suburbs should be safe at home. Both of these beliefs were tested.

It is not just the act of kidnapping that instills fear, it is what kidnapping represents: our inability to shield children from the dangers of the outside world. Kidnapped children force us to question our beliefs about childhood—if childhood really isn't always a time of carefree innocence, then what is it? More importantly, stranger abductions represent a breakdown in the assumption that parents have an absolute ability to protect their children or to exert complete control over their lives.

But rather than realistically recognize these beliefs as faulty, we try to cling to them even tighter. Books are sold, fingerprint fairs are held, and pundits talk of implanting microchips in kids to track them should they disappear. Safety and awareness are good things, but they can provide the illusion that if we just try harder we can cordon kids off from the world. Public attention should also focus on identifying and preventing people from preying on children. Abductions and homicides of children by strangers allow us to overlook a high prevalence of family violence and to provide a rationale for even greater parental control and monitoring in a world that feels out of control and unsafe for our children.

We have to realize that no matter how hard we try, we can't and shouldn't wall children off from the outside world. Trying to preserve our children's sense of innocence (or ignorance) about the realities of the world may feel comforting to us, but it does nothing to prepare young people to make successful choices and decisions, particularly pertaining to their safety. The innocence that we like to believe used to exist in the world is revisionist history: children have always faced both natural and human danger, and they have always needed to learn how to cope with both. Attempts to shield children from information will not protect them in the end.

Just as pre–September 11 America wasn't quite innocent when it came to experiencing the trauma of violence—millions of Americans in central cities have dealt with our own brand of urban terror for decades—children have never been quite as safe in their homes as we often believe. That is, if children have homes at all. In our despair over the lives of a few, we tend to ignore the despair of many children who are never afforded anything that comes close to our fantasy of innocence . . .

Discussion Questions

1. Although we pay a lot of attention to child abductions by strangers, what are more likely threats to children's safety in the United States?

2. Compare stories about kidnapping today with the ransom-based abductions of the past that the author discusses. Why do you think the nature of kidnapping has changed in the last hundred years?

3. Discuss some of the negative consequences of irrational fears about children's safety.

4. What roles do race, class, and gender play in stories about child abductions?

Notes

1. Timothy W. Maier, "Data Missing on Missing Children," *Insight on the News,* September 23, 2002.
2. Based on a Lexis-Nexis search of articles with *child* and *kidnap* in the headline or lead paragraph. The average number of stories was 95 in 2001, 116 in 2003, and 252 in 2002.
3. Paula S. Fass, *Kidnapped: Child Abduction in America* (New York: Oxford University press, 1997), 6.
4. Fass, *Kidnapped,* 250.
5. A Lexis-Nexis search was conducted in February 2003 for the period February 1–September 30 for all years noted.
6. These were the hits for the search string "child AND kidnap." A search for "child AND abduct" yielded a smaller number, several of which also appeared in the 608.

7. David Finkelhor and Richard Ormrod, "Kidnaping of Juveniles: Patterns from NIBRS," *Juvenile Justice Bulletin*, Office of Juvenile Justice and Delinquency Prevention, June 2000.

8. Andrea J. Sedlak, David Finkelhor, Heather Hammer, and Dana J. Schultz, "National Estimates of Missing Children: An Overview," *National Incidence Studies of Missing, Abducted, Runaway, and Throwaway Children*, Office of Juvenile Justice and Delinquency Prevention, October 2002, 9.

9. David Finkelhor, Heather Hammer, and Andrea J. Sedlak, "Nonfamily Abducted Children: National Estimates and Characteristics," *National Incidence Studies of Missing, Abducted Runaway, and Throwaway Children*, Office of Juvenile Justice and Delinquency Prevention, October 2002, 2.

10. Finkelhor, Hammer, and Sedlak, "Nonfamily Abducted Children." Calculations based on data from table 7. Total U.S. child population from table 2.

11. Based on an estimated 46 deaths within a population of 70,172,700.

12. Data from Centers for Disease Control and Prevention, National Center for Health Statistics, National Vital Statistics Program, "Child Mortality: Death Rates for Children Ages 5 to 14 by Gender, Race, Hispanic Origin, and Cause of Death, Selected Years 1980–2000," and "Adolescent Mortality: Death Rates Among Adolescents Ages 15 to 19 by Race, Hispanic Origin, and Cause of Death, Selected Years 1980–2000," http://childstats.gov (last accessed January 5, 2006). Note that data on adolescents does not include death by flu or pneumonia.

13. Federal Bureau of Investigation, *Uniform Crime Reports for the United States*, 1983–2002 (Washington, D.C.: U.S. Department of Justice, 2003).

14. Richard Rosenfeld, "Crime Decline in Context," *Contexts* 1 (2002): 25–34.

15. Federal Bureau of Investigation, *Uniform Crime Reports for the United States*.

16. Don Plummer, "Reported Kidnap Tries Leave Parents Fearful," *Atlanta Journal–Constitution*, September 26, 2002, 1JF.

17. Franci Richardson, "Defiant Auburn Girl, 4, Foils Abduction Attempt," *Boston Herald*, September 26, 2002, 10.

18. Brenda J. Buote, "Crimes against Children Common," *Boston Globe*, September 22, 2002, 7.

19. Tracy Connor, "Two Safe at Home," *Daily News* (New York), August 15, 2002, 6; Eddy Ramirez, "A Close Call Close to Home," *Plain Dealer*, August 9, 2002, B1; Kieran Nicholson, "Denver Girl Foils Kidnap Attempt," *Denver Post*, August 8, 2002, A1.

20. "Washington in Brief," *Washington Post*, September 11, 2002, A5; Leo Standora, "Drifter Held in Kidnap-Slay," *Daily News* (New York), July 27, 2002, 3.

21. "Difficult Days for Those Who Love Children," *San Diego Union–Tribune*, July 24, 2002, B9.

22. Terry Collins, "Witness Helps Police Nab Abduction Suspect," *Star Tribune* (Minneapolis), March 30, 2002, 6B.

23. Keith Morelli, "Child Abductors Just a Threat Here—So Far," *Tampa Tribune*, July 24, 2002, 2.

24. Sedlak et al., "National Estimates of Missing Children," table 3.

25. U.S. Department of Health and Human Services, *Child Maltreatment 2002* (Washington, D.C.: GPO, 2003).

26. U.S. Department of Health and Human Services, *Child Maltreatment 2002*.

27. Finkelhor and Ormrod, "Kidnaping of Juveniles."

28. Ed Hayward, "Southboro 4th-Grader Eludes Abuctor," *Boston Herald*, September 21, 2002, 4.

29. "Stafford Event to Include Bike Rodeo, Child-Safety Tips," *Houston Chronicle*, August 1, 2002, 9.

30. Deborah Ensor, "Body That of Missing Orange County Girl," *San Diego Union–Tribune*, July 18, 2002, A1; Valerie Alvord and Chuck Squatriglia, "Dragnet for Kid Killer," *San Francisco Chronicle*, July 18, 2002, A1.

31. Plummer, "Reported Kidnap Tries Leave Parents Fearful." Nicholson, "Denver Girl Foils Kidnap Attempt."

32. Stephanie Dunnewind, "Parent Panic," *Seattle Times*, September 10, 2002, E1.

33. Dunnewind, "Parent Panic."

34. Morelli, "Child Abductors Just a Threat Here."

35. Azell Murphy Cavaan, "Prevent Every Parent's Nightmare," *Boston Herald*, June 30, 2002, 63.

36. Plummer, "Reported Kidnap Tries Leave Parents Fearful."

37. Editorial, "All-Out Effort on Child Snatchers," *Omaha World–Herald*, August 3, 2002, 10b.

38. Patricia Davis, "Guarding Their Precious Ones," *Washington Post*, July 14, 2002, CI.

39. Children's Defense Fund, "2002 Facts on Child Poverty in America," Washington D.C., November 2003; Children's Defense Fund, "Children's Health Coverage in 2001," Washington, D.C., February 2003; U.S. Department of Health and Human Services, *Child Maltreatment 2002*.

40. U.S. Department of Health and Human Services, Adoption and Foster Care Analysis and Reporting System, *The AFCARS Report* (Washington, D.C.: GPO, March 2003).

41. Includes medical reasons, accidents, and homicide.

42. Robert Pear, "U.S. Finds Fault in All 50 States' Child Welfare Programs," *New York Times*, April 26, 2004.

43. Cheryl Wetzstein, "Lost in Foster Care?" *Washington Times*, April 29, 2001, A1.

44. Associated Press, "Florida Finds One of Its Missing Kids," *Los Angeles Times*, February 9, 2003, A26.

45. Based on a full-text Lexis-Nexis search on May 5, 2004, of each child's name the month following the date they disappeared.

46. Lila J. Mills and Sarah Hollander, "Missing Girl's Mom Gets Polygraph Text," *Plain Dealer*, September 29, 2003, B1.

47. Donna Lacoboni and Thomas J. Quinn, "Police Search for Girl Missing Since Saturday," *Plain Dealer*, September 16, 2003, B5.

PART TWO

Theorizing Childhood
How Do Social Scientists Think About Children?

How do we think about children? Typically, we think of childhood as a passing phase with adulthood the end result, rather than an important social category. Traditionally, the questions we have asked about children include:

- What are children learning and how do they learn?
- When do children develop emotional capabilities similar to adults?
- How do children process information?
- How do childhood experiences affect personality development?

While these are important questions, none consider race, class, or gender, or how children themselves understand their worlds. Traditional theories have tended to concentrate on how children are socialized into the broader society and influenced by the world around them, or how they take on proscribed roles. In nearly any introduction to sociology text, you will find a chapter on socialization that talks about the outside forces that influence children, such as parents, teachers, media, and peers, as well as life course milestones that people encounter at different ages. Children are often presumed to be passive absorbers of culture instead of active participants within society. Rarely do we study children's impact on adults or institutions, or think critically about the ways in which children are conceptualized in society.

THINKING ABOUT CHILDREN DIFFERENTLY

In her groundbreaking 1987 article, "Re-Visioning Women and Social Change: Where Are the Children?" sociologist Barrie Thorne criticized the tendency of social scientists to think about "women and children" as though the two groups were fundamentally inseparable. In fact, the interests of the two groups have traditionally been bound together, as women have largely been conceptualized as mothers, and children as members of families dependent (mostly on mothers) for their care. Additionally, women have historically been treated as dependent, the weaker sex both in need of protection and less deserving of full status as citizens.

While Thorne acknowledges that children are in fact often dependent and cannot be fully autonomous, she suggests that we grant children "conceptual autonomy." This means that at the very least we think about children as a separate social category. Recent work, asking different questions, has done that.

- Instead of asking only how children adapt to society, researchers have focused on how children themselves make sense of their lives.

- Rather than looking only at how young people internalize messages about gender and race, new questions ask how children recreate and negotiate these social categories.
- Further questions have recognized that children are a marginalized group, and considered how young people respond to their limited amount of social power.

To answer these questions, sociologists have sought new ways of thinking about children as a social group and childhood as a social construct.

CHILDREN'S ROLES IN SHAPING THEIR WORLDS

Just as children are shaped and influenced by the societies around them, they also exert important influences on their societies as well as their families and peers. We often hear new parents talk of how having children "changes everything," and through this example we can see that children are not just influenced by adults. Children play an active role in shaping the experiences of adults as well. Sociologist William Corsaro, author of "The Structure of Childhood and Children's Interpretive Reproductions," calls this interactive process "interpretive reproduction." Children, he argues, internalize meanings from adults and creatively reconstruct rules, ideas, and concepts. For instance, he discusses how preschool children he studied were taught that toys, gum, or any other distractions were forbidden. Yet they often brought in things from home and worked at concealing them, avoiding the conflict the teachers initially hoped to avoid. This led to a slight change in the rules in some cases. This example demonstrates how children's actions are important in shaping and defining important aspects of their daily lives. Children's play is another way that ideas from the "adult" world are not just adopted, but changed to meet the needs of the game.

Childhood is not just an experience, but a social institution itself—a stable, prominent, organizing feature of social life. Sara H. Matthews explores this idea in "A Window on the 'New' Sociology of Childhood." In her selection, Matthews also considers why many people are so often resistant to view children as full members of society and not members-in-training.

A NEW PARADIGM

Paradigms, or ways of seeing, are difficult to change. We are used to thinking about children as passive learners of adult culture, as sponges and absorbers rather than active social participants, and as Matthews discusses, nonmembers of society.

In their selection "A New Paradigm for the Sociology of Childhood?" Alan Prout and Allison James suggest that we consider a new way of understanding childhood within social science. They discuss six key components of this paradigm. First, childhood is not just a biological phase but something that we socially construct. Second, the experiences of childhood cannot be separated from class, gender, or ethnicity. There is no universal experience of childhood. Third, children, their relationships, and culture are topics worth studying. We should seek to understand children's experiences as important at present, not simply based on how they might "turn out" as adults. Fourth, we need to understand that children are active in constructing meaning and shaping the world around them, not simply passive. Fifth, ethnography (to be discussed in Part III) is an important way to learn about children and childhood, as it gives their experiences value and validity. Finally, changing how we think about children and how we study children will shift our social construction of childhood and we hope, broaden and expand our way of thinking about the experiences of children. This in effect could alter the way children themselves think about childhood.

I have found that many students have a hard time challenging the way that we think about children and childhood. If as you read these selections you feel resistant to the authors' ideas, ask yourself why. Why do we cling so tightly to ideas about childhood, and what does letting go of some of them mean?

Re-Visioning Women and Social Change: Where Are the Children?

BARRIE THORNE

INTRODUCTION

In this selection, adapted from a 1986 lecture, sociologist Barrie Thorne examines the strides that social scientists have made in studying women. Following the influence of feminist thought in the 1970s, women were no longer regarded simply as "non-men" in social science research. The author notes, however, that the same had not yet happened for children, who were still often regarded by researchers as "non-adults." In this piece, she suggests that research scholars recognize the "conceptual autonomy" of children: the need to think about children as a distinct social category, even if they are in many ways dependent on adults.

. . . Adult perspectives infuse three contemporary images of children: as threats to adult society, as victims of adults, and as learners of adult culture ("socialization"). We can bring children more fully into knowledge by clarifying ideological constructions, with attention to the diversity of children's actual lives and circumstances; by emphasizing children's agency as well as their subordination; and by challenging their conceptual privatization.

Critical scholars have revealed deep sources of bias masked by claims that knowledge is "objective" and without standpoint; the experiences and interests of the privileged have shaped not only the choice of topics but also conceptual frameworks and methods of study (Smith 1979). . . . But while feminists challenged the hegemony of men's experiences, we have often assumed the standpoints of white, class-privileged, heterosexual, and Euro-American women.[1] The process of critique . . . has become a complex project.

I want to add to that complexity by pursuing a relatively simple observation: Both feminist and traditional knowledge remain deeply and unreflectively centered around the experiences of adults. Our understanding of children tends to be filtered through adult perspectives and interests. How can we bring children more fully into our understanding of social life, including processes of social change? Because the fates and definitions of women and children have been so closely tied, our re-visioning of women may provide useful leads for recentering our knowledge of children . . . .

We need a similar re-visioning of children; their full lives, experiences, and agency have been obscured by adult standpoints. We may discover leads for rethinking children both by examining *parallels* between their situations and those of women, and by gaining clarity about ideological and actual *connections* between women and children. Finally, I will discuss limits of the analogy between our re-visioning of women and potential re-visioning of children. . . . I will try to clarify the discomfort that accompanies the granting of conceptual autonomy. . . .

PLACING WOMEN AT THE CENTER: THE RE-VISIONING OF WORK

Within traditional sociology, . . . men were granted a direct position in production and class struggle, and hence in the making of social change. . . .

Fuller attention to women's lives also encouraged more research on women's experiences in a variety of occupations (e.g., see Lopata, with Miller and Barnewolt 1984). This has included jobs in which women traditionally have predominated, such as clerical work, elementary school teaching, paid domestic labor, routine assembly work, and subsistence farm labor in developing countries, and the experiences of women tokens in male-dominated occupations such as police enforcement, construction work, law, and medicine. . . .

Feminists' efforts to understand the whole of women's lives also challenged the equation of work with paid work. Broadening their conception of "work," feminists illuminated various forms of unpaid "invisible labor" (Glazer 1984; Kahn-Hut et al. 1982). Such labor—housework, subsistence farming, the knitting together of kin, volunteering in community institutions, shopping for consumer goods, care of children and the frail elderly—tends to be overlooked and devalued in part *because* it is usually done by women. . . .

Women, in short, have been re-visioned as active, speaking subjects. Feminist re-visioning of women in varied economic, family, political, cultural, and social contexts has highlighted several basic themes:

1. Women's subordination to men is basic to their experiences. But women are not just passive victims; they are also agents, actors, creators of culture, and participants in the making of history. . . .
2. Like other subordinates, women have often been defined by their social category and treated as a singularity. . . .
3. Women are actors and participants in all social institutions, and the study of gender should be basic not only to conceptualizations of more "private" institutions such as family and community (with which women have ideologically been associated) but also to the study of more "public" institutions—the wage economy, bureaucracies, the state, and political movements (Stacey and Thorne 1985). . . .

HOW DO WE THINK ABOUT CHILDREN?

Children lurk at the edges of the knowledge I have briefly reviewed. They worked alongside women in the early textile mills, and in traditional thought, notions like "the family" and "the domestic" have encapsulated children along with women. Feminist challenges of public/domestic divisions have opened new angles of vision that have not been as fully developed for children as for women. . . . Adult interests and perspectives infuse three contemporary images of children: as threats to adult society, as victims of adults, and as learners of adult culture.

Children as Threats and as Victims

Within sociological, feminist, and popular thought, children rarely appear on *public* agendas unless they are defined as a social problem. Adults do the defining, using imagery that vacillates between two sometimes interrelated poles: children as a threat to adult society and children as victims of adults. In both views, the experiences of children are filtered through adult concerns.

In nineteenth-century England and the United States, state agencies first began to intervene in families in response to perceived problems of juvenile crime (Eekelar et al. 1982; Gordon 1988). Children, especially from working-class households, were seen as potential threats to social order. Emphasis on protection of adults *from* children later shifted to protection *of* children from specific adults—parents who abused and neglected them. . . . A variety of reformers—charity workers, evangelicals, municipal authorities, and feminists—shaped these changing definitions. Nineteenth-century feminists were especially active in movements to protect children from adult abuse (Gordon 1988).

In the changing construction of social problems, images of children as threats and as victims have continued to appear and reappear. In the United States in the 1950s, juvenile delinquency became a spectre in popular consciousness. The theme of children as menacing to adult society continued in images of "hippie" youth culture in the 1960s (in this case the imagery was of adolescents, who generally seem less innocent and more threatening than younger children). . . . The media, buttressed by social science findings, have given visibility to the problem of adult physical abuse of children, and, in recent years, . . . to the prevalence of adult sexual abuse of children (McCormack 1985). Startling statistics about the growing impoverishment of children in the United States add to a sense of alarm about the victimization of children.

The popular media use portrayals of victimized young children. . . to convey the severity of problems that adults often face as well. Since children are defined as innocent, their presence suggests that at least some of the victims cannot be blamed. For example, when the media began to emphasize the presence of children among the urban homeless, the reports assumed new urgency and a shift from victim blaming. . . .

A. . .wave of books with almost interchangeable titles—*The Disappearance of Childhood* (Postman 1982), *Children Without Childhood* (Winn 1983), *The Hurried Child* (Elkind 1981), *Our Endangered Children* (Packard 1983), *The Erosion of Childhood* (Suransky 1982)—portray contemporary children as generalized victims, deprived of adult protection and subjected to unhealthy competitive and bureaucratic pressures, sex, drugs, and too much television. These authors also believe children are victimized by divorce, (and) the large number of mothers in the work force. . . .

These are compelling issues, and my intent is not to undermine their importance. I want rather to observe that it is *adults* who construct the imagery of children both as quintessential victims *and* as threats to adult society. In both cases, children tend to be constructed as "the other," to be regarded with emotions of pity or fear. Neither portrayal allows much room for understanding children's consciousness and actions within their sometimes difficult circumstances. . . .

Children as Learners: The "Socialization" Approach

Apart from the social problems tradition, children have mostly been considered under the rubric of "socialization" in . . . traditional sociology. . . . The core insight is reasonable and even compelling: Born without language or knowledge of social organization, children become slowly inducted into the social worlds around them. This process of induction addresses a basic sociological question: How is society possible? The socialization answer posits that new members internalize culture and learn the rules of adult society. An enormous and in many ways useful body of research informs us about the ways children acquire language, conceptions of social organization, the capacity for friendship, religious beliefs, political attitudes, and the outlooks of their social class.

Mainstream sociologists and psychologists often give positive weighting to processes of socialization and "child development." Kagan et al. (1978, p. 5) observe that experts in child development usually assume "orderly, organized change toward a hypothetical ideal." . . . Developmental psychologists emphasize "flexibility, control, self-consciousness, strength, coordination, task competence, freedom of choice, and speed of cognitive processing," all of which seem to increase with age. The authors observe that "depression, chronic anxiety, guilt, ambivalence, insomnia, vacillation, and hatred" also become more common with age. But these more negative states are rarely assumed to be the endpoints of development.

Feminists have used the socialization approach . . . to demonstrate that gender divisions (man/woman; masculine/feminine) and male dominance are not "natural" and hence immutable, but are socially constructed. As learners of culture, children become drawn into, and thus help reproduce, the gender organization of their society. . . .

But "socialization" frameworks . . . embed what Matthew Speier (1976) calls "the adult ideological viewpoint." Children are imaged primarily as learners of adult culture, their experiences in the present continually referred to a presumed future, the endpoint . . . of adulthood.

Studies of the socialization of gender start with adult arrangements—feminine and masculine personalities, gendered divisions of labor, and gender hierarchies. Children's lives are then referred to that outcome, with the basic question: How do children become shaped by and inducted into the (adult) sex/gender system? The result is a conceptual double standard: Adults are understood by their present actions and experiences in the world; children are understood more by their becoming, as adults-in-the-making. . . .

They also assume . . . a division between the supposedly completed nature of the adult and the incomplete child (Jenks 1982). In a classic article, Ruth Benedict (1938) observed that in our culture, adults go to great extremes to define themselves as different from children. Adults consider themselves responsible, dominant, and sexual, and assume children to be irresponsible, submissive, and asexual. Earlier in Western history, adult/child dichotomies were less sharply drawn (Aries 1962). As Arlene Skolnick (1980) argues, our contemporary social practices, such as the restriction of children to age-graded institutions, may help to construct some of the very patterns psychologists have posited as universal "stages of development."

Jerome Kagan (1984) makes a related point: Cultures project onto infants and young children a nature opposite to the qualities prized in adults. Valuing independence, we define children as dependent; the task of socialization is to encourage independence. In the nineteenth century, when parental authority was idealized, adults defined children as willful, and the goal of socialization was to teach obedience. The Japanese, who value interdependence, define infants as too autonomous and needing to be tempted into dependence.

Thus, conceptions of adulthood and childhood vary cross-culturally and change historically. . . . But whatever the conception of children, adults do the defining. Currently, adults use children to define themselves, . . . analogous to the way in which men have defined women and colonialists have defined those they colonized, as "the other" (DeBeauvoir 1953; Fanon 1967). . . .

Socialization . . . is forward looking, taking a long temporal sweep by referring children's experiences in the present to their presumed distant futures. . . . This approach tends to be abstracted from historical time. It entails . . . a belief that "life is an unbroken trail" on which one can trace a particular quality or presumed outcome to its beginning. . . . Personal change is sometimes abrupt, due to biological maturation or unexpected social events. War, economic crisis, environmental disasters, and even a shift from the situations of elementary school to those of junior high, may quickly alter the behavior and experiences of people of any age. . . .

A growing number of researchers have used tools of ethnography, sociolinguistics, and open-ended interviewing to uncover the complex nature of children's experiences. They organize their insights around the theme of children's active participation in processes of socialization. For example, in empirical studies of children's interactions in same-gender play groups, Lever (1976) and Fine (1981) focus their analyses upon the question of what adult skills children's interactions teach. . . .

Some researchers have dislodged the conventional socialization framework by . . . asking not how adults shape children, but rather how children influence adults. . . .

RETHINKING IDEOLOGICAL CONSTRUCTIONS OF CHILDREN

How can we move beyond the limitations of adult-centered frame-works and bring children more fully into sociological and feminist thought, including our conceptions of human agency and social change? Because the fates and definitions of children have been closely tied with those of women, feminist re-visioning of women may provide leads for similar re-visioning of children. One fruitful source of insight comes from feminist analyses of gender ideologies, which are often intertwined with ideological constructions of children and adults. . . .

Feminists have traced the changing social and cultural construction of gender dualisms like man/woman and feminine/masculine. Age-based dualisms like adult/child are also socially constructed. . . .

Adult/child dualisms—especially the authority of parents (and within that, the authority of fathers) over children—are often invoked to justify other forms of social inequality. Different types of power—of kings over subjects, slave owners over slaves, and men over women—have been justified by defining the subordinates as "like children," inherently dependent and vulnerable, less competent, incapable of exercising full responsibility, and in need of protection. Each of these forms of domination and its supporting ideology has, in turn, been challenged; political subjects, blacks, and women are *not* "like children," and their subordination is not legitimate.

The use of adult/child dualisms to justify inequality should be pushed a step further. Do children—given their great variability in age, culture, and circumstance—have a singular "child-like nature" that legitimates their subordination to adults? . . . Definitions of children are socially constructed and historically changing; a . . . notion like "the child" should be critically examined. Furthermore, . . . challenging . . . women's subordination has led to questioning of family hierarchies and patterns of "intimate oppression" (see Thorne, with Yalom 1982), with important . . . implications for rethinking the subordination of children.[2]

In some ideological constructions, women are *likened to* children. In other constructions, women are *closely and unreflectively tied* with children; womanhood has been equated with motherhood in a mixing of identities that simply does not occur for men and fatherhood. . . . In the colonial period, women were depicted as wives and Christians, and motherhood was not idealized. Over the course of the eighteenth century, as men gradually shifted to wage labor, many women and children became economic dependents and public/domestic divisions became more sharply marked. A new maternal ideal gained ascendancy in the middle class, and women were increasingly defined by ideologies of motherhood and domesticity. . . . This altered view of women entailed a redefinition of children as domesticated, dependent, and needing constant maternal care.

Between 1870 and 1930 the ideology of domesticated mothers and children expanded across social classes, in a process analyzed by Viviana Zelizer (1985), who emphasizes changing definitions of children. Child labor laws and compulsory public schooling further privatized children. Through considerable conflict that often pitted working-class women and men against middle-class reformers, an earlier view of the useful wage-earning child was replaced by a view of the child as "economically worthless, but emotionally priceless" (Zelizer 1985, p. 21). Children became sentimentally defined, their "proper place" narrowed to families and schools. The field of child development also emerged in this period, providing "expert" definitions of the nature and needs of children, and charging mothers with the work of deliberately "developing" the child (Ehrenreich and English 1979; Kessen 1979).

Modern ideologies of motherhood and childhood are far from monolithic, but in various twists of definition and labeling—which in the United States often embed structures of social class and race—women and children have been repeatedly defined in terms of one another. . . . The labeling of "single mother" and "neglected child" developed as interrelated conceptions imposed by child welfare agencies between 1880 and 1920. Bias against single mothers, who violated ideals of family life, shaped definitions of child neglect. . . . Definitions of "the day care child" have been closely linked to constructions of "the working mother." . . .

Contemporary sentimental definitions trivialize and domesticate children's activities and objectify them as "cute." Conceptualizing children in terms of development and socialization imposes an adult-centered notion . . . upon children's experiences in the present. Both . . . tend to collapse children into a singularity—"the child" (perhaps subdivided into "developmental stages")—and deflect attention from children's varied circumstances, experiences, and social relations. These ideologies also mask the harsh realities of children's subordination: Placing children on the pedestal of sentimentality helps obscure the ways in which adults abuse and exploit them, and government policies contribute to their growing impoverishment. Conceptualizing children as victims *does* reveal these harsh realities, but that view—when it fails to acknowledge children's worlds of meaning and their capacities for action and survival—also distorts. . . . We need fuller understanding of the social contexts in which different . . . constructions of children are evoked, the effects of adult definitions on children's own experiences of themselves, and more attention to children's abilities to act within and upon the world.

RE-VISIONING CHILDREN

. . . Within sociology, the study of children has largely been confined to a few subfields: the family, education, and social psychology—arenas in which socialization frameworks flourish. Anne-Marie Ambert (1986) documents the near absence of children in writings of classical sociological theory, recent introductory sociology textbooks, and eight widely read sociology journals. At most, textbooks have one chapter on children, usually under the rubric of socialization. At the top of the journals in the proportion of space devoted to children, *Journal of Marriage and Family* had only 3.6 percent and *Sociology of Education* only 6.6 percent of articles on children. . . .

Children remain relatively invisible in most sociological *and* feminist literature. To bring children more fully into knowledge, we will need to rethink their conceptual privatization. Age relations, like gender relations, are built into varied institutions and social circumstances. The experiences of children may be illuminated by, and in turn may challenge, our frameworks for understanding not only families and schools but also politics, work, poverty, social class, organizations, bureaucracy, urban life, social stratification, and social change. One can argue, as Joan Kelly (1979, p. 21) did for women, that children's place is "not a separate sphere or domain of existence but a position within social existence generally."

Of course, in contemporary Western societies children are largely excluded from public politics and paid work; in many ways they are literally relegated to a separate sphere of family, neighborhood, and schooling. But in situations of intense political conflict, as in South Africa and Nicaragua, even young children may be directly involved in actions conventionally defined as "political." Children may also be canny political observers. Through respectful listening to children, Robert Coles (1971, 1986) has revealed complex political and ethical sensibilities that make psychologists' "stages of moral development" seem highly artificial. And in relations with adults, as well as within their social groups, children collaborate to further their interests, engaging in conflicts and gestures of partisanship that not only may be understood as socialization for later, more full-fledged political life but also as a form of politics itself (Maynard 1985). Attention to children may expand our overall notions of "the political."

In contemporary Western societies, children do relatively little paid work. But in studies of political economy and development, we should attend more closely to the productive labor of children in Third-World countries, in earlier historical times, and, in our own society, in contexts like those of migrant farming (Coles 1971). . . . Children also do invisible work; they nurture others (Boulding 1980); they construct culture and social organization (Corsaro 1985; Goodwin 1980; Maynard 1985); they participate in negotiations and conflicts about and in some of the actual doing of housework (Wittner 1980). As with adults, children's visible and invisible labor tends to be divided by gender (Medrich et al. 1982). These activities are not simply socialization for adult work life; they have their own consequence and meanings in the present and should become more central to our overall conceptualizations of work. . . .

We often assume that adults work and children "play," a conceptual separation that tends to bracket children's activity from "serious" life. Clinical psychologists and sociologists have called play "the work of little children" (Denzin 1977)—a shift of metaphors intended, like feminist renaming, to rescue activities from invisibility and trivialization. Indeed, children's play *is* often serious and purposive. But we should question the very dichotomy between work and play, a dichotomy, imposed by adults and perhaps distinctively Western, that masks great variety in the experiences of people of all ages. As Suransky (1982) observes, young children do not experience a play/work dichotomy; they work while playing and play while working. Wonderfully detailed studies of children at play (reviewed in Schwartzman 1978) reveal multiple layers of meaning in children's activities. Such complex phenomenological understanding—the result of revaluing children and attending closely to their experiences—may inspire fresh approaches to adult life.

Closer attention to children and their diversity can also deepen our understanding of social stratification. In an ethnographic study of working-class "lads" in a vocational school in England, Paul Willis (1977) connects daily interactions with the organization of institutions and with structural contradictions of age, social class, and gender. Resisting the authority structure of their school, the "lads" develop an oppositional culture of aggression and joking that resembles the masculine, working-class culture of factory work—their ultimate, albeit unintended destination. While they resist social-class domination, they ironically end up re-producing the class structure, and doing so partly through a specific form of masculinity.

Inspired by Willis's approach, later researchers have examined strategies of accommodation and resistance used by girls as well as boys, and they have begun to explore dimensions of race as well as social class (e.g., Anyon 1983; Connell et al. 1982; Fuller 1980). In these studies, children are not defined as undergoing socialization, but rather as human actors negotiating within and sometimes resisting institutional structures—schools, families, wage labor. These studies emphasize both agency and structure; they bridge between public and private institutions; and they trace complex, sometimes contradictory intersections of class, gender, race, and age. . . .

Epistemological Issues

It is not by chance that the most suggestive empirical research on children—revealing them to be complex actors, strategists, performers, users of language, creators of culture—is based on qualitative and interpretive approaches. Open-ended interviewing (e.g., Coles 1971, 1986; Wittner 1980), participant-observation (e.g., Willis 1977), and the tools of sociolinguistics (e.g., Corsaro 1985; Goodwin 1982; Maynard 1985) assume the importance of human action and the daily construction of meaning. They are especially helpful in uncovering experiences and forms of agency that have been suppressed by dominant ideologies.

Reflexive and interpretive approaches also help researchers grapple with a fundamental fact: "virtually all studies of children have been done by adults" (Boocock 1975, p. 426). Adult women, blacks, and Hispanics can bring their missing voices into knowledge by speaking and writing about their own experiences. But while children may help with research (Boocock 1981), they will never be in central positions of knowledge-creation. That fact suggests one limit to the analogy I have been pushing between the re-visioning of women and the re-visioning of children in knowledge. . . .

There is an added and distinctive twist in the study of children: All adults were once children themselves. Whereas those of different genders or races rarely cross social categories, in this case the subject/other division masks a running process: children, the subordinates and the other, are daily moving toward adulthood, the dominant position. And the dominants were once subordinates. This structure may hold special promise for understanding: Adults may know from their own experience what it is like to be a child. On the other hand, the child within—suffused with the distortions as well as insights of memory and threatening when it contradicts idealized adulthood—may also pose obstacles to seeing children clearly. Furthermore, the special ties of affection, power, and authority that mark relationships between adults and children may have profound effects on the construction of knowledge.

CONCLUSION: THE LIMITS OF AUTONOMY

My emphasis on conceptual autonomy may have glossed over the depth and intensity of young children's dependence upon, and relationships to, adults. The power of adults—partly inherent in greater physical capacities, but greatly magnified by economic and social organization and cultural beliefs—has both positive and negative dimensions. Having resources to provide responsible care to those who are more vulnerable and dependent (the positive side of greater adult power) is essential to ensuring children's survival and growth. But adults also use their greater power to dominate, exploit, and abuse children. Debates over "children's rights" divide on the problem of how to enhance adults' nurture, while diminishing their abuse of power.

Those who stress the oppression of children see "adult protection" as a euphemism for control. They advocate empowering children by granting them self-determination and "liberty rights." Others argue that when taken to an extreme, granting formal equality to children—in effect, treating them like adults—results in their exploitation. Children, especially young children (the issue of relative competence and vulnerability becomes crucial), are inherently dependent on adults. Children's needs for adult care and protection are best expressed through "claim rights" that place duties on adult caretakers and the state.

The most sensible writings I have seen on children's rights steer a course between these two positions. . . . In some circumstances, children may need more protection, but in others they benefit from autonomy. The often contradictory relationships between individuals, families, and the state must be carefully sorted out.

I mention the debate over children's rights mostly to suggest the complexity of power relations between adults and children, a complexity that needs to be taken into account in our re-visioning of children. The domination of men over women and of adults over children are both analogous *and* very different. . . .

The recent wave of books about "children without childhood" generally fall on the protect-the-child side of the debate over children's rights. To varying degrees, each of these books takes traditional gender divisions of labor for granted, holding mothers uniquely responsible for nurturing, caring for, and protecting children. Working mothers (but not working fathers) are included among the forces depriving contemporary children of their "right to childhood." This message echoes a theme dear to the heart of the New Right—that the autonomy of women is necessarily gained at the expense of children. . . .

The . . . Right assumes that "woman's place" should primarily be defined by motherhood, public/private divisions [and] male dominance in all institutions. . . . While the welfare of children *should* be a matter of widespread concern, to find solutions in "defense" of a romanticized nuclear family with a stay-at-home mother at its symbolic core, is to ignore reality (few households fit that model). . . . Improved understanding of children, in all their diversity and in varied institutional contexts, will strengthen feminist visions of and strategies for social change.

Granting women, and children, conceptual autonomy is essential if we are to bring their experiences into knowledge that has been shaped by dominant groups. . . .

If our theorizing began with selves defined through relationships with others, retaining full awareness of social hierarchies, and if that approach were developed into a full critique of existing institutions, we might thoroughly overturn traditional knowledge.

Discussion Questions

1. How does the author compare the status of children with that of women?

2. The author notes that children can never be fully independent, while women can be. How does she suggest we think about and study children, with this in mind?

3. What does the author mean when she suggests that we grant children "conceptual autonomy"?

4. Following the author's suggestions, how might researchers go about designing studies involving children?

Notes

1. Analyses of racist bias in feminist writings can be found in Hooks (1981) and Zinn et al. (1982). Rich (1980) discusses heterosexual bias; Nash and Fernandez-Kelly (1983) and Duley and Edwards (1986) point to questions raised by more global frameworks.
2. In a founding work of feminist theory, Shulamith Firestone (1970) argued that the oppression of children is tied to the oppression of women. There are many problems with her way of thinking about children (e.g., see criticisms in Suransky 1982). But in making the liberation of children a central concern, Firestone is relatively unusual among feminist writers (a point made by Jaggar 1985).

References

Ambert, Anne-Marie. 1986. "Sociology of Sociology: The Place of Children in North American Sociology." pp. 11–31 in *Sociological Studies of Child Development*. Vol. 1 edited by P. Adler and P. A. Adler. Greenwich, CT: JAI Press.

Anyon, Joan. 1893. "Intersections of Gender and Class: Accommodation and Resistance by Working-Class and Affluent Females to Contradictory Sex Role Ideologies." pp. 1–19 in *Gender, Class and Education*, edited by S. Walker and L. Barton. Sussex: Falmer Press.

Aries, Philippe. 1962. *Centuries of Childhood*. New York: Vintage Books.

Benedict, Ruth. 1938. "Continuities and Discontinuities in Cultural Conditioning." *Psychiatry* 1:161–67.

Boocock, Sarane Spence. 1975. "The Social Context of Childhood." *Proceedings of the American Philosophical Society* 119:419–29.

———— 1985. "The Life Space of Children." pp. 93–116 in *Building for Women*, edited by S. Keller. Lexington, MA: Lexington Books.

Coles, Robert. 1971. *Migrants, Sharecroppers, Mountaineers*. Boston: Little, Brown.

———— 1986. *The Political Life of Children*. Boston: Atlantic Monthly Press.

Connell, Robert W., Dean J. Ashenden, Sandra Kessler, and Gary W. Dowsett. 1982. *Making the Difference: Schools, Families, and Social Division*. Boston: Allen & Unwin.

Corsaro, William. 1985. *Friendship and Peer Culture in the Early Years*. Norwood, NJ: Ablex.

DeBeauvoir, Simone. 1953. *The Second Sex*. New York: Knopf.

Denzin, Norman K. 1977. *Childhood Socialization*. San Francisco: Jossey-Bass.

DuBois, Ellen, Gail Kelly, Elizabeth Kennedy, Carolyn Krosmeyer, and Lillian Robinson. 1985. *Feminist Scholarship: Kindling in the Groves of Academe*. Urbana: University of Illinois Press.

Duley, Margot I., and Mary I. Edwards, eds. 1986. *The Cross-Cultural Study of Women*. New York: Feminist Press.

Eekelaar, John M., Robert Dingwall, and Topsy Murray. 1982. "Victims or Threats? Children in Care Proceedings." *Journal of Social Welfare Law*: 68–82.

Ehrenreich, Barbara, and Deirdre English. 1979. *For Her Own Good*. Garden City, NY: Doubleday Anchor.

Elkind, David. 1981. *The Hurried Child*. Reading, MA: Addison-Wesley.

Fanon, Frantz. 1967. *Black Skin, White Masks*. New York: Grove Press.

Fine, Gary Alan. 1981. "Friends, Impression Management, and Preadolescent Behavior." pp. 29–52 in *The Development of Children's Friendships*, edited by Steven R. Asher and John M. Gottman. New York: Cambridge University Press.

Firestone, Shulamith. 1970. *The Dialectic of Sex*. New York: Morrow.

Fuller, Mary. 1980. "Black Girls in a London Comprehensive School." pp. 52–65 in *Schooling for Women's Work*, edited by R. Deem. London: Routledge & Kegan Paul.

Glazer, Nona Y. 1984. "Servants to Capital: Unpaid Domestic Labor and Paid Work." *Review of Radical Political Economics* 16:61–87.

Goodwin, Marjorie H. 1982. "He-Said-She-Said: Formal Cultural Procedures for the Construction of a Gossip Dispute Activity." *American Ethnologist* 7:674–95.

Gordon, Linda. 1985. "Single Mothers and Child Neglect, 1880–1920." *American Quarterly* 37:173–92.

———— 1988. Heroes of their Own Lives: The Politics of Family Violence. *Boston 1880–1960.* New York: Pantheon.

Harding, Sandra. 1986. *The Science Question in Feminism.* Ithaca: Cornell University Press.

Hooks, Bell. 1981. *Ain't I a Woman? Black Women and Feminism.* Boston: South End Press.

Jaggar, Alison M. 1985. *Feminist Politics and Human Nature.* Totowa, NJ: Rowman & Allenheld.

Jenks, Chris. 1982. "Introduction: Constituting the Child." pp. 9–24 in *The Sociology of Childhood,* edited by Chris Jenks. London: Batsford Academic.

Kagan, Jerome. 1984. *The Nature of the Child.* New York: Basic Books.

———— Richard B. Kearsley, and Philip R. Zelazo. 1978. *Infancy: Its Place in Human Development.* Cambridge, MA: Harvard University Press.

Kahn-Hut, Rachel, Arlene Kaplan Daniels, and Richard Colvard, eds. 1982. *Women and Work.* New York: Oxford University Press.

Kelly, Joan. 1979. "The Doubled Vision of Feminist Theory." *Feminist Studies* 5:216–27.

Kessen, William. 1974. "The American Child and Other Cultural Inventions." *American Psychologist* 34:815–20.

Lever, Janet. 1976. "Sex Differences in the Games Children Play." *Social Problems* 23:478–87.

Lopata, Helena, with Cheryl Miller and Debra Barnewolt. 1984. *City Women: Work, Jobs, Occupations, Careers.* Vol. I. New York: Praeger.

Maynard, Douglas. 1985. "On the Functions of Social Conflict Among Children." *American Sociological Review* 50:207–23.

McCormack, Mary. 1985. "Silenced No More: The Emergence of Child Sexual Abuse as a Social Problem." Unpublished paper, Sociology Department, Michigan State University.

Medrich, Elliott A., Judith Roizen, Victor Rubin, and Stuart Buckley. 1982. *The Serious Business of Growing Up.* Berkeley: University of California Press.

Millman, Marcia, and Rosabeth Moss Kanter, eds. 1975. *Another Voice: Feminist Perspectives on Social Life and Social Science.* Garden City, NY: Anchor Books.

Nash, June, and Patricia Fernandez-Kelly, eds. 1983. *Women, Men and the International Division of Labor.* Albany: SUNY Press.

Packard, Vance. 1983. *Our Endangered Children.* Boston: Little, Brown.

Postman, Neil. 1982. *The Disappearance of Childhood.* New York: Delacorte Press.

Rich, Adrienne. 1980. "Compulsory Heterosexuality and Lesbian Existence." *Signs: Journal of Women in Culture and Society.* 5:631–60.

Sherman, Julia, and Evelyn T. Beck, eds. 1979. *The Prism of Sex: Essays in the Sociology of Knowledge.* Madison: University of Wisconsin Press.

Schwartzman, Helen B. 1978. *Transformations: The Anthropology of Children's Play.* New York: Plenum Press.

Skolnick, Arlene. 1980. "Children's Rights, Children's Development." pp. 138–74 in *Children's Rights and Juvenile Justice,* edited by L. T. Empey. Charlottesville: University of Virginia Press.

Smith, Dorothy. 1979. "A Sociology for Women." pp. 135–87 in *The Prism of Sex,* edited by J. A. Sherman and E. T. Beck, Madison: University of Wisconsin Press.

Speier, Matthew. 1976. "The Adult Ideological Viewpoint in Studies of Childhood." pp. 168–86 in *Rethinking Childhood,* edited by A. Skolnick. Boston: Little, Brown.

Spender, Dale, ed. 1981. *Men's Studies Modified: The Impact of Feminism on the Academic Disciplines.* New York: Pergamon Press.

Stacey, Judith. 1983. "The New Conservative Feminism." *Feminist Studies* 9:559–83.

———— and Barrie Thorne. 1985. "The Missing Feminist Revolution in Sociology." *Social Problems* 32:301–16.

Suransky, Valerie Polakow. 1982. *The Erosion of Childhood.* Chicago: University of Chicago Press.

Thorne, Barrie, with Marilyn Yalom, eds. 1982. *Rethinking the Family: Some Feminist Questions.* New York: Longman.

Willis, Paul. 1977. *Learning to Labor.* New York: Columbia University Press.

Winn, Marie. 1983. *Children Without Childhood.* New York: Pantheon.

Wittner, Judith G. 1980. "Domestic Labor as Work Discipline: The Struggle over Housework in

Foster Homes." pp. 229–47 in *Women and Household Labor*, edited by S. F. Berk. Newbury Park, CA: Sage.

Zelizer, Viviana A. 1985. *Pricing the Priceless Child: The Changing Social Value of Children*. New York: Basic Books.

Zinn, Maxine Baca, Lynn Weber Cannon, Elizabeth Higginbotham, and Bonnie Thornton Dill. 1986. "The Costs of Exclusionary Practices in Women's Studies." *Signs: Journal of Women in Culture and Society* 11:290–303.

Children's Interpretive Reproductions

WILLIAM CORSARO

INTRODUCTION

Traditionally, social scientific thinking about children has overlooked that they are part of a social system and active agents in their own lives. In this selection, sociologist William Corsaro discusses the weaknesses of many traditional ways of understanding children within both psychological and sociological theories. He introduces the idea of interpretive reproduction, which posits that children take concepts from the world around them, use them in their play with peers, and create new shared meanings based on their interactions.

This chapter examines the reasons for the resurgent interest in children in society and, especially, in sociology. I review traditional theories of socialization and child development and examine basic assumptions in these theories that have now been called into question. Finally, I present an alternative theoretical approach to childhood, one that reconceptualizes the place of children in the social structure and stresses the unique contributions that children make to their own development and socialization.

SOCIOLOGY'S REDISCOVERY OF CHILDHOOD

As recently as 18 years ago there was a near absence of studies on children in mainstream sociology (Ambert, 1986). Today the situation is very different. A large and growing number of monographs, edited volumes, and journal articles address theoretical issues and report empirical findings related to the sociological study of children and childhood. Childhood socialization has been given expanded coverage in basic introductory texts in sociology; new journals and sections of national and international associations devoted to the sociology of childhood have been established; and courses on the sociology of childhood are now frequently offered in sociology.

These developments are long overdue and very encouraging. But why have children been so long ignored in sociology? Jens Qvortrup (1993a) aptly notes that children have not so much been ignored as they have been *marginalized*. Children are marginalized in sociology because of their subordinate position in societies and in theoretical conceptualizations of childhood and socialization. As I will discuss more fully in this chapter, adults most often view children in a forward-looking way, that is, with an eye to what they will become—future adults with a place in the social order and contributions to make to it. Rarely are they viewed in a way that appreciates what they are—children with ongoing lives, needs, and desires. In fact, the current lives, needs, and desires of children are often seen as causes for alarm by adults, as social problems that are threatening, that need to be resolved. As a result, children are pushed to the margins of the social structure by more powerful adults (including social theorists), who focus instead on the potential and the threat of children to present and future societies.

Another question prompted by the resurgence of interest in childhood is why ideas are now being put forth that reconsider, challenge, refine, and even transform traditional lay and theoretical approaches to children and childhood. One reason is that consideration of other subordinate groups by sociologists (for example, minorities and women) has drawn attention to the lives of children. Unlike other subordinate groups, children have no representatives among sociologists; however, the work of feminists and minority scholars has, at least indirectly, drawn attention to the neglect of children. Barrie Thorne notes that in some ideological constructions, "*women are closely and unreflectively tied* with children; womanhood has been equated with motherhood in a mixing of identities that simply does not occur for men and fatherhood" (1987, p. 96; emphasis in original). Indeed, feminists who find themselves labeled (most especially by political conservatives) as selfishly negligent of children have responded that children should be the responsibility of women and men. In their call for recognition of more diverse and equitable roles for women and men, feminists have been slow to note the marginalization of children in sociology. However, feminist analyses of gender ideologies have provided a lens for what Thorne (1987) has called the "re-visioning of children," resulting in a number of important recent studies of children, gender, and identity (Alanen, 1994; Eder, 1995; Mayall, 2002; Thorne, 1993).

New ways of conceptualizing children in sociology also stem from the rise of **constructivist and interpretive theoretical perspectives in sociology** (Connell, 1987; Corsaro, 1992, James, Jenks, & Prout, 1998). From these perspectives, assumptions about the genesis of everything from friendship to scientific knowledge are carefully examined as social constructions rather than simply accepted as biological givens or obvious social facts. What this means is that childhood and all social objects (including things like class, gender, race, and ethnicity) are seen as being interpreted, debated, and defined in processes of social action. In short, they are viewed as social products or constructions. When applied to the sociology of childhood, constructivist and interpretive perspectives argue that children and adults alike are active participants in the social construction of childhood and in the interpretive reproduction of their shared culture. In contrast, traditional theories view children as "consumers" of the culture established by adults.

TRADITIONAL THEORIES: SOCIALIZATION

Much of sociology's thinking about children and childhood derives from theoretical work on **socialization**, the processes by which children adapt to and internalize society. Most have focused on early socialization in the family, which views the child as internalizing society. In other words, the child is seen as something apart from society that must be shaped and guided by external forces in order to become a fully functioning member.

Two different models of the socialization process have been proposed. The first is a **deterministic model**, in which the child plays a basically passive role. In this view the child is simultaneously a "novice" with potential to contribute to the maintenance of society and an "untamed threat" who must be controlled through careful training. In the second, a **constructivist model**, the child is seen as an active agent and eager learner. In this view, the child actively constructs her social world and her place in it. Let's look first at the deterministic model.

The Deterministic Model: Society Appropriates the Child

Early theorists of socialization had a problem. In their day, the philosophy of individualism held sway; it was popular to focus on how individuals relate to society. And yet society was also recognized as a powerful determinant of individual behavior. How were these theorists to resolve the contradiction (Wentworth, 1980, pp. 38–39)? The solution to this problem was a theoretical view describing appropriation of the child by society.

Appropriation means the child is taken over by society; she is trained to become, eventually, a competent and contributing member. This model of socialization is seen as deterministic, because the child plays a primarily passive role. Within the deterministic model, two subsidiary approaches arose that differed primarily in their views of society. The functionalist models, on the one hand, saw order and balance in society and stressed the importance of training and preparing children to fit into and contribute to that order. The reproductive models, on the other hand, focused on conflicts and inequalities in society and argued that some children have differential access to certain types of training and other societal resources.

FUNCTIONALIST MODELS.   **Functionalist models**, which were popular in the 1950s and 1960s, focused on describing rather superficial aspects of socialization: what the child needed to internalize and which parental child-rearing or training strategies were used to ensure such internalization. Functionalists had little concern for why and how children become integrated into society. Alex Inkeles, for example, maintained that the study of socialization must be inherently "forward looking," specifying what the child must become to meet requisites for the continued functioning of society (1968, pp. 76–77).

The major spokesperson of the functionalist perspective, Talcott Parsons, set the tone for Inkeles's forward-looking view of socialization. In Parsons's view, the child is a threat to society; he must be appropriated and shaped to fit in. Parsons envisioned a society as an "intricate network of interdependent and interpenetrating" roles and consensual values (Parsons & Bales, 1955, p. 36). The entry of the child into this system is problematic because, although she has the potential to be useful to the continued functioning of the system, she is also a threat until she is socialized. In fact, Parsons likened the child to a "pebble 'thrown' by the fact of birth into the social 'pond'" (Parsons & Bales, 1955, pp. 36–37). The initial point of entry—the family—feels the first effects of this "pebble," and as the child grows older the effects are seen as a succession of widening waves that radiate to other parts of the system. In a cyclical process of dealing with problems and through formal training to accept and follow social norms, the child eventually internalizes the social system (Parsons & Bales, 1955, p. 202).

REPRODUCTIVE MODELS.   As sociological theory developed, the functionalist view of socialization lost favor. Some social theorists argued that the internalization of the functional requisites of society could be seen as a mechanism of social control leading to the social reproduction or maintenance of class inequalities (Bernstein, 1981; Bourdieu & Passeron, 1977). These **reproductive models**, as they are known, focus on the advantages enjoyed by those with greater access to cultural resources. For example, parents from higher social-class groups can ensure that their children receive quality education in prestigious academic institutions.

Reproductive theorists also point to differential treatment of individuals in social institutions (especially the educational system) that reflects and supports the prevailing class system.

WEAKNESSES OF THE DETERMINISTIC MODEL.   Reproductive theorists provide a needed acknowledgment of the effect of social conflict and inequality on the socialization of children. However, both functionalist and reproductive theories can be criticized for their overconcentration on the outcomes of socialization, their underestimation of the active and innovative capacities of all members of society, and their neglect of the historical and contingent nature of social action and reproduction. In short, these abstract models simplify highly complex processes and, in the process, overlook the importance of children and childhood in society.

A key question is: Where do children and childhood fit into these abstract theories of social structure? Not surprisingly, some of these social theorists downplayed the importance of children's activities, which they considered to be inconsequential or nonfunctional. Other determinists looked to theories of child development and learning that fit their views for explanations about the mechanisms of socialization. Parsons, for example, linked his views on socialization to Freud's theory of psychosexual development. In his model, socialization takes place as the child learns to act in accordance with social norms and values rather than according to innate sexual and aggressive drives. Inkeles opts for another type of determinism, behaviorism, and points to the importance of explicit training in the skills needed for living in society, supported by a system of rewards and punishments (1968, pp. 97–103).

Both functionalist and reproductive models overlook the point that children do not just internalize the society they are born into . . . Children act on and can bring about changes in society. Reproductive theorists are, however, more inventive than functionalists in their views of socialization. Bourdieu (1977), for example, offers the complex and intriguing notion of the habitus to capture how members of society (or social actors), through their continual and routine involvement in their social worlds, acquire a set of predispositions to act and to see things in a certain way. This set of predispositions, this habitus, is inculcated in early socialization and plays itself out reproductively through the tendency of the child and all social actors to maintain their sense of self and place in the world (Bourdieu, 1993).

Bourdieu is on a track that usefully leads us away from determinism and provides a more active role for the child. However, this conceptualization of socialization limits children's involvement to cultural participation and reproduction while ignoring children's contributions to cultural refinement and change. For a model that truly incorporates an active child, we must consider the rise of constructivism.

The Constructivist Model: The Child Appropriates Society

Much of the early sociological study of childhood socialization was influenced by the dominant theories in developmental psychology at the time. The theories that sociologists most often turned to, most especially varieties of behaviorism, relegate the child to a passive role. In these theories development is basically unilateral, with the child being shaped and molded by adult reinforcements and punishments. Many developmental psychologists, however, have come to see the child as active rather than passive, involved in appropriating information from her environment to use in organizing and constructing her own interpretations of the world.

PIAGET'S THEORY OF INTELLECTUAL DEVELOPMENT.   Perhaps the best representative of the constructivist approach is the Swiss psychologist Jean Piaget. He studied the evolution of knowledge in children, which was a way of integrating two of his enduring interests: biology and epistemology (the study of knowledge) (Ginsburg & Opper, 1988). Piaget's many empirical studies of children and their development had a major impact on the image of the child in developmental psychology. Piaget believed that children, from the first days of infancy, interpret, organize, and use information from the environment, and that they come to construct conceptions (known as **mental structures**) of their physical and social worlds.

Piaget is perhaps best known for his view that intellectual development is not simply an accumulation of facts or skills, but rather is a progression through a series of qualitatively distinct stages of intellectual ability. Piaget's notion of stages is important for the sociology of children because it reminds us that children perceive and organize their worlds in ways qualitatively different from adults. Consider, for example, the following incident, which occurred in my very first ethnographic study of young children. A three-year-old boy, Krister, drew a squiggly line on a chalkboard. I asked him what it was and he responded, "A snake." "A snake!" I replied and then asked, "Have you ever seen a snake?" "Sure," said Krister, pointing to his squiggly line, "right there!" I then realized that my perspective of the "squiggly line" as a representation of a snake was different than Krister's perspective of his creation, which was that the line was exactly what he said it was—a snake!

As a result of many similar experiences, I have gotten much better at adopting children's perspectives in my fieldwork. I have also come to appreciate, in line with Piaget's theory, that any sociological theory of children and childhood that attempts to explain children's understanding and use of information from the adult world, as well as children's participation in and organization of their own peer worlds, must consider the child's level of cognitive development. . . .

CHILDREN'S UNDERSTANDING OF CONSERVATION OF MASS

In a classic experiment, Piaget would present a child between the ages of four and nine with two identical balls of clay. The child would be asked if each ball contained the same amount of clay. If the child did not think so, he or she would be asked to take away or add some clay to make the balls identical. Then, Piaget would change one of the balls into a sausage shape as the child watched. The child would then be asked if the ball and sausage now contained the same amount of clay. This experiment can be seen as illustrating the process of equilibration, with the child attempting to compensate through a series of strategies. We can capture the nature of the series each child will go through by examining how children of different ages deal with the problem:

1. The very young child, age four or five, concentrates on one characteristic or dimension of the objects, usually length, and is apt to say with a great deal of conviction, "This one, 'cause it is longer!" The child is unaware of the notion of conservation of mass and refers only to one dimension. Again, the child shows a great deal of certainty, and there is limited mental activity or thinking. In fact, the child may even claim that the problem is too easy, silly, or possibly a trick.
2. The slightly older child, age six or seven, tends to reverse her original claim because she notices a second dimension (width or thinness). At this point a new strategy becomes probable because the uncertainty of the child leads to more activity in dealing with the intrusion. In thinking about the intrusion, the child oscillates back and forth in her thinking and may become vaguely

aware of the interdependence of the sausage's elongation and its thinness. Here a child might start out with confidence: "This one 'cause it's longer. No, no wait this one 'cause it's fatter. Oh, I don't know!"

3. The seven- to nine-year-old child acts on the insight of interdependence. She places a mental emphasis on the transformation rather than the static configuration with dimensions. She will make them both the same and will now claim that they are equal. Here the child will often be very careful, rolling the ball into a second sausage and holding the two next to each other to see if they match. If not, she will go back to work, shortening one or lengthening the other until she convinces herself that they are the same. Here there is a maximum of activity in the equilibration process as the child approaches the mental insight of conservation of mass.

4. For the nine- to eleven-year-old, the strategy begins with the discovery of the compensations of the transformation (that is, as clay lengthens it becomes thinner; as it broadens it becomes shorter). Here the child may scoff at the question, saying, "They are obviously the same!" or, "See, it makes no difference. I can make this ball a sausage or the sausage a ball," doing so as she talks. At this point, conservation is accepted and the child understands reversibility. Certainty now returns and related problems in the future will seem simple.

—Adapted from Piaget (1968: 112) and Ginsburg & Opper (1988: 150–151).

VYGOTSKY'S SOCIOCULTURAL VIEW OF HUMAN DEVELOPMENT.   Another important constructivist theorist is the Russian psychologist, Lev Vygotsky. Like Piaget, Vygotsky stressed children's active role in human development. Vygotsky, however, believed that children's social development is always the result of their collective actions and that these actions take place and are located in society. Therefore, for Vygotsky, changes in society, especially changes in societal demands on the individual, require changes in strategies for dealing with those demands. For Vygotsky, strategies for dealing with changes in societal demands are always collective; that is, they always involve interaction with others. These collective strategies are seen as practical actions that lead to both social and psychological development. In this sense, the child's interactions and practical activities with others lead to her acquisition of new skills and knowledge, which are seen as the transformation of previous skills and knowledge.

A key principle in Vygotsky's view is the individual's internalization or appropriation of culture. Especially important to this process is language, which both encodes culture and is a tool for participating in culture. Vygotsky argues that language and other sign systems (for example, writing, film, and so on), like tool systems (for example, material objects such as machines), are created by societies over the course of history and change with cultural development. Thus, argued Vygotsky, children, through their acquisition and use of language, come to reproduce a culture that contains the knowledge of generations.

Vygotsky offered a quite different constructivist approach to human development than that of Piaget. Although both theorists viewed development as resulting from the child's activities, Vygotsky made no nativistic assumption similar to Piaget's notion of equilibrium to account for the motivating factor that generates the child's activities. Vygotsky saw practical activities developing from the child's attempts to deal with everyday problems. Furthermore, in dealing with these problems, the child always develops strategies collectively—that is, in interaction with others. Thus, for Piaget, human development is primarily individualistic, whereas for Vygotsky it is primarily collective.

Other differences exist between the two theorists. Piaget concentrated more on the nature and characteristics of cognitive processes and structures, whereas Vygotsky emphasized their developmental contexts and history. As a result, rather than identifying abstract stages of cognitive development, Vygotsky sought to specify the cultural events and practical activities that lead to the appropriation, internalization, and reproduction of culture and society.

How, specifically, do these processes of internalization, appropriation, and reproduction occur? Two of Vygotsky's concepts are crucial. First is the notion of **internalization**. According to Vygotsky, "every function in the child's development appears twice: first on the social level, and later on the individual level; first, between people (interpsychological) and then inside the child (intrapsychological)" (1978, p. 57). By this, Vygotsky means that all our psychological and social skills (cognitive, communicative, and emotional) are always acquired from our interactions with others. We develop and use such skills at the interpersonal level first before internalizing them at the individual level.

Consider Vygotsky's conceptions of self-directed and inner speech. By self-directed speech, Vygotsky is referring to the tendency of young children to speak out loud to themselves, especially in problematic situations. Piaget saw such speech as egocentric or emotional and serving no social function. Vygotsky, on the other hand, saw self-directed speech as a form of interpersonal communication, except that in this case the child is addressing himself as another. In a sense, the child is directing and advising himself on how to deal with a problem. In experimental work, Vygotsky found that such speech increased when children were given a task like building a car with construction toys or were told to draw a picture. Vygotsky believed that, over time, self-directed speech was transformed or internalized from the interpersonal to the intrapersonal, becoming inner speech or a form of thought. We can grasp his ideas when we think about how we first learn to read. Most of our early reading as young children is done out loud as we read to ourselves and others. Over time we begin to mumble and then to mouth the words as we read, and eventually we read entirely at a mental level. In short, the intrapsychological function or skill of reading has its origins in social or collective activity—reading out loud for others and oneself. For Vygotsky, internalization occurs gradually over an extended period of time. . . .

WEAKNESSES OF THE CONSTRUCTIVIST MODEL.   Although the general acceptance of constructivism moved theory and research in developmental psychology in the right direction, its main focus still remains squarely on individual development. We can see this in repeated references to the *child's* activity, the *child's* development, the *child's* becoming an adult. In Piaget's theory, the focus is on the individual child's mastery of the world on her own terms. Constructivism offers an active but somewhat lonely view of children. Even when others (parents, peers, and teachers) are taken into account, the focus remains on the effects of various interpersonal experiences on individual development. There is little, if any, consideration of how interpersonal relations reflect cultural systems, or how children, through their participation in communicative events, become part of these interpersonal relations and cultural patterns and reproduce them collectively.

Another limitation of constructivist developmental psychology is the overwhelming concern with the endpoint of development, or the child's movement from immaturity to adult competence. Take, for example, research on friendship. The focus of nearly all of the research is on identifying stages in the child's abstract conceptions of friendship. These conceptions are elicited through clinical interviews, and their underdeveloped conceptions are compared to those of the competent adult (Damon, 1977; Selman, 1980). Yet few psychologists study what it is like to be or to have a friend in children's social worlds, or how developing conceptions of friendships are embedded in children's interactions in peer culture.

This emphasis on the endpoint of development is also apparent in many developmental psychologists' interest in Vygotsky's notion of internalization. As we saw previously, Vygotsky stressed both children's collective interactions with others at the interpersonal level and their internalization of these interactions at the intrapersonal level in his theory of children's appropriation of culture. Yet, much research by constructivists places so much emphasis on the second phase of internalization that many view the appropriation of culture as the movement from the external to the internal. This misconception pushes children's collective actions with others to the background and implies that an individual actor's participation in society occurs only after such individual internalization.

EXTENSIONS OF PIAGET AND VYGOTSKY.   Recent theoretical discussions and research by both Piagetians and sociocultural theorists influenced by Vygotsky have extended constructivist theory to focus more on children's agency in childhood and the importance of peer interaction. For example, Tesson and Youniss (1995) argue that there has been too much emphasis on the details of stages in developmental psychology. They maintain that Piaget did not place great importance on the stages and that his later work investigated the interrelationship between the logic and social qualities of children's thought. Expanding on Piaget's work on moral development, Tesson and Youniss argue that Piagetian operations enable children to make sense of the world as a set of possibilities for action. Thus Piaget attributed agency to children and further argued that children's relationships with peers were more conducive to the development of cognitive operations than the authoritative relationships with adults. Along these lines, Piaget made a distinction between practical and theoretical modes of behavior. "The practical occurs on the plane of direct action, the theoretical on the plane of consciousness. Piaget proposed a developmental relation between the two. First the child works out the conception of rules in the course of actual play with peers, then later the child grasps in consciousness a symbolic representation of this once practical concept" (Youniss & Damon, 1994, p. 277). As we will see later, the interpretive approach to childhood socialization gives special emphasis to children's practical activities in their production of and participation in their own peer cultures.

Recent work by sociocultural theorists develop the theoretical work of Vygotsky in a similar vein, also stressing children's collective activities with peers and others. Rogoff, for example, building on Vygotsky, argues that "human development is a process of *people's changing participation in sociocultural activities of their communities*" (2003, p. 32). To capture the nature of children's involvements in sociocultural activities, Rogoff (1996) suggests that they be studied on three different planes of analysis: the community, the interpersonal, and the individual. However, Rogoff notes that these processes must not be analyzed separately, but together in collective activities. In line with this view of human development, Rogoff introduces the notion of "participatory appropriation" by which she means that any event in the present is an extension of previous events and is directed toward goals that have not yet been accomplished (Rogoff, 1995, p. 155). Thus, previous experiences of collectively produced and shared activities are not merely stored in individual memory and called upon in the present; rather, the individual's previous participation contributes to and primes the event at hand by having prepared it.

Here again, in this extension of the constructivist approach, we see new emphasis on collective actions in social context as essential for the development of children and all humans. To capture more fully the importance of collective action and children's construction of their own peer cultures, we now turn to a discussion of the notion of interpretive reproduction.

INTERPRETIVE REPRODUCTION: CHILDREN COLLECTIVELY PARTICIPATE IN SOCIETY

Sociological theories of childhood must break free from the individualistic doctrine that regards children's social development solely as the child's private internalization of adult skills and knowledge. From a sociological perspective, socialization is not only a matter of adaptation and internalization but also a process of appropriation, reinvention, and reproduction. Central to this view of socialization is the appreciation of the importance of collective, communal activity—how children negotiate, share, and create culture with adults and each other (Corsaro, 1992; James, Jenks, & Prout, 1998).

However, to say that a sociological perspective of socialization stresses the importance of collective and communal processes is not enough in constructing a new sociology of childhood. The problem is the term *socialization* itself. It has an individualistic and forward-looking connotation that is inescapable. One hears the term, and the idea of training and preparing the individual child for the future keeps coming to mind (Thorne, 1993, pp. 3–6; also see James, Jenks, & Prout, 1998, pp. 22–26). Instead, I offer the notion of **interpretive reproduction**. The term *interpretive* captures the *innovative* and *creative* aspects of children's participation in society. In fact, as we shall see, children create and participate in their own unique peer cultures by creatively taking or appropriating information from the adult world to address their own peer concerns. The term *reproduction* captures the idea that children are not simply internalizing society and culture, but are actively *contributing to cultural production and change*. The term also implies that children are by their very participation in society, *constrained by the existing social structure and by societal reproduction*. That is, children and their childhoods are affected by the societies and cultures of which they are members. These societies and cultures have, in turn, been shaped and affected by processes of historical change.

Let's pursue this notion of interpretive reproduction further by looking at two of its key elements: the importance of language and cultural routines and the reproductive nature of children's evolving membership in their culture.

LANGUAGE AND CULTURAL ROUTINES.   Interpretive reproduction places special emphasis on language and on children's participation in cultural routines. Language is central to children's participation in their culture both as a "symbolic system that encodes local, social, and cultural structure" and as a "tool for establishing (that is, maintaining, creating) social and psychological realities" (Ochs, 1988, p. 210). These interrelated features of language and language use are "deeply embedded and instrumental in the accomplishment of the concrete routines of social life" (Schieffelin, 1990, p. 19).

Children's participation in **cultural routines** is a key element of interpretive reproduction. The habitual, taken-for-granted character of routines provides children and all social actors with the security and shared understanding of belonging to a social group. On the other hand, this very predictability empowers routines, providing a framework within which a wide range of sociocultural knowledge can be produced, displayed, and interpreted. In this way, cultural routines serve as anchors that enable social actors to deal with ambiguities, the unexpected, and the problematic while remaining comfortably within the friendly confines of everyday life (Corsaro, 1992).

Participation in cultural routines begins very early, almost from the minute children are born. Early in infancy, at least in Western societies, when children's language and communicative abilities are limited, social interaction proceeds in line with an **"as-if" assumption**. That is, infants are treated as socially competent ("as if" they are capable of social exchanges). Over time, because of this "as if" attitude, children move from limited to full participation in cultural routines.

Consider, for example, the well-known parent-infant game of "peekaboo." In their study of six mother-infant dyads, Bruner and Sherwood (1976) identified four basic phases in peekaboo: (1) initial contact or shared attention (usually established by the mother through vocalization and/or gaze); (2) disappearance (usually the mother hiding her or her child's face with her hands or a cloth, accompanied by vocalizations such as "Where's baby?"); (3) reappearance (removal of hands or cloth, usually by the mother); and (4) the reestablishment of contact (usually with vocalizations such as "boo," "there's the baby," and so on by the mother, gaining a response such as a smile or laugh from the child). Bruner and Sherwood note that what the child appears to be learning "is not only the basic rules of the game, but the range of variation that is possible with the rule set" (1976, p. 283). Thus, by participating in the routine, the children are learning a set of predictable rules that provide security, and they also are learning that a range of embellishments of the rules is possible and even desirable. In this way, children gain insight into the generative or productive nature of cultural participation in a play routine from which they derive great pleasure. Furthermore, we know from later work (Ratner & Bruner, 1977) that there is a movement from the "as if" function of these games in the first months of life, where children's participation is often limited to a responsive role, to a point where the same children at one year old are initiating and directing the games and even creating and participating in other types of disappearance-reappearance games alone and with others.

To say that adults always strive for shared understanding with children and that the adoption of an "as-if" attitude in parent-child games is crucial in attaining joint activity does not mean that shared understanding is always achieved and maintained in adult-child interaction. What is important is not that shared understanding is always achieved, but rather that attempts by both the adult and child to reach such understanding are always made. Often, especially in adult-child interaction, children are exposed to social knowledge and communicative demands they do not fully grasp. Interaction normally continues in an orderly fashion, and any persisting ambiguities must be pursued over the course of the children's experiences with adults and peers. . . .

From Individual Progression to Collective Reproductions

As we discussed earlier, many theories of child development focus on the individual child. These theories take a **linear view of the developmental process**. In the linear view, it is assumed that the child must pass through a preparatory period in childhood before he or she can develop into a socially competent adult. In this view, the period of childhood consists of a set of developmental stages in which cognitive skills, emotions, and knowledge are acquired in preparation for adult life.

Interpretive reproduction views children's evolving membership in their cultures as reproductive rather than linear. According to this reproductive view, children do not simply imitate or internalize the world around them. They strive to interpret or make sense of their culture and to participate in it. In attempting to make sense of the adult world, children come to collectively produce their own peer worlds and cultures. . . .

Until recently, sociology has paid relatively little attention to children and childhood. The neglect or marginalization of children in sociology is clearly related to traditional views of socialization, which relegate children to a primarily passive role. Most of these theories were based on behavioristic views of child development that have been severely challenged by the rise of constructivism in contemporary developmental psychology. Best represented in Piaget's cognitive developmental theory and Vygotsky's sociocultural approach, constructivism stresses the child's active role in her development and her eventual participation in the adult world. Although constructivist theories of individual human development provide sociology with a lens for refocusing our images of children as active agents, these theories until recently have focused primarily on developmental outcomes and failed to seriously consider the complexity of social structure and children's collective activities. Interpretive reproduction provides a basis for a new sociology of childhood. Interpretive reproduction replaces linear models of children's individual social development with the collective, productive-reproductive view. . . . Children spontaneously participate as active members of both childhood and adult cultures.

[Next, . . .] we will extend the notion of interpretive reproduction by examining its relationship to structural and relational approaches to children and childhood.

. . . As a group, children are in a subordinate position in society in relationship to other groups. Therefore, even though children are active agents, the nature of their activities, power, and rights must be considered in relation to their role as a generational group in society and their place in the generational order (Alanen, 2000; Mayall, 2002). To capture these generational relationships, we must examine childhood from a structural perspective.

ASSUMPTIONS OF THE STRUCTURAL PERSPECTIVE

In a series of theoretical papers stemming from his work on the international project "Childhood as a Social Phenomenon," the Danish sociologist Jens Qvortrup (1991, 1993a, 1993b, 1994a, 1994b) has outlined a structural perspective to the study of childhood. The approach is based on three central assumptions: (1) childhood constitutes a particular structural form; (2) childhood is exposed to the same societal forces as adulthood; and (3) children are themselves coconstructors of childhood and society. Let's examine each of these assumptions.

Childhood as a Structural Form

Childhood is both a period in which children live their lives and a category or part of society, like social class. . . . While childhood is a temporary period for children, it is a permanent structural category in society. Qvortrup further develops the notion of viewing childhood as a structural form by contrasting it with perspectives that focus on childhood only as a period of life. He places these perspectives in three general categories. The first is the typical psychological view, which is individual and personality oriented. In this view, childhood is forward looking or anticipatory, and is determined by an adult perspective. The second is the psychoanalytic view, which is also individual and personality oriented, but here the interest in individual adulthood requires the retrospective examination of the individual's childhood experiences. A third view is the life course perspective. This perspective is a mix of individual and nonindividual approaches, in that it follows single individuals from childhood to adulthood or vice versa while at the same time stressing the impact of historical and societal events. All of these views are similar to the traditional theories of socialization we discussed: . . . (1) they focus on the anticipatory outcomes of childhood (that is, children becoming adults), and (2) they consider childhood and adulthood as necessarily belonging to different historical periods.

Qvortrup argues that, by conceptualizing childhood as a structural form, we can move beyond these individualistic, adult-oriented, and time-bound perspectives to pose and answer a wide range of sociological questions. Consider just a few possibilities: How is childhood alike, different from, and related to other age groups at any given time and place? (For example, consider the interrelationships of childhood, adulthood, and old age in the 1950s compared to the 1980s in the United States.) How has the conception and nature of childhood changed over different historical periods in particular societies (for example, childhood in the 1890s compared to the 1990s in the United States)? How do conceptions and the nature of childhood vary across cultures at particular points in time (for example, childhood in the early years of the 21st century in Western industrial societies compared to non-Western developing societies)? . . .

Let's now move to a consideration of the general effects of societal forces on childhood.

Effects of Societal Forces on Childhood

A key feature of Qvortrup's structural approach is that it sees childhood as integrated in society (Qvortrup, 1991, p. 14). Children in their particular childhoods are, like adults, active participants in organized activities (for example, they engage in economic production and consumption). They both affect and are affected by major societal events and developments. Consider, for example, recent changes in Western societies such as higher divorce rates, greater female participation in the labor force, and lower fertility levels (especially among the middle and upper classes). Sociologists have increasingly documented the effects of these factors on the family and to some extent on individual children. But how are the lives of children—that is, contemporary children's childhoods—affected by such changes? Furthermore, how might children, through their collective activities, contribute to society's accommodation to such changes? . . .

Like most traditional sociological research that involves children, Cherlin and Furstenberg's study focuses on the effects of a social phenomenon (in this case grandparenting) on individual children. Although their acknowledgment of subtle forms of influence hints at the complexity of the worlds of children and their grandparents, the authors fail to push their study to fully consider children's perspectives. For example, they do not consider the possible counterpart of the conception of grandparenthood, which we can term "grandchildhood." Just as adults are grandparents, children are grandchildren, and as the nature of grandparenting changes so does the nature of being a grandchild. The very difficulty of the word, grandchildhood, is due to the tendency of social scientists to think of children as individually affected (as dependent variables) rather than as agents of complex collective actions.

Surely the intergenerational lives of grandchildren have changed in ways that parallel those of their grandparents. We can consider a whole new set of vantage points: styles of being a grandchild; grandchild careers; and variations in these styles and careers by gender, class, race, and ethnicity. An important factor to keep in mind in this regard is the influence of parents on their children's lives as grandchildren (or, for that matter, the lives of their parents as grandparents). At least for younger children, for instance, parents control access to grandparents, and they both actively and reactively support children in their interpretation and appreciation of their interactions with grandparents. Finally, children's interactions with grandparents occur often in multigenerational settings (for example, in the presence of grandparents, parents, aunts, uncles, and cousins). These occasions provide an ideal setting for priming activities in which children are prepared for transitions into a variety of social relations in their lives. One such family obligation—to serve as the adult child caretaker of elderly parents—may indeed be a long and demanding one for the present generation of children . . . .

Through their participation in such cultural routines in the family with parents and siblings, young children initiate their evolving membership in their culture. We can see this evolving membership as a process in which children refine and expand their place in the culture over time and with experience (Lave & Wenger, 1991). This process continues as children, from very young ages, begin to participate in cultural routines and other collective activities outside the family. By interacting with playmates in play groups and preschools, children produce the first in a series of peer cultures in which childhood knowledge and practices are gradually transformed into the knowledge and skills necessary to participate in the adult world . . . .

SUMMARY

In recent years we have seen the beginnings of a new sociology of childhood, one that breaks free from the individualistic doctrine that regards socialization as the child's private internalization of adult skills and knowledge. In this new approach the focus is on *childhood* as a social construction resulting from the collective actions of *children* with adults and each other. Childhood is recognized as a structural form and children as social agents who contribute to the reproduction of childhood and society through their negotiations with adults and through their creative production of a series of peer cultures with other children. This new view of childhood as a social phenomenon replaces the traditional notion of socialization with the concept of interpretive reproduction. Interpretive reproduction reflects children's evolving membership in their culture, which begins in the family and spirals outward as children create a series of embedded peer cultures based on the institutional structure of the adult culture. Overall, the notion of interpretive reproduction challenges sociology to take children seriously and to appreciate children's contributions to social reproduction and change.

Discussion Questions

1. Define interpretive reproduction.
2. What are the weaknesses of traditional theories of childhood development, according to the author?
3. The author provides some examples of interpretive reproduction—can you think of any others?

4. Can you think of any weaknesses to the theory of interpretive reproduction? If so, how would you improve this idea?

References

Alanen, L. (1994). Gender and generation: Feminism and the "child question." In J. Qvortrup, M. Bardy, & H. Wintersberger (Eds.), *Childhood matters: Social theory, practice and politics* (pp. 27–42). Brookfield, VT: Avebury.

Alanen, L. (2000). Visions of a social theory of childhood. *Childhood, 7*, 493–505.

Ambert, A. (1986). Sociology of sociology: The place of children in North American sociology. In P. Adler & P. Adler (Ed.), *Sociological studies of child development* Vol. 1 (pp. 11–31). Greenwich, CT: JAI Press.

Bernstein, B. (1981). Codes, modalities, and the process of cultural reproduction: A model. *Language in Society, 10*, 327–363.

Bourdieu, P. (1977). *Outline of a theory of practice.* New York: Cambridge University Press.

Bourdieu, P. (1993). Concluding remarks: For a sociogenetic understanding of intellectual works. In C. Calhoun, E. Lipuma, & M. Postone (Eds.), *Bourdieu: Critical Perspectives* (pp. 263–275). Chicago: University of Chicago Press.

Bourdieu, P., & Passeron, J. C. (1977). *Reproduction in education, society, and culture.* Beverly Hills, CA: Sage.

Bruner, J., & Sherwood, V. (1976). Peekaboo and the learning of rule structure. In J. Bruner, A. Jolly, & K. Sylva (Eds.), *Play: Its role in development and evolution* (pp. 277–285). New York: Basic Books.

Cherlin, A., & Furstenberg, F. (1986). *The new American grandparent: A place in the family, a life apart.* New York: Basic Books.

Connell, R. (1987). *Gender and power: Society, the person and sexual politics.* Stanford, CA: Stanford University Press.

Corsaro, W. (1992). Interpretive reproduction in children's peer cultures. *Social Psychology Quarterly, 55*, 160–177.

Corsaro, W., & Rosier, K. (1992). Documenting productive-reproductive processes in children's lives: Transition narratives of a Black family living in poverty. In W. Corsaro & P. Miller (Eds.), *Interpretive approaches to childen's socialization* (pp. 69–93). New Directions for Child Development, No. 58, San Francisco: Jossey-Bass.

Damon, W. (1977). *The social world of the child.* San Francisco: Jossey-Bass.

Eder, D. (1995). *School talk: Gender and adolescent culture.* New Brunswick, NJ: Rutgers University Press.

Ginsburg, H., & Opper, S. (1988). *Piaget's theory of intellectual development.* (3rd ed.). Englewood Cliffs, NJ: Prentice Hall.

Inkeles, A. (1968). Society, social structure and child socialization. In J. A. Clausen (Ed.), *Socialization and society* (pp. 73–129). Boston: Little, Brown.

James, A., Jenks, C., & Prout, A. (1998). *Theorizing childhood.* New York: Teachers College Press.

Lave, J., & Wenger, E. (1991). *Situated learning: Legitimate peripheral participation.* New York: Cambridge University Press.

Mayall, B. (2002). *Towards a sociology for childhood: Thinking from children's lives.* Philadelphia, PA: Open University Press.

Ochs, E. (1988). *Culture and language development: Language acquisition and language socialization in a Samoan village.* New York: Cambridge University Press.

Parsons, T., & Bales, R. F. (1955). *Family, socialization and interaction process.* New York: The Free Press.

Piaget, J. (1968). *Six psychological studies.* New York: Vintage.

Qvortrup, J. (1991). Childhood as a social phenomenon—An introduction to a series of national reports. *Eurosocial Report No. 36.* Vienna, Austria: European Centre for Social Welfare Policy and Research.

Qvortrup, J. (1993a). Nine theses about "childhood as a social phenomenon." In J. Qvortrup (Ed.), *Childhood as a social phenomenon: Lessons from an international project. Eurosocial Report No. 47* (pp. 11–18). Vienna, Austria: European Centre for Social Welfare Policy and Research.

Qvortrup, J. (1993b). Societal position of childhood: The international project childhood as a social phenomenon. *Childhood, 1*, 119–124.

Qvortrup, J. (1994a). Childhood matters: An introduction. In J. Qvortrup, M. Bardy, G. Sgritta, & H. Wintersberger (Eds.), *Childhood matters: Social theory, practice, and politics* (pp. 1–23). Brookfield, VT: Avebury.

Qvortrup, J. (1994b). A new solidarity contract?: The significance of a demographic balance for the welfare of both children and the elderly. In J. Qvortrup, M. Bardy, G. Sgritta, & H. Wintersberger (Eds.), *Childhood matters: Social theory, practice, and politics* (pp. 319–334). Brookfield, VT: Avebury.

Ratner, N., & Bruner, J. (1977). Games, social exchanges and the acquisition of language. *Journal of Child Language, 5,* 391–401.

Rogoff, B. (1995). Observing sociocultural activity on three planes: Participatory appropriation, guided participation, and apprenticeship. In J. Wertsch, P. del Rio, & A. Alvarez (Eds.), *Sociocultural studies of mind* (pp. 139–164). Cambridge: Cambridge University Press.

Rogoff, B. (1996). Developmental transitions in children's participation in socio-cultural activities. In A. Sameroff & M. Haith (Eds.), *The five to seven year shift: The age of reason and responsibility* (pp. 273–294). Chicago: University of Chicago Press.

Rogoff, B. (2003). *The cultural nature of human development.* New York: Oxford.

Schieffelin, B. (1990). *The give and take of everyday life: Language socialization of Kalui children.* New York: Cambridge University Press.

Selman, R. (1980). *The growth of interpersonal understanding.* New York: Academic Press.

Tesson, G., & Youniss, J. (1995). Micro-sociology and psychological development: A sociological interpretation of Piaget's theory. *Sociological Studies of Children and Youth, 7,* 101–126.

Thorne B. (1987). Re-visioning women and social change: Where are the children? *Gender & Society, 1,* 85–109.

Thorne, B. (1993). *Gender play: Girls and boys in school.* New Brunswick, NJ: Rutgers University Press.

Vygotsky, L.S. (1978). *Mind in society.* Cambridge, MA: Harvard University Press.

Wentworth, W. M. (1980). *Context and understanding: An inquiry into socialization theory.* New York: Elsevier.

Youniss, J., & Damon, W. (1994). Social construction and Piaget's theory. In B. Puka (Ed.), *Moral development*, volume 5, *New research in moral development* (pp. 407–426), New York: Garland.

A Window on the "New" Sociology of Childhood

SARAH H. MATTHEWS

INTRODUCTION

This article is intended as a window on the body of research that has come to be known as the "new sociology of childhood." To elucidate its underlying tenets, the author identifies three major weaknesses that scholars in the "new" sociology find in the "old" conceptualization— socialization—and discusses implications for doing research on children and childhood. Scholars in the United States are on a somewhat different path than their colleagues in other Western countries. . . . The view that children are not yet members of their societies is one that is difficult to undermine.

What has come to be known as the 'new sociology of childhood' emerged during the mid-1980s when scholars began to chide their colleagues for not taking seriously the study of children and childhood (Adler and Adler 1986; Alanen 1988; Ambert 1986; Jenks 1992; James and Prout 1990; Qvortrup et al. 1994; Thorne 1987; Waksler 1986). Since then, the number of scholars engaged in research on children has increased. Book series on children have been inaugurated (e.g. Routledge/The Falmer Press and Rutgers University Press). In 1992, Children became a section in the American Sociological Association and, in 1998, Childhood became a research committee in the International Sociological Association. Three new journals—*Childhood: A Global Journal of Child Research, Journal of Children and Poverty,* and *Childhood and Society*—were inaugurated in 1993, 1995, and 1996, respectively. In 1986, a review was launched, *Sociological Studies of Child Development,* later changed to *Sociological Studies of Children and Youth*, with the 11th volume published in 2005. Perhaps the best evidence of childhood's acceptance as a legitimate substantive field is that textbooks have begun to appear (e.g. Boocock and Scott 2005; Corsaro 2005; Mayall 2002; Wyness 2006).

This article is intended as a window on this new body of research. I begin by identifying three major weaknesses that scholars in the 'new' sociology of childhood find in the 'old' conceptualization of children as well as their suggestions for overcoming them. I then discuss implications for conducting research on children and childhood. Finally, I identify a difference in focus between research in the United States and other Western countries. Throughout the article I include references to various strands of the literature that readers may follow, depending on their specific interests.

There is some disagreement about whether children or childhood is the more appropriate designation for the field (Johnson 2001). Qvortrup (2002, 74) points out that unlike children, childhood 'is a *permanent form*, which never disappears, even if its members change continuously, and even if it is historically varied.' To make the same point, Sprey (2003) distinguishes between the cognitive and relational realities of institutions. As with most social science, research is more likely to focus . . . on children, rather than on . . . childhood. My use of childhood rather than children, then, is intended to acknowledge that the experiences of children cannot be divorced from the institution of childhood, which, as Qvortrup (2002) argues, is universal. Throughout history, across and even within societies there is no agreement on what constitutes childhood or when it ends. Nevertheless, every society that depends on procreation for its survival must take into account in its social organization that children initially require a great deal of care.

THE 'OLD' VERSUS THE 'NEW' SOCIOLOGY OF CHILDHOOD

In sociology, children traditionally have been understood primarily in terms of socialization (Handel et al. 2007). Under this rubric, childhood is envisioned as a stage in which the young acquire the requisite knowledge and skills to become competent members of society: 'The child is conceptualized as a lump of clay in need of being molded to fit the requirements of a social system' (Knapp 1999, 55). The socialization perspective defines children as 'incomplete' or 'in process' rather than as full members of the group and sees them as potential outcomes rather than as social actors who are not only affected by but also affect social structures and relationships. Except as future adults, children have been of little interest to sociologists (Ambert 1986). After reviewing the research literature on children in the United States prior to the advent of the 'new' sociology of childhood, Johnson (2001, 71–2) concludes, 'While it is important to acknowledge that work has been produced, it is just as important to acknowledge that *relative* to other sub-disciplines and more popular fields of study, literature on children has been slim.'

The 'new' sociology cannot deny the universality of the extreme dependence of human infants relative to other primates, a state that has been used to justify both socialization and child development as perspectives through which to view children. . . . The newest evidence suggests that socialization is very much dependent on interaction in which children, even infants, play an active role. In this section I choose three issues in the socialization perspective with which to highlight differences between the 'old' and the 'new' sociology of childhood.

Recognition of Children's Competence as Social Actors

The 'new' sociology sees children as social actors who are capable of making sense of and affecting their societies. A major concern is that socialization depicts children as passive recipients of the culture into which they are born (Waksler 1991). Until recently, sociologists have invested little time in documenting what is happening during this period of childhood socialization and have been content to view the process as a 'black box' (Mehan 1992; but see Mackay (1973) for an exception). Jenks (1996) compares the way sociologists have spoken of 'the child' to the way anthropologists in the early part of the last century spoke of 'the savage.' He reluctantly uses the term 'gerontocentrism' as a parallel to ethnocentrism to highlight general disdain for children's competence.

A growing body of literature, which explores the sense that children make of their worlds, provides evidence that children actively construct them. This research tends to focus on children's relationships with age peers (e.g. Adler and Adler 1998; Corsaro 2003; Fine 1987), those with whom children are likely to spend a great deal of time given the way childhood is structured in modern societies. From these studies evidence accrues that children are not simply being 'enculturated' by adults. . . .

Researchers willing to grant competence to children are discovering that they do not simply adopt the culture of adults who presumably are socializing them, but use it to create their own peer cultures. The 'new' sociology of childhood emphasizes that children are social actors who are capable of reflexivity. ✷ New.

Homogeneity or Heterogeneity?

A second concern is that the socialization perspective homogenizes children. This critique is leveled more strongly at child development, the dominant perspective through which children have been interpreted for the last century (Waksler 1991). Best (1994, 4) asserts that 'by largely ignoring younger children, sociologists have virtually surrendered the study of those children to child psychologists. . . ' . . .

Both the socialization and the developmental psychology perspectives push scholars to write about children as if all children were the same regardless of social location or context. The 'new' sociological perspective stresses 'the plurality of childhoods' not only within the same society but also across the settings in which children conduct their everyday lives (Jenks 1996, 121). Jenks (1996) advocates adding an 's' to 'childhood' to serve as a continual reminder of variety of children's experiences. ✷Old / New ✷

Historical and anthropological research provides strong evidence that the nature of childhood and children varies through time and across societies. Research builds on Aries' (1962) historical account of changes in the treatment of children in *Centuries of Childhood*: 'What Aries is illuminating is that the manner of [children's] recognition by adults, their representations, and thus the forms of their relationships with adults, has altered through the passage of time' (Jenks 1996, 63). . . . Jenks (1996) labels this the social constructionist view of children, as does Mayall (1999, 12): 'The 'new childhood studies' start from broadly social constructionist premises: that the child is not a natural category and that what a child is and how childhood is lived is structured by adult norms, aims and cultures.'

Using the social constructionist view, scholars focus on how particular cultural representations of children affect children's relationships, rights, and responsibilities. Scholars in the 'new' sociology advocate recognizing that children in different social locations have different childhoods and that their experience of childhood changes from one context to another. Although cultural representations of children typically are proposed to occur serially, representations of children compete within societies and are important sources of heterogeneity (e.g. Lareau 2003). In addition, the 'new' childhood scholars argue that different representations may be used in different social contexts (Mayall 1994), that childhood has many settings. Research on children in non-Western societies also contributes to awareness of heterogeneity among children and childhoods (Small 2001).

To counteract the assumption that simply describing social actors as children is adequate, the 'new' sociology of childhood advocates documenting the actual representations of children used in different social locations and settings. In short, statements about children are suspect if they are not grounded in a social context but instead claim to describe children in general.

Children's Relationships

A third reason the 'new' sociology of childhood scholars object to the socialization perspective's monopoly on interpreting children's lives is that, much like child development, it focuses on the individual child. The process of becoming adult is divorced from the social context of relationships in which it occurs. . . .

The 'new' sociology requires that adults and peers with whom childhood is experienced be taken into account.

Emphasized in the 'new' sociology is that the adults with whom children are in relationships typically have power over them.

Scholars argue that no matter how benign parents, teachers, and other adults may be, relationships between adults and children are characterized by differential power resources. Hence, depending on the situation, dependency in relationships with adults may capture the experience of children better than socialization, which characterizes children as deficient relative to adults rather than disadvantaged or oppressed by them. Jenks (1996, 41), for example, suggests that instead of a period of socialization, childhood might be thought of as 'development through dependency'. Qvortrup (2002, 71) writes, 'I would suggest characterising childhood as a minority category, the members of which are marginalized in relation to adult society and exposed to paternalistic treatment while their constructive ability is slighted.' Oldman (1994, 44) proposes that,

> we might consider adults and children as constituting classes, in the sense of being social categories which exist principally by their economic opposition to each other, and in the ability of the dominant class (adults) to exploit economically the activities of the subordinate class (children).

Power differences have been of considerable interest to sociologists. The application of theories of power to children's lives taps a rich theoretical and empirical vein. Much like Goode's (1982) application of the 'sociology of superordinates' to illuminate 'why men resist' gender equality, conceptualizing children as disadvantaged relative to adults or oppressed by them challenges taken-for-granted assumptions about children that are hidden in both the socialization and child development perspectives.

In summary, advocates of the 'new' sociology of childhood find the traditional socialization framework inadequate because it fails to recognize children's competence to interpret the social world and act on it. Second, seeing children through the lens of socialization homogenizes children, hiding the fact that children experience childhood differently depending on many factors, which require identification. Any statement that claims to describe children must deal with the question, 'Which children and under what circumstances?' Last, the 'old' frameworks fail to recognize that the everyday lives of children are experienced through social relationships with other children but perhaps more significantly with adults who control institutions that justify and support the type of dependency that children experience.

NEW METHODS

The questions Mayall raises call for carefully designed studies to explore the actual experience of childhood from children's points of view.

In the 'old' sociology of childhood, others have been allowed to speak for children, effectively silencing them. Oldman (1994, 44) writes, 'there is an absence of systematic information on the *experience* of childhood in any given society.' In research on children in families, for example, parents, typically mothers, routinely speak for their children about issues deemed important by adults. In research on school children, teachers assess children's personalities, abilities, and promise. Interaction among children is dismissed as merely play or as preparation for adulthood. The assumption that children cannot speak for themselves was rarely questioned because the voices of those not yet fully socialized were deemed not worth taking seriously.

Scholars of the 'new' sociology question the practice of privileging adults' views over children's about issues related to children's lives. These researchers advocate interacting directly with children. This injunction requires researchers to think carefully about suitable ways to gather data from children. A significant portion of the literature in the 'new' sociology of childhood focuses on appropriate ways to collect and interpret data (e.g. Christensen 2004; Christensen and James 2000; Christensen and Prout 2002; Davis 1998; Fine and Sandstrom 1988; Greene and Hogan, 2005; Hood et al. 1999).

Collecting data from children using questionnaires or traditional interviews is suspect because children, like others without power, are wise enough not to reveal information that might be used against them (Waksler 1996). Children are savvy and know both what adults want to hear and what they do not want to hear (Best 1983; Tobin 1995). Furthermore, due to different social locations, life experiences, and 'gerontocentrism' (Jenks 1996), adults are likely to have difficulty interpreting children's words.

Describing the program of research he directed, Prout (2002, 11) writes, 'Most of the research had a qualitative character . . .' James and Prout (1998, 8) suggest that, 'Ethnography is a particularly useful methodology for the study of childhood. It allows children a more direct voice and participation in the production of sociological data than is usually possible through experimental or survey styles of research.' Hutchby and Moral-Ellis (1998) advocate the use of a modified version of conversational analysis to capture children's experiences in everyday life. Most scholars, then, advocate using some form of carefully tailored qualitative research methods. . . .

Another concern is that the way demographic data are collected typically hides children within families, making it difficult to get a clear picture of them (Qvortrup 1990; Saporiti 2001). An important project in the 'new' sociology of childhood is making children visible through the way statistics are collected and reported.

A major problem encountered in applying the 'new' sociology of childhood perspective in research is that children may have no independent right to participate in research. Although in the United States children must *assent* to participate, their parents have the right of first refusal and can withhold *consent*. Research that encourages children to express their views of adults may have little appeal to parents, teachers, or any other adults who have power over them. It is not surprising that in the 'new' sociology research on children's family ties is less common than research on peer relationships. Even when school children are the focus, it is their relationships with one another rather than with teachers that are explored (Matthews 2003). In nations where issues related to children's rights are being addressed, researchers may have less difficulty with access.

DIFFERENCES IN FOCUS OF RESEARCH

Finally, I want to call attention to an apparent difference in focus between research in the United States and other Western countries that I am sensitized to through my research on inner-city children in the United States who tend to have highly authoritarian relationships with adults. My concern with power-dependent relationships may account for my attraction to the argument that children's dependence on adults be conceptualized in terms of dependency and oppression rather than deficiency (Jenks 1996; Mayall 1999; Oldman 1994; Qvortrup 2002), and to the argument that adults contribute to the 'hard times of childhood' because children do not have the power to correct adult's misunderstandings of them (Waksler 1996).

Some of the impetus for the 'new' sociology can be traced to the 1989 United Nations Convention on the Rights of the Child, which has been adopted by all countries except the United States: 'The interlocking Articles of the Convention offer children an internationally recognized set of rights that they can hold in independence of the interests and activities of the adults that directly surround them' (Lee 2001, 92). The proliferation of the 'new' sociology of childhood can be read as one result of scholars in various countries taking up the challenge of the UN Convention by thinking carefully about how children experience institutions controlled by adults. In fact, a multidisciplinary journal, *The International Journal of Children's Rights*, was inaugurated in 1993 to focus on these issues.

Guggenheim (2005) argues that failure of the United States to adopt the UN Convention is not an indication that the country is anti-child but that children's rights do not resonate in the United States in the same way they do in other countries. Perhaps this is why scholars of the 'new' sociology in the United States appear to be more reluctant to discard socialization (e.g. Cahill 2003; Corsaro and Fingerson 2003; Handel et al. 2007) than is the case in other Western nations. My reading is that research that explores the effects of the power differential between children and adults is rare in the United States, but central to the 'new' sociology in other Western countries. Compared to peer relationships, children's relationships with adults have received relatively little attention in the United States. . . . There is also a stronger affinity with the life course perspective, in which attempts are made to link past and current life events in individuals' lives. This may account for the fact that the Children section of the American Sociological Association added 'and Youth' to its name, which suggests a continued focus on stages of development. The section of the International Sociological Association chose Childhood, the cognitive rather than the relational form of the institution (Sprey 2003), and has not moved to change it. In terms of the three weaknesses identified earlier, compared to other Western countries, scholarship in the United States focuses more on children's competence and peer relationships and less on children's lack of power in relationships with adults.

CONCLUSION

There is no question that the field of sociology of childhood is growing rapidly and in many directions. Some scholars now describe recent research efforts as *social studies* of childhood, as evident in recent editorials in *Childhood* (see also Prout 2005). This designation draws in other disciplines, particularly anthropology and geography (Qvortrup 2002), but also history, cultural psychology, education, law, philosophy, and communication. Past and current scholarship in these fields, particularly when generated through qualitative research methods, clearly informs the 'new' sociology of childhood. . . .

This article is intended as a window on sociological research that moves beyond the socialization perspective to conceptualize children as active participants in their societies. This field, which has come to be known as the 'new' sociology of childhood, has grown rapidly over the last two decades as the substantive area has gained legitimacy through specialty journals, sections in professional organizations, and graduate students trained in the area. Although Thorne (2006) suggests that the field has reached middle age, in my view it is still coming of age. As Lee (2001) points out, what it means to take children seriously is still ambiguous. The view that children are not full-fledged members of society is entrenched in cultures and institutions. The ramifications of organizing societies in which children have rights and determining what those rights might be are only beginning to be explored. The process of reconceptualizing children and childhood is a challenging task that has only begun. The payoff for improving understanding of societies by including children and childhood seems worth the effort both for the field of sociology and for the welfare of children. . . .

Discussion Questions

1. Describe the "old" sociology of childhood.
2. How is the "new" sociology of childhood different from the "old"?
3. What does the author suggest that we can learn from children's relationships with one another?

4. Why do you think the author says that people might be resistant to viewing children as active members of society?

References

Adler, Peter and Patty Adler 1986. 'Introduction.' *Sociological Studies of Child Development* **1**: 3–10.

Adler, Peter and Patty Adler 1998. *Peer Power: Preadolescent Culture and Identity.* New Brunswick, NJ: Rutgers University Press.

Alanen, Leena 1988. 'Rethinking Childhood.' *Acta Sociologica* **31**: 53–67.

Ambert, Anne-Marie 1986. 'Sociology of Sociology: The Place of Children in North American Sociology.' *Sociological Studies of Child Development* **1**: 11–34.

Aries, Philippe 1962. *Centuries of Childhood.* New York: Vintage Books.

Best, Joel 1994. *Troubling Children: Studies of Children and Social Problems.* New York: Aldine de Gruyter.

Best, Raphaella 1983. *We've All Got Scars.* Bloomington, IN: Indiana University Press.

Boocock, Sarane Spence and Kimberly Ann Scott 2005. *Kids in Context: The Sociological Study of Children and Childhoods.* Lanham, MD: Rowman and Littlefield.

Cahill, Spencer 2003. '*Childhood.*' pp. 857–74 in *Handbook of Symbolic Interactionism,* edited by

Larry T. Reynolds and Nancy J. Herman-Kinney. Walnut Creek, CA: AltaMira Press.

Christensen, Pia Haudrup 2004. 'Children's Participation in Ethnographic Research: Issues of Power and Representation.' *Childhood and Society* **18**: 165–76.

Christensen, Pia and Alan Prout 2002. 'Working with Ethical Symmetry in Social Research with Children.' *Childhood* **9**: 477–97.

Christensen, Pia and Allison James 2000. *Research with Children: Perspectives and Practices.* New York: The Falmer Press.

Corsaro, William A. 2003. *We're Friends, Right? Inside Kid's Culture.* Washington, DC: Joseph Henry Press.

Corsaro, William A. 2005. *The Sociology of Childhood* (2nd edn). Thousand Oaks, CA: Pine Forge Press.

Corsaro, William A. and Laura Fingerson 2003. 'Development and Socialization in Childhood.' pp. 125–55 in *Handbook of Social Psychology,* edited by John Delamater. New York: Kluwer Academic/Plenum Publishers.

Davis, John M. 1998. 'Understanding the Meanings of Children: A Reflexive Process.' *Childhood and Society* **12**: 325–35.

Fine, Gary Alan 1987. *With the Boys*. Chicago, IL: University of Chicago Press.

Fine, Gary Alan and Kent L. Sandstrom 1988. *Knowing Children*. Newbury Park, CA: Sage Publications.

Goode, William 1982. 'Why Men Resist.' pp. 287–310 in *Rethinking the Family*, edited by Barrie. Thorne and Marilyn Yalom. Boston: Northeastern University Press.

Greene, Sheila and Diane Hogan 2005. *Researching Children's Experience*. Thousand Oaks, CA: Sage Publications.

Guggenheim, Martin 2005. *What's Wrong with Children's Rights*. Cambridge, MA: Harvard University Press.

Handel, Gerald, Spencer E. Cahill and Frederick Elkin 2007. *Children and Society: The Sociology of Children and Childhood Socialization*. Los Angeles: Roxbury Publishing Company.

Hood, Suzanne, Berry Mayall and Sandy Oliver 1999. *Critical Issues in Social Research: Power and Prejudice*. Philadelphia, PA: Open University Press.

Hutchby, Ian and Jo Moral-Ellis 1998. 'Situating Children's Social Competence.' pp. 7–26 in *Children and Social Competence: Arenas of Action*, edited by Ian Hutchby and Jo Moran-Ellis. Washington, DC: The Falmer Press.

James, Allison and Alan Prout 1990. *Constructing and Reconstructing Childhood: Contemporary Issues in the Sociological Study of Childhood*. New York: The Falmer Press.

James, Allison and Alan Prout 1998. *Constructing and Reconstructing Childhood* (2nd edn). Washington, DC: The Falmer Press.

Jenks, Chris 1992 [1982]. *The Sociology of Childhood: Essential Readings*. Hampshire, UK: Gregg Revivals.

Jenks, Chris 1996. *Childhood*. New York: Routledge.

Johnson, Heather Beth 2001. 'From the Chicago School to the New Sociology of Children: The Sociology of Children and Childhood in the United States, 1900–1999.' *Advances in Life Course Research* (*Children in the Millennium: Where Have We Come From, Where Are We Going?*) **6**: 53–93.

Knapp, Stan J. 1999. 'Facing the Child: Rethinking Models of Agency in Parent-child Relations.' *Contemporary Perspectives on Family Research* **1**: 53–75.

Lareau, Annette 2003. *Unequal Childhoods: Class, Race, and Family Life*. Berkeley: University of California Press.

Lee, Nick 2001. *Childhood and Society: Growing up in an Age of Uncertainty*. Philadelphia, PA: Open University Press.

Mackay, Robert W. 1973. 'Conceptions of Children and Models of Socialization.' pp. 27–43 in *Recent Sociology*, No. 5, edited by Hans Peter Dreitzel. New York: Macmillan.

Matthews, Sarah H. 2003. 'Counterfeit Classrooms: School Life of Inner-city Children.' *Sociological Studies of Children and Youth* **9**: 211–26.

Mayall, Berry 1999. 'Children and Childhood.' pp. 10–24 in *Critical Issues in Social Research: Power and Prejudice*, edited by Suzanne Hood, Berry Mayall, and Sandy Oliver. Philadelphia, PA: Open University Press.

Mehan, Hugh 1992. 'Understanding Inequality in Schools: The Contribution of Interpretive Studies.' *Sociology of Education* **65**: 1–20.

Oldman, David 1994. 'Adult-child Relations as Class Relations.' pp. 43–58 in *Childhood Matters: Social Theory, Practice and Politics*, edited by Jens Qvortrup, Marjatta Bardy, Giovanni Sgritta, and Helmut Wintersberger. Aldershot, UK: Avebury.

Prout, Alan 2005. *The Future of Childhood: Towards the Interdisciplinary Study of Children*. New York: Routledge/Falmer.

Qvortrup, Jens 1990. 'A Voice for Children in Statistical and Social Accounting: A Plea for Children's Right to be Heard.' pp. 78–98 in *Constructing and Reconstructing Childhood: Contemporary Issues in the Sociological Study of Childhood*, edited by Allison James and Alan Prout. New York: The Falmer Press.

Qvortrup, Jens 2002. 'Sociology of Childhood: Conceptual Liberation of Children,' pp. 43–78 in *Childhood and Children's Culture*, edited by Flemming Mouritsen and Jens Qvortrup. Esbjerg, Denmark: University Press of Southern Denmark.

Qvortrup, Jens, Marjatta Bardy, Giovanni Sgritta, and Helmut Wintersberger 1994. *Childhood Matters: Social Theory, Practice and Politics*. Aldershot, UK: Avebury.

Saporiti, Angelo 2001. 'A Methodology for Making Children Court,' pp. 243–72 in *Childhood in Europe*, edited by Manuela du Bois-Reymond, Heinz Sunker, and Heinz-Hermann Kruger. New York: Peter Lang.

Small, Meredith F. 2001. *Kids: How Biology and Culture Shape the Way We Raise Our Children*. New York: Doubleday.

Sprey, Jetse 2003. 'Do Institutions Mind? The Case of Marriage and the Family. ' Unpublished manuscript. Revision of paper presented at the Theory Construction and Research Methodology Workshop, Annual Meetings of the National Council of Family Relations, Houston, Texas, November 2002.

Thorne, Barrie 1987. 'Re-visioning Women and Social Change: Where Are the Children?' *Gender and Society* **1**: 85–109.

Thorne, Barrie 1993. *Gender Play: Girls and Boys in School*. New Brunswick, NJ: Rutgers University Press.

Thorne, Barrie 2006. 'Editorial: US Disasters and Global Vulnerability.' *Childhood* **13**: 5–9.

Tobin, Joseph 1995. 'Post-structural Research in Early Childhood Education.' pp. 223–44 in *Qualitative Research in Early Childhood Settings*, edited by J. Amos Hatch. Westport, CT: Praeger.

Waksler, Frances Chaput 1986. 'Studying Children: Phenomenological Insights.' *Human Studies* **9**: 71–82.

Waksler, Frances Chaput 1991. 'Beyond Socialization.' pp. 12–22 in *Studying the Social Worlds of Children: Sociological Readings*, edited by Frances Chaput Waksler. New York: The Falmer Press.

Waksler, Frances Chaput 1996. *The Little Trials of Childhood and Children's Strategies for Dealing with Them*. New York: The Falmer Press.

Wyness, Michael 2006. *Childhood and Society: An Introduction to the Sociology of Childhood*. New York: Palgrave McMillan.

A New Paradigm for the Sociology of Childhood?

ALAN PROUT AND ALLISON JAMES

INTRODUCTION

While children's biological immaturity is a fact of life, authors Alan Prout and Allison James contend that how we make sense of this immaturity is a cultural construction. In this selection, they critically examine taken-for-granted assumptions about children: that they are irrational, universal, and naturally progress toward adulthood at a particular pace. They argue that we must separate the social from biological development and recognize that social life is constantly created by interactions between people—including children. A new paradigm—or way of seeing— is necessary to begin to study and understand the depth of children's experiences.

INTRODUCTION: THE NATURE OF CHILDHOOD

. . . In this chapter we present . . . an emerging and not yet completed approach to the study of childhood. . . . The title encapsulates what we feel to be the nature of the social institution of childhood: an actively negotiated set of social relationships within which the early years of human life are constituted. The immaturity of children is a biological fact of life but the ways in which this immaturity is understood and made meaningful is a fact of culture (see La Fontaine, 1979). It is these 'facts of culture' which may vary and which can be said to make of childhood a social institution. It is in this sense, therefore, that one can talk of the social construction of childhood and also, as it appears in this volume, of its re- and deconstruction. In this double sense, then, childhood is both constructed and reconstructed both for children and by children.

Attempting to describe and analyze the quality of that experience, researchers have, over the years, begun to develop new approaches to the study of childhood. One of the fore-runners of this 'emergent paradigm', Charlotte Hardman, in 1973 compared her work on the anthropology of children to the study of women, arguing that 'both women and children might perhaps be called "muted groups" i.e., unperceived or elusive groups (in terms of anyone studying a society)' (1973: 85). . . . The history of the study of childhood in the social sciences has been marked not by an absence of interest in children—as we shall show this has been far from the case—but by their silence. What the emergent paradigm attempts to . . . regard . . . 'children as people to be studied in their own right, and not just as receptacles of adult teaching' (*ibid* 87).

In what follows we trace the origins of this approach, analyze its benefits and outline some issues confronted in its further development. We show the ways in which the socio-political context made possible alternative approaches to childhood study as the experience of childhood changed for children. We locate these changes in relation to the new theoretical directions taken by the social sciences, described by Crick as 'a shift from function to meaning' which made possible the study of social categories rather than groups (1976: 2). Finally we point to the potential which the 'emergent paradigm' has for future developments in childhood sociology.

At this juncture it is useful, therefore, to reiterate what we see as the key features of the paradigm:

1. Childhood is understood as a social construction. . . . It provides an interpretive frame for contextualizing the early years of human life. Childhood, as distinct from biological immaturity, is neither a natural nor universal feature of human groups but appears as a specific structural and cultural component of many societies.

2. Childhood is a variable of social analysis. It can never be entirely divorced from other variables such as class, gender, or ethnicity. Comparative and cross-cultural analysis reveals a variety of childhoods rather than a single and universal phenomenon.

3. Children's social relationships and cultures are worthy of study in their own right, independent of the perspective and concerns of adults.

4. Children are and must be seen as active in the construction and determination of their own social lives, the lives of those around them and of the societies in which they live. Children are not just the passive subjects of social structures and processes.

5. Ethnography is a particularly useful methodology for the study of childhood. It allows children a more direct voice and participation in the production of sociological data than is usually possible through experimental or survey styles of research.

6. . . . To proclaim a new paradigm of childhood sociology is also to engage in and respond to the process of reconstructing childhood in society.

It is not certain whether these constitute the radical break with the past, as is sometimes claimed by those who are perhaps a little too enthusiastic for the study of childhood to be given recognition and status within mainstream sociology. While it is certainly true that sociologists have devoted little attention to childhood as a topic of interest in itself and that many of the key concepts used to think about childhood are problematic, it is misleading to suggest that childhood is absent from the discourse of social scientists. On the contrary, 'the century of the child' can be characterized as such precisely because of the massive corpus of knowledge built up by psychologists and other social scientists through the systematic study of children. If the concept of childhood as a distinct stage in the human life cycle crystallized in nineteenth century western thought, then the twentieth century has seen that theoretical space elaborated and filled out with detailed empirical findings. . . . Psychological experiment, psychometric testing, sociometric mapping, ethnographic description and longitudinal surveys have all been applied to childhood and structured our thinking about children. They have also . . . led to the growing imposition of a particularly western conceptualization of childhood for all children which effectively conceals the fact that the institution of childhood is a social construction. It is our task here . . . to situate what is new in the context of what has passed in order to judge its efficacy for contemporary concepts of childhood.

The complexity of the background to the emergence of the 'new' paradigm necessitates that we adopt an essentially thematic rather than historical account of the developments which allowed for, and at times precluded, changes in thinking about childhood. It is clear that psychological explanations of child development, announced early on in the twentieth century, have until recently dominated childhood study. They both supported and were supported by child-rearing/training practices, bridging the gap between theory and practice, parent and child, teacher and pupil, politician and populace. It is therefore predominantly developmental psychology which has provided a framework of explanation of the child's nature and indeed justified the concept of the naturalness of childhood itself. During this period, however, alternative voices have been raised, in the ideologies of populist movements and from changing paradigms within the social sciences. But for a long time these have gone unremarked and unheard or, indeed, have been silenced. The question now arises as to their salience . . . when a reconstituted sociology of childhood has become more than the promise of a possibility. . . .

DOMINANT AND DOMINATING ACCOUNTS

A key concept in the dominant framework surrounding the study of children and childhood has been development and three themes predominate in relation to it: 'rationality', 'naturalness' and 'universality'. These have structured a mode of thought which stretches far beyond the disciplinary boundaries of psychology, influencing not only sociological approaches to child study but the socio-political context of childhood itself. The concept of 'development' inextricably links the biological facts of immaturity, such as dependence, to the social aspects of childhood.

This dominant developmental approach to childhood, provided by psychology, is based on the idea of natural growth (see Jenks, 1982). It is a self-sustaining model whose features can be crudely delineated as follows: rationality is the universal mark of adulthood with childhood representing the period of apprenticeship for its development. Childhood is therefore important to study as a presocial period of difference, a biologically determined stage on the path to full human status i.e., adulthood. The naturalness of children both governs and is governed by their universality. It is essentially an evolutionary model: the child developing into an adult represents a progression from simplicity to complexity of thought, from irrational to rational behavior. As an explanatory frame, it takes its inspiration from an earlier era, from the dawning of a scientific interest in society. During the nineteenth century western sociological theorists, the self-elected representatives of rationality, saw in other cultures primitive forms of the human condition. These they regarded as childish in their simplicity and irrational in their belief. . . . The 'savage' was seen as the precursor of civilized man, paralleling the way that the child prefigured adult life. . . .

The model of child development which has come to dominate western thought similarly connects biological with social development: children's activities—their language, play and interactions—are significant as symbolic markers of developmental progress. As activities they are seen to prefigure the child's future participation in the adult world. Little account is given of their significance to children's social life or to the variation which they reveal in the social context of childhood. The decreasing 'irrationality' of children's play as they mature is taken as a measure of an evolving 'rationality' of thought, charting the ways in which 'primitive' concepts become replaced by sophisticated ideas. The powerful and persistent influence of this explanatory framework can be illustrated through considering the impact of Jean Piaget's work on child development. . . . In Piaget's account, child development has a particular structure, consisting of a series of predetermined stages, which lead towards the eventual achievement of logical competence. This is the mark of adult rationality. Within such a conceptual scheme children are marginalized beings awaiting temporal passage, through the acquistion of cognitive skill, into the social world of adults. . . .

The scientific construction of the 'irrationality', 'naturalness' and 'universality' of childhood through psychological discourses was translated directly into sociological accounts of childhood in the form of theories of socialization during the 1950s. At a time when positivism gripped the social sciences it offered a 'scientific' explanation for the process whereby children learned to participate in society. Within structural functionalist accounts of society the 'individual' was slotted into a finite number of social roles. Socialization, therefore, was the mechanism whereby these social roles came to be replicated in successive generations. The theory puported to explain the ways in which children gradually acquire knowledge of these roles. However, it frequently failed to do so; 'how' socialization occurs was often ignored or glossed over. . . .

Traditional functionalist accounts of socialization conflate these distinctions and ultimately fail to satisfactorily explain the process by which 'the individual acquires personhood'. (*ibid:* 245) As Jenks puts it: 'the social transformation from child to adult does not follow directly from physical growth' as is logically the case in traditional accounts of socialization (1982: 12).

The implicit binarism of the psychological model was uncritically absorbed into classical socialization theory. In such an account children are regarded as 'immature, irrational, incompetent, asocial [and] acultural' with adults being 'mature, rational, competent, social and autonomous' (Mac Kay, 1973: 28). . . . Socialization is the process which magically transforms the one into the other, the key which turns the asocial child into a social adult. The child's nature is therefore assumed to be different; for the model to work indeed this must be the case. The child is portrayed, like the laboratory rat, as being at the mercy of external stimuli: passive and conforming. Lost in a social maze it is the adult who offers directions. The child, like the rat, responds accordingly and is finally rewarded by becoming 'social', by becoming adult. . . . Like a totalitarian regime of control, this model of socialization maintained the theoretical stability of functionalist accounts of society and indeed contributed to the production of the stasis of the functionalist world view. In so doing it generated a new series of problems related to the supposed failure of socialization in the everyday practices of some children.

Part of the reason for this mismatch between theory and practice is that the perspectives for the study of children derived from socialization theory were primarily based upon adult concern for the reproduction of social order. Children were of little account other than as passive representatives of the future generation which, as it turned out, was theoretically a heavy responsibility. Summarizing traditional approaches to socialization theory, Shildkrout comments that:

> . . . child culture is seen as a rehearsal for adult life and socialization consists of the processes through which, by one method or another, children are made to conform, in cases of 'successful' socialization or become deviants in cases of 'failed socialization' (1978: 109–10).

This neglect of the process of socialization, with undue emphasis placed upon its outcome, spawned a whole series of debates and moral panics about childhood. These focused upon the role of the family and the school as socializing agents with little weight given to consideration of the impact or meaning of these institutions in the lives of children. As important features in the social landscape of adults they were assumed, by adults, to be critical to the developmental progress of their children. Little attention was paid to the possibility of contradictions or indeed conflict in the socialization process. Tied to an implicit psychological model of child development, the sociological account of growing up was based on an inherent individualistic naturalism. All children who seemed to falter in the socialization process were potentially included in the new set of categories of 'child': school failures, deviants and neglected children. Failure to be harmoniously socialized into society's functioning meant, in effect, a failure to be human.

DISSENTING VOICES: A CHALLENGE TO ORTHODOXY

The persistence of psychological explanations of the sociality of children both fed on and was fed by their ubiquity. . . .

   The biological facts of life, birth and infancy, were constantly used to explain the social facts of childhood with little account taken of any cultural component. It was the gradual growth in awareness that the meanings attached to the category 'child' and 'childhood' might differ across time or in space which began to destabilize traditional models of child development and socialization. As Danziger (1970) notes, the traditional model of socialization developed in the west, contained an implicit cultural bias, making it of little use for comparative purposes. The emergent paradigm, in contrast, begins with the assumption that a child is socialized by belonging to a 'particular culture at a certain stage in its history' (Danziger, 1970: 18).

   . . . The growth of interpretive perspectives in the social sciences, . . . gave an impetus to new directions in the study of childhood. In particular, they fostered an interest in children as social actors and childhood as a particular kind of social reality. For example the preoccupation with the social activities of everyday life—a concern that became central to interactionist sociology—allowed for the possibility of questioning that which previously had been seen as unproblematic. Within the interpretive tradition aspects of everyday life which are taken for granted are examined. . . . The aim is to render them culturally strange by a process of detailed and critical reflection, thus bringing them into the sphere of sociological analysis. A second and crucial perspective is that social reality is not fixed, constant or unitary. Rather, social life is seen as being constantly created through the activities of social actors. It is an accomplishment of human beings and carried out on the basis of beliefs, perspectives and typifications which give rise to meaningful and intentional action. The explanation of social life requires grasping the meaning of it for participants in the context of its specific occurrence. These two features of interpretive sociology have combined to create a particular interest in the perspectives of low status groups in social organizations and settings. One such low-status group is, of course, children.

   In the 1950s and 60s, then, interpretive sociologies were a potent source for the critique of the then dominant paradigm of structural-functionalism, from which conceptions of child socialization derived. This general critique reversed the structural-functionalist relationship between structure and agency, with interpretivists stressing the role of creative individual activity in the constitution of human society. . . . It was only a short step from this to the suggestion that the concept of childhood within socialization theory was itself faulty. MacKay summarized his position:

   If the two claims are correct, that children are competent interpreters of the social world and that they possess a separate culture(s), then the study of adult-child interaction (formerly socialization) becomes the study of cultural assimilation, or, more theoretically important, the study of meaningful social interaction (1973: 31).

. . . Following the demolition of traditional models of socialization and critiques of child development,. . . these intellectual trends focused further attention on the ways in which processes of social classification not only structure the institutional arrangements of social life but our very mode of apprehending them. The possibilities of alternative world views, . . . paved the way for the suggestion that certain social groups might possess different views of the social world from the majority. . . .

Changes in the general intellectual climate during the 1970s initiated new directions in the study of childhood within many disciplines . . . Although by no means the first historian to propose a radical critique of concepts of childhood, the work of the French historian Philippe Aries had a major impact on the social sciences. His dramatic and boldly stated contention that 'in medieval society the idea of childhood did not exist' was eagerly taken up by sociologists (1962: 125). It quickly became incorporated as an example of the variability of human societies, all the more useful because it looked not to the 'exotic' or 'primitive' but to a familiar western European past.

Aries's challenge to orthodoxy lay in his suggestion that the concept of childhood emerged in Europe between the fifteenth and eighteenth centuries, thus blasting a large hole in traditional assumptions about the universality of childhood. Making extensive use of medieval icons he argued that, beyond the dependent stage of infancy, children were not depicted. They were there as miniature adults only. However, from the fifteenth century onwards children began to appear as children, reflecting their gradual removal from the everyday life of adult society. According to Aries this was first fostered through the growth of new attitudes of 'coddling' towards children, which stressed their special nature and needs. Second was the emergence of formal education and long periods of schooling as a prerequisite for children before they assumed adult responsibilities. Initially only economically and practically possible for the upper classes, who alone had the time and money for 'childhood', these trends diffused downwards through society. Childhood became institutionalized for all.

Aries's work stimulated a flurry of historical work in relation to children and the family. Some of it offered support to Aries's idea of 'the discovery of childhood' while other work rejected the challenge. Lloyd De Mause (1976) for example retained the notion of childhood as a human universal, preferring to characterize early child rearing practices as so brutal and exploitative that they bear little resemblance to those of modern western societies. Childhood, he argued, is the same; it is parents who have changed. Aries's thesis was also increasingly the subject of critical scrutiny by other historians in relation to his historical method, evidence, and interpretation. The debate continues but one of the more interesting critiques can be found in Pollock (1983). Using 415 primary sources between 1500–1900, she comments that,

> Many historians have subscribed to the mistaken belief that, if a past society did not possess the contemporary Western concept of childhood, then the society had no such concept. This is a totally indefensible point of view—why should past societies have regarded children in the same way as Western society today? Moreover, even if children were regarded differently in the past, this does not mean that they were not regarded as children (1983: 263).

This is far from the sensationalism of Aries' original work, and ends with the more modest claim that while western societies both past and present make a distinction between children and adults, and accord children characteristics and treatment different from adults, the particular form of modern childhood is nevertheless historically specific.

Although there is no acknowledged link, this less grandiose formulation of the contention that childhood is socially constructed is supported by the earlier work of social anthropologists involved in culture and personality studies. These studies . . . focused on variations in child rearing practices as the locus of difference. . . . Earlier, Margaret Mead (1928), the chief representative of the 'culture-personality' school had sought, through her Samoan work, to counter the psychologist Stanley Hall's suggestion that adolescence is a period of natural rebellion through showing its absence in Samoa. However, despite this emphasis on the variability of childhood, such writers retained a conventional view of socialization as a molding process carried out by adults. Little attention was paid to childhood as a phenomenon in itself or to children as active participants in their own rearing process.

Anthropological interest in age as a principle of social differentiation and stratification is less well known. But it could be argued that the body of theory and ethnographic material has had a more lasting impact on the current new thinking about childhood. Writing from the perspective of Parsonian structural functionalism, but borrowing heavily from anthropology, Eisenstadt (1956) suggests that strong age grades are functional to the social stability of contemporary societies. In particular he identifies youth subcultures as the means by which future adult familial and occupational roles can be both 'held at bay' and rehearsed in safety. This notion that strong age group affiliations among young people form a transitional stage which partially sequesters them from adult society reflects anthropological work on age systems cross-culturally.

From these beginnings the body of work on subculture was spawned. Functionalist theorists, such as Musgrove (1964), took Eisenstadt's suggestion further through arguing that young people were a consumer defined class outside the structured differentiations of capitalist society. This view was later rejected in the analyses emerging from the Center for Contemporary Cultural Studies (see Hall and Jefferson, 1976). . . . Writers within this tradition, on the contrary, saw youth subcultures as expressing the contradictions and conflicts of the class structure. The most celebrated example is Cohen's (1972) analysis of skinheads. With their boots, braces, collarless shirts and cropped hair, Cohen describes the skinheads as attempting to magically recover the traditional English working-class community life that was fast disappearing in sixties urban reconstruction.

The emergence and later analysis of working-class youth subcultures as social groups with specific ideologies sparked off sociological interest in 'age' as a principle of social classification in *western* societies. Other 'age' categories such as 'children' and 'the elderly' assumed new status as 'social problems' in the socio-political context of 'aging' populations and increasingly 'child-centered' societies. Paralleling the work on subcultural world views it was therefore suggested that younger children too might inhabit semi-autonomous social worlds whose meanings the adult world had yet to come to terms with . . .

Within psychology, which, as we have already shown, had always been the main arena for childhood research in the social sciences, doubting voices also began to be raised during the late 1960s. Here again interpretive perspectives combined with an awareness of cultural and historical relativism to produce a radical critique. . . .

These then are some of the intellectual trends which have created a theoretically plausible space called the 'social construction of childhood'. It would, however, be naive to imply that the establishment of such a space was made possible only by the community of social scientists. It is clear, for example, that the influence of interpretive philosophy within the social sciences was bolstered by the political possibilities which it seemed to offer. If social (and psychological) realities are constructions of human understanding and international activity then they can be unmade as well as made. The more optimistic versions of this . . . suffused the radical political movements of the 1960s and 70s and underpinned much of its 'counter-cultural' thinking. Anti-colonial, civil rights, anti-psychiatry and the women's movements all suggested that social relationships were not fixed by social and psychological laws but could be reconstituted (through various forms of social and political struggle) on a different basis. Although the optimism about social change may have diminished over the last decade, at its most powerful, it began to question even the most taken-for-granted social relationships. Children and childhood, although not central to this questioning, played a small part in, for example, an upsurge of interest in children's rights.

In considering the question of the relationship between the social sciences and society we have already pointed to the way in which Piagetian developmental psychology has shaped the practices of primary school teaching. In general, while sociology and psychology may seek only to understand the world as it is, their products, findings, terminology and ways of accounting for the world are nevertheless absorbed back into it and become constitutive of the societies into which they inquire. In this sense there can be no concepts of childhood which are socially and politically innocent. Where sixties radicalism saw itself as liberating children from oppression, we now see practitioners of the social sciences more cautiously acknowledging the role of their disciplines in the production of childhood in its present form.

OBSTACLES TO AND PROSPECTS OF CONSTRUCTING A NEW PARADIGM

First, it has to be recognized that the still dominant concepts of 'development' and 'socialization' are extraordinarily resistant to criticism. They persist despite all that has been said against them. Richards and Light (1986: 3), for example, lament that despite widespread discussion of the need for cognitive and developmental psychology to locate itself within a social and cultural context, only a minority of recently published empirical research even faintly considers this possibility. Similarly, in sociology, the concept of socialization continues to dominate theory and research about children. The lack of change here stands out particularly sharply in, for example, the sociology of the family. While thinking about women and the family has been revolutionized by feminist critiques, thinking about childhood remains relatively static, like the still point at the center of a storm. There are, for example, huge differences in the treatment of most topics between Morgan's excellent *Social Theory and the Family* (1975) and his publication of (the equally excellent) *Family, Politics and Social Theory* a decade later (1985). Childhood, however, remains more or less unchanged, and is, if anything, more marginal in the second than in the first work. . . .

Their continued dominance is, in part, the responsibility of those who (like ourselves) have talked long on the sociology of childhood but published little. This chapter is a partial remedy for that but it also has to be acknowledged that there are some deep-rooted sources of resistance to the reconceptualizing of childhood within sociology. Ambert (1986) uncovers some of these in her survey of childhood in North American sociology. She suggests that children's relative absence is rooted in the same factors which excluded attention to women (and gender): that is, a male-dominated sociology that does not give worth to child care and still less to the activities of children themselves. This, allied to conservativism and a male-oriented career structure means that: '. . . the gate-keepers of the discipline . . .

continue to place a high value on certain types of knowledge, data, theories and research methods. . . . One does not become a household name in sociology by studying children' (Ambert, 1986: 16).

Resistance to new ways of thinking about childhood extends beyond the confines of sociology. There is a correspondence between the concepts of the social sciences and the ways in which childhood is socially constructed. Notions like socialization are inscribed in the practices of teachers and social workers, for example, and this ensures that their critique extends into and meets a wider resistance. This is not simply a matter of habit, convenience, false consciousness or vested interests but of what Foucault refers to as 'regimes of truth' (1977). He suggests that these operate rather like self-fulfilling prophecies: ways of thinking about childhood fuse with institutionalized practices to produce self-conscious subjects (teachers, parents and children) who think (and feel) about themselves through the terms of those ways of thinking. 'The truth' about themselves and their situation is thus self-validating. Breaking into this with another 'truth' (produced by another way of thinking about childhood) may prove difficult. For example, the resilience of socialization as a dominant concept rests partly on the way in which notions of childhood are embedded within a tightly structured matrix of significations binding childhood with, and positioning it in relation to, the family. . . .

Unlocking these relationships is one of the main theoretical tasks for the development of an alternative framework.

How can this be best approached? In one sense the emergent paradigm outlined here is the start of this process. . . . For some time now it has been possible to think of a theoretical space in which, for example, children can be looked at as active social beings, constructing and creating social relationships, rather than as the 'cultural dopes' of socialization theory. Similarly, it is possible to posit age relationships as a serious dimension of analysis alongside those of class, gender and ethnicity. . . .

We believe, however, that it would be a mistake to think that the theorizing of childhood should, or can, take place outside of the theoretical debates of mainstream sociology. On the contrary, it needs to draw on the debates of the social sciences at large—and to contribute to them—if it is not to become an isolated and esoteric specialism. That outcome would be almost as damaging as no sociology of childhood at all, since it would relieve other branches of sociology from the necessity of thinking through the implications for their own treatment of childhood. The aim, rather, must be for a sociology of childhood which is coherent enough both to stand on its own but at the same time make a serious impact on other branches of the discipline. To achieve this its concerns must correspond and connect with wider sociological debates. . . .

Consideration of, for instance, the different physical size of children and their relative muscular weakness compared to adults (of either sex) are not relevant to sociological explanations of, for example, inequalities of power between children and adults. This, however, seems an absurd example of . . . 'cultural determinism', that is exempting human beings from the rest of the animal kingdom by denying *any* effects of our biological and physical being. But if we are to see childhood as *both* biological and social, as we argued at the outset of this chapter, what weight should be given to each factor? In some societies, for example, children are expected to do far more physically demanding work than they do in Europe and North America. Do we account for this as part of the cultural variability of childhood or do we accept that at some point biological facts constrain the argument and compel us to invoke ethical and political categories such as abuse and exploitation?

The second issue arises from the application of a strict logic to the notion that childhood is socially constructed, that is constituted in discourse. If this is so then there can be no such object as the 'real child' (or any variant on this theme such as 'the authentic experience of childhood'). Instead we must content ourselves with the analysis of how different discursive practices produce different childhoods, each and all of which are 'real' within their own regime of truth. This is difficult for many of those active within the sociology of childhood to accept. There is strong tendency to see the mission of sociology as debunking, demystifying and releasing childhood from the ideological distortions of dominant social theories and practices. Ethnographic methods, in particular, are advocated as means of getting nearer to the 'truth' about what childhood is like. . . . While not (usually) claiming to be privileged accounts of children's lives (and in this sense claiming authenticity), such work has, within the limits of any situated interpretation, given voice to the previously silent.

These questions of social construction, subjectivity and authenticity are intimately bound up in the major theoretical debate of contemporary sociology: that is, the problem of the relationship between agency (or 'action') and structure in social life. The debate has a particular salience for the sociology of childhood, since it was from interpretive sociology that much of the impetus to re-examine the role of children as active, meaning-producing beings came. Interpretive sociology stresses the creative production ('agency') of social life rather than the determination of social behavior by systems of social organization. For a period of time in the 1960s and 1970s there appeared to be two competing types of sociology: one stressed that the system of social relationships in society (the mode of production, power and domination, belief systems and ideology etc.); the other stressed the creative activity, purposes and negotiative interaction between individual actors. . . .

Some such view of how structure and agency complement each other seems be an essential component in any new sociology of childhood. It is important to recover children as social actors (and their activity as a source of social change); as interpretivists have insisted, this in itself is not adequate. We need also, however, to grasp childhood as a social institution that exists beyond the activity of any particular child or adult. There must be theoretical space for both the construction of childhood as an institution and the activity of children within and upon the constraints and possibilities that the institutional level creates. This does seem to be possible; in this volume for example, Kitzinger's analysis of child sexual abuse retains both structure and agency. By exploring the relationship between these two levels we can, then, begin to elucidate the links between given (and largely adult defined social institutions) and the cultures which children construct for and between themselves. This is important for at least two reasons. First, unless we do so, accounts of children's cultures will always run the risk of consigning themselves to the margins of both social and sociological concern. . . . Second, if we attempt to account for children as both constrained by structure and agents acting in and upon structure, we can make a plausible claim that such accounts, if rigorous, are 'authentic'. Not in the sense that they reveal some hitherto timeless 'essence' of childhood but rather that they accurately portray aspects of childhood as it is constituted at a particular moment in time and point in space.

Temporality, in fact, is a feature of childhood to which little attention has been paid. While it is. . . inherent to the notion of psychological development it appears there only as a natural constant, the background flow to the. . . unfolding of the child. In sociology, the concept of socialization acts as a kind of suppressor of childhood's present tense, orientating analysis either towards the past (what went wrong with socialization) or the future (what the goals of socialization should be). This neglect of the present is unusual since sociologists tend to conduct synchronic analyses, preferring to leave the succession of events in time to historians. One solution would be to fuse the historical and sociological enterprises. Fruitful though this may be, the resulting synthesis would probably also treat time as if it is simply the natural stuff within which events occur. What is needed is a more thoroughgoing analysis of time as a social construction during childhood. . . .

POLITICS AND ETHICS IN RESEARCHING CHILDHOOD

Finally, we turn to the importance of empirical studies of childhood, for despite the emphasis of this chapter, we believe it would be a mistake to see the way forward only in terms of theoretical development. Well conducted empirical studies . . . are essential counterparts to theoretical work. Quite apart from this symbiosis between theory and empirical enquiry, however, we believe that the sociology of childhood in particular needs many more studies which open up hitherto neglected topics—children and work, politics, health, food, and so on. These in themselves could begin to pry the sociology of childhood away from the stereotyped topics of the family and schooling.

　　Throughout this . . . chapter we have stressed that the social sciences are not neutral commentaries on childhood but active factors in its construction and reconstruction. The processes by which this occurs are complex. . . . Nevertheless, recognition of the socially constitutive role of the social sciences seems to require that attention be paid to the social implications of sociological work. It is far from clear, however, how these issues are best handled. The traditional notion of the detached scholar has collapsed, but what will replace it? This is not a question unique to the sociology of childhood but is an issue of current debate throughout the social sciences (Silverman, 1985). . . .

　　Although generally attractive, the application of this perspective to childhood presents some special problems. Despite our recognition that children are active social beings, it remains true that their lives are almost always determined and/or constrained in large measure by adults and there are few instances of children becoming organized at a 'grass roots' level to represent themselves independently. On the contrary, almost all political, educational, legal and administrative processes have profound effects on children but they have little or no influence over them. Child care proceedings, for example, are supposed to be taken 'in the best interests of the child' but the children concerned are frequently never consulted. . . . While independent political action by children is not unknown . . . , its history is frequently hidden or suppressed. This not only makes it difficult to incorporate into academic accounts but frustrates any continuity in children's political organization. Nevertheless, attempts by children to 'speak for themselves' persist. . . .

　　Sociologists need to find a relationship to both children's own activity and to the social processes which shape and constrain children's lives but in which they themselves are not necessarily involved. . . .

　　For example, the current concern with child sexual abuse centers on the need to protect children from sexual exploitation. But, as Kitzinger argues in this volume, many of the practices through which this protection is established themselves disable and depower children by confirming the traditional view of children as passive victims. How, then, can we contribute to combatting child abuse whilst at the same time questioning these assumptions? More generally, how can a sociology of childhood be practiced in a way which is sensitive to the political and ethical problems it inevitably entails?. . .

Discussion Questions

1. Discuss the six key features of the "new paradigm." What do each of them mean?
2. Why do the authors argue that by studying children differently we change the meaning of childhood itself?
3. According to the authors, what challenges do creating a new way of thinking present?
4. Do you think that there are more changes that need to be made in the way we understand children and childhood?

References

Ambert, A. M. (1986) 'The place of children in North American sociology'. In Adler, P. and Adler, P. (Ed) *Sociological Studies in Child Development,* Greenwich, Conneticut, JAI Press.

Aries, P. (1962) *Centuries of Childhood,* London, Jonathan Cape.

Cohen, P. (1972) *Subcultural Conflict and Working Class Community,* Birmingham, Centre for Contemporary Cultural Studies.

Crick, M. (1976) *Explorations in Language and Meaning,* London, Malaby Press.

Danziger, K. (Ed) (1970) *Readings in Child Socialization,* London, Pergamon Press Ltd.

De Mause, L. (Ed) (1976) *The History of Childhood,* London, Souvenir Press.

Eisenstadt, S. N. (1956) *From Generation to Generation,* London, Collier-Macmillan.

Foucault, M. (1977) *Discipline and Punish,* London, Allen Lane.

Hall, S. and Jefferson, T. (Eds) (1976) *Resistance Through Rituals: Youth Subculture in Postwar Britain,* London, Hutchinson.

Hardman, C. (1973) 'Can there be an anthropology of children?'. *Journal of the Anthropological Society of Oxford,* 4, 1, pp. 85–99.

Jenks, C. (1982) *The Sociology of Childhood: Essential Readings,* London, Batsford.

La Fontains, J. S. (1979) *Sex and Age as Principles of Social Differentiation,* London, Academic Press.

MacKay, R. (1973) 'Conceptions of children and models of socialization', In Dreitzel, H. P. (Ed) (1973) *Childhood and Socialization,* London, Collier-Macmillam, pp. 27–43.

Morgan, D. H. J. (1975) *Social Theory and the Family,* London, Routledge and Kegan Paul.

Morgan, D. H. J. (1985) *The Family, Politics and Social Theory,* London, Routledge and Kegan Paul.

Musgrove, F. (1964) *Youth and the Social Order,* London, Routledge and Kegan Paul.

Pollock, L. A. (1983) *Forgotten Children: Parent–Child Relations from 1500 to 1900,* Cambridge, Cambridge University Press.

Richards, M. and Light, P. (Eds) (1986) *Children of Social Worlds,* Cambridge, Polity Press.

Shildkrout, E. (1978) 'Roles of children in urban Kano', in La Fontaine, J. S. *Sex and Age as Principles of Social Differentiation,* London, Academic Press.

PART THREE

Studying Children
How Do Social Scientists Study Children and Childhood?

Children have long been the subjects of academic study. In the past their intelligence, their emotional, cognitive, and physical development have all been studied by researchers eager to understand how young people become adults. As we discussed in Part II, social scientists today are increasingly becoming interested in studying young people as they are, not for who they will become.

In researching young people, we aim to understand what some aspect of social life is like from their perspective. To do that, we try as best as we can to make their points of view central, rather than our own. Also, research on childhood now looks forward to see how young peoples' lives are influenced by broader social changes and how children shape the people and institutions around them.

METHODS OF STUDYING CHILDREN AND ADOLESCENTS

Researchers have several choices to make before beginning a study in order to decide what method will work best. Traditionally, researchers conducted experiments with children. You might be familiar with the work of Swiss psychologist Jean Piaget, who conducted a series of experiments with children, and ultimately used his findings to theorize how children's cognitive development happens in a series of stages. Other researchers have utilized surveys—often based on the responses of parents or teachers but not children.

While these methods have important uses, they are *researcher* centered. In other words, the adult researcher remains the expert, and children's interpretations are used only to compare to the adult perspective. As in Piaget's experiments, children's interpretations were measured as deficits compared with adult cognition instead of as alternative ways of seeing. Thus, children's inferiority is reconfirmed through these kinds of studies.

By contrast, many researchers now bring children to the center through a method called ethnography. Traditionally used within anthropology, ethnography involves studying people in their natural setting. Researchers employing this method do their best to observe, rather than manipulate or disrupt children's activities. For instance, researchers like William Corsaro, author of "Yeah, You're Big Bill," observe children as they play. By conducting child-centered research, we learn more about children's perspectives of their experiences, and how they interact with their peers. Corsaro discusses using the "reactive" method, which means observing kids without taking on the role of authority figure or rule enforcer. He recommends allowing children to make the decision to approach observing adults, rather than the more typical disruptive role adults play in children's everyday lives. In this type of research, children remain the experts of their own lives, which researchers hope to learn more about.

Of course this kind of research is a challenge if adults are in fact in positions of authority in a particular setting. Gary Alan Fine and Kent L. Sandstrom discuss the challenges and benefits of different roles adult researchers can take in "Researchers and Kids." In this selection, they discuss how being a group leader or authority figure may be a good way to gain access to a group of kids to study, but young people may not be as open with you if you are in a position to discipline them. Being a detached observer also has pros and cons: kids may behave more naturally once they get used to your presence, but they probably won't confide in you if they have had little interaction with you. Taking on a friend-like role has greater advantages. Though this role is the most difficult to cultivate in some circumstances, especially if there is a large age difference, once established, this role encourages greatest openness. However, there are ethical issues to consider particularly as the research process ends. You might also learn very private information that requires you to inform other adults, such as information about abuse or threats of violence.

Michael Wyness considers these and other concerns in his chapter, "Researching Children and Childhood." As children are a protected group, it is often difficult to conduct research with them in the first place. As such, it is vital to ensure anonymity whenever possible, particularly in any publication of your findings. Children should also have the right to decide whether they want to participate in research or not.

Wyness also discusses the possibility of children being researchers themselves, if not conducting their own studies, they certainly can be consulted with to discuss findings of research based on their lives. This practice is not uncommon when conducting ethnographic research with adults, and Wyness suggests that we consider affording children the same opportunity to comment on the analysis of their experiences.

Studying children can be challenging, but also fun and enlightening. As with any form of research, it requires patience. Most centrally, researching and writing about children's lives must be done respectfully. Just as if we were studying an ethnic group or culture different from our own, as researchers we have the responsibility not to demean our subjects by viewing them as inferior.

Yeah, You're Big Bill: Entering Kids' Culture

WILLIAM CORSARO

INTRODUCTION

Sociologist William Corsaro has conducted many ethnographic studies of children. In this excerpt, he describes how he was able to gain the trust of the preschoolers he studied in both the U.S. and Italy. He suggests that researchers should let go of the adult tendency to lead conversations with children by asking lots of questions and instead use a "reactive" method that encourages children to initiate conversations and reinforces the idea that kids are the experts of "kid" culture, not adult researchers.

I enter the outside play area of the preschool and walk up to two four-year-old girls, Betty and Jenny, who are sitting in the sandpile. As I get close to them, Betty says:

"You can't play with us!"

"Why not?" I ask.

"Cause you're too big," Betty replies.

"I'll sit down," I say as I plop down in the sand next to the girls.

"You're still too big," says Jenny.

"Yeah, you're Big Bill!" shouts Betty.

"Can I watch?" I ask.

"OK," says Jenny. "But don't touch nuthin'!"

"Yeah," says Betty. "You just watch, OK?"

"OK."

"OK, Big Bill?" asks Jenny.

"OK."

(Later Big Bill got to play.)

BECOMING AN ETHNOGRAPHER OF KIDS' CULTURES

Ethnography is the method anthropologists most often employ to study exotic cultures. The word "ethnography" is derived from "ethno" (people or culture) and "graphy" (the writing about or study of). You might have heard of the classic ethnographic study, *Coming of Age in Samoa,* by Margaret Mead. The ethnographic method demands that researchers enter, become accepted by, and participate in the lives of those they study. In this sense, ethnography involves "going native." As I noted in the preface, once I became convinced that children have their own cultures, I wanted to become part of those cultures and document them. To do this, I decided I had to enter into the children's everyday lives—to be one of the kids as best I could.

But how does a grown man go about being accepted into children's worlds? When I began my research, there were no established models to follow. So when I entered the first of many preschools I studied in the United States and Italy, I decided that the best way to become part of children's worlds was to "not act like a typical adult." In this chapter I describe how I went about doing this in several of the different early education settings I became part of and shared with kids, their teachers, and parents.

Let's start at the beginning, many years ago in Berkeley, California. I began in Berkeley because my dissertation director had a friend who agreed to sponsor my postdoctoral research and could also help me gain access to a preschool affiliated with the university.

Berkeley, California (1974–1975)—"A Big Kid"

In preparing for my research in Berkeley, I took the advice of one of the teachers and spent several weeks observing interactions in the school from a concealed observation area. The teacher, Margaret, told me that in the first weeks of school the children were still adjusting to the new setting, and parents and teachers were also a bit tense about the beginning of the new year. So she suggested that I observe from the one-way screened area that ran the length of the school's inside and outside. This viewing area was used by parents and for some observational research by developmental psychologists from a nearby university.

In my first days of observation, I was overwhelmed by the number, range, and complexity of the interactive events occurring before my eyes. On the first day, I had no clear idea of what to write in my field notes, so I just watched and tried to make general sense of things. In the following days, I began to focus on what happened when and where in the school and discovered a general routine. I made an inventory of the various activities in which the children participated, both those directed by the teachers and those they created themselves. I also gradually learned all the children's names and, to some extent, their various personalities.

During the third week I began to consider how I was going to enter into and be accepted by this group of kids who were becoming more familiar to me. Because I wanted to become involved directly in the kids' peer interactions, I knew that I did not want to be seen as a typical adult. The first step to discovering how to do this was to watch closely how the adults interacted with the children. Here is what I saw.

The adults were primarily active and controlling in their interaction with the kids. For example, parents and other adult visitors to the school often approached the kids, initiated interactions, and asked a lot of questions. Consider the following:

One day a visiting mother approaches a table where two girls are drawing. The mother watches for a while, bending over and looking down at the girls.

"What are you drawing?" she asks.

"A tree," one of the girls replies.

Now there's a silence as the girls continue their work.

"What color is the tree?" asks the mother.

"Green," says the girl, who does not look up but continues to draw.

"What else is green?" asks the mother.

Another silence and then the other girl says, "Grass."

The mother now straightens up, looks around the room, and moves off to another area.

Adults want to initiate conversations with children but are uncomfortable with the kids' minimal replies and their tolerance of what (to adults) seem to be long silences. Often, as in the previous example, adults start asking test questions (things to which they already know the answer, like the color of a tree) to see what children are thinking about, or what they are doing, or simply to make the exchange a learning experience.

The teachers also asked a lot of questions, but they were more sophisticated in developing the learning potential of their conversations and interactions with the kids. They also directed and monitored the kids' play, helped in times of trouble, and told them what they could or could not do. Finally, adults (teachers or visitors) restricted their contact with the kids to specific areas of the preschool. Adults seldom entered the playhouses, outside sandpile, climbing bars, or climbing house.

Seeing how active and controlling adults were in their interactions with kids, I adopted a "reactive" entry strategy. In my first week in the school, I continually made myself available in child-dominated areas of the school and waited for the kids to react to me. For the first few days, the results were not encouraging. Beyond several smiles and a few puzzled stares, the kids pretty much ignored me. Of all the hundreds of hours I have observed in preschools, these were the most difficult. I wanted to say something (anything) to the kids, but I stuck with my strategy and remained silent.

On my fourth afternoon in the preschool, I stationed myself in the outside sandpile directly behind a group of five kids who were digging in the sand with shovels. They were doing "construction work" with four workers and a boss (four boys and a girl). The construction involved two of the boys digging a trench in the sand and another boy filling it with water while the fourth boy (the "dam stopper") stuck, pulled out, and restuck his shovel at various points in the trench to create a dam. He did this upon the orders of the girl boss. I watched this complex play for more than 40 minutes. Then the first two of the boys and, shortly after, the remaining two stuck their shovels in the sand and ran inside the school with the boss following them. I suspected that they did not plan to return and that the construction project was abandoned.

I was feeling ill at ease and considering my next move when I noticed Sue. She was standing alone near the sandpile about 20 feet away, and she was definitely watching me. I smiled and she smiled back, but then to my dismay she ran over near the sandbox and stood watching a group of three other girls. I then heard a disturbance near the climbing bars. I looked over to see that Peter had stolen (or so Daniel claimed) Daniel's truck. I noticed that a teacher had arrived to settle the dispute. When I looked back to the sandbox, Sue was gone.

I started to get up to go inside the school, but then I heard someone say, "What'ya doing?" Sue had approached from behind and was now standing next to me in the sandpile.

"Just watching," I said.

"What for?" she asked.

"Cause I like to."

Then Sue asked my name. I said (and this turned out to be important), "I'm Bill and you're Sue."

Sue took two steps back and demanded, "How do you know my name?"

I now did something adults seldom do when talking to young children, especially if they think kids will not understand the answer. I told the truth with no attempt to simplify.

"I heard Laura and some other kids call you Sue."

"But how do *you* know *my* name?" Sue asked again.

Sticking to my guns, I repeated that I had heard other kids call her Sue. She gave me a puzzled look, twirled around, and ran into the school.

So here I was. After spending several days trying to become one of the kids, finally a child talks to me and I scare her off! But then Sue reemerged from the school and came running back to me with Jonathan by her side.

When they reached me, Jonathan asked, "What's my name?"

"Jonathan," I replied.

"How do you know my name?"

"I heard Peter [one of his frequent playmates] and some other kids call you Jonathan." I said.

"See, I told you he knows magic," said Sue.

"No, no, wait a minute," cautioned Jonathan. "Who're those kids over there?" he asked, pointing to Lanny and Frank.

"Lanny and Frank," I responded confidently. I knew all the kids.

Jonathan looked around, trying to find a hard kid and he then asked me to name three more. I identified them all easily.

With a sly smile Jonathan then asked, "OK, what's my little sister's name?"

Jonathan thought he had me. But I actually knew his sister's name. The secretary at the school had provided me with a roster that listed the names of the children, their parents, and their siblings. I memorized much of this information and, fortunately for me, I remembered Jonathan's sister's name.

"Alicia!" I declared. I was feeling good now.

Jonathan was very impressed. He looked at Sue and said, "I can't figure this guy out." He then ran off to tell Peter and Daniel.

Meanwhile, Sue handed me a shovel.

"You wanna dig?"

"Sure," I said, taking the shovel.

We shoveled sand into the buckets and soon we were joined by Jonathan, Peter, and Daniel. Peter and Daniel asked me if I knew their names. I did, of course, and told them. Then we all started to shovel and the kids organized another construction project and I was assigned the role of worker. Christopher and Antoinette also joined us and the play continued for 20 minutes or so until one of the teachers announced "clean-up time," whereupon we reluctantly put away our shovels and went inside for meeting time.

For several days after this breakthrough, the children began to react to my presence (ask who I was) and invite me into their play. Although I was able to observe, and in many cases participate to some degree in the kids' play, their acceptance of me was gradual. During the first month, the kids were curious about me and why I was around every day. They asked lots of questions that followed a general sequence: "Who are you?" "Are you a teacher?" "Are you gonna play a game with us?" (that is, ask them to be in one of the research experiments that occurred routinely in this lab school) "Are you a Daddy?" and "Do you have any sisters or brothers?" The pattern here is important. The children moved from general questions about adult characteristics to the last question about siblings, which is one kids typically ask of each other.

At the time of this first study, my answer to all the adult information questions was "No" because I was not a teacher, experimental researcher, or a father. But I do have siblings—seven of them! My having so many brothers and sisters piqued the kids' curiosity about me. However, they were hesitant to believe me, and some asked, "For real?" Then to their delight I named them all. Being from a big family helped solidify my acceptance and standing in the group.

I am not claiming that the kids quickly accepted me as one of them. I have not in all my many years in preschools ever been seen totally as one of the kids. Even in Italy where I was seen as an adult incompetent because of my limited knowledge of Italian, I was still an adult. I am just too big to be a kid. Thus, the nickname that surfaced near the end of the first month at Berkeley in the scene I described earlier is important. I became accepted as a different or atypical adult—a sort of big kid.

My status as a "big kid" was demonstrated in a number of ways in my initial ethnography. First, I was allowed to enter ongoing peer activities with little or no disruption. I could move into the playhouses, sandpile, and even climbing structure without much comment beyond a few smiles and some laughter. Second, I had little or no authority when compared to other adults. Given my desire to be part of the kids' culture, I refrained from controlling their behavior. However, on those few occasions when I feared for their physical safety my "Be careful" warnings were always countered with "You're not a teacher!" or "You can't tell us what to do!" Finally, throughout the school year, the kids demanded that I be a part of the more formal peer activities. At birthday parties, for example, the kids insisted that I sit with them (in a circle) rather than on the periphery with the teachers and parents. Also, several of the kids demanded that their mothers write my name, along with those of their playmates, on cookies, cupcakes, and valentines that were brought to school on special days.

Before leaving the Berkeley part of my story, I should note that as an atypical adult I came to have a special relationship with the kids, but this relationship varied from child to child. In all the settings certain kids became special friends. In Berkeley it was Martin. Martin took to me early on and often looked for me when deciding on a group to enter in free play. Noticing that Martin was becoming a bit too dependent on me, I often slipped away from certain play activities once Martin got involved. Soon I discovered that Martin was fine on his own, but he still considered me one of his best buddies.

One day this became very clear to me when his mother stayed around after bringing him to school to talk with one of the teachers.

"Which little boy is Bill?" she asked.

"We don't have a Bill," responded Margaret. "Except for Bill Corsaro, but he is here doing research."

"Oh, I remember now signing a consent from a William Corsaro," said Martin's mother. "But Martin talks about Bill all the time and a book he has, so I thought it was another boy in the class. Martin keeps asking if he can have a book like Bill's to bring to school."

The book Martin's mother was referring to was the small notebook I always carried in my back pocket. After observing an episode of peer interaction, I often slipped away to a secluded area of the school and jotted down a few notes to be expanded later that evening. Martin asked me about the notebook once and I told him that I liked to write things in it to remember what happened. He sort of shrugged at this explanation and did not mention the notebook again.

So when I talked with his mother that day, I explained all this and offered to bring a notebook for Martin the next day. He was all smiles when I gave it to him and helped him put it in the back pocket of his jeans. It was a snug fit in the small pocket, but Martin did not take it out once it was inside. He patted his pocket now and then throughout that first day and brought the notebook most days to keep in his pocket. In this way he could be like Bill, a sort of junior ethnographer!

Bologna, Italy (1983–1986)—"An Incompetent Adult"

I was apprehensive about field entry in the first Italian preschool I studied because of my limited abilities in conversational Italian at that time. As it turned out, this apprehension was short-lived. With the help of Italian colleagues I gained entry to a preschool and presented my research aims (basically, what was it like to be a child in the school) to the teachers. In Italy, preschool is government funded and more than 96 percent of Italian three- to five-year-olds attend before entering the first grade of elementary school at six years of age. The school I became a part of had 5 teachers and 35 children in a mixed age group of three- to five-year-olds.

On my first day at the preschool, the teachers introduced me to the kids as someone from the United States who would be coming to the school to be with them throughout the year. Relying on the "reactive" strategy of field entry I had first used in Berkeley, I entered play areas, sat down, and waited for the kids to react to me. It didn't take long. They began asking me questions, drew me into their play activities, and over time defined me as an atypical adult.

Somewhat to my surprise my acceptance by the Italian children was much easier and quicker than it had been by the American children. For the Italian kids as soon as I spoke in my fractured Italian I was unusual, funny, and fascinating. I was not just an atypical adult, but also an incompetent adult—not just a big kid but sort of a big dumb kid.

The first thing they noticed was my accent, but they quickly got used to it and then realized that I often used the wrong words (bad grammar) and more often than not made little sense (bad semantics). At first they had fun laughing at and mocking my mispronunciations. But soon they became little teachers, correcting my accent and grammar and even repeating and adjusting their own speech when I couldn't understand them. At times they acted out words and frequently consulted in small groups, often laughingly calling to others, "Guess what Bill said now!" Before long we were doing pretty well and my confidence in communicating with the kids grew. I specifically remember one small triumph.

I was sitting on the floor with two boys (Felice and Roberto) and we were racing some toy cars around in circles. Felice was talking about an Italian race car driver as we played, but because he was talking so fast I could understand only part of what he was saying. At one point, however, he raced his car into a wall and it flipped over. Then I clearly heard him say *"Lui è morto,"* and I knew this meant, "He's dead." I guessed that Felice must be recounting a tragic accident in some past Grand Prix event. At that moment I remembered and used a phrase that I had learned in my first Italian course: *"Che peccato!"* ("What a pity!"). Looking up in amazement, Felice said: "Bill! Bill! *Ha ragione! Bravo Bill!*" ("Bill! Bill! He's right! Way to go Bill!"). *"Bravo Bill!"* Roberto chimed in.

Then Felice called out to other children in the school. Several of the kids came over and listened attentively as Felice repeated the whole story of the tragic accident and then added: "And Bill said, *'Che peccato!'*" The small group cheered and some even clapped at this news. Not in the least embarrassed by all the attention, I *felt good—like one of the group*! I was no longer an adult trying to learn about kids' culture. I was in. I was doing it. I was part of the action!

Things were not going as well with the teachers. In fact, confusion and communication breakdowns were frequent during my first months in the school. There were a number of reasons for these problems. First, the teachers and I were self-conscious about these language problems. For the teachers, it was because they knew only one language and for me it was because my Italian was poor. Second, we tried to talk about rather abstract topics (like early education policy in the United States) in contrast to the more here-and-now conversations I had with the kids during their play. Third, the teachers were not as good at adjusting their speech as the kids were. They would start off talking slowly and were careful to avoid difficult constructions and idiomatic expressions. However, after a conversation was under way, things sped up, complicated phrases emerged, and I got confused. When I expressed confusion, the teachers often got a bit flustered and insisted we start over, and as a result, we seldom got very far in these early attempts.

Given our difficulties, the teachers were surprised by my apparent communicative successes with the kids. On several occasions I saw one or another of the teachers call children over to ask them what we had been talking about. The kids had no problem telling the teachers what they and I had said. These explanations prompted the teachers to ask me why I could communicate so well with the kids. I told them that the children and I talked about simpler and more direct things related to the kids' play. While still a bit perplexed, the teachers accepted this explanation, and over time as my Italian improved, so did my communications with the teachers.

Importantly, however, the children's discovery of my communicative problems with the teachers was a special aspect of our relationship. They could talk with me and I with them with little difficulty, but it was apparent to them that my communication with the teachers was not as easy. In fact, several parents told me that their sons or daughters came home and told them: "There is this American, Bill, at the school and we can talk to him, but the teachers can't!" In short, the children saw my relationship with them as a partial breakdown of the control of the teachers. . . .

. . . Several ethnographers of children have pointed to the importance of developing a participant status as an atypical, less powerful adult in research with young children. In this case, as I argued earlier, my very foreignness was central to my participant status. My limited competence in the Italian language and lack of knowledge of the workings of the school led the children to see me as an "incompetent adult" whom they could take under their wings to show the ropes.

A second important aspect of the story is its capturing of the importance of longitudinal ethnography when studying young children. Recent theoretical work in this area is critical of traditional theories of socialization and child development for their marginalization of children. Traditional views focus on individual development and see the child as incomplete—in the process of movement from immaturity to adult competence. The new approaches eschew the individualistic bias of traditional theories and stress the importance of collective action and social structure. Longitudinal ethnography is an ideal method for such a theoretical approach, particularly when it aims to document children's evolving membership in their culture and when focused on key transition periods in children's lives. . . .

Indianapolis Head Start (1989–1990)—"A New Friend"

Indianapolis is my hometown and when I met with the director of the Head Start center and the teachers I was to work with, we found that we shared many experiences growing up in the city. They were quick to accept me into the center. However, when I told them of my plans to visit the center twice a week over the school year to learn about the children's peer interaction and culture, one teacher was doubtful. "What do you want to do that for?" she asked. She was convinced that I would soon become bored or quickly find out all I needed to know. But after I had stayed true to my word for three weeks, the teachers began to look forward to my visits and we established a good rapport.

Things also went well with the children, who quickly pulled me into their play activities. However, my early experiences in the Head Start center were in one way completely novel for me. What was different about the Head Start study was that I was a white man in a world of mainly black women and children. For the first time in my life I was spending considerable time in a setting where I was a minority, as all but one of the teachers and staff in the center and the overwhelming majority of the children were African-American. Although I was very conscious of this fact, the kids seemed unconcerned. Over the first couple of weeks, several of the children asked me if I was Brandon's (a Latino boy's) father. I said I was not and that I was at the school to be and play with them. About two months into the study, one girl, Tamera, came up to me and said: "Bill, you're white!" Not knowing exactly what to say, I replied, "Yeah, I am." And that was that.

During the third week in the school something important for both the kids and the teachers happened with regard to my acceptance and participant status in the school. The Head Start center was located in an old elementary school and, unlike most preschools, there were no bathrooms for the children in the classrooms. Preschool children frequently need to use toilets and are too young to be allowed to travel to bathrooms located outside the classroom on their own.

Therefore, one of the teachers had to take the children as a group to centrally located bathrooms twice each session. I went along on these trips and watched as the teacher lined the children up along the wall outside the bathrooms. She then sent three or four boys into the boys' room and the same number of girls to the girls' room. She waited a few minutes, entered each bathroom, and hurried the children along, and then sent in the next group, until all the children had a turn. We then walked back to the classroom with the teacher reminding the children to stay in line, walk slowly, and be quiet so as not to disturb other classes.

I could tell that this was not a pleasant chore for the teachers. However, I was still surprised when one day in the morning group, a teacher asked me to take the children to the bathroom. This request seemed perfectly reasonable. After all, it was not a difficult task. Besides, if I was going to tag along when the teachers took the kids, why couldn't I take them down myself?

The problem was that I did not want to be seen as an authority figure by the children, and I had talked with the teachers about this aspect of my research. However, it was clear they did not think this small chore would cause me problems or they just didn't make the connection when they asked for the favor. I decided that it was best to agree to help out and hoped it would not be too much of a challenge to my relationship with the kids. It turned out I got much more than I bargained for, at least on our first trip to the bathrooms.

Things started out fine. I noticed a few smiles on the kids' faces when the teacher said I would be taking them. They were told to be on their best behavior as we exited the room. In the hallway and down the stairs they were like little angels. There was no talking or running; even the line was perfectly straight. They also were orderly as they lined up against the wall (boys near the boys' bathroom and girls near the girls').

I sent the first four boys in line (Charles, Luke, Joseph, and Antwaan) into the bathroom and also sent in four girls (Cymira, Tasha, Michelle, and Lamecca). After a few minutes I heard a lot of noise in the boys' bathroom.

"What are they doing in there?" asked Jeremiah. This was the same question I was asking myself. When I went in to find out, I immediately knew I was in trouble. Joseph had wadded up several paper towels and was throwing them at the other three boys. Antwaan was standing at the sink with the cold water on full blast while he flung his hand under and then upward to spray water around the room. Meanwhile Charles and Luke were laughing loudly as they stood at an angle over the urinals trying to pee over each other's streams into the adjoining urinals.

"Hey, you guys," I said. "Cut that out and come back outside."

"You can't tell us what to do," said Charles who had at least straightened around and was peeing in his own urinal.

"Yeah, he's right," added Antwaan. "You're not a teacher."

Now hearing a lot of noise outside, I ran back out there. All the children wanted to have their turns and asked me when they could go in. Brandon was the most insistent, moaning "I gotta pee!" I had to go myself, but that was the least of my worries. I went back in with the boys and realized that trying to be stern was not going to help. Charles and Luke had now joined Joseph in throwing the paper towels, one of which hit me in the back of the head as I stopped Antwaan from throwing water by shutting off the faucet.

Before the boys could challenge me, I said: "I'm not a teacher, but Mrs. Green's class will be coming soon. If you guys don't get back outside, *we'll all get in trouble.*"

"Yeah, Bill's right," said Charles. "We better go back out."

The other boys agreed and I quickly ushered in the remaining boys, including Brandon, who raced in as fast as he could go. Thank God he had not wet his pants. Now for the first time I realized that the first four girls had still not come out, and there was a lot of noise coming from the girls' bathroom. I ducked my head in, but Tasha shouted out "No boys allowed!" The teachers didn't have this problem as they entered the boys' room to hurry them along without concern. I decided to accept Tasha's warning. However, I was prepared to deal with the situation now.

"I think Mrs. Green and her class are coming," I said loudly.

"Uh-oh," I heard Michelle exclaim.

"Yeah, let's go," said Cymira. And soon all four of the girls were out and the rest of the girls were in.

The second shift of children played around a bit but were quick to heed my warning about Mrs. Green's class. Soon all the children were finished and we were lined up and ready to go. Several of the kids were smiling, and Charles said, "It's fun to go to the bathroom with Bill!" Now we started back to the room and the children were as well behaved as they were on the way down.

Back in the room, Mrs. Jones said, "You took a while. You better have not given Bill any trouble."

"We didn't," replied Charles looking at me with a smile.

"We like going with Bill," added Tasha.

I felt safe. I had cleaned up all the paper towels. The floor was still pretty wet in the boys' bathroom, but it would probably be dry by the time Mrs. Green's class got there.

After a few days the word spread to the afternoon class about my bathroom responsibilities and I was asked to take charge of bathroom time in that class as well. The kids gave me a hard time on the first trip, but now I was better prepared. Actually, this role brought me closer to the kids because they always knew they could play around a bit on these bathroom trips and could give me a bit of a hard time. Still, they realized that there was a limit to their horseplay. As was the case with the Italian children, we had certain experiences we shared away from the control of the teachers. Thus, my status as a special and fun adult was solidified. . . .

Discussion Questions

1. Corsaro was able to gradually gain the trust of children despite his adult status. What are the challenges he encountered in the process?
2. How did his experiences studying children vary based on the setting (in Berkeley, Indianapolis, and Bologna) of his research?
3. Do you think that his ability to gain the children's trust would have been more difficult if the children were older? If they were teens? Why?
4. If you were to begin ethnographic work with children, what do you think your biggest challenges might be? How would you attempt to address these challenges?

Researchers and Kids

GARY ALAN FINE
AND KENT L. SANDSTROM

INTRODUCTION

One of the biggest challenges in doing ethnographic research with children is the fact that the researchers almost never are children themselves. This makes it difficult to observe children's actual behavior with one another; instead researchers may get what kids interpret to be preferred behavior, or how adults think children should act. When studying children, our purpose is to learn about their real, uncensored behavior as much as possible. The authors discuss the different roles that researchers can take and why too much authority can diminish the opportunity to get a real look at children's interactions. Instead, they suggest taking the role of a friend; while adults can't pretend to be "one of them" we can gradually become trusted adults.

Like the white researcher in black society, the male researcher studying women, or the ethnologist observing a distant tribal culture, the adult participant observer who attempts to understand a children's culture cannot pass unnoticed as a member of that group.[1] The structure of age roles in American society (Davis, 1940; Parsons, 1942) makes impossible the enactment of the complete participant role (Gold, 1958). Patterns of age segregation in American society (Conger, 1971) mean that it is unexpected for an adult to "hang out" with children's groups; legitimate adult-child interaction depends on adult authority. The taken-for-granted character of this authority structure and the different worldviews that are related to it create unique problems for participant observation with children. While certain problems are applicable to research with other "protected groups" (e.g., the mentally retarded; Edgerton, 1984), other problems are distinctive because of the effects of the age difference between researcher and informant.

In traditional ethnographic settings, a common assumption is that one's research subjects are equal in status to oneself, or at least should be treated as such. For instance, ethnographers typically treat members of the underclass, criminals, the mentally ill, the sick, or the infirm with the same respect with which they treat their colleagues. While status is always an issue the sensitive researcher examines, the muting of status lines is more common than deepening or reinforcing them. Yet, in participating with children, such a policy is not fully tenable, because the social roles of the participants have been influenced by age, cognitive development, physical maturity, and acquisition of social responsibility.

In this chapter, we shall describe some of the fundamental problems that must be confronted by a researcher studying children of any age. More specifically, we will describe (1) research roles open to adults, (2) ethical implications of the research, (3) techniques for achieving rapport, and (4) general problems involved with understanding children's meanings. Obviously these are issues that emerge in research with adults, but the forms that they take in studying children are significantly different. Underlying this analysis is our claim that "normal" relationships between adult and child in American society must be taken into account in planning research.

RESEARCH ROLES

Roles that adults assume when they study children may be differentiated on two dimensions: (1) the extent of positive contact between adult and child, and (2) the extent to which the adult has direct authority over the child (Fine and Glassner, 1979). These dimensions are in reality not dichotomous, although, for this discussion, we will treat them as such. The roles presented are ideal types, seldom, if ever, found in practice. While there are many "roles" that characterize the relations that adults have with children, we find these two *dimensions* to be particularly central in depicting the possibilities for research. We do not claim that these role labels are absolute or "real" in any meaningful sense, although we believe that the dimensions that lie behind them seem to us to be characteristic of all contact with children.

It is the authority dimension, in particular, that separates research with adults from research with children. With the exception of some studies of the institutionalized "ill" or "protected" (e.g., Goffman, 1961), adult researchers are not in positions of direct, formal authority over adult informants. Only in research with children can authorities legitimately conduct ethnographic work with their charges. Although we shall focus on the role of the friend (positive affect and low authority) in this Chapter, we are not setting up the other roles as "straw men." They are legitimate research techniques, although, in their more extreme form, they pose problems different from the friend role.

Supervisor

In its pure form, the supervisor role (authority; no positive affective relations) seems incompatible with ethnographic research. Authorities who do not express positive feelings toward their charges are unlikely to write about their experiences. Such figures include authoritarian teachers, camp supervisors, and religious instructors. Generally this role provides access to a relatively restricted range of youthful behavior. Often in such situations, the child will behave in one way while being observed (and under coercion) and a quite different way when removed from the gaze of an authority. Thus children, particularly by the time they are able to attend school, have developed techniques of impression management that permit them to "get by" in front of disliked or feared authorities in order to avoid disapproval or reprimand. Although the level of dramaturgical skill and information control differs by age, the goal remains constant. The behaviors observed may be "natural," but these observations will only include a small portion of the children's behavior. Within the context of this role, it is unlikely that the barriers between adults and children will be breached. . . .

Leader

The leader can be differentiated from the supervisor by the presence of positive contact with the child, although legitimate authority remains. The leader role is seen most clearly in the many popular treatments of teacher-student contact (e.g., Kohl, 1967; Kozol, 1967, Richmond, 1973). In addition to teachers, other professionals who regularly deal with groups of children adopt this role—camp counselors, coaches, or scout troop leaders. Children have somewhat greater leeway for action in such relationships, and even when they overstep the line of proper behavior, tolerance will frequently be shown by the adult leader. The normative frame of reference, however, remains that of the adult. Children may even feel constrained to be on their "best behavior" so as not to embarrass their leader. Their affection and regard for their leader may prevent them from revealing private feelings or behavior, which may be contrary to the image that they wish to portray. This respect may serve as a barrier for research. The adult, in turn, is expected by his or her charges to behave like an adult. As a leader, he or she can never simply remain in the background and watch how children's culture develops.

Observer

The observer role is the inverse of the leader role. He or she is an adult without formal authority and affective relationships. Indeed, such a role is not consistent with *participant* observation, but it may be used where a record of overt behavior is more important than the rhetorics that children give to explain their behaviors. While children may not consciously behave so as to obtain approval, neither do they admit the observer into their confidences. Children have little or no motivation to allow the observer to learn the social contingencies by which their group operates. Because the observer is seen as an adult, they will hide those behaviors to which they think anonymous adults might object. For instance, preadolescent boys sometimes post a lookout for adults and quickly change the subject when an adult is present. Similarly, when children wish to engage in socially deviant acts, they often retreat to private locations where a stranger cannot follow. The pure observer is granted little more right to witness their behavior than any member of the general public, although this may vary depending upon how the researcher presents the study. Even if the observer witnesses normally "hidden" behavior, its meaning may remain opaque, and the children involved have little incentive to explain it. The meaning of the behavior may only become known (perhaps inaccurately) because of the overlap in shared culture between adult and child.

Being an outsider is difficult. It is natural to wish to establish friendly relations. Polansky and his colleagues (1949) attempted to employ this approach in observing early adolescents in a summer camp for disturbed children. They discovered that the observer role proved threatening to the children, and to some extent to the counselors as well, because of the anxiety involved in being observed without feedback. By the second week of camp, the researchers decided to humanize their role, and subsequently became observer-friends. Glassner encountered similar anxieties during his research at a St. Louis elementary school when he adopted a cross between the observer role and the friend role. He noted occasions when some of his subjects found it uncomfortable to be observed without a full explanation (Glassner, 1976, pp. 19–20). One boy even hid from the researcher and later cried violently about being observed—until he received an explanation of why Glassner was taking notes.

A particularly common type of observation involves watching children in a public area—such as a park, playground, or street. In such locales, one finds adults sitting and standing without providing a public explanation (Polgan, 1976; Dawe, 1934; St. J. Neil, 1976;

Sluckin, 1981). These studies provide much behavioral and descriptive data, but often the collection of explanations form the children's point of view is left to others.

Friend

The final major type of participant observation role . . . is to become a friend to one's subjects and interact with them in the most trusted way possible—without having any explicit authority role. As indicated earlier, in our view, this will always be an ideal type because of the demographic and power differences involved. Yet, some researchers emphasize the possibilities of a true equality of friendship between an adult and child (Goode, 1986)—the adoption of the least-adult role (Mandell, 1988).[2] We believe there is methodological value in maintaining the differences between sociologists and children—a feature of interaction that permits the researcher to behave in certain "nonkid" ways—such as asking "ignorant" questions.[3]

To the extent that the researcher can transcend age and authority boundaries, children may provide access to their "hidden" culture (Llewellyn, 1980; Knapp and Knapp, 1976). The friend role is conducive to the development of trust, although this trust must be cultivated by the researcher. As we shall discuss next, children create interpretations of who the researcher is and what he or she wants to know. Children may suspend their typical modes of dealing with adults, but this type of unique interaction takes time to develop. Often children will make note of this relationship (e.g., giving the researcher a nickname), so as to indicate its special nature. This was impressed on the senior author when he was studying preadolescent baseball teams, and one preadolescent labeled him an "honorary kid," to signal to a friend (with whom the senior author did not have a relationship) that they could talk in his presence.

The key to the role of friend is the explicit expression of positive affect combined with both a relative lack of authority and a lack of sanctioning of the behavior of those being studied. In turn, adopting the friend role suggests that the participant observer treats his or her informants with respect and that he or she desires to acquire competency in their social worlds.

DEVELOPING THE FRIEND ROLE

Given that the friend role is the basis of much participant observation, including that with children, how can it be cultivated? We will focus on how this role (and the research associated with it) is explained to children.

To be in any location, one needs a justification, an account for oneself. In much of our lives, these justifications are implicit. We walk on the street because streets are public arenas and we are going somewhere. We attend sports events because we enjoy watching those events and have paid for the right to be present. Of course, some locations call for a greater explanation. If an adult wishes to be present in a sixth-grade classroom, he or she cannot simply walk in and say that it is public space (which it is) or that he or she is interested in what is occurring (although he or she may be). Rather, one must provide gatekeepers of those locations with a credible account of one's presence. Access becomes a more difficult issue in relatively small and privately operated environments that are occupied by protected or deviant groups. On the other hand, access is more taken for granted in large, public places that are populated by heterogeneous crowd.

Yet, gaining access to a location does not mean that one will become part of a group. Simply to be near children does not mean that one will automatically become their friend. Further explanations are necessary to cultivate a relationship—that is, one needs a justification or "cover" (Fine, 1980, p. 122) for the unexpected social relationship. In nonresearch situations, one may be able to cite the sponsorship of an acquaintance or the existence of some biographical interest that legitimates one's presence. These natural explanations are routinized and conventionalized, and typically are not problematic. In natural interaction,[4] the explanation that is given will often be the one that the explainer privately accepts—it is the *real* reason for the person's presence. Justifications must be accepted both by the group and by the participant. This proffering of justifications may be particularly difficult in settings with several distinct groups of actors, as each group (adult guardians and children) may have their own criteria for acceptance and their own understandings. If the explanations are too much at variance (and are not backed up by appropriate behavior), either group may become suspicious of the researcher.

In response to these dilemmas, three basic approaches have been used by researchers to explain their presence. First, the participant observer may provide the research subjects with a complete and detailed explanation of the purposes and hypotheses of the research; this we term "explicit cover." Second, the researcher may explain that research is being conducted, but be vague or less than completely candid about its goals—"shallow cover." Finally, the researcher may deliberately hide the research form informants—"deep cover."

Explicit Cover

Although an explicit announcement of one's research might at first seem to be the most ethically responsible tactic, it also creates methodological problems. Even when the observer presents his or her role as "objectively" as possible, this does not mean that the children, who lack experience with sociological investigations, will understand this explanation "properly." There is also danger in telling informants too much about one's research goals, and this danger consists of more than the expectancy effect by which knowledgeable subjects attempt to confirm or deny the researcher's hypotheses. The explanation given may, if sufficiently explicit, limit what informants decide to share with their friend. Further, by presenting the research as more formal than it is (considering the flexible nature of grounded research; Glaser and Strauss, 1967), friendships may be less likely. The relationships that develop are likely to be utilitarian ones, based upon the formal research bargain. A good example of how limited research goals can be facilitated by a modified version of explicit cover is an ethnographic study of the social dynamics of a car pool (Adler and Adler, 1984). Here the topic was limited in scope and was not emotionally sensitive. Also, by virtue of being drivers, the researchers had the advantage of having legitimate relations with the informants separate from the research bargain.

Shallow Cover

The approach that the senior author used in his own research with Little League baseball players is "shallow cover"—an explanation most notable for its "sin" of omission. While explicitly mentioning and reaffirming that he was a social psychologist interested in observing the behavior of preadolescents, this was not expanded upon in detail. He claimed that he wished to discover what children said and did, and that he would spend as much time with them as possible (see also Cusick, 1973; Llewellyn, 1980; Hollingshead, 1975). This vague bargain permitted informal arrangements with many individuals—explanations that could differ substantially. Some players treated him as an intimate, sharing their dirty stories and vile exploits; others used him as a protector against the bullying of their peers. He also provided isolated boys with someone to talk to about their baseball concerns; and he was an audience for parents and coaches to describe their frustrations in raising children (Fine, 1987).

Shallow cover makes one's structural role explicit, and, as such, the researcher's credibility cannot be undermined. Yet, no matter how vague the researcher attempts to be, children develop ideas of what the researcher is looking for. These ideas can be cruelly or benignly disconfirmed and that disconfirmation may affect the researcher's access to the subjects. Shallow cover is perhaps the most frequent approach and may account for the fact that, occasionally, after a research account is published (Gallagher, 1964; Vidich and Bensman, 1964), informants will feel betrayed when the ambiguous explanation becomes clear in retrospect. Although the informants are not defrauded, in that they knowingly participated in research, the topics of study were not what they expected them to be. For instance, a researcher who is interested in sexism and interpersonal violence might avoid telling informants of this fact, and the publication of his or her conclusions may be traumatic for them.

Using shallow cover, one can create flexible research bargains. Because the researcher may initially have no firm hypotheses (a basis of inductive research), the research problem can be narrowed or shifted while maintaining the original research bargain. Thus, when the senior author expanded his focus from what occurred on baseball diamonds to what preadolescents did in their leisure time, he could successfully do this because it did not violate the original bargain.

Deep Cover

In research studies in which subjects are unaware that they are being observed, the researcher is operating in a manner analogous to an undercover intelligence agent—although perhaps with a more benign set of motives. Here one may witness a wide variety of behaviors, but may simultaneously find it difficult to inquire about any of these behaviors without arousing suspicion. A cover that is exposed in such a situation—when subjects discover that their new "friend" is actually a sociologist—may have profound implications. The exposure discredits not only the research, but also the researcher.

Deep cover is primarily an issue in research with late adolescents, where some possibility of "passing" can occur. One might also apply this approach, however, to legitimate authorities who are collecting data in their legitimate roles without informing subjects. For example, Muzafer Sherif portrayed a camp custodian in his summer camp studies (Sherif et al., 1961; Sherif and Sherif, 1953), while David Voigt and Lewis Yablonsky were actually coaches when they studied Little League baseball (Voigt, 1974; Yablonsky and Brower, 1979).

This kind of deception, while generally innocuous in its immediate moral consequences, typically can be sustained only for a short period because of (1) the frustrations that affect the researcher, and (2) the limitations that are built into the role in terms of lack of access to the meanings that the events have for participants. While "real" group members may believe that the researcher knows as much about the rules of the game as they do, he or she actually knows less and finds no easy path to discovery.

The research announcement made by the participant observer influences his or her ability to feel comfortable within the setting. Deep cover is clearly the most problematic in that the research is continually in danger of being unmasked. Discrediting or revealing information must be hidden. While explicit cover promotes personal comfort—because little discrepancy exists between public and private roles—a change in the research bargain may cause trouble and the observer must acquire new abilities (such as the ability to talk about preadolescent sexual behavior as well as baseball). . . . Shallow cover avoids having the research discredited, and, due to the open focus of the researcher's role, it allows for questioning of the rules and appropriate behaviors of the group, both in public and in private.

BUILDING TRUST

The nature of participant observation requires that the researcher gains access to settings— particularly those to which he or she would not "normally" have access as a member of the general public. This is achieved through gaining rapport with a group.

Not every researcher is suitable for every research setting. Each observer has strengths and weaknesses, preferences and fears—together these make up the researcher's personal equation. A basic requirement for a participant observer is that he or she emotionally empathizes and doesn't feel excessive personal anxiety becoming close to those being studied (Johnson, 1975). Most individuals are "comfortable" with some groups, and ill at ease with others. While liking is a part of this response, it also connects to the basic—and sometimes unstated and unrecognized—moral, social, or political values of the researcher. The senior author has found working with children exhilarating, although others might find that same research tiresome or anxiety-producing. In order to be a participant observer with children, one must be able to deal with them on a relatively equal footing and one must also have the ability and desire to listen to them. Further, this kind of research requires giving up some of one's adult prerogatives and occasionally shelving some of one's "adult" dignity.

Adults may place themselves in the same location with children, but this does not mean that children will reveal their secrets. Texts on how to conduct participant observation typically recommend that researchers remain passive and nondistracting (Taylor and Bogdan, 1984). Yet, adults are salient individuals in children's social worlds and are difficult to ignore due to the authority that usually accompanies their age. Whatever technique one adopts, the problem of reactivity must not be overlooked and all data collected from children must be examined for artifacts arising from adult presence.

Given these challenges, we argue that there are two general techniques that may be employed to increase rapport and access. The first is for the adult to adopt the behavior and values of the children—essentially having the adult become a "peer," and the second is for the adult to employ social rewards and material gifts to promote acceptance.

Shared Values and Behaviors

As tempting as it might be, "going native" is simply not viable. Yet, researchers may adopt many of the behaviors of the children and adolescents they study. Hollingshead (1975, p. 15) notes: "We 'ganged' and 'clowned' with the adolescents in their 'night spots' and favorite 'hangouts,' after the game, dance or show." He courteously refrained from observing lover's lanes, however. The senior author attempted to spend as much time with preadolescent baseball players as he could, but they and he felt that it would not be tactful if he were present when "moons were shining,"[5] at boy-girl parties, or when eggs were thrown at neighboring houses. He was, however, told about these events in great detail. He inquired about going with the boys when they played pranks or attended boy-girl parties, but this never happened. . . . Obviously, observation of preadolescent sexuality would involve very sensitive topics that are outside the normal sphere of adult-child interaction.

A fine line exists between what is considered appropriate behavior by the observer and what is awkward for both parties. Although one may wish to obtain as much data as possible to understand the world of these children, one should avoid behaving in ways that make one uncomfortable. Given the differences between acceptable adult and child behavior, this discomfort may occur when the adult strives to be a peer. Most children can sense whether a researcher looks like a good bet as a friend (Cottle, 1973) and will usually spot those who attempt to be something other than what they are and who make them uncomfortable. It was a memorable moment for the senior author when one boy told another about a mutual secret, "You can tell Gary. He's one of the boys." Being "one of the boys" was a mark of acceptance by these preadolescents.

While being approving, sympathetic, and supportive leads to increased rapport, a false attempt to be "with it" may backfire—not only making the researcher feel anxious, but also cutting off research opportunities. Children's slang is hard for an adult to master, and even when learned correctly, often sounds strange when uttered by an adult. . . Researchers, particularly those studying adolescents, may be offered drink or drugs, either as a test or an act of friendship, and the researcher must decide how to respond (Lowney, 1984). The key point is that intimacy cannot be rushed, and close relationships may never develop if pressured. Many researchers (e.g., Corsaro, 1985; Glassner, 1976; Fine, 1987) describe a period of some weeks in which they were treated as nonpersons before the long—and never-ending—road to acceptance began.

Aside from building trust with the children he or she is studying, a participant observer who lacks formal authority must also negotiate rapport with adult authorities or guardians who are present or who have responsibility for these children. A wise participant observer should carefully cultivate and maintain these relationships to prevent misunderstandings, such as the reaction of parents to one researcher who, as a girl scout leader, was accused of not sufficiently instilling discipline in her troop. These rapport-building contacts enable one to obtain an informative perspective, while simultaneously ensuring that no objections are being raised to one's actions. This should not affect one's research negatively, as children recognize the need for the adult to act both as a friend to them and as a friend to other adults.

Rewards and Gifts

Because adults have greater access to resources primarily—though not exclusively—pecuniary, the participant observer may feel that it is advantageous to use these resources to develop rapport. This technique can be successful, but it can also lead to difficulties. Researchers may offer many services to child informants, including companionship, educational expertise, praise, food, and monetary loans. A useful rule of thumb when the researcher is trying to be a friend is that one should behave as a good friend might. This involves establishing relations of mutuality and respect that implicitly involve boundaries for acceptable "exchanges."

When in a position of authority, one must avoid misusing responsibility merely to curry favor with the group. . . .

One wonders whether this manipulation by the children compromises the research. Certainly the researcher in turn manipulates the children for her own ends, but the protection she offers them may undermine justice within the school. It also poses ethical questions about what kind of favors an adult researcher should offer to children in the attempt to promote rapport or to gain access to information.

In his research, the first author did provide services for children. He provided rides for both Little Leaguers and fantasy gamers. He took the preadolescents out for ice cream, to movies, and to baseball games. Excellent data were collected in this way. While the behavior may not have been totally natural, the researcher could ask questions outside of the earshot of other adults whose presence would have inhibited the sharing of certain kinds of information.

In regard to utilizing money, we concur with Whyte (1955) and Wax (1971) that any type of financial arrangement between researcher and subjects has the potential to produce tension in the relationship, but that in some situations financial transactions are necessary to gain rapport. It is imperative, however, that loans not be *expected*. The senior author claimed on occasion that he was out of money when demands for loans were becoming too frequent. . . .

A danger exists in providing services, even those that are not monetary. Researchers may become accepted for what they can provide, not for what they are. They will be seen as useful only as long as they provide rewards. The relationship may become commodified and instrumental. The senior author experienced this problem in the opening weeks of his first season of Little League research. He carried sticks of chewing gum, careful to chew them in public, and was pleased to provide gum to whomever asked. While this allowed him to become acquainted with the players, it also led to insistent demands for gum. This demand became contrary to his research goals, and after a few days on which the gum was conveniently "forgotten," the requests ceased.

In extreme cases, children may attempt to "blackmail" the researcher into helping them, against his or her best judgment. One of Jules Henry's research assistants reported a dramatic example of this in his study of Rome High School:

> Lila [attempted] to blackmail the Researcher into writing a term paper for her. During the Christmas season when Bill [Lila's brother] took advantage of the mistletoe above the Greene doorway to kiss the [female] Researcher, Lila took a picture of it, and she then threatened to give it to [Bill's girlfriend] if the Researcher refused to write the paper. The Researcher solved this problem by staying away from the Greene house until after the paper was due [Henry, 1963, pp. 208–209].

Such difficulties may not be typical, but, as in the Researcher's example, they may disrupt the research. Some informants are willing to use the researcher for what they can get, just as some researchers use their informants. When researchers are asked to help in criminal activities (see Lowney, 1984; Polsky, 1967), the issues of rapport may become legal and ethical issues as well.

ADULT-ROLE-RELATED ETHICAL ISSUES

Typically when ethical issues are discussed in the literature on ethnography or participant observation, they are discussed in light of relations between peers—actual or theoretical equals. Even when we consider oppressed groups, there is no debate that these individuals should be treated as equals. Yet, let us not pretend that either adults or children would be comfortable if full equality were expected. While it is desirable to lessen the power differential between children and adults, the difference will remain and its elimination may be ethically inadvisable.

If one accepts this perspective, several ethical issues emerge. Researchers must remember that children are "immature" (if only in that their behavior differs from what those in power think of as "adult" or morally proper) and, further, they are not at the age of legal responsibility. A participant observer can justify not interfering with the actions of deviant adults, but such a justification is more problematic when the informants are minors. The ethical implications of participant observation research differs with the age of the children. . . . Here we shall focus broadly on three issues that emerge in qualitative research:

(1) the responsibility of the adult in dealing with possibly harmful situations;
(2) the implications of the adult "policing role"; and
(3) the problems of obtaining informed consent from one's informants and explaining the research in a comprehensible fashion.

Adult Responsibility

In dealing with children in unstructured situations or when there is no clear adult authority, one may have to make quick decisions in order to protect the children involved. Children are mischievous, sometimes aggressive, and occasionally cruel. What is the responsibility of the participant observer in that situation? The ethical guidelines of the American Sociological Association (ASA, 1968) claim that the researcher should ensure that research subjects do not suffer harm as the result of their participation, but this refers to circumstances in which the researcher is actively doing something to the subjects. Does it apply to participant observation in which informants are encouraged to behave naturally? Yet, this naturalism is not clear-cut either. Observation is always reactive to some degree. In some situations, an observer's presence may increase the display of aggression among minors (Polsky, 1962; Glassner, 1976)—this gratuitous display of aggression may be a way to "test" the researcher. Can we ever know what are the "real" motivations of our informants?

The judgment as to whether intervention is appropriate should depend at least somewhat on the situation. Children can place themselves in danger. In that event, an adult participant observer has a moral obligation to assist them in a way that is "protective":

> A flight nearly started between Wiley and Bud. At the beginning of the game Wiley has walked along the Rangers' bench knocking off caps from the heads of his teammates. Later, when the Rangers were losing, Bud attempted to get even by knocking off Wiley's baseball cap, and Wiley got angry. I was worried about this because Bud, who was known for his violent temper, was holding an aluminum bat. They pushed each other, but didn't come to blows. I suggested that they should keep their attention on the game and the situation ended [Fine, 1987, p. 229].

Other adults, who might intervene if the researcher were not present, might refrain, believing that the children are under adult supervision. If a possibility of serious physical injury exists, an adult participant observer may need to intervene, even though he or she will thereby alter the behavior of the group.

Few situations are physically dangerous. Boys frequently get into fights, and on occasions girls do as well. In instances of "normal" or "playful" aggression, peer jurisprudence often is able to handle the situation. Many children's groups contain members whose role involves breaking up fights, minimizing the dangers in which others place themselves, and even serving as counselors or amateur medics. High-status boys, secure in their position of peer authority, also have the ability to tell others to "knock it off."

Yet, if a fight had become sufficiently serious, moral concern would have demanded interference. Had a fight caused permanent damage to one or more of the participants, the observer would have rightly been held in part responsible—morally, and, if the observer had a position of authority, legally as well. While this intervention becomes more problematic as the children grow older, the observer has a special role as long as the children are below the age of legal responsibility. The ideal of not influencing natural behavior is just that—an ideal.

There are other circumstances that are not physically dangerous, but reveal behaviors that are generally condemned: racism and theft. On one occasion, the senior author accompanied some Little Leaguers to an ice cream parlor. While there, he noticed to his acute discomfort that the . . . players ware stealing candy. A first reaction was that he had the obligation to stop them and insist that they return what they had stolen. This emotion was partly attributable to generalized ethical concerns, the desire to teach these preadolescents what was morally proper, and the personal fear that he might be blamed and publicly embarrassed if these boys had been seen. Yet, he realized that had he made a public display, their behavior would likely not have changed, but he would have excluded himself from witnessing these behaviors again. As a result, the chance to observe this form of preadolescent deviance, rarely examined, would have been lost. In addition, he had by that time become friends with these boys, and reporting them might cause them embarrassment or legal trouble. One tends to protect one's friends in one's research (Johnson, 1975). In fact, the decision to do nothing was based as much on indecision as on moral certainty. It is difficult to make complex moral decisions in the rush of events. Regardless, the decision ultimately was methodologically sound. On the drive home, the boys discussed what had occurred and, by nonevaluative probing, the researcher learned the extent of stealing (or "ripping off") in other circumstances.

The degree of direct involvement in directing the behavior of children may depend on the individual researcher—we all must live up to our personal standards (Polsky, 1962). Gold (1958) has suggested that on occasion it may be necessary to subordinate the self to the role in the interest of research, but, even so, in dealing with children there will be occasions when one's authority should be used to enforce moral imperatives of the self.

Adult Policing Role

To what extent should adult participant observers allow themselves to police the behavior of their informants on a regular basis? This issue may arise even when the informants are late adolescents. . . . Many groups are concerned about the use of the information that they provide, and the observer rarely gains full access to the private behaviors of the group until they feel that the observer is trustworthy. These first few days and weeks are crucial in determining the success of the research. . . . "Testing" the researcher is a common phenomenon. . . .

Problems of access and trust stem not only from the children's suspicions of participant observers. Adult authority figures may also pose challenges when they attempt to use participant observers for their own ends. . . .

The senior author felt . . . pressured when asked to run practices, umpire, and once to coach a team when its regular coaches had to be out of town. At several times during the research, he was asked for advice about children with minor behavior problems. Although desiring to help, he felt unable to divulge any information. Neither did he feel it appropriate to enforce the rules that the coaches had established. He had made this clear to the Little League coaches before the season and the issue was never explicitly raised; still, he had the impression that other adults would have liked him to take a more active role in disciplining the children. Because of the participant observer's refusal to discipline the children, he or she may be seen as the good guy, while the adult authority is seen as the heavy. The presence of an noncensorious adult in these situations may make salient the fact that the coach is a harsh disciplinarian. Indeed, the members of one team wished that the senior author could become their coach. The presence of an nondisciplining adult can thus complicate the life of the adult authority.

The solution for the researcher embracing the "friend role" is to emphasize to both adults and children that he or she will not be a disciplinarian, and to back that up with consistent behavior. . . .

Informed Consent

When the observer is not in position of authority (and even in certain instances in which he or she has authority), informants must be informed about the nature of the research. We have touched on this issue earlier when considering the participant observer's research role. Here we want to focus more directly on what the informants understand. The need for (and desirability of) informed consent has perhaps not always been sufficiently recognized in participant observation, where secrecy is still common and decisions about permitting the researcher access are seen as the prerogative of adult guardians.[6] In situations where the adult researcher has little authority, it is desirable that he or she provide a credible and meaningful explanation of his or her research intentions.

Even with the best explanation, children will fit the observer's behavior into their own view of the world and will construct that role through gossip (Murphy, 1985). Thus the senior author was asked if he were a reporter, writing a movie like "the Bad News Bears," or with Little League headquarters. In one league, it was even rumored that he was a drug dealer, just as Robert Everhart was accused of being a narc by his high school informants (Everhart, 1983, p. 287). Observers working in school systems are first assumed to be teachers of some kind (Glassner, 1976; Corsaro, 1985; Everhart, 1983). In general, explanations are easier to make to adolescents who may have some vague notions of "research," but can be quite a challenge among younger children.

During the first year the senior author studied Little League players, he was a graduate student, and he explained to them that he was there as part of a school project. This account seemed to satisfy the children. In fact, one preadolescent friend commented that the researcher's teacher had better give him an A "or else!" Children can identify with doing "homework," and explanations of this kind seem to be generally understandable (e.g., Gordon, 1957). Other years, he told the children (and later the adolescent Dungeons & Dragons players) that he was writing a book about them. As is typical in such situations, he was told that he should be sure to include certain events in the book. At times it seemed as if he was treated as the "official" historian of the league.

Perhaps the major theoretical problem that relates to informed consent with children is how to handle confidentiality. Confidentiality is assumed to be necessary in order to hide the identity of specific persons who might be subject to reprisals or embarrassment. The dilemma in the Little League research was that many players preferred, and in some cases insisted, that their real names be used. The possibility of fame outweighed potential embarrassment in their minds. Most players were enthusiastic about being depicted in the book, and some wondered whether they would become famous. Although some of the players were concerned about their parents learning of things they did, most were not. . . .

Despite the senior author's sense that Little League players preferred to have their names used, he decided to use pseudonyms. He considered using the real names of those who requested it, but concluded they were not sufficiently aware of the possible ramifications of their decisions. Several informants made remarks with aggressively sexual or racial content, and, even after several years, they might be blamed for these statements.

While a verbal account is important, actions speak louder than words in informed consent. The actions of the participant observer will be the central way in which children learn of the researcher's intentions. The questions asked, and the situations during which the observer scribbles furiously in his or her notepad, will highlight the observer's true interests.

Informed consent, of course, implies informed rejection. Children must be given a real and legitimate opportunity to say that they do not want to participate in the research. While it is not possible for the researcher to leave the setting simply because of the refusal of one or a few individuals to participate, these individuals should not be questioned, their actions should not be recorded, and they should not be included (even under a pseudonym) in any book or article. To be sure, when these individuals are part of a group, they may be included as part of a collectivity; still, their legitimate rights should be respected. Often these rejections are a result of mistrust of the researcher; at some later time when the researcher has gained rapport with the group, these individuals can be approached again—tactfully and privately—and asked if they have changed their minds. While it is tempting to pressure these individuals, such pressure is unethical. In the senior author's research, he has never had an informant refuse to be observed, and only a few refused to be interviewed.

When one obtains informed consent with children, one will also need to obtain consent and support from adults. This can be more complicated than obtaining consent from children. Indeed, adults often are more concerned about what researchers write than are children (Everhart, 1983, p. 282). To gain access to a league, the senior author first approached the president of the Little League he wished to study. He explained that he wished to examine how Little League baseball players played the game and what they did in their leisure. He described the basic plan of the research—he would observe but would not be actively involved in the league structure as an umpire, coach, or grounds keeper. When he gained the league president's approval, he asked to meet the coaches and other adults involved with the league. This was done at league board meetings or at the baseball tryouts. At that time, he explained the goals of the research—finding out about preadolescent behavior—and told the coaches they could request that he not study their teams—either on specific occasions or for the whole season (this happened only once; described in Fine, 1987, pp. 237–238). He emphasized that he would not undermine their authority. Gaining the approval of the coaches, he asked for permission to explain the research to players. At the end of the talk, each player was handed a letter to give to his parents; it explained the central focus of the research, invited parents to call or speak to him with any questions, and informed them that, if they had objections to their child's participation in the study, their wishes would be respected. Only two parents (neither on teams studied intensively) registered objections, and their children were not interviewed or given questionnaires.

Several coaches admitted after the season that they were hesitant about the research, afraid—in the words of one coach—that Fine "would blow things out of proportion." Coaches (and perhaps parents) were afraid that he would conduct a "hatchet job" on them; eventually they decided that he was "on their side."

On some occasions, attitudes of adults have disrupted research. . . . We live in a society in which parents are concerned about strangers kidnapping and abusing their children (see Best and Horiuchi, 1985). The ease we had researching children in the late 1970s probably could not be duplicated today. The creation of the "stranger" (or "stranger danger") as a major social concern with parents has posed new and challenging problems for those who wish to understand the world of children. Researchers have the obligation to understand how the concerns of parents affect what can be done with their children, given the images of social problems in society. Likewise, as the legal environment has changed in the United States, researchers may find themselves more responsible for what happens when they are present. The fact that one is conducting research (and being "passive") may still leave one open to the charge of negligence. To the best of our knowledge, such a case has not occurred—yet.

UNDERSTANDING THE WORLD OF CHILDHOOD

Understanding what children say would, on its surface, appear to be a simple task, but it proves to be deceptively complex. Children have a subculture of their own—a culture of childhood (Speier, 1976; Goode, 1986; Silvers, 1976). . . .

This culture, like many grounded in closed communities, has elements that are "secret." It is what Glassner (1976) termed "Kid Society."

Although this situation is somewhat analogous to that of any group that hides its behavior because of possible repercussions, what makes the research challenging is that all adults have passed through childhood, and, as a result, may believe that they have a greater knowledge of children's culture than they actually do. This sense of déjá vu may be deceptive, presenting an obstacle to successful research—in that children's behavior may be interpreted through old frames of reference.[7] For example, the behavioral referents of preadolescent male talk about their "sexual conquests" are different (and somewhat more "advanced") than the behavioral referents of similar talk when we were their age. Because this topic is usually handled obliquely, it may be difficult to discover precisely what behaviors are being referenced. Only after developing trust with the preadolescents could they be questioned. Still, because of the delicacy of the subject matter, and the uncertainty of the children as to what they really meant, the questioning had to be done tactfully.

In addition, because children live within the mainstream of society, there is a tendency to believe that their culture is highly similar to adult culture. While children's culture is similar in some ways, as researchers, we should not take this for granted, and it is wrong to assume that our social meanings are the same as the social meanings of children. Our spatial proximity to children may lead us to believe that we are closer to them than we really are[8]— only differing in that (adults claim) children are still growing up ("developing") and are often wrong ("lack understanding") (see Waksler, 1986). . . . Much of the unique contribution of participant observation is lost if we ignore or dismiss our informants' social meanings.[9] Likewise, the questions that we adults ask during interviews presuppose an implicit adult theory of childhood or adolescence (Baker, 1983; see also Tammivaara and Enright, 1986).

The situated character of children's meanings is perhaps most evident in the world of insults. Insults are spoken frequently by children with a wider range of meanings than adults might guess: to indicate friendship, status, or disdain. An adult who examines these words on the basis of the expectations of adult society, assuming the standard denotative and connotative meanings that adults give these words (e.g., *fag, dip,* or *whore*), may overlook their implications when spoken by children (Fine, 1981). To complicate matters further, one should not assume that these meanings remain constant over generations—or even between curricular cohorts of a single academic year. Meanings can also differ between communities. For example, the senior author noticed that the obscenity "cocksucker" was considered much more hostile when used by preadolescent boys in one community than in another. In one case, it was a fighting word; in the other, it was an amusing obscenity.

Assumptions that might seem valid because we believe that we know and understand children, both because we were children once and because we see them so often, present a methodological problem. Essentially this is a problem of ethnocentrism, but it is compounded because often we do not recognize that it is problematic. Only by attempting to bracket our commonsense understandings and thereby making these neighbors into strangers (and, in turn, making these strangers into peers by taking their roles) can we begin to get a sense of what it means to be a child.

Discussion Questions

1. The authors discuss four possible roles a researcher can take when studying children. Describe the roles and the advantages and disadvantages of each.
2. What obstacles might researchers face in getting started in participant observation research with children?
3. How do the authors suggest handling rewards for children participating in research?
4. When studying children, what are the ethical considerations?

Notes

1. An exception to this statement are those studies of late adolescence in which observers pretend to be full, hidden members of that culture. In such studies, typically conducted by pop journalists, the observer pretends to be a newly arrived member of a high school class (see Tornabene, 1967; Owen, 1981; Crowe, 1981).
2. For a contrary view of the possibilities of interpersonal closeness, see Damon (1977).
3. Authority lines can be vague at times as in cases of "opportunistic" research in which a researcher has contact with a group of children because of circumstance, rather than a formal authority. Those adults who meet children by virtue of being kin, neighbors, or friends of their parents are not in authority roles, but still have some residual authority by being "adults in the community."
4. Here we do not consider the various types of fabrications that Goffman (1974) addresses. All the world can be an arena for espionage.
5. "Moons are shining" was an expression used by preadolescents in one suburb to describe the childhood custom of "mooning." Mooning has many variants, but essentially it refers to the act of showing one's buttocks in public. In this community, it typically involved a group of boys pulling down their pants and underwear in unison while facing away from a major street. The "moons" shine for no more than a few seconds.
6. The issue of informed consent of children in medical settings is sensitively treated by Langer (1985).

She argues that it is important for doctors to seriously consider the wishes of children in planning their medical treatment.
7. Sometimes children may "perform" information gained from one adult in front of another adult from the same background—thus convincing that second adult that children really are knowable and haven't changed that much after all (Peter Adler, personal communication, 1986).
8. A similar argument is made by Peshkin (1984) in studying a fundamentalist Baptist school. Despite the similarity of the school in some ways to secular American society, the differences were dramatic and capable of leading to profound misunderstandings. The children Peshkin studied, although neighbors of "normal" (i.e., secular) children, were very different in beliefs and values.
9. Goode (1986, p. 94), studying a deaf-blind girl, attempted to understand her world by empathizing with her: "Through unique research techniques (mimicking, remaining passively obedient during interaction, prolonged observation, video taping interaction and simulated deaf-blind experiences) I discovered that many of her seemingly pathological behaviors had a definite purposiveness and rationality. The more I 'saw' things from her point of view, the more I realized that because the staff and other professionals had operated with culturally dominant adultcentric conceptions of human competence, they incorrectly faulted these residents."

References

Adler, P. and P. Adler. 1984. "The Carpool: A Socializing Adjunct to the Educational Experience." *Sociology of Education* 57: 200–210.

ASA. 1968. "Toward a Code of Ethics for Sociologists." *American Sociologist* 3:316–318.

Baker, C. D. 1983. "A 'Second Look' at Interviews with Adolescents." *Journal of Youth and Adolescence* 12:501–519.

Best, J. and G. T. Horiuchi. 1985. "The Razor Blade in the Apple: The Social Construction of Urban Legends." *Social Problems* 32:488–499.

Conger, J. J. 1971. "A World They Never Knew: The Family and Social Change." In *Twelve to Sixteen: Early Adolescence*, edited by J. Kagan and R. Coles. New York: Norton.

Corsaro, W. A. 1985. *Friendship and Peer Culture in the Early Years*. Norwood, NJ: Ablex.

Cottle, T. 1973. "The Life Study: On Mutual Recognition and the Subjective Inquiry." *Urban Life and Culture* 2:344–360.

Crowe, C. 1981. *Fast Times at Ridgemont High*. New York: Simon & Schuster.

Cusick, P. A. 1973. *Inside High School*. New York: Holt, Rinehart & Winston.

Damon, W. 1977. *The Social World of the Child*. San Francisco: Jossey-Bass.

Davis, K. L. 1940. "The Sociology of Parent-Youth Conflict." *American Sociological Review* 5:523–535.

Dawe, H. C. 1934. "An Analysis of Two Hundred Quarrels of Preschool Children." *Child Development* 5:139–157.

Edgerton, R. B. 1984. "The Participant Observer Approach to Research in Mental Retardation." *American Journal of Mental Delinquency* 88:498–505.

Everhart, R. 1983. *Reading, Writing and Resistance*. Boston: Routledge & Kegan Paul.

Fine, G. A. 1980. "Cracking Diamonds: Observer Role in Little League Baseball Settings and the Acquisition of Social Competence." In *The Social Experience of Field-Work*, edited by W. Shaffir, A. Turowetz, and R. Stebbins. New York: St. Martin.

————1981. "Friends, Impression Management, and Preadolescent Behavior." In *The Development of Children's Friendships*, edited by S. R. Asher and J. M. Gottman. Cambridge: Cambridge University Press.

————1987. *With the Boys*. Chicago: University of Chicago Press.

————and B. Glassner. 1979. "Participant Observation with Children: Promises and Problems." *Urban Life* 8:153–174.

Gallagher, A. 1964. *Plainvitte: Twenty Years After*. New York: Columbia University Press.

Glaser, Barney and Anselm Strauss. 1967. *The Discovery of Grounded Theory*. Chicago: Aldine.

Glassner, B. 1976. "Kid Society." *Urban Education* 11:5–22.

Goffman, E. 1961. *Asylums*. Garden City, NY: Doubleday.

————1974. *Frame Analysis*. Cambridge, MA: Harvard University Press.

Gold, R. L. 1958. "Roles in Sociological Field Observations." *Social Forces* 36:217–223.

Goode, D. A. 1986. "Kids, Culture and Innocents." *Human Studies* 9: 83–106.

Gordon, Wayne. 1957. *The Social System of the High School*. Glencoe, IL: Free Press.

Henry, J. 1963. *Culture Against Man*. New York: Random House.

Hollingshead, A. B. 1975. *Elmtown's Youth and Elmtown Revisited*. New York: John Wiley.

Johnson, J. M. 1975. *Doing Field Research*. New York: Free Press.

Knapp, M. and H. Knapp. 1976. *One Potato, Two Potato. . . . The Secret Education of American Children*. New York: Norton.

Kohl, H. 1967. *36 Children*. New York: New American Library.

Kozol, J. 1967. *Death at an Early Age*. Boston: Houghton-Mifflin.

Langer, D. 1985. "Children's Legal Rights as Research Subjects." *Journal of the American Academy of Child Psychiatry* 24:653–662.

Llewellyn, M. 1980. "Studying Girls at School: The Implications of Confusion." In *Schooling for Women's Work*, edited by R. Deem. London: Routledge & Kegan Paul.

Lowney, J. 1984. "The Role of a Nonparticipant Observer in Drug Abuse Field Research." *Adolescence* 19:425–434.

Mandell, N. 1988. "The Least-Adult Role in Studying Children." *Journal of Contemporary Ethnography* 16:433–467.

Murphy, M. D. 1985. "Brief Communications." *Human Organization* 44:132–137.

Owen, D. 1981. *High School*. New York: Viking.

Parsons, T. L. 1942. "Age and Sex in the Social Structure of the United States." *American Sociological Review* 7:604–616.

Peshkin, A. 1984. "Odd Man Out: The Participant Observer in an Absolutist Setting." *Sociology of Education* 57:254–264.

Polansky, N., W. Freeman, M. Horowitz, L. Irwin, N. Papania, D. Rapaport, and F. Whaley. 1949. "Problems of Interpersonal Relations in Groups." *Human Relations* 2:281–291.

Polgar, S. K. 1976. "The Social Context of Games: Or When Is Play Not Play?" *Sociology of Education* 49:265–271.

Polsky, H. 1962. *Cottage Six*. New York: John Wiley.

Polsky, N. 1967. *Hustlers, Beats and Others.* Garden City, NY: Doubleday.

Richmond, G. 1973. *The Micro-Society School.* New York: Harper & Row.

Sherif, M., O. J. Harvey, B. J. White, W. R. Hood, and C. Sherif. 1961. *Intergroup Conflict and Cooperation: The Robbers Cave Experiment.* Norman: Oklahoma Book Exchange.

Sherif, M. and C. Sherif. 1953. *Groups in Harmony and Tension.* New York: Harper.

Silvers, R. J. 1976. "Discovering Children's Culture." *Interchange* 6:47–52.

Sluckin, A. 1981. *Growing Up in the Playground.* London: Routledge & Kegan Paul.

Speier, Matthew. 1976. "The Adult Ideological Viewpoint in Studies of Childhood." pp. 168–186 in *Rethinking Childhood,* edited by Arlene Skolnick. Boston: Little, Brown.

St. J. Neil, S. R. 1976. "Aggressive and Non-Aggressive Fighting in Twelve- to Thirteen-Year-Old Pre-Adolescent Boys." *Journal of Child Psychology and Psychiatry* 17:213–220.

Tammivaara, J. and D. Scott Enright. 1986. "On Eliciting Information: Dialogues with Child Informants." *Anthropology and Education Quarterly* 17:218–238.

Taylor, S. and R. Bogdan. 1984. *Introduction to Qualitative Research Methods.* New York: John Wiley.

Tornabene, L. 1967. *I Passed as a Teenager.* New York: Simon & Schuster.

Vidich, A. J. and J. Bensman. 1964. "The Springdale Case: Academic Bureaucrats and Sensitive Townspeople." In *Reflections on Community Studies,* edited by A. J. Vidich, J. Bensman, and M. R. Stein. New York: John Wiley.

Voigt, D. 1974. *A Little League Journal.* Bowling Green, OH: Popular Press.

Waksler, F. C. 1986. "Studying Children: Phenomenological Insights." *Human Studies* 9:71–92.

Wax, R. H. 1971. *Doing Fieldwork.* Chicago: University of Chicago Press.

Whyte, W. F. 1955. *Street Corner Society.* Chicago: University of Chicago Press.

Yablonsky, L. and J. J. Brower. 1979. *The Little League Game.* New York: Times Books.

Researching Children and Childhood

MICHAEL WYNESS

INTRODUCTION

Studying children is both an exciting and challenging undertaking. Author Michael Wyness provides suggestions on how to work best with children in the research process. First, he suggests taking the "least adult role" with children so that the researcher's status as an adult does not prevent children from sharing information. Some other challenges include negotiating relationships and dealing with a power imbalance, particularly with very young children. Wyness notes that children can also be collaborators in the research process, rather than simply objects of study. Finally, he explains some of the very important ethical considerations researchers must take into account.

INTRODUCTION

. . . There is now potential to think of children as active research collaborators. The dominant framework . . . assumes that research is done 'on' children as part of a process of measuring and normalizing childhood, evaluating children's socialization, their progress towards full personhood. . . . The recent reconceptualizing of childhood has challenged the basis to adult/child relations and, in the process, led to a reappraisal of relations between adult researchers and child respondents. There has been a . . . shift from working 'on' children to working 'with' children (Mayall 2002, p. 121). Children viewed as research subjects rather [than as] research objects captures a new . . . interest in children's knowledge and understanding, prioritizing the idea that children have subjective worlds worth researching.

In this chapter . . . I explore the research process at various levels and from various vantage points. . . . If we can now deploy . . . methods in measuring and comparing various aspects of children's lives rather than simply their rate of development, then we are starting to recognize children as full members of society. Nevertheless, . . . more has been written about qualitative approaches that privilege the understanding of children in local settings. For some, uncovering children's social worlds has become a social as well as sociological imperative. . . .

Researchers in recent years have been committed to understanding children's social worlds. Researchers have drawn on a range of techniques for getting at children's meanings and allowing children more participation within the research process. At the same time, they encounter a series of methodological issues that confront most researchers within the field of 'qualitative' research, but which I would argue are magnified and compounded by the involvement of children. In the first section of the chapter I examine some of these issues in terms of methodology. This is followed by a discussion of the ethical dimension to child research. As child professionals have become more sensitive to the needs and interests of children in recent years, so researchers have had to think about how common research practices affect children as respondents. In particular I address one key question: should our conduct within the research process with children follow general ethical guidelines that cover all research within the social sciences, or are there separate moral and legal considerations that affect our research practices with child respondents?

In the final section of the chapter I explore the possibilities for viewing children as researchers. While up-to-date research has tended to assume that children are capable or playing a full research part as meaning-making respondents, a few adult researchers have experimented with using children in a researching rather than researched capacity. I will draw on some of these projects that illuminate a variety of research roles taken up by children.

RESEARCHING CHILDREN'S SOCIAL WORLDS: METHODOLOGICAL ISSUES

Playing the 'Least Adult' Role

One of the problems with the ethnographic approach, a potentially more intractable problem when working with children, is the multiple and often conflicting roles that researchers play. From the child's perspective, the researcher's adult status can easily be construed as the 'master status'. Especially with younger children, the sheer physical presence of the adult researcher can be a considerable obstacle to entering children's cultures. Mandell (1991) in her research with preschool children tries to overcome this problem by taking the 'least-adult' role. Mandell adopted various strategies in trying to minimize the significant differences between herself and her research subjects. Thus she assumed the role of learner by staying close to the children, watching their movements and initially saying very little until she thought she was being accepted as a child participant. Mandell (1991) eschewed contact with the teachers, gatekeepers or colleagues, preferring to gain entry into the children's worlds via the children themselves. She refused to do what she called 'teacherly' things, often ignoring requests from the children for help, guidance and support, 'suspending all adult-like characteristics except physical size' (1991, p. 40).

Thorne (1993) devotes a chapter of her book, entitled 'Learning from Kids', to try to come to terms with her master status as an adult. Like Mandell (1991), she was attempting to understand children's cultures from the inside. In particular, she was trying to enter the world of the elementary classroom and playground as a way of examining the processes through which children shape their gendered identities. Within the context of the school, Thorne tries at first to conceal a variety of perspectives that she brings to the research as an adult. She goes on in her chapter to talk about her research experiences as a process through which she was forced to reflect on her adult role: if anything, her interactions in the playground with the children magnified her adult status. As an adult she was often mistaken for a teacher. She was sometimes seen as a protector, sometimes a custodian and on occasion an associate of the teachers in school. The very language she used with the children served to heighten her authority:

> During one of my first forays on the Oceanside (school) playground, a boy came
> over and asked, 'What ya writing?' 'I'm interested in what you children are like',

I responded; 'I'm writing down what you are doing. Do you mind?' He warily edged away. 'I didn't do anything', he said. Another of my early explanations— 'I'm interested in the behavior of children'—also brought defensive responses. I came to see that verbs like 'doing' and 'behaving', which figure centrally in the language of social science, are also used by adults to sanction children. The social sciences and child-rearing are both practices geared to social control. (1993, p. 17)

Thorne also reflects on how the research brought out the 'mothering' aspects of her identity. Thus the physical nature of child's play in the playground sometimes generated protective responses. . . . There is also a continual tension between the need to allow children to express themselves in their own physical terms and the demands of a broader social order that emphasizes personal individual space. Mandell (1991), for example, found it difficult to shake off her adult/maternal perspective in that she initially found children's interactions to be chaotic. Similarly, Thorne documents her urge to intervene and regulate these 'collisions' while at the same time becoming sensitive to the notion that the physical in the child's world is part of the social and should simply be seen in these terms. She had to learn to step back and recognize what Cullingford (1991, p. 88) has called the 'volatile underworld of school', that children's worlds are more brutal and physical and that children have a potentially different and collective sense of what constitutes aggression or bullying than adults. Unlike Mandell, Thorne reflects on the impossibility of trying to pass herself off as a new member of the children's world. Mayall (1996, p. 15) comments on the futility of the least-adult role: we are continually brought back to the power and status differences between adults and children that no amount of effort on the part of the researcher can conceal.

Corsaro and Molinaro (2000) take a quite different approach by using their master statuses as adults as a way of immersing themselves within their cultures. Researchers use their 'foreignness', their distinctiveness from the children, as a means of entering their social worlds. In Corsaro's case, working with groups of Italian children, this meant his nationality as an American as well as his adult status. The children would consciously introduce him to their norms, routines and language as an 'incompetent adult'. Children's familiarity with their school accentuated the researcher's foreignness, with the latter using this as a further pretext for his induction into the group.

Alliances with Respondents

A second role confusion, a perennial one in ethnographic research, is the tension between the researcher as ally and as dispassionate observer of the social scene.[1] In the first case, the ability to enter the researched communities' worlds, or at the very least to get a sense of how others view these worlds, depends on the researcher building up a relationship of trust and empathy between himself or herself and the community being studied. In the latter case, the researcher might have to shift his or her ground to be able to take a more objective line. In the case of researching children, the difficulties are compounded by the 'dispassionate researcher' position being construed as an authoritarian one. John Davis (Davis, Watson and Cunningham-Burley 2000) demonstrates this point in recounting his research experiences with a group of schoolchildren with learning difficulties. Davis consciously eschewed the authority role in trying to build up a rapport with the youngsters. There were two reasons behind this. First, their learning difficulties sometimes made conventional discourse difficult. Davis wanted to learn ways of communicating with these children as a practical means of entering their social worlds. This involved the patient development of friendship-type relations with the children. More significantly for

Davis, learning a new language was a way of giving the children a voice within their community. The staff in the school often interpreted the children's lack of linguistic skills to mean that they were incapable of communicating, and they routinely made decisions for them. In relation to the adult staff, Davis became an advocate for the children, constantly reaffirming what they were trying to communicate. In the case of one boy, Bobby, he became the main medium through which communication took place. This rapport with the children was openly if unintentionally undermined by the teachers who would occasionally ask Davis to control or discipline the children, sometimes putting him in an ambiguous position with regard to his young respondents.

As I have already stated, researchers are constantly made aware of their power with regard to child respondents. However, children are in quite a strong position to dictate the flow of interactions with the researcher, especially where he or she is committed to the least-adult role. Mandell (1991) and Thorne (1993) were conscious of the way that their roles were continually being tested by the children, with children intermittently breaking rules in front of them in the playground and in the classroom. These situations were more acute when it became evident to the staff that the researchers were aware of this deviance. Thorne's vantage point at the back of the class gave her access to children's cultures and on occasion she was drawn in to this underworld as the children were aware of her surveillance. The alliances that researchers are trying to develop with children are often in conflict with the professional and collegiate relations that they have with the teachers. With teachers in the position of ultimate gatekeepers, there is a need to maintain a precarious balance between the demands of the children and the demands of the 'responsible adults'.

Interviewing Children

Ethnographies, as we have seen, rely on the insider role of the researcher as a participating observer of children's cultures. In turning to other less intrusive research techniques such as interviewing, there is less stress placed on the impact of the researcher within the researched community. Scott (2000) refers to a number of ways in which children can be interviewed, including one-to-one encounters, with their parents, in pairs or groups, through focus groups and by using the 'walkman' method. In the last case, Scott used this approach as part of the British Household Panel Survey (BHPS), an annual survey of 'microsocial change in Britain' (Scott 2000, p. 110). This allowed a sample of around 800 children aged between 11 and 15 to respond privately to a series of questions through an audio tape machine in their own homes. The children were 'interviewed' on issues relating to health, family life and leisure.

Other smaller-scale pieces of research have used interview-based techniques in trying to make sense of what it is like to be a child. Mayall (2000) talks about 'conversations' with children as the basis for revealing children's knowledge of their social lives. Her research focus was the 'generational order': how children in a number of different contexts made sense of their social positions as part of the younger subordinate generation. Solberg (1996), similarly, interviewed a sample of Norwegian children as a means of understanding the roles that children played in negotiating the generation order as a series of routines within their families.

However, as with the ethnography, the adult interviewer/child interviewee relationship generates methodological considerations. Various researchers have looked at the interview relationship in terms of power (Oakley 1981b). Thus the typical characteristics of the researcher as educated, white and middle-class influence the nature of the data, with interviewees providing accounts that accord with what they think is expected of them from the interviewer rather than in their own terms. If there is a perceived power relationship between the researcher and researched here, it compromises the sense of ownership that the latter has of their understanding of the world. Power here is attributed to an unequal relationship to knowledge, with the researcher monopolizing the situation. Attempts are made to counter this by matching adult interviewees with researchers in terms of gender, ethnicity and social class. In theory, this 'matching' puts the researcher in a better position to empathize with the respondent and gain a more authentic understanding of their social worlds. While it does not and cannot break down the power relationship between researcher and researched, this matching is also less threatening for the respondent.[2] With child interviewees this is much more difficult for, as was mentioned earlier, there is limited scope in presenting oneself in the 'least-adult role'. The power relationship between adult and child is more evident and visible, with physical size providing continual evidence of the power imbalance. Hood, Kelley and Mayall (1996) try to get around this by manipulating other research variables. Children can be interviewed in pairs or in groups—the numerical advantage of the interviewees, to some degree, counteracting the power of the single, adult interviewer. . . . We might also return to Mayall's conversations with children on the generational order: in some cases, her young respondents adapted to the interview situation to meet their own conversational needs rather than simply to respond at the appropriate points in the interview to the adult interviewer's requests. When referring to an interview with two 6-year-old girls, she commented, 'they [the two girls] were sufficiently at ease with each other that they could, at some points, set aside the generational order of my conversation with them' (2000, p. 126).

One variable over which the child respondents have little control is the location of the interview. Some researchers have argued that this is a crucial consideration because children's personalities are context-dependent (Scott 2000, p. 103). If we compare their home and school environments, children probably have a different relationship with each other and with adults in these environments. Whether children are any less centered in terms of identity and personality than adults is a moot point. Nevertheless, the location of the research is important because we generally tend to think that the respondent is more likely to feel in control of the research situation where they are familiar with the surroundings and where there is a degree of privacy. . . . Privacy is a common good to which adults have access. Children have to negotiate access according to age-related criteria, determined by their adult caretakers. Older children can expect more private space than younger children. This places considerable limits on children being able to choose an interview location. The researcher's awareness of this problem does not necessarily make things any easier: while the adult researcher might think that privacy restricts the direct surveillance of their caretakers, it places more onus on the researcher to act as a surrogate caretaker, thus shifting the 'protective' burden from parent and teacher to researcher. Thus the more private the research context, the more likely adult researchers will have to assume the role of guardian. Nevertheless, having access to some place where there is less adult regulation can help to downplay the 'adultness' of the researcher and provide a less inhibiting context for the research.[3]

Child-Centered Research Techniques

In many cases ethnographers will adopt a multimethod approach in uncovering children's understandings and social worlds. . . . Pollard and his colleagues (1999) used a biographical-case-study approach. Primary school children's school lives were tracked over time—the children were actively involved throughout the research. Among other things they constructed sociometric maps of their friendship networks and kept diaries of their everyday activities, as well as taking part in interviews. In turning to another example, a vignette approach has been used to elicit children's definitions of family. In two separate projects, O'Brien, Alldred and Jones (1996) asked 460 children aged between 7 and 16 to comment on a series of hypothetical family situations in order to elicit their views on the meaning of family.

Conversational techniques are central to a qualitative approach, for they highlight the respondents' understandings of themselves and their social worlds. The general feeling is that the most direct . . . research techniques allow the respondent a degree of autonomy in producing more authentic accounts of their social worlds. Other researchers have produced innovative methods as a way of engaging with young people and alleviating the power differences between researcher and researched. Samantha Punch (2002) used a 'secret box' . . . and a variety of stimulus material to connect with her young sample, making the research more interesting and relevant to their lives.

However, a child-centered approach to research has often led to child-specific research techniques being deployed, which imply that children are not quite capable of sustaining a more conventional verbal account. The assumption is still that young children can only express complex thoughts and ideas indirectly through role-play, games or drawings. Hill, Laybourn and Borland (1996) were aware of this tension and sought a balance between what they called 'ordinary methods' (interviews) and 'special measures' (child-centered methods). Their research focused on primary-aged children's (5–11) understandings of their emotional well-being. The project was concerned to demonstrate children's social competence through interviews. At the same time, the researchers asserted that younger children are used to child-specific modes of expression in school, such as drawing, games and physical exercises. These more familiar techniques were used to maintain children's interest in the research project.

ETHICAL CONSIDERATIONS

A key theme in this chapter is that the neglect of children as research subjects is reflected in their general invisibility. Their lack of personhood has often meant that children simply do not come into the reckoning where organizations involved with research are forced to take account of the dispositions and feelings of certain groups. The ethical dimension to child-focused research is no exception here, with a low priority attached to regulating the general conduct of researchers working with children.

Informed Consent

If we concentrate for the moment on informed consent—a key principle within most professions' ethical guidelines—it is clear that, for many researchers working with children, adult gatekeepers remain the last point at which access to a child population may or may not be granted. . . .

Research participants need to be fully informed before the research can take place. . . . As the field of children and childhood research continues to grow, a number of commentators and organizations are starting to examine the ethical position of children and adult researchers. One important principle established is the . . . status of the child within the research process, with a commitment to allowing children to opt out of participation in a research project. . . . The consent of the child should be sought in addition to that of the parent. . . .

Children need to be fully briefed at the beginning of the research. Among other things, children need to know what the research is about, the significance of their roles as respondents and any possible outcomes of the research. Once it has been established that potential child respondents are fully aware of the aims of the research, then they are in a position to decide whether or not to take part.

This does not dispose of the problem of disagreements between child and caretaker, particularly where the caretaker refuses the child access in cases where the child is willing. For example, Mason and Falloon's (2001) research on children's conceptions of child abuse set out to challenge the adult-centered nature of the discourse on abuse. Thus the importance of treating their child sample as the sole 'definers' within their project meant that there was a high premium placed on the children themselves opting into the project. However, their employers, the University of Western Sydney, insisted that they gain consent from the parents as well as the respondents. According to the researchers, this resulted in some children who were willing to take part being excluded from the project.[4]

An analysis of the ethics of child research thus brings to the surface ambiguities surrounding the treatment of children. Children can opt out, but there is a lack of clarity as to whether they can opt in. . . . Children are . . . established as full members of society; at the same time children's status within the social structure is as lesser members of society. In terms of the research process, children are established as agents who can choose to take part in research. Their status as agents assures them of a place within what Hood, Kelley and Mayall (1996) call a 'hierarchy of gate-keepers', but located firmly on the bottom rung. Parents and, to a lesser extent, teachers are still the dominant reference points when negotiating access, reflecting their structurally superior position within the hierarchy.

Formal principles that foreground the child as a key research participant are important in establishing a formal research agenda. However, the organizational structures which researchers have to negotiate and the character of the dynamics between the various participants in the research often determine the outcome of issues of consent. Even where we can establish children's consent, they may feel compelled to take part; the presence of a teacher or parent can imply to the child that they ought to help the researcher. Again I come back to the implicit power of the adult over the child. An illustration from my own experience as a researcher might help here. With a colleague I carried out interviews with primary school children in the mid-1990s. The interviews were part of a broader examination of key educational actors' perceptions of values, choice and accountability in English primary schools (Wyness and Silcock 1999). The pupils were interviewed after we had gained the views of teachers, heads and inspectors. In one of the schools we had developed good relations with the teaching staff, who were quite happy to offer us access to the pupils. We emphasized to the staff how important it was that the pupils should feel free to opt out if they were not happy taking part. On the day of the interviews, the head teacher produced groups of children who were waiting quietly in his office to be interviewed. Before starting the interviews we gave the children the information on the project and the opportunity to opt out. We also assumed that the children had been briefed by the head teacher. While all of the children seemed keen to take part, any of the children in the head's office would have found it very difficult to opt out. We had no reason to think that these children had been forced or even persuaded to take part. Nevertheless, the position of the head, and the knowledge the pupils had that the interviews were taking place in the head's office, probably made it less likely that any of them were in a strong enough position to opt out. It was clearly in our interests to obtain a sample of children. At the same time, our interests in collecting good data needed to be set against the . . . right to be in a position to make a relatively free choice. . . .

We need to be careful when assuming that children in school are bound to say yes to researchers even when they want to say no. A culture of obedience may dominate the decision-making processes of young children in school. However, the point that I want to make is that the context within which decisions are made by research participants is important and, in some cases, the presence of an adult researcher may have an opposite effect on the decisions that children make. France, Bendelow and Williams (2000) tried to explain the lack of participation of some pupils in their research on children's perceptions of health because of a more instrumental view among pupils. Hence some pupils refused to become involved in the research because in their opinion there was really nothing in it for them. Moreover, the researchers imply that children view this instrumental culture in school as an unfair exchange, with students continually getting very little back for their deference. As the authors argue, 'Young people are expected to be good citizens but little attention is paid to their own needs as citizens' (France, Bendelow and Williams 2000, p. 158). It may be that the two examples here reflect different school-age populations—a younger, more deferent group in my own case, and an older, more assertive group in the second example. Nevertheless, the context of the school is significant in generating willing and unwilling samples of children.

Confidentiality

It is common practice to assure any sample of adults that what they say and reveal in the research is confidential, with names and places being changed. Where research findings are likely to be read by a much larger or wider audience, consideration has to be given to whether the research community needs to be consulted before publication. . . . In turning to child respondents, the same demands are made of researchers to maintain confidentiality. In Sam Punch's (2002) research into how 13–14-year-olds cope with problems, the respondents saw confidentiality as a precondition of their involvement. As I mentioned earlier, one of the author's innovative techniques was a 'secret box' which she used to try and assure her young respondents of the confidentiality of their accounts. Respondents were asked to write down on a blank piece of paper any problems they had experienced or were experiencing. They were to omit their names and post these pieces of paper in a secret box. The researcher assured the respondents that she would not be able to put a name to these problems or trace the handwriting. The researcher was able to collate and categorize the different problems without being able to link them to specific respondents. In one sense there is nothing particularly child-centered about this approach. Adults as well as children experience things that they are unwilling to divulge to an interviewer unless confidentiality is guaranteed. In principle we might use this technique with an adult sample. Where confidentiality is particularly an issue for children is when it can conflict with demands placed on professionals, including researchers, to protect children. Wherever possible, children should be afforded the same level of integrity as adults with reference to the confidential nature of their testimony. In some instances, children are likely to feel inhibited when they feel that what they say to a researcher is likely to be passed on to someone else in authority. This was the case with Punch's sample. Yet Masson (2000) talks . . . about researchers having limited legal liability. That is, researchers may be legally bound to disclose this testimony to the appropriate agencies when the researcher believes that the child is disclosing information about abuse or exploitation. At a minimum, researchers cannot guarantee child respondents absolute confidentiality because they have a duty to act on any information given to them by the child relating to abuse, irrespective of the effects this has on the integrity of the research.

Some researchers have argued that the ethical dimension goes much further than any legal obligation to inform the appropriate authorities (Alderson 1995). Thus while researchers cannot guarantee confidentiality, at the outset they are morally obliged to tell the child respondent that they might have to disclose information given to them. Moreover, where the researcher feels obliged to pass the information to other professionals, wherever possible the researcher will discuss this disclosure with the child first before taking any action. The aim here is to encourage the children themselves to seek help from the appropriate agencies. In some instances, child researchers have a professional background in counseling children. In returning briefly to Mason and Falloon's (2001) research, their own backgrounds in child protection equipped them with the skills to deal with any possible disclosures when interviewing children about child abuse. But balancing the integrity of the interview with the responsibility to protect often makes researching with children a 'risky business'.

The Effects of Research

A third ethical issue, again underpinned by the imperative to protect, is the 'effects' of research on children. Ever since the notorious experiments into obedience conducted by Milgram in the 1960s, researchers have been grappling with the potential impact of certain types of research on their respondents (Baumrind 1964). Will children's participation in a research project harm them in any way? Do we need to debrief children once the interview or experiment has finished? Alderson (1995) goes further in linking 'effects' to the theoretical basis of the research. She argues that the outcomes of the research can be linked to the theoretical assumptions made about the children being researched. . . . The researcher who makes assumptions about the child's level of social learning or development works within a dominant framework which perpetuates the subordinate position of children. In relation to research that explores the subjective realm, this has often meant that researchers rely on proxy adults for accounts of children's understandings rather than sampling the children themselves. In effect, Alderson (1995) is encouraging researchers to reflect on their theoretical models in terms of how they confirm and sustain particular social conceptions of childhood. Thus rather than focus on the . . . short-term impact of research on individual children, the effects of research are seen to be much broader in terms of the structural position of children. . . .

CHILDREN AS RESEARCHERS

Up until now I have concentrated on children as 'meaning-making' respondents within the research process. The broad thrust of child-focused research has been for adults to generate the ideas and the funding, manage the field work and bring children in as willing and capable respondents. . . . I want now to turn to the more challenging notion of children as researchers. In principle there are different levels of involvement on the 'research' side. Hart's (1997) 'ladder of children's participation' sets out a hierarchy of children's involvement in a range of projects and activities. At the bottom we have forms of 'non-participation', claims made by adults about children's involvement that are in reality marginal, contrived and tokenistic. Thus very young children being taken to a street demonstration wearing T-shirts with political statements on them comes into the category of 'decorative participation'. At the upper end of the ladder, we have children initiating and controlling their affairs, with adults playing a lesser role. The further up the ladder we go, the more likely we are to find child-initiated projects. At this upper end, Hart (1997, p. 23) refers to the Earthnauts, a democratic structure for children's participation in local matters based in Austin, Texas. The board of directors is made up equally of adults and children, and the leadership of specific local projects is shared between the children and the adults.

Adapting the upper end of the ladder to the research context would mean children setting up their own project, conducting the research and publishing the results (Alderson 2000). The nearest we get to a situation where the children were instrumental from inception to publication is the 'Everybody In?' project involving young disabled people.[5] Three young male collaborators worked alongside the 'adult' researchers in examining the perceptions of disabled and non-disabled students on policies of inclusion (Roberts 2000). One of the material outcomes was a report co-written by the young people and the professional researchers (Ash et al. 1997). More recently the Open University in England has set up the Children's Research Center where children generate the research topics, undertake the research and write up and publish their research on their own (childrens-research-centre.open.ac.uk). Examples of research papers found on the center's website include:

- 'Hey I'm nine not six!' A small-scale investigation of looking younger than your age at school (Anna Carlini and Emma Berry, aged 10)
- How does death affect children? (Paul O'Brien, aged 12)
- Girls want to play too! Investigating the views of 9–11-year-old pupils about mixed-gender football (Ben Davies and Selena Ryan-Vig, aged 10).

It is in the middle range of the ladder of participation where we find most examples of children as researchers. Children's standpoints and life worlds are prioritized within these projects. Ethically, children who play a more 'collegiate' role in the research will have much fuller information about the aims and objectives of the research process. Thus the problem of informed consent becomes less of a problem, with children in a much better position to weigh up their involvement. Beyond these broad principles, children are playing different roles within the research enterprise as researchers.

Adults' Research Project, Children as Consultants

Here adults by and large determine the broad parameters of the research and play a more regulative role, but children have some influence over the methods used, the questions asked and the general conduct of the research. If we return to the research into children's perceptions of child abuse by Mason and Falloon (2001), their 'collaborative' approach meant that the small sample of children determined the form and membership of the 'focus groups' utilized, as well as the timing and location of the interviews. Interestingly, the researchers were keen to feed back the transcripts of the taped material and their interpretations to the children. The children, on the other hand, saw little value in this process and eschewed the feedback. The researchers speculate that one reason for this is that children have little sense of owning knowledge and are not used to being asked to comment on data. Being marginal to the production of knowledge in school, children's full involvement in the research process here comes up against a still-dominant culture of exclusion.

Adults' Research Project, Children as Fieldworkers

I have emphasized the principled involvement of children at various levels of the research process. There is also a more pragmatic basis to 'employing' child researchers. First of all, children are more actively involved in the research process because they may be the most effective observers of children's worlds within an educational context, what I referred to earlier as the hidden 'underworld' of schooling (Cullingford 1991, p. 58). Children may thus be employed as researchers in an attempt to solve Mandell's (1991) problem of the 'least-adult' role of the researcher. Secondly, where the research is problem-driven, for example work on bullying or sexism, children in school tend to consult with their peers first before approaching teaching staff (Cullingford, 1991). Children as researchers or reporters of incidents may be more effective in that they bring to the surface a range of issues and problems that may remain hidden from adult purview. Thirdly, children who act as researchers are likely to develop a range of skills that improve their levels of self-esteem and commitment to schoolwork. . . .

If we take seriously the view that children can undertake research, we need to address the various legal restrictions (Masson 2000). One issue is whether child research assistants should be construed as employees in the same way as their adult counterparts. How are children to be rewarded for their work? Should child researchers be paid? Within the school context, research is normally subsumed within their education, and payment is rarely an issue. Nevertheless, the 'innovative' nature of employing child researchers needs to be set against the cost to the researcher of having to employ an adult research assistant in more conventional research. . . .

CONCLUSION

I have argued that, in line with a more child-focused sociology, 'working with children' signals an important shift in viewing children as research subjects rather than research objects. 'Working *with* children' rather than 'working *on* children' at a very basic level means drawing horizontal rather than vertical lines of interaction between researcher and researched. This might imply degrees of collegiality and equality in the way that researchers relate to the researched community. Researchers are now engaging with children in the research process as respondents and, to a limited extent, as co-researchers. . . . The binary divide between children and adults breaks down as both inhabit life worlds that generate social meaning. Researchers assume that these symbolic worlds are now open to both adults and children, which in turn produces a commitment on the part of the researcher to understand these symbolic worlds.

I referred to the way that researchers generate children's accounts of the social world through interviews. These accounts are important but they are abstracted from their everyday routines. Children tell us about their social worlds at a given time and place and, by virtue of our powerful positions, children, like adults, from time to time tell us what we want to hear. What the researcher misses is an interactive and collective component of children's worlds. In trying to capture this, equality with children necessitates a movement 'downwards' for many researchers. As we saw earlier children are seen to be meaning-makers in their own terms, and within their own worlds and cultures. Ethnographers adopt various positions ranging from the empathetic to the 'least adult'. Understanding children's life worlds here means gaining access to children's worlds. Equality in these terms means being childlike, becoming an honorary member of a secret society or tribe where children routinely negotiate their own rules and relations. . . .

This creates a dilemma for the researcher: do we protect children from the rigors of conventional research methods and risk patronizing them as research respondents, or do we engage children fully in the research as competent actors and risk alienating them from the research by utilizing what are seen by the child respondents to be adult methods? While we cannot envision a wholly democratic relationship between researcher and researched, from within the new sociology of childhood we have identified the quintessentially reflexive nature of research with children.

Discussion Questions

1. What are the special ethical concerns researchers must consider when studying children?
2. Describe how children may act as collaborators and consultants in the research process.

3. If you were to design a study of children, what do you think your biggest challenges would be?
4. Why is it important to consider what children themselves think about the research process?

Notes

1. Mahon et al. (1996) refer to a third 'therapeutic' role.
2. But see Finch (1984) for some of the drawbacks to this approach.
3. Within childhood geography, for example, researchers utilize the 'walking interview', whereby children can be interviewed on the move with the children determining the physical direction of the interview and in many cases its content. See Driskell (2002).
4. One recent commentary suggests that we should always err on the side of the guardian (France, Bendelow and Williams 2000).
5. The collaborators were over 18.

References

Alderson, P. (1995) *Listening to Children: Ethics and Social Research*, Barkingside: Essex.

Alderson, P. (2000) 'Children as Researchers: The Effects of Participation Rights on Research Methodology', in P. Christensen and A. James (eds) *Research with Children: Perspectives and Practices,* London: Falmer.

Ash, A., Bellew, J., Davies, M., Newman, T. and Richardson, M. (1997) 'Everybody in? The Experience of Disabled Students in Colleges of Further Education', *Disability and Society*, 12, 4, pp. 605–21.

Baumrind, D. (1964) 'Some Thoughts on Ethics of Research: After Reading Milgram's "Behavioural Study of Obedience"', *American Psychologist*, 19, pp. 421–3.

Corsaro, W. and Molinaro, L. (2000) 'Entering and Observing Children's Worlds: A Reflection on a Longitudinal Ethnography of Early Education in Italy', in P. Christensen and A. James (eds) *Research with Children: Perspectives and Practices*, London: Falmer.

Cullingford, C. (1991) *The Inner World of the School*, London: Cassell.

Davis, J., Watson, N. and Cunningham-Burley, S. (2000) 'Learning the Lives of Disabled Children: Developing a Reflexive Approach', in

P. Christensen and A. James (eds) *Research with Children: Perspectives and Practices*, London: Falmer.

Driskell, R. (2002) *Creating Better Cities with Children*, London: Earthscan.

France, A., Bendelow, G. and Williams, S. (2000) 'A Risky Business: Researching the Health Beliefs of Children and Young People', in A. Lewis and G. Lindsay (eds) *Researching Children's Perspectives*, Buckingham: Open University Press.

Hart, R. (1997) *Children's Participation: The Theory and Practice of Involving Young Citizens in Community Development and Environmental Care*, London: Earthscan.

Hill, M., Laybourn, A. and Borland, M. (1996) 'Engaging with Primary-aged Children about their Emotions and Well-being: Methodological Considerations', *Children and Society*, 10, 2, pp. 129–44.

Hood, S., Kelley, P. and Mayall, B. (1996) 'Children as Research Subjects: A Risky Enterprise', *Children and Society*, 10, 2, pp. 117–28.

Mahon, A., Glendinning, C., Clarke, K. and Craig, C. (1996) 'Researching Children: Methods and Ethics', *Children and Society,* 10, 2, pp. 145–54.

Mandell, N. (1991) 'The Least Adult Role in Studying Children', in F. Waksler (ed) *Studying the Social Worlds of Children*, London: Falmer Press.

Mason, J. and Falloon, J. (2001) 'Some Sydney Children Define Abuse: Implications for Agency in Childhood', in L. Alanen and B. Mayall (eds) *Conceptualising Child–Adult Relations,* London: RoutledgeFalmer.

Masson, J. (2000) 'Researching Children's Perspectives: Legal Issues', in A. Lewis and G. Lindsay (eds) *Researching Children's Perspectives*, Buckingham: Open University Press.

Mayall, B. (1996) *Children, Health and the Social Order*, Buckingham: University Press.

Mayall, B. (2002) *Towards a Sociology of Childhood: Thinking from Children's Lives,* Buckingham: Open University.

Oakley, A. (1981b) *Sex, Gender and Society*, 2nd edn, London: Maurice Temple Smith.

O'Brien, M., Alldred, P. and Jones, D. (1996) 'Children's Constructions of Family and Kinship', in J. Brannen and M. O'Brien (eds) *Children in Families*, London: Falmer.

Punch, S. (2002) 'Interviewing Strategies with Young People: The "Secret Box", Stimulus Material and Task-based Activities', *Children and Society*, 16, 1, pp. 45–56.

Roberts, H. (2000) 'Listening to Children: And Hearing Them', in P. Christensen and A. James (eds) *Research with Children: Perspectives and Practices*, London: Falmer.

Scott, J. (2000) 'Children as Respondents: The Challenge for Quantitative Methods', in P. Christensen and A. James (eds) *Research with Children: Perspectives and Practices*, London: Falmer.

Solberg, A. (1996) 'The Challenge in Child Research: From "Being" to "Doing"', in J. Brannen and M. O'Brien (eds) *Children in Families: Research and Policy*, London: Falmer.

Thorne, B. (1993) *Gender Play: Girls and Boys in School*, Milton Keynes: Open University Press.

Wyness, M. and Silcock, P. (1999) 'Market Values, Primary Schooling and the Pupils' Perspective', in D. Lawton, J. Cairns and R. Gardner (eds) *Values and the Curriculum: The School Context*, Occasional Paper, London: Institute of Education.

PART FOUR

Relationships
How Do Children Actively Negotiate Relationships with Friends and Family?

Children actively negotiate relationships with friends and family, despite the long-standing tendency to view kids as merely affected by the people around them. Typically, when we think about children's relationships with peers we look for negative influences; the term *peer pressure* connotes that any influence children have over one another is dangerous. But as with adults' relationships with one another, children's relationships are complex and not as simple as we often presume.

Schools are a primary setting to observe children's relationships with one another; three of the selections in this section are based on observations of kids at school. Authors Patricia A. Adler and Peter Adler observed their own preadolescent children and their children's friends in middle school to better understand how children carve their identities through interacting with one another. In their selection, "Popularity," they discuss how status is produced within peer culture. They find that the process of popularity is distinctly different for boys than it is for girls, who attain status by seeming more disconnected and cool—they would often demonstrate this by appearing less interested in school. The Adlers found that regardless of gender, kids whose parents provide less supervision tend to be more popular.

Understanding how kids create status is very important, as is *why* young people create status hierarchies amongst their peers. In "Exchanges, Labels, and Put-Downs" Murray Milner, Jr., takes a more macro-level look at status and popularity, and concludes that in a closed system, such as school, kids have a limited degree of freedom and power. By creating their own hierarchies of power, young people manufacture the power they mostly lack in society as a whole.

Kids reproduce other power inequities through their interactions. Donna Eder, Catherine Colleen Evans, and Stephen Parker observed middle school students and noted the ways in which gender and sexuality are used as tools by kids to recreate the meanings of both, all while creating their own status system. In "Crude Comments and Sexual Scripts" the authors observe that challenging the heterosexual appeal of both boys and girls is a central way for a child to reduce another child's status. They observed how boys competed with one another to appear to be the most sexually knowledgeable and the most emotionally disconnected from the girls they claimed involvement with. By contrast, girls might gain status with one another by being considered attractive to boys, but they were still marginalized by boys—and by teachers—the authors note.

In addition to schools, researchers also study children's experiences in their families. While we tend to think of children as more or less passive recipients of "parenting," in reality children are active contributors to their families in ways we often overlook. Abel Valenzuela studied the children of Mexican immigrants, and found that these children are vital in the settlement process. For one, many families decide to immigrate in hope of providing more opportunities for their children. Children also help their parents navigate American social institutions, such as school, work, and health care, often as translators. In "Gender Roles and Settlement Activities Among Children and Their Immigrant Families," Valenzuela finds that the children of immigrants, beyond helping their parents with English, are often central in helping their parents understand their rights in the workplace, and they become essential in the family decision-making process.

It's not just children of immigrants who shape their families' everyday lives. Annette Lareau conducted ethnographic research in a dozen families and found that more affluent families' lives tend to be structured around their children's leisure and enrichment activities. In "Concerted Cultivation and the Accomplishment of Natural Growth," Lareau considers how a family's socioeconomic status shapes parents perspective on how children should spend their time outside of school. For the middle- and upper-middle class families, children were very busy participating in structured, organized adult-run activities in order to help them "cultivate" specific skills. By contrast, lower-income families enrolled their children in fewer organized activities; in part because of the high cost and limited time parents had to shuttle kids around, but also because of the belief that children should have plenty of free time, what she calls "accomplishment of natural growth." Her piece informs us not only of how children may significantly shape the way families spend their time, but also how assumptions about childhood itself vary based among different economic classes.

Popularity
PATRICIA A. ADLER AND PETER ADLER

INTRODUCTION

Researchers Patricia A. Adler and Peter Adler conducted an ethnographic study of their preadolescent children's peer cultures. In this selection they consider the role that popularity plays, examining what makes some children more popular than others. They note that differences based on gender are highly important. For boys, being athletic was a major contributor, while excelling academically was not. For girls, their family's wealth and their appearance were very important. The authors also conclude that children with more lax parents were more likely to be popular.

O ne of the strongest dimensions of life that preadolescents wrestle with is popularity. They are forever talking about who is popular, who is unpopular, and why they are popular. Children strive, much to parents' chagrin, to enhance their own popularity, often at considerable expense. In this effort, there are some things that they can influence, and others that fall beyond their control. Factors affecting children's popularity and unpopularity are different for boys and girls. These are rooted in the strong gendered peer cultures that arise during youth, as children attempt to discern the contours of adult gender dimensions and adapt them, as relevant, to their own age cultures. Segregated . . . cultures have been observed as early as preschool (Berentzen 1984; Cahill 1994; Corsaro 1985; Gunnarsson 1978; Joffe 1979), as boys and girls separate and begin to evolve their own interests and activities. . . .

In educational institutions, children develop a stratified social order determined by their interactions with peers, parents, and other social elements (Passuth 1987). According to Corsaro (1979), children's knowledge of social position is influenced by their conception of status, which may be defined as popularity, prestige, or "social honor" (Weber 1946). In the school environment, boys and girls have divergent attitudes and behavioral patterns in their gender role expectations and the methods they use to attain status, or popularity among peers.

In this chapter, we examine differences in the factors affecting girls' and boys' popularity in their gendered peer cultures.

BOYS' POPULARITY FACTORS

Boys' popularity, or rank in the status hierarchy, was influenced by several factors. Although the boys' popularity ordering was not as clearly defined as the girls', there was a rationale underlying the stratification in their daily interactions and group relationships.

Athletic Ability

The major factor affecting boys' popularity was athletic ability.[1] This was so critical that individuals who were proficient in sport attained both peer recognition and upward social mobility. In several schools we observed, the best athlete was also the most popular boy in the grade.

Two third- and fourth-grade boys considered the question of what makes kids popular:

NICK: Craig is sort of mean, but he's really good at sports so he's popular.

BRIAN: Everybody wants to be friends with Gabe, even though he makes fun of most of them all the time. But they still all want to pick him on their team and have him be friends with them because he's a good athlete, even though he brags a lot about it. He's popular.

In the upper grades, the most popular boys all had a keen interest in sports even if their athletic skills were not very adept. Those with moderate ability and interest in athletic endeavors fell primarily into lower-status groups. Those least proficient athletically were potential pariahs.

Because of their physicality, contact sports occasionally degenerated into conflicts between participants. Fighting, whether formal fights or informal pushing, shoving, or roughhousing, was a means to establish a social order for the boys. More popular boys often dispensed these physical actions of superiority, while the less popular boys were often the recipients. The victors, although negatively sanctioned by the adults in the school, attained more status than the defeated, who lost considerable status. Less popular boys were the ones most frequently hurt and least frequently assisted during games on the playground. For example, Mikey, an unpopular boy with asthma who was fairly uncoordinated and weak, was often the victim of rough playground tackles in football or checks in soccer. Boys knew they could take the ball away from him at will. When he was hurt and fell down crying, he was blamed for the incident and mocked.

Coolness

For boys, being "cool" generated a great deal of peer status. As Lyman and Scott (1989, 93) note, "a display of coolness is often a prerequisite to entrance into or maintenance of membership in certain social circles." Cool was a social construction whose definition was in constant flux. Being cool involved individuals' self-presentational skills, their accessibility to expressive equipment, such as clothes, and their impression management techniques (Fine 1981).

Various social forces were involved in the continual negotiation of cool and how the students came to agree upon its meaning. As Mrs. Slade, a sixth-grade teacher, commented: "The popular group is what society might term 'cool.' You know, they're skaters, they skateboard, they wear more cool clothes—you know, the 'in' things you'd see in ads right now in magazines. If you look at our media and advertising right now on TV, like the Levi commercials, they're kinda loose, they skate, and they're doing those things. The identity they created for themselves, I think, has a lot to do with the messages the kids are getting from the media and advertising as to what's cool and what's not cool." . . .

Toughness

In most of the schools we studied, the popular boys, especially in the upper grade levels, were defiant of adult authority, challenged existing rules, and received more disciplinary actions than boys in the other groups. They attained a great deal of peer status from this type of acting out. This defiance is related to what Miller (1958) calls the "focal concerns" of lower-class culture, specifically "trouble" and "toughness." Trouble involves rule-breaking behavior and, as Miller (1958, 176) notes, "in certain situations, 'getting into trouble' is overtly recognized its prestige conferring." Boys who exhibited an air of nonchalance in the face of teacher authority of disciplinary measures enhanced their status among their peers, as witnessed by Fine (1987) in his study of Little League boys.

Two fourth-grade boys described how members of the popular group in their grade acted:

ANDY: They're always getting into trouble by talking back to the teacher.

TOM: Yeah, they always have to show off to each other that they aren't afraid to say anything they want to the teacher, that they aren't teachers' pets. Whatever they're doing, they make it look like it's better than what the teacher is doing, 'cause they think what she's doing is stupid.

ANDY: And one day Josh and Allen got in trouble in music 'cause they told the teacher the Disney movie she wanted to show sucked. They got pink [disciplinary] slips.

TOM: Yeah, and that's the third pink slip Josh's got already this year, and it's only Thanksgiving.

Toughness involved displays of physical prowess, athletic skill, and belligerency, especially in repartee with peers and adults. In the status hierarchy, boys who exhibited "macho" behavioral patterns gained recognition from their peers for being tough. Often, boys in the high-status crowd were the "class clowns" of "troublemakers" in the school, thereby becoming the center of attention.

In contrast, boys who demonstrated "effeminate" behavior were referred to by pejorative terms such as "fag," "sissy" and "homo", and consequently lost status (cf. Thorne and Luria 1986). One boy was constantly derided behind his back because he got flustered easily, had a "spaz" (lost his temper, slammed things down on his desk, stomped around the classroom), and then would start to cry.

Two fifth-grade boys described a classmate they considered the prototypical fag:

TRAVIS: Wren is such a nerd. He's short and his ears stick out.

NIKKO: And when he sits in his chair, he crosses one leg over the other and curls the toe around under his calf, so it's double-crossed, like this [shows]. It looks so faggy with his "girly" shoes. And he always sits up erect with perfect posture, like this [shows].

TRAVIS: And he's always raising his hand to get the teacher to call on him.

NIKKO: Yeah, Wren is the kind of kid, when the teacher has to go out for a minute, she says, "I'm leaving Wren in charge while I'm gone."

Savoir Faire

Savoir faire refers to students' sophistication in social and interpersonal skills. These included interpersonal communication skills such as being able to initiate sequences of play and other joint lines of action, affirmation of friendships, role-taking and role-playing abilities, social knowledge and cognition, providing constructive criticism and support to one's peers, and expressing feelings in a positive manner. Boys used their social skills to establish friendships with peers and adults both within and outside the school environment, thereby enhancing their popularity.

Many of the behaviors composing savoir faire depended on students' maturity, adroitness, and awareness of what was going on in the social world around them. Boys who had a higher degree of social awareness knew how to use their social skills more effectively. This manifested itself in a greater degree of sophistication in communicating with peers and adults.

Miss Hoffman, a fourth-grade teacher, commented on some of the characteristics she noted in the group leaders: "Interpersonal skills, there's a big difference there. It seems like I get a more steady gaze, more eye contact, and more of an adult response with some of the kids in the popular group, one-on-one with them. The ones who aren't [in the popular group] kind of avert their gaze or are kind of more fidgety; they fidget a little more and are a little more uneasy one-on-one."

A parent also remarked on this difference between popular leaders and less popular followers in discussing a burglary attempt that had been inadvertently foiled by a group of third-grade boys who returned home early one day and surprised some thieves in the house: "They all got a good look at the pair, but when the police came, only Kyle and Devin were able to tell the police what went on. The rest of the boys were all standing around, pretty excited and nervous, and they couldn't really explain what had happened or understand what had happened. . . . And when the police took them down to the station to give a description and to look through the mug books, Kyle and Devin did all of the talking. I know my kid could not have done what they did. He's a little more in outer space somewhere. Kyle, especially, has always been more mature than the rest."

Many boys further used their savoir faire to their social advantage. In their desire to be popular, they were often manipulative, domineering, and controlling. They set potential friends against each other, vying for their favors. They goaded others into acting out in class and getting into trouble. They set the attitudes for all to follow and then changed the rules by not following them themselves. One mother sighed about her son Trevor's friendship with Brad. . . , the leader of the popular group: "I'm glad they're not in the same class together this year. Every year he [her son] has chased after Brad, trying to be his best friend. He has gotten into a lot of trouble and put himself into a lot of competition with other kids over Brad. And then he's been left high and dry when Brad decided he wanted to be best friends with someone else."

Group leaders with savoir faire often defined and enforced the boundaries of an exclusive social group. While nearly everyone liked them and wanted to be in their group, they only included the kids they wanted. . . . They communicated to other peers, especially unpopular boys, that friendships did not exist or that play sessions were temporary. This maintained social boundaries by keeping others on the periphery and at a marginal status. These kinds of social skills did not seem to emerge along a developmental continuum, with some children farther along than the rest. Rather, certain individuals seemed to possess a more proficient social and interactional acumen, and to sustain it from year to year, grade to grade.

In contrast, those with extremely poor savoir faire had problematic social lives and low popularity. . . . Their interpersonal skills were awkward or poor, and they rarely engaged in highly valued interaction with their peers. Some of them were either withdrawn or aggressively antisocial. Others exhibited dysfunctional behavior and were referred to as "bossy" or mean. These individuals did not receive a great deal of peer recognition yet often wanted acceptance into the more prestigious groups.

A group of second-grade boys discussed these behaviors in regard to their classmate Bud:

STEVE: Bud, he's the worst bugger in the whole school. He always bugs people a lot.

TIMMY: And he always pushes all of us around, and he calls us all names.

Q: *Is Bud popular?*

ALL: NO.

SAM: Because he calls everybody names and kicks everybody and pushes us.

STEVE: You know what he's best at? *["No, what"]* Annoying people.

Many of the students who lacked savoir faire to an extreme were disagreeable in conversations with their peers. Not only did they lack the social skills necessary to making it in the popular group, they could not maintain relationships with other less popular individuals.

Cross-Gender Relations

Although cross-gender friendships were common in the preschool years, play and games became mostly gender-segregated in elementary school and there was a general lack of cross-gender interaction in the classroom . . . After kindergarten and first grade, boys and girls became reluctant to engage in intergender activities. Social control mechanisms, such as "rituals of pollution" and "borderwork" (Thorne 1986), reinforced intragender activities as the socially acceptable norm.[2] Also, peers often viewed intergender activities as romances, which made them highly stigmatized and therefore difficult to maintain. Elementary school boys sometimes picked out one girl that they secretly "liked," but they were reluctant to spend much time talking with her or to reveal their feelings to anyone for fear of being teased. When these secrets did get out, children were made the butt of friends' jokes. Most boys, whatever their popularity, were only interested in the select girls from the popular group.

Sometime during the fourth or fifth grade, both male and female students began to renegotiate the social definition of intergender interactions. . . . During the later elementary years it generally became more socially acceptable for the members of male and female groups to engage in intergender interactions. This took the form of boys talking with girls in the protected enclave of their social group. They would tease girls or ask them silly or awkward questions. They sometimes wrote anonymous prank letters with their friends to girls they secretly liked, asking or challenging these girls about "mysterious" features of puberty.

By the sixth grade, boys began to display a stronger interest in girls, and several—usually the most popular boys—initiated cross-gender relations. As Mr. Clark, a fifth-grade teacher, remarked: "The big thing I think is that they are with the girls. They've got some relationships going with the girls in the class, whereas the less popular group does not have that at all."

As Fine (1987) notes, sexual interest is a sign of maturity in preadolescent boys, yet it is problematic for inexperienced boys who are not fully cognizant of the norms involved. For safety, boys often went through intermediaries (cf. Eder and Sanford 1986) in approaching girls to find out if their interests were reciprocated. Rarely were such dangerous forays made face-to-face. Boys gathered with a friend after school on the phone to call girls for each other, or passed notes or messages from friends to the girl in question. When mutual interest was confirmed, they then asked the girl to "go" with them. . . .

Boy-girl relations posed considerable risks by representing "innovative situations" (Lyman and Scott 1989) that called for displays of coolness. Yet when a boy went with a girl, he was free to call her on the phone at home and to invite her to a boy-girl party, to a movie, or to the mall with another couple or two.

Once the connection was established, boys pressured each other to "score" with girls. Boys who were successful in "making out" with girls (or who claimed that they were) received higher status from their friends. . . .

Boys who were successful in getting girls to go with them developed the reputation of being a ladies' man and gained status among their peers.

Academic Performance

The impact of academic performance on boys' popularity was negative for cases of extreme deviation from the norm, but changed over the course of their elementary years for the majority of boys from a positive influence to a potentially degrading stigma.

At all ages, boys who were skewed toward either end of the academic continuum suffered socially. Thus, boys who struggled scholastically, who had low self-confidence in accomplishing educational tasks, or who had to be placed in remedial classrooms lost peer recognition. One third-grade boy, for example, who went to an after-school tutoring institute shielded this information from his peers, for fear of ridicule. Boys with serious academic problems were liable to be called "dummies." At the other end of the continuum, boys who were exceedingly smart but lacking in other status-enhancing traits such as coolness, toughness, or athletic ability were often stigmatized as "brainy" or "nerdy."

The following discussion, by two fifth-grade boys, highlighted the negative status that could accrue to boys with excessive academic inclinations and performance:

GLEN: One of the reasons they're so mean to Seth is because he's got glasses and he's really smart. They think he's a brainy-brain and a nerd.

SETH: You're smart too, Glen.

GLEN: Yeah, but I don't wear glasses, and I play football.

SETH: So you're not a nerd.

Q: *What makes Seth a nerd?*

GLEN: Glasses, and he's a brainy-brain. He's really not a nerd, but everybody always makes fun of him 'cause he wears glasses.

In the early elementary years, academic performance in between these extremes was positively correlated with social status. Younger boys took pride in their work, loved school, and loved their teachers. Many teachers routinely hugged their students at day's end as they sent them out the door. Yet sometime during the middle elementary years, by around third grade, boys began to change their collective attitudes about academics. This coincided with a change in their orientation, away from surrounding adults and toward the peer group. Their shift involved the introduction of a potential stigma associated with doing too well in school. The macho attitudes embodied in the coolness and toughness orientations led them to lean more toward group identities as renegades or rowdies. This stance affected their exertion in academics, creating a ceiling level of effort beyond which it was potentially dangerous to reach. Boys who persisted in their pursuit of academics while lacking other social skills were subject to ridicule as "cultural dopes" (Garfinkel 1967). Individuals who had high scholastic aptitudes, even with other culturally redeeming traits, became reluctant to work up to their full potential for fear of exhibiting low-valued behavior. By diminishing their effort in academics, they avoided the disdain of other boys. One fifth-grade boy explained why he put little more than the minimum work into his assignments: "I can't do more than this. If I do, then they'll [his friends] make fun of me and call me a nerd. Jack is always late with his homework, and Chuck usually doesn't even do it at all [two popular boys]. I can't be the only one."

Not only did this diminished academic effort preclude boys' ostracism from popular groups, it also demonstrated support and solidarity for others less able than themselves. This functioned as a technique of collective face-saving. The group identity was managed so that "low achievers" were able to occupy positions of high status. Discussing the dynamics of boys' groups, Miss Moran, a fourth-grade teacher, stated: "It was like they all had that identity and they all hung together like none of us do it, none of us are gonna do it. If we do it, it's gonna be half, and if we do any better than half the job, then we're gonna give it to you on the slide."

Some boys who were scholastically adept tried to hide their academic efforts or to manage good performance in school with other status-enhancing factors so as to avoid becoming stigmatized. They gave their friends answers when friends were called on by the teacher, and were disruptive and off-task during instructional periods, socializing with their friends and occasionally playing the class clown. These behaviors nullified the label of "goody-goody" or "teacher's pet" by demonstrating a rebellious attitude to adult authority. Thus, by the second half of elementary school, the environment provided more of a social than the educational function for them, and this had a negative effect on their desire for academic success (cf. Coleman 1961).

GIRLS' POPULARITY FACTORS

The major distinction between the boys' and girls' status hierarchies lay in the factors that conferred popularity. Although some factors were similar, girls used them in a different manner to organize their social environment. Consequently, they had different effects on their status hierarchies.

Family Background

As with the middle school girls studied by Eder (1985), elementary school girls' family background was one of the most powerful forces affecting their attainment of popularity. Their parents' socioeconomic status and degree of permissiveness were two of the most influential factors.

SOCIOECONOMIC STATUS (SES). Maccoby (1980) suggests that among the most powerful and least understood influences on a child are the parents' income, education, and occupation. In general, many popular girls came from upper- and upper-middle-class families. These students were able to afford expensive clothing, which was socially defined as stylish and fashionable. These "rich" girls had a broader range of material possessions, such as expensive computers or games, a television in their room, and/or designer phones in their room with their own separate line (some girls even had a custom acronym for the number). They also participated in select extracurricular activities, such as horseback riding, skiing, and vacation travel to elite locations. Some girls' families owned second homes in resort areas to which they could invite their friends for the weekend. Their socioeconomic status gave these girls greater access to highly regarded symbols of prestige. While less privileged girls often referred to them as "spoiled," they secretly envied their lifestyle and possessions.

Two fourth-grade girls in the unpopular group discussed the issue of popularity versus unpopularity:

ALISSA: If your mom has a good job you're popular, but if your mom has a bad job then you're unpopular.

BETTY: And if, like, you're on welfare, then you're unpopular because it shows that you don't have a lot of money.

ALISSA: They think money means that you're great, you can go to Sophia's [a neighborhood "little store" where popular people "hang out"] and get whatever you want and stuff like that. You can buy things for people.

BETTY: I have a TV, but if you don't have cable [TV] then you're unpopular, because everybody that's popular has cable.

Family background also influenced girls' popularity indirectly, through the factor of residential location. Neighborhoods varied within school districts, and girls from similar economic strata usually lived near each other. Not only did this increase the likelihood of their playing together, and not with girls from other class backgrounds, but the social activities in which they engaged after school were more likely to be similar, and their parents more apt to be friends. In addition, the differences in their houses could be considerable, intimidating some and embarrassing others. One girl, who lived in one of the poorer areas in the district, referred to the houses of her classmates as "mansions." When she invited these girls over to her house, she had difficulty bringing them into her room, since her clothes were kept in cardboard Pampers boxes, out of which her mother had fashioned a dresser. As her mother remarked: "I think sometimes it's a lot easier for Angela to just play with the neighborhood girls here than to try to make friends with some of the other girls in her class. They're popular, and they do all the fun things that Angela wants to get involved with, but it's hard for her when they come over here and stare. . . . And she knows she can't afford to do all the things they do, too."

Thus, although there were some popular girls who were not affluent, for the most part they came from families with high socioeconomic status. Girls believed that having money influenced their location in the social hierarchy.

LAISSEZ-FAIRE.   Laissez-faire refers to the degree to which parents closely supervised their children or were permissive, allowing them to engage in a wide range of activities. Girls whose parents let them stay up late on sleepover dates, go out with their friends to all kinds of social activities, and who gave them a lot of freedom while playing in the house were more likely to be popular. Girls who had to stay home (especially on weekend nights) and "get their sleep," who were not allowed to go to mixed-gender parties, who had strict curfews, or whose parents called ahead to parties to ensure that they would be adult "supervised" were more likely to be left out of the wildest capers and the most exclusive social crowd.

Whether for business, social, or simply personal reasons, permissive or absentee parents oversaw the daily nuances of their children's lives less closely. They had a less tightly integrated family life and were less aware of their children's responsibilities, activities, and place in the social order. These girls had a valuable resource, freedom, that they could both use and offer others. They were also the most likely to spend time socializing away from the house or to organize activities with their friends that others perceived as fun and appealing. Their freedom and parental permissiveness often tempted them to try out taboo activities, which was a source of popularity among peers. Their activities sometimes served to make the group a wild or fast crowd, further enhancing their status.

In some instances, girls who received less support or supervision in their home lives developed an "external locus of control" (Good and Brophy 1987) and became major figureheads in the popular crowd. Using the peer group as a support mechanism, they manipulated others in the group to establish their central position and to dominate the definition of the group's boundaries. These ringleaders could make life difficult for members of their own clique, as Diane, one member of the fifth-grade popular group. . . , lamented:

"I've really been trying to break away from Tiffany this year because she can be so mean, and I don't know when I go in to school everyday if she's been calling up other girls talking about me behind my back and getting everybody against me or not. Like, if I don't call everyone in my clique every night, I might find myself dropped from it the next day. Or she might decide at school that I've done something she doesn't like and turn everyone against me. That's why I'd like to break away from her, but I'm afraid, because she controls everybody and I wouldn't have any friends."

Physical Appearance

Another powerful determinant of girls' location in the stratification system was their physical attractiveness.[3] Others have noted that appearance and grooming behavior are not only a major topic of girls' conversation but also a source of popularity.[4] The norms of popular appearance included designer clothing, such as Calvin Klein, Gap, Banana Republic, and J. Crew. In the upper grades, makeup was used as a status symbol, but as Eder and Sanford (1986) note, wearing too much makeup could inhibit a girl's social mobility since other members of the group were highly critical of this practice. Finally, girls who were deemed pretty by society's socially constructed standards were attractive to boys and had a much greater probability of being popular. . . .

A group of five second-grade girls had bad feelings about another girl in their class because they felt that she was popular and they were not:

JEN: It's just that she has a lot of money but we don't, so it's like that's why she has the prettiest clothes and, you know, the prettiest makeup.

LIZ: And she thinks, like, she's the prettiest girl in the whole school. Just because she's blond and all the boys like her.

ANITA: And she thinks only she can have Erin [a well-liked girl] as her friend and not even us, she doesn't even play with us, and that's not very nice.

The perception that popularity was determined by physical traits was fully evidenced by these second graders. These aspects of appearance, such as clothing, hairstyles, and attractiveness to boys, were even more salient with the girls in the upper grades. As an excerpt from one of our field notes indicated: "I walked into the fifth-grade coat closet and saw Debby applying hairspray and mousse to Paula's and Mary's hair. Someone passed by and said, 'Oh, Mary I like your hair,' and she responded, 'I didn't do it, Diane did it.' It seemed that Diane, who was the most popular girl in the class, was socializing them to use the proper beauty supplies which were socially accepted by the popular clique. I asked what made girls unpopular, and Diane said, 'They're not rich and not pretty enough. Some people don't use the same kind of mousse or wear the same style of clothing.'" . . .

Social Development

As with the boys, the most precocious girls achieved dominant social position but they were also more sensitive to issues of inclusion and exclusion. Precocity and exclusivity were crucial variables in influencing girls' formation of friendships and their location on the popularity hierarchy.

PRECOCITY.   Precocity refers to girls' early attainment of adult social characteristics, such as the ability to express themselves verbally, an understanding of the dynamics of intra- and intergroup relationships, skills at convincing others to see things their way and manipulating them into doing what they want, and an interest in more mature social concerns (such as makeup and boys). As with the boys, these social skills are only partly developmental; some girls just seem more precocious from their first arrival in kindergarten.

Mrs. Appleyard, a teacher, discussed differences in girls' social development and its effects on their interactions: "Communication skills, I can see a definite difference. There is not that kind of sophistication in the social skills of the girls in the unpopular group. The popular kids are taking on junior high school characteristics pretty fast just in terms of the kinds of rivalries they have. They are very active after school, gymnastics especially. Their conflicts aren't over play as much as jealousy. Like who asked who over to their house and who is friends. There is some kind of a deep-running, oh, nastiness as opposed to what I said before. The popular group, they seem to be maturing; I wouldn't call them mature, but their behavior is sophisticated. The unpopular girls seem to be pretty simple in their way of communicating and their interests."

The most precocious girls showed an interest in boys from the earliest elementary years.[5] They talked about boys and tried to get boys to pay attention to them.[6] This group of girls was usually the popular crowd, with the clothes and appearance that boys (if they were interested in girls) would like. These girls told secrets and giggled about boys, and in class and in the halls they passed them notes that embarrassed but excited the boys. They also called boys on the phone, giggling at them, asking them mundane or silly questions, pretending they were the teacher, singing radio jingles to them, or blurting out "sexy" remarks.

When Larry. . . was in third grade, he described the kinds of things a group of popular girls said to him when they called him on the phone: "Well, usually they just call up and say like, 'This is radio station KNUB, and we're here to call you,' but sometimes they say things like, 'Babe will you go out with me tonight,' or one time Jim [his brother] answered the phone and they said, 'Get your sexy brother on the phone right now.' And one time last year when we were out to dinner, they called and filled up our whole phone machine with messages, around twenty of them, and my mom had to call their moms and tell them to stop it."

Girls who did not participate in these kinds of interactions often looked down on these girls as boy-crazy, but the interactions sharpened the interest of the boys. While boys could not let their peers know they liked this, they appreciated the attention. The notice they repaid to the girls then enhanced these girls' popularity (cf. Schofield 1981).

By around fourth to sixth grade, it became more socially acceptable for girls to engage in cross-gender interactions without being rebuked by peers. The more precocious girls began to experiment further with flirting with boys, calling them on the telephone, "going" with them, going to parties, and, ultimately, dating. Although some were adventurous enough to ask a boy out, most girls followed traditional patterns and waited for boys to commit themselves first. Kara, a popular fourth grader, described what it meant to "go" with a boy: "You talk. You hold hands at school. You pass notes in class. You go out with them, and go to movies, and go swimming. . . . We usually double-date."

In the upper grades, if a girl went with a popular boy, she was able to achieve a share of his prestige and social status. Several girls dreamed of this possibility and even spoke with longing or anticipation to their friends about it.[7] When popular girls went with popular boys, this reinforced and strengthened both parties' status. This was the most common practice, as one fifth-grade girl noted, "It seems that most of the popular girls go out with the popular boys; I don't know why." One fourth-grade girl referred to such a union as a "Wowee" (a highly prestigious couple), because people would be saying "Wow!" at the magnitude of their stardom.

Yet to go out with a lower-status boy would diminish a girl's prestige. Three fourth-grade girls responded to the question "What if a popular girl went with an unpopular boy?"

ALISSA: DOWN! The girl would move down, way down.

BETTY: They would not do it. No girl would go out with an unpopular boy.

LISA: If it did happen, the girl would move down and no one would play with her either.

A high-status girl would be performing a form of social suicide if she interacted with a low-status boy in any type of relationship whatsoever. While girls acknowledged themselves as very sensitive to this issue, they doubted that a popular boy's rank in the social hierarchy would be affected by going with a girl from a lower stratum. They thought that boys would not place as much weight on such matters.

EXCLUSIVITY.   Exclusivity refers to individuals' desire, need, and ability to form elite social groups using negative tactics such as gossiping, rumormongering, bossiness, and meanness. There were one or two elite groups of girls in each of the grade levels who jointly participated in exclusionary playground games and extracurricular activities. This formed clearly defined social boundaries because these girls granted limited access to their friendship circles.

In one fourth-grade class, a clique of girls had such a strong group identity that they gave themselves a name—the Swisters—and a secret language. Three of the members talked about their group:

ANNE: We do fun things together, the Swisters here, um, we go roller skating a lot, we walk home together and have birthday parties together.

CARRIE: We've got a secret alphabet.

ANNE: Like an "A" is a different letter.

DEBBIE: We have a symbol and stuff.

ANNE: But we don't sit there and go like mad and walk around and go, "We're the Swisters and you're not, and you can't be in and anything."

CARRIE: We don't try to act cool; we just stick together, and we don't sit there and brag about it.

This group of girls restricted entrée to their play and friendship activities, although they did not want to be perceived as pretentious or condescending. Many girls in the less popular groups did not like the girls in the highest-status crowd, even though they acknowledged their popularity (cf. Eder 1985). One sixth-grade girl, Melody, who was in an unpopular group remarked that "with a few exceptions, most of the girls in the fifth grade are snobby, and with the sixth grade most of them are snobby too, especially Carol, but they're popular. That might be what makes them popular."

Two lower-status fourth-grade girls commented further on the girls' social hierarchy:

BETTY: The popular girls don't like the unpopular girls.

Q: *Why not?*

LAUREN: Because they don't think they look good and don't dress well, and Anne, Carrie, Debbie, and all those guys have an attitude problem.

Q: *What do you mean?*

ALISSA: An attitude problem is just coming in to impress people and like beating people up constantly or being really mean.

BETTY: If you're not popular, you mostly get treated like you're really stupid. They stare at you and go, "Uhhh." Like if someone does something bad, then the popular girl will tell all the other popular girls, and they'll go, "Oh, I hate you, you're so immature." Then they'd tell their whole gang, and then their whole gang won't like you one bit.

Thus, one of the most common forms of boundary maintenance among friendship groups, both intra- and interclique, involved the use of rumors and gossip (Parker and Gottman 1989). Shared secrets were passed among friends, cementing their relational bonds (Simmel 1950), while derisive rumors were told about outsiders. During class, many of the girls were preoccupied with passing notes to one another. These behaviors primarily involved the girls in the popular cliques, who often derided the girls in the unpopular groups. Such tactics served not only to separate the groups but also to maintain the popular crowd's position at the top of the social hierarchy. As Simmel (1950, 314) notes, "The lie which maintains itself, which is not seen through, is undoubtedly a means of asserting intellectual superiority and of using it to control and suppress the less intelligent (if intelligence is measured as knowledge of the social situation)."

Academic Performance

In contrast to the boys, elementary school girls never seemed to develop the machismo culture that forced them to disdain and disengage from academics. While not all popular girls were smart or academic achievers, they suffered little stigma from performing well scholastically. Throughout elementary school, most girls continued to try to attain the favor of their teachers and to do well on their assignments. They gained status from their classmates for getting good grades and performing difficult assignments. The extent to which a school's policies favored clumping students of like abilities in homogeneous learning groups or classes affected the influence of academic stratification on girls' cliques. Homogeneous academic groupings were less common during the early elementary years but increased in frequency as students approached sixth grade and their performance curve spread out wider. By fifth or sixth grade, then, girls were more likely to become friends with others of similar scholastic levels. Depending on the size of the school, within each grade there might be both a clique of academically inclined popular girls and a popular one composed of girls who did not perform as well and who bestowed lower salience on schoolwork.

These findings on gendered peer cultures accord well with other research. Studies of elementary school children have pointed out that girls value social and nurturant roles (Best 1983; Borman and Frankel 1984) while beginning to focus on appearance and romantic issues (Eisenhart and Holland 1983). Boys have been found to gain status from competitive and aggressive achievement-oriented activities, with an emerging interest in the later grades in romance (Best 1983; Eisenhart and Holland 1983; Goodwin 1980a, 1980b, Lever 1976). Yet our research suggests that many of these peer focal concerns arise and become differentiated earlier than has been previously shown—in elementary school rather than adolescent gendered cultures. Thus, girls we observed were already deriving status from their success at grooming, wearing the "right" clothes, and other appearance-related variables; social sophistication and friendship ties; romantic success as measured through popularity and going with boys; affluence and its correlates of material possessions and leisure pursuits, and academic performance. Boys, even in the predominantly white, middle-class schools that we studied, were accorded popularity and respect for distancing themselves from the deference to authority and investment in academic effort, and for displaying traits such as toughness, troublemaking, domination, coolness, and interpersonal bragging and sparring skills.

Discussion Questions

1. Why do you think that popularity is measured so differently for boys and girls?
2. What do the authors mean by savior faire? Why do you think it was important for boys?
3. Why do you think that girls are less likely to be penalized socially for academic performance?
4. Were the factors discussed by the Adlers similar to your preadolescent experience of popularity? Were there other important factors that the authors did not observe in their study?

Notes

1. Many other scholars also note the importance of athletic ability to popularity; see Coleman (1961), Eder and Parker (1987), Eitzen (1975), Fine (1987), Schofield (1981).
2. Rituals of pollution refer to inter-gender activities where each gender accuses the other of having "germs" or "cooties." Thorne (1986, 174–175) notes that girls are perceived as being more polluting than boys, and this anticipates and influences cross-cultural patterns of feminine subordination.
3. Dion and Berscheid (1974) note that friendship choices are often based on physical attractiveness. Dodge (1983) and Young and Cooper (1944) correlate low physical attractiveness with social rejection.
4. See Coleman (1961), Eder and Sanford (1986), Eder and Parker (1987), and Schofield (1981).

5. Simon, Eder, and Evans (1992) note that having a boyfriend enhances girls' popularity.
6. In the second grade, a group of popular girls, whose ringleader was extremely precocious, phoned boys on a regular basis. They asked them silly questions, giggled, and left long messages on their telephone answering machines. At one school outing, the dominant girl bribed a boy she liked with money and candy to kiss her, but when he balked at the task (after having eaten the candy and spent the money), she had to pretend to her friends that he had, so as to avoid losing face.
7. One girl even lied to her friends, pretending that she was going with a popular boy. When they found out that she had fabricated the story, they dropped her; so she lost both her status and her friends.

References

Berentzen, Sigurd. 1984. *Children's Constructing Their Social Worlds*. Bergen, Norway: University of Bergen.

Best, Raphaela. 1983. *We've All Got Scars*. Bloomington: Indiana University Press.

Borman, Kathryn M., and J. Frankel. 1984. "Gender Inequalities in Childhood Social Life and Adult Work Life." In *Women in the Workplace*, edited by S. Gideonse. Norwood, N.J.: Ablex. pp. 55–83.

Cahill, Spencer. 1994. "And a Child Shall Lead Us? Children, Gender, and Perspectives by Incongruity." In *Symbolic Interaction: An Introduction to Social Psychology*, edited by N. J. Herman and L. T. Reynolds. Dix Hills, N.Y.: General Hall. pp. 459–469.

Coleman, James. 1961. *The Adolescent Society*, Glencoe: Free Press.

Corsaro, Willam A. 1985. *Friendship and Peer Culture in the Early Years*. Norwood. N.J.: Ablex.

——— 1979. "Young Children's Conceptions of Status and Role." *Sociology of Education* 52:46–59.

Dion, Karen K. and Ellen Berscheid. 1974. "Physical Attraction and Peer Perception among Children." *Sociometry* 37:1–12.

Dodge, Kenneth A. 1983. "Behavioral Antecedents of Peer Social Status." *Child Development* 53:1386–1399.

Eder, Donna (with Catherine C. Evans and Stephen Parker). 1985. "The Cycle of Popularity: Interpersonal Relations among Female Adolescents." *Sociology of Education* 58:154–165.

Eder, Donna, and Maureen T. Hallinan. 1978. "Sex Differences in Children's Friendships." *American Sociological Review* 43:237–250.

Eder, Donna, and Stephanie Sanford. 1986. "The Development and Maintenance of Interactional Norms Among Early Adolescents." In *Sociological Studies of Child Development*, vol. 1, edited by P. A. Adler and P. Adler. Greenwich, Conn.: JAI. pp. 283–300.

Eisenhart, Margaret A., and Dorothy C. Holland. 1983. "Learning Gender from Peers: The Role of Peer Groups in the Cultural Transmission of Gender." *Human Organization* 42:321–332.

Eitzen, D. Stanley. 1975. "Athletics in the Status System of Male Adolescents: A Replication of Coleman's *The Adolescent Society*." *Adolescence* 10:267–276.

Fine, Gary Alan. 1981. "Friends, Impression Management, and Preadolescent Behavior." In *The Development of Children's Friendships*, edited by S. Asher and J. Gottman. New York: Cambridge University Press. pp. 29–52.

——— 1987. *With the Boys*. Chicago: University of Chicago Press.

Garfinkel, Harold. 1967. *Studies in Ethnomethodology*. Englewood Cliffs, N.J.: Prentice-Hall.

Good, Thomas L., and Jere E. Brophy. 1987. *Looking in Classrooms*, 4th ed. New York: Harper and Row.

Goodwin, Marjorie H. 1980a. " 'He-Said-She-Said:' Formal Cultural Procedures for the Construction of a Gossip Dispute Activity." *American Ethnologist* 7:674–695.

——— 1980b. "Directive/Response Speech Sequences in Girls' and Boys' Task Activities." In *Women and Language in Literature and Society*, edited by S. McConnell-Ginet, R. Borker, and N. Furman. New York: Praeger. pp. 157–173.

Gunnarsson, L. 1978. *Children in Day Care and Family Care in Sweden*. Stockholm, Sweden: Department of Educational Research.

Joffe, Carol. 1971. "Sex Role Socialization and the Nursery School: As the Twig Is Bent." *Journal of Marriage and the Family* 33:467–475.

Lever, Janet. 1976. "Sex Differences in the Games Children Play." *Social Problems* 23:478–487.

Lyman, Stanford, and Marvin Scott. 1989. *A Sociology of the Absurd*. 2d ed. Dix Hills, N.Y.: General Hall.

Maccoby, Eleanor. 1980. *Social Development*. New York: Harcourt Brace Jovanovich.

Miller, Walter. 1958. "Lower Class Culture and Gang Delinquency." *Journal of Social Issues* 14:5–19.

Parker, Jeffrey G., and John M. Gottman. 1989. "Social and Emotional Development in a Relational Context." In *Peer Relationships in Child Development*, edited by T. J. Berndt and G. W. Ladd. New York: Wiley. pp. 95–131.

Passuth. Patricia. 1987. "Age Hierarchies within Children's Groups." In *Sociological Studies of Child Development*, vol. 2, edited by P. A. Adler and P. Adler. Greenwich, Conn.: JAI. pp. 185–203.

Schofield, Janet W. 1981. "Complementary and Conflicting Identities: Images and Interaction in an Interracial School." In *The Development of*

Children's Friendships, edited by S. Asher and J. Gottman. New York: Cambridge University Press. pp. 53–90.

Simmel, Georg. 1950. *The Sociology of Georg Simmel*, translated and edited by K. Wolff. New York: Free Press.

Simon, Robin, Donna Eder, and Cathy Evans. 1992. "The Development of Feeling Norms Underlying Romantic Love among Adolescent Females." *Social Psychology Quarterly* 55:29–46.

Thorne, Barrie. 1986. "Girls and Boys Together, But Mostly Apart: Gender Arrangements in Elementary Schools." In *Relationships and Development*, edited W. Hartup and Z. Rubin. Hillsdale, N.J.: Lawrence Erlbaum. pp. 167–184.

Thorne, Barrie, and Zella Luria. 1986. "Sexuality and Gender in Children's Daily Worlds." *Social Problems* 33:176–190.

Weber, Max. 1946. "Class, Status, and Party." In *From Max Weber*, edited by H. Gerth and C. W. Mills. New York: Oxford University Press.

Young, L. L., and D. H. Cooper. 1944. "Some Factors Associated with Popularity." *Journal of Educational Psychology* 35:513–535.

Exchanges, Labels, and Put-Downs
MURRAY MILNER, JR.

INTRODUCTION

The difficulty of negotiating cliques and peer groups in early adolescence has been well documented. In his ethnographic study within a school, Murray Milner applies sociological concepts of status and mobility to understand why kids can be cruel to one another. Not unique to kids' experience, Milner explores how being in the closed social system of a school means that the opportunities for status are limited. Rather than simply being mean-spirited, young people jockey for position in a unique social environment.

My life has been full of incident: I have met well-known people, including Salvador Dali (mad, but shrewd) and Prince Charles (shorter than you would imagine), many exciting women (including an actress who almost received an Oscar), yet here in Hollybush [Michigan] my whole life is seen to be defined by the high school senior trip of 1966.

—JUSTIN CARTWRIGHT, 1998

From The Lunchroom: Melanie began telling stories about talent show auditions. Apparently, she is in charge . . . of choosing the acts. She made fun of an [Asian] Indian girl who did a dance, saying it didn't even look like an Indian tribal dance at all, and standing up and imitating her. She said the girl had bells on her skirt and an Indian costume where you couldn't see her face . . . She and two other girls "couldn't look at each other or else they would start cracking up." Melanie also talked about other acts . . . including a freshman named Patrick who apparently wears a skirt to school. She said he played a guitar and sang. Then she imitated how horrible he was. She talked about a girl [singer] . . . "She is the one who" and then made a gesture imitating big breasts. "They call her Foxy Brown." Boy #1 said, "No, they should call her Big and Brown." [The observer remarks]: " . . . they are probably one of the more popular junior groups . . . They talked about people behind their backs; ritually insulated, and imitated people during most of the lunch period." . . .

INALIENABILITY

If a robber says, "Your money or your life," most people hand over their cash. But if a robber says, "Your status or your life," people are likely to become very apprehensive—he must be insane. They could not give him their status if they wanted to. In this sense, status is inalienable. In high schools, the handsome football player or the beautiful cheerleader cannot give someone else their status—much less sell it to them. Stated in other terms, changing or exchanging status is difficult, and therefore converting other resources directly into status is problematic. One can, of course, gain or lose status by acquiring a status-relevant social position, but the status acquired is compromised if it is gained by illegitimate means. The nobleman who gains the crown by murdering the existing king and his heirs, the bourgeoisie who buys a title of nobility, or the candidate who wins by bribing election officials are looked upon with suspicion and disdain. Or conversely, the opposition leader or social critic who is imprisoned for obvious political reasons may officially be a criminal, but in the eyes of many becomes a hero. The point is not that economic and political resources are never used to manipulate status, but that the very nature of status makes this problematic.

This relative inalienability of status has several important implications for the nature of the social structure. First, it is the reason that social exchange in status systems is both limited and tends to be implicit or indirect. Second, it is one reason that status systems tend to be stable and have restricted mobility.

Exchange, Conversion, and Money

A note is required about the significance of exchange, conversion, and money. Clearly, having the resources to buy fashionable clothes, drive a cool car, and go to the "in" places is a big advantage. But it is important to see that economic resources are primarily a means and not the basis of status. The student who goes to school waving his bank statement around and bragging that he or his family has lots of money, only lowers his status. Wealth is an effective means to status only when converted into appropriate status symbols. Even then simply buying the right things is not enough. One must be able to develop the right personal style and the appropriate associations to be accepted. As one student noted, "Buying the right clothes did not automatically increase your status, but it served as one way to keep some people out. People who believed that they were cool simply because they wore expensive clothes were often the butt of many private jokes." Moreover, exchanges between individuals must be implicit. The boy who is too blatant about wooing girls with gifts and lavish entertainment becomes suspect—not to mention the girl who is too obviously influenced by such things or resorts to such tactics herself.

In the case of exchange and conversion, approvals or disapprovals that are bought or coerced are greatly devalued if not meaningless. Those who hire yes-men and flatterers are looked upon with derision, as are those who sell their services in this way. The same is true of prostitutes and their clients, and regimes that use torture to get confessions or pay for false testimony. The motives of the beautiful young woman who marries the rich old man are suspect, and there is "no fool like an old fool." These various examples indicate that for status to be valuable, it must be rooted in relatively authentic expressions of approval and disapproval. Consequently, conversion of force or material resources into status is problematic. A well-known movie among teenagers is entitled *Can't Buy Me Love*.[1] Made and set in the 1980s, it is the story of the stereotypical nerd who hires the beautiful popular girl to go out with him. His status skyrockets and he becomes one of the coolest guys in the school. They begin to fall in love—transforming their "arrangement" into an authentic relationship—only to be disgraced when their peers discover how the whole thing started. Of course, in good Hollywood fashion, they work through this trouble and supposedly live happily ever after. Even the Hollywood versions of adolescent culture recognize the limitations on exchange and conversion of other resources into status.

None of this is to argue that wealth is not important or that the class and status of a student's family are irrelevant. Rather, I am arguing that the effect of these background resources on a student's status *within a given school status structure* are mainly indirect and mediated through conformity to the student norms in a particular school. Obviously, family resources play a crucial role on where you live and which school you are likely to attend. They also affect a student's ability to engage in implicit exchange with other students; the low-income student cannot offer friends a ride in a new cool car. Nonetheless the link between family background characteristics and status among one's peers is not especially strong and is largely mediated through lifestyle norms.

Stability and Mobility

Once status systems become well established, they are relatively stable. Adolescents repeatedly report the difficulty of changing their status once their peers have categorized them. There is general agreement that "a person's rank was mainly determined during their first year" [of high school]. A girl from a District of Columbia suburb reports, "Social groups within the freshman classes started to be formed. These groups remained relatively stable throughout all four years . . ." Another student qualifies this slightly: "By sophomore year, the [high-status group] had basically determined who was going to be 'cool' for the next three years." A sophomore in high school says: "I don't really think that there is a way to change your status because who you start to hang out with when you begin high school is who you end up with at graduation . . . Once you are labeled by the students and the teachers as belonging to one group or another group, that status does not change throughout your high school experience." A student from an all-girls Catholic high school reports, "At the beginning of the freshman year there were not too many bonds formed, so mobility and change was widely accessible. But as the years passed, accessibility became more difficult for those few that wanted to change groups." A student who attended an all-male Catholic school reports the same: "It is hard to think of how hard it was to move from one group to another." Like in the caste system, and apparently most institutionalized status systems, mobility is highly restricted. Frequently, however, the stability and the absence of mobility are exaggerated. There were cases of women who "bloomed" or men who became star athletes rather late, and consequently experienced considerable upward mobility. Occasionally, popular students disgraced themselves. Most of the mobility that does occur involves movement from middle status categories to categories just above or below. As we shall see later, boundaries weaken as students move into higher grades and are less salient in certain more pluralistic schools. For the most part, however, after the first year or so, status is relatively fixed for most people in most schools.[2] What is even clearer is that many students perceive that changing identities and crossing boundaries is difficult.

There is an individual and psychological aspect of this tendency toward stability. The initial rejections that many adolescents experience in middle school and the early years of high school shape how these students see themselves. If someone is a late bloomer and not particularly attractive their freshman year, this objective reality limits their opportunity to conform to the norms of their peers. Typically they are excluded from the highest status, most popular groups. This initial objective experience then shapes their subjective sense of themselves, which may in later years limit them as much or more than their own looks or the actions of others. . . . One student describes how early social definitions become personal identities.

> Early definitions of the groups were hard to overcome. I know that by my senior year, I would have interacted well with the popular group, and I also know that they would have been fairly accepting. Despite these two facts, I never made much of an effort to break into that social crowd because I still felt a distinctive separation from it . . . In my mind the popular group was inherently exclusive and I therefore did not have a chance of successfully interacting within it. Because I had this prejudice, I did not even try to break into the group. I ended up excluding myself.

This is the report of a white middle-class student from Alaska. It seems likely that these effects are even stronger for those from lower-class or minority backgrounds, who have often experienced a long history of being rejected by those of higher status.[3]

This stability, however, involves more than limited mobility for individuals. Rarely are there dramatic changes in the relative status of different categories. In no school that we know about are cheerleaders and athletes the "in crowd" one year, only to be replaced by computer geeks and drama students the next year. The categories and the relationship between categories are relatively stable over time. None of this means that there is no mobility or that the rankings of social categories are natural or immutable. Nor am I suggesting that an individual's status cannot change quickly, for example, by being disgraced or winning a famous prize. In most situations, however, the inalienability of status makes status systems *relatively* stable.

INEXPANSIBILITY

. . . The total amount of status available to a group. . . (is) largely inexpansible, in contrast to goods and services or force. Status is primarily a relative ranking. If everyone received A's or had Mercedes these would not have much status value.

More on Mobility

The concept of inexpansibility of status further enriches our understanding of several of the key characteristics of high school status systems. First, in conjunction with the notion of inalienability, it helps us comprehend why mobility is so difficult in high school status systems. Because status is relatively inexpansible, those who initially gain high status are very reluctant to improve the status of inferiors by associating with them. Intuitively they know that allowing others to move up threatens their own position. So, the concepts of inexpansibility and inalienability help us to see why, in most high schools, very few people are able to change their status or their group ties after the first or second year.

This is not to say that people do not try to change their status. A few succeed as the following account indicates:

> My friend had been a member of the Brain groups since elementary school, but beginning in the eighth grade and continuing through high school, he persistently pursued acceptance by the Preps. His family background and dress were quite similar to theirs, yet they were reluctant to accept him. He was fairly good friends with a couple of Prep girls, but still not a group member. In an effort to prove to

them he could be like them, he changed his appearance slightly by wearing nicer shirts, such as polos and oxfords . . . He gradually distanced himself from his old friends and continually "kissed-up" to the Preps . . . He spent two and a half years striving to become one of the Preps. Surprisingly enough, he was successful and became one of them by the time we reached the end of junior year. His success became evident when he won a spot on the student council and was the student announcer for the morning announcements our senior year.

Clearly one of the prerequisites of this success was a willingness to distance himself from old friends.

Another girl, in a quite different school, reports on a similar attempt that was less successful:

As we got older, about the end of the tenth grade, a group of girls began to move ourselves away from our normal crowd . . . My two best friends, Sarah and Marry, and I were getting bored with hanging out at the mall and going to the movies every weekend. The three of us and a few other girls felt the draw of the popular crowd. We were ready to drink and socialize with the popular girls and date the more attractive guys. Unfortunately, it was not easy to break into the popular crowd. We attended a couple of the popular crowd's parties because we would tag along with Mary's popular older brother John when he went out. But we never reached the stage where we felt that we could just show up at parties and be accepted as regular members.

She goes on to recount how this attempt at upward mobility involved not only withdrawing from old relationships, but also denigrating former friends and contributing to their downward mobility.

For us to move up, we felt that we had to distance ourselves from our former friends and push them down. My friends and I would not defend our old friends when the popular kids called them dorks merely because they did not drink or because they attended the Governor's magnet school . . . for science. We just laughed . . . and agreed with their insults. We wanted to distance ourselves from our old friends so that the popular kids would see that we were nothing like them. In the end, I think my friends and I that broke away merely reestablished ourselves as the normal group and . . . downgraded our friends to the smart nerd category. . . .

Put-Downs and "Small Cruelties"

The fact that status is inexpansible has an additional implication. If lowers moving up threaten those above, the inverse is true; you can move up by putting others down. This is one reason put-downs are such a common phenomenon among adolescents. In his book *Cool*, Marcel Danesi notes the prevalence of "small cruelties." He focuses on those that involve the criticism of someone's body, for example, "Hey, fatso."[4] While these "small cruelties" often refer to characteristics of the body, the phenomenon is much more general and fundamental. Terms like "put down," "make fun of," "trash," and "dump on" . . . occur with considerable regularity in school settings. More accurately, most local adolescent cultures have more "up-to-date" synonyms for these concepts.

Both (my) observations . . . and the descriptions from other high schools provide many examples of this phenomenon. On the mild side was the treatment of low-status peers who showed up in public places frequented by the elite: "Those who were not 'cool', that showed up at the park, were not included, ostracized, and even teased." The treatment of others is frequently much harsher. One girl from an East Coast metropolitan area reports, "The struggle for popularity was a harsh one, with back-stabbing by supposed 'friends' . . . and the banishment of one person by another based on the need to find one's own level of popularity."

Most common is the tendency of friends and clique members to say snide things about those who are not members of their group. Even if the outsiders are not present, such put-downs lower their status and discourage those who are present from associating with them, or even treating them with routine respect. One of our field observers recorded the following incidents:

> Kate and Ellen were joking with Robert about having found him a date for the dance. I did not catch the name of the girl they were making fun of, but they told him that he could go with "that big, fat, blonde girl." This inspired Robert to start making jokes about the trouble he would have wrapping his arms around the girl and to laugh about how she would roll over him.

This was a put-down of both the "fat blonde girl," but also a subtle dig at Robert. He ignores the innuendo by playing along with the "joke." While Kate may have been particularly inclined to put others down, it was by no means restricted to her. Our field observer continues, "There was an overweight girl whom I have never seen before who was sitting at the table for the first few minutes of the period. After she left, everyone expressed their gratitude that 'the bitch was gone . . .'" These incidents are reported from a school that, relatively speaking, is low on hierarchy and status differentiation.

Such behavior is not restricted to the inner-city or public schools. A student who attended a relatively small and well-to-do Christian academy in a major Southern capital reports:

> Ritual insulting was common. The most popular boys were capable of cleverly using language to formulate the perfect insult. They devised nicknames for everyone they did not like. These nicknames brought individuals into the spotlight and heavily influenced their status. "Betty Spaghetti" went on to a successful social career. "Yoshi" and "Salmon Boy" became isolates . . . Low-status boys . . . participated in ritual insulting in a more vicious and indiscriminate way.

Nor was viciousness in this school restricted to the boys. The popular girls "practiced ritual insulting, mocking each other and those less popular, attractive, or fashionable." The former student of this Christian academy was struck by what she called "the brutality of their commentary." Physical aggression was also used to keep people in their place. High-status boys would gang-tackle and rough-up others "in an isolated hallway out of the view of the administration . . ." "New football players were cruelly hazed and freshman boys tried to avoid locker rooms where they could be cornered and dunked in a toilet."

Predictably the tendency is for those of higher status to insult those of lower status and this motivated the latter to minimize interaction. A young woman from a small coastal town in the East says, "If a higher status person talked to a lower status person then they were usually out to embarrass them. A lower status person usually avoided high status people for this reason."

Harassing the Weak

Preps often make fun of nerds. A northern Virginia female says, "The 'cool kids' had many ways of making themselves distinctive; the first and most obvious was labeling everyone else . . . with names like prude, dork, geek, dweeb, bamma . . . which instantly made you a social outcast."

More generally those who are most vulnerable usually receive the most verbal and physical harassment. In some situations, students officially designated as academically weak were stigmatized. A student from a small rural community says that the "slow" students

> . . . were made to attend classes separate from the rest of the students and were given various labels that coincided with each new trend developed by educators to make them feel less inferior . . . [T]hese labels were used by other students to demean the "slow" students and differentiate them from "normal" students. It is no surprise that many of these students eventually dropped out.

One of the most troubling things is the aggressive harassment of the physically or mentally handicapped. A student from Texas reports:

> The retarded students socialized only with each other, and were pretty much made fun of by all the normal students. For example, during class changes, all of the retarded students stood outside their classroom and watched everyone walk by. The sad part is that they were oblivious to the fact that almost everyone passing by made fun of them in some sort of way. They tried to participate in extracurricular activities, such as going to the Homecoming Dance and football games, but yet again just hung around each other. Most students felt they had special needs and should not be in public schools as they were.

In the relatively egalitarian school in which we conducted extensive fieldwork, an observer reports: "Then a mentally disabled boy walked by who Angela called 'Funky Butt' because of the way he walked. She then started to make up songs about him."

A female with a physical handicap from a well-to-do community in New Jersey reports, "Those students with physical disabilities tend to be mocked . . . The learning disabled are not popular and are seen as stupid dorks who wear ugly clothes. Special education students have classes in a separate part of the school, and teachers assume they are troublemakers."

On theoretical grounds, I would predict that harassment of the weak is more common from those just above them or those who are wannabes rather than from the highest status students. The top elites of a social system rarely carry out the persecution of the lowly—even though they may instigate it. One of the points of being elite is to have stooges do the dirty work for you. We did, however, observe cases where relatively high status students engage in this behavior. Overall our data is ambiguous on this point and further research is needed to clarify the matter.

In short, "small cruelties" and "meanness" are extremely common.[5] Why are teenagers so mean? This is due to the centrality of peer status in school settings and the competition that results for a largely inexpansible resource.[6] In the competition for status, people (especially leaders), often vacillate between being nice and being mean, depending on whether they see the other person as a supporter or as a threat. Conversely, followers are usually nice to those above them in the hope of being accepted as an intimate, and hence raising their status. At the same time, they often resent the deference they have to show. Frequently, those with high status are talked about and envied, but disliked.[7] From the leader's point of view, followers of high status are essential, but they pose a threat and from time to time must be "put in their place." This, of course, may turn them into enemies rather than supporters. To further complicate things, if those of high status hold others at too much of a distance, they run the risk of being labeled snobs. In sum, high status requires the careful management of social distance and intimacy. These contradictions and dilemmas often lead to treating others positively in one context and negatively in another. Often this involves two-facedness and backbiting.

My key point, of course, is that such behavior is not primarily rooted in a particular stage of biological and psychological development, but is largely the result of the social context.[8]

But if teenagers are mean to those who are roughly equals because they are competitors for an inexpansible resource, why are they mean to those who offer no threat at all? Some of the most demeaning behavior is directed toward those who are the weakest and most vulnerable. Why does cruelty to the handicapped raise someone else's status? Beating a much weaker team does not raise the status of the victor much. I suspect that the primary motivation for picking on the weak is not because it directly raises the aggressor's status. One psychological and two social processes probably contribute to the victimization of the weak. First, in an atmosphere where put-downs and verbal aggression are common, there is probably a definite tendency to displace hostility by scapegoating the vulnerable.[9] This mechanism has been widely alluded to as a reason for the persecution of minority groups.[10] Second, in a context where verbal aggression is common and even admired, the vulnerable offer an opportunity to hone and display one's skills without risking significant retaliation. Third, in a system where the content of many of the norms is obviously highly arbitrary—as is the case with fashion and style—an even higher value is placed on conformity. Deviance must be persecuted lest it call into question the basic assumptions of the normative structure. Many handicapped students do deviate considerably from the norms of other students. Apparently, this is seen as highly threatening and is punished. These ideas are offered as tentative hypotheses to explain what seem like "senseless" cruelties. The broader theoretical point is that the inexpansibility of status has a number of direct and indirect consequences on behavioral patterns. None of this means that such cruelties are unavoidable or inevitable, but it does suggest that they are likely, given how we currently organize our schools.[11]

Exclusion and Inclusion of the Weak

There is also a tendency for the weakest members of the group to be the most isolated. This is not limited to the handicapped. In August B. Hollingshead's classic study *Elmtown's Youth*, which was initiated in the 1940s, he reports:

> [P]ersons in each class try to develop relations with persons a class higher in the status structure than themselves. Conversely, the higher-class person, on average, tries to limit his contact with persons of lower status than himself in order to not be criticized for "lowering himself." This process operates in all classes, but it is especially noticeable in contacts with class V. This class is so repugnant socially that adolescents in higher classes avoid clique and dating ties with its members.[12]

The treatment of Untouchables in the Indian caste system is an even more extreme version of this. In the past they were forced to live outside the village, excluded from temples, forbidden to use the village wells, and forced to carry out the most menial tasks, such as removing dead animals and cleaning out latrines. In general, they were shunned by everyone else. . . .

On the other hand, rarely is the isolation of the lowly solely a matter of persecution; they often do deviate in ways that are at best insensitive to others. This is not infrequently true of handicapped students. A fieldworker reports on an incident involving a special education student who had some kind of mental handicap:

> One specific incident that occurred toward the end of the period while the girls were around was the ridicule of Louis. Louis was distinct in the group because he was the only black person and overweight. When I asked a girl who he was she said, "He is Louis. No one really likes him, but he always hangs around during

lunch. He is foul." Louis had been the center of ridicule throughout lunch but he seemed to bring it on to himself. At one point, Louis pulled out a condom. He started to swing it around and got the girls worked up and the boys laughing. He then put his mouth to it and blew it up like a balloon. All of the girls shrieked and the boys thought that that was so funny. Word got around to the whole group, even those who were not watching the incident. Laura stood up and told a friend who was approaching the group to let her know what Louis had done. Louis then dropped the condom and walked away. An adult walked up to the area and Louis nonchalantly picked up the condom and threw it away in the trashcan. The adult remained standing in the area for most of the remaining lunch period.

Hence, reducing the exclusion and isolation of the lowest strata—even handicapped students in schools—is rarely simply a matter of reducing inequality and changing the prejudices of higher status strata. This is, however, a crucial prerequisite to greater inclusion and solidarity.[13]

Gossip

Gossip is a particularly common and powerful means to inflict small cruelties. . . . Others have studied the content and structure of gossip in some detail.[14] Gossip is evaluative talk about a person who is not present. . . . Unless a high status member of the group immediately contradicts a negative remark, it tends to be seconded and elaborated by other members of a group, both those of high status and those of low status. An obvious question is why gossip tends to be so negative and often malicious—even when it is about close intimates. Why do people rarely gossip about how well someone else did on a quiz or how pleasant he or she is? First, if one is inclined to praise someone, it can be done in public—even with the person present; it does not require their absence, as is the case with gossip. Second, because of the in-expansibility of status, praise of others tends to lower one's own status. Conversely, putting them down tends to accomplish the opposite—especially if others join in.

If the point is to raise one's own status, put-downs are most useful if they lower the status of those who are status equals or superiors. But publicly criticizing such people can be dangerous; it motivates them to retaliate. Precisely because they have equal or superior status their put-downs are as likely to be just as successful as the instigator's. Hence, secrecy is needed. This encourages people to be two-faced and go behind others' backs. If others really respect someone, criticizing them can be a risky act of deviance. Hence, the company of those who are likely to agree is needed. Consequently, most gossip occurs between those who are relatively intimate and considered trustworthy.

A very important kind of respect and status comes from one's close peers, and the rivalry can be intense. Sibling rivalry is the most obvious case, but gossip about close friends is another. The result is that gossip is often about another intimate who is not present, and is frequently associated with backstabbing and backbiting. A fieldworker reports:

> This group almost always had gossip, often about their own members who weren't there at the time. This was not done only playfully, but often was somewhat malicious. For instance, when it was discovered that Karen had egged Kate's car, everyone turned against [Kate] and insulted her seeming inability to stand up for herself. Yet, the next week, Susan was talking about [Kate] as if they were great friends again. I found it sort of odd that so much backbiting went on within this seemingly close-knit group.

Not all gossip is about close friends. Frequently, gossip is a form of forced intimacy, that is, people being intimate when it is not wanted. Gossip does not involve forced physical intimacy, as in the case of throwing food, but rather forced cognitive and emotional intimacy. But what is the motivation for such behavior? Why would people want to be intimate with someone who rejects them? There seem to be two key motivations. One is to reduce the status of someone by making public his or her deviant behavior. This is usually directed toward rivals or high status individuals who are viewed as snobbish and as needing to be "brought down a notch or two." An alternative motivation is to raise one's own status by publicly displaying one's intimacy with someone of higher status. Even if the person who spreads the gossip does not have direct contact with the high status person, it shows that they have their "sources"—that is, they are tied into the network of higher status people.

Web-based bulletin boards are becoming a new means of public ridicule popular among teenagers. This is, of course, a great magnification of gossip written on the walls of toilet stalls. These means of gossip do not require that it be restricted to trusted intimates because retaliation is unlikely since the perpetrator is anonymous. Such Websites often amount to near-permanent public slander, which is potentially available to large audiences. It is becoming an increasing matter of concern to students, teachers, and parents.[15]

Gossip and storytelling are closely related. Having gossip or a juicy story to tell is also a way of gaining the group's attention and making one's self the center of the group's activities, as well as lowering someone else's status. I recorded the following in my field notes:

> About this time John asked Linda whether she likes Luke. She said, "Well, not really. He treats me nice but we're not really friends." John then said, "Well, you'll like to hear this because he's really 'going down.'" He repeated the theme of "going down" several times laughing about it. When they asked why, he said that Luke's girlfriend was going to beat him up. Apparently on a band [bus] trip . . . someone suggested . . . that they share their most secret fantasies [by writing them down] . . . Luke wrote down, "Every night I dream of fucking Sally [someone other than his girlfriend]." Predictably—and maybe this was part of a plot all along—the paper was grabbed and passed around the bus. John took great relish in recounting these various events of the bus trip. Jane expressed the general opinion of the group that anyone who would write down such fantasies was stupid and deserved to be embarrassed.

This incident illustrates in a slightly different way the significance of gossip and storytelling and how one blends into the other. Telling a good story is, in part, a source of status for the storyteller, but it is also usually a way to lower the status of someone else.

In sum, like earlier work we found that gossip was common and usually negative. This is rooted in the struggle for status and respect—even among intimates—that is accentuated because of the relative inexpansibility of status.

Group Mobility: The Effect of Age and Grade

Earlier I discussed the difficulty most individuals face in changing their initial status or crowd—due to the inalienability and inexpansibility of status. On the other hand, the distribution of status across grades, and the fact that most students will change grades each year, means that there are certain forms of built-in mobility.

David Kinney's study of "Nerds to Normals" looked at students' transition from middle school to high school.[16] In middle school, students were either members of the popular crowd or they were shunned and excluded and given a negative label such as nerds or geeks. But when these same students made the move to high school many of the former nerds were able to make the transition to normals. Because of the greater number and variety of both students and extracurricular activities there was a larger array of peer groups, while those who had been nerds could find friends that would treat them as normal. Moreover, high school students were generally less judgmental of their peers than middle school students. This same decline in the intensity of status differences seems to continue as students move through high school.

Not surprisingly, students are especially preoccupied with their status during the early years of high school. A girl from suburban Boston says:

> During the first two or three years of high school students, were very conscious of the status of the particular group to which they belonged, and various groups did very little intermingling. For instance, a "cooler" or more popular student rarely formed a friendship or even acknowledged a friendship with a less popular student . . . The strict barriers around different cliques made it very hard for students to get to know students [from other social groups] well.

Even some freshmen are aware of this pattern:

> Susan began to explain to me how the freshmen class was very clique-oriented and that although the different groups sometimes associated with one another, there was often tension between them. She seemed very mature and said that, "By the time the students reached their senior year, the cliques became less apparent and the class interacted more as a whole." She said that she was friends with many upperclassmen, and that "on the whole, they were much more accepting of each other." She explained, "You don't have to look or act a certain way to be someone's friend by the time you enter twelfth grade."

Part of this anticipated change will result from physical and psychological maturation.[17] In addition to physical and psychological considerations, the social status of freshmen is relatively fluid. Students see both great opportunity and danger, and hence are more concerned about their status. But these well-known factors are exacerbated by a structural consideration that is often overlooked: First- and second-year students as a group have low status relative to other students and so collectively these lower grades have less status to go around. This makes the competition for that status especially intense. As time goes on their status becomes crystallized and they become resigned, if not reconciled, to their social position. But in addition, the competition and emphasis on differentiation lessens as the status of the class as a whole gradually increases. A student from Pennsylvania makes the following observations about her senior year: "The senior class as a whole became such a high status group that even [vocational/technical students] and nerds were reassimilated back into the general fold of simply 'a senior' . . . [T]here was just less drive to increase individual status as the class as a whole was so high . . ." This student attended a medium-sized, rural high school. The shift toward class solidarity may have been more extensive than in other settings, but students in most schools report these same tendencies. In short, because status is relatively inexpansible, and because its distribution is skewed in favor of the upper grades, competition and preoccupation are especially acute in the early years of high school and less so in later years. Data dealing with a different aspect of school life supports this interpretation. Anthropologist Frances Schwartz found that students in high ability classes were much more cooperative and less hostile toward one another than students in low ability classes.[18] Obviously various things could contribute to this. Nevertheless, the relative inexpansibility of status and scarcity of respect for students in lower-status classes almost certainly adds to their competitiveness and aggressiveness.

The higher status of older students is probably the most important social factor affecting the declining significance of status. A second social factor is the extensive common activities and rituals of solidarity during the senior year: senior trips, senior-class gifts to the school, senior picnics, the senior prom, and usually a whole array of graduation-related events. A girl from an urban Catholic school in Texas recalls, "As senior year rolled around the groups became more welcoming and open because of the bonding events that the school sponsored, such as retreats, community days, and intramurals [i.e., competitions between the senior and junior classes]."[19]

A third important consideration is a shift in the types and arenas of power that are relevant. Most seniors have more money to spend than in previous years, in part because many have part-time jobs. Many become eligible to vote. Some are courted by colleges and offered scholarships. That is, status in their peer group is no longer the only kind of power that is available. A key assumption of the theory is that the patterns associated with status groups and caste will be especially strong where status is insulated from other forms of power. As this condition begins to break down, the power of these patterns declines accordingly. Stated in slightly different terms, seniors begin to both acquire and anticipate other forms of power, and hence the relevance of the high school status system declines.

To summarize, the behaviors characteristic of status systems in general and teenagers in particular occur because of the nature of status as a resource. Status is relatively inalienable. It cannot be easily appropriated or simply transferred from one person to another. Because status is relatively inalienable, status identities and status systems tend to be relatively stable once they have become well established. Therefore changing status or status groups after the first or second year in a school is difficult.

Status is also relatively inexpansible. If someone moves up in the status structure, someone else will have to move down. Similarly if a social category gains higher status, another category will lose status. Conversely, one way to move up is to put others down. These characteristics of status help explain a number of behaviors typical of status systems in general and teenagers in particular, including: extreme concern to maintain boundaries and limit mobility; the "small cruelties" toward those who are vulnerable, including the handicapped; the frequent use of negative and even malicious gossip—even about close intimates; and the greater concern with status and cliques. The theory of status relations, and more specifically the concepts of the inalienability and inexpansibility of status, offers systematic explanations for all of these phenomena in the sense that they can be seen as parts of a broader pattern rooted in the nature of status and status groups.

Discussion Questions

1. How are status systems established in school?
2. What is "inexpansibility" according to the author?
3. According to the author, what are the purposes of gossip and put-downs?
4. Was the social environment in the school Milner studied similar to your experience? If so, why, and if not, why not?

Notes

1. Touchstone Pictures, 1987, starring Patrick Dempsey and Amanda Peterson, directed by Steve Rash.
2. One longitudinal study found that between the 7th grade and the 12th grade, more than 50 percent of the students changed crowds, though this may or may not be representative of most schools. Cited in Brown, Mory, and Kenney (1994), "Casting Adolescent Crowds in a Relational Perspective," 161. The data collected at two points in time by Franzoi and his colleagues (1994), "Two Social Worlds," indicates that there is very low downward mobility out of the highest groups and very little upward mobility out of the highest groups and very little upward mobility out of the lowest groups, but considerable mobility between the middle groups and those above and below. The findings from Franzoi et al. are, however, built upon a sociometric measure of status that divides groups into the categories of popular, controversial, average, neglected, and rejected. It is doubtful, however, that the findings are solely due to this measure. The pattern that is reported roughly parallels what we know about occupational mobility in modern societies. See David L. Featherman and Robert M. Hauser (1978), "A Refined Model of Occupational Mobility," chap. 4. The rates of entry and exit to the top and bottom are even lower in high school status structures, which are rooted in interpersonal status differences and less tied to income and political power. This is what the theory of status relations would lead us to expect.
3. In addition to the language often associated with symbolic interactionism, which often focuses on the social construction and interpretation of social and personal identities, most introductory psychology textbooks have discussions of the "primacy effect," and other psychological mechanisms that bias actors' cognitions, attitudes, and behaviors. See, for example, Wortman, Loftus, and Weaver, III (1997), *Psychology*. These are probably some of the psychological and cognitive mechanisms that operate in the processes described by reproduction theory that reinforce restricted social mobility. I do *not*, however, mean to suggest that the social expectations or self-image of lower status students' personal identities are the key source of the low rates of mobility that could be remedied by various techniques aimed at increasing self-esteem.
4. Danesi (1994), *Cool*, 49.
5. The most extensive studies of bullying have been carried out by Olweus (1993), *Bullying at School,* in Norway. He found that bullying is more common among girls than boys and that it declines with the age of the student. Between 5 and 6 percent of students in grades 7–9 reported being bullied, but nearly 12 percent of boys in secondary school reported that they engaged in bullying others. There was a clear tendency for smaller, weaker, and shy students to be victims. While Olweus did not find

that academic competition led to bullying, he did not specifically look at competition for informal peer status. With respect to girls, see Simmons (2002), *Odd Girl Out*, and the journalistic account by Talbot (2002), "Mean Girls and the New Movement to Tame Them."
6. Adler and Adler's (1998), *Peer Power*, an account of behavior in the preadolescent years, portrays behavior that seems to be at least as mean and cruel as that characteristic of adolescents. It is clear from their account that most of this is rooted in the struggle for status and social relationships. What appears to be different is that the norms of "niceness"— which make the most blatant forms of nastiness counterproductive—are less developed prior to secondary school. This may well be due to the fact that the cliques and crowds are much more gender segregated than in high school.
7. See Eder and Kinney (1995), "Effects of Extracurricular Activities on Adolescents' Popularity," and Eder et al. (1995), *School Talk*, esp. chap. 4, for a discussion of the ambiguous feelings students have about those who are popular.
8. Merten (1997), "The Meaning of Meanness," has identified similar processes among Junior high school girls and has discussed these in terms of "the meaning of meanness." See also Eder et al. discussion of "targeting the low end of the hierarchy" in (1995), "Effects of Extracurricular Activities on Adolescents' Popularity," 49–54. My discussion is certainly indebted to their work.
9. Allport defines scapegoating in (1948), *ABC's of Scapegoating*, as "a phenomenon wherein some of the aggressive energies of a person or a group are focused upon another individual, group, or object; the amount of aggression and blame being either partly or wholly unwarranted." See also Allport (1954), "Choice of Scapegoats," esp. chap. 15.
10. While scapegoating is often directed toward economic or political competitors, it is nearly always expressed in terms of status considerations. The discrimination against blacks by white workers is usually justified in terms of the moral failings of blacks: They are characterized as lazy, dirty, immoral, unreliable, etc.
11. Children in many less developed countries who are physically deformed are severely teased and harassed. An organization named Operation Smile is specifically devoted to providing reconstructive surgery to children in such situations primarily because of the intense harassment they suffer from peers. Apparently this tendency of children and adolescents to attack the vulnerable is extremely widespread—cutting across cultures and historical periods. This does not mean that it is impossible to reduce the rates of such behavior.
12. Hollingshead (1975), *Elmtown's Youth*, 178.
13. Over the last quarter century, there has been a strong movement to integrate students with various kinds of mental and physical disabilities into the

general school population. The intent, of course, is to reduce their isolation and sense of being "other." For a moving portrayal of the need to treat the mentally handicapped as "normal" human beings, see Edgerton (1993), *The Cloak of Competence*.

Given adolescents' (1) acute status consciousness, (2) judgmental attitudes toward most kinds of nonconformity, and (3) reluctance to associate with anyone of lower status, it is at least debatable whether this move toward inclusion of "special education" students in comprehensive high schools has increased or decreased the negative stigmatization they experience. As the above description indicates, such students can be aggressive in seeking attention and contribute to some of the very stereotypes that their integration with the general school population was intended to overcome. These comments are not intended to argue for the isolation of such students, but rather to point to the very mixed consequences of such policies—given the current structure of most high schools.

14. While my discussion focuses on different issues, it is highly indebted to Eder and Enke's (1991), "Structure of Gossip." Because we were not allowed to record conversations, I did not attempt to replicate or extend their approach.

15. Guernsey (2003), "High School Confidential, Online."

16. Kinney (1993), "Nerds to Normals."

17. It is usually assumed that as adolescents mature, they are less insecure about their own personal identity, and hence less judgmental of others and less concerned about being exclusively identified with the "right" social group. It seems likely that this is the case. See Kinney (1993), "Nerds to Normals." This may be less important than is assumed. Brown, Eicher, and Petries (1986), "The Importance of Peer Group Affiliation in Adolescence," studied variation in attitudes toward crowd membership by age and gender. They found that the importance of the crowd declined as the students aged. However, the importance of crowd affiliation was *not* related to the students' sense of identity, but was related to their willingness to conform and their position in the crowd. This may suggest that social factors may have more impact on the importance of crowd affiliation than psychological attributes, though this is a very tentative hypothesis.

18. Schwartz (1981), "Supporting or Subverting Learning."

19. Collins's (1988), *Sociology of Marriage and Family* theory of interaction ritual is again relevant here.

Crude Comments and Sexual Scripts

DONNA EDER, CATHERINE COLLEEN EVANS, AND STEPHEN PARKER

INTRODUCTION

Eder and her colleagues conducted an ethnographic study at a midwestern middle school and found that the environment was laden with sexual teasing. They note that through interaction with their peers, males gradually learn that acceptance means talking about females and sex in a very aggressive manner. Being masculine in this environment means being sexually dominant and viewing females as objects. In this setting girls also learn that status comes from sexual teasing, especially of boys and girls who are less popular and do not conform to gender norms.

Many of the boys in [our] study were beginning to define themselves in relation to girls in the school or to girls more generally. We will see later that girls were developing a view of male–female relationships that both challenged and conformed to traditional heterosexual relationships. We saw fewer challenges to stereotypical notions on the part of boys, however. We also found that their shared orientation toward girls was primarily based on sexuality and that only a few boys admitted to having romantic or affectionate feelings toward girls.

Many studies have commented on the sexual (as opposed to romantic) focus of boys' orientation toward girls in adolescence. What was striking in our study was the *nature* of this sexual focus and the ways in which the boys were actively shaping each others' views about sexuality. It was clear that many boys began adolescence with a nonaggressive orientation toward sexuality that took the social context into account. In the following episode one of the most verbally aggressive boys in the school, Hank, reveals some sensitivity to the importance of situational factors when discussing sexuality. However, the pressures to be sexually active and competitive transform his orientation into a much more impersonal one.

Sam was acting as a messenger from Hank to the girls. They wanted him to come down to their group, but he didn't want to. Joe told Hank that he was crazy not to; that she [Cindy] might want to fuck him on the other side of the school. Hank said he [Joe] was stupid; that wasn't going to happen and that nothing was going to happen. He added that it might if they were alone, but not with everyone around. Someone said that he didn't know how and didn't even want to fuck her. Hank got mad and said, "I'll fuck her anytime—right here, right now, any time, anyplace." [Steve's notes]

At first Hank indicated that the public setting of the school is not appropriate for sexual intercourse. After someone challenged his sexual abilities and interests, he moved to a much more impersonal and aggressive stance regarding sexuality, where timing and location become irrelevant. Since Hank had a reputation for being tough and competitive, it is not surprising that he responded so strongly when accused of lacking sexual knowledge and interest. It is likely that Hank's reaction was based largely on fear of losing status among his peers. This illustrates the way in which even boys who may appear to be inherently aggressive are influenced to become even more aggressive, in this case in the sexual arena, through insults and challenges from peers.

These boys' view of sexuality is clearly being shaped by their more general view that boys should be tough and domineering. The sensitivity Hank initially demonstrated was replaced by a much more impersonal stance toward sexuality, one in which the feelings of girls are disregarded in the attempt to demonstrate one's sexual prowess and aggressiveness. This corresponds with the general competitive orientation of "winning at all costs." It also reflects the perceived lack of need to be sensitive to other people's feelings. Now this attitude is being transferred to boys' newly developing relationships with girls.

Boys were also expected to defend their "sexual property" aggressively. This further reflects the tendency to define sexual activity as another type of rivalry in which boys compete with other boys for conquests. Within this framework it is acceptable for boys to make sexual advances toward other boys' girlfriends, since it is up to the boys whose "property" has been invaded to defend their territory. In the following episode, a boy who fails to stand up to a competitor is negatively evaluated by his peers.

Perry and Richard walked over behind Tammy, and Perry acted like he was grabbing her bottom. Richard went ahead and actually did it. She turned around, but didn't retaliate in any way. They came back over to the table and retold what had happened. The point they stressed was that Carl (who was going with Tammy) was standing there when they grabbed her. After Richard grabbed her, Carl took a step toward Richard and said his name. Richard stuck his chest forward and said, "What?" Carl just backed down. Consensus was that Carl was a pussy. Hank and Joe were the most outspoken about this. [Steve's notes]

Even though Carl made some initial attempt to defend his girlfriend from unwelcome sexual advances, he was criticized for not continuing to stand up to a possible confrontation with Richard. At the same time, Richard was not criticized for making a sexual advance toward someone else's girlfriend. These responses support sexual prerogative and promiscuity for boys, while reinforcing a view that girls are sexual objects to be fought over. The responses also illustrate how girls are viewed as territorial property to be violated when challenging another boy's masculinity.

These boys appear to be applying the standards of aggressiveness and competition which they have learned to their newly formed relationships with girls. Studies of older male athletes and fraternity members found that women were often referred to as objects of sexual conquests and were the targets of antagonistic sexual jokes.[1] Apparently this competitive, conquest orientation toward women continues to be the main orientation for many older male athletes and fraternity men. As girls and women are increasingly forced into the narrow, male-defined role of objects to be conquered and boasted about, they are at considerable risk of being the targets of displaced male aggression.[2]

SEXUAL TEASING

As mentioned previously, boys are expected to demonstrate their masculinity by controlling their emotions during insult exchanges. According to Peter Lyman, sexual teasing is also part of learning to keep one's cool.[3] Many of the boys in this study had learned how to keep their cool during insult exchanges, but few were able to control their anger over sexual teasing.

Teasing routines were typically more flexible than insult exchanges: teasing involved a much wider range of playful behavior, including mock threats, mock challenges, and imitations of verbal and nonverbal behavior. As with ritual insulting, the nature of the response to a teasing comment played a critical role in determining whether a playful tone was maintained.[4] There was a wider range of possible responses, from joking denials to self-mocking remarks, but the greater flexibility of teasing routines, as well as their less competitive structure, may have made it difficult for boys to know how to respond to their peers' teasing comments. Thus, in many cases boys responded to such remarks by getting angry and/or leaving the interaction.

> Kevin and Tom were both giving Mike a hard time about Patty wanting to go with Mike. He denied it, but he wasn't very convincing. Kevin said that he knew he was interested . . . , but Kevin and others just laughed and Kevin imitated Patty saying, "Oh Mike, don't leave. Stay with me and I'll let you do anything." Mike looked angry and walked away. [Steve's notes]

While overtly sexual teasing was most common, boys were also sensitive to being teased about their romantic interest in girls, especially if it included letting the girl involved know of their interest.

> Joe and Hank were asking Sam if he really liked some girl. I asked who it was and Eric told me I didn't want to know, insinuating that she was ugly. Sam denied all of this. Then Joe and Hank left the table to tell her that Sam liked her. This upset Sam, who called them assholes and said he was going to kick their butts. Joe ignored it, and Hank told him he could try if he wanted to. Later Sam was eating by himself at a table, and Joe asked why. Hank said it was because he was pissed about the girl. Sam said it was only because he was hungry and decided to get something to eat. Joe said, "Aah, poor Sam. Eating by himself cause his friends did him wrong." Then Hank and Joe sighed together a couple of times in fake sympathy. Sam acted like he didn't notice any of their actions. [Steve's notes]

While girls relied on empathy to limit the extent of unpleasant teasing, most boys appeared to believe that it was up to the target of the teasing to manage any unpleasant feeling that arose. Although Sam tried to let his friends know that they had taken the teasing too far, they ignored his physical threats and made fun of him for being so upset that he needed to isolate himself from the group. Again, the orientation toward "being tough" and "keeping one's cool" prevailed.

At times boys also made sexually teasing and insulting comments directly to girls. These comments implied that the only interest they or their friends had in girls was as sexual objects.

Cindy came over to the table and wanted to know who was throwing stuff. She addressed herself to Eric. Eric grabbed her arms when she got close. Joe told her that he wanted to eat her and grabbed her waist. She told him to let go. Joe said he changed his mind and walked away. Eric started pulling her down on his lap and told her, "Just a little more. I can almost see down your shirt." She got away, and, before she attacked Eric, Bobby called her over and started talking to her. She calmed down immediately. [Steve's notes]

Through their aggressive sexual comments and behaviors, these boys displayed their group's increasingly aggressive stance toward sexuality. These behaviors appeared to anger Cindy, who was about to respond by confronting Eric. Just at this point, a boy from a different peer group intervened and kept the interaction from escalating.

Barrie Thorne found that the elementary students in her study often had different interpretations of the same male-female interaction. What girls defined as a serious violation, boys often viewed as "just playing." It is likely that Cindy's view of Eric and Joe's behavior differed significantly from their view of it as "playful, harmless behavior." As Thorne notes, these differences persist—adult men and women often disagree about what should be viewed as sexual harassment and/or abuse.[5]

Sometimes the aggressive sexual stance demonstrated by boys made the targets so angry that potential romantic connections were broken. For example, one day a boy prevented a girl from responding to his friend's request to "go with him" by treating her as a sexual object.

She [Tammy] stopped at our group to say "hi" and waited until Richard said "hi" as well. She stood there smiling, and finally Richard said, "Well, what do you say—yes or no? Are you going to go with me? Come on and go with me." Sam then said, "Yeah, go with him. He just wants some." Tammy got mad and tried to hit Sam saying, "I'll give you some." She then turned and walked away from the group. Richard never got his answer. [Steve's notes]

Tammy offered a very effective response to Sam's sexual reference to Richard "wanting some" by transforming the meaning of "some" to her physical attack on Sam. However, while Tammy clearly let Sam know his comment made her angry, none of the boys, including Richard, sanctioned Sam's behavior. Instead, Richard missed out on an opportunity to form a relationship with Tammy, largely because his group's approach to sexuality was one that is alienating to most girls.[6]

In his study of fraternities, Lyman found that some men thought that sexual jokes are vulgar but necessary for strengthening male bonds. They did, however, feel it was a mistake to reveal their "crudeness" to women, since they did not think women were as accustomed to such lewd remarks. However, many sexual jokes and comments about girls and women such as those described here are not only lewd but also sexually oppressive in that they portray females as passive objects of male sexual desire and aggression.[7]

Occasionally, boys in the school commented on the crude or "gross" nature of another boy's remark. Since boys did not believe that others should limit their teasing or insulting remarks, the comments seldom had any effect on their behavior, as the next episode illustrates.

Kevin, Bobby, and Johnny were on one side of the group. Bobby got the attention of a girl who was sitting in another part of the cafeteria. When she looked at him, he said that Kevin liked her and wanted to get to know her. Kevin just ducked down so that he couldn't be seen. . . . Bobby kept this up and Johnny joined in. Then Joe

> joined in, saying "He likes you and wants your body. He wants your ass." Kevin said that was gross. Joe continued telling her that Kevin "wanted to put his prick up her shithole." Bobby and Johnny stopped talking to the girl at this point. I don't think they wanted to be connected with Joe's comments. Joe turned to Eric and asked if he had heard him. Eric said no and Joe repeated it. [Steve's notes]

Joe appears to have used this interaction as an opportunity to show off his ability to make crude and aggressive sexual comments to a girl, since he made a point of reporting his behavior to Eric. He was not willing to modify his behavior when Kevin told him he was being "gross," because he apparently saw more advantage in impressing other boys with the extent of his grossness. In this case, the girl was reduced to an object through which Joe could display his sexually aggressive stance. Because Joe's comments depersonalized Kevin as well the girl he was interested in and reduced the chances of a relationship starting, it is evident that boys as well as girls can be the victims of dominant boys' aggressive talk. Also, since Joe's behavior was unaffected by Kevin's sanction, the only option left for boys who have negative reactions to sexually aggressive talk is to distance themselves from the interaction.

In his study of older athletes, Michael Messner also found that some disapproved of the way girls were treated like objects, judged by their appearance, and spoken about in abusive language. Rather than trying to voice their complaints about these behaviors to the boys involved, however, they distanced themselves more from the jock culture during their later years in high school.[8] Again, the norms against setting limits on dominant boys' verbal behavior appear to be so strong that those boys who do object to the treatment of girls usually remain silent. Also, given the power of these norms, a boy would need to have extremely high status within a peer group in order to be able to challenge them successfully.[9]

GIRLS AS TEASERS AND INSULTERS

Boys tended to take the initiative in incidents of cross-sex insulting, but occasionally boys who were the only male members of girls' groups found themselves the targets of sexual teasing or insulting. Since teasing typically consisted of mocking comments, whether threats, challenges, or other remarks, girls frequently used teasing to make fun of traditional images of romantic and/or sexual relationships. Thus, just as collaborative storytelling was sometimes used by boys to resist traditional gender messages, girls frequently used teasing as a collective means for expressing resistance of and detachment from traditional roles. For example, one day several girls developed an extensive teasing episode based on the imaginary fatherhood of a male friend.

> The major joke that came up this period was that Laura had gotten pregnant and that Jerry was the father. All the girls kept saying this loudly and laughing about the idea. Some of them told Jerry. He yelled down toward them, asking them to clarify what they were saying about Laura. They said, "Laura's pregnant." Then he asked who they were saying was the father. They told him, "It's you; you are the father." Jerry immediately turned red and his eyes got bigger, though he was giggling. He said it wasn't true and was laughing as he did because the idea was such a ridiculous one. Given Jerry's small size, he obviously hasn't entered into puberty yet. Laura is rather tall and hefty and definitely looks several years older than Jerry. Then Laura came over and sat by Jerry. She teased him, too, by saying that everyone was embarrassing Jerry and that they should leave him alone. She grabbed him in a rather rough, yet teasing, manner as she said this. Everyone was laughing a lot. A male teacher came by and asked Jerry, "What kind of trouble

are you causing this time?" Several girls told him that "He got Laura pregnant." The teacher opened his mouth and pretended to be shocked. This made everybody laugh louder and made Jerry blush. [Cathy's notes]

Immediately after this episode, Laura took Jerry by the hand and pretended to be his mother, dragging him around as she might a small child, first jerking him in one direction and then in another. They continued to find amusement in this gender reversal, as did their peers.

In this case, the peer group used teasing to mock traditional sexual relationships by pretending that an older and larger girl has been sexually involved with a small boy. Following this scenario with a contrasting one—that of a mother with a small boy—underscores the mockery of the first scenario. Also, because it is clear that the girl has a greater power advantage in the mother role-play, the coupling of these two scenarios allows the girls to create an even safer context for experimenting with future male-female sexual roles.

In contrast to teasing, the sexual insults that girls directed toward boys were more likely to reinforce stereotypical gender concerns. As shown previously, girls as well as boys used homosexual labels to insult boys who did not appear to be tough or who spent time with girls rather than with their male peers. They also insulted boys by referring to their sexual inadequacy, including the small size of their genitals, as in the following example.

> Paul mentioned getting hit somewhere twice before today and Ali said, "Oh do you have anything worth getting hurt?" Ali thought this was really funny and repeated the episode to both me and to Patty. Paul was sort of embarrassed about this. Later on she said something else to him, and he said, "Oh, you've gone too far now." [Donna's notes]

It was ironic that even the boys whose company and attention the girls liked were at times insulted for the very behavior of sitting with them. In the following episode, Natalie initiated an insult exchange with Jimmy, a boy she was coupled with for a short time several weeks previously and would like to go with again. Several of the other girls in the group also liked this boy and had been playfully teasing him during much of the lunch period. While the flexibility of teasing routines easily allowed for many group members to join in, these girls found a way to make ritual insulting a more collaborative endeavor, with several girls constructing the insults aimed indirectly or directly at Jimmy.

Eighth Grade

NATALIE: How come he don't ruin your family life—is he sterile?

ELLEN: No, we was t—[Ellen breaks into laughter before finishing her sentence. Everyone else laughs too.]

NATALIE: Well? [Giggles]

GWEN: I don't know, ask him.

NATALIE: Jimmy, do you feel weird sittin' around with a bunch of girls?

ELLEN: Well, he's never gotten me pregnant yet so maybe he is.

RHODA[?]: No, he feels right at home. [Sentence less audible]

NATALIE: Okay, but

ELLEN: Natalie.

NATALIE: *Why?* You're around your own kind.

GWEN: He likes it. [Ellen and Rhoda repeatedly try to get Natalie's attention by saying her name.]

JIMMY: [to Natalie] Huh?

TRICIA: That's an insult. [There is a brief side conversation between Rhoda and Natalie.]

JIMMY: That would make you guys bad.

This insulting exchange was transformed into a collaborative activity by Natalie's first insult concerning Jimmy's sexual inadequacy, in the form of a question addressed to both Ellen and Gwen rather than being addressed directly to Jimmy. Before Ellen could finish her response, Natalie offered a second insult, this time about the weirdness of Jimmy's association with girls. Although this second insult was in the form of a question addressed to Jimmy, it was also responded to and expanded upon by other girls, including the questioner herself. All of the comments serve to further develop the theme of association with girls, saying "he feels right at home," that "you're around your own kind," and that "he likes it." Jimmy eventually offered a counterinsult, "that would make you guys bad," implying that they have incriminated themselves by claiming he is around his own kind. This insult turns the theme of similarity away from gender to being "bad," thus casting everyone into a deviant role.

This particular insult exchange is important in that it shows the creative way adolescents can alter the structure of insulting from a one-on-one duel to a more collaborative endeavor, with several girls uniting against one boy. The basic structure of responding to an insult with a counterinsult still remains, however, and thus this exchange serves to convey rather than challenge the message that there is something wrong with not always being sexually potent or with a boy choosing the company of girls.

It is somewhat surprising that girls would insult boys (especially boys they like) about spending time with girls. However, girls and boys seem to have some awareness of each others' main concerns and use these as the basis for their insults. Thus, girls as well as boys often fail to reflect on the messages implicit in the content of standard insults and therefore help to maintain the negative orientation toward girls that is a central aspect of some male peer cultures. In addition, they are reinforcing boys' concerns with heterosexuality and sexual performance in relationships with girls. By encouraging boys to avoid informal contact with girls and to prove themselves sexually, girls are negating the value of female companionship and reinforcing the primacy of boys as sexual actors. This shows that both girls and boys contribute to maintaining beliefs about male-female relationships that ultimately limit the options for everyone. . . .

A CULTURE OF SEXUAL AGGRESSION

Thus, many boys were developing a view of girls as sexual objects, not sexual actors. To the extent that girls become objectified, it is even easier to discount their feelings, including possible feelings of discomfort and humiliation. It is important to note that boys with very high status as well as those with low status developed this orientation toward girls. This finding seems to contrast with research on working-class Chicano men, which has claimed that negative views toward women and a machismo view of men are due largely to channeling social class conflict into the arena of gender.[10] If sexual aggression toward women is due only to suppressed anger from being at the bottom of a social hierarchy, we would expect to see such behavior predominantly on the part of the lower-status boys and men.

Instead, it appears that when toughness and competition are valued, boys and men at high as well as low status levels are encouraged by some of their peers to approach male-female relations competitively and/or aggressively. According to Victor Seidler, having sex is a way of proving one's masculinity. For many men, sex becomes another form of achievement as well as a way to assert power over women. Furthermore, Seidler claims that masculinity must continually be proven, since it relies on external validation rather than an inner sense of self. Thus, even high-status men might feel a need to prove their masculinity continually by having new sexual conquests.[11]

All these informal activities create taken-for-granted notions about male sexuality. Because the activities themselves are so routine, the messages they convey are often viewed as being "natural" or "typical" orientations toward sexuality and are seldom challenged. The only evidence of collective challenges we saw at Woodview was through the teasing routines initiated by girls, who used the mocking nature of this activity to make fun of stereotypical male-female sexual roles. While boys in the medium-high-status groups were much less likely than those in higher- or lower-status groups to engage in aggressive sexual behavior and, in general, were more sensitive to girls' concerns, they found few successful ways to challenge the sexist behaviors of their peers. On occasion they were berated for not being more aggressive in defending their "sexual property," and when their attempts to curtail the crude remarks of other boys proved ineffective, they tended to distance themselves from such behavior by sitting apart from them rather than persist in trying to stop it. At this age, at least, it appears that boys have few opportunities to effectively challenge messages regarding male sexuality as another arena for competition.

Only recently have researchers begun to identify these and similar behaviors in school settings from elementary to college level as being part of a culture of rape and sexual aggression. Nan Stein found that sexual harassment is a frequent public occurrence in elementary and secondary schools across the country, in small towns and large cities alike. "Examples of sexual harassment that happen in public include attempts to snap bras, grope at girls' bodies, pull down gym shorts, or flip up skirts; circulating 'summa cum slutty' or 'piece of ass of the week' lists; designating special weeks for 'grabbing the private parts of girls'; nasty, personalized graffiti written on bathroom walls; sexualized jokes, taunts, and skits that mock girls' bodies, performed at school-sponsored pep rallies, assemblies, or halftime performances during sporting events; and outright physical assault and even rape in school."[12] Like our findings, which link sexual aggression to other forms of aggressive behavior within the school environment, Stein sees these acts of sexual harassment as an extension of bullying behavior in which boys as well as girls are targets.

The girls Stein studied report having few effective strategies for dealing with sexual harassment. Their own attempts to end it are often unsuccessful, and adults often fail to take the problem seriously, or else ignore it altogether. As one fifteen-year-old wrote, "It was like fighting an invisible, invincible enemy alone. I didn't have a clue as to what to do to stop it, so I experimented [with] different approaches. Ignoring it only made it worse. It made it easier for them to do it, so they did it more. Laughing at the perpetrators during the assaults didn't dent the problem at all, and soon my friends became tired of doing this. They thought it was a game. Finally I wrote them threatening letters. This got me in trouble. But perhaps it did work. I told the school administrators what had been happening to me. They didn't seem to think it a big deal, but they did talk to the three biggest perpetrators. The boys ignored the administrators and it continued. And they were even worse."[13] Faced with little official response to this problem and limited options for dealing with it, girls as young as fourteen become resigned to sexual harassment. "I felt like the teacher (who was a man) betrayed me and thought I was making a big deal out of nothing. But most of all, I felt really bad about myself because it made me feel slutty and cheap. It made me feel mad too because we shouldn't have to put up with that stuff, but no one will do anything to stop it. Now sexual harassment doesn't bother me as much because it happens so much it almost seems normal. I know that sounds awful, but the longer it goes on without anyone doing anything, the more I think of it as just one of those things that I have to put up with."[14] . . .

Discussion Questions

1. How does this study demonstrate the importance of peers in understanding sexuality?
2. Based on the fact that both males and females used sexual teasing to bolster their status with peers, what do we learn about gender from this research?
3. Do you think the interactions in this middle school constitute sexual harassment? Why? If so, what do you think ought to be done about it?
4. Do you recall a similar level of sexual teasing in your early adolescence? If so, what impact did it have on your experience in school?

Notes

1. Michael Messner, "Like Family: Power, Intimacy, and Sexuality in Male Athletes' Friendships," in *Men's Friendships*, ed. Peter Nardi (London: Sage, 1992), 215–237; Lyman, "The Fraternal Bond as a Joking Relationship," 148–163.
2. Messner, "Like Family"; Lyman, "The Fraternal Bond as a Joking Relationship."
3. Lyman, "The Fraternal Bond as a Joking Relationship."
4. In her research on elementary students, Thorne found that teasing exchanges could move from being playful to being irritating or malicious and then back to being playful again (*Gender Play*). She notes that the multiple layers of meaning in teasing provide opportunities to try out certain messages while keeping the option of following back on other, safer meanings.
5. Ibid.
6. It is also possible that Sam purposely used this tactic of insulting a potential girlfriend to keep Richard from gaining status within this peer group through this new relationship.
7. Lyman, "The Fraternal Bond as a Joking Relationship."
8. Messner, "Like Family."
9. In contrast to our findings and those of others regarding boys' willingness to act aggressively toward girls as well as toward other boys at school, Canaan found that boys were only aggressive toward low-status boys (and not toward girls) in her study of a predominantly middle-class school ("Passing Notes and Telling Jokes"). She attributes this to the fact that girls were considered of only marginal interest to boys in this middle school and thus primarily served as an audience for observing male insulting and joking. The disparity between the findings in her study and ours could also reflect differences resulting from social class background, with sexual harassment and insulting beginning at earlier ages in mixed-class and working-class schools than in predominantly middle-class schools.
10. Maxine Baca Zinn, "Chicano Men and Masculinity," in *Men's Lives*, ed. M. Kimmel and M. Messner (New York: MacMillan, 1992), 67–77; Manuel Pena, "Class, Gender, and Maschismo," *Gender and Society* 5 (1991): 30–46.
11. Seidler, *Rediscovering Masculinity*.
12. Nan Stein, "No Laughing Matter: Sexual Harassment in K–12 Schools," in *Transforming a Rape Culture*, ed. Emile Buchwald (Minneapolis: Milkweed Editions, 1993), 313–314.
13. Ibid.
14. Ibid.

Gender Roles and Settlement Activities Among Children and Their Immigrant Families

ABEL VALENZUELA

INTRODUCTION

This article explores how girls and boys facilitate the establishment of permanent settlement in Mexican immigrant households. Through analysis of 68 interviews, the authors identify . . . three primary roles that children play: (a) tutors, when children serve as translators and teachers for their parents and younger siblings: (b) advocates, when children intervene or mediate on behalf of their households during difficult transactions or situations: and (c) surrogate parents, when children undertake nanny or parent-like activities. In addition, . . . girls participate more than boys in tasks that require detailed explanations or greater responsibility. Boys, despite their involvement in household activities, did not have the same responsibility roles as girls did. Finally, the eldest child, regardless of gender, often took the lead role in assisting and caring for younger siblings. . . .

This article explores the gendered ways in which girls and boys facilitate the establishment of permanent settlement among Mexican immigrant households. Immigrant settlement is a complicated process involving different circumstances, social ties, strategies, and economic well-being. With a few exceptions (Alarcón, 1995; Chávez, 1992; Hondagneu-Sotelo, 1994), we know little with regard to familial or household activities that help immigrant families settle in a new country, city, or community. We know even less about the role that children undertake in this process. Focusing on the specific roles that boys and girls undertake in aiding their household settlement helps us understand the role of children in different settlement processes and, equally important, how gender interacts with immigration. . . .

MEXICAN IMMIGRANT SETTLEMENT

Mexican immigration to the United States has been occurring, at least in a technical sense, since the Treaty of Guadalupe Hidalgo was signed at the termination of the Mexican and American war in 1848, which among many things, created the state of California. Since then, several important waves have characterized immigration from Mexico to the United States. At least since World War II, migration of people from Mexico has occurred in unprecedented numbers. In part, the Bracero Program,[1] which began in 1942 and terminated in 1964, helps us understand the large number of Mexican immigrants who attempted to migrate to the United States after 1965 when Congress terminated the National Origins Act that until then severely restricted legal immigration from the Western Hemisphere. As a result of these and other factors, Mexican immigration to the United States has been immense. Los Angeles is second only to Mexico City in the number of Mexicans residing in this metropolitan region. California, our country's most populous state by at least 10 million residents, has the largest number of Mexican- and Latino-origin people, which accounts for well over 29% of the total (State of California, Department of Finance, 1998). As a result, immigration studies have produced at least two strands of research: The first strand looks specifically at issues of Mexican immigrant settlement, and the second consists of generation studies that analyze outcomes (e.g., education, employment, psychological, incorporation) and other processes of the children of Mexican and other immigrants. . . .

Research on first-generation immigrant children or second-generation children (children born in the United States to immigrant parents) has similarly garnered . . . attention. Most of the work in this area looks at assimilation and adaptation processes of school-age children (Gibson, 1988; Portes, 1996; Rumbaut, 1997; Zhou, 1997), educational outcomes (Olsen, 1988; Rumbaut, 1990, 1996; Rumbaut & Cornelius, 1995; Vernez & Abrahamse, 1996), and psychological determinants, motivations, and achievement patterns as a result of immigration status (Suárez-Orozco & Suárez-Orozco, 1995). This last body of research does an exemplary job of exploring gender differences.

However, both of these two frameworks and their studies ignore children as actors in the day-to-day activities as well as in the more complex scenarios that immigrant households confront as families become settled and Americanized. For example, even though Chávez (1992) and Hondagneu-Sotelo (1994) analyze the processes of settlement and family formation, both ignore children's participation. Similarly, second-generation studies are preoccupied with exploring outcomes and processes that happen to children after immigration and settlement. As a result, they pay little attention to factors leading to the decision to immigrate and of course, the varied and complex activities that children undertake as active participants in the actual settlement process. How might children of Mexican origin undertake important roles and activities in assisting their immigrant parents and households to settle? In addition, how salient is gender in the allocation and carrying out of the various activities that assist settlement?

CHILDREN AND SETTLEMENT

To conceptualize the processes through which children become major actors in their households regarding settlement and other important household developments, I reflected on my own upbringing and engaged in classroom discussion on this topic in several immigration classes at the University of California, Los Angeles (UCLA). Born in the United States to immigrant parents from Mexico, my second-generation status allowed me to compare my household responsibilities and roles with those of first-generation immigrant students, many of whom enroll in my immigration classes. I was always impressed with the number of different stories, activities, roles, and events that students discussed in my classroom regarding their participation in their families' settlement. My students believed, and rightfully so, that they were major players in their households, at least when it came to assisting their parents in specific settlement types of activities, such as translating, teaching, or caring for younger siblings. I wondered if the immigrant children of today serve in roles similar to those of their earlier cohorts who, for example, arrived in the United States before 1965 or during the mid- to late 1980s when the United States experienced unprecedented numbers of newcomers.

When an immigrant family arrives in the United States is important because it allows us to explore whether there might be differences in the degree to which children assist their households to settle based on the availability of local or regional institutional resources. To assist with their settlement, immigrants are able to use both community-based and familial/kin resources at much higher rates today than, for example, during the immediate post–World War II immigrant era in which immigration was not nearly as high as in the post-1965 era. Today, at least in Los Angeles and in other immigrant-rich cities, there exists a number of immigrant advocacy agencies, community-based organizations, bilingual education programs and sources of information, immigrant-sensitive elected officials, and of course, large immigrant communities, which makes initial settlement perhaps less reliant on children than in years past. As a result, I would argue that families who immigrated to the United States prior to 1965 relied on their children to a larger degree because of the fewer immigrant resources available to newcomer households in Los Angeles during that era. Here, I do not mean to suggest that immigration is an easy process in the 1990s but, rather, that the context of a receiving community is much different and perhaps allows for less reliance on children to perform complex tasks and interventions as parents and households maneuver through settlement.

I also wondered if there was something specific to Mexican immigrants that might account for children undertaking very specific and important roles and activities in assisting their immigrant parents and households settle. We know for example that many Mexican immigrants to the United States come from rural or agrarian backgrounds where the meaning of what it is to be a child is different from that of Mexicans from urban centers or even Mexicans living in Los Angeles. Viviana Zelizer (1985), in her classic study on the social value of children, teaches us about the transformation in the economic and sentimental value of children. Basically, she argues that children in postindustrial societies are in a strict sense economically "worthless" but emotionally "priceless." That is, Zelizer teaches us how, over time, the role that children undertake in their families has changed from "contributors" to "sentimental" objects of affection. The important roles that immigrant children of Mexican origin undertake in their households challenge Zelizer's notion that their contributions, even in a strict economic sense, are nil. My study shows that immigrant children and young teenagers, in addition to contributing financially to their households, undertake other important activities that assist their families' settlement.

For example, in my study, I was able to identify three broad but nevertheless primary roles and a series of activities and actions that children undertake in helping their parents and siblings adjust to and settle in a new country. Some of these tasks include serving as translators or interpreters, as financial consultants, as teachers, as mediators, or in parentlike activities. Indeed, children are important actors in their household settlement, a process I clearly document later in this article.

GENDER AND CHILDREN'S ROLES

Barrie Thorne (1995) provides us with an excellent framework to understand how gender might interact with children's roles as they assist their immigrant households to settle in the United States. She does not look at children so much as individuals but rather in group situations with social relations, through the organization and meanings of social situations, and in the collective practices through which children and adults create and re-create gender in their daily interactions. In shifting the focus from individuals to social relations, Thorne moves away from the question, Are boys and girls different? Instead, she wants to explore how children actively come together to help create, and sometimes challenge, gender structures and meanings. Her logic is that children's collective activities should weigh more fully in understanding gender and social life. This framework helps me understand how gender might also interact in familial or group (brothers and sisters) settings in households engaged in day-to-day activities and other complex situations related to settlement. Perhaps more important, it helps me place children and gender at the center of immigrant settlement. . . .

In this article, I challenge the notion that settlement can be adequately understood as only an adult process, one devoid of the younger members of an immigrant household. I also attempt to identify patterns of immigrant settlement by gender; this is, Do boys undertake settlement roles or tasks that are qualitatively different from the activities that girls undertake? And if so, why? . . .

Studies show that the presence of children in a family contemplating immigration greatly influences the decision to leave (Chávez, 1988; Hondagneu-Sotelo, 1994) or to stay. We also know that once in the United States, immigrants who might have contemplated returning to their countries of origin may not do so as a result of family formation. Chávez (1988), for example, argues that even for undocumented workers, the formation of a family begins a process that leads to eventual permanent settlement. The families often become binational because they straddle the very difficult reality of unauthorized immigration status among the adult parents and citizenship status among their children and all the rights pertaining to them. Children are important factors in the decision to immigrate and in subsequent decisions to remain permanently in the new country of origin. Not well known, however, are the specific roles and gendered patterns that children undertake in assisting their parents and younger siblings with day-to-day activities and larger familial responsibilities related to immigrant settlement. This study is the first, to my knowledge, that attempts to document this process.

DESCRIPTION OF RESEARCH

During the summer and fall of 1996, with the assistance of three UCLA students, I developed a questionnaire guideline and interviewed 44 adult heads of immigrant households. From these households, we then conducted another 24 interviews with the children of the adult respondents.[2] Together, these 68 in-depth interviews, which averaged 2 to 3 hours each, constitute the empirical database for this article. The data used in this article are part of a larger study in which I investigate how children facilitate their immigrant families' initial settlement into the United States. When we interviewed the adult household heads, we were interested in learning how they perceived their children's assistance to family integration into U.S. culture and society in general. Similarly, when we interviewed their adult children, we wanted to learn what roles and activities they recalled undertaking in helping their newly arrived households to settle.[3]

Funding restrictions limited our interviews to Mexican-origin households. Our respondents were found through a nonrandom snowball sampling method (Biernacki & Waldorf, 1981; Van Meter, 1990; Watters & Biernacki, 1989) undertaken in the greater Los Angeles metropolis. Each participant in the study was provided with a $25 incentive. . . .

We began the interviews by first asking the adults to list or describe the most important ways in which their children assisted them in their everyday lives as members of recently arrived immigrant households. Thereafter, we probed the different possible roles that children might have undertaken in helping their families navigate in different institutional settings such as the schools, the labor market, church, politics, legal and financial institutions, recreation and social occasions, health services, and a host of miscellaneous situations not easily categorized. . . .

The data and findings culled from this study add to the complexity of our perceptions regarding what children do in assisting their families in day-to-day activities. More important, they show how varied immigrant settlement actually is and how children of these families actually contribute significantly to this process.

RESEARCH FINDINGS

Besides the many different activities that children of immigrant families undertake in helping their households to settle, several notable patterns did emerge. First, young girls seemed to participate at higher rates than boys in those tasks that required detailed explanations or translations. Second, boys, even though they assisted their households in numerous activities related to settlement, did not have the same responsibility roles or influence as did the girls in this study. Third, the eldest child, regardless of gender, often took the lead role in assisting younger siblings with what is usually done in the household by the mother, such as feeding and caring for younger siblings, getting the brothers and sisters dressed for school, transporting them to and from school, and baby-sitting.

In addition to the gender patterns above, three primary tasks summarize the roles that children undertake in assisting their household settlement. The first is as *tutors*—children served as translators, interpreters, and teachers for their parents and younger siblings. From our interviews, we documented many different instances in which children performed tutorial types of activities in day-to-day circumstances. Perhaps the most common form of tutoring involved basic translation from English to Spanish and vice versa. Translation spanned different activities including television news, important government documents and other mail, newspapers, ordering food or other services at restaurants or stores, and basic communication with English-speaking merchants and/or officials. Often intermingled with translation activities was the role of interpreting. That is, children, in addition to translating from one language to another, found themselves having to interpret and explain in better detail particularities or difficult issues that might arise in basic translations. Children became the go-between for their Spanish-speaking parents and English-speaking officials in difficult or hard-to-explain situations such as physician visits or parent-teacher appointments involving an unruly child or disciplinary matter. Finally, children often found themselves teaching their parents certain skills or activities that ranged from the filing of taxes to explaining a difficult-to-read employment manual or discussing political or legal issues related to immigration.

A second important activity that children undertake in assisting their immigrant households to settle is as *advocates*, a role in which children intervene, mediate, or advocate on behalf of their parents or their households during difficult financial, legal, or other complicated transactions or situations. Children were sometimes asked or forced to take on important roles and activities that required some type of intervention, mediation, and/or clarification. As a result, children in their role of mediating or advocating on behalf of a younger sibling or a parent often had to confront rude salespersons, school officials, bankers, or other important people who showed little patience toward their parents or siblings. In most instances, language or the inability to clearly communicate between the parents or a younger sibling and an English-speaking official was clearly the major reason prompting intervention. This situation however differs from the role of tutor or translator in that the section described here is much more than basic translation or even interpretation and includes active engagement and mediation on the part of the child.

Third and last, children actively participate in their household settlement as *surrogate parents* in which they undertake nanny or parentlike activities in the caring of younger household members and in other household tasks. Activities children performed in this realm included cooking, dressing, bathing, transporting, baby-sitting, caring, and providing for younger siblings. In addition to these parentlike activities, children would often be consulted by their parents in dealing with disruptive or disciplinary matters involving younger siblings. Children were likewise consulted on other matters relating to their younger siblings or on issues having to do with household decisions such as paying bills or purchasing large consumer goods.

The precarious situations that Mexican immigrants find themselves in are varied and complex. For example, undocumented status is an added factor that greatly complicates settlement and causes strain on families and children. Many children of undocumented families are legal (i.e., they were born in the United States) but, nevertheless, function in their day-to-day activities as illegal as a result of their parents' status. The data collected for this study show that children actively participated in legalization processes and that, to a large degree, children were primarily responsible for getting their parents through the naturalization process either as financial or moral supporters or by prodding their parents to become legal residents or naturalized citizens.

In the sections that follow, I look at four specific institutional settings and/or scenarios that immigrants confront on an almost daily basis: (a) schools, (b) financial resources and complex transactions, (c) labor markets and legal and political institutions, and (d) health services. In each of these sections, I explicate the three different gender patterns described above and the three primary roles (tutor, advocate, and surrogate parent) and activities that children undertake in assisting their immigrant households to settle.

SCHOOLS

On their arrival to the United States, immigrant families with young children are quickly introduced to the U.S. decentralized school system. Learning about a school system is not easy nor does it follow a set pattern or prescribed path. For example, school districts vary in enrollment periods, start days, and placement requirements and in Los Angeles, year-round schooling[4] only adds to the confusion, not to mention the numerous school districts that blanket this large metropolis.[5] For newcomers attempting to locate housing, working in several jobs, or being preoccupied with other day-to-day activities, learning about the school system is often doled out to the eldest or another sibling in the household. Here, I do not suggest that schooling has a lower priority for immigrant families but, rather, that children, in attending school on a daily basis, are more apt to deal with irregularities or regular activities related to schools than are their working parents. Children walk with their older siblings to school, act as interpreters between teachers and their parents, and often take a larger role among their siblings in school success or failure. Parents were not, however, completely uninvolved in their children's school activities.

Interfacing with the school system was, in many instances, relegated to mothers and the eldest children. This was evident from our sample, where fathers tended to relegate the responsibility of schooling in the household to their spouses or to their children's mother. One school-age respondent remarked that getting her father to attend the school-related activities was difficult. "When they [parents] did go, we had to persuade them. We had to drive them to the conferences. Especially my father, he never wanted to go to the parent conferences. 'Let your mother take care of that, why do I need to be there for?' " In addition to explicit commentary about the minimal role of fathers in the school system, such as the above, female respondents consistently made reference to school activities or school-administrated functions that involved the mother rather than the father, suggesting a larger level of involvement for females.

Parental involvement in the schooling activities of nonimmigrant families is also gendered, with mothers usually undertaking the bulk of tending to their children's educational needs and the day-to-day school activities and administrative requirements such as enrollment, parent-teacher conferences, after-school activities, and homework. Although the schooling responsibilities of children clearly fell on mothers a majority of the time, gender does not seem to be a factor in children assuming these tasks for their parents. That is, both boys and girls undertook this role on a regular basis.

The one pattern, however, that was evident was the role that the eldest undertook in caring for the younger brothers and sisters in the day-to-day activities related to school, such as supervising homework, transporting to or picking up younger siblings from school, and making sure that younger brothers or sisters were fed and clothed in preparation for school that day. An adult respondent describes her eldest son's role in this regard:

> He would help me in the morning by driving them to school, pushing them to go to school. . . . He was 9 years old when I brought him here, and he always helped his brothers put on clothes in the morning, he would feed them and then driving them to school, and bringing them back. Jaime would wake up and help his younger brothers change their clothes and get them ready for school.

In a similar pattern, another adult respondent describes the role of her eldest daughter: "When the children were younger, Martina was the one who translated at school and helped with the children's schooling the most." Martina, on the other hand, describes her role in her siblings' education as a bit more involved:

> There was always more involvement, there were always open houses, and there was always someone at school who didn't behave the emergency cards, or lunch school applications. Any form that came from school, year round, I had to do that. I had to be involved in it. Or any questions regarding whatever, I had to be involved with it. 'Well it is your sister's graduation next week. What kind of dress do you think we should get her?' Or, 'Is it true that your sister is graduating next week, or is the lying to us?' 'Is it true that your brother or sister has to stay after school because the teacher said they need to do something more?' It was always, 'What do you think?' and it was always me.

This last commentary suggests that parents, although they might not have been directly involved in the day-to-day activities of their children, nevertheless did attempt to keep abreast of their school-age children by communicating or assessing their children's progress or school activities via an older child. This older child, in essence, almost became an equal at least in regard to parents asking his or her opinion about younger siblings' school performance or day-to-day activities.

Immigrant children undertake an important role in assisting their households to adapt to or become integrated in the U.S. school system. Their role is perhaps similar to families with few financial resources, to large families, or to families with two breadwinners—situations that all require that children undertake greater degrees of responsibility in their households. Immigrant families are often poor or have two adults working to make ends meet, or they merely do not understand the particularities and varied processes of schooling in the United States. In addition, immigrant families, in the process of adapting to a new host society, relegate certain tasks and responsibilities to their children that distribute household responsibilities among different members. As a result, immigrant children become intimately involved in their younger siblings' education.

FINANCIAL RESOURCES AND COMPLEX TRANSACTIONS

Perhaps the biggest challenge awaiting newcomers on arrival to the United States is obtaining financial resources necessary for survival. This is often accomplished through employment and to a lesser extent through kin, loans, or saved capital from the country of origin. Through social networks and other methods of job search, immigrants in Los Angeles and elsewhere in the United States are quite successful in procuring jobs, albeit often in low-paying and low-skilled occupations. Obtaining a job is really the first step in establishing some form of household stability that allows newcomers to ease into other settlement processes such as obtaining shelter, clothing, and nourishment. However, because immigrants are mostly employed in low-paying occupations, household financial resources are stretched; spouses are forced to work at home, maintaining the household, and outside so as to contribute monetarily to the home; and immigrant children fully cognizant of the household financial situation feel pressured to also contribute to making ends meet. As a result, children of immigrant households play a significant role in their financial stability.

There are two ways that children of immigrant households are immersed in assisting their parents financially—first as monetary contributors and second as mediators of complex financial transactions. Both are extremely important, and both were evident in many of the households interviewed for this study. In addition, a gender pattern clearly emerged with girls undertaking a larger role than boys in assisting their households both as financial contributors and as interlopers in complex transactions.

In strict economic terms, household members can serve both as financial resources and as expenditures. Children in the postindustrial United States however are rarely thought of as financial resources or expenses but, rather, as sentimental or emotionally "priceless" children. (Zelizer, 1985). Nevertheless, immigrant children, teenagers actually, performed paid labor functions so as to contribute to familial resources. Of course, not all children of immigrant households work or, for that matter, work so as to contribute to their families' households, but in several instances, older children toiled to assist their parents. The two examples come from two respondents recalling their work contributions to their households as teenagers.

> As soon as I was 16, I started working. But they [parents] never really asked us to contribute to the house economically. It was more if you wanted to give. If you wanted to contribute to the family that's fine. But I did contribute, 'Well here's half of my paycheck.' If you think about it, I was in high school, there isn't that many expenses except for your senior year with prom, yearbook and stuff. I worked during the weekends. . . . I would just give half of my paycheck to the house.
>
> During the summer of 1988 I held two jobs—that's when I was really contributing to the household. Any bills or anything that needed to be paid, I paid them.

Other children respondents remembered working alongside their parents assisting them in their jobs, often receiving little or no pay. This ostensibly would free up time for the father to either work at another job or spend time at home with the family.

> I remember that when I was younger, we used to work. We were in junior high, and my sister and I would go clean offices with my father. We would be out there until 11 at night. We cleaned the offices, throwing trash away, dusting, things like that. And sometimes we had to talk to the managers to get supplies and things like that.

Girls in immigrant households often served as go-betweens in complex financial matters such as the purchasing of a home, the filing of income taxes, or the controlling of the financial duties of the household. Most of the respondents who answered that they had assisted their parents either financially or through financial institutions were female. This is not to suggest that boys did not contribute to household finances but that clearly the girls in my sample were the overwhelming contributors. Little reference however was made to their gender as a possible explanation as to why it was the females who undertook this important familial role. Nevertheless, more often girls rather than boys undertook this role. As Xochitl remarked,

> If something needed to be bought I took it upon myself to purchase it. I just took the initiative and if I saw that there was something needed in the household I would do it. I did manage the house and the household finances for a time when my dad was not working. It was actually for a long time. I would basically pay the bills.

The adult respondents also commented on the role that their daughters played in assisting their families with large financial transactions such as purchasing a home or a new car or filling out credit card applications. As adult respondent, Paula, describes the role that her daughter Martha undertook:

> When we refinanced this house, Martha was the one in charge of all the paperwork because the first time we did it, we were taken for $18,000. She looked at the papers and said that our payments weren't paying for the house, we were just paying interest. When she found out, Martha at the age of 16 took 2 days to call different places and to find out information. She arranged to have our home refinanced by a different bank so that we could save money from a lower interest rate.

Whatever the outcome of their assistance, girls provided either financial support through direct monetary contributions, by assistance at work, or by providing invaluable information or mediating transactions that are complex or that require a large degree of translation and academic background. Having another family member explain complex financial transactions serves a very important function in any family attempting to settle in a foreign country. In the case of immigrant households, young girls seem to be undertaking this role to a larger degree than boys are. The anxiety that any new homeowner confronts when making such a large purchase is great, and the frustration that emanates from not understanding printed material is large, even among U.S.-born English-speaking Americans. The role that children from immigrant households undertake in assisting their parents financially is great and helps lower levels of frustration but, perhaps more important, facilitates permanent settlement in the United States.

LABOR MARKETS AND LEGAL AND POLITICAL INSTITUTIONS

Mexican immigrants come to the United States primarily to seek jobs. The role of social networks is extremely important in disseminating job information and in procuring jobs for recent arrivals (Chávez, 1988; Massey et al., 1987). For many Mexican immigrants, job procurement comes by word of mouth from extended kin or compatriots from the same village or town in Mexico. Indeed, the role of social networks is well established in helping us understand how many Mexican immigrants obtain jobs almost immediately after arriving in the United States. Little, however, is known regarding the role of children in the process of securing jobs or, as this section describes, in maintaining job stability.

Children have little to contribute in assisting their parents secure employment. No respondents spoke of their children actually helping them get jobs. However, I did find that children play an important role in their parents' employment stability by informing them about worker's rights, taxes, benefits, and other personnel issues related to their jobs. Once again, it appears to be primarily the girls who undertake this role of worker advocate or interloper on behalf of working parents.

A typical response from a mother describing the role of her young daughter regarding a personnel issue provides a good example of how children translated, but more important, how they explained and taught their parents about the regulations contained in an unwieldy personnel manual.

> In my husband's job, for example, if there was a policy or regulations about the company. Then we would ask Patty—for example, in the policy [manual] it said you can't go this fast on the forklift—regulations like that [help] to avoid accidents. To make sure we understood it. It wasn't just one little paper, it was a big book that said what should be done and what shouldn't be done.

The stress involved in not being able to understand job descriptions or safety regulations while on the job is large for recent arrivals. The important role of Patty and other children who do more than merely translate is lost in simple descriptions of reading or translating to Spanish a new company letter or regulation, as one teenage daughter describes:

> My dad would get letters from work and he didn't understand what they were about so I had to kind of translate or I would tell him what they were asking for or what they were all about, but it wasn't just about reading the letter. . . . Yeah, translation and interpretation. There is lots of things that my parents didn't understand. As far as like technical terms like my dad's job. Because they always sent him information and he didn't know what it was about and I had to educate him.

Mexican immigrant workers occupy the worst paying and perhaps the most abusive jobs in Los Angeles's labor market. As a result, they confront poor working conditions and are exposed to work hazards with much greater risks than nonimmigrants are (Mozingo, 1997). For employers, one of the attractions of hiring immigrant labor is the immigrants' tolerance for difficult or hazardous work sites where they can be easily injured. In several interviews, adult respondents underlined how their children intervened on their behalf to prevent abuses and injuries at the workplace.

> I had an accident at my job. Both of my children helped me. They interpreted for me when I went to the doctors. I was under medical supervision. And they would read the papers and tell me where to go. They would tell me not to go to work because I was so sick. They said I should not go to work. I told them that the

company doctor said I could work, that I was fine, that there was no reason not to work. They (my daughters) said, 'No, even if the doctor told you, if you don't feel well, why should you go?' They gave me advice to look for an attorney. My children also told me to get another doctor. One that wasn't associated with the company. They helped me find a doctor and then an attorney.

Similar to intervening on behalf of their parents on issues of worker rights, young children, again mostly the daughters, were involved in assisting their parents or their parents' friends with legal issues.

Once a friend of the family had a problem with the law. My daughters called around and found out the means to resolve this problem. Another time, a woman we know had a problem with a ticket and a warrant. My daughter called and took her where she needed to go in order to resolve the problem.

The political participation (voting, registration, parties) of immigrants is low, perhaps due to multiple reasons such as lack of citizenship, thus the inability to vote; general disdain for politics, which in Mexico is often linked to corruption; and of course, the same reasons that apply to the 80% or so of the American populace that does not participate in politics. After reviewing the responses to queries about politics, I was impressed by the level of interaction between parents and their children over issues such as U.S. presidential elections, local elections, and issues related to civil rights or Mexican American/Chicano politics. "My parents wanted to know what was going on . . . so they would ask, 'Who's the presidential candidate, what does he represent, what does he offer?' "

Several (6) of the children that we interviewed had gone to college and obtained bachelor's or associate's degrees. During college, some had participated in student advocacy or politically oriented organizations, and they would share their experiences with household members. Of the 6 students who attended college, 2 were women, and it was only these 2 that participated to any degree in politics at their respective universities. In fact, they participated a great deal in politics, one actually being arrested for protesting and the other assuming a leadership role in a Latina-only organization that advocates on behalf of other Latinas. Their discussions at home of campus political involvement on their part was well received perhaps because both women had taken on leadership positions or were convincing about the worthiness of their causes. The one student who was arrested even influenced her mother and father to protest at a large rally and march against California's Proposition 187.[6]

HEALTH SERVICES

Children also assisted their parents with the health care system. Almost all of the adult respondents reported that their children had assisted them in various capacities related to health services. These activities included accompanying them to yearly doctor visits, translating professional diagnoses from English to Spanish, and caring for ill parents at home. In the arena of health services, no clear gender difference emerged. Both the boys and the girls were involved in translating either for the father or the mother. However, unlike translating school concerns, personnel manuals, or even complex financial transactions, the respondents voiced a certain level of difficulty in explaining medical ailments to doctors and then explaining the doctor's responses or questions back to their parents. For example, Jose describes his role as a young teenager translating for his mother.

My mom has heart problems. And I remember as a kid, it was a little bit scary, and she had an episode where she got pretty sick, so I couldn't exactly communicate what she was feeling to the doctor. The doctor would ask her in English, she could understand herself but just couldn't communicate, and I would translate for her but it just wasn't a complete communication with the doctor. So it did affect her a lot. Because the doctors wanted to know exactly what you're feeling.

Although translations are often awkward, those undertaken in a hospital or doctor's office seemed to be especially embarrassing, difficult, and dehumanizing for boys and girls. Angelo describes his experience as a young boy accompanying his mother to visit a doctor over an illness she wanted checked.

We always went with our parents. We always had to be the ones telling the doctor what was going on. Tell the doctors that we didn't have insurance. And we pretty much did all the talking. As soon as the doctor walked in they would notice that my parents didn't speak English. They would ask the first question like what was wrong or this and that. And the minute I would answer—from that point on—they wouldn't really look at my parent. The minute they asked the first question I would answer it and from that point on they wouldn't really make eye contact with my mom, they would just tell us. The only time they would turn to them was when they saw me ask my mom something, then they would look at her to see what she said to me, and then they looked at me when I answered.

Girls similarly undertook these important roles and also experienced embarrassing or difficult situations when it came to translating difficult information regarding a parent's health condition. Marta describes one particular visit, accompanying her father to a doctor's office, in which she became frustrated over her struggle with English and having to nevertheless interpret:

And sometimes the Anglo doctors and nurses would get upset with me because I would speak English in a broken king of English and I was barely like 6 or 7. So, I would get really upset or nervous. And my dad would get upset because I'm not translating right, and the doctor would get upset because I'm not translating right. So sometimes the hospital staff would get mad.

There is no denying that children assisted their immigrant parents greatly in the provision and translation of health services. It is also evident that both boys and girls assisted their parents in this role without any clear gender pattern (e.g., girls assisting only their mothers or boys assisting only their fathers). Below, I discuss the implications of my findings and attempt to explain why certain gender patterns exist in some institutions and why they do not exist in others.

DISCUSSION AND CONCLUSION

The results of this study point to important roles that children undertake in caring and providing for immigrant households as they navigate through the process of settlement. Table 1 summarizes the different institutional settings in which children contribute significantly in assisting their parents and households to settle. In addition, Table 1 identifies those settings in which a gender pattern emerged.

The data from the in-depth interviews suggest gender patterns, with girls undertaking specific roles more often than boys do. This was not always the case, however, especially

TABLE 1 Children's Roles in the Settlement of Mexican Immigrant Households

	Role	Gender Patterns
School settings	Tutors	In the household, mothers clearly took on this role.
	Surrogate parents	Among children, no clear gendered pattern emerged.
Financial resources and complex transactions	Financial contributors Mediators in complex transactions Advocates	Girls clearly undertook these role more frequently than boys did.
Employment-related issues	Tutors Advocates	Girls clearly undertook these roles more frequently than boys did.
Legal institutions and issues	Advocates	Girls clearly undertook these roles more frequently than boys did.
Political involvement	Tutors Advocates-activists	Girls clearly undertook these roles more frequently than boys did.
Health services	Tutors Advocates Care given	There was no clear gender pattern.

when age surfaced as the primary indicator as to who would care for younger siblings and/or parents. In addition, both boys and girls also participated more equally in translating difficult medical jargon and accompanying their parents in visits to health providers.

When an immigrant arrived in the United States (pre-1965, 1965–1985, or after 1985) was not a significant factor in determining whether parents and immigrant households relied less or more on their children for assistance. This suggests that perhaps immediate household members rely on each other initially to a greater extent for support, at least in regard to the institutions that I analyzed in this study, regardless of whether community and social network resources exist or if they arrived during a different decade. Children were as likely to participate in important household settlement activities (e.g., translating, care giving, contributing financially) whether they immigrated to Los Angeles with their families prior to 1965 or after 1985.

What explains the larger roles that girls undertake in four out of the six institutional settings that I studied for this article? Several factors help us understand these processes. First, although assistance from children was expected, girls undertook these expectations more readily and in turn were rewarded with a modicum of independence. Similar to Hondagneu-Sotelo's (1994) important finding that women move toward more egalitarian relationships with their spouses after immigrating to the United States, girls likewise are given more credibility, responsibility, and thus a greater degree of independence, perhaps similar to that of their brothers. That is, girls, given their important roles in their households as translators, interlopers, mediators, and especially, surrogate parents, are seen by both their younger and even older siblings and by their parents performing under difficult and strenuous circumstances. These girls in turn are able to exert some degree of independence or authority, certainly with their siblings, over certain household privileges or tasks. This of course is tempered somewhat; after all, they are still children or young teenagers under the tutelage of their parents, and the roles that girls undertake in an immigrant Mexican household are by and large well defined and secondary to those of the boys.

Second, the parents and the children in larger households (e.g., where several siblings, both boys and girls, live) may have participated in a double standard of sorts with regard to household activity assignments. Girls, given predefined roles that relegate them to household or home activities, participated to a much larger degree than did boys in institutional matters that could easily be completed at home. With the exception of financially contributing to the household, the roles in which girls were clearly in charge were in the home. In contrast, the two institutional settings outside of the home (schooling and health) showed no clear gender patterns and required larger degrees of independence and adultlike responsibilities. In these settings, boys as much as girls undertook important roles with their younger siblings and parents. Girls, to a greater degree than boys, undertook certain roles and tasks in assisting their households to settle, in part because of predetermined roles that girls and boys have in Mexican households.

Third, even though the findings clearly suggest a gender pattern in who assisted their siblings and parents, boys were not completely devoid of assistance, they just assisted less frequently in home-type activities. There were some instances in which boys undertook important roles in their households, roles that I have characterized as being girl dominated. For example, although caring for younger siblings in school settings meant meeting with teachers, walking the kids to school, and participating in school activities, boys also helped in girl- or woman-defined domestic activities such as preparing the children for school by getting them dressed, feeding them, or making sure their homework was complete. Nevertheless, because school and health settings in which children played important roles were outside of the household or "girl" domain, boys and girls equally participated. This clearly indicates that when boys did participate in important settlement activities it was to a much larger degree outside of the household rather than inside of it.

Several important factors support my primary finding that girls, more so than boys, assist their families' settlement in household-related activities. Research on Latino families (Zambrana, 1995) and Chicana feminism (Garcia, 1989) clearly documents the traditional roles that women and, by extension, girls are relegated to in their households. Similarly, double standards also exist between boys and girls, in which boys are allowed to venture outside of the household whether it be for labor, recreation, or household responsibilities. Girls in Mexican-origin families are usually spatially bound and are not permitted to venture too far from the home for a number of different cultural and structural reasons. For example, a father and mother often wish to protect or guard their daughter's virginity. Likewise, parents insist that their daughters need to stay at home to care for younger siblings or even older brothers or that they need to assist with other household duties. College admissions officers often point to the difficulty in matriculating Latinas due to parents' cultural fears and notions that either their daughters do not need a college education or that they can enroll in the local junior college or university.

Through this article, I have explored the ways in which girls and boys facilitate the establishment of permanent settlement in Mexican immigrant households. The findings help us better understand the role of children in different settlement processes and, equally important, how gender interacts with immigration. The patterns, roles, and activities that I culled from this study add to the complexity of what children do in assisting their families in day-to-day activities. More important, they show how varied immigrant settlement actually is and the significance of children in this process. As a result of undertaking active roles and activities in their households, girls are challenging to some degree some of the cultural and patriarchal legacies described earlier.

Discussion Questions

1. How does the settlement process challenge the idea that children are "economically useless"?
2. Describe the ways in which children assisted their parents in the settlement process.

3. Why do you think that daughters often had more responsibilities in assisting their parents?
4. Discuss how this study challenges popular beliefs about immigration and about children.

Notes

1. The Bracero Program was a legal agreement between the United States and Mexico that provided for Mexican nationals to work in the United States as temporary workers; that is, workers were recruited and contracted to work for a period of time, and then they returned to Mexico.
2. Most of the "children" interviews were actually interviews with adults who we queried about their childhood contributions to their households. Thus, when I make reference to children respondents, I am not referring to them as children in the literal sense but, rather, based on their recollections to their experiences as children in their particular households.
3. At the outset, I would like to emphasize that this study was unfortunately not intended to investigate how boys and girls, within a specific gender context, assisted their immigrant households to settle. As a result, questions were not asked regarding gender-specific tasks, activities, and roles and on how gender interacts with children in settlement. My findings for this study are derived from carefully culling a difficult database and putting together gender trends, activities, and roles among

children that emerged from this database from hours of research.
4. Several years ago, most of the schools in the Los Angeles Unified School District moved away from typical 9-month school years (e.g., September to June) to year-round school years to account for overenrollment that is in part the result of increased immigration and other demographic factors.
5. Southern California, which often includes in its definition the counties of Los Angeles, Ventura, San Bernardino, Riverside, and Orange, provides a massive landscape from which to navigate between city services, educational resources and institutions, and of course, school districts. Together, these five counties account for many different school districts, each with its own set of regulations, requirements, and structures.
6. This proposition, which won decisively in the electorate but failed in the courts, denies access to publicly funded social services to undocumented California residents through five measures regarding the provision of education, health care and other social services, law enforcement and the use of false immigration, social security, and citizenship documents.

References

Alarcón, R. (1995). *Immigrants or transnational workers? The settlement process among Mexicans in rural California* (Report to the California Institute for Rural Studies, P.O. Box 2143, Davis, CA 95617).

Biernacki, P., & Waldorf, D. (1981). Snowball sampling: Sampling and techniques of chain referral sampling. *Sociological Methods and Research, 10,* 141–163.

Chávez, L. (1988). Settlers and sojourners: The case of Mexicans in the United States, *Human Organization, 47*(2), 95–108.

Chávez, L. R. (1992). *Shadowed lines: Undocumented immigrants in American society.* San Diego, CA: Harcourt Brace Jovanovich.

Garcia, A. (1989). The development of Chicana feminist discourse, 1970–1980. *Gender & Society, 3*(2), 217–237.

Gibson, M. (1988). *Accommodation without assimilation: Sikh immigrants in an American high school.* Ithaca, NY: Cornell University Press.

Hondagneu-Sotelo, P. (1994). *Gendered transitions: Mexican experiences of immigration,* Berkeley, CA: University of California Press.

Massey, D., Alarcón, R., Durand, J., & González, H. (1987). *Return to Aztlan: The social process of international migration from western Mexico,* Berkeley, CA: University of California Press.

Mozingo, J. (1997, November 25). Injured worker finds little aid. *The Los Angeles Times,* Metro Section, p. 1.

Olsen, L. (1988). *Crossing the school house border: Immigrant students in the California public schools* (Policy research report). San Francisco: California Tomorrow.

Portes, A. (Ed.). (1996). *The new second generation.* New York: Russell Sage.

Rumbaut, R. (1990). *Immigrant students in California public schools: A summary of current knowledge* (Report No. 11). Baltimore: Center for Research on Effective Schooling for Disadvantaged Students, Johns Hopkins University.

Rumbaut, R. (1996). *The new Californians: Assessing the educational progress of children of immigrants* (California Policy Seminar, Vol. 8, No. 3). Berkeley: University of California.

Rumbaut, R. (1997). *Passages to adulthood: The adaptation of children of immigrants in Southern California.* Unpublished Report to the Russell Sage Foundation Board of Trustees.

Rumbaut, R. & Cornelius, W. (1995). *California's immigrant children: Theory, research, and implications for educational policy.* San Diego: Center for U.S. Mexican Studies, University of California.

State of California, Department of Finance. (1998). *Race/ethnic population estimates: Components of change by race, 1990–1996.* Sacramento: Author.

Suárez-Orozco, M., & Suárez-Orozco, C. (1995). *Trans-formations: Migration, family life, achievement, motivation among Latino adolescents.* Palo Alto, CA: Stanford University Press.

Thorne, B. (1995). *Gender play: Girls and boys in school.* New Brunswick, NJ: Rutgers University Press.

Van Meter, K. M. (1990). Methodological and design issues: Techniques for assessing the representativeness of snowball samples, In E. Y. Lambert (Ed.), *The collection and interpretation of data from hidden populations* (National Institute on Drug Abuse Research Monograph 98, pp. 31–43). Washington, DC: US Government Printing Office.

Vernez, G., & Abrahamse, A. (1996). *How immigrants fare in U.S. education.* Santa Monica, CA: RAND.

Watters, J. K., & Biernacki, P. (1989). Targeted sampling: Options for the study of hidden populations. *Social Problems, 36,* 416–430.

Zambrana, R. E. (Ed.). (1995). *Understanding Latino families: Scholarship, Policy, and Practice.* Thousand Oaks, CA: Sage.

Zelizer, V. A. (1985). *Pricing the priceless child: The changing social value of children.* New York: Basic Books.

Zhou, M. (1997). Growing up American: The challenge confronting immigrant children and children of immigrants. *Annual Review of Sociology, 23,* 62–95.

Concerted Cultivation
and the Accomplishment
of Natural Growth

ANNETTE LAREAU

INTRODUCTION

Sociologist Annette Lareau conducted an ethnographic study of family life in families from a variety of economic backgrounds. In this excerpt, she discusses how families structure their time differently based on their socioeconomic status. More affluent parents tend to enroll their children in many organized activities and spend much of their free time shuttling kids from lessons to games. She calls this mode of family life concerted cultivation, *the belief that children need to have as many opportunities in a formal setting to develop their personal interests as possible. Families with less income cannot afford to place their children in as many activities, but also believe that children need to learn to occupy themselves during free time, which Lareau calls* accomplishment of natural growth. *She observes that each mode of childhood has both positives and negatives, but ultimately each serves to perpetuate class differences.*

L aughing and yelling, a white fourth-grader named Garrett Tallinger splashes around in the swimming pool in the backyard of his four-bedroom home in the suburbs on a late spring afternoon. As on most evenings, after a quick dinner his father drives him to soccer practice. This is only one of Garrett's many activities. His brother has a baseball game at a different location. There are evenings when the boys' parents relax, sipping a glass of wine. Tonight is not one of them. As they rush to change out of their work clothes and get the children ready for practice, Mr. and Mrs. Tallinger are harried.

Only ten minutes away, a Black fourth-grader, Alexander Williams, is riding home from a school open house.[1] His mother is driving their beige, leather-upholstered Lexus. It is 9:00 P.M. on a Wednesday evening. Ms. Williams is tired from work and has a long Thursday ahead of her. She will get up at 4:45 A.M. to go out of town on business and will not return before 9:00 P.M. On Saturday morning, she will chauffeur Alexander to a private piano lesson at 8:15 A.M., which will be followed by a choir rehearsal and then a soccer game. As they ride in the dark, Alexander's mother, in a quiet voice, talks with her son, asking him questions and eliciting his opinions.

Discussions between parents and children are a hallmark of middle-class child rearing. Like many middle-class parents, Ms. Williams and her husband see themselves as "developing" Alexander to cultivate his talents in a concerted fashion. Organized activities, established and controlled by mothers and fathers, dominate the lives of middle-class children such as Garrett and Alexander. By making certain their children have these and other experiences, middle-class parents engage in a process of *concerted cultivation*. From this, a robust sense of entitlement takes root in the children. This sense of entitlement plays an especially important role in institutional settings, where middle-class children learn to question adults and address them as relative equals.

Only twenty minutes away, in blue-collar neighborhoods, and slightly farther away, in public housing projects, childhood looks different. Mr. Yanelli, a white working-class father, picks up his son Little Billy, a fourth-grader, from an after-school program. They come home and Mr. Yanelli drinks a beer while Little Billy first watches television, then rides his bike and plays in the street. Other nights, he and his Dad sit on the sidewalk outside their house and play cards. At about 5:30 P.M. Billy's mother gets home from her job as a house cleaner. She fixes dinner and the entire family sits down to eat together. Extended family are a prominent part of their lives. Ms. Yanelli touches base with her "entire family every day" by phone. Many nights Little Billy's uncle stops by, sometimes bringing Little Billy's youngest cousin. In the spring, Little Billy plays baseball on a local team. Unlike for Garrett and Alexander, who have at least four activities a week, for Little Billy, baseball is his only organized activity outside of school during the entire year. Down the road, a white working-class girl, Wendy Driver, also spends the evening with her girl cousins, as they watch a video and eat popcorn, crowded together on the living room floor.

Farther away, a Black fourth-grade boy, Harold McAllister, plays outside on a summer evening in the public housing project in which he lives. His two male cousins are there that night, as they often are. After an afternoon spent unsuccessfully searching for a ball so they could play basketball, the boys had resorted to watching sports on television. Now they head outdoors for a twilight water balloon fight. Harold tries to get his neighbor, Miss Latifa, wet. People sit in white plastic lawn chairs outside the row of apartments. Music and television sounds waft through the open windows and doors.

The adults in the lives of Billy, Wendy, and Harold want the best for them. Formidable economic constraints make it a major life task for these parents to put food on the table, arrange for housing, negotiate unsafe neighborhoods, take children to the doctor (often waiting for city buses that do not come), clean children's clothes, and get children to bed and have them ready for school the next morning. But unlike middle-class parents, these adults do not consider the concerted development of children, particularly through organized leisure activities, an essential aspect of good parenting. Unlike the Tallingers and Williamses, these mothers and fathers do not focus on concerted cultivation. For them, the crucial responsibilities of parenthood do not lie in eliciting their children's feelings, opinions, and thoughts. Rather, they see a clear boundary between adults and children. Parents tend to use directives: they tell their children what to do rather than persuading them with reasoning. Unlike their middle-class counterparts, who have a steady diet of adult organized activities, the working-class and poor children have more control over the character of their leisure activities. Most children are free to go out and play with friends and relatives who typically live close by. Their parents and guardians facilitate the *accomplishment of natural growth*.[2] Yet these children and their parents interact with central institutions in the society, such as schools, which firmly and decisively promote strategies of concerted cultivation in child rearing. For working-class and poor families, the cultural logic of child rearing at home is out of synch with the standards of institutions. As a result, while children whose parents adopt strategies of concerted cultivation appear to gain a sense of entitlement, children such as Billy Yanelli, Wendy Driver, and Harold McAllister appear to gain an emerging sense of distance, distrust, and constraint in their institutional experiences.

America may be the land of opportunity, but it is also a land of inequality. This chapter identifies the largely invisible but powerful ways that parents' social class impacts children's life experiences. It shows, using in-depth observations and interviews with middle-class (including members of the upper-middle-class), working-class, and poor families, that inequality permeates the fabric of the culture. . . . I report the results of intensive observational research for a total of twelve families when their children were nine and ten years old. I argue that key elements of family life cohere to form a cultural logic of child rearing.[3] In other words, the differences among families seem to cluster together in meaningful patterns. In this historical moment, middle-class parents tend to adopt a cultural logic of child rearing that stresses the concerted cultivation of children. Working-class and poor parents, by contrast, tend to undertake the accomplishment of natural growth. In the accomplishment of natural growth, children experience long stretches of leisure time, child-initiated play, clear boundaries between adults and children, and daily interactions with kin. Working-class and poor children, despite tremendous economic strain, often have more "childlike" lives, with autonomy from adults and control over their extended leisure time. Although middle-class children miss out on kin relationships and leisure time, they appear to (at least potentially) gain important institutional advantages. From the experience of concerted cultivation, they acquire skills that could be valuable in the future when they enter the world of work. Middle-class white and Black children in my study did exhibit some key differences; yet the biggest gaps were not within social classes but, as I show, across them. It is these class differences and how they are enacted in family life and child rearing that shape the ways children view themselves in relation to the rest of the world.

CULTURAL REPERTOIRES

Professionals who work with children, such as teachers, doctors, and counselors, generally agree about how children should be raised. Of course, from time to time they may disagree on the ways standards should be enacted for an individual child or family. For example, teachers may disagree about whether or not parents should stop and correct a child who mispronounces a word while reading. Counselors may disagree over whether a mother is being too protective of her child. Still, there is little dispute among professionals on the broad principles for promoting educational development in children through proper parenting.[4] These standards include the importance of talking with children, developing their educational interests, and playing an active role in their schooling. Similarly, parenting guidelines typically stress the importance of reasoning with children and teaching them to solve problems through negotiation rather than with physical force. Because these guidelines are so generally accepted, and because they focus on a set of practices concerning how parents should raise children, they form a *dominant set of cultural repertoires* about how children should be raised. This widespread agreement among professionals about the broad principles for child rearing permeates our society. A small number of experts thus potentially shape the behavior of a large number of parents.

Professionals' advice regarding the best way to raise children has changed regularly over the last two centuries. From strong opinions about the merits of bottle feeding, being stern with children, and utilizing physical punishment (with dire warnings of problematic outcomes should parents indulge children), there have been shifts to equally strongly worded recommendations about the benefits of breast feeding, displaying emotional warmth toward children, and using reasoning and negotiation as mechanisms of parental control. Middle-class parents appear to shift their behaviors in a variety of spheres more rapidly and more thoroughly than do working-class or poor parents.[5] As professionals have shifted their recommendations from bottle feeding to breast feeding, from stern approaches to warmth and empathy, and from spanking to time-outs, it is middle-class parents who have responded most promptly.[6] Moreover, in recent decades, middle-class children in the United States have had to face the prospect of "declining fortunes."[7] Worried about how their children will get ahead, middle-class parents are increasingly determined to make sure that their children are not excluded from any opportunity that might eventually contribute to their advancement.

Middle-class parents who comply with current professional standards and engage in a pattern of concerted cultivation deliberately try to stimulate their children's development and foster their cognitive and social skills. The commitment among working-class and poor families to provide comfort, food, shelter, and other basic support requires ongoing effort, given economic challenges and the formidable demands of child rearing. But it stops short of the deliberate cultivation of children and their leisure activities that occurs in middle-class families. For working-class and poor families, sustaining children's natural growth is viewed as an accomplishment.[8]

What is the outcome of these different philosophies and approaches to child rearing? Quite simply, they appear to lead to the *transmission of differential advantages* to children. In this study, there was quite a bit more talking in middle-class homes than in working-class and poor homes, leading to the development of greater verbal agility, larger vocabularies, more comfort with authority figures, and more familiarity with abstract concepts. Importantly, children also developed skill differences in interacting with authority figures in institutions and at home. Middle-class children such as Garrett Tallinger and Alexander Williams learn, as young boys, to shake the hands of adults and look them in the eye. In studies of job interviews, investigators have found that potential employees have less than one minute to make a good impression. Researchers stress the importance of eye contact, firm handshakes, and displaying comfort with bosses during the interview. In poor families like Harold McAllister's, however, family members usually do no look each other in the eye when conversing. In addition, as Elijah Anderson points out, they live in neighborhoods where it can be dangerous to look people in the eye too long.[9] The types of social competence transmitted in the McAllister family are valuable, but they are potentially less valuable (in employment interviews, for example) than those learned by Garrett Tallinger and Alexander Williams.

The white and Black middle-class children in this study also exhibited an emergent version of the *sense of entitlement* characteristic of the middle-class. They acted as though they had a right to pursue their own individual preferences and to actively manage interactions in institutional settings. They appeared comfortable in these settings; they were open to sharing information and asking for attention. Although some children were more outgoing than others, it was common practice among middle-class children to shift interactions to suit *their* preferences. Alexander Williams knew how to get the doctor to listen to his concerns (about the bumps under his arm from his new deodorant). His mother explicitly trained and encouraged him to speak up with the doctor. Similarly, a Black middle-class girl, Stacey Marshall, was taught by her mother to expect the gymnastics teacher to accommodate her individual learning style. Thus, middle-class children were trained in "the rules of the game" that govern interactions with institutional representatives. They were not conversant in other important social skills, however, such as organizing their time for hours on end during weekends and summers, spending long periods of time away from adults, or hanging out with adults in a nonobtrusive, subordinate fashion. Middle-class children also learned (by imitation and by direct training) how to make the rules work in their favor. Here, the enormous stress on reasoning and negotiation in the home also has a potential advantage for future institutional negotiations. Additionally, those in authority responded positively to such interactions. Even in fourth grade, middle-class children appeared to be acting on their own behalf to gain advantages. They made special requests of teachers and doctors to adjust procedures to accommodate their desires.

The working-class and poor children, by contrast, showed an emerging *sense of constraint* in their interactions in institutional settings. They were less likely to try to customize interactions to suit their own preferences. Like their parents, the children accepted the actions of persons in authority (although at times they also covertly resisted them). Working-class and poor parents sometimes were not as aware of their children's school situation (as when their children were not doing homework). Other times, they dismissed the school rules as unreasonable. For example, Wendy Driver's mother told her to "punch" a boy who was pestering her in class; Billy Yanelli's parents were proud of him when he "beat up" another boy on the playground, even though Billy was then suspended from school. Parents also had trouble getting "the school" to respond to their concerns. When Ms. Yanelli complained that she "hates" the school, she gave her son a lesson in powerlessness and frustration in the face of an important institution. Middle-class children such as Stacey Marshall learned to make demands on professionals, and when they succeeded in making the rules work in their favor they augmented their "cultural capital" (i.e., skills individuals inherit that can then be translated into different forms of value as they move through various institutions) for the future.[10] When working-class and poor children confronted institutions, however, they generally were unable to make the rules work in their favor nor did they obtain capital for adulthood. Because of these patterns of legitimization, children raised according to the logic of concerted cultivation can gain advantages, in the form of an emerging sense of entitlement, while children raised according to the logic of natural growth tend to develop an emerging sense of constraint.[11]

SOCIAL STRATIFICATION AND INDIVIDUALISM

Public discourse in America typically presents the life accomplishments of a person as the result of her or his individual qualities. Songs like "I Did It My Way," memoirs, television shows, and magazine articles celebrate the individual. Typically, individual outcomes are connected to individual effort and talent, such as being a "type A" personality, being a hard worker, or showing leadership. These cultural beliefs provide a framework for Americans' views of inequality.

Indeed, Americans are much more comfortable recognizing the power of individual initiative than recognizing the power of social class. Studies show that Americans generally believe that responsibility for their accomplishments rests on their individual efforts. Less than one-fifth see "race, gender, religion, or class as very important for 'getting ahead in life.'"[12] Compared to Europeans, individuals in the United States are much more likely to believe they can improve their standard of living. Put differently, Americans believe in the American dream: "The American dream that we were all raised on is a simple but powerful one—if you work hard and play by the rules, you should be given a chance to go as far as your God-given ability will take you."[13] This American ideology that each individual is responsible for his or her life outcomes is the expressed belief of the vast majority of Americans, rich and poor.

Yet there is no question that society is stratified. . . . Highly valued resources such as the possession of wealth; having an interesting, well-paying, and complex job; having a good education; and owning a home are not evenly distributed throughout the society. Moreover, these resources are transferred across generations: One of the best predictors of whether a child will one day graduate from college is whether his or her parents are college graduates. Of course, relations of this sort are not absolute: Perhaps two-thirds of the members of society ultimately reproduce their parents' level of educational attainment, while about one-third take a different path. Still, there is no question that we live in a society characterized by considerable gaps in resources or, put differently, by substantial *inequality*. . . . However, reasonable people have disagreed about how best to conceptualize such patterns. They also have disagreed about whether families in different economic positions "share distinct, life-defining experiences."[14] Many insist that there is not a clear, coherent, and sustained experiential pattern. . . . Cultural logic of child rearing . . . tends to differ according to families' social class positions. I see these interweaving practices as coming together in a messy but still recognizable way. In contrast to many, I suggest that social class does have a powerful impact in shaping the daily rhythms of family life.

THE STUDY

It is a lot of work to get young children through the day, especially for their parents. When I embarked on this study, I was interested in understanding that labor process. In choosing to look at families, rather than just at children or parents, I hoped to capture some of the reciprocal effects of children and parents on each other. My approach also meant moving beyond the walls of the home to understand how parents and children negotiate with other adults in children's lives.

My study is based on intensive "naturalistic" observations of twelve families (six white, five Black, and one interracial) with children nine and ten years old. The twelve families are part of a larger study of eighty-eight children from the middle-class, working-class, and poor.[15] . . . I met most of these children when I visited their third-grade classrooms in an urban school, Lower Richmond, and a suburban school, Swan. . . . With the help of white and Black research assistants, I carried out interviews first with the mothers and then with many of the fathers of these children. To better understand the expectations that professionals had of parents, I also interviewed the children's classroom teachers and other school personnel.

From this pool of children the research assistants and I selected twelve families for intensive observations.[16] We generally visited each family about twenty times in and around their home, usually in the space of one month. We followed children and parents as they went through their daily routines, as they took part in school activities, church services and events, organized play, kin visits, and medical appointments. Most visits lasted about three hours; sometimes, depending on the event (e.g., an out-of-town funeral, a special extended family event, or a long shopping trip), we stayed much longer. In most cases, we also arranged one overnight visit in each family's home. Often, especially after the families got used to us, we carried tape recorders.

When we introduced ourselves to each family, we said that, following a famous study, we wanted to be treated like "the family dog."[17] We wanted parents to step over and ignore us, but allow us to hang out with them. In reality, our presence had a more active character. Still, after some initial chatter, we often slipped into the background, letting the children and their parents set the pace. In the house, we sat on the floor with children and, as a rule, insisted on sitting in the backseat of cars when we rode along on family outings. Outside, we played ball with children or hung around while they played with their friends. Middle-class children, especially, spent quite a bit of time waiting for adults. We waited, too. . . . The rule of thumb was not to criticize and not to intervene unless a child was in imminent danger. We encouraged families not to worry about entertaining us, we told children to feel free to curse in front of us if they would do so normally, and we asked that other normal "guest" rules be dissolved.

Unquestionably, our presence changed the dynamics as we were sitting in living rooms watching television, riding along in the backseat of the car to a soccer game, watching children get into their pajamas, or sitting in church with them. Over time, however, we saw signs of adjustment (e.g., as families got used to us, yelling and cursing increased). Many families reported that, especially after the initial adjustment, their behavior changed only in modest ways, if at all.

The children found participating in the project enjoyable. They reported it made them feel "special." They were demonstrably happy to see the field-workers arrive and, at times, were reluctant to let them leave. Some parents also, at times, said they "had fun." Delight in the study was clearly stronger in the working-class and poor families, possibly because it was rare for these children to meet adults outside of their extended family, neighbors, and teachers. In middle-class families, children routinely interacted with nonfamilial adults outside of the home environment or school.

ENDURING DILEMMAS

. . . Some reviewers worried that given the contested character of race relations in the United States, the behavior patterns described in this study might reinforce negative stereotypes of certain groups. The results could be taken out of context and exploited by others, particularly political conservatives. Some early readers encouraged me *not to report* results that might be used to reinforce negative images of, for example, poor Black families. The fact that the manuscript includes portraits of poor white families as well as Black families did not completely assuage these concerns. A key problem is that most readers will be middle class or, as college students, on the road to becoming middle class, even if they had working-class or poor origins. As readers, they will have their own childhoods and their own lives as parents or future parents as a base for what they consider appropriate. This cultural and historical frame can become the basis for interpreting the discussion. Indeed, some (middle-class) readers of earlier drafts felt that a child's life that consists of watching television all day would be "boring" or "bad" for the child. This interpretation, though, is rooted in a particular vision of childhood—one involving development and concerted cultivation. The historical and cultural character of readers' beliefs often are thrown into relief only through sharp cross-cultural or historical comparisons.[18]

In sum, the fear is that some readers will project their own cultural beliefs on the material. This pattern of projection makes it difficult to "see" alternative conceptions of child rearing as legitimate. As a result, although I make an assiduous effort to report the complexity of family life, at times I spend more time pointing out drawbacks of middle-class child rearing than I do drawbacks of working-class and poor families' approach. Still, it is in fact possible that the results of this study could be distorted or used to promote political positions that I find repugnant. But squelching results due to fears about how they could be interpreted (particularly worries that the examples could reinforce "deficit" theories of social life) seems wrong. Thus, although urged to do so, I have not omitted data on this criterion.

. . . In sum, I see it as a mistake to accept, carte blanche, the views of officials in dominant institutions (e.g., schools or social service agencies) regarding how children should be raised. Indeed, outside of institutional settings there are benefits and costs to both of these logics of child rearing. For example, concerted cultivation places intense labor demands on busy parents, exhausts children, and emphasizes the development of individualism, at times at the expense of the development of the notion of the family group. Middle-class children argue with their parents, complain about their parents' incompetence, and disparage parents' decisions. In other historical moments, a ten-year-old child who gave orders to a doctor would have been chastised for engaging in disrespectful and inappropriate behavior. Nor are the actions of children who display an emerging sense of entitlement intrinsically more valuable or desirable than those of children who display an emerging sense of constraint. In a society less dominated by individualism than the United States, with more of an emphasis on the group, the sense of constraint displayed by working-class and poor children might be interpreted as healthy and appropriate. But in this society, the strategies of the working-class and poor families are generally denigrated and seen as unhelpful or even harmful to children's life chances. The benefits that accrue to middle-class children can be significant, but they are often invisible to them and to others. In popular language, middle-class children can be said to have been "born on third base but believe they hit a triple." . . .

Discussion Questions

1. What are some examples of *Concerted Cultivation* in this article? *Accomplishment of Natural Growth?*

2. Would you describe your childhood experiences as more similar to *concerted cultivation* or the *accomplishment of natural growth* (or a combination of both)? How do you think this shaped your childhood?

3. Why do you think that more affluent families favored the *Concerted Cultivation* approach?

4. If you were to study children in their families, how would you go about it?

Notes

1. Choosing words to describe social groups also becomes a source of worry, especially over the possibility of reinforcing negative stereotypes. I found the available terms to describe members of racial and ethnic groups to be problematic in one way or another. The families I visited uniformly described themselves as "Black." Recognizing that some readers have strong views that Black should be capitalized, I have followed that convention, despite the lack of symmetry with the term white. In sum, alternate between the terms "Black," "Black American," "African American," and "white," with the understanding that "white" here refers to the subgroup of non-Hispanic whites.

2. Some readers have expressed concern that this phrase, "the accomplishment of natural growth," underemphasizes all the labor that mothers and fathers do to take care of children. They correctly note that working-class and poor parents themselves would be unlikely to use such a term to describe the process of caring for children. These concerns are important. As I stress in my book (especially in the chapter on Katie Brindle, Chapter 5) it does take an enormous amount of work for parents, especially mothers, of all classes to take care of children. But poor and working-class mothers have fewer resources with which to negotiate these demands. Those whose lives the research assistants and I studied approached the task somewhat differently than did middle-class parents. They did not seem to view children's leisure time as their responsibility; nor did they see themselves as responsible for assertively intervening in their children's school experiences. Rather, the working-class and poor parents carried out their chores, drew boundaries and restrictions around their children, and then,

within these limits, allowed their children to carry out their lives. It is in this sense that I use the term "the accomplishment of natural growth."

3. I define a child-rearing context to include the routines of daily life, the dispositions of daily life, or the "habitus" of daily life. I focus on two contexts: concerted cultivation and the accomplishment of natural growth. In my book, I primarily use the concept of child rearing, but at times I also use the term *socialization*. Many sociologists have vigorously criticized this concept, noting that it suggests (inaccurately) that children are passive rather than active agents and that the relationship between parents and their children is unidirectional rather than reciprocal and dynamic. See, for example, William Corsaro, *Sociology of Childhood*; Barrie Thorne, *Gender Play*; and Glen Elder, "The Life Course as Development Theory." Nonetheless, existing terms can, ideally, be revitalized to offer more sophisticated understandings of social processes. Child rearing and socialization have the virtue of being relatively succinct and less jargon laden than other alternatives. As a result, I use them.

4. For discussions of the role of professionals, see Eliot Freidson, *Professional Powers;* Magali Sarfatti Larson, *The Rise of Professionalism;* and, although quite old, the still valuable collection by Amitai Etzioni, *The Semi-Professionals and Their Organizations*. Of course, professional standards are always contested and are subject to change over time. I do not mean to suggest there are not pockets of resistance and contestation. At the most general level, however, there is virtually uniform support for the idea that parents should talk to children at length, read to children, and take a proactive, assertive role in medical care.

5. Sharon Hays, in her 1996 book *The Cultural Contradictions of Motherhood*, studies the attitudes of middle-class and working-class mothers toward child rearing. She finds a shared commitment to "intensive mothering," although there are some differences among the women in her study in their views of punishment (with middle-class mothers leaning toward reasoning and working-class women toward physical punishment). My study focused much more on behavior than attitudes. If I looked at attitudes, I saw fewer differences; for example, all exhibited the desire to be a good mother and to have their children grow and thrive. The differences I found, however, were significant in how parents *enacted* their visions of what it meant to be a good parent.

6. See Urie Bronfenbrenner's article, "Socializations and Social Class through Time and Space."

7. Katherine Newman, *Declining Fortunes*, as well as Donald Barlett and James B. Steele, *America: What Went Wrong?* See also Michael Hout and Claude Fischer, "A Century of Inequality."

8. Some readers expressed the concern that the contrast to natural would be "unnatural," but this is not the sense in which the term *natural growth* is used here. Rather, the contrast is with words such as cultivated, artificial, artifice, or manufactured. This contrast in the logic of child rearing is a heuristic device that should not be pushed too far since, as sociologists have shown, all social life is constructed in specific social contexts. Indeed, family life has varied dramatically over time. See Philippe Aries, *Centuries of Childhood*, Herbert Gutman, *The Black Family in Slavery and Freedom, 1750–1925,* and Nancy Scheper-Hughes, *Death without Weeping*.

9. Elijah Anderson, *Code of the Street;* see especially Chapter 2.

10. For a more extensive discussion of the work of Pierre Bourdieu see the theoretical appendix; see also David Swartz's excellent book *Culture and Power*.

11. I did not study the full range of families in American society, including elite families of tremendous wealth, nor, at the other end of the spectrum, homeless families. In addition, I have a purposively drawn sample. Thus, I cannot state whether there are other forms of child rearing corresponding to other cultural logics. Still, data from quantitative studies based on nationally representative data support the patterns I observed. For differences by parents' social class position and children's time use, see especially Sandra Hofferth and John Sandberg, "Changes in American Children's Time, 1981–1997." Patterns of language use with children are harder to capture in national surveys, but the work of Melvin Kohn and Carmi Schooler, especially *Work and Personality*, shows differences in parents' child-rearing values. Duane Alwin's studies of parents' desires are generally consistent with the results reported here. See Duane Alwin, "Trends in Parental Socialization Values." For differences in interventions in institutions, there is extensive work showing social class differences in parent involvement in education. See the U.S. Department of Education, *The Condition of Education, 2001*, p.175.

12. In my book, unless otherwise noted, the statistics reported are from 1993 to 1995, which was when the data were collected. Similarly, unless otherwise noted, all monetary amounts are given in (unadjusted) dollars from 1994 to 1995. The figure reported here is from Everett Ladd, *Thinking about America*, pp. 21–22.

13. This quote is from President Bill Clinton's 1993 speech to the Democratic Leadership Council. It is cited in Jennifer Hochschild, *Facing Up to the American Dream*, p. 18.

14. Paul Kingston, *The Classless Society*, p. 2.

15. As I explain in more detail in my book's methodological appendix, family structure is intertwined with class position in this sample. The Black and white middle-class children that we observed all resided with both of their biological parents. By contrast, although some of the poor children have regular contact with their fathers, none of the Black or white poor children in the intensive observations had their biological fathers at home. The working-class families were in between. This pattern raises questions such as whether, for example, the pattern of concerted cultivation depends on the presence of a two-parent marriage. The scope of the sample precludes a satisfactory answer.

16. As I explain in my book's Appendix A, three of the twelve children came from sources outside of the schools.
17. Arlie Hochschild, *The Second Shift.*

18. See Julia Wrigley. "Do Young Children Need Intellectual Stimulation?" and Linda A. Pollock, *Forgotten Children.*

References

Alwin, Duane F. 1984. "Trends in Parental Socialization Values." *American Journal of Sociology* 90(2): 359–82.

Anderson, Elijah, 1990. *Streetwise.* Chicago: University of Chicago Press.

Anderson, Elijah, 1999. *Code of the Street: Decency, Violence, and the Moral Life of the Inner City.* New York: W. W. Norton.

Aries, Philippe. 1962. *Centuries of Childhood: A Social History of the Family,* New York: Basic Books.

Barlett, Donald L., and James B. Steele. 1992. *America: What Went Wrong?* Kansas City: Andrews and McMeel.

Bronfenbrenner, Urie. 1966. "Socialization and Social Class through Time and Space." pp. 362–77 in *Class, Status, and Power,* edited by R. Bendix and S. M. Lipset. New York: The Free Press.

Corsaro, William A. 1997. *The Sociology of Childhood.* Thousand Oaks, Calif.: Pine Forge.

Elder, Glen H., Jr. 1998. "The Life Course as Development Theory." *Child Development* 69(1): 1–12.

Etzioni, Amitai, ed. 1969. *The Semi-Professions and Their Organizations: Teachers, Nurses, Social Workers.* New York: The Free Press.

Freidson, Eliot. 1986. *Professional Powers: A Study of the Institutionalization of Formal Knowledge.* Chicago: University of Chicago Press.

Gutman, Herbert G. 1976. *The Black Family in Slavery and Freedom, 1750–1925.* New York: Vintage.

Hays, Sharon. 1996. *The Cultural Contradictions of Motherhood.* New Haven: Yale University Press.

Hochschild, Arlie Russell. 1989. *The Second Shift.* New York: Viking.

Hochschild, Jennifer L. 1995. *Facing Up to the American Dream: Race, Class, and the Soul of the Nation.* Princeton, N.J.: Princeton University Press.

Hofferth, Sandra L., and John Sandberg. 2001. "Changes in American Children's Time, 1981–1997." In *Children at the Millennium: Where Have We Come From, Where Are We Going?* edited by Sandra L. Hofferth and Timothy J. Owens. Vol. 6 of Advances in life Course Research. Oxford: JAI.

Kingston, Paul W. 2000. *The Classless Society.* Stanford: Stanford University Press.

Kohn, Melvin L., and Carmi Schooler, eds. 1983. *Work and Personality: An Inquiry into the Impact of Social Stratification.* Norwood, N.J.: Ablex.

Ladd, Everett. 1993. "Thinking about America." *The Public Perspective* 4(5): 19–34.

Larson, Magali Sarfatti. 1977. *The Rise of Professionalism: A Sociological Analysis.* Berkeley: University of California Press.

Massey, Douglas, and Nancy Denton. 1993. *American Apartheid.* Cambridge: Harvard University Press.

Neckerman, Kathleen, and Joleen Kirschenmann. 1991. "Hiring Strategies, Racial Bias, and Inner-City Workers." *Social Problems* 38 (November): 433–47.

Newman, Katherine S. 1993. *Declining Fortunes: The Withering of the American Dream.* New York: Basic Books.

Pollock, Linda A. 1983. *Forgotten Children: Parent-Child Relations from 1500 to 1900.* Cambridge: Cambridge University Press.

Scheper-Hughes, Nancy. 1992. *Death without Weeping: The Violence of Everyday Life in Brazil.* Berkeley: University of California Press.

Swartz, David. 1997. *Culture and Power: The Sociology of Pierre Bourdieu.* Chicago: University of Chicago Press.

Thorne, Barrie. 1993. *Gender Play: Girls and Boys in School.* New Brunswick, N.J.: Rutgers University Press.

U.S. Department of Education. 2001. *The Condition of Education,* 2001. Washington, D.C.: National Center for Educational Statistics.

Wrigley, Julia. 1989. "Do Young Children Need Intellectual Stimulation? Experts' Advice to Parents, 1900–1985." *History of Education Quarterly* 29(1): 41–75.

PART FIVE

Constructing Race, Ethnicity, and Gender
Beyond Socialization and Imitation

Traditionally, social scientists have looked at race and gender as things that children were either simply born with or acquired through socialization by adults. Either way, this presumes that children passively absorb their racial/ethnic or gender identity from the world around them. More recently, researchers studying children have sought to understand what role children themselves play in actively constructing the meanings of race, ethnicity, and gender in their lives.

Once again, the most common way that social scientists have understood the process of how children construct meanings of race, ethnicity, and gender has been through ethnography. By observing young people in their daily lives, researchers have been able to note several of the ways that children negotiate, apply, and re-create race and gender as they work to construct a sense of identity.

Certainly adults play an important role in children's constructions of race and gender; kids receive many cues about racial, ethnic, and gender hierarchies that they apply to their own interactions. Debra Van Ausdale and Joe R. Feagin found in their ethnographic study of preschool children that children don't merely repeat concepts of race and ethnicity, but use them to create a sense of inclusion and exclusion with other children. In their selection, "Using Racial and Ethnic Concepts: The Critical Case of Very Young Children," the children they studied were very astute about the subtle markers of race and ethnicity and applied them in their play with one another. For instance, hair is a common marker of race; one child observed Van Ausdale's braided hair and presumed that she must be Native American. Rather than simply note how children "misunderstand" race, which is itself a slippery social construction, Van Ausdale and Feagin examine how adults often overlook the complexity with which very young children comprehend difference.

Adults, of course, play active roles in this process too. Amanda E. Lewis observed students in elementary schools and described the interactive nature of how children construct race. Rather than simply adopt the attitudes of the adults around them, children actively negotiate the meaning of race with both adults and one another. Her selection, "Constructing and Negotiating Racial Identity in School," considers the process of identity construction. Valerie Ann Moore, author of "The Collaborative Emergence of Race in Children's Play: A Case of Two Summer Camps," looks at older children's play and finds that the meanings of race shift for children based on social context. For example, being African American in a predominantly white camp often meant being invisible—to both other campers and counselors. As an African-American researcher, Moore found that the white children asked her to explain her "difference." By contrast, in a camp with many African-American children, being black was constructed as "cool," and kids deemed not "black enough" often found themselves isolated. Thus, hierarchies of race shift based on the situation.

Likewise, hierarchies related to gender shift based on the context of children's circumstances. In her study of elementary school kids, Barrie Thorne found that gender is not always a dividing line between children, but sex segregation is situation specific. Classrooms are one place where "borderwork", or crossover interaction is common between boys and girls. Yet she observed that oftentimes teachers will redefine the boundary by referring to students as "boys and girls" or by creating teams or seating charts based on gender. Her selection, "Constructing Opposite Sides," illustrates how gender divisions are not necessarily natural or inevitable, but again based on the particular context.

While children are active in shaping the multiple meanings of gender in their lives, we can see reflections of the larger world in their play as well. Thorne found that boys often monopolized space on the playground, and sometimes invaded girls' games in order to disrupt them. In her study there was one girl who was widely accepted by both girls and boys' in their games, but this was a rarity.

It is not uncommon for adults to point to the differences in the ways in which boys and girls at early ages behave and presume that distinctions are natural and biological. But it is important not to overlook the fact that children, even at very early ages, are social beings. They are not just influenced by the world around them, but make sense of it themselves, often in unique ways.

Peers are incredibly important in constructing the meaning of gender. Michael A. Messner observed children playing American Youth Soccer Organization (AYSO) soccer. While gender was not always a salient factor, particularly since teams were gender-segregated, he did observe moments when the importance of gender became magnified. In his selection, "Barbie Girls Versus Sea Monsters: Children Constructing Gender," he describes one such moment, which happened during the league's opening day celebration. Each team paraded their mascot, and when the "Barbie Girls" team joyously passed by a group of young boys, they spontaneously began to chant "no Barbie!" While some of the parents commented on how "natural" gender divisions between very young boys and girls seemed to be, Messner examines the performative nature of gender, or how masculinity is something boys frequently feel compelled to demonstrate to *one another*. In one of his examples, Messner notes that boys who may express interest in playing with dolls might have the support and encouragement of their parents, but the condemnation of their peers sends a powerful message to conform.

Finally, it is important to consider that the social categories of race, ethnicity, and gender do not exist in a vacuum—they are interlocking and intersecting, and we can understand these categories better when we examine the intersections more closely. Julie Bettie observed high school students to better understand how girls from a variety of racial, ethnic, and socioeconomic backgrounds make sense of their current social status and future opportunities. Her selection, "Girls, Race, and Identity: Border Work Between Classes," discusses the very important issue of social class, specifically, how those from wealthier, white backgrounds understand their privilege. Likewise, she explores how those labeled "working class" negotiate their sense of self in school, where they are often expected not to excel.

All of these selections remind us that children's experiences vary by race, ethnicity, gender, and social class, and there is no singular definition of what it means to be a child. Children actively make sense of their social position and sometimes defy the expectations of their peers and of the adults in their lives.

Using Racial and Ethnic Concepts: The Critical Case of Very Young Children

DEBRA VAN AUSDALE AND JOE R. FEAGIN

INTRODUCTION

Debra Van Ausdale and Joe R. Feagin examine the racial and ethnic concepts and related actions of very young children in a preschool setting. Breaking with much of the conventional literature on the cognitive development of preschool children, the authors argue that young children engage in interaction involving clear and often sophisticated understandings of racial and ethnic concepts and meanings. They discuss: (1) how racial and ethnic concepts are used to exclude or include others; (2) how racial or ethnic concepts are used to define oneself and others; (3) how power and control link to racial and ethnic understandings; and (4) how adults misperceive the racial and ethnic language and activities of children.

Since the 1930s social science has examined children's attitudes toward race. Research has focused on situations in which race has meaning for children and on how children form racial identities (Clark and Clark 1939; Spencer, Brookins, and Allen 1985), create in-group racial and ethnic orientations (Aboud 1977; Cross 1987; Spencer 1987), form attitudes toward others (Williams and Morland 1976), and use race in friend selection (Schofield and Francis 1982). The literature clearly demonstrates that racial identification and group orientation are salient issues for children (Ramsey 1987).

Cognitive development theories propose stage models to explain children's acquisition of racial and ethnic knowledge (Aboud 1977; Porter 1971). These models assume an age-related progression in children's ability to interpret racial and ethnic information, usually depicting children as proceeding in linear fashion toward cognitively mature adulthood. Most research focuses on children over five years of age; very young children are rarely studied. Research on racial and ethnic views generally uses one of three methods. Techniques include picture or doll-choice tests to secure information on children's racial identities (Clark and Clark 1939), brief observations of children's behavior in controlled situations (Dunn,

Slomkowski, and Beardsall 1994), and third-party (e.g., parent or teacher) reports of children's behavior (Cross 1981; Parcel and Menaghan 1994; Hallinan 1994).

Researchers have rarely sought children's views directly, beyond recording brief responses to tests. Few have interviewed children or made in-depth, long-term observations to assess social attitudes, limiting the ability to investigate more fully the nature of children's lives. Children's abilities have been seriously underestimated by reliance on techniques that do not make real-life sense to children (Donaldson 1978). Investigations often have assumed that young children are incapable of using abstract concepts (Holmes 1995). An emphasis on psychological testing is often coupled with the notion that children have limited understandings of race and ethnicity (Goodman 1964; Katz 1976; Porter 1971). Children are typically assumed to have temporary or naive views about social concepts until at least age seven. Prior to that age, children's use of concepts differs from that of adults in form and content.

Little attention has been devoted to how children create and assign meaning for racial and ethnic concepts. Conventional thinking about children draws on traditional cognitive theories (Katz 1976; Piaget 1926, 1932, 1973; Piaget and Inhelder 1969). Research that explores children's attitudes toward race often relies heavily on Piagetian theories (Aboud 1987, 1988; Allport 1954; Holmes 1995; Ramsey 1987; Wardle 1992) and assumes that because young children's minds are egocentric they cannot handle complex abstractions like race and ethnicity. Under this perspective, race and ethnicity have little meaning until children are able to use these concepts as adults would. Wardle (1992) summarizes cognitive theory as depicting three- to seven-year-olds as egocentric, relying on concrete information rather than abstract knowledge, and possessing no complex ideas about racial identities. In general, Piagetian theory accents each individual child's development and neglects children's social worlds.

Several researchers have broken with the mainstream Piagetian perspective and expanded developmental theory toward a better understanding of the social-cultural contexts of child socialization. While this interpretive theory does not reject Piagetian theories, it argues for greater attention to collective, interpretive reproduction (Corsaro 1992). Vygotsky (1978) places children in a social world in which interactions are the source of mental functioning (Peterson and McCabe 1994) and meanings for social concepts. Spencer (1987) points out that framing children's attitudes as immature limits knowledge of their attitudes. Several researchers stress the need for child-centered research. Corsaro (1979) has pioneered in showing how young children are informed actors within in the social production of everyday life. Sullivan, Zaitchik, and Tager-Flusberg (1994) demonstrate that three-year-olds maintain complex mental-belief systems. Dunn (1993) shows how children create complex networks of relationships. Corsaro and Miller (1992), who demonstrate the effectiveness of interpretive approaches for understanding how children develop meanings, propose a multidimensional theory emphasizing children's collective participation in culture-making.

Although Maccoby's (1988) research demonstrates children's complex knowledge of gender, this new sociology of the child has not systematically examined racial behaviors. We provide data indicating that racial concepts are employed with care by children as young as age three. Research based on the conception of children as incapable of understanding race (Menter 1989) presents as incorrect image of children's use of abstractions. Drawing on Willis (1990) and Thorne (1993), we suggest that notions of race and ethnicity are employed by young children as integrative and symbolically creative tools in the daily construction of social life.

THE RESEARCH APPROACH

We gathered experiential data on how children use racial and ethnic understandings in every-day relationships. Influenced by Dunn's 1993 approach, we made unstructured field observations and recorded everyday behaviors. Our data come from extensive observations of 58 three-, four-, and five-year-old children in a large preschool in a southern city. The school employed a popular antibias curriculum (Derman-Sparks 1989). Over an 11-month period in 1993, we systematically observed everyday interactions in one large classroom containing a very diverse group of children. The center's official data on the racial and ethnic backgrounds of children in the classroom are: White = 24, Asian = 19, Black = 4, biracial = 3, Middle Eastern = 3, Latino = 2, and other = 3.

Children's racial and ethnic designations, which were given by parents, were supplemented with information that we gained through classroom observation of a few children with mixed ethnic identities. We use a shorthand code to describe the racial and ethnic backgrounds of the children. For example, Rita is described as (3.5: White/Latina), indicating that she is three and one-half years old, was initially registered as White, but was later discovered to have a Latino heritage. Michael is listed as (4: Black), indicating that he is four years old, was registered as Black, and that no additional racial or ethnic information was revealed through further observation. This code attempts to illustrate the complex identities of many of the children. In a few cases we have used a broad designation (e.g., Asian) to protect a child's identity. Children with multiple identities are somewhat overrepresented here but not in the larger work from which this study is drawn. These children were adept at negotiating racial and ethnic identities and their activities provided us with clear data on how the complexities of race and ethnicity shaped their daily interactions.

Like the children and teachers, the senior author (hereafter Debi), a White woman, was usually in the classroom all day for five days a week. As observer and playmate, Debi watched the children and listened to them in their free play and teacher-directed activities. Over 11 months Debi observed 370 significant episodes involving a racial or ethnic dimension, about 1 to 3 episodes per day. When children mentioned racial or ethnic matters, Debi noted what they said, to whom they spoke, and the context of the incident. Extensive field notes were entered immediately on a computer in another room when the children were otherwise occupied. This was done to preserve the details of any conversations and the accuracy of the data.

Using an approach resembling that of the "least-adult role" (Corsaro 1981; Mandell 1988), Debi conducted extensive participant observation. When children or adults asked, Debi identified herself as a researcher, and she consistently assumed the role of a nonauthoritarian observer and playmate. She was soon accepted as such by children and teachers, and the children spoke freely, rarely ceasing their activities when she was present. Children's interactions with her differed from their interactions with teachers and parents. Our accounts make clear Debi's natural, nonsanctioning role in discussing racial and ethnic matters initially raised by the children. In no case did Debi ask predetermined questions. Racial and ethnic issues arose naturally. Although Debi sometimes asked questions that might have been asked by other adults, she never threatened the children with a sanction for their words or actions. Thus, our interpretations of children's attitudes and behavior evolved gradually as Debi observed the children in natural settings.

We began with the assumption that very young children would display no knowledge of racial or ethnic concepts and that any use of these concepts would be superficial or naive. Our data contradicted these expectations.

USING RACIAL AND ETHNIC CONCEPTS TO EXCLUDE

Using the playhouse to bake pretend muffins, Rita (3.5: White/Latina) and Sarah (4: White) have all the muffin tins. Elizabeth (3.5: Asian/Chinese), attempting to join them, stands at the playhouse door and asks if she can play. Rita shakes her head vigorously, saying, "No, only people who can speak Spanish can come in." Elizabeth frowns and says, "I can come in." Rita counters, "Can you speak Spanish?" Elizabeth shakes her head no, and Rita repeats, "Well, then you aren't allowed in."

Elizabeth frowns deeply and asks Debi to intercede by telling her: "Rita is being mean to me." Acting within the child-initiated framework, Debi asks Rita, "If only people who speak Spanish are allowed, then how come Sarah can play? Can you speak Spanish, Sarah?" Sarah shakes her head no. "Sarah can't speak Spanish and she is playing," Debi says to Rita, without suggesting she allow Elizabeth in. Rita frowns, amending her statement: "OK, only people who speak either Spanish or English." "That's great!" Debi responds, "because Elizabeth speaks English and she wants to play with you guys." Rita's frown deepens. "No," she says. Debi queries, "But you just said people who speak English can play. Can't you decide?" Rita gazes at Debi, thinking hard. "Well," Rita says triumphantly, "only people who speak two languages."

Elizabeth is waiting patiently for Debi to make Rita let her play, which Debi has no intention of doing. Debi then asks Rita: "Well, Elizabeth speaks two languages, don't you Elizabeth?" Debi looks at Elizabeth, who now is smiling for the first time. Rita is stumped for a moment, then retorts, "She does not. She speaks only English." Debi smiles at Rita: "She does speak two languages—English and Chinese. Don't you?" Debi invites Elizabeth into the conversation. Elizabeth nods vigorously. However, Rita turns away and says to Sarah, "Let's go to the store and get more stuff."

Language was the ethnic marker here. Rita defined rules for entering play on the basis of language—she was aware that each child not only did not look like the others but also spoke a different language. From a traditional Piagetian perspective, Rita might be seen as egocentric and strongly resistant to alternative views. However, here we see the crucial importance of the social-cultural context, in particular the development of racial and ethnic concepts in a collaborative and interpersonal context. Defending her rules, Rita realized her attempts to exclude Elizabeth by requiring two languages had failed. This three-year-old child had created a social rule based on a significant understanding of ethnic markers. The final "two languages" rule did not acknowledge the fact that Sarah only spoke English. Rita's choice of language as an exclusionary device was directed at preventing Elizabeth from entering, not at maintaining a bilingual play space.

Exclusion of others can involve preventing associations with unwanted others, as in Rita's case, or removing oneself from the presence of unwanted others, as in this next instance. Carla (3: White) is preparing herself for the resting time. She picks up her cot and starts to move it. The head teacher, a White woman, asks what she is doing. "I need to move this," explains Carla. "Why?" asks the teacher. "Because I can't sleep next to a nigger", Carla says, pointing to Nicole (4.5: African/biracial) on a cot nearby. "Niggers are stinky. I can't sleep next to one." Stunned, the teacher's eyes widen, then narrow as she frowns. She tells Carla to move her cot back and not to use "hurting words." Carla looks amused and puzzled but complies. Nothing more is said to the children, but the teacher glances at Debi and shakes her head.

Three-year-old Carla's evaluation of the racial status of another young child was sophisticated and showed awareness not only of how to use racial epithets but also of the negative stigma attached to black skin. Like most children we observed, Carla was not the unsophisticated, naive child depicted in the mainstream literature. She used material (e.g., the epithet) that she undoubtedly had learned from other sources, probably in interaction with other children or adults, and she applied this material to a particular interactive circumstance.

Later, after the children have been wakened and have gone to the playground, the center's White director approaches Debi and says, "I have called Carla's parents and asked them to come to a meeting with me and Karen [the teacher] about what happened." Neither Debi nor the director feel a need to clarify what he is referring to, as he adds: "If you want to attend I would really like to have you there. Karen will be there too." Debi tells him she will attend. "I suppose this is what you're looking for," he continues with a smile. "Well, no, not exactly," Debi replies, "but of course it is worth noting, and I am interested in anything that the kids do with race." "Well," he shot back, "I want you to know that Carla did not learn that here!"

Although the observed children rarely used explicit racial slurs, the director's remark about the origin of Carla's epithet is typical of the responses adults gave when children at the center used negative terms. The center's staff was extremely interested in limiting children's exposure to prejudice or discrimination and used a multicultural curriculum to teach children to value diversity. The center's adults often seemed more concerned with the origins of child-initiated race-relevant behaviors than with the nuanced content or development of those behaviors.

The meeting with Carla's parents was informative. Carla's mother is biracial (Asian and White), and her father is White. Both parents are baffled when told of the incident. The father remarks, "Well, she certainly did not learn that sort of crap from us!" The teacher immediately insists that Carla did not learn such words at the center. Carla's father offers this explanation: "I'll bet she got that ["nigger", comment] from Teresa. Her dad is really red." When Debi asks what he means, the father responds, "You know, he's a real redneck." Then the director steps in: "It's amazing what kids will pick up in the neighborhood. It doesn't really matter where she learned it from. What we need to accomplish is unlearning it." He suggests methods for teaching Carla about differences and offers her parents some multicultural toys.

The reactions of the key adults illustrate the strength of adult beliefs about children's conceptual abilities. Their focus was on the child as imitator. The principal concern of teacher, parents, and administrator was to assure one another that the child did not learn such behavior from them. Thus adults reshape their conceptions as children do, collaboratively. Acting defensively, they exculpated themselves by suggesting someone else must be responsible. The director ended the blaming by attributing the source of the child's behavior to neighborhood—a diffuse, acceptable enemy—and initiated the task of unlearning.

USING RACIAL AND ETHNIC CONCEPTS TO INCLUDE

The children also used racial and ethnic understandings and concepts to include others—to engage them in play or teach them about racial and ethnic identities.

Ling (5: Asian/Chinese) has a book that teaches the Chinese language. She announces to Debi that her grandmother has given her the book and that she is learning Chinese. Debi asks if she is making progress. "Oh yes," Ling says happily, "I have already learned many characters. They're called characters, you know." She points out several. "What does that say?" Debi asks, pointing to one. "Cat!" Ling beams. Debi and Ling spend some time reading from Ling's book, then Ling leaves to show off her reading prowess to another child.

Over several weeks, Ling's behavior underscores for the observer how racial and ethnic understandings develop in social contexts. Ling engages numerous others in reading Chinese with her. Carrying the book everywhere, she earnestly tries to teach others to read and write Chinese characters. Chinese characters appear on other children's drawings and on the playground. Other children actively embrace these new characters and concepts and incorporate them into their activities, a clear indication of how children learn ethnic ideas from each other. Ling's efforts demonstrate that she is aware that non-Chinese, including adults, do not know how to read Chinese. Clearly she is aware that Chinese is distinct from the experience of most people around her, and she recognizes this even though she herself is just learning to read Chinese.

Jewel (4: Asian/Middle Eastern) uses her knowledge of different languages to draw an adult into a child-initiated game. Jewel, Cathie (4: White), and Renee (4.5: White) are trying to swing on a tire swing. Rob, a White college work-study student, has been pushing them but leaves to perform another task. Jewel starts to chant loudly, "Unche I, Unche I!" (an approximation of what she sounded like to Debi). The other girls join in, attracting Rob's attention. He begins to push the girls again. With a smile, he asks, "What are you saying?" Jewel replies, "It means 'pants on fire'!" All three girls roar with laughter. Rob smiles and urges Jewel, "Say it again." She begins to chant it again, now drawing Rob into the play. Rob asks, "Tell me some more." Jewel shakes her head, continuing to chant "Unche I!" and to laugh. Rob persists, asking Jewel to teach him how to "talk." Jewel obliges, making up new chants and repeating them until the others get them, then changing the words and repeating the behavior again. Cathie and Renee are delighted. The playing continues for a while, with the girls chanting and Rob pushing them on the swing.

Later, Debi learned that Jewel had developed sophisticated ethnic play around her understanding of language. When Jewel translated "Unche I" as "pants on fire," Rob accepted this and the game continued. Several weeks later, however, Debi heard Jewel's mother greet her daughter at the door by saying "Unche I!" It seemed strange that a mother would say "pants on fire" to greet her child, and Debi noted the incident in her field notes. Some time later, when Debi presented this scene to graduate students in a seminar, one student laughed, informing her that as far as he could tell Jewel was saying her own name. The phrase meant "Jewel."

Jewel's use of her native name illustrates Willis's (1990) notion of symbolic creativity among children. Jewel was able to facilitate and increase interaction with an adult of another cultural background by choosing word symbols that intrigued the adult. As the interaction continued, she elaborated on that symbol, creating a new world of ethnic meanings that accomplished her goal. She successfully shaped an adult's actions for some time by catching his attention with language she realized he did not understand. This required that she understand his perspective and evaluate his knowledge of language, activities requiring considerable interpretive capability.

USING RACIAL AND ETHNIC CONCEPTS TO DEFINE ONESELF

The use of racial and ethnic concepts to include or exclude others is often coupled with the use of these concepts to describe and define oneself. For most children, racial and/or ethnic identity is an important aspect of themselves, and they demonstrate this in insightful ways in important social contexts.

Renee (4.5: White), a very pale little girl, has been to the beach over the weekend and comes to school noticeably tanned. Linda (4: White) and Erinne (5: biracial) engage her in an intense conversation. They discuss whether her skin would stay that color or get darker until she became, as Linda says, "an African American, like Charles" (another child). Renee denies she could become Black, but this new idea, planted in her head by interaction with the other children, distresses her. On her own initiative, she discusses the possibility with Debi and her mother, both of whom tell her the darker color is temporary.

Renee was unconvinced and commented on her racial identity for weeks. She brought up the issue with other children in many contexts. This linking of skin color with racial identity is found in much traditional literature on children's racial understandings (Clark and Clark 1940). But this racial marking was more than a fleeting interest, unlike the interest mainstream cognitive theorists might predict for such a young child. Renee reframed the meaning of skin color by questioning others on their thoughts and comparing her skin to others'.

Corinne (4: African/White) displays an ability to create meaning by drawing from her personal world. Corinne's mother is Black and is from an African country; her father is a White American. Corinne speaks French and English and is curious about everything at the center. She is a leader and often initiates activities with other children. Most children defer to her. One day Corinne is examining a rabbit cage on the playground. A teacher is cleaning out the cage and six baby bunnies are temporarily housed in an aluminum bucket that Corinne is holding. Three bunnies are white, two are black, and one is spotted black and white.

As Corinne is sitting at a table, Sarah (4: White) stuck her head into the bucket. "Stop that!" Corinne orders. Sarah complies and asks, "Why do you have the babies?" "I'm helping Marie [teacher]," says Corinne. "How many babies are there?" Sarah asks Corinne. "Six!" Corinne announces, "Three boys and three girls." "How can you tell if they're boys or girls?" Sarah questions. "Well," Corinne begins, "my daddy is White, so the white ones are boys. My mommy is Black, so the black ones are girls." Sarah counts: "That's only five." The remaining bunny is black and white. "Well, that one is like me, so it's a girl," Corinne explains gently. She picks up the bunny and says, "See, this one is both, like me!" Sarah then loses interest, and Corinne returns to cooing over the bunnies.

This four-year-old's explanation incorporates an interesting combination of color, race, and gender. While her causal reasoning was faulty, she constructed what for her was a sophisticated and reasonable view of the bunnies' sexes. She displayed an understanding of the idea that an offspring's color reflects the colors of its parents, a knowledge grounded in her experience as a biracial child. Strayer (1986) underscores how children develop appropriate attributions regarding situational determinants. Corinne's use of parental gender to explain the unknown gender of the bunnies was an appropriate explanation of how bunnies got certain colors. Skin color was a salient part of her identity, and it was reasonable in her social world to assume that it would be salient for the identity of others, even animals.

In the literature on childhood, the nature of a child's interaction with a peer is often analyzed in terms of how effective the outcome is for the child (Lee 1975). Exchange theory analysis ignores the often playful nature of children's interactions. For Corinne, comparing parents' skin colors to the rabbits' colors solved the dilemma of the bunnies' sexes. The interactive prodding of another child about the gender of the spotted bunny became an occasion for creativity and delight for Corinne. That her answers about race and gender were not correct is not as important as her ability to handle questions of race and gender. Most importantly, perhaps, the answers made sense to Corinne and Sarah.

Racial and ethnic understandings involve many aspects of one's culture. Jie (4.5: Asian/Chinese) brought her lunch of homemade Chinese dishes to school. When David, a White student employee, asks her what she has, she replies, "I brought food for Chinese people." Pointing to containers of Chinese food, she explains, "Chinese people prefer Chinese food." When David asks for a taste, she hesitates. "Well," she offers, "you probably won't like it."

You're not Chinese." Here are the beginnings of explanations for differences between racial and ethnic groups.

Jie demonstrated not only that she recognized the differences between racial and ethnic groups, but also that she understood the socially transmitted view that physical differences are accompanied by differences in cultural tastes and behavior. Her interaction with the adult revealed a strong understanding of her culture by referring to her food as "for Chinese people" and wondering if non-Chinese people would enjoy it. Her explanation indicated that she was aware of what is *not* a part of her culture as much as what *is* a part of it, and that it is possible that outsiders would not enjoy Chinese food.

In another setting, Corinne (4: African/White) provides an example of the complexity of young children's racial understandings: She refines the nature of racial identity during a hand-painting activity. The children have taken a field trip and are asked to make a thank-you poster for their host, a poster constructed of a large sheet of paper featuring handprints of the children. Children are asked by the teacher to choose a color that "looks just like you do." The paints are known as "People Colors," and are common at daycare centers concerned with diversity issues. The activity was designed to increase appreciation of differences in color among the children (Derman-Sparks 1989).

The six paints ranged from dark brown to pale pink. The handprint poster activity is familiar to the children, and the teacher asks Debi to help. Debi accepts but keeps her involvement to a minimum. Several children wait in line to participate in this desirable activity. Each chooses paint according to the teacher's criterion, has Debi apply the paint to the palm of one hand, and then presses the painted hand onto the poster. Debi then writes the child's name next to the handprint. Some children point out how closely the paint matches their skin color or ask Debi if she thought the choice was "right."

Corinne approaches the table, and Debi says, "OK, which color is the most like you? Which color matches your skin?" Corinne looks over the bottles carefully and chooses pale brown. "This one for one hand," she replies, continuing to scan the bottles, "and this one for the other hand," she concludes, choosing a second, dark brown color. When Debi asks if that color matches her skin, Corinne calmly replies, "I have two colors in my skin." Debi smiles and paints one of her palms pale brown and the other dark brown. Corinne places both hands on the poster, making two prints. Debi then writes Corinne's name between the two handprints. "Perfect!" Corinne says.

This four-year-old chose appropriately for her understanding of the situation. That the paints she picked did not exactly match her skin color was not important to her because she was thinking in terms of her parents' different racial identities. Corinne insisted that she be allowed to choose two colors to reflect her biracial origin. For her, choosing two colors is not an example of cognitive confusion or inconsistency (as a mainstream analysis might see it), but rather her innovative way of recognizing that her mother is dark brown ("Black") and her father is pale brown ("White"). These examples show that children's abilities exceed what would be predicted from the mainstream research perspective.

USING RACIAL AND ETHNIC CONCEPTS TO DEFINE OTHERS

We observed many examples of children exploring the complex notions of skin color, hair differences, and facial characteristics. They often explore what these things mean and make racial and/or ethnic interpretations of these perceived differences. Mindy (4: White) insists that Debi is Indian. When queried, Mindy replies that it is because Debi is wearing her long dark hair in a braid. When Debi explains that she is not Indian, the child remarks that maybe Debi's mother is Indian.

These statements show not only awareness of the visible characteristics of race and ethnicity but also insight into how visible markers are passed from generation to generation. They demonstrate a child's ability to grasp salient characteristics of a racial and/or ethnic category not her own and apply them to others in a collaborative and evolving way.

In another episode, Taleshia (3: Black) approaches the handpainting table. Asked if she wants to make a handprint, she nods shyly. A child with dark brown skin, Taleshia scans the paint bottles and points to pale pink. Curious about her preference, Debi asks, "Taleshia, is this the color that looks like you?" Taleshia nods and holds out her hand. Behind her, Cathie (3.5: White) objects to Taleshia's decision. "No, no," Cathie interjects, "She's not that color. She's brown." Cathie moves to the table. "You're this color," Cathie says and picks out the bottle of dark brown paint. Cathie is interested in helping Taleshia correct her apparent mistake about skin color. "Do you want this color?" Debi asks Taleshia. "No," she replies, "I want this one," touching the pink bottle. Regarding Taleshia with amazement, Cathie exclaims, "For goodness sake, can't you see that you aren't pink?" "Debi," Cathie continues to insist, "you have to make her see that she's brown." Cathie is exasperated and takes Taleshia by the arm. "Look," she instructs, "you are brown! See?" Cathie holds Taleshia's arm next to her own. "I am pink, right?" Cathie looks to Debi for confirmation. "Sure enough," Debi answers, "you are pink." "Now," Cathie continues, looking relieved, "Taleshia needs to be brown." Debi looks at Taleshia, who is now frowning, and asks her, "Do you want to be brown?" She shakes her head vigorously and points to pale pink, "I want that color."

Cathie is frustrated, and trying to be supportive, Debi explains that "Taleshia can choose any color she thinks is right." Cathie again objects, but Taleshia smiles, and Debi paints her palm pink. Then Taleshia makes her handprint. Cathie stares, apparently convinced that Taleshia and Debi have lost touch with reality. As Taleshia leaves, Cathie takes her place, remarking to Debi, "I just don't know what's the matter with you. Couldn't you see that *she is brown!*" Cathie gives up and chooses pale pink for herself, a close match. Cathie makes her handprint and says to Debi, "See, I am *not* brown."

Taleshia stuck to her choice despite Cathie's insistence. Both three-year-olds demonstrate a strong awareness of the importance of skin color, and their views are strongly held. This example underscores the importance of child-centered research. A traditional conceptualization of this Black child's choice of skin color paint might suggest that the child is confused about racial identity. If she chose pink in the usual experimental setting (Clark and Clark 1940; Porter 1971), she would probably be evaluated as rejecting herself for a preferred whiteness. Debi had several other interactions with Taleshia. The three-year-old had, on other occasions, pointed out how pale Debi was and how dark her own skin was. She had explained to Debi that she was Black, that she thought she was pretty, and that pink was her favorite color. One possible explanation for her choice of pink for her skin color in the handpainting activity relies on Debi's knowledge of Taleshia's personality, family background, and previous interactions with others. Taleshia may have chosen pink because it is her favorite color, but this does not mean that she is unaware that most of her skin is dark. Another explanation for Taleshia's choice of skin color representation is that, like other African Americans, Taleshia's palms are *pink* while most of her skin is very dark. Perhaps she was choosing a color to match the color of her palms, a reasonable choice because the task was to paint the palms for handprints. The validity of this interpretation is reinforced by another episode at the center. One day Taleshia sat down and held Debi's hands in hers, turning them from top to bottom. Without uttering a word, she repeated this activity with her own hands, drawing Debi's attention to this act. The three-year-old was contrasting the pink-brown variations in her skin color with Debi's pinkish hand color. This explanation for the child's paint choice might not occur to a researcher who did not pay careful attention to the context and the child's personal perspective. Taleshia's ideas, centered in observations of herself and others, were more important to her than another child's notions of appropriate color. Far from being confused about skin color, she was creating meaning for color based on her own evaluations.

USING RACIAL CONCEPTS TO CONTROL

The complex nature of children's group interactions and their solo behaviors demonstrates that race and ethnicity are salient, substantial aspects of their lives. They understand racial nuances that seem surprisingly sophisticated, including the power of race. How children use this power in their relationships is demonstrated in two further episodes.

Brittany (4: White) and Michael (4: Black) come to Debi demanding that she resolve a conflict. Mike tearfully demands that Debi tell Brittany that he "does too have a white one." As he makes this demand, Brittany solemnly shakes her head no. "A white what?" Debi asks. "Rabbit!" he exclaims. "At home, in a cage." Brittany continues shaking her head no, infuriating Mike. He begins to shout at the top of his lungs, "I do too have a white one!" Debi asks Brittany, "Why don't you think he has a white rabbit at home?" "He can't," she replies, staring at Mike, who renews his cries. Debi tries to solve the mystery, asking Mike to describe his bunny. "She white," he scowls at Brittany. "You do not," she replies. Mike screams at her "I DO TOOO!" Debi hugs Mike to calm him and takes Brittany's hand. Brittany says, "He can't have a white rabbit." Debi asks why, and the child replies, "Because he's Black." Debi tells Brittany, "He can have any color bunny he wants." Mike nods vigorously and sticks his tongue out at Brittany, who returns the favor. "See," he says, "you just shut up. You don't know." Brittany, who is intensely involved in baiting Mike, shakes her head, and says "Can't." She sneers, leaning toward him and speaking slowly, "You're Black." Mike is angry, and Debi comforts him.

Then Debi asks Brittany, "Have you been to Mike's house to see his bunny?" "No," she says. Debi asks, "Then how do you know that his bunny isn't white?" Debi is curious to find out why Brittany is intent on pestering Mike, who is usually her buddy. "Can't *you* see that he's Black?" she gazes at Debi in amazement. Debi replies, "Yes, of course I can see that Mike is Black, but aren't we talking about Mike's rabbit?" Debi is momentarily thrown by the child's calm demeanor. Brittany again shakes her head slowly, watching Debi for a reaction all the while. "Mike is Black." she says, deliberately forming the words. She repeats, "He is Black." Debi tries again, "Yes, Mike is Black and his bunny is white," now waiting for her response. Brittany shakes her head. "Why not?" Debi tries. "Because he is *Black*," Brittany replies with a tone suggesting that Debi is the stupidest person she has ever met. "Have you been to his house?" Debi asks her again. She shakes her head no. "Then," Debi continues, "how do you know that his bunny isn't white?" "I know," Brittany replies confidently. "How?" Debi tries one last time. "He can't have just any old color rabbit?" Debi asks. "Nope." Brittany retorts firmly, "Blacks can't have whites."

Brittany insisted that Mike could not own a white rabbit because he is Black. She "knew" it and belabored this point until he was driven to seek adult intervention. His plea for intercession was unusual because he is a large boy who was normally in charge of interactions with peers. In this instance, however, he was driven to tears by Brittany's remarks. "Blacks can't have whites" was her social rule. The power of skin color had become a tool in Brittany's hands that she used to dominate interaction with another child.

Brittany's ideas are strong—she creates a similar confrontation with a different child a week later. In this later case, Brittany and Martha (3.5: Black/White) are discussing who will get to take which rabbit home. Martha states that she will take the white one. Brittany again starts the "Blacks can't have whites" routine that she so successfully used with Michael. Martha becomes upset, telling Brittany she is stupid. This scene lasts about 10 minutes until it escalates into shouting, and Joanne, a teacher, breaks up the fight. Neither girl will explain to Joanne what the trouble is. They both just look at her and say "I don't know" when Joanne asks what is going on. Joanne tells them that friends don't yell at each other. When the teacher leaves, Martha takes a swing at Brittany, who runs away laughing and sticking out her tongue.

Thus Brittany engaged two Black children in heated interactions based on skin color. In the classical Piagetian interpretation, she would be seen as egocentric and resistant to other interpretations. Contesting her social rule on skin color creates a disequilibrium for her that would somehow be worked out as she seeks a rational, adult perspective on skin color. However, an interpretive analysis underscores the crucial collaborative context. Brittany's use of racial concepts involves her in intimate interaction with two other children. When a teacher got involved, Brittany stopped, and she and her victim refused to offer an explanation. In the first episode Brittany was willing to engage Debi, who was not a sanctioning adult, in a detailed discussion, taking valuable play time to explain her reasoning. When confronted by a teacher, Brittany withdrew, refusing to disclose what was going on between her and the Black girl. Brittany had created a tool to dominate others, a tool based on a racial concept coupled with a social rule. In addition, all three children were highly selective about the adults with whom they shared their racially oriented views and behavior.

In another encounter, this time among three children, a White child demonstrates her knowledge of broader race relations, demonstrating her grasp of race-based power inequalities. During play time Debi watches Renee (4: White) pull Ling-mai (3: Asian) and Jocelyn (4.5: White) across the playground in a wagon. Renee tugs away enthusiastically. Suddenly, Renee drops the handle, which falls to the ground, and she stands still, breathing heavily. Ling-mai, eager to continue this game, jumps from the wagon and picks up the handle. As Ling-mai begins to pull, Renee admonishes her, "No, no. You can't pull this wagon. Only *White Americans* can pull this wagon." Renee has her hands on her hips and frowns at Ling-mai. Ling-mai tries again, and Renee again insists that only "White Americans" are permitted to do this task.

Ling-mai sobs loudly and runs to a teacher, complaining that "Renee hurt my feelings." "Did you hurt Ling-mai's feelings?" the teacher asks Renee, who nods, not saying a word. "I think you should apologize," the teacher continues, "because we are all friends here and friends don't hurt each others feelings." "Sorry," mutters Renee, not looking at Ling-mai, "I didn't do it on purpose." "OK," the teacher finishes, "can you guys be good friends now?" Both girls nod without looking at each other and quickly move away.

This interaction reveals several layers of meaning. Both children recognized the implications of Renee's harsh words and demands. Renee accurately underscored the point that Ling-mai, the child of Asian international students, was neither White nor American. Her failure to be included in these two groups, according to Renee's pronouncement, precluded her from being in charge of the wagon. Ling-mai responded, not by openly denying Renee's statements, but by complaining to the teacher that Renee had hurt her feelings. Both children seem knowledgeable about the structure of the U.S. and global racial hierarchy and accept the superior position accorded to Whites. The four-year-old child exercised authority as a White American and controlled the play with comments and with her stance and facial expressions. Our findings extend previous research on young children's knowledge of status and power (Corsaro 1979; Damon 1977) by showing that children are aware of the power and authority granted to Whites. The children were not confused about the meanings of these harsh racial words and actions.

ADULT MISPERCEPTIONS

Children's use of racial and ethnic concepts often goes unnoticed, even by adults in daily contact with them. This is illustrated by the responses of classroom teachers and the center director to preliminary reports on our research. Debi wrote two research reports, one for the classroom teachers and one for the director. After reading the reports, the teachers insisted to Debi that she must have been observing "some other children" and that "these are not our kids." The director seemed determined to "guess" the identity of children whose incidents Debi described at a meeting. Throughout the episodes Debi described, he interrupted with remarks like "I'll bet that's Sarah you're talking about, isn't it?" His determination to attach names to the children revealed his investment in "curing" racism. He seemed determined to discover the culprits so unlearning might begin.

Adults' strong need to deny that children can use racial and ethnic concepts is also revealed in the next account. Here two children are engaged in a discussion of "what" they are. Debi is sitting with all the children on the steps to the deck playing "Simon Says." "Simon," a child selected by teachers to lead the game, directs the main action, while Debi observes that Rita (3.5: White/Latina) and Louis (4: Black) are engaged in their own private side activity. While the game continues, Rita and Louis discuss what they are. "What are you?" Louis asks Rita, and without waiting for her reply announces, "I'm Black and you're White." "No," she retorts, correcting him, "I'm not White, I'm mixed." Louis regards her curiously, but at this moment Joanne, the lone Black teacher in the classroom, intervenes. "You're not mixed, Rita, you're Spanish," she informs the child. "What race am I?" Joanne continues, trying to get the children to change the subject and glancing over at me anxiously. Rita replies, "Mixed." "Mixed!?" Joanne, laughing, responds, "Mixed with what?" "Blue," Rita says, looking only at her hands. Joanne is wearing a solid blue outfit. "Oh no, honey," Joanne says, "I'm Black too, like Louis, not mixed. What an interesting conversation you guys are having." Rita says nothing in response, and Louis remains silent throughout Joanne's attempt at dialogue. Suddenly, "Simon Says" ends and the kids run to the playground, escaping Joanne's questions. Joanne smiles and remarks to Debi, "Boy, it's really amazing what they pick up, isn't it?"

When Joanne intervened, Rita and Louis had to refocus their attention from a discussion between themselves about what they "are" to responding to Joanne's questioning. The adult interruption silenced Louis completely and made Rita defensive and wary. As other research has demonstrated, adult involvement in children's discourse can result in changes in the nature of the children's relations (Danielewicz, Rogers, and Noblit 1996). Rita realized that she must avoid sanctions when Joanne introduced her own racial identity into the game, attempting to distract the children from what Joanne perceived as an argument based on racial differences. However, the children were engaged in an appropriate discussion about their origins. Rita is indeed a "mixed" Latina, for her mother is from one Latin American country and her father is from another Latin American country. Rita understood this and had on other occasions described trips to visit her father's home. Louis is indeed Black and views Rita as White. Rita seemed to be trying to extend the concept beyond skin color and thus to educate Louis, until the teacher interrupted. Joanne's assumption seemed to be twofold: that Rita was confused and that as a teacher Joanne must act preventively. Here the teacher focused on quashing prejudice rather than seizing an opportunity to listen to the children and discuss their racial and ethnic perspectives. Adults tend to control children's use of racial and ethnic concepts and interpret children's use of these concepts along prejudice-defined lines. Clearly, the social context of children's learning, emphasized in the interpretive approach, includes other children and adults, but our accounts also demonstrate the way in which children's sophisticated understandings are developed without adult collaboration and supervision.

Jason (3: White) and Dao (4: Chinese) have developed a friendship over a period of several weeks, despite the fact that Dao speaks almost no English and Jason speaks no Chinese. The two are inseparable. The adults at the center comment on the boys' relationship, wondering aloud about their communication. Yet the boys experience little trouble in getting along and spend hours engaged in play and conversation.

As this friendship develops, Jason's mother, several months pregnant at the time, comes to the head teacher with a problem. "Jason has begun to talk baby talk," she informs the teacher. "Oh, I wouldn't worry about it," the teacher reassures her. "Kids often do that when their mom is expecting another baby. It's a way to get attention." Jason's mother seems unconvinced and asks the teachers to watch for Jason's talking "gibberish" and to let her know about it.

Jason and Dao continue their friendship. Teachers remark on their closeness despite Dao's extremely limited command of English. One afternoon, Dao and Jason are playing with blocks near Debi. Deeply involved, they chatter with each other. Debi does not understand a single word either of them are saying, but they have no difficulty cooperating in constructing block towers and laugh together each time a tower collapses. Jason's mother arrives to take him home. He ignores her and continues to play. The head teacher joins the scene and begins a conversation with Jason's mother. When Jason finally acknowledges his mother's presence, he does so by addressing her with a stream of words that make no sense to the nearby adults.

"See, see? That's what I mean," Jason's mother says excitedly. "He talks baby talk. It's really getting bad." The teacher remarks that perhaps after the baby's arrival this will disappear. Debi, after a moment's thought, says to Jason, "Honey, would you say that again in English?" Jason nods and responds, "I want to check out a book from the library before we go home." The teacher and Jason's mother look at him and then at Debi. "Oh, my goodness!" the teacher exclaims, "How did you know to ask him that?" Debi gestures toward the boys and says, "It seemed reasonable. They talk all the time." "That's amazing," Jason's mother shakes her head. "What language do you think they are speaking?" she asks Debi. "I don't know," Debi responds. "I don't understand a word of it. Maybe it's invented."

With the cooperation of Dao's father, who listened in on the boys, Debi finally determined that Jason had learned enough Chinese from Dao, and Dao had learned enough English from Jason to form a blended language sufficient for communication. What adults thought was "baby talk"—and what was thought by the teacher to be jealousy toward an unborn sibling—was an innovative synthesis of two languages formed by young children maintaining a cross-ethnic friendship. This is a normal human phenomenon and, if the boys were adults, would likely have been interpreted as a pidgin language—the simplified language that develops between peoples with different languages living in a common territory.

One of the powerful ethnocultural definers of Dao's social life was his inability to speak English, which caused him grief because it kept him from following teachers' directions promptly. He experienced difficulty in creating friendships, for most other children were not patient enough to accommodate him. Dao was a quiet and cautious child, particularly when teachers were nearby. Jason's ability to develop a language in interaction with Dao was empowering for Dao: the language was the cement that bonded the boys together. The boys' collaborative actions were not only creative, but also reveal one of the idealized (at least for adults) ways that human beings bridge ethnic and cultural differences. The boys were natural multiculturalists.

CONCLUSION

Through extensive observation, this study has captured the richness of children's racial and ethnic experiences. The racial nature of children's interactions becomes fully apparent only when their interactions are viewed over time and in context. Close scrutiny of children's lives reveals that they are as intricate and convoluted as those of adults.

Blumer (1969:138) suggests that any sociological variable is, on examination, "an intricate and inner-moving complex." Dunn (1993) notes that children's relationships are complex and multidimensional, even within their own families. In the case of Jason and Dao, for example, the interactions were not only complex and incomprehensible to adults, but also evolved over time. By exploring the use of racial concepts in the child's natural world, instead of trying to remove the child or the concepts from that world, we glean a more complete picture of how children view and manipulate racial and ethnic concepts and understandings.

For most children, racial and ethnic issues arise forcefully within the context of their interaction with others. Most of the children that we observed had little or no experience with people from other racial or ethnic groups outside of the center. For these very young children, who are having their first extensive social experiences outside the family, racial and ethnic differences became powerful identifiers of self and other. Whether this is also true for children who do not experience such a diverse range of exposure to racial and ethnic concepts is beyond the scope of this project. However, over the 11 months we observed dozens of slowly evolving transformations in these children's racial and ethnic explorations and understandings. For many children, racial and ethnic awareness increased. Some, like Taleshia, regularly explored racial identities by comparing their skin color with that of others. Others, like Renee, faced crises over identity. For still others, racial and/or ethnic matters arose intermittently, but these matters did not seem to be central to the children's explorations. Children varied in how often they expressed or indicated racial or ethnic understandings, but we were unable to observe each child constantly and cannot make a more detailed judgment on this issue.

To fully understand the importance of children's racial and/or ethnic understandings, the nuanced complexity and interconnected nature of their thinking and behavior must be accepted and recognized. Measures of racial and ethnic awareness should consider not only children's cognitive abilities but also the relationships that children develop in social situations.

Corsaro (1981) proposes that conventional cognitive-developmental models do not offer much analysis of children's communicative skills in regard to status issues. Peer interaction is critical for children exploring social status. Children can explore the meaning of social authority, social rules, and status when separated from adults and older siblings they are in contact with at home. Social status and its accompanying power and prestige become important to very young children at a preschool. In the classroom hierarchy, teachers have the highest status, and children acknowledge this by acquiescing to teachers. However, much research suggests that children behave differently when an adult is present than they do when they are involved with only other children (Danielewicz, Rogers and Noblit 1996). Debi's usual position as playmate-observer was affirmed periodically; Debi was not a teacher in the children's eyes. When Debi approached children playing, they usually did not alter their activity, even if the activity was one that would be sanctioned by a teacher. In contrast, children either stopped what they were doing or changed the nature of such activities when teachers entered the scene.

Regarding the racial and ethnic hierarchy, young children understand that in U.S. society higher status is awarded to White people. Many understand that simply by virtue of their skin color, Whites are accorded more power, control, and prestige. Very young children carry out interactions in which race is salient. Racial knowledge is situational, and children can interact in a race-based or race-neutral manner, according to their evaluations of appropriateness. In children's worlds race emerges early as a tool for social interaction and quickly becomes a complex and fluid component of everyday interaction.

The behaviors of the children in this preschool setting are likely to be repeated in other diverse settings. The traditional literature accepts that children display prejudice by the time they arrive at school, but offers no explanation about the acquisition of this prejudice beyond it being an imitation of parental behavior. We expect continuity of children's racial and ethnic categories across settings, for children reveal a readiness to use their knowledge of race and ethnicity.

The observed episodes underscore problems in traditional theories of child development. When children fail cognitive tasks framed in terms of principles such as conservation and reciprocity, researchers often conclude that children lack the cognitive capability to understand race. However, surveys and observations of children in natural settings demonstrate that three-year-old children have constant, well-defined, and negative biases toward racial and ethnic others (Ramsey 1987). Rather than insisting that young children do not understand racial or ethnic ideas because they do not reproduce these concepts on adult-centered cognitive tests, researchers should determine the extent to which racial and ethnic concepts—as used in daily interaction—are salient definers of children's social reality. Research on young children's use of racial and gender concepts demonstrates that the more carefully a research design explores the real life of children, the more likely that research can answer questions about the nature of race and ethnicity in children's everyday lives.

Discussion Questions

1. How have researchers traditionally studied racial concepts in children? How does this study differ?

2. How did children use racial concepts to include other children in play? To exclude other children?

3. In what way did children use racial concepts to help construct their own sense of identity?

4. What does this study tell us about how children actively make sense of the concepts of race? What do adults typically not understand about children's use of racial concepts?

References

Aboud, Frances E. 1977. "Interest in Ethnic Information: A Cross-Cultural Developmental Study. *Canadian Journal of Behavioral Science* 9:134–46

———. 1987. "The Development of Ethnic Self-Identification and Attitudes." pp. 32–55 in *Children's Ethnic Socialization: Pluralism and Development,* edited by J. S. Phinney and M. J. Rotheram, Newbury Park, CA: Sage.

———. 1988. *Children and Prejudice.* New York: Blackwell.

Allport, Gordon W. 1954. *The Nature of Prejudice.* Cambridge, MA: Addison-Wesley.

Blumer, Herbert. 1969. *Symbolic Interactionism: Perspective and Method.* Englewood Cliffs, NJ: Prentice-Hall.

Clark, Kenneth B. and Mamie P. Clark. 1939. "The Development of Consciousness of Self and the Emergence of Racial Identification in Negro Preschool Children." *Journal of Social Psychology,* SPSSI Bulletin 10:591–99.

———. 1940. "Skin Color as a Factor in Racial Identification and Preference in Negro Children." *Journal of Negro Education* 19:341–58.

Corsaro, William A. 1979. "We're Friends, Right?" *Language in Society.* 8:315–36.

———. 1981. "Entering the Child's World: Research Strategies for Field Entry and Data Collection in a Preschool Setting." pp. 117–46 in *Ethnography and Language in Educational Settings*, edited by J. Green and C. Wallat. Norwood, NJ: Ablex.

———. 1992. "Interpretive Reproduction in Children's Peer Cultures." *Social Psychology Quarterly* 55:160–77.

Corsaro, William A. and Peggy J. Miller. 1992. *Interpretive Approaches to Children's Socialization.* New Directions for Child Development Series, Number 58, Winter. San Francisco, CA: Jossey-Bass Publishers.

Cross, William E., Jr. 1981. "Black Families and Black Identity Development." *Journal of Comparative Studies* 12:19–50.

———. 1987. "A Two-Factor Theory of Black Identity: Implications for the Study of Identity Development in Minority Children." pp. 117–33 in *Children's Ethnic Socialization: Pluralism and Development*, edited by J. S. Phinney and M. J. Rotheram. Newbury Park, CA: Sage.

Damon, William. 1977. *The Social World of the Child.* San Francisco, CA: Jossey-Bass.

Danielewicz, Jane M., Dwight L. Rogers, and George Noblit. 1996. "Children's Discourse Patterns and Power Relations in Teacher-Led and Child-Led Sharing Time." *Qualitative Studies in Education* 9:311–31.

Derman-Sparks, Louise. 1989. *Anti-Bias Curriculum: Tools for Empowering Young Children.* Washington, DC: National Association for the Education of Young Children.

Donaldson, Margaret. 1978. *Children's Minds.* London, England: Fontana.

Dunn, Judy. 1993. "Young Children's Understanding of Other People: Evidence from Observations within the Family." pp. 97–114 in *Young Children's Close Relationships: Beyond Attachment*, edited by J. Dunn. Newbury Park, CA: Sage.

Dunn, Judy, Cheryl Slomkowski, and Lynn Beardsall. 1994. "Sibling Relationships from the Preschool Period through Middle Childhood and Early Adolescence." *Developmental Psychology* 30:315–24.

Goodman, Mary E. 1964. *Race Awareness in Young Children.* New York: Crowell-Collier.

Hallinan, Maureen T. 1994. "Effects of Tracking on Achievement of Black and White Students: A Longitudinal Study." Paper presented at the annual meeting of the American Sociological Association, August 4–10, Los Angeles, CA.

Holmes, Robyn M. 1995. *How Young Children Perceive Race.* Thousand Oaks, CA: Sage.

Katz, Phyllis A. 1976. "The Acquisition of Racial Attitudes in Children." pp. 125–54 in *Towards the Elimination of Racism,* edited by P. A. Katz. New York: Pergamon.

Lee, Lee C. 1975. "Toward a Cognitive Theory of Interpersonal Development: Importance of Peers. pp. 207–21 in *Friendship and Peer Relations,* vol. 4, edited by M. Lewis and L. A. Rosenblum. New York: Wiley.

Maccoby, Eleanor E. 1988. "Gender as a Social Category." *Developmental Psychology* 24:755–65.

Mandell, Nancy. 1988. "The Least-Adult Role in Studying Children." *Journal of Contemporary Ethnography* 16:433–67.

Menter, Ian. 1989. " 'They're Too Young to Notice': Young Children and Racism." pp. 91–104 in

Disaffection from School? The Early Years, edited by G. Barrett. London, England: Falmer.

Parcel, Toby L. and Elizabeth G. Menaghan. 1994. *Parents' Jobs and Children's Lives.* New York: Aldine de Gruyter.

Peterson, Carole and Allyssa McCabe. 1994. "A Social Interactionist Account of Developing Decontextualized Narrative Skill." *Developmental Psychology* 30:937–48.

Piaget, Jean. 1926. *The Language and Thought of the Child.* London, England: Kegan Paul.

———. 1932. *The Moral Judgment of the Child.* Glencoe, IL: Free Press.

———. 1973. *The Child and Reality.* New York: Viking.

Piaget, Jean and Barbel Inhelder. 1969. *The Child's Conception of Space.* New York: Norton.

Porter, Judith D. R. 1971. *Black Child, White Child: The Development of Racial Attitudes.* Cambridge, MA: Harvard University.

Ramsey, Patricia A. 1987. "Young Children's Thinking about Ethnic Differences." pp. 56–72 in *Children's Ethnic Socialization: Pluralism and Development,* edited by J. S. Phinney and M. J. Rotheram. Newbury Park, CA: Sage.

Schofield, Janet W. and William D. Francis. 1982. "An Observational Study of Peer Interaction in Racially-Mixed 'Accelerated' Classrooms." *Journal of Educational Psychology* 74:722–32.

Spencer, Margaret B. 1987. "Black Children's Ethnic Identity Formation: Risk and Resilience of Castelike Minorities." pp. 103–16 in *Children's*

Ethnic Socialization: Pluralism and Development, edited by J. S. Phinney and M. J. Rotheram. Newbury Park, CA: Sage.

Spencer, Margaret B., Geraldine K. Brookins, and Walter R. Allen. 1985. *Beginnings: Social and Affective Development of Black Children.* New York: Erlbaum.

Strayer, Janet. 1986. "Children's Attributions Regarding the Situational Determinants of Emotion in Self and Others." *Developmental Psychology* 22:649–54.

Sullivan, Kate, Deborah Zaitchik, and Helen Tager-Flusberg. 1994. "Preschoolers Can Attribute Second-Order Beliefs." *Developmental Psychology* 30:395–402.

Thorne, Barrie. 1993. *Gender Play: Girls and Boys in School.* New Brunswick, NJ: Rutgers University Press.

Vygotsky, Lev S. 1978. *Mind in Society: The Development of Higher Psychological Processes,* edited by M. Cole, V. John-Steiner, S. Scribner, and E. Souberman. Cambridge, MA: Harvard University Press.

Wardle, Francis. 1992. "Supporting Biracial Children in the School Setting." *Education and Treatment of Children* 15:163–72.

Williams, John E. and John K. Morland. 1976. *Race, Color, and the Young Child.* Chapel Hill, NC: University of North Carolina Press.

Willis, Paul. 1990. *Common Culture: Symbolic Work at Play in the Everyday Cultures of the Young.* Buckingham, England: Open University Press.

Constructing and Negotiating Racial Identity in School

AMANDA E. LEWIS

INTRODUCTION

Author Amanda E. Lewis conducted an ethnographic study in elementary schools in order to understand the ways in which children construct racial identities. She examines how race shapes interactions between children and adults (and with one another). Through observations and interviews, she describes how people come to understand their experiences through the lenses of race.

. . . Lily and Kate, two fourth-grade girls, stand on the schoolyard talking. As part of a class presentation that morning, Lily had described her ethnic heritage as "Mexican American and European American." She is asking Kate about her own background—"just Caucasian." Seeing Benjamin (a biracial/bicultural Columbian and Indonesian fifth-grader) sitting nearby eating his morning snack, Lily turns to him and asks, "What are you?" He looks at the two girls for several moments without replying. Eventually he responds that he would "rather not say." Trying to be helpful, one of the girls offers, "You're Chinese, right?" When he does not respond to either confirm or deny their suggestion, the girls turn away.

Like Benjamin, all adults and children must contend with others' racial ascriptions—external racial identifications that may or may not match individuals' own self-identifications. In daily interactions like the one here, people regularly go through the same process as Lily and Kate—they work with available racial categories and meanings, draw on available cues, and make decisions about who they think someone is, where in the racial schema the person they are observing fits. In this chapter I discuss these issues of racial signification as they operated in . . . three school communities. By *racial signification*, I mean the way race comes to affect our understandings of ourselves and others and how, as part of that process, it simultaneously shapes our interactions and opportunities.

Schools provide a venue in which to study larger social processes as well as a unique setting in which to study identity formation—they are one of the central places where notions of self are formed. Confrontations over difference often happen for the first time in school, and they tend to happen over an extended period. The data collected in this study give us a window into racialization processes, and they allow us to examine these processes at work in the place where we often first learn about difference and about who we are in the larger world. Schools are the context in which we land when we first leave the family. Moreover, because the schools in this study are elementary schools, we are able to study them as communities in which families are still integrally involved. In this way I am envisioning schools as functioning in relation to family rather than separately from family. Thus, in this chapter, I draw on data not only from interviews and observations within school buildings but also from interviews with parents and other school community members.

. . . Race is part of the normal operation of schools; as Omi and Winant (1994: 60) describe it, race is "a way of comprehending, explaining, and acting in the world." Race, for example, shapes how teachers understand and interact with the children in their classrooms, how adults and children make decisions about who would make a good friend, classmate, or neighbor, and, as in the earlier example, how peers make sense of each other. In this chapter I analyze how racialization processes played out in . . . three school communities. These processes include how people get racially categorized; how boundaries between racial categories are formed, negotiated, and interpreted; and how those first two processes (racialization and boundary formation) affect interactions and opportunities. Drawing on observational and interview data from all three schools, I analyze the ways race shapes interpretations of the world and how people understand their experiences in racial terms.

RACIAL-ASCRIPTION PROCESSES

Racial-ascription processes are in operation most of the time; they are part of the backdrop to interpersonal interactions. We utilize familiar social categories to anticipate what to expect from strangers and strange situations. "The ability to identify unfamiliar individuals with reference to known social categories allows us at least the illusion that we know what to expect from them" (Jenkins 1996: 83). Categorization usually takes place automatically and unconsciously except when we confront someone who is racially ambiguous; in such cases categorization becomes more conscious and deliberate. As in the well-known *Saturday Night Live* skit involving a character named Pat, who has a number of ambiguous gender characteristics, when we encounter people who seem to straddle several racial categories or who do not easily fit into our existing schema, we draw on all available information to try to determine where they fit. The process of racial categorization in such situations is not necessarily different from the more common unconscious and automatic processes taking place when someone's race is seemingly obvious, but it is more explicit. Therefore these ambiguous situations often provide insight into how categorization works more generally—what cues or indicators we look for, how we interpret them, what we do with conflicting information. Once categorization is complete, once we have utilized available clues or signs to decide where someone fits, we have, in fact, created a relationship with that person—one imbued with perceived lines of sameness and difference, in which the person is variously "like us" or "different."

In addition to categorizing others, we must, both interpersonally and in our interactions with official institutions, contend with others' evaluations of who or what we are. For example,

Rodney, an African American fourth-grader at West City, made the following evaluation of his Latino fifth-grade peer Mike:

> AMANDA: What about Mike, what is he?
>
> RODNEY: White.
>
> AMANDA: He's white?
>
> RODNEY: He white to me.

It is safe to say that Mike would have been quite upset had he heard Rodney's ascription of majority identity to him. Yet in his use of the phrase "He white to me," Rodney astutely recognized the reality that external racial ascriptions in many ways matter as much as one's self-identification, if not more. Thus though what Mike thought (how he self-identified) mattered, it did not necessarily trump the identity ascribed to him externally. Rodney was reading the world and mapping those he saw into the schema as he understood it, and as far as he was concerned, Mike was white. As Jenkins (1996: 2) states, "Identity is often in the eye of the beholder." Though Rodney's reading may have mattered less to Mike than that of Mike's teacher, a store owner, or a future employer, peer judgments of racial categorization and performance are far from unimportant or meaningless.[1]

The examples of Lily, Kate, and Benjamin from Metro2 and of Mike and Rodney from West City illustrate the kinds of external ascriptions that are a daily part of peer interactions in school. Racial ascriptions also are a part of interactions between teachers and students. In a case involving Metro2 school personnel, Ms. Lawrence discussed her son Héctor's struggle to be "recognized" at school. In my interview with him, Héctor had unequivocally identified himself as Latino, but as his mother reported, he was not necessarily read as Latino at school.

> Well, let's see, well his father is originally from El Salvador and Héctor, Spanish is really his first language, although I've never been able to convince anybody at Metro2 of that. I think they look at him and they think he's white, basically and don't want to hear otherwise. . . . My concerns stem more from, have people been able to see my son as I see him or how I think he is? And I don't think that's always happened. . . . He had two kindergarten teachers, one of them didn't even know that he spoke Spanish . . . and they're suppose to assess him and they're like writing a report card, you know, "Spanish coming along . . ." and to me that is just so annoying and I try to talk to them but it's like they think he's white. Whenever [my ex-husband and I] talk to him about being in two different cultures, Héctor goes "yes, but I'm not white, look at my skin," his skin's like very very pale but he's saying it's brown.

As we can see from Ms. Lawrence's discussion of her son's defense of his own self-identification, skin color was a key factor both in his teachers' identifying him as white and in his own claims to be otherwise. That skin color was used both in the teachers' reading of him as white and in his own defense of his brownness highlights the often subjective quality of this category. Yet, skin color is not the only factor at play in racial ascription. As Héctor's relationships with his teachers illustrate, language is closely linked to, and often works in interaction with, readings of external physical features (phenotype). Héctor's teachers' mistaken assumptions about his Spanish-language proficiency were tightly interwoven with their reading of him as white (a speculation on Mrs. Lawrence's part that my observations largely affirmed). Language and physical features often interact with other factors to mark someone as similar or different ("of color").

Markers of Difference/Otherness

. . . In making decisions about who is white and who is not, language, accent, cultural performances, and other signals of social location regularly come into play. All these are somehow indicators of difference and perhaps nonwhiteness. These various markers of otherness operate interactively to move people further or closer on the continuum of difference. For example, when I asked Anne Velez, the white mother of Jorge, a biracial white/Latino fifthgrader at Metro2, how he racially self-identified, she raised issues of cultural performance as key to racial identification. Initially she signaled her son's Latino-ness by stating, "Well, he's a *Velez.*" Almost immediately, however, she began to backtrack as she remembered a recent incident. Ms. Velez's Latina sister-in-law, Aunt Maribel, took Ms. Velez's boys and her own children to the amusement park every summer; in the past Jorge had had trouble getting on the roller coasters because of his height. This year Maribel gelled Jorge's hair back to make him appear taller. As Ms. Velez stated, "It worked, and he got on, and it was fabulous." Yet, as she reported, when he looked at himself in the mirror with his new hairdo, Jorge's reaction was to laugh as he said, " 'I look like a Latino kid,' and [his aunt] goes, 'Well what do you think you are?' " This incident highlights the performative nature of race; when it comes to everyday interactions, certain kinds of performances, styles, or costumes may determine what one "is" or how one is seen and categorized as much as if not more than "blood," ancestry, or phenotype.

As Figure 1 shows, a collection of factors provides the information for making racial identifications. The thicker arrow connecting skin color to ascription points to the fact that in many ways phenotype functions as a trump card: skin color and other physical features can

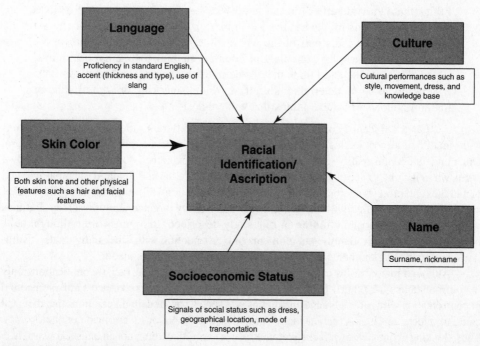

FIGURE 1 Markers of Racial Difference.

unambiguously mark one as being racially other. In these unambiguous cases other factors are not unimportant; they often function as modifiers, answering the question "how other" or "how different." These factors may shape the kinds of racial stereotypes that come into play; for example, dress, language, and style may affect whether an Asian teenager is read as a dangerous gang-banger or a brainy overachiever. However, as many African Americans experience daily, in many situations (say, trying to hail a cab) few factors besides skin tone matter much at all (dress, language, and other indicators cannot protect one from negative outcomes of racial categorization). . . .

As these examples demonstrate, racialization processes are often easiest to see and identify at the borders between categories. In these cases such processes become conscious, and explanation is required. In regard to both self-identification and the categorization of others, processes that are in effect in all cases become more self-evident and explicit as people navigate through ambiguous racial terrain. Thus, though I give many examples of biracial children and multiracial families who exist on the borders between racial categories, the process they grapple with is operating in interpersonal interactions generally—although it may be only implicit or assumed.[2]

THE CONFRONTATION OF INTERNAL AND EXTERNAL IDENTIFICATIONS

Choices about self-identification must necessarily be made in interaction with an external world that regularly assigns identities. Omar, a Metro2 fifth-grader whose father was Latino and whose mother was German, struggled with these issues. His experience exemplifies some of the complexity in the confrontation of internal and external identifications. Omar's father, Mr. Morales, who was Latino, described his son's self-identification:

> I think that Omar identifies himself more with Latinos, in part because he lives with me, and all his life he has lived with me, so, you can't obviate that fact. At the same time, he feels part of the whole American culture. He speaks more English than Spanish, for example. But I don't even think that he has determined what he wants to be, and I think that it's definitely up to him, and what he wants. If he wants to be, to determine himself as white, American, or white-Latino or Latino-Latino, or Hispanic, I think that will come later.

. . . Omar did identify as both white and Latino in different moments, but he was externally identified almost exclusively as Latino. He was, in practice, not really able to choose. Omar understood this reality to some extent. As his father explained, Omar recognized his own status when it came to various political issues. For example, he and his father had participated in marches and protests against the anti-immigrant Proposition 187, and Omar, despite his U.S. citizenship, had identified with the group being collectively targeted and unwanted—Latinos.

As many adults and children in this study described, they most often thought self-consciously about their identities in moments of confrontation with other individuals, institutions, or situations—moments where an external identification was made. . . .

Although many whites explained that they thought about their racial identifications only in confrontations with others, for many African Americans and dark-skinned Latinos this kind of confrontation with external racial ascriptions was such a part of daily interactions that they had come to understand it as a regular factor—whether the ascriptions were made explicit or not. Thus, thinking about their own racial identities was an everyday thing, not an unusual occurrence.

Both positively (e.g., having pride in their racial heritage) and negatively (e.g., dealing with racism), they had come to understand their racial identity as a part of daily life.

RACIAL BOUNDARY FORMATION

The various interactions described earlier—between Lily and Kate and Benjamin, between Héctor and his teachers—are skirmishes along the borders between racial categories. As categories are applied in interpersonal interactions, the boundaries between categories are simultaneously created or reinforced. One cannot determine who one is without determining simultaneously who one is not and in some manner, at least metaphorically, drawing a boundary. But these racial boundaries are not fixed. They are in flux, the ongoing products of social interaction in which identities are produced and reproduced.

The borders between groups were not the same in each school. As Figure 2 illustrates, some of the schools had a fair amount of fluidity between certain racial categories, a moderate amount of border crossing, while at others boundaries were more fixed and borders were less permeable. For example, at West City racial categorization was an either/or process of identifying which single category a person belonged to. In contrast, both Metro2 and Foresthills had some room for movement between white and Asian and white and Latino categories. In every context however, white and black still functioned as mutually exclusive and distinct categories, with little to no crossing or fluidity, and thus no overlap. For example, Sylvie was a black child regardless of the fact that she had a white mother. Enrique, at Metro2, was a black child no matter how he self-identified ethnically. Moreover, white and black were still the primary referential categories—the two poles that other categories were defined in reference to. For example, when Crystal, a white Foresthills fourth-grader, described several of her classmates she said: "Well Cedric [a Filipino fourth-grader] is kind of black. Unless he's really tan, but . . . um . . . otherwise that's kind of it. Jake [a Korean fourth-grader] is

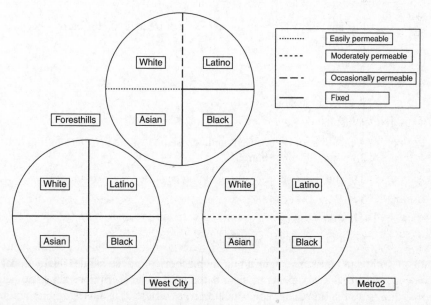

FIGURE 2   **Racial Boundaries in the Three Schools.**

kinda white. But kinda tan, but he's more on the white side kind of." Whether students were seen as kind of white or kind of black depended not only on phenotypic variation but also on relative acculturation and socioeconomic status—all those factors indicated in Figure 1 that play into racial identification and serve as markers of racial difference.

RACIAL MEANING, POWER, AND EXCLUSION

In regard to race, the delineation of same and different that transpires during ascription is not a neutral or benign process but one imbued with power. People experience not merely being identified or labeled but, as boundaries are drawn, being simultaneously included or excluded—they are treated in a particular way because someone has identified them as a member of a particular racial group. Racial identifications thus are not merely about thought processes but about action; acts of inclusion and exclusion are part of the racialization process. These acts range from explicit exclusion or racial violence (e.g., racial discrimination) to subtle inclusion. . . . In truth, the process of being confronted with external ascriptions and the many accompanying stereotypes and assumptions is one that we all deal with but it affects various groups quite differently. Racial minorities are much more often confronted with negative assumptions and exclusionary practices as a result of racial-ascription processes, while whites often reap advantages from their categorization.

One Latina mother, Ms. Carillo, described what often happened when her Latino-ness was recognized: "Oh, yes, yes, right off the bat [people] recognize the Latino, don't you think? The Hispanic. Not that one feels bad about it, you know, but some people give us bad looks sometimes or . . . or they do not answer the way they should. I have seen racism in that sense particularly. A certain look sometimes says it all." This subtle exclusion plays out not only in "a certain look" but also at times in a certain tone of voice. As London, an African American nine-year-old explained, sometimes a way of speaking says it all:

AMANDA: Has anybody ever been mean to you or treated you differently because of your color?

LONDON: Yeah.

AMANDA: How so?

LONDON: People in the store.

AMANDA: What happened?

LONDON: A month ago. He accused me because he just, he just start yelling but I don't know why though.

AMANDA: Do you think he was yelling at you because you were black?

LONDON: Yes.

AMANDA: How do you know?

LONDON: I don't know, it just sounded like it.

Ms. Carillo and London recognized through subtle (or not so subtle) interactional cues that someone had made assessments of them based on a racial ascription. They had behaved or appeared in ways that marked them as qualitatively different, as lesser. In these cases the subjects became aware of ways that others had read them racially and the maltreatment that followed. These kinds of daily microaggressions take a toll on those who experience them (Lewis, Chesler, and Forman 2000; Solórzano, Ceja, and Yosso 2000). . . .

These experiences, in which youth learn what it means to be black and Latino, provide further evidence of the role of schools in shaping racial identities and understandings. These kinds of memories of school as a place of injustice and pain necessarily made parents cautious and concerned when thinking about their own children's schooling. Although they recognized that times had changed, that some improvements had been made, they generally believed that the situation had not changed as much as they had hoped. As a result, they felt that one of their jobs as parents was to prepare their children for the racism they would inevitably face. . . .

It is not merely that poverty, danger, and other negative characteristics are associated with being of color, but that power, wealth, and other characteristics of high status are associated with being white. This is a set of understandings that whites and people of color shared. . . . Students also regularly talked about whites as people with money and authority. At one point Rodney, an African American fourth-grader, tried to explain what he would do if he were going to imitate a white person: "I would just put some white make-up on and dress up kind of like." When I asked him why he would dress up, he replied, "Because white people have more money."

Racialized understandings shape our impressions not only of other groups but also of our own, as in Rodney's explanation of why he thought white people had more money:

AMANDA: Why do you think [white people have more money]?

RODNEY: Because mostly black people is on the streets and white people have cars, houses, big houses, and everything.

AMANDA: Why do you think they have big houses and stuff though?

RODNEY: Because they have money.

AMANDA: Where do they get the money?

RODNEY: Job, working, or . . .

AMANDA: Why do black people have less money?

RODNEY: Because mostly black people is [too] lazy to go find something else so they can get something.

. . . Rodney . . . explained his understanding that "all black men" must go to prison at some point in their lives and his opinion that it was better to go before college.

Children, like adults, are working to make sense of the world around them. They are reading the world, taking in what they see and experience and interpreting the meaning, the patterns, and the order. Rodney's belief that "all black men" must go to prison at some point in their lives, though troubling to his teachers, was merely part of his strategic attempts to assess the world he had to negotiate. Race is one lens through which this reading of the world occurs: it is at least in part how we decide who is friend or foe or, as Peshkin (1991) talked about it, who is a friend and who is a stranger.

THE INFLUENCE OF CONTEXT

Though racialization processes exist in all settings, they do not operate uniformly across time and space. Thus, local contexts, although existing within a larger racial formation, have some impact on the shape of racial boundaries and on how they operate in everyday life. The way people get categorized varies from setting to setting (e.g., the same person may be read differently in different settings). And the meaning of particular labels (e.g., the meanings associated with *black* or *Latino*), as well as the experiential aspects of group membership (e.g., how Latino-ness or blackness is experienced), varies from place to place. Being black in a setting where you are one of many is quite different from being one of eight black students in a school of six hundred. Context clearly matters in at least three ways: spaces themselves can be racially coded, local contexts and institutions can have both direct and indirect influences on identification processes, and the effects of being categorized as well as understandings of the meaning of race can vary by context.

Racially Coded Spaces

People frequently talked about schools as racially coded institutions. At different times each school in this study was described as a socially or culturally "white" space (even if it was not demographically white). In this way, all institutions, neighborhoods, parks, and cities function as racial spaces with their own set of dynamics, rules, associated meaning structures, and cultural repertoires. . . . Schools are not only racial spaces but also spaces in which racial politics are fought out. . . .

Self-Identification

Context shapes not only how we think about others but also how and whether we think about our own racial identities. . . .

A number of Latino parents also discussed being surrounded primarily by those who were "the same" (because they lived in socially isolated, segregated neighborhoods) as a reason race didn't come up much. Race did arise in relation to a larger context in which hostile laws were contested or in interactions with large public institutions outside the immediate neighborhood; but in daily, local interactions with other Latinos, it was almost a nonissue. Several parents whose children were among the few white students at West City also reflected on their children's "minority" experience as the key factor that had led to their children's awareness of their own whiteness.

In light of these contextual issues, it was no surprise that the majority of white parents, children, and teachers in predominantly white Foresthills did not think much about their own whiteness and were mostly unable to talk about race in relation to their own lives. When I asked parents whether they ever thought about their own racial identity, it was not unusual to have someone respond, "Well I just haven't been around it too much." In this case, race appeared to them to have meaning only in relation to others. Yet, parent's comments made clear that their own race and the race of those around them mattered as a signifier of who would, for instance, make a good neighbor. But they regarded looking for sameness, or choosing to be around people they were comfortable with and could relate to, as distinct from avoiding difference or excluding others. . . . What her racial identity meant and how relevant it felt for her experientially thus varied across time and space.

For some children racial identity was different at home than at school—not only the specific category of identification but the content of what that identity meant.[3] For Sylvie, the biracial (black/white) student at Foresthills, her blackness felt different to her when she was staying with her African American father in the largely black town nearby than it did when she was with her white mom and sister at home in Sunny Valley or when she was "the black kid" at school. For some of the Latino children, the meaning of identity at home in either an all-Latino or all-white setting differed from the meaning at school, where they were surrounded by African American, lower-income Latino, or white children.

The Meaning of Race

Different environs also can lead to different understandings of what race means. As Forman (2001a) demonstrates, local school contexts shape children's understandings about race. Metro2 students tended to have much more complex understandings of the relationship between race and social structure. Metro2 students generally understood that race and racism affected peoples' lives and opportunity structures. In answering a question about why some people are rich and others poor, one Metro2 student responded, "Some people have families that got more money than other families so they just passed on the money when they died . . . [and] because maybe their race. Because maybe they don't get the job opportunities as another race." Metro2 students also tended to have some understanding of the impact of the past on the present. But although many white Metro2 students were able to recognize the impact of race beyond the school, they continued to perceive their school as an ideal community that was above or separate from an unfair world. They said that students "here" would never be mean to other students because of their race or color. "Because, the teachers have taught us well . . . equality . . . yeah . . . to be fair to everybody."

Others at Metro2, primarily the black and dark-skinned Latinos, described school as a place where racialized behavior was still very much in place, where they were still likely to confront racial antagonism in the schoolyard. For example, an African American fifth-grader and I had the following exchange:

AMANDA: Why do you think that some kids don't like to play with other kids?

VANESSA: Maybe because they think that they're different in some way and maybe because they don't like them for some reason.

AMANDA: Do you think that happens here?

VANESSA: Yeah.

AMANDA: In what kind of ways?

VANESSA: In what kind of ways like, "oh, you're black, you can't play," or "you're Mexican, you can't play," or "you're Latino, you can't play." "No Latinos allowed" and stuff like that.

AMANDA: Why do you think they feel that way?

VANESSA: Maybe because they think like that different colors are more important than other ones [because they think] one color is better than another color.

AMANDA: Is it one group that mostly does it to other kids or is it everybody that does it?

VANESSA: Um, not to be racist or anything but I think that sometimes . . . most of the time it's white people, white kids.

At West City, understandings of race were more mixed, based not only on students' own race but also on their class status. Many of the working-class and the few middle-class black and Latino children had sophisticated understandings of the relationship between race, structure, and opportunity, while poor black and Latino children had more traditional explanations for social inequality. For example, Rodney (who lived in a large housing project) explained black poverty as result of laziness, while Darnell, the son of a nurse, suggested the following:

DARNELL: White people are supposed to be real good, they're supposed to be the best people in the world.

AMANDA: Well do you think that white people are the best people in the world?

DARNELL: No.

AMANDA: When you say "the best" do you mean like all uptight or actually the best?

DARNELL: They're like on top of everything, they're prefect. They don't get any of their math problems wrong. They read on seventh-grade levels.

AMANDA: Do you think that's true?

DARNELL: Well for some white people, yeah. But they have a better start than we do.

AMANDA: So you think white people read better because they have a better start in life, what do you mean by that?

DARNELL: I mean like white people when they're younger their parents teach them how to read at like one year old. They start better and some black people don't care if they read or don't read. But my mom taught me to read when I was about five or six. She taught me to read and I read and I'm reading well. If like 50 percent of like every black person did that, then it would be a better place.

AMANDA: Why do you think some parents don't teach their kids how to read when they're young?

DARNELL: Because they probably live in a poor neighborhood and they're working two jobs and they don't have time.

AMANDA: Do you think most black people work pretty hard?

DARNELL: Yeah a lot of black people work very hard. Almost every black person works hard, they work hard whatever they do. Selling drugs, they probably work hard, nurses work hard.

AMANDA: Why do you think more black people are poorer than white people?

DARNELL: Because we started off wrong with like racism and stuff. If we didn't start off like that we would probably be at the same place where white people were.

Darnell understood the role of history, resources, and access in shaping outcomes. It was not, as he talked about it, an issue of hard work—black people (even drug dealers) worked hard—but a matter of opportunity.

Although white children at West City recognized that racism still existed and that it existed locally, in their own school, they were likely to see themselves as victims of it as much as blacks or Latinos. They had, for instance, heard black and Latino children called names, just as they themselves had been called "whitey" during recess. They did not have any way of differentiating these experiences or any frame for understanding their schoolyard experiences as different in nature from other forms of racism.

Finally, in Foresthills . . . with the exception of Sylvie and one Latino son of immigrants, most students were unable to talk about race. Many children did not know what race or racism was. As one student stated when I asked her what she would say if someone asked her what race she was, "I don't know. I don't [know] what race means." Moreover, those who did know what prejudice and racism were thought they were remnants of the past that were no longer relevant. Whiteness was quite clearly still normatively in the center as both white and nonwhite children talked about difference as not applying to whites.

CHALLENGING BOUNDARIES

A few school community members were actively engaged in challenging racial boundaries with the expressed interest of creating a more just world. Ms. Wilson, at Metro2, described one of her classroom practices, the "culture bag," as a way to get children to understand that they were all both similar and different:

> "Culture bag" is about unveiling the mysteries, it's about kids having the opportunity to see that kids in their classes that they may not have thought were like them are really like them in a lot of ways. That everybody has a baby blanket even though they're from totally different backgrounds or different colors. That everybody's got some favorite stuffed animal just about or some family members that they love. I wanted them to see what was alike about them and I wanted them to appreciate what was different about each other.

In observing a number of these "culture-bag" events, in which children brought artifacts from their culture to share in class, I regularly heard students murmuring to themselves. "Oh I have one of those," visibly enthralled by something they had not known about. In this way they were encouraged both to see continuities among themselves and to value differences. Also, their assumptions were regularly tested as they shared who they were in a mostly unfiltered fashion. Thus, when Vanessa shared aspects of her Jamaican ethnic heritage, students became aware of her as more than black; they became aware of diversity within the category black. Another time, the entire class was surprised as a student who most had assumed was white shared that he was part French, part Irish, part Latino, and part African American. Thus automatic racial readings based on visible physical features were made problematic if not challenged. . . .

In another example, Mr. Morales, who is Latino, talked about his son Omar learning to stand up for his rights. His son had found out about the lawsuit against Denny's food chain for discriminating against blacks and Latinos. As Mr. Morales summarized it, "There was a group of people who took this restaurant chain to court and it was very prominent in all [the state]." One day, after Mr. Morales picked Omar up from the airport, they passed by a Denny's. Omar's response was to enthusiastically suggest they go there. "He said, 'Denny's! That's the restaurant! Why don't we go there?' We had talked about how no one should exclude you, and if someone does then we have to do something about it. So then we went there and I liked his attitude about how he didn't let himself be inhibited. 'Let's go, and we are going to buy something there and they are going to treat us well.'"

CONCLUSION

Race is continually at play inside and outside schools. It is present in the "hidden curriculum," in explicit historical lessons, in discipline practices, and in interpersonal relations; race is a part of what is happening in schools as much as it is anywhere else. It is one lens through which people read the world around them and make decisions on how to act, react, and interact. Using data from ethnographic research in three school communities, I've attempted to demonstrate how racialization processes work. These processes describe the ways racial identities are assigned to individuals and how racial categories are mapped onto groups. These ascriptive processes work primarily through interpersonal interactions in which we attempt to assess what we know about another person, first through the instantaneous reading or interpreting of available clues (e.g., visible cues such as skin color or facial features, auditory cues such as accent, spatial cues such as neighborhood), and second through rereading or reinterpreting initial assumptions as additional information becomes available. These processes operate in a largely relational manner: some people are determined to be "same" (or "like me") and others are determined to be "different."

At all steps, institutional processes and dynamics affect these racial interactions and interpretations. Both racial ascription and racial self-identification are contextual processes influenced by local meaning systems, rules, demographics, relationships, and structures. For example, . . . blackness took on specific meanings at West City in relation not only to a larger culture but also to a specific set of practices within that school. At Metro2, white students' sophisticated understanding of the relationship between race and structure was not accidental but seemed at least partially related to a school context in which racism, power, and equity were an explicit part of the curriculum. Foresthills students' limited language for talking about race was understandable in the context of dominant local racial discourses of color blindness, which framed race as largely irrelevant.

Racial ascriptions are also not solely about deciding what category an individual belongs to but also about the mapping of systems of meaning onto individuals. A person categorized as black, white, or Asian is being linked with a category already imbued with meanings. The sameness or difference ascertained is not a neutral measure like shoe size or ear shape but a central clue about who a person is. The moment of identification is also a moment of inclusion or exclusion; an understanding is not merely formed but in many cases is subtly or explicitly acted on. Inclusion or exclusion can take form in how one is treated in a particular context (e.g., the slightly cool treatment of a waitress or the particularly welcoming greeting from a new neighbor) or in concretely material processes of who gets access to what kind of resources (e.g., what mortgage rate a bank offers).

Everyday interactions, the moments in which the social category "race" takes shape and is given meaning in social interaction, are the means through which boundaries between groups are created, reproduced, and resisted. One is a member of a particular group at least in part because one is not a member of another. Systems of social inclusion and exclusion are organized (to some extent) around the resulting racial categories and the boundaries between them.[4] Racialization thus involves the assignment of bodies to racial categories and the association of symbols, attributes, qualities, and other meanings with those categories (which then are understood to belong to those bodies in a primordial or natural way). Racial categorizations are used to decide who is similar and different; opportunities and resources are then distributed along racial lines as people are included in or excluded from a range of institutions, activities, or opportunities because or their categorization.

Although racial categorization is not externally imposed in an uncomplicated or automatic way, the range of available racial categories and the meanings associated with them necessarily shape and limit the kinds of racial identifications that are possible. As Benjamin's failed efforts to reject identification (cited at the beginning of the chapter) illustrate, one cannot decide to opt out altogether. Yet collective action can alter the content or boundaries of categories (e.g., black efforts during the 1960s to redefine blackness—"black is beautiful"). And individual interventions are not meaningless; when, Benjamin, a multiracial (and visually racially ambiguous) child, resists identifications. He is at once illuminating the idiocy of a process that tries to find a singular and simple place for him and affirming the power of a process that works hard to pigeonhole him. What one is able to claim for oneself is clearly limited by context and the available categories. Though Tiger Woods created the racial/ethnic category Cablinasian to describe himself, the category was not widely (or even narrowly) accepted. His actions did, however, encourage an occasionally more complex reading of his person, which otherwise (and most often) is still read as black.

The state historically has played an important role in the creation and alteration of categories, usually in interaction with the groups involved (Almaguer and Jung 1999). For instance, efforts on the part of multiracial groups and Asian–Pacific Islanders among others have led to new census categories that allow for different or multiple racial designations (Wright 1994). These individual claims and state actions may be a sign of changes to come. However, their only moderate success may be an indicator of just how entrenched current racial categories are. At issue are not only the borders between categories—whether they exist, what shape they take, whether they are permeable or fixed—but also the content of the categories themselves. What does it mean to be white, black, Latino, Asian? Who decides what category a person belongs to? Are these categories mutually exclusive?

In practice, these questions have no single answer. What the boundaries are and how they work are not established and universally consistent social facts. Nor is the content and meaning of any racial category consistent across space, culture, or time. This indefiniteness lies at the heart of what it means to talk about race as a social construction. Though the idea that race is a social construction is widely accepted, the reality of race in daily life has received little attention.

The lack of fixed and permanent markers and the flexibility of meanings may not, however, signal the declining significance of race. Although I find evidence of confusion, indefiniteness, and disagreement about racial identities and their meaning, I find little evidence of any weakening of the racial-ascription process or of the power of race to shape opportunities and outcomes. Possibly the patterns I identify are a sign of new times. However, they may well be just a sign of new configurations, of adaptations in the making that will yield a slightly different but still powerful and entrenched racial system.

Discussion Questions

1. According to the author, how do children ascribe racial identities to themselves and their peers?
2. How did children form racial boundaries in the elementary schools the author studied?
3. What is the importance of context in how children make sense of racial categories?
4. How did children challenge the boundaries of racial categories?

Notes

1. These judgments are what social psychologists such as Rob Sellers and Jennifer Crocker refer to as "Public Regard." See Sellers et al. 1998 and Luhtanen and Crocker 1992.
2. For more on this process, see Reskin 2002.
3. Harris and Sim (2000) discuss this issue in relation to students' self-identifications on a survey instrument. Students did not all claim the same racial identities in school as they did at home.
4. As Hall (1980, 1986a) describes it, when the signifying system of race is joined with power, it becomes an organized system of inclusion and exclusion that shapes social life and profoundly affects both identity and life chances. Systems of inclusion and exclusion are also organized around other social categories (e.g., gender).

References

Almaguer, Tomas, and Moon-Kie Jung. 1999. "The Enduring Ambiguities of Race in the United States." In *Sociology for the Twenty-First Century*, edited by J. L. Abu-Lughod. Chicago: University of Chicago Press.

Forman, Tyrone. 2001a. "Social Change, Social Context and White Youth's Racial Attitudes." Ph.D. diss., Department of Sociology, University of Michigan, Ann Arbor.

Hall, Stuart. 1980. "Race, Articulation and Societies Structured in Dominance." In *Sociological Theories: Race and Colonialism*. Paris: UNESCO.

———. 1986a. "Gramsci's Relevance for the Study of Race and Ethnicity." *Journal of Communication Inquiry* (Special Issue) 10: 5–27.

Harris, David R., and Jeremiah Joseph Sim. 2000. "Who Is Mixed Race? Patterns and Determinants of Adolescent Racial Identity." Research Report 00–452. Ann Arbor: University of Michigan Population Studies Center.

Jenkins, Richard. 1996. *Social Identity*. New York: Routledge.

Lewis, Amanda, Mark Chesler, and Tyrone Forman. 2000. "The Impact of 'Colorblind' Ideologies on Students of Color: Intergroup Relations at a Predominantly White University." *Journal of Negro Education* 69:74–91.

Luhtanen, Riia, and Jennifer Crocker. 1992. "A Collective Self-Esteem Scale: Self-Evaluation of One's Social Identity." *Personality & Social Psychology Bulletin* 18(3): 302–318.

Omi, Michael, and Howard Winant. 1994. *Racial Formation in the United States: From the 1960s to the 1990s*. New York: Routledge.

Peshkin, Alan. 1991. *The Color of Strangers, the Color of Friends: The Play of Ethnicity in School and Community*. Chicago: University of Chicago Press.

Reskin, Barbara. 2002. "Retheorizing Employment Discrimination and Its Remedies." In *The New Economic Sociology: Developments in an Emerging Field*, edited by M. Guillen, R. Collins, P. England, and M. Meyer. New York: Russell Sage Foundation.

Sellers, Robert M., Mia A. Smith, Nicole J. Shelton, Stephanie A. Rowley, Tabbye M. Chavous. 1998. "Multidimensional Model of Racial Identity: A Reconceptualization of African American Racial Identity." *Personality & Social Psychology Review* 2(1): 18–39.

Solórzano, Daniel, Miguel Ceja, and Tara Yosso. 2000. "Critical Race Theory, Racial Microaggressions, and the Campus Racial Climate: The Experiences of African American College Students." *Journal of Negro Education* 69: 60–73.

Wright, Lawrence. 1994. "One Drop of Blood." *New Yorker*, July 25, pp. 46–55.

The Collaborative Emergence of Race in Children's Play: A Case of Two Summer Camps

VALERIE ANN MOORE

INTRODUCTION

This study . . . explores the . . . use of concepts of race in preadolescents' . . . peer cultures. . . . Using an interactionist approach, [Valerie Ann & Moore showed] how the ways in which kids established and negotiated race category membership and then evaluated each other's actions accordingly, and informed how they used clique dynamics in structuring peer relations in two racially varied recreational settings. Children in the predominantly white setting and the multiracial setting appropriated, used, and negotiated race somewhat similarly, particularly regarding the invisibility . . . of whiteness as a racial category and the assumption of a shared culture and connection among kids of color. They differed, though, in how they . . . resisted race-based clique dynamics. Because of the presence of kids of color, the greater range of relational options available to youths in the multiracial setting introduced a wider range of power dynamics into clique structures and more . . . fluidity into conceptions of race, thus disrupting easy definitions of in-group and out-group membership and affecting the . . . negotiation of identity in the children's peer cultures.

STUDYING THE RACIAL PRACTICES OF KIDS

Studies of children often underestimate their capacity to understand nuanced conceptions of race (Hatcher and Troyner 1993; Van Ausdale and Feagin 1996, 2001). Many researchers approach youngsters from developmental or socialization models, focusing on the progressively sophisticated, stable and orderly *individual* acquisition of identity, such that the *social* negotiation of identity is viewed as immaturity and incompetence, especially as compared with adult identity (Thorne 1993; Van Ausdale and Feagin 1996, 2001). There is, however, a growing body of work in the sociology of children and youth focusing on . . . their collaborative peer cultures and the negotiation of identities and relations in which they engage (see Adler and Adler 1998; Corsaro 1988, 1992; Eder 1995; Fine 1987; Holmes 1995; Thorne 1993; Van Ausdale and

Feagin 1996, 2001). . . . Little . . . literature, though, focuses . . . upon the emergence and use of race in kids[1] collaborative peer cultures. My research seeks to begin to fill this gap.

West and Fenstermaker's (1993, 1995a, 1995b) ethnomethodological work and Corsaro's (1992, 1997) interactionist studies nicely ground this analysis of my observations of the peer cultures of preadolescents in two racially varied, recreational, summer day camp settings. My findings demonstrate that, in contrast to the predominantly white setting, the greater range of relational options available to kids in the multiracial setting introduced a wider range of power dynamics into clique structures and more . . . fluidity into conceptions of race, thus disrupting easy definitions of in-group and out-group membership and affecting the social negotiation of identity in the children's peer cultures. . . .

First, from their . . . studies of gender, West and Fenstermaker (1993, 1995a, 1995b; see also West and Zimmerman 1987) . . . argued that race is an accomplishment, something we "do," rather than something we are or have. The concept of "doing" race (West and Fenstermaker 1995a, 1995b) elaborates the ways in which we continue the fiction of race. Culturally, we have constructed boundaries that separate people into racial groupings. We categorize ourselves, we categorize others, and others categorize us into these racial groupings. Then, in our interactions with others, "persons involved in virtually any action may be held accountable for their performance of that action as members of their race category" (1995a:23). We are evaluated and evaluate others according to . . . conceptions of what is appropriate for members of these racial categories in specific circumstances. These evaluations ultimately emphasize and legitimate differences among people we consider to be of "different" races. Conceptualizing race as something we "do" allows us to see kids as active agents who form their own constructions of race and who influence and are influenced by their peers, adults, and the larger social structures around them. It allows us to see how concepts of race *emerge* in the children's interactions. Moreover, it forces us to observe and talk to kids in their "natural" settings.

Second, from his studies of children, Corsaro (1992, 1997) developed an "interpretive reproduction" standpoint, noting that kids appropriate and transform information from the adult world in the creation of their own "locally shared peer cultures," cultures created from situated, face-to-face interaction. The children's norms for evaluating each other's performance based upon perceived race category membership (West and Fenstermaker 1995a, 1995b), then, are uniquely their own, though reflective of and influential toward adult cultures. Further, Corsaro finds that preadolescents tend to stratify their peer groups by status, status that sometimes invokes racial categories and their evaluations. Thus, race categorization and evaluation are not merely outcomes (West and Fenstermaker's focus) of kids' interactions, but are also means for establishing other processes (such as hierarchical peer status). Using "interpretive reproduction" to frame my analysis allows me to address one criticism of which some scholars have accused processual approaches to understanding race: that these approaches ignore the power dynamics inherent in the structural nature of these categorizations (Collins, et al. 1995). Corsaro (1992, 1997) suggests that interpretive reproduction focuses our attention precisely upon how children incorporate cultural and structural dimensions of

---

[1] I prefer using the term "kids," instead of "children," because that is how kids refer to themselves. Moreover, "children" is a top-down term, implying beings still in development; "kids" implies active social actors (Thorne 1993). To make the chapter easier to read, however, I alternate between terms such as "kids," "children," and "campers."

adult culture into their own peer cultures, and how they use those structures in their interactions involving status and control. Recognizing race categorization . . . as a means for establishing peer status, as well as an outcome itself, highlights how the structural power of race plays out in kids' everyday interactions.

More and more . . . studies are seeking to build upon . . . "interpretive reproduction" . . . in order to study children as competent . . . social actors. Using this type of perspective in their longitudinal study of preadolescents, Adler and Adler (1998) identified several interactional features of the stratified cliques that kids created and the dynamics kids used to maintain the cliques, including "exclusivity, power and dominance, status stratification, cohesion and integration, popularity, submission, and in-group and out-group relations" (1998:71). In their study, leaders of popular cliques maintained their status and control over groups by manipulating dynamics of membership inclusion, encouraging out-group stigmatization, and reminding subordinates of their ever-tenuous group membership. The dynamics of inclusion and exclusion practiced by the popular cliques held group members, and kids wanting to be group members, to stringent and frequently capricious norms of behavior, in the name of status and popularity. In the stratified hierarchy of kids' peer groups, however, although children in the middle level friendship groups had lower prestige, they also had more secure relationships without the group manipulations characteristic of popular cliques. Further, the youths in Adler and Adler's study might temporarily include the isolated kids in a particular activity, but isolates usually were marked as "different" and excluded from regular membership in any friendship group.

My work elaborates upon these clique dynamics, showing how preadolescents in two different day camps used race-based dynamics of inclusion and exclusion to establish and negotiate their peer relations. Campers, however, used somewhat different criteria for organizing these clique dynamics depending upon the camp setting. . . .

METHODOLOGY

I chose two very different summer day camps as the settings for my observations. Summer camps provide activities initiated and directed by *kids*, giving campers some control and power in their choice and manner of activity, while also providing *adult*-initiated activities and . . . routines in which campers participate. Camps also provide regular and predictable camper attendance. These features made day camp a better setting for my purposes than the possible free-form spontaneity of playgrounds or neighborhoods (see Adler and Adler 1998). While I did not have access to data by which I could accurately assess the class status of all of the kids, both camps I chose drew their camper population from a wide class range.[2] I chose camps that differed in their policies toward kids' racial practices: one being a rather "typical"[3] camp and the other being a "cultural awareness" camp (for more detail, see Moore 1997).

---

[2] For example, some families needed the camp voucher program in order to cover camp fees for their children: others did not. I also personally knew some of the parents of the campers. Among them were a co-parenting executive director of an agency, a single parent restaurant worker, and a single parent receiving public assistance.

[3] Given my 10 years of experience being involved with summer camps (not including my years of being a camper) and based upon interviews with camp directors, this setting seems "typical" of camps that present themselves as generalist (non-specialized) recreational day camps in its structure, activities and rules. Thus, I use the shorthand label "typical" camp, which seems an especially apt comparison to the distinctly non-typical "cultural awareness" camp.

The "typical" camp was a "generalist" program located on the grounds of a middle school. Sports activities, team games, hikes and scavenger hunts, crafts, singing, and swimming figured prominently in the camp day. The "cultural awareness" camp was based at an elementary school, though two afternoons a week the campers were bussed to the local town pool for swim, playground, crafts, and sports activities. The brochure advertised the camp as a "cultural awareness program in the arts," with morning art, music, and theater activities focused on the experiences of people living in a particular culture, thereby "helping to foster respect and appreciation for cultural diversity." Afternoon recreational activities resembled those of an after-school program: games on the playground equipment or in the gym, swimming or water slide play, watching movies, playing table games or reading, arts and crafts, and outdoor sports.

The "typical" camp separated camp groups by gender as well as by age: three girls' groups and three boys' groups. In contrast, unlike most camps, the "cultural awareness" camp did not separate kids into camp groups for recreational activities. Ostensibly then, campers could choose any of the offered activities that they wanted. Moreover, the parent handbook for the after-school program affiliated with the camp, which camp directors provided as part of the training materials for counselors, described the program as "committed to providing a non-sexist and non-racist environment . . . to foster appreciation for the multitude of cultures . . . in the world." . . . Thus, camp routines and rules of behavior explicitly sought to challenge racial stereotypes and the significance of racial distinctions. Camp staff enforced these non-stereotypical routines and rules when they could. For example, they made sure campers followed the rule asking them to allow anyone who wanted to participate in any recreational activity to do so, even if kids would have preferred to limit participation, especially along category lines of gender, age or race. Staff also engaged campers in discussions of inequality often. Consequently, even when staff was not present, kids frequently followed the rules. There were times, though, when their practices did not match camp expectations.

Since the "cultural awareness" camp focused on racial differentiation and evaluation as problematic, this camp setting proved a useful comparison to the "typical" camp setting, where race was an identity taken for granted. Campers in both settings ranged from ages 6 to 12. For this chapter, I will follow the camps' designation of the 6- to 9-year olds as "younger" and the 10- to 12-year olds as "older." My observations focus on the older preadolescents.

I was merely an observer at the "typical" camp: floating between groups or activities, observing many of the kids at various times, but not interacting in an authoritative role. I also did informal, unstructured interviews with kids and staff during advantageous moments— such as when I joined a camper playing by herself—and when I had questions about what they were doing or had said. It took some time, but the children came to trust that I was not someone who would hold them to camp rules, censure their speech, limit their behavior or "get them into trouble." In contrast, the way I gained access to the "cultural awareness" camp was to work as a camp counselor: an authority figure who could either sanction or punish certain acts and speech. I, therefore, consciously worked hard to avoid inhibiting what campers felt free to disclose to me or exhibit around me. One way I minimized my authority was by claiming ignorance of camp rules (ignorance that was often genuine, since I had never worked at this camp before). I was at least partially successful in minimizing my authority because, toward the end of summer, while sitting with some campers—one of whom was straddling the line between acceptable and unacceptable camp language—an older camper said to me, "I like you Val; you don't do anything" in response to my lack of action toward that camper. At least some of the time then, the kids saw me as a safe person around whom they could continue to interact with their peers in peer-approved ways. . . .

Since I am a black woman, kids—particularly white kids—also may have hidden "racist" language and sentiments from me, either to avoid punishment or to avoid hurting my feelings. Still, given my success at mitigating my authority, it is likely that my observations underestimate merely the intensity or frequency of these types of remarks, but not their existence. For example, a group of white girls felt free to discuss a comment one of their grandmothers had made—that the girl in question had "nigger lips"—with me standing nearby (Moore 1997). . . . My race category membership affected the ways kids formed relationships with me. Though that relationship sometimes affected the ways in which kids formed relationships with each other, it did so as an afterthought. For example, one black girl turned to me for friendship, but did so only after finding herself shut off from friendship with white campers. . . . However, this also happened with a few isolated white girls. Furthermore, I kept close contact with counselors and camp directors, many of whom were white, during my research. Given their support of my research, they made sure to mention to me interactions I may have missed, including troublesome conflicts due to race category membership. Thus my observations remain sound, though they may underplay the more virulently racist language and behavior of kids.

Two observations about language must precede my analysis of the campers' interactions. . . . I try to use the race categorization language that I observed the kids using, quoting them when I do so. There are times, though, when I observed patterns that the kids did not articulate explicitly. Then, I must use my own language. The "cultural awareness" camp posed the greatest challenge, since older black and Latino campers grouped as "kids of color," but did not refer to themselves this way. That is, they did not explicitly acknowledge the ways they used this broader race categorization by using this pan-ethnic label. Indeed, they referred to each other by name. I try to be accurate to the kids' *sense* of meaning through my use of this language: sometimes referring to "the black kids"; sometimes to "the kids of color." . . . In the everyday day negotiation of racialized meanings and group boundaries, however, people often racialize ethnic concepts. One reason for this conflation rests with the shared history of people treated as members of the same race category who then create their own culture at least partially in response to their treatment as a race category (Omi and Winant 1986). . . . I found that the kids used matters more accurately related to culture in their race categorizations and evaluations, matters such as language/speaking Spanish and changing one's first name.

RACIAL STRUCTURE OF BOTH SETTINGS

The two settings differed in their racial contexts and policies. At the "typical" camp, race was not explicitly mentioned by staff or by policy. This was so, at least partially, because it was a predominantly white setting. Fifteen counselors at the "typical" camp were white; the one Latino counselor left after first week of camp due to injury. The majority of campers also were white: approximately 70 out of 80 campers; the rest were black. The camp directors mentioned that it would have been nice to have more staff of color, but did not go to extraordinary lengths to ensure that counselors of color were present. They did not see them as serving a needed or required function for campers of color *or for white campers.*

Race seemingly became a non-issue because the vast majority of people present were white. This is not, however, a racially neutral composition. Some scholars have noted that dominant whites typically equate race with people of color, making "whiteness" an invisible racial category (Frankenberg 1993; McIntosh [1988] 1998). . . . In this predominantly white camp setting, then, staff experienced whiteness as an invisible race category. Paradoxically, their silence around whiteness still created and reproduced racial distinctions, for constructing whiteness as an invisible category marked "other" experiences as the only ones defined as racial experiences, as experiences worth exploring. . . . Moreover, staff did not make race categorization explicitly problematic. That is, the very few times that staff mentioned race, I heard no questioning of the ways we categorize people into races nor the ways we assume similarity and connection among people we assign to the same racial category.

In contrast, the . . . after-school "cultural awareness" program affiliated with the camp had been started by several black parents concerned about their kids' racial well-being in the predominantly white community in which the school and camp were located. The parents designed a program where kids explored the experiences of people in a multitude of world-wide cultures, including those in the U.S. Kids also discussed issues of oppression, racial and otherwise: examining its dimensions, discussing ways it had been dealt with in the past, exploring ways to deal with it in the future. . . . The directors classified would-be campers and staff as members of particular race categories. They then implemented admissions and hiring policies ensuring a "racially diverse" camp population, with an even mix of campers who identified as white and campers who were children of color—mostly black, with a few Latinos and a few Asians—and adults who identified as white, black, Latino, Asian and "mixed-race." Additionally, camp directors hired staff carefully to ensure fit with the goals and philosophy of the program, including a personal commitment to eradicating prejudice and to valuing "diversity" in its manifestations at camp. . . .

Parents and staff at the "cultural awareness" camp agreed that campers categorized as white kids and kids of color should feel free to interact as equals. Simultaneously, though, anti-racism in a predominantly white context, such as the surrounding community, involved letting the kids of color feel part of the smaller "community" of people of color. Thus, some parents and camp staff identified increased peer interaction among the children of color as a positive goal. Indeed, they assumed that "kids of color" would be a relevant categorization for the children that they categorized that way. They approved, then, when the "kids of color" sought out only each other for friendship when they chose to do so. Thus, staff at the "cultural awareness" camp explicitly held kids accountable to race category membership . . . . They encouraged campers to resist finding significance in categorizing each other by race, while simultaneously validating the self-segregation practices of the kids of color, based upon their understanding of the current significance of race category membership in the larger culture.

REINFORCEMENTS OF AND DISRUPTIONS TO IN- AND OUT-GROUP MEMBERSHIP BY RACE

My observations show that the less stable that race was in the children's peer cultures, the less likely they were to reinforce in- and out-group membership by race. Moreover, that stability of race varied by camp setting. . . .

. . . Exclusionary Tactics

. . . Campers created new peer cultures delimiting peer status, control over participation in activities, and norms of communal sharing at both camps. . . . At both camps, kids engaged in exclusionary clique dynamics (Adler and Adler 1998), holding each other accountable for race category membership as they reinforced in- and out-group membership.

At the "typical" camp[4] I observed that the white girls isolated and neglected the black girls more often and for longer periods of time than they did other white girls. That is, black girls had more episodes where they were "loners," standing or sitting by themselves, looking for a pal, and remaining marginal to the action. One example of this dynamic occurred on a day when each camp group was to dress in the color they had chosen the previous day. The older girls decided to wear white shorts. A counselor talked to the girls about who was and was not wearing white shorts, but no one mentioned that the one black girl in the group had them on. The counselor even enumerated the girls who wore white shorts, but left the black girl off of the list. None of the girls called attention to her, and she did not call attention to herself. Even though another black girl eventually became friends with her white group mates— with them periodically including her in their clique activities—the girl often sat alone during lunchtime and craft time.

Racial isolation, as in these cases, often resulted in a seeming invisibility. . . . Unlike the sustained ridicule of isolates that some researchers have found in kid's peer cultures (see Adler and Adler 1998; Eder 1995), these "inconsequential" black camper isolates most often experienced mere neglect, a status commonly found for blacks who are a small minority of a population (Eder). In her review of some of the isolate literature, Eder found that kids tend to create highly competitive peer cultures in schools, using the typically few highly visible extracurricular activities present to bolster their status. In these peer cultures, isolates are treated harshly. Camp, however, is a different sort of setting, with fewer structural opportunities than schools have for a group of kids to enforce rigid hierarchies of status. For example, camp attendance fluctuated daily or by camp session. Counselors often asked kids from different clique or friendship groups to play on the same team for a whole camp unit activity or multiple camp unit games. Campers with different status frequently interacted amicably when they participated in the same activities from the limited choice of individual activities available. Thus, the ways in which camp structures were looser than school structures made it harder for campers to use structured activities to establish status. . . .

Campers at the "typical" camp also used exclusionary clique dynamics to reinforce in- and out-group membership by verbally marking some race boundaries and leaving others unmarked. . . . Through these conversations, the white kids clearly treated whiteness as an unmarked racial category, a tendency enhanced by predominantly white settings (Frankenberg 1993). Most of these articulations involved white kids asking black kids "who-are-you" questions, questions through which the white kids tried to understand how being black differed from their own experience. Though these kids were sometimes merely seeking information, the questioning also clearly delineated the black kids and lone black adult at camp as members of a "different" race category, one that merited exploration. For example, on a particularly sweltering day when everyone was complaining about the heat, one white girl asked me if I got hot. Though I said yes, she responded "oh, maybe the heat just reflects off of your black head," almost as if she had not heard my response. On another day, one of the older black girls had her hair in "corn rows," little braids that were tight against her scalp in waves, with the ends hanging down. Several of the white girls were fascinated with her hair, exclaiming, "Oh, look at your hair," touching it and asking her all sorts of questions about it: "How'd you do that?" "How come it stays at the bottom?" "Do you wash your hair that way?" After a

---

[4] There was only one black boy at the "typical" camp. As I had few opportunities to observe him in interaction, I leave him out of this discussion.

couple of attempts to explain, she finally told one girl that her hair stayed braided because it was "french-braided." That was a characterization of the process that she thought the white girl would recognize and understand. Though the braiding techniques are quite similar, cornrows are a style associated with blacks, while french braids are associated with whites. Thus, the black girl used vocabulary more associated with the hair care of white people to foster understanding.

Other "who-are-you" questions assumed a shared connection between blacks or people of color, for example when "typical" camp white campers asked me if I was the sister or mother of a couple of the black girls. They did not ask similar questions of the white adults regarding white campers. Indeed, it would be a random and, therefore, ridiculous question to ask a white counselor if he or she was related to a white camper, unless some other indication of connection existed. However, some white campers found it reasonable to ask me. Thus, white campers at the "typical" camp implicitly held "non-whites" accountable for their "oddness" and "difference" and illustrated the ongoing assignment and evaluation of race as a "natural" difference and mechanism for delineating in- and out-going membership.

At the "cultural awareness" camp, it was the older kids of color who often separated themselves from the older white campers, thus establishing a race-based clique. . . . Interaction between older white kids and older kids of color were often antagonistic—sometimes teasing, sometimes more explicitly hostile—though there were times when the joy or fun of an activity took precedence (for example, all of the kids were friends on the water slide). Much of the time, though, the older kids held each other accountable for organizing along a racial boundary: the older kids of color always sat together at one table during lunch and never invited or were asked to allow an older white kid to join them. The older kids of color were seen by everyone at camp as the "coolest" campers, an evaluation they worked to cultivate through their style of dress, knowledge of popular culture (especially black popular culture), athletic skill and interest (especially basketball), avoidance of adults and circumvention of adult rules. Thus, it was the kids of color in the "cultural awareness" camp who fit Adler and Adler's (1998) definition of a popular, status-dominant clique, since they were the ones who generally excluded other children, particularly white kids from their interactions.

Moreover, we can see the ways in which these top-tier popular kids of color organized gender differently than did the second-tier popular cliques and middle level friendship groups of the white campers. The gendered racial dynamics for the white campers at the "typical" camp were similar to the boundary maintenance between girls and boys that Thorne (1993) found. . . . For kids of color at the "cultural awareness" camp, however, race was the salient category of differentiation. They grouped together as *kids* of color, and only occasionally invoked gender as an appropriate category of difference. . . .

Kids of color at the "cultural awareness" camp, though, did verbally mark race boundaries in other, exclusionary ways. For example, on the bus one day a young black boy got another young black boy to participate in a "trick": first he held his two hands up and close together, and said to his friend "open the refrigerator door," meaning his hands. His friend hesitantly did so. Then he instructed "get a Coke." "Close the door." "Open the bottle." "Take a sip." His friend pantomimed all of this. Then he said, in sing-song, "Me Chinese, me play joke, me make pee-pee in your Coke!" And the two boys laughed. A counselor nearby talked to the boys about the inappropriateness of this joke. Yet, during an activity later on in the day, I heard the two boys repeat the trick to each other again. The two black boys seemed to be bonding together racially at the expense of a "racial other," though that someone else was more hypothetical in the situation than real. That is, though there were a few Asian-American campers present, they were not nearby during this play, and I did not observe these boys harass or antagonize them during the summer. In these kinds of situations, kids constructed (and tried to hide from adults) racial evaluations ridiculing specific others constructed as on the other side of the boundary, thus reaffirming separate racial categories. Moreover, campers used this separation and ridiculing evaluation to maintain an elevated peer status over those "racial others" and to delineate in- and out-group membership. Thus, as Corsaro (1992, 1997) suggests, racial differentiation and evaluation were both an outcome of the kids' interactional articulations and a means for establishing peer status. . . .

. . . Inclusive Tactics

While campers at the "typical" camp stigmatized black girls by the ways in which they organized and reinforced boundaries of group membership, these black girls found ways to negotiate for higher status. Occasionally the black girls spoke up and made their presence felt. They sometimes actively pursued friendships with the white girls: initiating conversations, going over to them when they were discussing matters to be kept secret from adults and non-clique (white) girls, sharing lunch food. . . . Yet, the black girls also found ways to use the camp peer culture's exclusionary sense of race to their benefit. They created an alternative peer culture that emphasized an inclusive blackness as a way to resist their isolation. . . . Though few of the older (white) girls physically attached themselves to counselors on a regular basis, the black girl who was in the group for most of the summer was often in physical contact with me. Day after day, she never tired of hugging me, climbing on my back, leaning against me or sitting on my lap. Though she was in physical contact with other adults, she was much more "familiar" with me than with the others. In fact, she began to blur my adult status and to treat me like a camper. Whenever I went with her group on a hike, she always chose me as her buddy (every camper had to have a buddy) and held my hand during the hike (most older girls did not hold their buddy's hand). Many girls shared a locker room changing stall with a trusted camp friend; this girl brought me into her stall several times as that friend. I was also the first person she came to see when she arrived at camp.

Isolates often rely on adults who presumably will not turn them away (though see Thorne 1993). The black girls who turned to me, however, treated me differently—more familiarly—than the way they treated the other (white) adults at camp. Moreover, white girls—even isolated ones—from the middle group did not hold my hand, spontaneously sit next to me during free time and activities, or deliberately walk and talk with me on hikes like the middle group black girls did. Further, if a black girl came over while the white campers were talking to me, they would defer to the black camper, allowing her to interrupt and reassert that special claim to me that the white kids presumably did not share. This action by the black girls may have been an indirect attempt to ingratiate themselves to clique elites (Adler and Adler 1998): if they could join my conversation or activity with white campers due to their recognized claim to me, maybe then white campers would see those black girls as worthy enough to join their friendship groups. Even if this bid to curry favor with white campers failed, though, attention from me and the temporary inclusion in our activity worked to ameliorate the black girls' isolation. . . . While the black girls in the "typical" camp were isolated and, thereby neglected, they also constructed a peer culture that provided them with alternatives to rejection and granted them active peer culture participation.

Because of the wider range of peer groups at the "cultural awareness" camp, I did not observe kids there engaging in inclusive practices as a response to rejection in the same way that campers in the "typical" camp did. There were more levels of race-based cliques and friendship groups at the "cultural awareness" camp because there were kids from more race categories present. Thus, for example, the three younger Asian campers played with everyone equally until a young Asian man joined camp staff. Those children then spent the majority of their camp time with him and with each other as a group. . . .

Complicating Race-Based Clique Dynamics

. . . Campers at the "cultural awareness" camp . . . did not always ground their assessment of racial differentiation in the physical body, but developed their own distinctive classification and evaluation schemes to include and exclude others. For example, a former counselor told me how some of the black kids told her that, in church and at home, they were taught not to trust white people. So, when faced with a camp problem or concern, they were to go only to counselors of color. Interestingly, the counselor they reportedly told this to was white, yet they went to her with their problems. When she asked one of the kids about this discrepancy, he looked her in the eye and insisted that "you're not white." Though she pointed out the she was, indeed, white, he continued to insist that she was not white. He categorized her according to his needs, presumably because he liked and trusted this white counselor and wanted to continue his relationship with her.

Clearly, the black kids in this example created their own sense of race out of contradictory information in their social world. Here, the racial intentions of parents, family, and church contradicted those of the camp. By simultaneously insisting upon the lack of trustworthiness of whites while, in fact, trusting a counselor who categorized herself as white and, hence, by changing her race category membership in their eyes, the black kids "did" race in the way they saw fit. They took seriously both their parents' cautions about whites *and* the camp's emphasis on racial integration and equality and created race categories in ways that fit and yet resisted both sets of these adult "instructions." They still used race, but complicated how they constructed it, disrupting easy delineation of in- and out-group membership. . . . According to my findings, black campers at the "cultural awareness" camp also did not take the physiological basis for race categorization for granted. By categorizing the counselor as "not white" (instead of other alternatives: black, Latina, Asian), they created a unique race category within their locally shared peer culture, one that seemed to put "exceptions to the rule" in a category limbo (not like those bad white people, not quite one of us, but close).

The older kids of color also used their own criteria for race to exclude some campers who categorized themselves as kids of color from their popular clique. Not all of the older kids of color passed the accountability test, therefore, a few were branded "not black enough." The criteria for excluding two boys in particular indicate the older kids of color's conceptions of race that made these boys marginal. They teased one boy, sometimes a part of their group, for not being dark enough to be "black." Several counselors who had observed these kids during the after-school program associated with the camp noted that what they called the boy's "biracial" parentage encouraged the older kids of color to find reasons to exclude him from full group participation. Though some kids of color in the group were also "mixed" (their language) and had light skin color, they could not "pass for white," as could this boy. Also, unlike this boy, many of these kids of color lived in the same neighborhood. Residential association and familiarity, bolstered by their parents' familiarity, seemed parts of what the kids of color used to hold each other accountable to "minority" race category membership. In response, the boy changed his name, from a typically Anglicized name to one that could be identified as sounding more black, Latino, or Italian. This kind of effort on his part helped maintain his membership in the group, tenuous and variable though it was.

The other excluded boy was dark enough that people easily categorized him as black. However, the group never claimed him as a member. While one counselor described the boy's exclusion as a problem of "not being hip enough," another counselor confided that the boy had a learning disability, of which some of the older kids of color were aware. Though high functioning, the boy sometimes talked and laughed too loudly and was easily frustrated and angered. The older kids of color were sometimes entertained and amused by his reactions, but never considered him a peer. Being "cool" was an important part of being black for these kids. Thus, dark skin color was not enough for them to include him in their group. Even the counselors' encouragement of the boy to seek out the kids of color only resulted in him sitting next to them. They did not interact with him. Having categorized this boy as black, the kids of color held him accountable for his lack of "coolness," a normative conception of one attitude appropriate for black kids. They, therefore, excluded him from their activities on an ongoing basis, thereby complicating the inclusion criteria for race category membership in ongoing interaction with him.

Since all of the older kids of color were included in the clique, to not include these two boys required justification. Just as the counselor the kids deemed as "not white" enjoyed a positive relationship with clique members, the kids deemed "not black enough" were stigmatized by the campers' evaluation of race category membership. The campers' actions suggest that, in this peer culture, "coolness" was more important to kids' conceptions of "blackness" than was mere skin color and familiarity. "Coolness" itself, though, was not enough for membership in this popular clique *of color*. Thus, the kids of color deemed the leader of the top white girls' clique cool enough to join the group's conversation about puberty one day, especially since she had information . . . that the other kids did not have. However, though she was seen as cool, the kids of color did not include her in their other activities; she did not gain membership into their clique. Another black boy that the kids of color perceived as "uncool" maintained clique inclusion because his brother was a clique leader. He paid for this inclusion, though, through frequent marginalizing and stigmatizing teasing by his brother, who called him names like "baby" and "copycat." Though "uncool," his race category membership and sibling connection made him a regular, though stigmatized, clique member.

Another example of how the older black kids at the "cultural awareness" camp negotiated complicated race categorization . . . emerged from how they held the Latino kids accountable for the use of Spanish, which they contested as a normative conception of an appropriate activity. Whenever an adult spoke Spanish to or in front of the "kids of color," the black children felt left out and asked the Latino kids what was being said and why Spanish was being spoken in that instance. This questioning erected a new racial divide, complicating previously established race category membership. Ordinarily, the Latino kids and the black kids identified themselves as part of the same group, the more inclusive, "kids of color." But when adults used Spanish, they categorized campers more specifically as "black kids, who (presumably) did not speak Spanish," and "Latino kids, who (presumably) spoke Spanish."[5] This narrower race categorization had an antagonistic edge. Though the Latino kids knew more about what was

---

[5] While there is no necessary link between language and race—not all Latinos speak Spanish and many non-Hispanic blacks do—"language is an important identifying characteristic" for Latinos living in the U.S. today (Trudgill 1983:53).

happening in these situations than did the black kids, the narrower race categorization involved a loss of power for the Latino kids, as it extracted them from the larger group, "kids of color," made up primarily of black kids. Seeking inclusion, the Latino kids tried to avoid that kind of accountability by never speaking Spanish in front of the black kids on their own.

By avoiding the use of Spanish, the Latino campers adhered to the "clique of color's" inclusionary . . . criteria by maintaining race category membership solidarity. . . . In the multiracial setting, constructions of race category membership became less stable. As kids complicated race category membership, they disrupted easy assignment of in- and out-group membership, thus requiring much more active negotiation of identity in their interactions. . . .

There were, however, more instances at the "cultural awareness" camp in which kids struggled with challenging race category membership as a legitimate means for establishing in- and out-group membership. One such occurrence took place during an altercation on the playground. A mixed-age group of girls were going to engage in fantasy play, whereby every girl was to be a certain character and they would make up a story as they went along, following each other's lead. The group consisted of about five white girls and a Korean-American girl, with one white girl taking more of a leadership role: setting the parameters of play, deciding the initial plot line, and so forth. A young black girl asked the group if she could join. The leader said no. Immediately, the rest of the girls argued that camp rules stated that anyone who wanted to play could do so and they questioned the leader: why did she not want the girl to play? The leader did not answer, but kept insisting that she could not play. After a few minutes, the girls agreed that they would not play with the leader if she would not let the black girl play and they began to walk away from her. She called to them and acquiesced: the black girl could play, but only if she followed the leader's lead and did not add to the story line herself. The other girls deemed that restriction unfair and told the leader that she had to be allowed to play like everyone else. Eventually, the leader blurted out, "but she's not pretty enough to play!" The girls questioned her: "What do you mean? What do you mean, 'she's not pretty?'" The leader answered, "She's not pretty enough to play! She's black!" . .

They rejected the leader's attempt to organize group solidarity through racial stratification. Indeed, the girls used the "cultural awareness" camp's philosophy to structure these more inclusive practices.

As the interaction continued, the game was forgotten and the leader's comments began a new discussion. The girls told the leader that she was wrong, and some of them talked to the black girl, making sure her feelings were not hurt. I followed the conversation of the leader and the Korean-American girl in the group, a conversation that the Korean-American girl turned into a bias intervention. She suggested that the leader would not like it if someone said something like that to or about her, and described her own experiences with kids in school teasing her, calling her "Chinese," and making fun of her based on her ethnicity. She said that it sometimes hurt her feelings, but she knew it was their problem and not hers. The leader eventually admitted that she had wanted to hurt the black girl's feelings, presumably so that she would not want to play.

The kids involved in this altercation took on the "cultural awareness" camp's philosophy as their own and tried to pressure their friend, the leader, to do the same. They challenged her attempt to use race differentiation and evaluation to establish peer status and insisted upon the more egalitarian and democratic relations characteristic of mid-level friendship group dynamics. Thus, the girls disrupted establishing in- and out-group membership by race, reproducing a peer culture that mirrored and maintained the alternative culture that the camp adults sought to establish.

Other "cultural awareness" camp interactions indicated that the campers were beginning to challenge the validity of assigning race category membership itself to each other, further resisting race-based groupings and interactions. In one incident, the kids were playing a game where one person left the room, someone in the room was designated as "it," and, when the camper came back into the room, he or she asked questions in order to guess which person was "it." When the black boy designated to leave the room came back, he would not ask the race category membership of the person who was "it." He asked about other physical attributes, such as hair color and hair length. He also asked about gender. Somehow, though, he perceived directly asking the race category membership of the kid designated as "it" to be inappropriate.

There were also times when adults at the "cultural awareness" camp struggled with the question of whether or not it was appropriate to mention someone's race. At a staff meeting, a camp director told staff members to make sure one of the kids ate everything in her lunch. The kid she was talking about, a young and little white girl, had the same first name as another camper, a young and little black girl, and staff was not sure about which girl she was talking. Using her last name did not help because the counselors did not yet know the kids' last names. Saying she was little, or the littler one, did not help; they were both petite. And they both had two pigtails. Finally, a counselor blurted out, "You mean the white one?" The director said yes, and the meeting continued. . . .

CONCLUSION

Kids came to camp with ideas regarding race, but those ideas became realized only as they negotiated peer relations with other kids in the immediate setting (Fine 1987). These negotiations yielded two outcomes: collaborative conceptions of race categories and evaluations (West and Fenstermaker 1995a); and peer cultures using those evaluations to establish and negotiate clique and friendship group formation (Adler and Adler 1998). The kids' collaborative local peer cultures reflected the influence of the larger adult culture and community around them, but they were also unique and not merely imitative (Corsaro 1992, 1997). The kids did not merely reproduce their parents' or counselors' or the camps' race categorization schemes and assessments. The camp interactions in this study, then, elaborate further the *social* negotiation of identity in which kids engaged.

The contrasting demographics of the two camps help explain the differences in the children's peer cultures. My observations indicate that the wider range of people from different race categories present at the "cultural awareness" camp meant that kids saw they had choices about splits and alliances they could form along pan-ethnic lines. Campers at the "typical" camp saw two race category options: majority white and minority black. Campers at the "cultural awareness" camp, however, saw that they had more race categories that they could appropriate, evaluate and use: white, black, Latino, Asian, "mixed," "not white," "of color." Thus, the few older Latino kids categorized themselves with the older black kids, not with the older white campers and not by themselves. The resultant group is best described as the older "kids of color" and my observations show that they acted as such. . . .

More research on kids' peer cultures in multiracial settings not guided by "anti-oppression" principles and in other predominantly monoracial settings can help us better assess these influences upon children's collaborative practices and conceptions. . . . In other words, the ways in which kids of color differentiate and assess others by race category membership varies substantially from how white kids do so. Further work on children in recreational settings would help us evaluate the accuracy of this conclusion.

Discussion Questions

1. What assumptions about whiteness as a racial category did the author observe?
2. How did the campers use race as a category to create inclusion? Exclusion?
3. How was the author's own race an important part of this study? Discuss how race

is an important factor for researchers conducting ethnography.

4. What does the author mean by "doing race"? What does this tell us about how children actively shape and create meanings of race in their peer groups?

References

Adler, Patricia A., and Peter Adler. 1998. *Peer Power: Preadolescent Culture and Identity.* New Brunswick, NJ: Rutgers University Press.

Collins, Patricia Hill, Lionel A. Maldonado, Dana Y. Takagi, Barrie Thorne, Lynn Weber, and Howard Winant. 1995. "Symposium: On West and Fenstermaker's 'doing difference.'" *Gender & Society* 9, 4:491–513.

Corsaro, William A. 1988. "Routines in the peer culture of American and Italian nursery school children." *Sociology of Education* 61, 1:1–14.

———— 1992. "Interpretive reproduction in children's peer cultures." *Social Psychology Quarterly* 55, 2:160–177.

———— 1997. *The Sociology of Childhood.* Thousand Oaks, CA: Pine Forge.

Eder, Donna (with Catherine C. Evans and Stephen Parker). 1995. *School Talk: Gender and Adolescent School Culture.* New Brunswick, NJ: Rutgers University Press.

Fine, Gary Alan. 1987. *With the Boys: Little League Baseball and Preadolescent Culture.* Chicago: University of Chicago Press.

Frankenberg, Ruth. 1993. *White Women, Race Matters: The Social Construction of Whiteness.* Minneapolis: University of Minnesota Press.

Hatcher, Richard, and Barry Troyner. 1993. "Racialization and children." In *Race, Identity and Representation in Education*, Cameron McCarthy and Warren Crichlow, eds. New York: Routledge.

Hooks, Bell. 1992. *Black Looks: Race and Representation.* Boston: South End Press.

McIntosh, Peggy. [1988]. "White privilege and male privilege: A personal account of coming to see correspondences through work in women's studies." In *Race, Class and Gender*, Margaret L. Andersen and Patricia Hill Collins, eds. Boston: Wadsworth.

Moore, Valerie Ann. 1997. "How kids create and experience gender and race." Ph.D. dissertation, University of Massachusetts, Amherst.

———— 2001a. "Children's use of race to establish and negotiate peer relations." Presented at the American Sociological Association Annual Meetings, Anaheim, CA, August.

———— 2001b. "'Doing' racialized and gendered age to organize peer relations: Observing kids in summer camp." *Gender & Society* 15, 6: 835–858.

Omi, Michael, and Howard Winant. 1986. *Racial Formation in the United States: From the 1960's to the 1980's.* New York: Routledge.

Thorne, Barrie. 1993. *Gender Play: Girls and Boys in School.* New Brunswick, NJ: Rutgers University Press.

Trudgill, Peter. 1983. *Sociolinguistics: An Introduction to Language and Society.* London: Penguin.

Van Ausdale, Debra, and Joe R. Feagin. 1996. "Using racial and ethnic concepts: The critical case of very young children." *American Sociological Review* 61:779–793.

———— 2001. *The First R: How Children Learn Race and Racism.* New York: Rowman and Littlefield.

West, Candace, and Sarah Fenstermaker. 1993. "Power, inequality, and the accomplishment of gender: An ethnomethodological view." In *Theory on Gender/Feminism on Theory*, Paula England, ed. New York: Aldine de Gruyter.

———— 1995a. "Doing difference." *Gender & Society* 9, 1:8–37.

———— 1995b. "Reply: (Re)doing difference." *Gender & Society* 9, 4:506–513.

West, Candace, and Don H. Zimmerman. 1987. "Doing gender." *Gender & Society* 1:125–51.

Constructing "Opposite Sides"

BARRIE THORNE

INTRODUCTION

Based on participant observation in elementary schools, Barrie Thorne found that children are active in constructing meanings of gender through their interactions with one another and adults. In this selection, she describes how children in school come to see boys and girls as on "opposite sides." Rather than as a natural or inevitable outcome, Thorne's piece details how the children and teachers actively create gender divisions through their work and play. Contests, chasing, cootie rituals, and invasions of space are a few ways that gender differences take on more meaning. However, there are many social contexts when gender divisions fade away.

It's like girls and boys are on different sides.

—HEATHER, AGE ELEVEN, DISCUSSING HER EXPERIENCES AT SCHOOL

When I first began to wander the Oceanside School playground, with gender on my mind, I came upon a noisy group at the edge of a grassy playing field. A tall, brown-haired girl leaned toward two shorter boys and yelled, "You creeps! You creeps!" Then she laughingly pretended to hide behind a much shorter girl at her side. As one of the boys moved toward them, he asked, "What did you call me?" "Creep!" the tall girl, Lenore, repeated emphatically as she turned and slowly began to run. The boy, Ronnie, loped after her for about fifteen feet and grabbed her ponytail, while she shrieked. Lenore then spun around, shook loose, and reversed the direction of the chase, setting out after Ronnie. In the meantime, Sherry chased after Brad with her arms extended. As they ran, Brad called, "Help, a girl's chasin' me!" When Sherry approached him, she swung her right leg into the air and made an exaggerated karate kick. Then they reversed directions, and Brad started running after Sherry.

I could tell from the laughter and stylized motions that this was a form of play, and I immediately recognized the genre from my own childhood schoolyard days: boys-chase-the-girls/girls-chase-the-boys. This kind of encounter, when "the girls" and "the boys" become defined as separate and opposing groups, drew me like a magnet: it seemed like the core of their gender relations. I gradually came to see that the occasions when boys and girls interact in relaxed and non-gender-marked ways are *also* significant, although, and this bears thought.

It is more difficult to analyze and write about the relaxed situations within the rubric of "gender." Gender is often equated solely with dichotomous difference, but . . . gender waxes and wanes in the organization and symbolism of group life, and that flux needs close attention.

. . . This chapter . . . examines boys' and girls' experiences of varied situations of "together" and "apart." It explores the ways in which boys and girls interact to create, and at other points to dismantle, group gender boundaries, or a sense of "the boys" and "the girls" as separate and opposing sides. It also probes the magnetism of gender-marked events for observers, for participants, and in the realms of memory.

BORDERWORK

Walking across a school playground from the paved areas where kids play jump rope and hopscotch to the grassy playing field and games of soccer and baseball, one moves from groups of girls to groups of boys. The spatial separation of boys and girls constitutes a kind of boundary, perhaps felt most strongly by individuals who want to join an activity controlled by the other gender. When girls and boys are together in a relaxed and integrated way, playing a game of handball or eating and talking together at a table in the lunchroom, the sense of gender as boundary often dissolves. But sometimes girls and boys come together in ways that emphasize their opposition; boundaries may be created through contact as well as avoidance.

The term "borderwork" helps conceptualize interaction across—yet interaction based on and even strengthening—gender boundaries. This notion comes from Fredrik Barth's analysis of social relations that are maintained across ethnic boundaries . . . without diminishing the participants' sense of cultural difference and of dichotomized ethnic status.[1] Barth focuses on more macro, ecological arrangements, whereas I emphasize face-to-face behavior. But the insight is similar: *although contact sometimes undermines and reduces an active sense of difference, groups may also interact with one another in ways that strengthen their borders.* One can gain insight into the maintenance of ethnic (and gender) groups by examining the boundary that defines them rather than by looking at what Barth calls "the cultural stuff that it encloses."[2]

When gender boundaries are activated, the loose aggregation "boys and girls" consolidates into "the boys" and "the girls" as separate and reified groups. In the process, categories of identity that on other occasions have minimal relevance for interaction become the basis of separate collectivities. Other social definitions get squeezed out by heightened awareness of gender as a dichotomy and of "the girls" and "the boys" as opposite and even antagonistic sides. Several times I watched this process of transformation, which felt like a heating up of the encounter because of the heightened sense of opposition and conflict.

On a paved area of the Oceanside playground a game of team handball took shape (team handball resembles doubles tennis, with clenched fists used to serve and return a rubber ball). Kevin arrived with the ball, and, seeing potential action, Tony walked over with interest on his face. Rita and Neera already stood on the other side of the yellow painted line that designated the center of a playing court. Neera called out, "Okay, me and Rita against you two," as Kevin and Tony moved into position. The game began in earnest with serves and returns punctuated by game-related talk—challenges between the opposing teams ("You're out!" "No, exactly on the line") and supportive comments between team members ("Sorry, Kevin," Tony said, when he missed a shot: "That's okay," Kevin replied). The game proceeded for about five minutes, and then the ball went out of bounds. Neera ran after it, and Tony ran after her, as if to begin a chase. As he ran, Rita shouted with annoyance, "C'mon, let's play." Tony and Neera re-turned to their positions, and the game continued.

Then Tony slammed the ball, hard, at Rita's feet. She became angry at the shift from the ongoing, more cooperative mode of play, and she flashed her middle finger at the other team, calling to Sheila to join their side. The game continued in a serious vein until John ran over and joined Kevin and Tony, who cheered; then Bill arrived, and there was more cheering. Kevin called out, "C'mon, Ben," to draw in another passing boy; then Kevin added up the numbers on each side, looked across the yellow line, and triumphantly announced, "We got five and you got three." The game continued, more noisy than before, with the boys yelling "wee haw" each time they made a shot. The girls—and that's how they now seemed, since the sides were increasingly defined in terms of gender—called out "Bratty boys! Sissy boys!" When the ball flew out of bounds, the game dissolved, as Tony and Kevin began to chase after Sheila. Annoyed by all these changes, Rita had already stomped off.

In this sequence, an earnest game, with no commentary on the fact that boys and girls happened to be on different sides, gradually transformed into a charged sense of girls-against-the-boys/boys-against-the-girls. Initially, one definition of the situation prevailed: a game of team handball, with each side trying to best the other. Rita, who wanted to play a serious game, objected to the first hint of other possibilities, which emerged when Tony chased Neera. The frame of a team handball game continued but was altered and eventually overwhelmed when the kids began to evoke gender boundaries. These boundaries brought in other possibilities—piling on players to outnumber the other gender, yelling gender-based insults, shifting from handball to cross-gender chasing—which finally broke up the game.

Gender boundaries have a shifting presence, but when evoked, they are accompanied by stylized forms of action, a sense of performance, mixed and ambiguous meanings (the situations often teeter between play and aggression, and heterosexual meanings lurk within other definitions), and by an array of intense emotions—excitement, playful elation, anger, desire, shame, and fear. I will elaborate these themes in the context of several different kinds of borderwork: contests; cross-gender rituals of chasing and pollution; and invasions. These stylized moments evoke recurring themes that are deeply rooted in our cultural conceptions of gender, and they suppress awareness of patterns that contradict and qualify them.

Contests

Girls and boys are sometimes pitted against each other in classroom competitions and playground games. Since gender is a relatively unambiguous and visible category of individual identity that divides the population roughly in half, it is a convenient basis for sorting out two teams. When girls and boys are on separate teams, gender may go unremarked as a grounds of opposition, as in the beginning of the team handball game; but more often gender, marked by talk and other actions, becomes central to the symbolism of the encounter. In the Oceanside fourth-fifth-grade classroom, where regular seating was almost totally divided by gender, the students talked about a boys' side and a girls' side. Drawing on and reinforcing the kids' self-separation, Miss Bailey sometimes organized the girls and the boys into opposing teams for spelling and math competitions.

Early in October, Miss Bailey introduced a math game. She would write addition and subtraction problems on the board, and a member of each team would race to be the first to write the correct answer. She designated the teams with two score-keeping columns on the blackboard: "Beastly Boys" . . . "Gossipy Girls." Several boys yelled, "Noisy girls! Gruesome girls!" and some of the girls laughed in response. Shaping themselves into a team, the girls sat in a row on top of their desks; sometimes they moved their hips and shoulders from side to side in a shared rhythm and whispered "pass it on." The boys stood along the wall, with several reclining against their desks. When members of either group came back victorious from the front of the room, they passed by their team members and did a "giving five" handslap ritual with each in turn.

By organizing boys and girls into separate teams and by giving them names with (humorously) derogatory gender meanings. Miss Bailey set up a situation that invited gender antagonism. Disparaging the other team/gender and elevating one's own became a running joke. A few weeks later, when the teacher once again initiated the math game, Tracy ran to the board, grabbed the chalk, and wrote two column heads: "Boys" . . . "Great Girls." Then Bill ran up, erased the "Great," and substituted "Horrible."

When teachers organize gender-divided classroom contests, students pick up on and elaborate the oppositional and antagonistic meanings. When free to set up their own activities, kids also sometimes organize girls-against-the-boys games, especially of kickball. Compared with games where each side has a mix of girls and boys, these gender-divided games are highly unstable, which may, of course, be the intention and much of the fun. As in the team handball example, the participants usually end up tugging the thread of gender and sexual meanings and thereby unraveling the ongoing game.

For example, on the fifth-sixth-grade side of the Ashton playground, I came upon a kickball game with all boys in the field and all girls up to kick; about a fourth of the players on each side were Black and the rest were white, but the emphasis on gender seemed to submerge potential racial themes. As the game proceeded, it was punctuated by episodes of cross-gender chasing. When one of these episodes involved a boy chasing a girl who had the rubber ball, the game changed into an extended version of "keepaway," with girls and boys on opposite sides, and a lot of chasing, pushing, screaming, and grabbing.

Chasing

Cross-gender chasing dramatically affirms boundaries between boys and girls. The basic elements of chase and elude, capture and rescue are found in various kinds of tag with formal rules, as well as in more casual episodes of chasing that punctuate life on playgrounds.[3] These episodes begin with a provocation, such as taunts ("You creep!"; "You can't get me!"), bodily pokes, or the grabbing of a hat or other possession. A provocation may be ignored, protested ("Leave me alone!"), or responded to by chasing. Chaser and chased may then alternate roles. Christine Finnan, who also observed schoolyard chasing sequences, notes that chases vary in the ratio of chasers to chased (e.g., one chasing one, or five chasing two), the form of provocation (a taunt or a poke); the outcome (an episode may end when the chased outdistances the chaser, with a brief touch, wrestling to the ground, or the recapturing of a hat or a ball); and in use of space (there may or may not be safety zones).[4] Kids sometimes weave chasing with elaborate shared fantasies, as when a group of Ashton first- and second-grade boys played "jail," with "cops" chasing after "robbers," or when several third-grade girls designated a "kissing dungeon" beneath the playground slide and chased after boys to try to throw them in. When they captured a boy and put him in the dungeon under the slide, two girls would guard him while other boys pushed through the guards to help the captured boy escape.

Chasing has a gendered structure. Boys frequently chase one another, an activity that often ends in wrestling and mock fights. When girls chase girls, they are usually less physically aggressive; for example, they less often wrestle one another to the ground or try to bodily overpower the person being chased. Unless organized as formal game like "freeze tag," same-gender chasing goes unnamed and usually undiscussed. But children set apart cross-gender chasing with special names. Students at both Oceanside and Ashton most often talked about "girls-chase-the boys" and "boys-chase-the girls"; the names are largely interchange-able, although boys tend to use the former and girls the latter, each claiming a kind of inno-cence. At Oceanside I also heard both boys and girls refer to "catch-and-kiss," and at Ashton, older boys talked about "kiss-or-kill," younger girls invited one another to "catch boys," and younger girls and boys described the game of "kissin'." In addition to these terms, I have heard reports from other U.S. schools of "the chase," "chasers," "chase-and-kiss," "kiss-chase," and "kissers-and-chasers." The names vary by region and school but always contain both gender and sexual meanings.[5]

Most informal within-gender chasing does not live on in talk unless something unusual happens, like an injury. But cross-gender chasing, especially when it takes the form of ex-tended sequences with more than a few participants, is often surrounded by lively discussion. Several parents have told me about their kindergarten or first-grade children coming home from school to excitedly, or sometimes disgustedly, describe "girls-chase-the-boys" (my chil-dren also did this when they entered elementary school). Verbal retellings and assessments take place not only at home but also on the playground. For example, three Ashton fourth-grade girls, who claimed time-out from boys-chase-the-girls by running to a declared safety zone, excitedly talked about the ongoing game: "That guy is mean, he hits everybody"; "I kicked him in the butt."

In girls-chase-the-boys, girls and boys become, by definition, separate teams. Gender terms blatantly override individual identities, especially in references to the other team ("Help, a girl's chasin' me!"; "C'mon Sarah, let's get that boy"; "Tony, help save me from the girls"). Individuals may call for help from, or offer help to, others of their gender. And in acts of treason, they may grab someone from their team and turn them over to the other side. For example, in an elaborate chasing scene among a group of Ashton third-graders, Ryan grabbed Billy from behind, wrestling him to the ground. "Hey girls, get 'im," Ryan called. . . .

VARIATIONS BY AGE.   Although the basic patterns of cross-gender chasing are remarkably persistent across all age levels, I noticed some variations by age. Several times I saw younger children go through a process of induction, as in the early fall at Ashton when a second-grade boy taught a kindergarten girl how to chase. He slowly ran backward, beckoning her to pursue him, as he called, "Help, a girl's after me." She picked up the loping movement and paced her-self behind him, as he looked back to make sure she was following. Then he slowly veered around and said, "Now I'll chase you."

Chasing often mixes with fantasy scenarios in the play of younger kids. An Ashton first-grade boy who said he was a "sea monster" made growling noises and curled his fingers like claws at the end of his outstretched arms as he stalked groups of girls. "There's a sea monster, c'mon, we gotta save our other friend, you know, Denise," Bonnie said to the three other girls beside her on the sidewalk. They ran from "the sea monster" to grab Denise's hand and then move into the safety of their "steel house." By the fourth and fifth grades, chasers have per-fected the exaggerated movements and sounds—stalking, screams, karate kicks—that accom-pany scenes of chasing among older girls and boys, and that help frame them as play.

Sexual meanings, highlighted by names like "chase-and-kiss" and "kissers-and-chasers," infuse cross-gender chasing at every age. The threat of kissing, most often girls threatening to kiss boys, is a ritualized form of provocation, especially among younger kids. When Shana, a third-grader, brought a tube of lipstick from home, she and her friends embellished games of kissin' by painting their lips dark red and threatening to smear the boys with kisses. This caused an uproar on the playground, and both boys and girls animatedly talked about it afterward. "The kiss gives you cooties," a boy explained to me.

I only once saw kisses used as a weapon in within-gender relations, when Justin, a second-grade boy, puckered his lips and told another boy that he would kiss him if he didn't leave him alone; the threat worked, and the other boy left. I never saw a girl use a kiss to threaten another girl, although young girls sometimes kissed one another with affection.

At both schools overt threats of kissing were more prevalent among younger kids, but they sometimes appeared in the play of fourth-, fifth-, and sixth-graders. At Oceanside I watched Lisa and Jill pull along Jonathan, a fourth-grade boy, by his hands, while a group of girls sitting on the jungle gym called out, "Kiss him, kiss him." Grabbing at his hair, Lisa said to Jill, "Wanna kiss Jonathan?" Jonathan wrenched himself away, and the girls chased after him. "Jill's gonna kiss your hair," Lisa yelled.

Sexual meanings may extend beyond kisses to other parts of the body. Margaret Blume, who observed on the Oceanside playground several years after I did, recorded a variant of chasing that the third-and fourth-graders called "scoring high with the girls."[6] When Margaret talked with a group who had been playing the game, a girl named Becky exclaimed, "They're trying to pinch our butts!" "Do you pinch them back?" Margaret asked. "No, I scratch; I hit them." A boy bragged, "I got fifty [pinches] now." "I guess we're popular," Becky said to Lois, as they both giggled.

Among fifth- and sixth-graders, cross-gender chasing involves more elaborate patterns of touch and touch avoidance than among younger kids. As I watched the stylized motions of grabbing at girls in ways that avoided their fronts, it seemed to me that older chasers often took account of girls' "developing" (or soon-to-be-developing) bodies, especially the growing visibility of their breasts. Principals, teachers, and aides generally ignored cross-gender chasing among younger kids, unless it got physically rough. Sometimes adults found it amusing, as when a first-grade teacher came up to me on the playground and, teasing the little girls who were standing next to her, told me, "Write down that first-grade girls kiss the boys." But if a fourth-, fifth-, or sixth-grade girl and boy ended a chase by wrestling on the ground (an infrequent occurrence; that sort of physical pummeling between boys and girls diminished with age), playground aides were quick to intervene, even when it was clear the tussle was being enacted in a mode of play. The Ashton principal told the sixth graders that they were not to play "pom-pom tackle," a complicated chasing game, because it entailed "inappropriate touch" between boys and girls. . . .

"Cooties" and Other Pollution Rituals

Episodes of chasing sometimes entwine with rituals of pollution, as in "cooties" or "cootie tag" where specific individuals or groups are treated as contaminating or carrying "germs." Cooties, of course, are invisible; they make their initial appearance through announcements like "Rochelle has cooties!"[7] Kids have rituals for transferring cooties (usually touching someone else, often after a chase, and shouting "You've got cooties!"), for immunization (writing "CV"—for "cootie vaccination"—on their arms, or shaping their fingers to push out a pretend immunizing "cootie spray"), and for eliminating cooties (saying "no gives" or using "cootie catchers" made of folded paper).[8] While girls and boys may transfer cooties to one another, and girls may give cooties to girls, boys do not generally give cooties to other boys.[9] Girls, in short, are central to the game.

Either girls or boys may be defined as having cooties, but girls give cooties to boys more often than vice versa. In Michigan, one version of cooties was called "girl stain"; the fourth-graders in a school on the East Coast used the phrase "girl touch."[10] And in a further shift from acts to imputing the moral character of actors, individuals may be designated as "cootie queens" or "cootie girls."[11] Cootie queens or cootie girls (I have never heard or read about "cootie kings" or "cootie boys") are female pariahs, the ultimate school untouchables, seen as contaminating not only by virtue of gender, but also through some added stigma such as being overweight or poor.[12] And according to one report, in a racially mixed playground in Fresno, California, "Mexican" (Chicano/Latino) but not Anglo children gave cooties; thus inequalities of race, as well as of gender and social class, may be expressed through pollution games.[13] In situations like this, different sources of oppression may compound one another.

I did not learn of any cootie queens at Ashton or Oceanside, but in the daily life of schools *individual* boys and girls may be stigmatized and treated as contaminating. For example, a third-grade Ashton girl refused to sit by a particular boy, whom other boys routinely pushed away from the thick of all-male seating, because he was "stinky" and "peed in his bed." A teacher in another school told me that her fifth-grade students said to newcomers, "Don't touch Phillip's desk; he picks his nose and makes booger balls." Phillip had problems with motor coordination, which, the teacher thought, contributed to his marginalization.

But there is also a notable gender asymmetry, evident in the skewed patterning of cooties; *girls as a group are treated as an ultimate source of contamination*, while boys as boys—although maybe not, as Chicanos or individuals with a physical disability—are exempt. Boys sometimes mark hierarchies among themselves by using "girl" as a label for low-status boys and by pushing subordinated boys next to the contaminating space of girls. In Miss Bailey's fourth-fifth–grade class other boys routinely forced or maneuvered the lowest-status boys (Miguel and Alejandro, the recent immigrants from Mexico, and Joel, who was overweight and afraid of sports) into sitting "by the girls," a space treated as contaminating. In this context, boys drew on gender meanings to convey racial subordination. In contrast, when there was gender-divided seating in the classroom, lunchroom, music room, or auditorium, which girls sat at the boundary between groups of girls and groups of boys had no apparent relationship to social status.

Boys sometimes treat objects associated with girls as polluting; once again, the reverse does not occur. Bradley, a college student, told me about a classroom incident he remembered from third grade. Some girls gave Valentine's Day cards with pictures of Strawberry Shortcake, a feminine-stereotyped image, to everyone in the class, including boys. Erik dumped all his Strawberry Shortcake valentines into Bradley's box; Bradley one-upped the insult by adding his own Strawberry Shortcake valentines to the pile and sneaking them back into Erik's box.

Recoiling from physical proximity with another person and their belongings because they are perceived as contaminating is a powerful statement of social distance and claimed superiority. Pollution beliefs and practices draw on the emotion-laden feeling of repugnance that accompanies unwanted touch or smell. Kids often act out pollution beliefs in a spirit of playful teasing, but the whimsical frame of "play" slides in and out of the serious, and some games of cooties clearly cause emotional pain. When pollution rituals appear, even in play, they frequently express and enact larger patterns of inequality, by gender, by social class and race, and by bodily characteristics like weight and motor coordination. When several of these characteristics are found in the same person, the result may be extreme rituals of shaming, as in the case of cootie queens. Aware of the cruelty and pain bound up in games of pollution, teachers and aides often try to intervene, especially when a given individual becomes the repeated target.

What is the significance of "girl stain," of the fact that girls, but not boys, become cast as an ultimate polluting group? Beliefs in female pollution, usually related to menstruation and reproductive sexuality, can be found in many cultures but not, at least from the reports I've been able to find, among prepubertal children. Cooties, which is primarily played by first-, second-, and third-graders (or kids ages six to nine), is therefore unusual. These pollution rituals suggest that in contemporary U.S. culture even young girls are treated as symbolically contaminating in a way that boys, as a group, are not. This may be because in our culture even at a young age, girls are sexualized more than boys, and female sexuality, especially when "out of place" or actively associated with children, connotes danger and endangerment. Furthermore, even before birth girls are, on the whole, less valued than boys; it is still the case, for example, that prospective parents more often wish for a son than a daughter. Pollution rituals connect with themes of separation and power, to which I will return later in the chapter.

Invasions

In contests and in chasing, groups of girls and groups of boys confront one another as separate "sides," which makes for a kind of symmetry as does the alternation of chasing and being chased. But rituals of pollution tip the symmetry, defining girls as more contaminating. Invasions, a final type of borderwork, also take asymmetric form; boys invade girls' groups and activities much more often than the reverse. When asked about what they do on the playground, boys list "teasing the girls" as a named activity, but girls do not talk so routinely about "teasing boys."[14] As in other kinds of borderwork, gendered language ("Let's spy on the girls"; "Those boys are messing up our jump rope game") accompanies invasions, as do stylized interactions that highlight a sense of gender as an antagonistic social division.

On the playgrounds of both schools I repeatedly saw boys, individually or in groups, deliberately disrupt the activities of groups of girls. Boys ruin ongoing games of jump rope by dashing under the twirling rope and disrupting the flow of the jumpers or by sticking a foot into the rope and stopping its momentum. On the Ashton playground seven fourth-grade girls engaged in an intense game of foursquare; it was a warm October day, and the girls had piled their coats on the cement next to the painted court. Two boys, mischief enlivening their faces, came to the edge of the court. One swung his arm into the game's bouncing space; in annoyed response, one of the female players pushed back at him. He ran off for a few feet, while the other boy circled in to take a swipe, trying to knock the ball out of play. Meanwhile, the first boy kneeled behind the pile of coats and leaned around to watch the girls. One of the girls yelled angrily, "Get out. My glasses are in one of those, and I don't want 'em busted." A playground aide called the boys over and told them to "leave the girls alone," and the boys ran off.

Some boys more or less specialize in invading girls, coming back again and again to disrupt; the majority of boys are not drawn to the activity.[15] Even if only a few boys do most of the invading, disruptions are so frequent that girls develop ritualized responses. Girls verbally protest ("Leave us alone!"; "Stop it, Keith!"), and they chase boys away. The disruption of a girls' game may provoke a cross-gender chasing sequence, but if girls are annoyed, they chase in order to drive the boy out of their space, a purpose far removed from playful shifting between the roles of chaser and chased. Girls may guard their play with informal lookouts who try to head off trouble; they are often wary about letting boys into their activities. And they sometimes complain to playground aides. . . .

IS BORDERWORK "ALL IN PLAY"?

I once asked Jeremy, one of the Oceanside fifth-graders, why girls and boys in Miss Bailey's class formed separate lines. "So they won't fight so much," he promptly replied. A variety of terms—"fighting," "teasing," "hassling," "bothering"—have been used to suggest the heightened emotions and the playful and real conflict that characterize borderwork.[16] Are the various incidents I have described really "fighting?" Or are they mostly "play?" When a girl repeatedly yells "You creep!" at a boy, is she insulting him or just fooling around? When a boy and a girl chase each other and wrestle on the ground, are they fighting, or expressing real sexual desire, or is it "all in fun?" Of course it all depends on context, and meanings are often mixed. Ambiguity is a feature of all types of borderwork and contributes to their volatility. . . .

All forms of borderwork partake, to varying degrees, in the frame or mode of "play." Some types of borderwork, like boys against the girls in kickball or in classroom math competitions, are organized as games, a rule-governed type of play. Episodes of chasing and cooties are more informal; participants signal the play frame by using scripted talk ("Help! A girl's chasin' me!"), laughter, stylized movements, and exaggerated kicks in the air. And when they disrupt a game of jump rope, boys often wear playful expressions and bend over with laughter when the jumper gets tangled in the rope. . . .

The Theme of Aggression

I have already touched on varied kinds of aggression, ranging from verbal insults to outright physical coercion, that thread through incidents of borderwork. When girls and boys confront one another as rival groups, their boundaries defined by gender, the situation invites verbal insults, like those that accompanied the math game in Miss Bailey's class. Sometimes kids voice insults in anger, as when Rita, Neera, and Sheila yelled, "Bratty boys! Sissy boys!" in the heated-up game of team handball. At other times, the rivalry may be more playful and almost ritualized, as when three girls, sitting in one of the waiting lines that crisscrossed the Ashton lunchroom floor, chanted in cheery unison, "Girls are smart, boys are bogue" ("bogue" means "stupid and uncool"). The boys across from them smiled and, quickly fishing for a retort, came up with "Boys are better, girls are dumb."

Kids often carry out episodes of playground chasing in a whimsically scripted way, providing many cues that "this is play." But in both same-gender and cross-gender chasing, provocations that violate bodies, possessions, and selves may not be intended or perceived as very playful, and they may spur an angry pursuit. In the course of my fieldwork one of the few times I heard overtly racist insults was during episodes of cross-gender chasing; "Na, na, colored boy," a white third-grade girl at Ashton School yelled at an African-American boy, who then chased her. At Oceanside Lenore, a fifth-grade white girl, repeatedly yelled "Mexican monkey" as she chased with a Chicano boy. Chasing sequences may contain physical as well as verbal aggression, with the chased being pummeled to the ground, tripped, and sat upon. This kind of "play fighting" sometimes shades into "real fighting," especially among boys, whose chasing tends to be quite physical. In cross-gender chasing, when girls complain to aides that the boys are getting too rough, or on the rarer occasions when boys complain, the frame of play breaks down and the issue of aggression comes to the fore.

In the charges and countercharges that attend some episodes of tattling, one party may define the situation as a serious violation, while the other party insists that they were "just playing." This pattern recurs in the wake of playground invasions; boys, far more often the invaders, often claim a play frame, but girls, more often the targets of invasion, refuse to accept that definition. The asymmetry increases with age; many fourth- and fifth-grade girls see male invasions as a playground nuisance that simply makes them angry. This pattern resembles the structuring of sexual harassment. The harasser, nearly always male, often claims that verbal and physical intrusions into the target's personal space are "all in fun," while the target, usually female, sees it as unwanted and even coercive attention. Hierarchies help determine whose version of reality will prevail.[17]

Kids and adults often use the word "teasing" to describe episodes of chasing and invasion; "teasing" suggests targeted humor, with an angry or aggressive edge. This mix again provides multiple possibilities for action and interpretation. Teasing may express affection and solidarity, but, as Freud persuasively demonstrated, humor may also be a guise for hostility. The ambiguity titillates, and the possibly serious import of humor may be raised for negotiation.[18]

Sexual and Romantic Themes

The ambiguities of borderwork allow the signaling of sexual or romantic, as well as aggressive, meanings, and the two often mix together. If a girl repeatedly chases a particular boy, or vice versa, it may be taken as a sign of "liking." Participants are fully aware of this potential interpretation, as shown during one vivid incident when a participant suddenly, teasingly named that tune. On the Ashton playground. Ken, a third-grader, growled and stalked after two of his classmates, Sharon and Jenny, who ran to the proclaimed safety of "the cage," as they called the area by the bars. Lisa came over and taunted, "Ken can't get me," and Ken chased her while she screamed. Then Ken circled back to the area of the bars and, his arms outflung, ran after Sharon and Jenny. The pursuit ended when Ken grabbed Jenny, and they ended up face-to-face with his arms around her. Jenny suddenly, teasingly said, "What you huggin' me for?" "I'm not," he replied in a slightly stunned voice, while she flashed a triumphant smile. Ken quickly let go.

Running after someone, pinning their arms from the front or behind, or verbally insulting them may all be intended and/or interpreted as positive signs of attention. A woman college student remembered "antagonizing guys" in fifth grade; "you chased them, yelled at them, and called them shocking names, but you really liked the guy. . . ."

Other researchers have pondered the mix of aggression and liking that infuses boundaries between boys and girls. In her research in a desegregated junior high, Janet Schofield observed a lot of physical "bothering" and "pushing" not only between girls and boys, but also between Blacks and whites. But she argues that these forms of hassling differ in fundamental ways: "Whereas relations with gender outgroups are fundamentally influenced by the knowledge of future positive ties, relations between blacks and whites are fundamentally shaped by the history and present existence of racial separation, hostility and discrimination in our society.[19]

Schofield's argument about the history and structure of race relations, and racism, in the United States is well taken. But this interpretation tends to naturalize gender relations instead of observing that they are *also* shaped by history and by patterns of separation, hostility, and discrimination. Adult cross-gender relations cannot be chalked up simply as "future positive ties"; not everyone is heterosexual, and the "liking" relations of adults, as well as of fifth-graders and junior high students, mix caring and antagonism, pleasure and hostility. These patterns should not be taken for granted: gender relations, like race relations, are always changing, and . . . they can be deliberately altered.

Issues of Power

Power is another consequential structure that moves in and out of the leavening frame of "play." Much borderwork is symmetrical—girls and boys both avoid one another, exchange insults, square off as separate sides in games of math or kickball, or alternate roles in games of chasing. But telling asymmetries skew the marking of gender difference toward patterns of male dominance among children as well as, although generally less than, among adults.

Space, an especially valuable resource in the crowded environment of schools, is the locus of one basic asymmetry between girls and boys. On school playgrounds boys control as much as ten times more space than girls, when one adds up the area of large playing fields (plus basketball courts and, at Oceanside, skateball courts) and compares it with the much smaller areas (for jump rope, hopscotch, foursquare, and doing tricks on the bars) where girls predominate.[20] In addition to taking up more space, boys more often see girls and their activities as interruptible; boys invade and disrupt all-female games and scenes of play much more often than vice versa. This pattern, coupled with the much larger turf under boys' control, led Zella Luria, another playground observer, to comment that playgrounds are basically male turf; even girls' smaller enclaves are subject to invasion.[21]

Boys' control of space can be seen as a pattern of claimed entitlement, perhaps linked to patterns well documented among adults in the same culture. For example, there is ample evidence, reviewed and analyzed by Nancy Henley, that adult men take up more personal and public space than adult women. Furthermore, men more often interrupt or violate the space, as well as talk, of women.[22]

Beliefs about female pollution also express and help maintain separation between the genders, and female subordination, in the social relations of U.S. elementary school children as well as in cultures of the Mediterranean and of highland New Guinea.[23] But, as anthropologists have recently argued, pollution beliefs have multiple and even contradictory dimensions.[24] In some contexts women, and girls, may use belief in female contamination to further their own ends and even as a source of power. Male susceptibility to female pollution can be experienced as a source of vulnerability; if a girl is designated as having cooties or threatens to plant a dangerous kiss, it is the boy who has to run.[25] In complex dialectics of power, boys treat girls' spaces, activities, and sheer physical presence as contaminating, but girls sometimes craft their perceived dangerous qualities into a kind of weapon. Several of the third-grade boys who talked about the "lipstick girls who gave cooties" seemed not only excited but also a little fearful. Furthermore, on some occasions girls and boys who *share* other features in the crisscross mix of social identities—who, for example, are Anglos (rather than Chicanos) or who are not cootie queens—unite in treating some "Other" as polluting. In these contexts, "sides" shift, and being a girl or boy becomes less important than *not* being the school pariah or a member of a racially marginalized group. Gender dominance is only one strand of an intricate mesh of power relationships.

The dynamics of power in children's social relationships are extremely complex, and in many ways, in the words of a playground aide, "girls give as well as get." Girls sometimes turn pollution into a weapon; they challenge and derogate boys; they guard their own play and respond angrily to invasions; they stave off provocations by ignoring them; they complain to adults. But in several notable ways, girls act from a one-down position, a pattern both enacted and dramatized in the processes of borderwork.

WHY IS BORDERWORK SO MEMORABLE?

The imagery of "border" may wrongly suggest an unyielding fence that divides social relations into two parts. The image should rather be one of many short fences that are quickly built and as quickly dismantled. Gender boundaries are episodic and ambiguous, and *the notion of "borderwork" should be coupled with a parallel term—such as "neutralization"—for processes through which girls and boys (and adults who enter into their social relations) neutralize or undermine a sense of gender as division and opposition.*[26] The situations (e.g., less crowded in space, with fewer potential witnesses and participants) and practices (e.g., teachers or children organizing encounters along lines other than gender) that draw girls and boys together are a first step. But these "with" situations can go in varied directions: when girls and boys are together, gender may be marked and boundaries evoked, the theme of this chapter, or gender may become muted in salience.

At the beginning of the chapter I described a team handball game in which gender meanings heated up. Heated events also cool down. After the team handball game transmuted into a brief scene of chasing, the recess bell rang and the participants went back to their shared classroom. Ten minutes later the same girls and boys interacted in reading groups where gender was of minimal significance. Gender boundaries may also be dismantled on the playground, as when boys and girls left their mostly gender-divided activities while defending Don against mistreatment by a teacher who was on "yard duty." In that incident, girls and boys found another source of solidarity—being in the same class and chafing under the authority of the adult "yard duty"—and gender divisions receded in importance.

Here I must stress *levels of analysis*. As *individuals*, we are (with a few ambiguous exceptions, such as transsexuals) each assigned to a fixed gender category, and by age three we develop relatively firm individual identities as either girls or boys. Over the course of our lives we continually enact and construct individual gender (being a male, being a female, with multiple styles of masculinity and femininity) through talk, dress, movement, activities.[27] But when the level of analysis shifts from the individual to *groups and situations*, gender becomes more fluid. A boy may always be a "boy," and that fact will enter into all of his experiences. But in some interactions he may be much more aware of that strand of his identity than in others, just as his ethnicity or age may be more relevant in some situations than in others. Multiple identities may also compound one another; sometimes it is highly salient that one is an African-American boy.

The salience of gender may vary from one situation to another, and gender and other social divisions (age, ethnicity, social class) may, depending on the context, "abrade, inflame, amplify, twist, dampen, and complicate each other" (in the phrasing of R. W. Connell and his colleagues).[28] Given these complexities, why are the occasions of gender borderwork so compelling? Why do episodes of girls-chase-the-boys and boys-against-the girls *seem* like the heart of what "gender" is all about? Why do kids regard those situations as especially newsworthy and turn them into stories that they tell afterward and bring home from school? And why do adults, when invited to muse back upon gender relations in their elementary school years, so often spontaneously recall "girls-chase-the-boys," "teasing girls," and "cooties," but less often mention occasions when boys and girls were together in less gender-marked ways? (The latter kinds of occasions may be recalled under other rubrics, like "when we did classroom projects.")

The occasions of borderwork may carry extra perceptual weight because they are marked by conflict, intense emotions, and the expression of forbidden desires. These group activities may also rivet attention because they are created by kids themselves, and because they are ritualized, not as high ceremony, but by virtue of being stylized, repeated, and enacted with a sense of performance.[29] I have described the scripted quality of contests, chasing, invasions, and tattling. This ritual dimension, as Mary Douglas has written, "aides us in selecting experiences for concentrated attention" and "enlivens the memory."[30] Cross-gender chasing has a name ("chase-and-kiss"), a scripted format (the repertoire of provocations and forms of response), and takes shape through stylized motions and talk. The ritual form focuses attention and evokes dominant beliefs about the "nature" of boys and girls and relationships between them. . . .

Games of girls-against-the-boys, scenes of cross-gender chasing and invasion, and episodes of heterosexual teasing evoke stereotyped images of gender relations. Deeply rooted in the dominant culture and ideology of our society, these images infuse the ways adults talk about girls and boys and relations between them; the content of movies, television, advertising, and children's books; and even the wisdom of experts, including social scientists. This hegemonic view of gender—acted out, reinforced, and evoked through the various forms of borderwork—has two key components:

1. ***Emphasis on gender as an oppositional dualism.*** Terms like "the opposite sex" and "the war between the sexes" come readily to mind when one watches a group of boys invade a jump rope game and the girls angrily respond, or a group of girls and a group of boys hurling insults at one another across a lunchroom. In all forms or borderwork boys and girls are defined as rival teams with a socially distant, wary, and even hostile relationship: heterosexual meanings add to the sense of polarization. Hierarchy tilts the theme of opposition, with boys asserting spatial, physical, and evaluative dominance over girls.

2. ***Exaggeration of gender difference and disregard for the presence of crosscutting variation and sources of commonality.*** Social psychologists have identified a continuum that ranges from . . . the "interpersonal extreme," when interaction is largely determined by *individual* characteristics, to the "intergroup extreme," when interaction is largely determined by the *group membership* or social categories of paicipants.[31] Borderwork lies at the intergroup extreme. When girls and boys are defined as opposite sides caught up in rivalry and competition, group stereotyping and antagonism flourish. Members of "the other side" become "that boy" or "that girl." Individual identities get submerged, and participants hurl gender insults ("sissy boys," "dumb girls"), talk about the other gender as "yuck," and make stereotyped assertions ("girls are crybabies"; "boys are frogs; I don't like boys").

Extensive gender separation and organizing mixed-gender encounters as girls-against-the-boys set off contrastive thinking and feed an assumption of gender as dichotomous and antagonistic difference. These social practices seem to express core truths: that boys and girls are separate and fundamentally different, as individuals and as groups. Other social practices that challenge this portrayal—drawing boys and girls together in relaxed and extended ways, emphasizing individual identities or social categories that cut across gender, acknowledging variation in the activities and interests of girls and boys—carry less perceptual weight. As do efforts by kids and adults to challenge existing gender arrangements. . . . *But the occasions where gender is less relevant, or contested, are also part of the construction of gender relations.*

I want to conclude by raising another interpretive possibility. The frames of "play" and "ritual" set the various forms of borderwork a bit apart from ongoing "ordinary" life. As previously argued, this may enhance the perceptual weight of borderwork situations in the eyes of both participants and observers, highlighting a gender-as-antagonistic-dualism portrayal of social relations. But the framing of ritualized play may also give leeway for participants to gain perspective on dominant cultural images. Play and ritual can comment on and challenge, as well as sustain, a given ordering of reality.[32]. . .

Discussion Questions

1. How do contests, often structured by adults, reaffirm the idea that boys and girls are on "opposite sides"?
2. Discuss the heterosexual rituals Thorne observed at the elementary schools she studied. How do children actively create meanings of heterosexuality?

3. What is borderwork? What does it tell us about the limitations of seeing boys and girls as on "opposite sides"?
4. Were any of these rituals similar to your elementary school experiences? What are other ways, in which children actively make meanings about gender?

Notes

1. Fredrik Barth, "Introduction" to *Ethnic Groups and Boundaries.* I am grateful to Fred Erickson for suggesting the relevance of Barth's analysis. Sandra Wallman's writing (e.g., "The Boundaries of Race") on the process of marking race and ethnic boundaries is also suggestive. Several years after I had worked out the significance of Barth's insight for understanding children's gender relations. I discovered a similar project in Berentzen's ethnography of a preschool in Norway, *Children Constructing Their Social World.*
2. Barth, "Introduction," p. 15.
3. For a taxonomy of children's games that distinguishes chasing from other forms, see Brian Sutton-Smith, "A Syntax for Play and Games."
4. Christine R. Finnan, "The Ethnography of Children's Spontaneous Play."
5. For brief descriptions of cross-gender chasing on school playgrounds, see ibid, (observations in Texas); Raphaella Best, *We've All Got Scars: What Boys and Girls Learn in Elementary School* (the Central Atlantic region); Kathryn M. Borman, "Children's Interactions in Playgrounds" (the Midwest); Corsaro, *Friendship and Peer Culture* ("cross-gender approach-avoidance" play, including chasing, in a nursery school on the West Coast); Sue Parrott, "Games Children Play: Ethnography of a Second-Grade Recess" (second-grade boys in Minnesota tell about playing "girls-catch-the-boys"); Andy Sluckin, *Growing Up in the Playground* ("kiss-chase" in a British school); and Stephen Richert, *Boys and Girls Apart: Children's Play in Canada and Poland* ("kissing girls," a children's chasing game in Ottawa, Canada, and "kisser catchers," in the Bahamas).

6. I would like to thank Margaret Blume for sharing her fieldnotes and giving me permission to cite this example.
7. The word "cooties" may have its origins among soldiers in foxholes in World War I, who used the term for head lice (Robert L. Chapman, *New Dictionary of American Slang*). When the soldiers returned home, some playfully called their wives and other women "cooties," and "The Cooties" was the name of at least one Veterans of Foreign Wars women's auxiliary club. Since the late 1940s a toy company has marketed a children's game called Cooties, which involves rolling a dice to draw body pieces and constructing an antlike plastic creature. Iona Opie and Peter Opie (*Children's Games in Street and Playground*) have recorded versions of cootie tag from England, Spain, Madagascar, and New England. With new times come new forms of contamination; I recently heard reports of children saying to one another, "Don't touch me; I don't want your AIDS."
8. Cootie catchers are a variant of the fortune-telling devices made of folded paper that are described and illustrated in Mary Knapp and Herbert Knapp, *One Potato, Two Potato: The Secret Education of American Children,* pp. 257–259 and in Iona Opie and Peter Opie, *The Lore and Language of Schoolchildren,* pp. 341–342.
9. This pattern was also found by Sue Samuelson, a folklorist, who gathered reports about how the game has been played ("The Cooties Complex").
10. Kevin Karkau "Sexism in Fourth Grade." Richert (*Boys and Girls Apart*) reports Canadian children talking about "girl germs" but not "boy germs."

11. Thanks to Bob Emerson for this insight.
12. College students have told me about cootie queens in the elementary schools they attended; one reported that she had been a cootie queen when she was in fourth grade, a memory fraught with shame and suffering. She speculated that the stigma was related to her being over-weight, as well as new to the school.
13. Samuelson, "The Cooties Complex." A friend of mine relayed a student's description of interactions in a school in a Canadian community divided between whites and more impoverished Native Americans. If a white girl accidentally touched a "native" girl, the white girl would quickly say "superstuff" and run to touch another white girl or boy to pass on, and thereby undo, the pollution.
14. I observed this in casual conversations at Ashton and Oceanside; the pattern also emerged in the memories of college students: both men and women recalled "chasing," but men talked more generally about "teasing girls." In extensive observations of elementary school children in West Germany, Oswald and his colleagues ("Gaps and Bridges") found a lot of mutual "bothering" between first-grade boys and girls. By fourth grade, boys bothered girls much more than the reverse; girls coped by complaining to adults and by ignoring or rebuking the botherers.

   In a study of U.S. first-graders, Linda Grant ("Black Females' 'Place' in Desegregated Classrooms") found that where an initiator could be discerned, boys were responsible for 59 to 90 percent of physically aggressive encounters between boys and girls. Ruth G. Goodenough ("Small Group Culture and the Emergence of Sexist Behavior: A Comparative Study of Four Children's Groups") computed the ratio of negative to positive behavior in relations between the genders in four different kindergartens. She found a wide range, from one classroom with a relatively even balance of negative and positive behaviors to one where boys' negative behaviors to girls outweighed their positive behaviors by a ratio of thirty-one to one. In that classroom, boys repeatedly disrupted girls' play, while girls rarely disrupted the activities of boys. The girls in that classroom were generally more timid and less spontaneous than girls in the more egalitarian kindergarten.

   Patricia S. Griffin ("Gymnastics Is a Girl's Thing: Student Participation and Interaction Patterns in a Middle School Gymnastics Unit"), who observed in a coed gymnastics class at a U.S. middle school, also found a dramatic gender asymmetry. Boys, as individuals and in groups, hassled girls (by getting in their way, butting into line, giving orders, teasing, mimicking, yelling and laughing at them) much more than the reverse. The girls responded by physically moving away, acquiescing (e.g., letting boys butt into line), ignoring, and asking the boys to stop. Boys generally interacted with girls only to hassle them; girls generally interacted with boys only when they responded to being hassled.
15. In quantified observations among elementary school children in West Germany, Oswald and his colleagues ("Gaps and Bridges") also found that a few boys—four out of fourteen in a group of fifth-graders—were responsible for most of the "bothering"; they made "plaguing girls" into a kind of sport. This pattern may relate to the emergence of school "bullies," although that topic has been studied more in the context of boy-boy than of boy-girl (or girl-girl) relationships.

   Dan Olweus *(Aggression in the Schools)* found that of one thousand Swedish boys, ages twelve to sixteen, 4 to 6 percent were, in the perceptions of teachers and other students, extreme bullies; another 4 to 6 percent were "whipping boys," or frequent targets of bullying. In research in Norway Olweus found that boys engaged in three times a much bullying as girls; girls' bullying tended to be more subtle, like spreading rumors. In 1983 the Norwegian government, with Olweus's help, launched a national campaign to end bullying in elementary an junior high schools. Educational materials about the bully problem were given to school staff and families, and teachers were urged to give a clear message that bullying is not acceptable, to initiate talks with victims and bullies, and to give generous praise when rules were followed. When rules were violated, teachers and parents were advised to consistently use nonhostile, noncorporal punishment. According to Olweus, this national campaign reduced bullying by as much as half (Peter Freiberg, "Bullying Gets Banned in Norway's Schools").
16. Perhaps because most of the students at both Oceanside and Ashton were white and working-class, I witnessed little systematic hassling along lines of race and/or social class. Researchers in schools with larger proportions of students from different races and social classes have found those boundaries marked by teasing and bothering, with gender cutting across. Judith Lynne Hanna *(Disruptive School Behavior: Class, Race, and Culture)* observed in a recently desegregated "magnet" elementary school composed mostly of Black working-class and white middle-class students. She found recurring patterns of verbal and physical aggression that the children called "meddlin," including insults and taunts, menacing body postures, pushing, hitting, poking, and fighting. Working-class Black boys most often engaged in meddlin, and Black girls did more meddlin, especially in response to provocation, than white girls. The targets of meddlin were sometimes social equals of the aggressor but were most often the vulnerable: newcomers, children with physical handicaps or unusual dress, poor athletes, or those afraid to stand up to provocation. Some white and more Black children responded to meddlin by reciprocating; middle-class children, Black and white, were more likely to comply with demands or to disengage by using humor, negotiation, withdrawal, or the mediation of a teacher or another child. Hanna connects this use of verbal and physical aggression to patterns of bodily self-assertion in African-American culture; she also suggests that when children lack material or academic

resources, they may resort to physical means to gain power. Meddlin took place mostly among Blacks and was not specifically targeted against whites as a group, but whites were put off by it and more often saw it as aggression rather than play, a perception that contributed to racial separation.

In observations in a desegregated junior high school, Schofield (*Black and White in Conflict*) also found an association between being Black, working-class, and male, and engaging in physical hassling. Targets who were white were quicker than those who were Black to interpret the hassling as intimidation.

17. See Nancy Henley and Cheris Kramarae, "Miscommunication, Gender, and Power."
18. Sigmund Freud, *Jokes and Their Relation to the Unconscious*, and Emerson, "Negotiating the Serious Import of Humor."
19. Janet Schofield, "Complementary and Conflicting Identities: Images of Interaction in an Interracial School," p. 85.
20. A pattern of boys having access to more space than girls of the same age can also be found in research on the daily lives of kids outside school. Roger Hart (*Children's Experiences of Place*) gathered information on the space traversed by forty-seven boys and forty girls, ages five through twelve, in a town in New England. At all ages, boys traveled almost twice as far as girls; for example, among fifth- and sixth-graders, boys averaged a distance of almost half a mile, and girls around one fourth of a mile. Parents gave boys permission to roam more freely than girls and were more likely to turn an eye when a son rather than a daughter broke the rules.

In a study of 764 sixth-graders in California, Medrich and his colleagues (*The Serious Business of Growing Up*) found boys were more physically mobile than girls, with some striking individual variations; for example, girls who played team sports were more physically mobile than other girls. They also found African-Americans were more physically mobile than whites or Asian-Americans; African-American boys roamed the farthest of any gender/ethnic group. Lever ("Sex Differences in the Games Children Play") found, as have other researchers, that when they are not in school, fifth-grade boys more often play in out-of-door activities, and girls are more likely to play in and around their houses. In a comparative study of six cultures, Whiting and Edwards (*Children of Different Worlds*)

found that boys more often traveled beyond the immediate neighborhood except in one culture, the Taira in Okinawa, where, at an early age, girls, as well as boys, were allowed to roam freely throughout the community.

21. Personal communication from Zella Luria.
22. Nancy Henley, *Body Politics: Power, Sex, and Nonverbal Communication*; also see Thorne et al., eds., *Language, Gender, and Society*.
23. In a classic statement, Mary Douglas argued that "pollution is a type of danger which is not likely to occur except where the lines of structure, cosmic or social, are clearly defined" (*Purity and Danger*, p. 113). Thus, depending on the context, pollution rituals may help sustain social divisions along lines of gender, race, ethnicity, social class, or age. For writings on female pollution beliefs and rituals in varied cultures, see Thomas Buckley and Alma Gottlieb, eds., *Blood Magic: The Anthropology of Menstruation*.
24. Buckley and Gottlieb, *Blood Magic*.
25. Feminist psychoanalytic theories, may help explain why males may feel threatened by females and "things feminine" and thus may treat girls as polluting. Chodorow's theory (*The Reproduction of Mothering*) may also help account for a related asymmetry: to say that a boy is "like a girl" is more insulting and personally threatening than to say that a girl is "like a boy." In the repertoire of children's teases I sometimes heard the taunting charge that a given boy "is" a girl ("Ben is a girl 'cause he's sitting at the girls' table"), but I never saw kids tease a girl for "being" a boy.
26. The process I am calling "neutralization" is called "decategorization" in Marilyn B. Brewer and Norman Miller, "Beyond the Contact Hypothesis: Theoretical Perspectives on Desegregation." In the process of decategorization, social categories like Black and white are made less salient than in "category-based contact."
27. See West and Zimmerman, "Doing Gender."
28. See Connell et al., *Making the Difference*, p. 182.
29. For a review of debates about use of the term "ritual," see Sally F. Moore and Barbara Myerhoff, eds., *Secular Ritual*.
30. Douglas, *Purity and Danger*, pp. 63–64.
31. Henri Tajfel, "Social Psychology of Intergroup Relations."
32. See Schwartzman, *Transformations*.

Barbie Girls Versus Sea Monsters: Children Constructing Gender

Michael A. Messner

INTRODUCTION

Recent research on children's worlds has revealed how gender varies . . . across social contexts. Building on this observation [Michael A. Messner] examines a . . . gendered moment of group life among four- and five-year-old children at a youth soccer opening ceremony, where gender boundaries were activated and enforced in ways that constructed an apparently "natural" categorical difference between the girls and the boys. The author . . . explores (1) how children "do gender" at the level of interaction or performance, (2) how the structured gender regime constrains and enables the actions of children and parents, and (3) how children's . . . immersion in popular culture provides symbolic resources with which children and parents actively create (or disrupt) categorical differences. The article ends with a discussion of how gendered interactions, structure, and cultural meanings are intertwined, in both mutually reinforcing and contradictory ways.

I n the past decade, studies of children and gender have moved toward greater levels of depth and sophistication (e.g., Jordan and Cowan 1995; McGuffy and Rich 1999; Thorne 1993). In her groundbreaking work on children and gender, Thorne (1993) argued that previous theoretical frameworks, although helpful, were limited: The top-down (adult-to-child) approach of socialization theories tended to ignore the extent to which children are active agents in the creation of their worlds—often in direct or partial opposition to values or "roles" to which adult teachers or parents are attempting to socialize them. Developmental theories also had their limits due to their tendency to ignore group and contextual factors while overemphasizing "the constitution and unfolding of *individuals* as boys or girls" (Thorne 1993, 4). In her study of grade school children, Thorne demonstrated a dynamic approach that examined the ways in which children actively construct gender in specific social contexts of the classroom and the playground. . . . Thorne developed the concept of "gender play" to analyze the social processes through which children construct gender. Her level of analysis was not the individual but "*group life*—with social relations, the organization and meanings of social situations, the collective practices through which children and adults create and recreate gender in their daily interactions" (Thorne 1993, 4).

A key insight from Thorne's research is the extent to which gender varies . . . from situation to situation. Sometimes, children engage in "relaxed, cross sex play"; other times—for instance, on the playground during boys' ritual invasions of girls' spaces and games—gender boundaries between boys and girls are activated in ways that variously threaten or (more often) reinforce and clarify these boundaries. However, these varying moments . . . are not free-floating; they occur in social contexts such as schools and in which gender is formally and informally built into the division of labor, power structure, rules, and values (Connell 1987).

The purpose of this article is to use an observation of a . . . moment of group life among four- and five-year-old children as a point of departure for exploring the conditions under which gender boundaries become activated and enforced. I was privy to this moment as I observed my five-year-old son's first season (including weekly games and practices) in organized soccer. Unlike the long-term, systematic ethnographic studies of children conducted by Thorne (1993) or Adler and Adler (1998), this article takes one moment as its point of departure. I do not present this moment as somehow "representative" of what happened throughout the season; instead, I examine this as an example of what Hochschild (1994, 4) calls "magnified moments," which are "episodes of heightened importance, either epiphanies, moments of intense glee or unusual insight, or moments in which things go intensely but meaningfully wrong. In either case, the moment stands out; it is metaphorically rich, unusually elaborate and often echoes [later]." A magnified moment in daily life offers a window into the social construction of reality. It presents researchers with an opportunity to excavate gendered meanings and processes through an analysis of institutional and cultural contexts. The single empirical observation that serves as the point of departure for this article was made during a morning. Immediately after the event, I recorded my observations with detailed notes. I later slightly revised the notes after developing the photographs that I took at the event.

I will first describe the observation—an incident that occurred as a boys' four- and five-year-old soccer team waited next to a girls' four- and five-year-old soccer team for the beginning of the community's American Youth Soccer Organization (AYSO) season's opening ceremony. I will then examine this moment using three levels of analysis.

The interactional level: How do children "do gender," and what are the contributions and limits of theories . . . in understanding these interactions?

The level of structural context: How does the . . . larger organizational level of formal sex segregation of AYSO, and the concrete, momentary situation of the opening ceremony provide a context that variously constrains and enables the children's interactions?

The level of cultural symbol: How does the children's shared immersion in popular culture (and their differently gendered locations in this immersion) provide symbolic resources for the creation, in this situation, of apparently categorical differences between the boys and the girls?

Although I will discuss these three levels of analysis separately, I hope to demonstrate that interaction, structural context, and culture are simultaneous and mutually intertwined processes, none of which supersedes the others.

BARBIE GIRLS VERSUS SEA MONSTERS

It is a warm, sunny Saturday morning. Summer is coming to a close, and schools will soon reopen. As in many communities, this time of year in this small, middle- and professional-class suburb of Los Angeles is marked by the beginning of another soccer season. This morning, 156 teams, with approximately 1,850 players ranging from 4 to 17 years old, along with another 2,000 to 3,000 parents, siblings, friends, and community dignitaries have gathered at the local high school football and track facility for the annual AYSO opening ceremonies. Parents and children wander around the perimeter of the track to find the assigned station for their respective teams. The coaches muster their teams and chat with parents. Eventually, each team will march around the track, behind their new team banner, as they are announced over the loudspeaker system and are applauded by the crowd. For now though, and for the next 45 minutes to an hour, the kids, coaches, and parents must stand, mill around, talk, and kill time as they await the beginning of the ceremony.

The Sea Monsters is a team of four- and five-year-old boys. Later this day, they will play their first-ever soccer game. A few of the boys already know each other from preschool, but most are still getting acquainted. They are wearing their new uniforms for the first time. Like other teams, they were assigned team colors—in this case, green and blue—and asked to choose their team name at their first team meeting, which occurred a week ago. Although they preferred "Blue Sharks," they found that the name was already taken by another team and settled on "Sea Monsters." A grandmother of one of the boys created the spiffy team banner, which was awarded a prize this morning. As they wait for the ceremony to begin, the boys inspect and then proudly pose for pictures in front of their new award-winning team banner. The parents stand a few feet away—some taking pictures, some just watching. The parents are also getting to know each other, and the common currency of topics is just how darned cute our kids look, and will they start these ceremonies soon before another boy has to be escorted to the bathroom?

Queued up one group away from the Sea Monsters is a team of four- and five-year-old girls in green and white uniforms. They too will play their first game later today, but for now, they are awaiting the beginning of the opening ceremony. They have chosen the name "Barbie Girls," and they also have a spiffy new team banner. But the girls are pretty much ignoring their banner, for they have created another, more powerful symbol around which to rally. In fact, they are the only team among the 156 marching today with a team float—a red Radio Flyer wagon base, on which sits a Sony boom box playing music, and a 3-foot-plus-tall Barbie doll on a rotating pedestal. Barbie is dressed in the team colors—indeed, she sports a custom-made green-and-white cheerleader-style outfit, with the Barbie Girls' names written on the skirt. Her normally all-blonde hair has been streaked with Barbie Girl green and features a green bow, with white polka dots. Several of the girls on the team also have supplemented their uniforms with green bows in their hair.

The volume on the boom box nudges up and four or five girls begin to sing a Barbie song. Barbie is now slowly rotating on her pedestal, and as the girls sing more gleefully and more loudly, some of them begin to hold hands and walk around the float, in sync with Barbie's rotation. Other same-aged girls from other teams are drawn to the celebration and, eventually, perhaps a dozen girls are singing the Barbie song. The girls are intensely focused on Barbie, on the music, and on their mutual pleasure.

As the Sea Monsters mill around their banner, some of them begin to notice, and then begin to watch and listen as the Barbie Girls rally around their float. At first, the boys are watching as individuals, seemingly unaware of each other's shared interest. Some of them stand with arms at their sides, slack-jawed, as though passively watching a television show. I notice slight smiles on a couple of their faces, as though they are drawn to the Barbie Girls' celebratory fun. Then, with side-glances, some of the boys begin to notice each other's attention on the Barbie Girls. Their faces begin to show signs of distaste. One of them yells out, "NO BARBIE!" Suddenly, they all begin to move—jumping up and down, nudging and bumping one other—and join into a group chant: "NO BARBIE! NO BARBIE! NO BARBIE!" They now appear to be every bit as gleeful as the girls, as they laugh, yell, and chant against the Barbie Girls.

The parents watch the whole scene with rapt attention. Smiles light up the faces of the adults, as our glances sweep back and forth, from the sweetly celebrating Barbie Girls to the aggressively protesting Sea Monsters. "They are SO different!" exclaims one smiling mother approvingly. A male coach offers a more in-depth analysis: "When I was in college," he says, "I took these classes from professors who showed us research that showed that boys and girls are the same. I believed it, until I had my own kids and saw how different they are." "Yeah," another dad responds, "Just look at them! They are so different!"

The girls, meanwhile, show no evidence they hear, see, or are even aware of the presence of the boys who are now so loudly proclaiming their opposition to the Barbie Girls' songs and totem. They continue to sing, dance, laugh, and rally around the Barbie for a few more minutes, before they are called to reassemble in their groups for the beginning of the parade.

After the parade, the teams reassemble on the infield of the track but now in a less organized manner. The Sea Monsters once again find themselves in the general vicinity of the Barbie Girls and take up the "NO BARBIE!" chant again. Perhaps put out by the lack of response to their chant, they begin to dash, in twos and threes, invading the girls' space, and yelling menacingly. With this, the Barbie Girls have little choice but to recognize the presence of the boys—some look puzzled and shrink back, some engage the boys and chase them off. The chasing seems only to incite more excitement among the boys. Finally, parents intervene and defuse the situation, leading their children off to their cars, homes, and eventually to their soccer games.

THE PERFORMANCE OF GENDER

In the past decade, especially since the publication of Judith Butler's highly influential *Gender Trouble* (1990), it has become increasingly fashionable among academic feminists to think of gender not as some "thing" that one "has" (or not) but rather as situationally constructed. . . . The idea of gender as performance analytically foregrounds the agency of individuals in the construction of gender, thus highlighting the situational fluidity of gender: here, conservative and reproductive, there, transgressive and disruptive. Surely, the Barbie Girls versus Sea Monsters scene described earlier can be fruitfully analyzed as a moment of . . . gender performances: The girls—at least at first glance—appear to be performing (for each other?) a conventional four- to five-year-old version of emphasized femininity. At least on the surface, there appears to be nothing terribly transgressive here. They are just "being girls," together. The boys initially are unwittingly constituted as an audience for the girls' performance but quickly begin to perform (for each other?—for the girls, too?) a masculinity that constructs itself in opposition to Barbie, and to the girls, as not feminine. They aggressively confront—first through loud verbal chanting, eventually through bodily invasions—the girls' ritual space of emphasized femininity, apparently with the intention of disrupting its upsetting influence. The adults are simultaneously constituted as an adoring audience for their children's performances and as parents who perform for each other by sharing and mutually affirming their experience-based narratives concerning the natural differences between boys and girls.

In this scene, we see children performing gender in ways that constitute themselves as two separate, opposed groups (boys vs. girls) and parents performing gender in ways that give the stamp of adult approval to the children's performances of difference, while constructing their own. . . . narrative that naturalizes this categorical difference. In other words, the parents do not seem to read the children's performances of gender as social constructions of gender. Instead, they interpret them as the inevitable unfolding of natural, internal differences between the sexes. . . . (But) as Walters (1999, 250) argues,

> The performance of gender is never a simple voluntary act. . . . Theories of gender as play and performance need to be intimately and systematically connected with the power of gender (really, the power of male power) to constrain, control, violate, and configure. Too often, mere lip service is given to the specific historical, social, and political configurations that make certain conditions possible and others constrained.

Indeed, feminist sociologists operating from the traditions of symbolic interactionism . . . have anticipated the recent interest in looking at gender as a dynamic performance. As early as 1978, Kessler and McKenna developed a sophisticated analysis of gender as an everyday, practical accomplishment of people's interactions. Nearly a decade later, West and Zimmerman (1987) argued that in people's everyday interactions, they were "doing gender" and, in so doing, they were constructing masculine dominance and feminine deference. As these ideas have been taken up in sociology, their tendencies toward a celebration of the "freedom" of agents to transgress and reshape the fluid boundaries of gender have been put into play with theories of social structure (e.g., Lorber 1994; Risman 1998). In these accounts, gender is viewed as enacted or created through everyday interactions, but crucially, as Walters suggested earlier, within "specific historical, social, and political configurations" that constrain or enable certain interactions.

The parents' response to the Barbie Girls versus Sea Monsters performance suggests one of the main limits and dangers of theories of performativity. Lacking an analysis of structural and cultural context, performances of gender can all too easily be interpreted as free agents' acting out the inevitable . . . natural inner essence of sex difference. An examination of structural and cultural contexts, though, reveals that there was nothing inevitable about the girls' choice of Barbie as their totem, nor in the boys' response to it.

THE STRUCTURE OF GENDER

In the entire subsequent season of weekly games and practices, I never once saw adults point to a moment in which boy and girl soccer players were doing the *same* thing and exclaim to each other, "Look at them! They are *so similar!*" The actual similarity of the boys and the girls, evidenced by nearly all of the kids' routine actions throughout a soccer season—playing the game, crying over a skinned knee, scrambling enthusiastically for their snacks after the games, spacing out on a bird or a flower instead of listening to the coach at practice—is a key to understanding the salience of the Barbie Girls versus Sea Monsters moment for gender relations. In the face of a multitude of moments that speak to similarity, it was this anomalous Barbie Girls versus Sea Monsters moments—where the boundaries of gender were so clearly enacted—that the adults seized to affirm their commitment to difference. It is the kind of moment—to use Lorber's (1994, 37) phrase—where "believing is seeing," where we selectively "see" aspects of social reality that tell us a truth that we prefer to believe, such as the belief in categorical sex difference. No matter that our eyes do not see evidence of this truth most of the rest of the time.

In fact, it was not so easy for adults to actually "see" the empirical reality of sex similarity in everyday observations of soccer throughout the season. That is due to one overdetermining factor: an institutional context that is characterized by . . . sex segregation among the parent coaches and team managers, and by formally structured sex segregation among the children. The structural analysis developed here is indebted to Acker's (1990) observation that organizations, even while appearing "gender neutral," tend to reflect, re-create, and naturalize a hierarchical ordering of gender. Following Connell's (1987, 98–99) method of structural analysis, I will examine the "gender regime"—that is, the current "state of play of sexual politics"—within the local AYSO organization by conducting a "structural inventory" of the formal and informal sexual divisions of labor and power.[1]

Adult Divisions of Labor and Power

There was a clear—although not absolute—sexual division of labor and power among the adult volunteers in the AYSO organization. The Board of Directors consisted of 21 men and 9 women, with the top two positions—commissioner and assistant commissioner—held by men. Among the league's head coaches, 133 were men and 23 women. The division among the league's assistant coaches was similarly skewed. Each team also had a team manager who was responsible for organizing snacks, making reminder calls about games and practices, organizing team parties and the end-of-the-year present for the coach. The vast majority of team managers were women. A common slippage in the language of coaches and parents revealed the ideological assumptions underlying this position: I often noticed people describe a team manager as the "team mom." In short, as Table 1 shows, the vast majority of the time, the formal authority of the head coach and assistant coach was in the hands of a man, while the backup, support role of team manager was in the hands of a woman.

These data illustrate . . . that sexual divisions of labor are interwoven with, and mutually supportive of, divisions of power and authority among women and men. They also suggest how people's choices to volunteer for certain positions are shaped and constrained by previous institutional practices. There is no formal AYSO rule that men must be the leaders, women the supportive followers. And there are, after all, *some* women coaches and *some* men team managers.[2] So, it may appear that the division of labor among adult volunteers simply

TABLE 1 Adult Volunteers as Coaches and Team Managers, by Gender (in percentages) (*N* = 156 teams)

	Head Coaches	Assistant Coaches	Team Managers
Women	15	21	86
Men	85	79	14

manifests an accumulation of individual choices and preferences. When analyzed structurally, though, individual men's apparently free choices to volunteer disproportionately for coaching jobs, alongside individual women's apparently free choices to volunteer disproportionately for team manger jobs, can be seen as a logical collective result of the ways that the institutional structure of sport has differentially constrained and enabled women's and men's previous options and experiences (Messner 1992). Since boys and men have had far more opportunities to play organized sports and thus to gain skills and knowledge, it subsequently appears rational for adult men to serve in positions of knowledgeable authority, with women serving in a support capacity (Boyle and McKay 1995). Structure—in this case, the historically constituted division of labor and power in sport—constrains current practice. In turn, structure becomes an object of practice, as the choices and actions of today's parents re-create divisions of labor and power similar to those that they experienced in their youth.

The Children: Formal Sex Segregation

As adult authority patterns are informally structured along gendered lines, the children's leagues are formally segregated by AYSO along lines of age and sex. In each age-group, there are separate boys' and girls' leagues. The AYSO in this community included 87 boys' teams and 69 girls' teams. Although the four- to five-year-old boys often played their games on a field that was contiguous with games being played by four- to five-year-old girls, there was never a formal opportunity for cross-sex play. Thus, both the girls' and the boys' teams could conceivably proceed through an entire season of games and practices in entirely homosocial contexts.[3] In the all-male contexts that I observed throughout the season, gender never appeared to be overtly salient among the children, coaches, or parents. It is against this backdrop that I might suggest a working hypothesis about structure and the . . . salience of gender: The formal sex segregation of children does not, in and of itself, make gender overtly salient. In fact, when children are absolutely segregated, with no opportunity for cross-sex interactions, gender may appear to disappear as an overtly salient organizing principle. However, when formally sex-segregated children are placed into immediately contiguous locations, such as during the opening ceremony, highly charged gendered interactions between the groups (including invasions and other kinds of border work) become more possible.

Although it might appear to some that formal sex segregation in children's sports is a natural fact, it has not always been so for the youngest age-groups in AYSO. As recently as 1995, when my older son signed up to play as a five-year-old, I had been told that he would play in a coed league. But when he arrived to his first practice and I saw that he was on an all-boys team, I was told by the coach that AYSO had decided this year to begin sex segregating all age-groups, because "during halftimes and practices, the boys and girls tend to separate into separate groups. So the league thought it would be better for team unity if we split the boys and girls into separate leagues." I suggested to some coaches that a similar dynamic among racial ethnic groups (say, Latino kids and white kids clustering as separate groups during halftimes) would not similarly result in a decision to create racially segregated leagues. That this comment appeared to fall on deaf ears illustrates the extent to which many adults' belief in the need for sex segregation—at least in the context of sport—is grounded in a mutually agreed-upon notion of boys' and girls' "separate worlds," perhaps based in ideologies of natural sex difference.

The gender regime of AYSO, then, is structured by formal and informal sexual divisions of labor and power. This social structure sets ranges, limits, and possibilities for the children's and parents' interactions and performances of gender, but it does not determine them. Put another way, the formal and informal gender regime of AYSO made the Barbie Girls versus

Sea Monsters moment possible, but it did not make it inevitable. It was the agency of the children and the parents within that structure that made the moment happen. But why did this moment take on the symbolic forms that it did? How and why do the girls, boys, and parents construct and derive meanings from this moment, and how can we interpret these meanings? These questions are best grappled within in the realm of cultural analysis.

THE CULTURE OF GENDER

The difference between what is "structural" and what is "cultural" is not clear-cut. For instance, the AYSO assignment of team colors and choice of team names (cultural symbols) seem to follow logically from, and in turn reinforce, the sex segregation of the leagues (social structure). These cultural symbols such as team colors, uniforms, songs, team names, and banners often carried encoded gendered meanings that were then available to be taken up by the children in ways that constructed (or potentially contested) gender divisions and boundaries.

Team Names

Each team was issued two team colors. It is notable that across the various age-groups, several girls' teams were issued pink uniforms—a color commonly recognized as encoding feminine meanings—while no boys teams were issued pink uniforms. Children, in consultation with their coaches, were asked to choose their own team names and were encouraged to use their assigned team colors as cues to theme of the team name (e.g., among the boys, the "Red Flashes," the "Green Pythons," and the blue-and-green "Sea Monsters"). When I analyzed the team names of the 156 teams by age-group and by sex, three categories emerged:

1. *Sweet names:* These are cutesy team names that communicate small stature, cuteness, and/or vulnerability. These kinds of names would most likely be widely read as encoded with feminine meanings (e.g., "Blue Butterflies," "Beanie Babes," "Sunflowers," "Pink Flamingos," and "Barbie Girls").
2. *Neutral or paradoxical names:* Neutral names are team names that carry no obvious gendered meaning (e.g., "Blue and Green Lizards," "Team Flubber," "Galaxy," "Blue Ice"). Paradoxical names are girls' team names that carry mixed (simultaneously vulnerable *and* powerful) messages (e.g., "Pink Panthers," "Flower Power," "Little Tigers").
3. *Power names:* These are team names that invoke images of unambiguous strength, aggression, and raw power (e.g., "Shooting Stars," "Killer Whales," "Shark Attack," "Raptor Attack," and "Sea Monsters").

As Table 2 illustrates, across all age-groups of boys, there was only one team name coded as a sweet name—"The Smurfs," in the 10- to 11-year-old league. Across all age categories, the boys were far more likely to choose a power name than anything else, and this was nowhere more true than in the youngest age-groups, where 35 of 40 (87 percent) of boys' teams in the four-to-five and six-to-seven age-groups took on power names. A different pattern appears in the girls' team name choices, especially among the youngest girls. Only 2 of the 12 four- to five-year-old girls' teams chose power names, while 5 chose sweet names and 5 chose neutral/paradoxical names. At age six to seven, the numbers begin to tip toward the boys' numbers but still remain different, with half of the girls' teams now choosing power names. In the middle and older girls' groups, the sweet names all but disappear, with power

TABLE 2 Team Names, by Age-Groups and Gender

	4–5		6–7		8–13		14–17		Total	
	n	%	n	%	n	%	n	%	n	%
Girls										
Sweet names	5	42	3	17	2	7	0	0	10	15
Neutral/paradoxical	5	42	6	33	7	25	5	45	23	32
Power names	2	17	9	50	19	68	6	55	36	52
Boys										
Sweet names	0	0	0	0	1	4	0	0	1	1
Neutral/paradoxical	1	7	4	15	4	12	4	31	13	15
Power names	13	93	22	85	29	85	9	69	73	82

names dominating, but still a higher proportion of neutral/paradoxical names than among boys in those age-groups.

Barbie Narrative Versus Warrior Narrative

How do we make sense of the obviously powerful spark that Barbie provided in the opening ceremony scene described earlier? Barbie is likely one of the most immediately identifiable symbols of femininity in the world. More conservatively oriented parents tend to happily buy Barbie dolls for their daughters, while perhaps deflecting their sons' interest in Barbie toward more sex-appropriate "action toys." Feminist parents, on the other hand, have often expressed open contempt—or at least uncomfortable ambivalence—toward Barbie. This is because both conservative and feminist parents see dominant cultural meanings of emphasized femininity as condensed in Barbie and assume that these meanings will be imitated by their daughters. Recent developments in cultural studies, though, should warn us against simplistic readings of Barbie as simply conveying hegemonic messages about gender to unwitting children (Attfield 1996; Seiter 1995). In addition to critically analyzing the cultural values (or "preferred meanings") that may be encoded in Barbie or other children's toys, feminist scholars of cultural studies point to the necessity of examining "reception, pleasure, and agency," and especially "the fullness of reception contexts" (Walters 1999, 246). The Barbie Girls versus Sea Monsters moment can be analyzed as a "reception context," in which differently situated boys, girls, and parents variously used Barbie to construct pleasurable intergroup bonds, as well as boundaries between groups.

Barbie is plastic both in form and in terms of cultural meanings children and adults create around her (Rogers 1999). It is not that there are not hegemonic meanings encoded in Barbie: Since its introduction in 1959, Mattel has been successful in selling millions[4] of this doll that "was recognized as a model of ideal teenhood" (Rand 1998, 383) and "an icon—perhaps *the* icon—of true white womanhood and femininity" (DuCille 1994, 50). However, Rand (1998) argues that "we condescend to children when we analyze Barbie's content and then presume that it passes untransformed into their minds, where, dwelling beneath the control of consciousness or counterargument, it generates self-image, feelings, and other ideological constructs." In fact, people who are situated differently (by age, gender, sexual orientation, social class, race/ethnicity, and national origin) tend to consume and construct meanings around Barbie variously. For instance, some adult women (including many feminists) tell retrospective stories of having rejected (or even mutilated) their Barbies in favor of boys' toys, and some adult lesbians tell stories of transforming Barbie "into an object of dyke desire" (Rand 1998, 386).

Mattel, in fact, clearly strategizes its marketing of Barbie not around the imposition of a singular notion of what a girl or woman should be but around "hegemonic discourse strategies" that attempt to incorporate consumers' range of possible interpretations and criticisms of the limits of Barbie. For instance, the recent marketing of "multicultural Barbie" features dolls with different skin colors and culturally coded wardrobes (DuCille 1994). This strategy broadens the Barbie market, deflects potential criticism of racism, but still "does not boot blond, white Barbie from center stage" (Rand 1998, 391). Similarly, Mattel's marketing of Barbie (since the 1970s) as a career woman raises issues concerning the feminist critique of Barbie's supposedly negative effect on girls. When the AAUW recently criticized Barbie, adult collectors defended Barbie, asserting that "Barbie, in fact, is a wonderful role model for women. She has been a veterinarian, an astronaut, and a soldier—and even before real women had a chance to enter such occupations" (Spigel 2004). And when the magazine *Barbie Bazaar* ran a cover photo of its new "Gulf War Barbie," it served "as a reminder of Mattel's marketing slogan: 'We Girls Can Do Anything' " (Spigel 2004). The following year, Mattel unveiled its "Presidential Candidate Barbie" with the statement "It is time for a woman president, and Barbie had the credentials for the job." Spigel observes that these liberal feminist messages of empowerment for girls run—apparently unambiguously—alongside a continued unspoken understanding that Barbie must be beautiful, with an ultraskinny waist and long, thin legs that taper to feet that appear deformed so that they may fit (only?) into high heels.[5] "Mattel does not mind equating beauty with intellect. In fact, so long as the 11½ inch Barbie body remains intact, Mattel is willing to accessorize her with a number of fashionable perspectives—including feminism itself" (Spigel 2004).

It is this apparently paradoxical encoding of the all-too-familiar oppressive bodily requirements of feminine beauty alongside the career woman role modeling and empowering message that "we girls can do anything" that may inform how and why the Barbie Girls appropriated Barbie as their team symbol. Emphasized femininity—Connell's (1987) term for the current form of femininity that articulates with hegemonic masculinity—as many Second Wave feminists have experienced and criticized it, has been characterized by girls' and women's embodiments of oppressive conceptions of feminine beauty that symbolize . . . a thoroughly disempowered stance. . . . To many Second Wave feminists, Barbie seemed to symbolize all that was oppressive about this femininity—the bodily self-surveillance, accompanying eating disorders, slavery to the dictates of the fashion industry, and compulsory heterosexuality. But Rogers (1999, 14) suggests that rather than representing an unambiguous image of emphasized femininity, perhaps Barbie represents a more paradoxical image of "emphatic femininity" that

> takes feminine appearances and demeanor to unsustainable extremes. Nothing about Barbie ever looks masculine, even when she is on the police force. . . . Consistently, Barbie manages impressions so as to come across as a proper feminine creature even when she crosses boundaries usually dividing women from men. Barbie the firefighter is in no danger, then, of being seen as "one of the boys." Kids know that; parents and teachers know that; Mattel designers know that too.

Recent Third Wave feminist theory sheds light on the different sensibilities of younger generations of girls and women concerning their willingness to display and play with this apparently paradoxical relationship between bodily experience (including "feminine" displays) and public empowerment. In Third Wave feminist texts, displays of feminine physical attractiveness and empowerment are not viewed as mutually exclusive or necessarily opposed realities, but as lived (if often paradoxical) aspects of the same reality (Heywood and Drake 1997). This embracing of the paradoxes of post–Second Wave femininity is manifested in many punk, or Riot Grrrl, subcultures (Klein 1997) and in popular culture in the resounding late 1990s' success of the Spice Girls' mantra of "Girl Power." This generational expression of "girl power" may today be part of "the pleasures of girl culture that Barbie stands for" (Spigel 2004). Indeed, as the Barbie Girls rallied around Barbie, their obvious pleasure did not appear to be based on a celebration of quiet passivity (as feminist parents might fear). Rather, it was a statement that they—the Barbie Girls—were here in this public space. They were not silenced by the boys' oppositional chanting. To the contrary, they ignored the boys, who seemed irrelevant to their celebration. And, when the boys later physically invaded their space, some of the girls responded by chasing the boys off. In short, when I pay attention to what the girls *did* (rather than imposing on the situation what I *think* Barbie "should" mean to the girls), I see a public moment of celebratory "girl power."

And this may give us better basis from which to analyze the boys' oppositional response. First, the boys may have been responding to the threat of displacement they may have felt while viewing the girls' moment of celebratory girl power. Second, the boys may simultaneously have been responding to the fears of feminine pollution that Barbie had come to symbolize to them. But why might Barbie symbolize feminine pollution to little boys? A brief example from my older son is instructive. When he was about three, following a fun day of play with the five-year-old girl next door, he enthusiastically asked me to buy him a Barbie like hers. He was gleeful when I took him to the store and bought him one. When we arrived home, his feet had barely hit the pavement getting out of the car before an eight-year-old neighbor boy laughed at and ridiculed him: "A *Barbie*? Don't you know that Barbie is a *girl's toy*?" No amount of parental intervention could counter this devastating peer-induced injunction against boys' playing with Barbie. My son's pleasurable desire for Barbie appeared almost overnight to transform itself into shame and rejection. The doll ended up at the bottom of a heap of toys in the closet, and my son soon became infatuated, along with other boys in his preschool, with Ninja Turtles and Power Rangers.

Research indicates that there is widespread agreement as to which toys are appropriate for one sex and polluting, dangerous, or inappropriate for the other sex. When Campenni (1999) asked adults to rate the gender appropriateness of children's toys, the toys considered most appropriate to girls were those pertaining to domestic tasks, beauty enhancement, or child rearing. Of the 206 toys rated, Barbie was rated second only to Makeup Kit as a female-only toy. Toys considered most appropriate to boys were those pertaining to sports gear (football gear was the most masculine-rated toy, while boxing gloves were third), vehicles, action figures (G. I. Joe was rated second only to football gear), and other war-related toys. This research on parents' gender stereotyping of toys reflects similar findings in research on children's toy preferences (Bradbard 1985; Robinson and Morris 1986). Children tend to avoid cross-sex toys, with boys' avoidance of feminine-coded toys appearing to be stronger than girls' avoidance of masculine-coded toys (Etaugh and Liss 1992). Moreover, preschool-age boys who perceive their fathers to be opposed to cross-gender-typed play are more likely than girls or other boys to think that it is "bad" for boys to play with toys that are labeled as "for girls" (Raag and Rackliff 1998).

By kindergarten, most boys appear to have learned—either through experiences similar to my son's, where other male persons police the boundaries of gender-appropriate play and fantasy and/or by watching the clearly gendered messages of television advertising—that Barbie dolls are not appropriate toys for boys (Rogers 1999, 30). To avoid ridicule, they learn to hide their desire for Barbie, either through denial and oppositional/pollution discourse and/or through sublimation of their desire for Barbie into play with male-appropriate "action figures" (Pope et al. 1999). In their study of a kindergarten classroom, Jordan and Cowan (1995, 728) identified "warrior narratives . . . that assume that violence is legitimate and justified when it occurs within a struggle between good and evil" to be the most commonly agreed-upon currency for boys' fantasy play. They observe that the boys seem commonly to adapt story lines that they have seen on television. Popular culture—film, video, computer games, television, and comic books—provides boys with a seemingly endless stream of Good Guys versus Bad Guys characters and stories—from cowboy movies, Superman and Spiderman to Ninja Turtles, Star Wars, and Pokémon—that are available for the boys to appropriate as the raw materials for the construction of their own warrior play.

In the kindergarten that Jordan and Cowan studied, the boys initially attempted to import their warrior narratives into the domestic setting of the "Doll Corner." Teachers eventually drove the boys' warrior play outdoors, while the Doll Corner was used by the girls for the "appropriate" domestic play for which it was originally intended. Jordan and Cowan argue that kindergarten teachers' outlawing of boys' warrior narratives inside the classroom contributed to boys' defining schools as a feminine environment, to which they responded with a resistant, underground continuation of masculine warrior play. Eventually though, boys who acquiesce and successfully sublimate warrior play into fantasy or sport are more successful in constructing what Connell (1989, 291) calls "a masculinity organized around themes of rationality and responsibility [that is] closely connected with the 'certification' function of the upper levels of the education system and to a key form of masculinity among professionals."

In contrast to the "rational/professional" masculinity constructed in schools, the institution of sport historically constructs hegemonic masculinity as *bodily superiority* over femininity and nonathletic masculinities (Messner 1992). Here, warrior narratives are allowed to publicly thrive—indeed, are openly celebrated (witness, for instance, the commentary of a televised NFL [National Football League] football game or especially the spectacle of televised professional wrestling). Preschool boys and kindergartners seem already to know this, easily adopting aggressively competitive team names and an us-versus-them attitude. By contrast, many of the youngest girls appear to take two or three years in organized soccer before they adopt, or partially accommodate themselves to, aggressively competitive discourse, indicated by the 10-year-old girls' shifting away from the use of sweet names toward more power names. In short, where the gender regime of preschool and grade school may be experienced as an environment in which mostly women leaders enforce rules that are hostile to masculine fantasy play and physicality, the gender regime of sport is experienced as a place where masculine styles and values of physicality, aggression, and competition are enforced and celebrated by mostly male coaches.

A cultural analysis suggests that the boys' and the girls' previous immersion in differently gendered cultural experiences shaped the likelihood that they would derive and construct different meanings from Barbie—the girls through pleasurable and symbolically empowering identification with "girl power" narratives; the boys through oppositional fears of feminine pollution (and fears of displacement by girl power?) and with aggressively verbal, and eventually physical, invasions of the girls' ritual space. The boys' collective response thus constituted them differently, *as boys*, in opposition to the girls' constitution of themselves *as girls*. An individual girl or boy, in this moment, who may have felt an inclination to dissent from the dominant feelings of the group (say, the Latina Barbie Girl who, her mother later told me, did not want the group to be identified with Barbie, or a boy whose immediate inner response to the Barbie Girls' joyful celebration might be to join in) is most likely silenced into complicity in this powerful moment of border work.

What meanings did this highly gendered moment carry for the boys' and girls' teams in the ensuing soccer season? Although I did not observe the Barbie Girls after the opening ceremony, I did continue to observe the Sea Monsters' weekly practices and games. During the boys' ensuing season, gender never reached this "magnified" level of salience again—indeed, gender was rarely raised verbally or performed overtly by the boys. On two occasions, though, I observed the coach jokingly chiding the boys during practice that "if you don't watch out, I'm going to get the Barbie Girls here to play against you!" This warning was followed by gleeful screams of agony and fear, and nervous hopping around and hugging by some of the boys. Normally, though, in this sex-segregated, all-male context, if boundaries were invoked, they were not boundaries between boys and girls but boundaries between the Sea Monsters and other boys' teams, or sometimes age boundaries between the Sea Monsters and a small group of dads and older brothers who would engage them in a mock scrimmage during practice. But it was also evident that when the coach was having trouble getting the boys to act together, as a group, his strategic and humorous invocation of the dreaded Barbie Girls once again served symbolically to affirm their group status. They were a team. They were the boys.

CONCLUSION

The overarching goal of this article has been to take one empirical observation from everyday life and demonstrate how a multilevel (interactionist, structural, cultural) analysis might reveal various layers of meaning that give insight into the everyday social construction of gender. This article builds on observations made by Thorne (1993) concerning ways to approach sociological analyses of children's worlds. The most fruitful approach is not to ask why boys and girls are so different but rather to ask how and under what conditions boys and girls constitute themselves as separate, oppositional groups. Sociologists need not debate whether gender is "there"—clearly, gender is always already there, built as it is into the structures, situations, culture, and consciousness of children and adults. The key issue is under what conditions gender is activated as a salient organizing principle in social life and under what conditions it may be less salient. These are important questions, especially since the social organization of categorical gender difference has always been so clearly tied to gender hierarchy (Acker 1990; Lorber 1994). In the Barbie Girls versus Sea Monsters moment, the performance of gendered boundaries and the construction of boys' and girls' groups as categorically different occurred in the context of a situation systematically structured by sex segregation, sparked by the imposing presence of a shared cultural symbol that is saturated with gendered meanings, and actively supported and applauded by adults who basked in the pleasure of difference, reaffirmed.[6]

I have suggested that a useful approach to the study of such "how" and "under what conditions" questions is to employ multiple levels of analysis. At the most general level, this project supports the following working propositions.

Interactionist theoretical frameworks that emphasize the ways that social agents "perform" or "do" gender are most useful in describing how groups of people actively create (or at times disrupt) the boundaries that delineate seemingly categorical differences between male persons and female persons. In this case, we saw how the children and the parents interactively performed gender in a way that constructed an apparently natural boundary between the two separate worlds of the girls and the boys.

Structural theoretical frameworks that emphasize the ways that gender is built into institutions through hierarchical sexual divisions of labor are most useful in explaining under what conditions social agents mobilize variously to disrupt or to affirm gender differences and inequalities. In this case, we saw how the sexual division of labor among parent volunteers (grounded in their own histories in the gender regime of sport), the formal sex segregation of the children's leagues, and the structured context of the opening ceremony created conditions for possible interactions between girls' teams and boys' teams.

Cultural theoretical perspectives that examine how popular symbols that are injected into circulation by the culture industry are variously taken up by differently situated people are most useful in analyzing how the meanings of cultural symbols, in a given institutional context, might trigger or be taken up by social agents and used as resources to reproduce, disrupt, or contest binary conceptions of sex difference and gendered relations of power. In this case, we saw how a girls' team appropriated a large Barbie around which to construct a pleasurable and empowering sense of group identity and how the boys' team responded with aggressive denunciations of Barbie and invasions.

Utilizing any one of the previous theoretical perspectives by itself will lead to a limited, even distorted, analysis of the social construction of gender. Together, they can illuminate the complex, multileveled architecture of the social construction of gender in everyday life. For heuristic reasons, I have falsely separated structure, interaction, and culture. In fact, we need to explore their constant interrelationships, continuities, and contradictions. For instance, we cannot understand the boys' aggressive denunciations and invasions of the girls' space and the eventual clarification of categorical boundaries between the girls and the boys without first understanding how these boys and girls have already internalized four or five years of "gendering" experiences that have shaped their interactional tendencies and how they are already immersed in a culture of gendered symbols, including Barbie and sports media imagery. Although "only" preschoolers, they are already skilled in collectively taking up symbols from popular culture as resources to be used in their own group dynamics—building individual and group identities, sharing the pleasures of play, clarifying boundaries between in-group and out-group members, and constructing hierarchies in their worlds.

Furthermore, we cannot understand the reason that the girls first chose "Barbie Girls" as their team name without first understanding the fact that a particular institutional structure of AYSO soccer preexisted the girls' entrée into the league. The informal sexual division of labor among adults, and the formal sex segregation of children's teams, is a preexisting gender regime that constrains and enables the ways that the children enact gender relations and construct identities. One concrete manifestation of this constraining nature of sex segregated teams is the choice of team names. It is reasonable to speculate that if the four- and five-year-old children were still sex integrated, as in the pre-1995 era, no team would have chosen "Barbie Girls" as its team name, with Barbie as its symbol. In other words, the formal sex segregation created the conditions under which the girls were enabled—perhaps encouraged—to choose a "sweet" team name that is widely read as encoding feminine meanings. The eventual interactions between the boys and the girls were made possible—although by no means fully determined—by the structure of the gender regime and by the cultural resources that the children variously drew on.

On the other hand, the gendered division of labor in youth soccer is not seamless, static, or immune to resistance. Once of the few woman head coaches, a very active athlete in her own right, told me that she is "challenging the sexism" in AYSO by becoming the head of her son's league. As post–Title IX women increasingly become mothers and as media images of competent, heroic female athletes become more a part of the cultural landscape for children, the gender regimes of children's sports may be increasingly challenged (Dworkin and Messner 1999). Put another way, the dramatically shifting opportunity structure and cultural imagery of post–Title IX sports have created opportunities for new kinds of interactions, which will inevitably challenge and further shift institutional structures. Social structures simultaneously constrain and enable, while agency is simultaneously reproductive and resistant

Discussion Questions

1. How do parents and others reinforce the idea that gender differences are both strong and inevitable?
2. According to the author, how do children actively "do gender"?

3. What role does social structure play in how children "do gender"?
4. How do children use popular culture to construct meanings of gender with their peers?

Notes

1. Most of the structural inventory presented here is from a content analysis of the 1998–99 regional American Youth Soccer Organization (AYSO) yearbook, which features photos and names of all of the teams, coaches, and managers. I counted the number of adult men and women occupying various positions. In the three cases where the sex category of a name was not immediately obvious (e.g., Rene or Terry), or in the five cases where simply a last name was listed, I did not count it. I also used the AYSO yearbook for my analysis of the children's team names. To check for reliability, another sociologist independently read and coded the list of team names. There was disagreement on how to categorize only 2 of the 156 team names.

2. The existence of some women coaches and some men team managers in this AYSO organization manifests a less extreme sexual division of labor than that of the same community's Little League baseball organization, in which there are proportionally far fewer women coaches. Similarly, Saltzman Chafetz and Kotarba's (1999, 52) study of parental labor in support of Little League baseball in a middle-class Houston community revealed an apparently absolute sexual division of labor, where nearly all of the supportive "activities off the field were conducted by the women in the total absence of men, while activities on the field were conducted by men and boys in the absence of women." Perhaps youth soccer, because of its more recent (mostly post–Title IX) history in the United States, is a more contested gender regime than the more patriarchally entrenched youth sports like Little League baseball or youth football.

3. The four- and five-year-old kids' games and practices were absolutely homosocial in terms of the kids, due to the formal structural sex segregation. However, 8 of the 12 girls' teams at this age level had male coaches, and 2 of the 14 boys' teams had female coaches.

4. By 1994, more than 800 million Barbies had been sold worldwide. More than $1 billion was spent on Barbies and accessories in 1992 alone. Two Barbie dolls were purchased every second in 1994, half of which were sold in the United States (DuCille 1994, 49).

5. Rogers (1999, 23) notes that if one extrapolates Barbie's bodily proportions to "real woman ones," she would be "33-18-31.5 and stand five feet nine inches tall, with fully half of her height accounted for by her 'shapely legs.' "

6. My trilevel analysis of structure, interaction, and culture may not be fully adequate to plumb the emotional depths of the magnified Barbie Girls versus Sea Monsters moment. Although it is beyond the purview of this article, an adequate rendering of the depths of pleasure and revulsion, attachment and separation, and commitment to ideologies of categorical sex difference may involve the integration of a fourth level of analysis: gender at the level of personality (Chodorow 1999). Object relations theory has fallen out of vogue in feminist sociology in recent years, but as Williams (1993) has argued, it might be most useful in revealing the mostly hidden social power of gender to shape people's unconscious predispositions to various structural contexts, cultural symbols, and interactional moments.

References

Acker, Joan. 1990. Hierarchies, jobs, bodies: A theory of gendered organizations. *Gender & Society* 4:139–58.

Adler, Patricia A., and Peter Adler. 1998. *Peer power: Preadolescent culture and identity.* New Brunswick, NJ: Rutgers University Press.

Attfield, Judy. 1996. Barbie and Action Man: Adult toys for girls and boys, 1959–93. In *The gendered object,* edited by Pat Kirkham, 80–89. Manchester, UK, and New York: Manchester University Press.

Boyle, Maree, and Jim McKay. 1995. "You leave your troubles at the gate": A case study of the exploitation of older women's labor and "leisure" in sport. *Gender & Society* 9:556–76.

Bradbard, M. 1985. Sex differences in adults' gifts and children's toy requests. *Journal of Genetic Psychology* 145:283–84.

Butler, Judith. 1990. *Gender trouble: Feminism and the subversion of identity.* New York and London: Routledge.

Campenni, C. Estelle. 1999. Gender stereotyping of children's toys: A comparison of parents and nonparents. *Sex Roles* 40:121–38.

Chodorow, Nancy J. 1999. *The power of feelings: Personal meanings in psychoanalysis, gender, and culture.* New Haven, CT, and London: Yale University Press.

Connell, R.W. 1987. *Gender and power.* Stanford, CA: Stanford University Press.

———. 1989. Cool guys, swots and wimps: The interplay of masculinity and education. *Oxford Review of Education* 15:291–303.

DuCille, Anne. 1994. Dyes and dolls: Multicultural Barbie and the merchandising of difference. *Differences: A Journal of Cultural Studies* 6:46–68.

Dworkin, Shari L., and Michael A. Messner. 1999. Just do . . . what?: Sport, bodies, gender. In *Revisioning gender,* edited by Myra Marx Ferree, Judith Lorber, and Beth B. Hess, 341–61. Thousand Oaks, CA: Sage.

Etaugh, C., and M. B. Liss. 1992. Home, school, and playroom: Training grounds for adult gender roles. *Sex Roles* 26:129–47.

Heywood, Leslie, and Jennifer Drake, Eds. 1997. *Third wave agenda: Being feminist, doing feminism.* Minneapolis: University of Minnesota Press.

Hochschild, Arlie Russell. 1994. The commercial spirit of intimate life and the abduction of feminism: Signs from women's advice books. *Theory, Culture & Society* 11:1–24.

Jordan, Ellen, and Angela Cowan. 1995. Warrior narratives in the kindergarten classroom: Renogotiating the social contract? *Gender & Society* 9:727–43.

Kessler, Suzanne J., and Wendy McKenna. 1978. *Gender: An ethnomethodological approach.* New York: John Wiley.

Lorber, Judith. 1994. *Paradoxes of gender.* New Haven, CT, and London: Yale University Press.

McGuffy, C. Shawn, and B. Lindsay Rich. 1999. Playing in the gender transgression zone: Race, class and hegemonic masculinity in middle childhood. *Gender & Society* 13:608–27.

Messner, Michael A. 1992. *Power at play: Sports and the problem of masculinity.* Boston: Beacon.

Pope, Harrison G., Jr., Roberto Olivarda, Amanda Gruber, and John Borowiecki. 1999. Evolving ideals of male body image as seen through action toys. *International Journal of Eating Disorders* 26:65–72.

Raag, Tarja, and Christine L. Rackliff. 1998. Preschoolers' awareness of social expectations of gender: Relationships to toy choices. *Sex Roles* 38:685–700.

Rand, Erica. 1998. Older heads on younger bodies. In *The children's culture reader,* edited by Henry Jenkins, 382–93. New York: New York University Press.

Risman, Barbara. 1998. *Gender Vertigo: American families in transition.* New Haven and London: Yale University Press.

Robinson, C. C., and J. T. Morris. 1986. The gender-stereotyped nature of Christmas toys received by 36-, 48-, and 60-month-old children: A comparison between nonrequested vs. requested toys. *Sex Roles* 15:21–32.

Rogers, Mary F. 1999. *Barbie culture.* Thousand Oaks, CA: Sage.

Saltzman Chafetz, Janet, and Joseph A. Kotarba. 1999. Little League mothers and the reproduction of gender. In *Inside sports,* edited by Jay Coakley and Peter Donnelly, 46–54. London and New York: Routledge.

Seiter, Ellen. 1995. *Sold separately: Parents and children in consumer in culture.* New Brunswick, NJ: Rutgers University Press.

Spigel, Lynn. 2004. Barbies without Ken: Femininity, feminism, and the art-culture system. In *Sitting room only: Television, consumer culture and the suburban home,* edited by Lynn Spigel. Durham, NC: Duke University Press.

Thorne, Barrie. 1993. *Gender play: Girls and boys in school.* New Brunswick, NJ: Rutgers University Press.

Walters, Suzanna Danuta. 1999. Sex, text, and context: (In) between feminism and cultural studies. In *Revisioning gender,* edited by Myra Marx Ferree, Judith Lorber, and Beth B. Hess, 222–57. Thousand Oaks, CA: Sage.

West, Candace, and Don Zimmerman. 1987. Doing gender. *Gender & Society* 1:125–51.

Williams, Christine. 1993. Psychoanalytic theory and the sociology of gender. In *theory on gender, gender on theory,* edited by Paula England, 131–49. New York: Aldine.

Girls, Race, and Identity: Border Work Between Classes

JULIE BETTIE

INTRODUCTION

Julie Bettie conducted an ethnographic study at a northern California high school to better understand how students make sense of social class. In addition, she looked at the role that race played in their upward mobility. Through her conversations with girls from a variety of racial-ethnic and socioeconomic backgrounds, she discovered that they often viewed these categories in complex ways. She concludes that aside from a few exceptions, family income plays a tremendous role in whether these girls will ultimately be able to attend college.

M any school ethnographies are comparative studies of students across class categories and make generalizations about the experiences of middle-class students and of working-class students. In order to speak about these class categories as if they are two clearly distinct peer groupings, one must ignore many students who are exceptions to the rule that class origin equates to class future. While the correlation is strong between parents' socioeconomic status and a student's membership in a middle- or working-class peer group, tracking experience, academic achievement, and consequent class future, it is imperfect, and there are always at least a handful of working-class students who are college-prep and upwardly mobile and a handful of middle-class students who are on the vocational track and downwardly mobile. Nonetheless, because research generally tends to highlight patterns, such cases are typically ignored, precisely because they are exceptions to the rule....

In this chapter I want to focus on those few girls, both white and Mexican-American, who were from working-class origins but who were upwardly mobile middle-class performers in high school, en route to achieving a university education, and to ask what we might learn from their exceptionalism. Foregrounding these exceptions to the rule, I explore what their experience might reveal about the way in which race ethnicity and gender, as autonomous axes of social inequality, intersect with class....

The ... question is *how* they do it. How do they negotiate the disparity between the working-class identity acquired from home and the performance of a middle-class identity at school, the disparity between their family lives and the family lives of their middle-class peers? What is the subjective experience of class passing, of "choosing" upward mobility and all that comes with it? . . .

WHITE GIRLS: CONTINGENT ROUTES TO MOBILITY

I met Staci during a slow day in the yearbook class. Most of the students were working on various aspects of pulling that year's annual together, but Staci felt she needed to put her energy elsewhere on this day and was headed to the library to look up some information for a history paper due at the end of the week. Staci's membership in the prep crowd was unusual, given her parents' economic and cultural capital. Her father worked "doing maintenance" at a retirement community. But the fact that her mother worked for a time in the kitchen at the private elementary school in town enabled Staci to receive a subsidized private school education, and she ran with the most academically elite crowd of girls at the school.

Like Staci, Heather had also attended private school but not with a subsidy, and it was difficult to understand how her parents could have afforded it. Her father worked as a mechanic and her mother as a nurse's aide. Between them they were nearing middle-income, but most Waretown families in this category were not sending their kids to private schools. As I pushed for a clearer explanation, she indicated that her parents experienced great financial sacrifice in order to send her to school, even borrowing money from relatives, but they felt it was worth it. According to her, her parents wanted to segregate her from "bad influences." This turned out to be a euphemism for Mexican-American students.

Likewise, Jennifer told me that while her parents had been able to afford to send her to private elementary school, they could not afford to send her brother too. Instead, they arranged for him to attend school in a neighboring town, and, once again, the reason was to avoid "bad influences." . . .

Mandy was also college-prep, although her membership among these girls was even more difficult to explain. She had not attended private elementary school yet did reasonably well academically in junior high and managed to get in with the prep crowd by high school. . . .

At times, . . . an individual girl's academic motivation seemed to come from defining herself in opposition to older brothers who were labeled delinquent and who, as the girls had witnessed, caused their parent(s) angst. It seemed that feminine norms sometimes allowed girls to forgo the delinquent paths their brothers might have felt compelled to follow as working-class boys, the need to engage in rituals of proving masculinity. I heard this story frequently enough, among both white and Mexican-American girls, that I began to suspect that working-class girls might experience a certain advantage over their male counterparts as a consequence of being girls. The social pressure for girls to conform and follow rules as part of the definition of femininity makes it a possibility that they might do better in school than working-class boys, for whom defining manhood includes more pressure to engage in risk-taking behavior and overt resistance to control. Girls may not only be less likely to engage in such activities but are relatively less likely to be labeled and punished as delinquents if they do (although this was somewhat less true for Mexican-American girls). That working-class girls might actually do better academically than working-class boys is a possibility easily missed by those taking an additive analytical approach to race, class, and gender as social forces. Such an approach would simply presume that girls' educational experiences and opportunities are in all cases "worse" than boys', rather than exploring the unique set of challenges girls face. . . .

Liz articulated yet another route to mobility. When I asked how it was that she came to be a part of her college-prep friendship circle, she explained that early on she discovered that she was good at basketball, and it was through this sport that she met and began to spend time with girls who were far more privileged than she was. Through association with high achievers, she was exposed to information that helped her get ahead. Overhearing conversations about college requirements and college-prep courses made her aware of the existence of two tracks of schooling and what she was missing out on. She clung to a middle-class girl, Amber, her best friend, hoping, it seemed, that she might "catch" the middle-classness Amber took for granted. Unable to name her desire as class envy, she simply said, "I'd like to be in a situation like that." . . .

WHITE GIRLS: BECOMING UPWARDLY MOBILE

Common among those girls whose families were much more working-class than the families of their closest friends was their nascent awareness of the difference between these class cultures. Class is a relational identity; awareness of class difference is dependent upon the class and race geography of the environment in which one lives and moves. While the community of one's formative years and schooling experiences, in particular, may be key shapers of one's perceptions of class difference, awareness of one's location in a class hierarchy is an ongoing and context-specific process. Beverley Skeggs (1997), in her semi-autobiographical book, explains that because her childhood was spent in a class-segregated community, "My first real recognition that I could be categorized by others as working-class happened when I went to university. . . . For the first time in my life I started to feel insecure. All the prior cultural knowledge [capital] in which I had taken pride lost its value, and I entered a world where I knew little and felt I could communicate even less." The working-class, upwardly mobile girls I met, by virtue of their location in mixed-class peer groups, had an earlier awareness of class distinctions, although they did not often name those differences as such.

In other words, upward mobility might occur at various points in life. As they acquire cultural and economic capital at different ages, upwardly mobiles begin passing in middle-class contexts at different times. Where Skeggs only began passing upon entry into college, some of the girls I knew began in junior high, and those with private school educations, in elementary school. Given that Staci has been part of a middle-class peer group since her private elementary school education, even though she is from a working-class family, her experience of college will likely be far different than the one Skeggs describes for herself. . . .

Geographic variability shapes the likelihood of class mobility. Being working-class and attending a well-funded school with a middle-class clientele where a curriculum of knowledge that is highly valued by society is made available is a far different experience than attending school in an isolated working-class community where the mere exposure to a college-prep curriculum is limited. Upwardly mobile girls from Waretown will likely develop an even greater awareness of class difference when they leave this agricultural community behind.

Due to their location in a college-prep rather than a vocational curriculum, these upwardly mobile working-class girls at times showed a clearer understanding of the fact of class differences than did their vocational counterparts. Liz was one of very few students I met who actually named herself as "working-class."

> JULIE: You said you were "working-class" earlier. Where did you get that term, what does it mean?
>
> LIZ: I learned it in a social science class or maybe in history. Working-class is like the serfs you know, the working-class are the majority, blue-collar versus the college-educated. . . .

Unlike working-class girls who were segregated in vocational tracks and so were rarely in mixed-class settings or peer groups, those working-class girls who were middle-class performers were not *as* mystified by the success of preps. By virtue of crossing, they could see the advantages and privileges their middle-class friends experienced. They were more acutely aware of the cultural differences based on class, as they found themselves exposed to the children of middle-class professionals in the college-prep curriculum, on the basketball court, in student government, and in middle-class homes. They could see the reasons why they had to work harder, and they were less likely to attribute friends' success to some innate difference between them. . . .

These girls also perceived that they had to work exceptionally hard to earn their high school diploma and to get into college relative to their middle-class friends. As Staci said,

They've always been kind of handed everything, that they've never really had to think about their future, and I was always, like, I don't want my future to be like my parents. And, I mean, that was like a big influence on me, I mean, my goal is I don't ever want to have to worry about money, like we have all my life. My friends never had to deal with that or anything and, it's just like everything has always been handed to them, and they, I mean, they never knew anything else.

I want to go to college and get a good education so I can have a better life, and they have always had a good life. I work my butt off, but it just seems easier for them. It's just always everything has always kinda been there for them. . . .

Moreover, these girls were aware of the fact that they exceeded their parents' educational level early on, and they perceived the fact that their parents were unable to help them with school as a handicap. As Mandy explained,

Ever since I've been in honors classes, I've always been around these people, you know, their parents have advanced degrees and everything else. My parents were never able to help me out with math. Once I entered algebra, that was it, that was as far as they could help me. I remember one time in this one class we had this project, we had to build something. One girl's father was an architect, and her father designed and basically built the entire project for her. We all had these dinky little things, and she's got this palace!

Later, however, she attempted to define her parents' lack of education as an asset.

I mean, I was never mad at my parents because they couldn't help me. I was actually happy, because once we get to college, you're not gonna call your parents up and say "Hey, Dad, can you design this for me?" You're on your own then. And so I've always had to work on my own with my schoolwork, it was always on my own, whereas other students, they always had their parents standing right there, you know?. . .

These middle-class-performing working-class girls were . . . readily able to see the differences between their own parents and those of their friends. They were painfully aware of the fact that their friends' parents viewed their own parents with indifference at best, disdain at worst.

. . .I sat next to Heather at a girls' basketball game one evening. She was sitting on the bleachers with the rest of her prep friends, front and center, cheering on the team, many of whom were part of their peer group. She kept glancing at the corner of the gym where several adults were standing, people who had come after halftime (when admission was free) to watch for a few minutes but weren't committed enough to staying to take a spot on the bleachers. I asked her if she was expecting someone, and she whispered, "My dad said he might stop by and check the score. I hope he doesn't.". . .

Where I first thought the idea of her father attending the game represented the standard embarrassment teens experience in relationship to having their parents near them at social events, I recognized later that its meaning went beyond this for her. In the middle-class milieu of the school, some parents are more embarrassing than others.

MEXICAN-AMERICAN GIRLS: CONTINGENT ROUTES TO MOBILITY

There was a small group of Mexican-American girls, mostly second generation but also including two girls who had immigrated, who were from poor and working-class families and who were exceptional in that they did not identify with the [vocational students] but rather were middle-class performers on the college-prep track. . . .

As with the white girls, it is difficult to account for upwardly mobile Mexican-American girls' exceptional status, but there are a variety of enabling conditions for each of these individual girls' mobility. Although the experience of exceptionalism that these girls articulated in some ways paralleled white working-class girls' accounts, in other ways the two groups' experiences diverged, revealing the racial/ethnic specificity of their early mobility experiences.

Like Liz, Adriana's location in the college-prep curriculum seemed in part to be linked to organized sports. She showed a talent for soccer early on and received much support for it from home, because her father was a big fan. ("Soccer is always on our TV," she said. "He gets cable just for the soccer.") Adriana's friendship group in junior high thus included many of the college-prep girls who tend to dominate organized sports. Like Liz, through association with preps, she experienced the benefit of the privileged treatment by teachers and counselors that is often reserved for college-prep students. But while she was friendly with these girls in the classroom and on the playing field, she primarily located herself in a peer group of other working-class Mexican-American girls who were middle-class performers.

Like the white working-class girls, these girls at times told stories of defining self in opposition to delinquent brothers. . . .

But more often they told stories of older siblings as the source of help and inspiration to go to college. Usually, but not always, these older siblings were sisters, generally an older sister who had finally managed, through a long and circuitous route that included junior college and many part-time and full-time jobs, to attend a four-year school. The older sisters sought to help their younger siblings manage more easily by advising them on the importance of getting the courses required for state university or UC admission done in high school (rather than in junior college), on taking SAT tests, and on filling out applications for financial aid and admissions on time. Luisa had two older sisters attending state schools, and she had been accepted to three university campuses. . . .

When I asked her if she had understood the differences between attending a junior college versus a state university or UC school, she said,

> Yeah, just from my sister. She always taught me what, you know, she's the one who told me what the differences were, and she helped me figure out that I wanted to go to UC, because I didn't want to go spend two yews at a JC and

> [then] like go for four more years, because I thought that was like a waste of two years."

Although Angela did not have older siblings guiding her, she clearly saw it as her job to help her five younger siblings. When I asked her about her social life, she said,

> Well, I don't spend time like I used to, with friends so much. My family, my little brothers and sister are more important than friends. They need to get ahead. And I don't want them to get behind or something. I want to help them do well.

Because she had so many younger siblings to help, who took energy away from her own schooling and who would need to use the family's economic resources, I had doubts that Angela's college dream would be realized, but it seemed likely that her siblings would benefit from her sacrifices. Indeed, this was a factor for Victoria, whose mobility was fostered by having older siblings—much older, in fact, since her mother was forty-two when Victoria was born. Not only were these older siblings able to advise her, but by the time she was ready to go to college many of them were established and could help her financially.

In short, older siblings who were the first in the family to go to college turned out to be important sources of insider information already known to students whose parents were college-educated, providing cultural and social capital not available from parents, and at times economic capital as well.

Two of the girls in this middle-class performing group were immigrants, and explaining their exceptionalism requires other considerations. These two girls were fluent enough in English to be able to complete college-prep courses. The remainder of immigrant girls in the senior class were on the vocational track. Many authors have noted the greater educational success of immigrant students compared to their second- and third-generation counterparts. It was Waretown school counselors' subjective impression that immigrant students "do better" in school. . . .

One explanation for the achievement of these two immigrant girls is that their parents had some other benefits and resources that enabled them to be more mobile than their vocational track counterparts. In her work on the educational mobility of low-income Chicana/os, Patricia Gándara (1995) asks not why low-income Chicana/os fail, but why those who experience class mobility succeed. She suggests that "family stories" can work as a kind of cultural capital for these students. The people in her study told stories of coming from families that were well-to-do or had achieved high levels of education in Mexico, or of families that had lost their fortunes—and so their status and financial well-being—in fleeing Mexico because they were on the losing side in the Mexican revolution.

When I asked Lupita, who had immigrated at thirteen, had quickly learned English, was an academic star at the school, and had been admitted to several University of California campuses, why she was different from the other students in her neighborhood, she explained that while their families had immigrated from rural areas of Mexico, her family had come from an urban environment where there was greater access to education. In fact, she had an older sibling who had received a college degree in Mexico. . . .

The girls I studied were fully aware of the fact that the status of Mexican-Americans was not on a linear progression upward and that their lives might not be any easier, even given the Mexican-American civil rights movement. In just the past five years, they had witnessed the passage of three ballot measures in California that put clear brakes on the possibility of mobility for Mexican Americans. Proposition 187, passed in 1994, took social services such as public health care and public school education away from undocumented immigrants.

Proposition 209, passed in 1996, eliminated affirmative action and thus encouraged other states to do the same. Proposition 227, passed in 1998, formally ended bilingual education in the state of California, re-igniting an English-only movement that spread throughout the country.

I began to identify an "immigrant orientation" (Ogbu and Matute-Bianchi 1986) that existed among some girls, regardless of whether they were immigrants or not, meaning they employed as a mobility strategy the belief in the classical immigrant story of using education as a route to the American dream of upward mobility. . . . This group of working-class college-prep students engaged this strategy, holding out hope for education as their route to mobility, more than did vocational students. . . , who were far more cynical about their ability to achieve success via education. However, these college-prep girls were not blind to the barriers that exist or to new ones that were currently being created by the state legislature. They were in fact, neither duped by achievement ideology or blindly assimilated, but rather were able to hold both hope and a practical cynicism in their minds simultaneously.

If . . . working-class students of color at times have higher aspirations than white working-class students, this does not mean that those higher aspirations result in higher achievement; a variety of structural barriers remain in place that inhibit their mobility. In the cases of Lupita and Angela, while family benefits, whether real or imagined, shape student aspirations, they do not dictate outcomes. Lupita did appear to come from an educated extended family in Mexico, and her college-educated sibling provided her with cultural capital that would possibly benefit her. But with five younger siblings, no health care, and a sick mother, Angela remains less likely to reap the benefits of her higher aspirations. Even though she was admitted to a UC campus, she was hoping to attend a nearby junior college:

> That's the only place I can go, because I can't afford to go away.

And when I asked Lupita about her family's income, she explained,

> Oh, you know how Mexican families are, a little bit from here, a little bit from there. My dad pays the rent, mom buys the food, my little brother pays the phone bill, and I'm responsible for the gas bill. My uncles fill in whatever else is needed.

Adriana cannot afford not to live at home, and her family cannot spare her economic contribution to the household.

MEXICAN-AMERICAN GIRLS: BECOMING UPWARDLY MOBILE

As with white working-class upwardly mobiles, these Mexican-American middle-class performers could see the differences between themselves and middle-class preps (mostly white) somewhat more clearly than their vocational counterparts could. But where whites articulated their difference from preps in veiled class term, Mexican-American girls articulated their difference clearly in terms of race. For example, Luisa commented:

> I think it is harder for Mexican-American students, because I think most white people have, like, money, like their parents, they went to college, and they have money. They have an education. But, you know, I'm not saying, well, you know, it's my mom's fault that she didn't go to college. She could have, you know, but I don't know, it's just, like, that's just what it is, kind of. The white students don't understand because, you know, their parents got to go to college, you know, had an education, they all have jobs.

Like white girls, Mexican-American girls wanted to point to the importance of mobility, yet did not want this to mean that their parents' lives were without value. They thus expressed a certain amount of ambivalence toward mobility and/or the acquisition of the middle-class cultural forms that accompany mobility. . . .

Mobility experiences can never be understood outside of their racial/ethnic specificity. Like white working-class girls, these girls were well aware of having exceeded their parents' abilities. But for them the acquisition of middle-class cultural forms also meant becoming bilingual, while their parents remained primarily Spanish speakers.

Where white working-class girls would say generally that they didn't want to struggle for money the way their parents did, Mexican-American girls were cognizant of the correlation between being Mexican-American and being poor and were more likely to name the specific occupations that the poorest people in their community worked and identified their motivation to escape these kinds of work. Angela declared:

> I don't want to be like everyone else, I want to, I want something better. I hate working in the fields, that's not for me, and I don't want to do that. It is minimum wage and I don't want to work for that. . . .

Unlike third-generation girls of middle-class origin who struggled hard in this particular context with being at once Mexican-American and middle-class and who tended at times to buy into the idea that to be authentically Mexican one must adopt working-class cultural forms, the college-prep working-class girls discussed here refused to interpret mobility as assimilation to whiteness and were not apologetic about their mobility; they did not feel any "less Mexican" for being college bound. John Ogbu and Maria Eugenia Matute-Bianchi (1986) suggest there is a difference between students who adopt an immigrant orientation toward schooling and those who adopt a caste-like orientation. A caste-like orientation equates schooling with a loss of racial/ethnic identity (i.e., "acting white") and leads to an adaptive strategy of resistance (often resulting in school failure). . . . The exact reason why some students of color equate educational mobility with acting white while others do not and instead formulate a bicultural identity is unclear. . . .

This handful of working-class college-prep girls enacted a different strategy than students who experienced or feared school success as assimilation. The former saw themselves as disproving white stereotypes about Mexican-Americans through their hard work and success, and they took pleasure from that. They adopted a strategy of "accommodation without assimilation," meaning that in the face of racial conflict and inequality, they made accommodations "for the purpose of reducing conflict," yet at the same time allowed their "separate group [identity and culture] to be maintained" (Gibson 1988, 24–25). In this formulation it is indeed possible to do well in school and not objectively be assimilated or "acting white." In short, they found ways to reject assimilation without resisting educational mobility. . . .

The correlation of race and poverty promotes the common-sense belief that middle-class and whiteness are one and the same; as a result Mexican-American students must negotiate educational mobility with the broader social perception that this mobility represents assimilation to whiteness. This assimilation is resisted and gets played out as intraethnic tension, as vocational Mexican-American students accuse college-preps of "acting white." These working-class upwardly mobiles did occasionally receive such accusations from their working-class peers, but they interpreted this as a joke, which though painful at times, was not taken as a real challenge, and their racial/ethnic identity remained unthreatened by their college-prep status . . . .

The fact that upwardly mobile students grew up working-class meant that their identity as Mexican-American was consistent with the common understanding of race and class as correlated. Their Mexican identity appeared less challenged (both internally and externally) than was the case for some middle-class Mexican-American girls, whose middle-class status made them appear to themselves and to others as acculturated. This, even though they were not so far removed from Mexican-American cultural forms. Some of their grandparents, with whom they had much contact, were immigrants; their parents were fluent in Spanish; and parents' work (as an ethnic studies professor, a labor lawyer, and a university administrator of minority programs, for example) promoted or at least made available a cultural and political racial/ethnic identity. Perhaps they were not "actually" or "really" more acculturated, but they were more middle-class, and this affected their view of themselves and others' view of them. . . .

RACE MATTERS

While all of these girls, across race/ethnicity, have not articulated their early mobility as particularly painful, it is likely to become more so as they (if they) proceed into college, which will take them much further away culturally from family and community than mere high school mobility could. Many have written of the pain that working-class upwardly mobile people experience when leaving their community behind and/or the difficulty of finding ways to reconcile the discord between class background and present status due to mobility. This experience differs, of course, for whites and people of color, as racial/ethnic groups of color are more consciously aware of themselves as a community of people because of a common history of colonization and oppression that results from being historically defined as a racial group. Alternatively, an aspect of whiteness is that whites often do not immediately experience themselves as members of the racial/ethnic category "white," but as individuals, and, without a cultural discourse of class identity, they do not readily experience themselves as members of a class community either. Evidence of this can be seen in the way white working-class college-prep girls expressed their experience of and concern over how education was distancing themselves from their parents. They did not articulate this as a distancing from their working-class *community;* their pain was more often articulated in relationship to an *individual* family, not a people. In short, these white working-class girls were not routinely accused of acting "too bourgeois" the way that middle-class performing Mexican-American girls were accused of acting "too white," because such clear language for class difference was unavailable. Their mobility appears less complicated because they are not made to feel that they are giving up racial/ethnic belonging in the process. . . . In a way, the lack of class discourse may be either a hindrance or a help for white working-class students. On the one hand, because class is unarticulated, they have only individual characteristics to blame for their class location: their status is a consequence of the fact that they and/or their parents are just "losers." On the other hand, their mobility may be made easier since they did not experience the same intra-ethnic tension or antagonism within their community over the link between mobility and assimilation that Mexican-American girls did.

As we have seen, being brown or black tends to signify working-class in the United States, given the high correlation between race and class. Consequently, for white working-class upwardly mobiles, the class referent is escapable precisely because of their whiteness. For whites, class does not as easily appear encoded onto the body (although it certainly can be and often is). White working-class upwardly mobiles can pass as middle-class more readily. At school, where no one necessarily knew where working-class white students lived or what their parents looked like, their classed identities could be invisible if they worked at it and learned how to pass, as many do. The possibility of, and perhaps ease of, upward mobility favor white working-class students may also be greater, given that Mexican-American girls were more likely to experience tracking as a consequence of counselors' perceptions and stereotypes. The correlation between race/ethnicity and class means that counselors are likely to assume that brown students are from low-income families (even when they are not) and therefore to make assumptions about what educational resources they need and can handle. White working-class students can escape tracking more easily because their color does not stand in for or signify lowness. . . .

The experiences of these girls reveal that, in order not to be vulnerable to tracking, a Mexican-American student has to be phenomenally good academically, perform a school-sanctioned femininity that signifies middle-classness to school personnel, and have no transgressions or slip-ups along the way. . . .

Discussion Questions

1. Describe some of the privileges the author found that girls from middle-class families frequently had.
2. What did it mean for the girls in this study when they were labeled as "working class"?
3. How did some girls become "exceptions to the rule" and become upwardly mobile despite their origins?
4. What role does race play in one's ability to move up, according to this study? What role does immigration status play, based on the author's findings?

References

Gándara, Patricia, 1995. *Over the Ivy Walls: The Educational Mobility of Low-Income Chicanos.* Albany: State University of New York Press.

Gibson, Margaret A. 1988. *Accommodation without Assimilation: Sikh Immigrants in an American High School.* Ithaca, N.Y.: Cornell University Press.

Ogbu, John V., and Maria Eugenia Matute-Bianchi, 1986. "Understanding Sociocultural Factors: Knowledge Identity and School Adjustment." In *Beyond Language: Social and Cultural Factors in Schooling Language Minority Students,* developed by the Bilingual Education Office, California State Department of Education, 73–142. Los Angeles: Evaluation Dissemination and Assessment Center, California State University, Los Angeles.

Skeggs, Beverley. 1997. *Formations of Class and Gender: Becoming Respectable.* London: Sage.

PART SIX

Popular Culture, Consumption, and Play
The Importance of Play and Popular Culture

Play is often seen as an imperative of childhood, the embodiment of the fun, and carefree experience often associated with childhood. We view play as the opposite of work, the perceived domain of adulthood, as something frivolous and inconsequential. *Child's play*, a phrase that connotes something simple or easy, is indicative of adults' tendency not to take children's activities seriously.

"Play" as an expected childhood pastime is an economically and historically situated concept. For children in developing countries, there may be little time for leisure, just as there wasn't in preindustrial times in the West. Children often had responsibilities of taking care of their younger siblings, cleaning, cooking, working on family farms, or learning trades. Author Hilary Levey describes how involvement in competitive sports has also been linked with social class. While organized sports are a central part of middle-class or affluent children's experiences today, at the start of the twentieth century organized sports grew out of concerns about how low-income immigrant children would spend their free time. "Outside Class: A Historical Analysis of American Children's Competitive Activities" details how sports and other competitive activities like spelling bees were considered ways to teach skills like hard work and respect for authority, thought to be lacking in children of poor immigrants.

Just as involvement in competitive activities has links with socioeconomic status, the creation of special toys for children also has economic roots. Until the late nineteenth century, it was rare that toys were actually purchased. When they were, they were often considered family heirlooms. The widespread marketing of toys grew with industrialization and the expansion of the middle classes at the beginning of the twentieth century. Toys were sold not just as amusement for children, but as representations of childhood itself. At a time when domesticity was idealized, removing women and children from the paid labor force came to symbolize the new conception of the family. Toys represent the growth of a leisure class, starting first with children. Around this same time, holidays like Christmas and rituals such as birthday parties became redefined as celebrations of both childhood and consumption. Christmas and Halloween, once associated with rowdy, drunken revelry, became redefined as celebrations of childhood in the late nineteenth century as the notion of childhood innocence began to prevail.

CHILDREN AS CONSUMERS

Other rituals, like the "arrival" of the Tooth Fairy after a child loses a tooth, are also consumption-centered. Author Cindy Dell Clark interviewed parents and children about this ritual, and in "Flight Toward Maturity: The Tooth Fairy" she notes how the exchange of the lost tooth for money helps alleviate the pain and fear associated with losing a body part. She also explores how through the construction of this mythical character, much like with Santa Claus and the Easter Bunny, parents can feel as though their children are still naive enough to believe in fantasy.

Yet many adults are concerned that the use of consumer purchases is an empty and superficial way of constructing a sense of self or belonging. This is a valid point, but one which is almost exclusively focused on children's consumption, rather than adults'. Fears about kids and consumption tend to be based on assumptions that children are easily manipulated, they don't know what they really want, and that they are particularly vulnerable to advertising.

It is true that sometimes we do not do enough to prepare young people to be savvy consumers (because many adults are not exactly wise consumers themselves). But rarely do critics about children and consumption base their claims on child-centered studies. Viviana Zelizer studied how children in the United States, Europe, and Asia spend their money. She challenges many taken-for-granted beliefs about child consumers in "Kids and Commerce," where she describes how children are not simply passive consumers—they are also producers and distributors, other forms of economic activity.

Likewise, shopping is a process, one that Christine L. Williams observed in "Kids in Toyland," an ethnographic study in toy stores. She noticed that while the activity of being in a toy store offered parents the chance to teach their kids how to shop, children also negotiated with their parents to maximize their gains. While many parents may not appreciate the skills their children develop—especially if they continually win during negotiation—her findings remind us that kids are not merely passive victims of the consumer marketplace. And just as Clark found in her study of the tooth fairy, parents also use toy purchases to feel as though they are contributing to their children's happiness. While this may be a temporary, if not superficial measure of happiness, in a consumer-based society purchases are regarded as prizes. Otherwise, government officials wouldn't encourage us to keep shopping to keep our consumer-dependent economy rolling.

And yet we rarely make the connection between the political economy of consumption and concerns about children being "too materialistic." If we question the latter, we must certainly question the former, but we seldom do. Children value consumer goods as part of a deeply materialistic society, where being a "good citizen," following the terrorist attacks on September 11, 2001 and in times of economic downturn, involves going to the mall, according to politicians, anyway.

Sarah Banet-Weiser critically examines the definition of citizenship in the United States in her piece "We Pledge Allegiance to Kids: Nickelodeon and Citizenship." Children are rarely considered citizens—they cannot vote, and they are typically used as symbols of innocence, danger, or victimhood in political campaigns. Banet-Weiser studied the *Nick News* online message board and found that many kids are both interested and knowledgeable about politics. Yet at the same time, Nickelodeon is well known for its heavily marketed merchandising that accompanies its programming. Banet-Weiser concludes that these contradictions remain within Nickelodeon's programming . . . just as they do within American life.

To many critics and parents, television does not just encourage children to buy, but encourages them to "grow up too fast." This fear presumes first that there is a "natural" pace at which young people should mature. As we discussed in Part I, this pace is constantly in flux. Nonetheless, sexual content in popular culture, particularly television, has generated a great deal of concern. Fears about what information about sex might "do" to young people presume that children are passive absorbers of media content. Yet researchers Peter Kelly, David Buckingham, and Hannah Davies talked with children about television and found that the idea of the passive child is too simple. Their selection, "Talking Dirty: Children, Sexual Knowledge, and Television" is based on their discussions about what makes some shows "for adults" compared with others. The children they spoke with offered multiple levels of analysis of what's on TV. First, claiming to know more about "adult" sitcoms and other shows was a way that the kids tried to elevate their status with one another. And second, young boys in particular expressed disdain about shows with too much romance in them. The children's responses help us to understand the ways in which they make sense of television in the context of their lives.

Outside Class: A Historical Analysis of American Children's Competitive Activities

HILARY LEVEY

INTRODUCTION

There is no shortage of complaints about kids today being "overscheduled" with many organized after-school activities filling their days. While many American children do not share this experience today, in the past the emphasis on organized competitive activities was not as great. Author Hilary Levey explores how competition came to characterize many children's lives. She cites changes in education, families, and leisure organizations as central to understanding why these kinds of activities have become so predominant in middle-class children's lives. Additionally, she notes that the orientation toward competition and achievement exacerbates existing inequalities.

Middle-class children's lives are filled with adult-organized activities, while working-class and poor children fill their own days with free play and television-watching. This is one of the central observations of Annette Lareau's ethnographic study of twelve families from different classes, raising third grade children around Philadelphia (Lareau 2003). Lareau's findings about the way children from middle-class families use their time is consistent with popular conceptions of over-scheduled kids from well-off families who are chauffeured from activity to activity on a daily basis (for examples see *New York Times* articles like Appleborn 2006, Kilborn 2005, and Tugend 2005).

Nowadays, these "over-scheduled" elementary school-age children (Rosenfeld 2001) not only participate in their myriad after-school activities, but they also compete. They tryout for all-star teams, travel to regional and national tournaments, and clear off bookshelves to hold all of the trophies they have won. Many Little League fields and dance studios have been transformed from environments that emphasized learning skills, personal growth, and simple fun to competitive cauldrons in which only a few succeed.

It has not always been this way. About a hundred years ago, it would have been the lower class children competing under adult supervision, with their upper class counterparts participating in non-competitive activities centered around the home. Children's tournaments, especially athletic ones, came first to poor, often immigrant children, in big cities. It was not until after World War II that these competitive endeavors began to be dominated by children from the middle and upper middle classes. The 1970s saw an explosion of growth in both the number of participants and the types of competitive opportunities available. Not surprisingly, participation in the activities became more and more expensive, crowding out many who could not pay to play.

Over time children's lives have become more organized and focused on winning, though in many ways the United States has always been, as Janet Spence explained in her presidential address to the American Psychological Association, "a success-oriented society whose attitudes toward achievement can be traced to our Protestant heritage with its emphasis on individualism and the work ethic (Spence 1985, 1285)." Yet if the playing field was ever level, it certainly is no longer. This orientation toward success and achievement in childhood reinforces inequalities, like those based on class. Today it costs to participate in competitive circuits and tournaments. For future Michelle Wies there is a youth PGA (Hack 2005), for future Dale Earnhardts there is a kids' NASCAR circuit (Gupta 2005), and for future Davy Crocketts there are shooting contests (Belluck 2005). The forces that have led to increasing inequality in other spheres—education, the workplace, wages—have come to the world of "play".

What are the social forces that have shaped the evolution of these children's competitive activities from roughly the turn of the twentieth century up to the present? In the following pages I detail why organized, competitive children's activities developed for elementary school-age kids, how they have changed over time, and when they became more prevalent among middle class children than amongst their lower class counterparts. This story is linked to major changes in three social institutions: the family, the educational system, and the organization of competition and prizes in the United States. I begin by providing a history of the development of competitive children's activities.

COMPETITIVE AFTER-SCHOOL HOURS OVER TIME

Beginning in the late nineteenth century, compulsory education had important consequences for families and the economy. Children experienced a profound shift in the structure of their daily lives, especially in the social organization of their time. Compulsory education brought leisure time into focus; since "school time" was delineated as obligatory, "free time" could now be identified as well (Kleiber and Powell 2005, 23). What to do with this free time? The question was on the minds of parents, social workers, and "experts" that doled out advice on child-rearing. The answer lay partly in competitive sports leagues, which started to evolve to hold the interest of children, the first phase in the development of the competitive children's activities. Overall, we can identify three key periods of development. The first runs roughly from the Progressive era through the Second World War; the second moves from post-World War II to the 1970s; and the last takes us from the 1980s into the present time.

SEEDS OF COMPETITION. The Progressive era, with its organizational and reform impulses, inevitably focused on children's lives and gave rise to some of the earliest competitions among American children. For example, reformers, concerned about the health of babies, started better baby contests (1908–1952), . . . *primarily* as a way to teach immigrant and lower class mothers the values of hygiene and nutrition. The contests were often held at state fairs and judges evaluated children along several dimensions, including weight, measurements, and appearance in order to find the "healthiest" or the "most beautiful" baby (Dorey 1999). These contests required little more of the baby than to submit to being poked, prodded, and put on display. The competition was really amongst adults. With respect to older children, reformers were concerned about how children were spending their after-school hours, and this period witnessed the establishment of many after-school activities, which quickly developed competitive elements, along with the establishment of competitive leagues, especially in urban areas.

Urban reformers were particularly preoccupied with poor, immigrant boys, who because of overcrowding in tenements were often on the streets (Halpern 2002, 180). With the simultaneous rise of mandatory schooling and laws restricting child labor (Zelizer 1994), worry mounted over the idle hours of children, which many assumed would be filled with delinquent or self-destructive activities. Initial efforts to deal with this problem focused on the establishment of parks and playgrounds, but attention soon shifted to sports.[1]

Sports were seen as important in teaching "American" values like cooperation, hard work, and respect for authority. Progressive reformers thought athletic activities could prepare the children for the "new industrial society that was emerging" (Halpern 2002, 181), one that would require them to be laborers. Playgrounds, schools, and a few nationally organized youth groups, like the YMCA, took on the responsibility of providing children with sports activities (Berryman 1988). By 1903 New York City's Public School Athletic League for Boys was established and contests between children, organized by adults, emerged as a way to keep the boys coming back to activities and clubs. Competition ensured participation.[2] Settlement houses and ethnic clubs followed suit. The number of these boys' clubs grew rapidly through the 1920s, working in parallel with school leagues, like the Public School Athletic League in New York City.

By the 1930s this pattern began to shift as school philosophies changed. Physical education professionals stopped supporting high level competition for children because of concerns that leagues only supported competition for the best athletes, leaving the others behind. "By allowing highly organized children's sport to leave the educational context," Jack Berryman, a medical historian, explains, "professional educators presented a golden opportunity to the many voluntary youth-related groups in America" (1988, 5). During the Depression many clubs with boys' competitive leagues suffered (Halpern 2002) and poorer children from urban areas began to lose sites for competitive athletic contests organized by adults. Fee-based groups like the YMCA and others began to fill the void—but usually only middle-class kids could afford them (Clement Ferguson 1997, 162).

In the same historical moment, athletic organizations that later formally instituted competitive tournaments for young kids were founded. Pop Warner football and Little League baseball came into being in 1929 and 1939 respectively. Two strains of organization emerged amongst the organizations: the first was focused on social control and the second on opportunity

---

[1] This is also the time when the Boy Scouts, Campfire Girls, and Girl Scouts, were founded. With their focus on patches and achievement hierarchies, some could define these activities as competitive, though they are not explicitly so.

[2] Of course, athletic contests are inherently competitive, with there usually being a winner and a loser. Organized leagues keep track of winners and there are often "championships" where a team emerges as the ultimate winner.

enhancement (Kleiber and Powell 2005, 25). This division was based on class lines, with the former corresponding to lower class children's activities and the latter for more middle-class children.

For example, . . . a non-athletic competitive activity, like the national spelling bee for children grew in popularity at this time. Spelling bees, also known historically as fights or parties, are an American folk tradition. Throughout the 1700s they were part of the typical Colonial education and by the 1800s they had developed into community social events (Maguire 2006, 56). By the turn of the twentieth century spelling bees had evolved into a competitive educational tool. In her history of American childhood from 1850–1950, Priscilla Ferguson Clement explains, "Individual competition was also a constant in [late] nineteenth-century schools. In rural areas, teachers held weekly spelling bees in which youngsters stood in a line before the teacher (toed the line) and vied to be at the head of the line rather than at the foot (1997, 89)." The purpose of the bees was to promote achievement, not social control. Around the turn of the century a social movement formed to promote a national student-only bee and the first nationwide bee was held on June 29, 1908. Due to racial tensions, after a young black girl won, the next national student spelling bee was not held until the 1920s; by 1925 the national student spelling bee as we know it had taken shape, complete with corporate sponsorship (Maguire 2006, 68).

Not only did turn-of-the-century school children participate in bees, both in rural and urban areas, but children from more comfortable families also received a variety of lessons thought to enhance their social skills and prospects. In a history of children from different class backgrounds in the United States, Harvey Graff wrote of one family, the Spencers: "The Spencer children went to dancing school, dressing the part and meeting their peers of the opposite sex. The girls were given music lessons, with varying degrees of success" (1995, 271). These activities were organized and overseen by adults, but were not yet competitive.

Previously, middle-class children had participated in personal growth activities, like the Spencer children [did, but] had not encountered much organized competition, even in school; the activities were, more than anything, a form of social grooming. That changed with the development of compulsory schooling, as there now had to be a way to distinguish the achievements of children from different classes. Historian Peter Stearns explains that this impulse partially explains the development of report cards as standard practice in the 1920s, the introduction of the SAT in 1926, and the rise of standardized testing in general. He explains, "Schools used aptitude tests widely in the 1920s to sort populations, often heavily immigrant, into educational tracks . . . Middle-class parents largely accepted the tests, assuming their own children would naturally do well, but the result put pressure on these same parents to anticipate and promote good results (2003, 99)." Not surprisingly, the 1930s also saw the development of gifted programs (Margolin 1994). As school became more competitive, so too did the time children spent outside of school—particularly for those from upwardly mobile families.

GROWTH OF COMPETITION.   Children from varied class backgrounds continued to participate in competitive athletic leagues following the Second World War and for the next two decades, into the 70s, which witnessed "explosive growth" (Passer 1988, 203) in the number of activities and participants. In the decades following WWII, a variety of competitive activities began to be dominated by children of the middle class as the activities themselves became more competitive and organized. As this occurred the competition intensified *within* the middle class, not just between different classes.

One of the first children's activities to become nationally organized in a competitive way, and certainly the most well-known and successful youth sports program, is Little League baseball (Fine 1987, 4). Founded in 1939, shortly before the war, the League would hold its first World Series only a decade later, in 1949. The following decades saw a huge expansion in the number of participants, including participants from around the world. As children's participation moved to this model of membership in a national league organization, fees to play increased. With the success of national programs like Little League, which charged for participation, it became more difficult to sustain free programs, especially since most elementary schools no longer sponsored their own leagues due to concerns over the effects of competition on children.[3] Private organizations rushed to fill the void, as parents seemed to increasingly want more competitive activities for their children, and were willing to pay for it.

By the 1960s, highly organized sport competition for children had grown to include Pop Warner football, Biddy basketball, Pee Wee hockey, and others. The 60s also saw the growth of more involved parents, as opposed to adults who were unrelated. With respect to sports this may partly have been due to increasing awareness of athletics as a viable professional choice for adults (Berryman 1988, 12), but parents were also getting more involved with school and community activities for their children, like soapbox derbies, so it appears to be a broader trend (Stearns 2003). Even non-team sports were growing and developing their own competitive circuit. For example, Double Dutch jump-roping, an activity dominated by girls, started on playgrounds in the 1930s and 40s; 1975 saw the formation of the American Double Dutch League to set formal rules and sponsor competitions (Chudacoff 2007, 133).

Non-athletic competitions for children also began to take off in this time period. One example is child beauty pageants. The oldest continuously running child beauty pageant in the United States, "Our Little Miss," started in 1961. This pageant was modeled on . . . the Miss America Pageant, with local and regional competitions followed by a national contest. Throughout the 1960s and 1970s a variety of child beauty pageants, in addition to Our Little Miss, began "mushrooming at an unbelievably fast rate" (Stanley 1989, 265). By the late 1970s there was even a media-recognized "pageant circuit." A *Chicago Tribune* story reported in 1977, "Youngsters who travel the circuit learn how to fill the bill whenever they are, acting naïve and spontaneous here and knocking them dead with vampiness there" (Gallagher 1977).

Whether based on academics, athletics, or appearance, by the 1970s, parents, mostly those who were upwardly-mobile, wanted their children to "be better than average in all things, so they tried to provide them with professionally run activities that would enrich their minds, tone their bodies, inculcate physical skills, and enhance their self-esteem" (Chudacoff 2007, 165). National organizations went along with this middle-class impulse to be better than average by instituting national guidelines and contests. Even programs that had a philosophy of "everyone plays" contradicted themselves by hosting elimination tournaments where there was only one victor. These competitions began to be geared to children of younger and younger ages at this time (Seefeldt 1998, 337).

Some observers have argued that the rise of these adult-organized competitive activities for children can partly be explained by the decrease in safe areas for children to play on their own (Kleiber and Powell 2005, 28). While there is some validity to this argument, as safe play space for children in both urban and suburban areas was declining, this argument does not explain the trend toward increased competition. In fact, there was an alternative from

---

[3] The desire to dampen overt competition in schools was part of the self-esteem movement that started in the 1960s in schools, which focused on building up children's confidence and talents without being negative or comparing them to others. The self-esteem movement did not similarly affect outside activities, like music and sports (Stearns 2003, 118).

the competitive path. At the same time that upwardly mobile parents clamored to have their children involved in activities that would brand them as "above-average", adults involved with less advantaged children focused on inclusiveness and not competition. Those involved with "preventing such youngsters from being lured into gangs, drug use, and other antisocial behavior, steered children into organized activities sponsored by churches, schools, YMCAs and YWCAs, and boys' and girls' clubs" (Chudacoff 2007, 165–6).

The same YMCAs and boys' clubs that had been the first movers in organized competition several decades before had changed in the opposite direction. The activities provided were organized by adults, but little of the tournament impulse remained. Instead, these children's better-off peers were now the competitive ones, working to ensure their superiority in school, on fields, and in auditoriums. As the price of such competitive success continued to increase, even for younger children, less advantaged children were largely pushed out of the competitive space.

EXPLOSION OF HYPER-COMPETITIVENESS.   Along with increasing costs of participation in competitive children's activities, the period from the 1980s to the present also saw increased professionalization and the rise of hyper-competition. Consistent with Annette Lareau's findings, Peter Stearns describes the 1980s and 90s as a time when, "Overorganized kids seemed to supplant the underorganized, particularly in the middle class, during the two-decade span" (2003, 9). In addition, the distance between middle-class children and others continued to grow in terms of the amount of competition, with the middle class being more competitive (Grasmuck 2005).

Many explanations for the growth of organized activities during this time focus on increases in maternal employment. With both parents outside of the home in the after-school hours, children need to be supervised (i.e. Halpern 2002, 201). But competitive activities actually create additional work for parents and take time away from other household tasks, as parents have to shuttle kids back and forth to various lessons, practices, and tournaments, in addition to making sure uniforms and other equipment are clean and ready for each occasion (Bianchi, Robinson, and Milkie 2006). [Members of the Baby] Boom . . . [generation] know what their children must do in order to succeed in an increasingly competitive society, but as they themselves are often so busy working that they do not have time to run the PTA or lead the Scout troop, as their mothers did (Newman 1994, 82). Not surprisingly, parents turn to "experts" to help prepare their children to succeed in life, just as they have outsourced more mundane tasks like cleaning or cooking (Hochschild 2001). It seems that as the parental "second shift" continues to grow (Hochschild 1989) a second shift for children is emerging—one that is suffused with competition rather than mere participation as kids balance practices, competitions, and schoolwork.

The professionalization of many competitive children's activities, but especially youth sports, started in the 1980s and it reflects the adult aspects of a children's second shift. In a variety of ways, but most notably with respect to their focus on professional aspirations and long-term skill development, children's activities can be thought of as a form of children's work (Levey, forthcoming). The Adlers refer to "children's careers" in more competitive activities (Adler and Adler 1994) and Fine discusses the "worklike components" of Little League in the 1980s (Fine 1987). Parents and children themselves often use work language to describe kids' participation; for example, it is common when a successful child quits an activity to say that s/he has "retired."

There are three key ways in which children's competitive youth sports have become more and more professionalized in the past three decades (Brower 1979), not all of which have had positive consequences, as they have sometimes led to parents lying about children's ages along with fistfights between parents (Powell 2003, xv). The first way in which youth sports have professionalized has to do with the development of elite programs (which encompasses travel, select, premier, all-star, and Olympic development programs), especially during the 1990s (Engh 2002). To incorporate the growing stratification there are now many categories of play, ranging from recreational up to elite (Averbuch and Hammond 1999). Children usually have to "work their way up" through these divisions, with the goal being the top level team in their geographic area.

Another way in which youth sports has become professionalized is the rise of the paid youth sport coach and very specialized trainers (for examples see Saint Louis 2007 and Sheff 2006). For most of the elite programs described earlier having a paid "professional" coach is de rigueur. Parent and volunteer coaches often only exist in "rec" leagues and some elite clubs explicitly forbid parents from having any coaching responsibilities. When a team must pay for full-time coaches or trainers, who often charge over $20,000 for a season, the costs will outstrip the budgets of all but the wealthiest families.

Finally, youth sports have become professionalized with the rise of the year-round season (see Bick 2007). In the past, soccer dominated the fall, basketball the winter, and baseball the spring. Now, at the competitive level, teams practice all year, often requiring a permanent commitment from families (Pennington 2003). With indoor training facilities and specialized camps held during school vacations, children are asked as early as ages nine and ten to commit to a single sport. This has the consequence, unintended or otherwise, of forcing children to specialize early in a particular sport, also a professional marker.

As part of this process, hyper-competitiveness has burst onto the scene as well. Indeed since the 1980s we have seen the development of complex, competitive circuits in a variety of activities; a great number of participants with higher stakes at the elite level; and competition reaching down into younger and younger age groups even in activities traditionally associated with older and more mature players. Looking for and labeling children . . . prodigies is a new [pastime.]

Cheerleading is a good example of the first trend—the growth of complex, competitive circuits. Cheerleading has a long history in this country, starting with men as the first participants in the late nineteenth century. Women became cheerleaders in the 1920s and have dominated the activity since then. It has often been associated with small-town local pride, national patriotism, and school promotion. A few scholastic-based competitions were held for older cheerleading squads—at the high school and collegiate level—in the period following WWII. In the 1990s private, competition-only squads, tied neither to scholastic nor civic identities, began to emerge as a variety of private cheer competitions started. Now teams like "The Hotties, The Firecrackers and The Flames . . . [compete] at [events like] the American Showdown, a giant, 'Bring It On'-style tournament where more than 60 of the top cheerleading teams from Kindergarten-12th grade vie for cash and prizes" (*The Insider* 2005). Video games are now the subject of a new . . . competition circuit, in which children as young as five competing against adults for money and endorsement deals (Lambert 2007). A separate children's-only video game circuit is not far behind.

The number of competitors at the highest levels has also increased, especially in the 1980s and 1990s as the rewards for winning increased. Gymnastics and figure skating are good examples, as detailed by Joan Ryan in her 2000 book *Little Girls in Pretty Boxes*, which describes the efforts of young girls and their families to fight time and puberty in an attempt to reach the Olympics in their respective sports. Ryan details how more and more families pushed their daughters into elite competition, often moving across the country to work with particular coaches. She describes one father, Bill Bragg, who actually gave up custody of his daughter to her figure skating coach, hoping that would help young Hollie become an Olympic ice princess. Ryan explains his motivation:

> Bragg himself had been a swimming coach, but swimming held no magic. It couldn't turn milkmaids into princesses. To him, skating was more than a sport. To succeed in skating was to succeed in life. It was a road to riches and recognition, and perhaps more important, it was a road to respectability. Skating offered a life of restaurants with cloth napkins, hotels with marble lobbies, a life where a girl from the wrong side of the tracks could be somebody (2000, 142).

Other competitive sports and activities also come with promises of riches and recognition now, especially in the form of endorsements. This is another way in which hyper-competition has permeated children's activities and promoted competition for younger and younger children. A 2003 *New York Times Magazine* piece focused on four-year-old champion skateboarder Dylan, who already was being touted as the "next big little thing" by promoters, merchandisers, and his parents (Talbot 2003). Even in historically established sports, like golf, young children who succeed competitively garner publicity, attention, and hence money. Twelve year-old Alexis Thompson made headlines in the summer of 2007 when she became the youngest qualifier ever for the US Women's Open in golf (AFP 2007). Touted as a "pre-teen prodigy," endorsement deals began coming in.

This proclivity for naming children prodigies happens not only in sports, but even more often in music. In a 2000 book that highlights the young string students who attend Julliard's Saturday pre-college program, music writer Barbara Sand explains that parents and students are so anxious to keep a "prodigy" label that they will often lie about a child's age (Sand 2000, 157). Being named a prodigy (defined as a child who displays "talents that are only supposed to be the province of gifted and highly trained adults" [Feldman 1991, 4]) confers status, but also money and attention. At the same time, with so many competitive circuits available, high performers almost expect to be declared prodigies, just as middle class parents in the 1970s expected their children to be above average (Quart 2006). Accordingly, those unable to claim the prodigy label constitute a failure in the current professionalized, hyper-competitive environment of competitive children's activities, now dominated by children of the middle and upper-middle classes. . . .

DISCUSSION: CHANGES IN FAMILIES, EDUCATION, AND PRIZES

A concatenation of reasons explains why competitive activities have developed in the way they have over the past century. These reasons primarily involve changes around the family, education, and prizes. Class is an important factor as well, overlaying the historical narrative and influencing the contemporary situation and its outcomes.

In their study of why American families are so busy in the early twenty-first century, anthropologists Darah Freeman and English-Lueck suggest that:

> Smaller family sizes, the reluctance of parents to permit unsupervised children's play, and preferences for structured, formalized children's activities require adults to transport and supervise their children. Many parents have also become more involved in their children's education and recreational activities reflecting

shifting norms of good parenting . . . This intensification of activities or performance standards may extend beyond parenting. Family members often emphasized one aspect of their lives or another, trying to reach the highest standard of excellence, either as connoisseurs or performers (2007, 49).

Embedded in these reasons for the increase in busyness are some of the reasons for the increase in competition in children's lives.

Demographic changes, like fewer children in each family, profoundly affect the tenor of parenting. Parents can devote more time and attention to their children in smaller families; this also means that there is even more parental anxiety since there are fewer chances to see children succeed (Stearns 2003). More mothers now work outside the home as well, which affects childcare arrangements. Working mothers in particular can produce parental guilt, as some delegation of socialization tasks occurs. This in turn may lead some parents to indulge children in their competitive or organized activities more than they might have otherwise (or to over-compensate for less physical time at home by being over-involvement in other ways).

Likely the most significant demographic change that has affected competitive children's activities are the population booms—the Baby Boom and its Echo Boom. While Baby Boom parents are actually the best-educated and wealthiest generation ever seen in the US, that enormous cohort has overwhelmed every social sorting institution it has come in contact with, from preschool classrooms to retirement homes. Hence the cultural experience of competition, of an insufficient supply of spots for the size of the group seeking them, has predisposed Boomers to see life as a series of contests (Newman 1994). With their children's cohort—the Echo Boom—if anything the competitive landscape is getting more crowded than it was in the Boomers' formative years and the stakes are even higher because bottlenecks are growing tighter.

This is especially true when it comes to higher education. The 1960s saw "a growing competitive frenzy over college admissions as a badge of parental fulfillment" (Stearns 2003, 100). Parental anxiety reached a new level because the surge in attendance by Boomers had strained college facilities and it became increasingly clear that the top schools could not keep up with the demand, meaning that students might not be admitted to the level of college they previously expected, given class backgrounds. Parents took on the responsibility of ensuring their children were successful in the college admissions process.

Interestingly, the competitive frenzy over college admissions did not abate in the 1970s and 80s, when it was actually easier to gain admission to college, given the decline in application numbers after the Baby Boomers. Instead, more aware of the stakes, families became more competitive. Now, with the Echo Boom in the late 1990s and early 2000s, it actually is once again harder to get into a "top" college (Stearns 2003, 104). This reality, combined with the existing tension around college admissions, has created an incredibly competitive atmosphere for families—which starts at younger and younger ages now, as parents start earlier and earlier in their children's lives on the long march to college admission. How early one starts seems to be related to class position, as those from higher classes start grooming their children for competitive preschool admissions in some parts of the country (for examples see Boncompagni 2006 and Willen 2003).

Part of this story now includes after-school activities to supplement in-school achievement and test scores. Performing well in activities that many parents perceive as integral to, but not entirely synonymous with, the formal educational system is seen as crucial (Kaufman and Gabler, 2004). Competitive activities are particularly appealing to parents, and admissions officers, because they can help children develop skills and learn life lessons that have both indirect and direct effects on their ability to navigate credentials bottlenecks. Indirect pathways involve the creation of a certain kind of cultural capital: the confident competitor. The direct avenues to the top have children competing to achieve special distinction in sports, intellectual tournaments, and creative arts that adults believe enhance children's prospects for admission to elite universities. Because there is unequal access to these activities only some children, whose families are already well off socio-economically, get through the financial filter and can apply their newly acquired skills to gaining admission to elite society (Golden 2006). Certain sports, like squash and fencing, are especially helpful, as they signal elite status in the college admissions process (Williams 2007).

Adults know that these educational credentials do in fact matter. . . . Randall Collins explained their importance this way: "The rise of a competitive system for producing an abstract cultural currency in the form of educational credentials has been the major new force shaping stratification in twentieth-century America" (1979, 94). This new stratification connected to existing inequalities based on class. The initial rise of competitive activities for children was also connected to class issues, but in a different way than it is now. That impulse was also tied to a major change in the educational system, the rise of the compulsory education, so class and education are inextricably linked in the historical development of competitive children's activities.

It is also important to note that there has been a general increase in both forming and joining competitive organizations and in winner-take-all "prize frenzy" in the US throughout this time period, with a greater emphasis on a high standard of excellence, as Darrah et al mentioned in the previous quote. For instance, the late nineteenth century saw the establishment of several different types of competitions that still exist today. In 1874 the first Kentucky Derby was held; 1876 witnessed the inaugural Westminster dog show; and in 1913 the first rose flower competitions were held in the US. The early twentieth century also saw the development of American sporting culture. The NCAA was established in 1910 and a variety of professional sports leagues grew at the same time. Scholars Markovits and Hellerman note that sports foster American's predilection for rankings and quantifications: "America's fetishism and obsession with rankings have made two ostensibly conflicting, yet essential, American values comparable: that of competition and fairness" (Markovits and Hellerman 2001, 50).

The value of competition in general intensified in the second half of the twentieth century. James English describes the 1970s as the most intense period of prize creation, with tremendous growth in every field, particularly when fields often added to existing prize systems (2005, 72). These prizes included music competitions, art awards, televised ceremonies for movies and television shows, and so on. Since that time, prizes have become increasingly fashionable and they are broadly publicized in a variety of fields, including sports and literary awards (Anand and Watson 2004, 60).

So while some changes, like those in the family and the educational system, had direct effects on children and their experiences with competition through activities, it is necessary to contextualize these changes in the broader competitive spirit of the US at this time. Competition and prize frenzy has increased over time, which has surely impacted the terrain of competitive children's activities. What is notable about this development is that earlier forms of competition were dominated by adults, so the number of opportunities for children to compete now is increasing, with implications for children's long-term development and for . . . inequality.

CONCLUDING THOUGHTS: THE FUTURE OF COMPETITIVE CHILDREN'S ACTIVITIES

Competitive children's activities have certainly evolved since they began in late nineteenth-century America—there are more activities, a greater number of competitions, and a profound change in the class backgrounds of competitors. These changes can be understood in terms of changes in families, the educational system, and the prize structure. In connecting the beginnings of children's competitive activities to the present, Kleiber and Powell state, "Turn-of-the-century reformers responded to a variety of social changes by trying to increase the social capital among young people at the time; the emerging significance of the after-school period provides a similar opportunity at this point in time" (2005, 40).

While there is an opportunity to once again involve less advantaged children in competitive activities—one example of this is occurring with scholastic chess in Harlem, the Bronx, and other urban centers which have non-profits supporting gifted children financially so they can train and travel—it is clear that the middle and upper-middle classes still dominate these activities and their children are often successful in the long march to college because of the ways in which they connect participation to the formal educational system. As paid coaches and fees for participation in activities and competitions continue to predominate, those who are not able to pay are pushed out of the system, at least when they are elementary school-age. There are opportunities for participation in school-sponsored activities in middle school and high school, but without specialized training at a young age, it is difficult to compete with those who have had such training. For the foreseeable future, it seems that the children from the middle and upper-middle classes will continue to dominate competitive children's activities.

Given the number of children who participate in organized competitive activities in the present, we need to understand the structure of the activities and their potential long-term affects, particularly in terms of the role they play in the sorting process that leads to higher education and hence lucrative occupations. Understanding the historical evolution of these activities is a first step, but we must also understand how parents and children conceptualize the place of these activities in their lives and the role that inequality plays in providing or constraining opportunities for children outside of the classroom.

Discussion Questions

1. What historical reasons does the author provide for the introduction of competitive children's activities?
2. How and why has the emphasis on organized activities shifted from lower income to upper income children?

3. Why has competition come to characterize so many of children's leisure activities?
4. Did you participate in many organized and/or competitive activities growing up? How did this shape your experience of childhood?

Works Cited

Adler, Patricia A. and Peter Adler. 1994. "Social Reproduction and the Corporate Other: The Institutionalization of Afterschool Activities." *The Sociological Quarterly.* 35(2): 309–328.

AFP. June 26, 2007. "Pre-teen prodigy makes US Women's Open history."

Anand, N. and Mary R. Watson. 2004. "Tournament Rituals in the Evolution of Fields: The Case of the Grammy Awards." *Academy of Management Journal.* Vol. 27 (1): 59–80.

Averbuch, Gloria and Ashley Michael Hammond. 1999. *Goal! The Ultimate Guide for Soccer Moms and Dads.* Emmaus, PA: Rodale Press.

Belluck, Pam. September 18, 2005. "Girls and Boys, Meet Nature. Bring Your Gun." *The New York Times.*

Berryman, Jack W. 1988. "The Rise of Highly Organized Sports for Preadolescent Boys." pp. 3–16 in Frank L. Smoll, Richard A. Magill, Michael J. Ash (eds). *Children in Sport* (3rd Edition). Champaign, IL: Human Kinetics Books.

Bianchi, Suzanne M., John P. Robinson, and Melissa A. Milkie. 2006. *Changing Rhythms of American Family Life.* New York, NY: Russell Sage Foundation.

Bick, Julie. February 25, 2007. "Looking for an Edge? Private Coaching, by the Hour." *The New York Times.*

Boncompagni, Tatiana. May 11, 2006. "Baby Shall Enroll: Mommy Knows." *The New York Times.*

Brower, Jonathan J. 1979. "The Professionalization of Organized Youth Sport: Social Psychological Impacts and Outcomes." *Annals of the American Academy of Political and Social Sciences.* 445: 39–46.

Chudacoff, Howard P. 2007. *Children at Play: An American History.* New York: New York University Press.

Clement, Priscilla Ferguson. 1997. *Growing Pains: Children in the Industrial Age, 1850–1950.* New York: Twayne Publishers.

Collins, Randall. 1979. *The Credential Society.* New York: Elsevier.

Darrah, Charles N., James M. Freeman, and J. A. English-Lueck. 2007. *Busier than Ever! Why American Families Can't Slow Down.* Stanford, CA: Stanford University Press.

Dorey, Annette K. Vance. 1999. *Better Baby Contests: The Scientific Quest for Perfect Childhood Health.* Jefferson, NC: McFarland & Company.

Engh, Fred. 2002. *Why Johnny Hates Sports: Why Organized Youth Sports are Failing Our Children and What We Can Do About It.* Garden City Park, NY: Square One Publishers.

English, James F. 2005. *The Economy of Prestige: Prizes, Awards, and the Circulation of Cultural Value.* Cambridge, MA: Harvard University Press.

Feldman, David Henry. 1991. *Nature's Gambit: Child Prodigies and the Development of Human Potential.* New York: Teachers College Press.

Fine, Gary Alan. 1987. *With the Boys: Little League Baseball and Preadolescent Culture.* Chicago, IL: University of Chicago Press.

Gallagher, Jim. July 28, 1977. "Pageants: Little Misses, Big Dreams (for their Mommies)." *The Chicago Tribune.* Pg. A1.

Golden, Daniel. 2006. *The Price of Admission: How America's Ruling Class Buys Its Way into Elite Colleges—and Who Gets Left Outside the Gates.* New York: Brown.

Graff, Harvey J. 1995. *Conflicting Paths: Growing Up in America.* Cambridge, MA: Harvard University Press.

Grasmuck, Sherri. 2005. *Protecting Home: Class, Race, and Masculinity in Boys' Baseball.* New Brunswick, NJ: Rutgers University Press.

Gupta, Sanjay. October 13, 2005. "NASCAR ride 'More than a Little Terrifying.'" CNN.

Hack, Damon July 3, 2005. "Youth is Served Earlier in LPGA." *The New York Times.*

Halpern, Robert. 2002. "A Different Kind of Child Development Institution: The History of After-School Programs for Low-Income Children." *Teachers College Record.* 104(2): 178–211.

Hochschild, Arlie and Anne Matchung. 1989. *The Second Shift: Working Parents and the Revolution at Home.* New York: Avon.

Kaufman, Jason and Jay Gabler. 2004. "Cultural Capital and the Extracurricular Activities of Girls and Boys in the College Attainment Process." *Poetics.* Vol. 32: 145–168.

Kleiber, Douglas and Gwynn M. Powell. 2005. "Historical Change in Leisure Activities During After-School Hours." pp. 23–44 in Joseph L. Mahoney, Reed W. Larson, and Jacqeulynne S. Eccles (eds). *Organized Activities as Contexts of Development: Extracurricular Activities, After-School and Community Programs.* Mahwah, NJ: Lawrence Erlbaum Associates.

Lambert, Bruce. June 7, 2007. "He's 9 Years Old and a Video-Game Circuit Star." *The New York Times.*

Lareau, Annette. 2003. *Unequal Childhoods: Class, Race, and Family Life.* Berkley, CA: University of California.

Levey, Hilary. Forthcoming. "Pageant Princesses and Math Whizzes: Understanding Children's Activities as a Form of Children's Work." *Childhood*.

Maguire, James. 2006. *American Bee: The National Spelling Bee and the Culture of Word Nerds, The Lives of Five Top Spellers as they Compete for Glory and Fame*. New York: Rodale.

Margolin, Leslie. 1994. *Goodness Personified: The Emergence of Gifted Children*. New York: Aldine.

Markovits, Andrei S. and Steven L. Hellerman. 2001. *Offside: Soccer and American Exceptionalism*. Princeton, NJ: Princeton University Press.

Newman, Katherine S. 1994. *Declining Fortunes*. New York: Basic Books.

Passer, Michael. 1988. "Determinants and Consequences of Children's Competitive Stress." Pg. 203–227 in Frank L. Smoll, Richard A. Magill, Michael J. Ash (eds). *Children in Sport* (3rd Edition). Champaign, IL: Human Kinetics Books.

Pennington, Bill. November 12, 2003. "As Team Sports Conflict, Some Parents Rebel." *The New York Times*. Section A, Page 1, Column 4.

Powell, Robert Andrew. 2003. *We Own This Game: A Season in the Adult World of Youth Football*. New York: Grove Atlantic.

Quart, Alissa. 2006. *Hothouse Kids: The Dilemma of the Gifted Child*. New York: The Penguin Press.

Rosenfeld, Alvin. 2001. *The Over-Scheduled Child*. New York: St. Martin's Press.

Ryan, Joan. 2000. *Little Girls in Pretty Boxes: The Making and Breaking of Elite Gymnastics and Figure Skaters*. New York: Warner Books.

Sand, Barbara Lourie. 2000. *Teaching Genius: Dorothy DeLay and the Making of a Musician*. Pompton Plains, NJ: Amadeus Press.

Saint Louis, Catherine. July 19, 2007. "Train Like a Pro, Even if You're 12." *The New York Times*.

Seefeldt, Vern. 1998. "The Future of Youth Sport in America." Pg. 335–348 in Frank L. Smoll, Richard A. Magill, Michael J. Ash (eds). *Children in Sport* (3rd Edition). Champaign, IL: Human Kinetics Books.

Sheff, David. July 20, 2006. "For 7th Grade Jocks, Is There Ever an Off-Season?" *The New York Times*.

Spence, Janet T. 1985. "Achievement American Style: The Rewards and Costs of Individualism." *American Psychologist*. 40(12): 1285–1295.

Stanley, Anna. 1989. *Producing Beauty Pageants: A Director's Guide*. San Diego, CA: Box of Ideas Publishing.

Stearns, Peter N. 2003. *Anxious Parents: A History of Modern Childrearing in America*. New York: New York University Press.

Talbot, Margaret. September 21, 2003. "Why, Isn't He Just the Cutest Brand-Image Enhancer You've Ever Seen?" *The New York Times Magazine*.

The Insider. March 11, 2005. "Tiny Texas Cheerleaders!"

Willen, Liz. February 14, 2003. "New Yorkers Queue to Buy their Kids a Future." Bloomberg.

Williams, Alex. December 9, 2007. "And for Sports, Kid, Put Down 'Squash.'" *The New York Times*.

Zelizer, Viviana A. 1994. *Pricing the Priceless Child*. Princeton, NJ: Princeton University Press.

Flight Toward Maturity: The Tooth Fairy

Cindy Dell Clark

INTRODUCTION

Did you welcome the tooth fairy when you lost your first teeth? Through interviews with children and parents, author Cindy Dell Clark takes an up close look at this widely practiced ritual. She finds that it serves the needs of both children and their parents. On the one hand, the money that the tooth fairy brings might offer comfort to a child who has experienced the pain and fear associated with losing a tooth. But by encouraging their children to believe in a fictional character, parents can reassure themselves that their child still believes in fantasy and has not totally "grown up" just yet.

. . . MAGICAL HEALING TO THE RESCUE

A better informant could not have been found to tell us about the contemporary American Tooth Fairy than Jimmy, a seven-and-a-half-year-old middle-class boy of Italian-Irish extraction living on Chicago's northwest side. Jimmy had lost his front tooth (the sixth baby tooth—or as they say, "milk tooth"—he had lost) about two weeks before I interviewed him at home one autumn day. Jimmy's mother alerted me to the situation. This last tooth was wiggling for a couple of weeks, and he wanted it out in the worst way. It was bothering Jimmy. Then one morning, getting ready to leave for school, he was in the back bathroom brushing his teeth. His mother called to him to come so she could brush his hair. All of a sudden she heard a scream, then tears and crying. He had been brushing his teeth when the bothersome tooth had fallen out and gone down the bathroom drain.

Jimmy's tears didn't surprise his mother:

> He couldn't leave his tooth for the Tooth Fairy if he didn't have the tooth. . . . And I said, "It's OK, Jimmy, I'll call Uncle Joe . . . and maybe he could take the sink apart and get the tooth." I wasn't really going to ask him to take the sink apart, but he had to get to school. And then I told him that night that "they couldn't get it apart. But it happened to a friend of ours, when they did take it apart, they couldn't find the tooth anyway. But maybe if you left a letter for the Tooth Fairy." So he did and taped it to the front door.

Taping the note to the front door (for the Tooth Fairy to see as she "flies by") seemed to do the trick. "She gave me the money and everything," Jimmy explained to me—and he still had the dollar squirreled away in a drawer. What Jimmy didn't know was that his mother had saved the note he wrote and had tucked it in her wallet along with her mercenary "valuables." Penned in Jimmy's own printing, the note read:

> Dear The Tooth Fairy,
> Sorry the tooth can't come because I was brushing my teeth and it fell down the drain.
> Love, Jimmy

Jimmy was sure that the Tooth Fairy is a she, as most children I've interviewed would agree, even though he had not personally seen her. With exceptional imagination, Jimmy speculated that the Fairy might live in "some dentist's office" hiding somewhere unbeknownst to the dentist. ("If she's an inch small like I think she is, she'd be in a drawer somewhere.") It was no coincidence that the Fairy was associated, in Jimmy's mind, with a dentist: Her job has to do with the trauma of losing a tooth and children's fear of toothlessness.

CDC: If you were going to talk to somebody like your little brother, and they never lost a tooth before and they didn't know anything at all about the Tooth Fairy, what would you tell them about it?

JIMMY: I might tell them that when you lose your tooth, you put it under the pillow. The next morning you'll get something for it. And not to worry because you'll get another tooth. You won't be toothless after you lose all your teeth.

CDC: It's important to know you're not going to be toothless, a kid should know that part?

JIMMY (nodding): The tooth they lost, I think they'll understand it better and not think it'll hurt or anything.

CDC: You think kids think it might hurt?

JIMMY (nodding): The fairy godmother, if they never saw the tooth, I think they might [think that].

CDC: What if the Tooth Fairy stopped coming? What if the Tooth Fairy said, "I'm tired of doing this. . . . I'm not going to come any more when kids lose their teeth? How would that be?"

JIMMY: I'd just glue the tooth back into my mouth. I'd leave it glued. And you don't really deserve any money for it, just a tooth.

CDC: What's more important, getting the money or getting another tooth?

JIMMY: Getting another tooth.

From a child's perspective, the Tooth Fairy is a way to handle the *loss* of the tooth—far more than many parents realize. This aspect is foregrounded in Jimmy's case because Jimmy had experienced a double loss: losing the already lost tooth down the bathroom drain. In turn, Jimmy's transaction with the Tooth Fairy centers on loss: "Sorry the tooth can't come because I was brushing my teeth and it fell down the drain" is Jimmy's explicit message to the Tooth Fairy. "Sorry you lost your tooth, but you'll get another one, and here's some money in the meantime" is the Tooth Fairy's implicit message to Jimmy.

So important is the easing of this loss that Jimmy guesses that God himself gave the Tooth Fairy her job.

CDC: How did the Tooth Fairy get started doing this, do you suppose?

JIMMY: Probably God made them. . . . One day Adam or Eve, either one, lost their tooth, and didn't know what to do with it. So God spoke to them, and she told them, put your tooth when you're sleeping and it'll go away and you'll get something for it.

CDC: How come God knew they'd need to do that? . . . How do you think he thought they'd feel?

JIMMY: He figured, toothless! Then they might not be able to bite so well.

CDC: So God made the Tooth Fairy and said, put the tooth under your pillow, and that's that? What did the Tooth Fairy think about getting the job?

JIMMY: Happy, . . . because not too many people get to see God while they're living, and then the Tooth Fairy got to see him any time that she wanted to, if she had any questions or anything. And she was a very special person because people wouldn't want to be toothless.

Spiritual intervention to reassure kids that tooth loss won't hurt and won't be permanent is warranted, as far as Jimmy is concerned. His case is not exceptional. Children described to me a host of physical displeasures that can accompany losing a tooth. There is bleeding and discomfort when too much pressure is applied to the loose tooth, as when eating or when someone pulls a tooth. There is the potential of swallowing the tooth, which happened to a few young unfortunates. And there can be difficulty in talking. (The lisp lampooned in the song "All I Want for Christmas Is My Two Front Teeth" is indeed a reality for some kids; by some cruel mistiming of speech development, many kids begin to make sounds such as "th" just when they lose the teeth needed to make these sounds.) Children are enthusiastic about getting "big teeth" or "grown-up teeth," but there's certainly need for a lot of reassurance along the way.

Being reassured about losing one's teeth is undoubtedly a deep human need. In literature (including biblical literature) and folklore, teeth have long been characterized as representing potency, beauty, and pain. A terrible Old Testament curse was to appeal to God to break the teeth of one's enemies. Toothlessness is a state associated with helpless dependency, exemplified in infants and the elderly. Such expressions as "arming ourselves to the teeth" "fighting tooth and nail," and "escaping by the skin of our teeth" reveal the risk to power that the loss of teeth represents.[1]

Dreams of losing teeth are widely reported among adults, as Freud and others have noted, not only in Western culture but around the world. During an interview, one mother reported with a white-faced look of shock and fear a recent dream: She had dreamt of all her bottom teeth coming out, one by one. Years earlier, she dreamed she was appearing on the Johnny Carson show as the teeth fell out of her mouth and everyone stared. . . .

That tooth loss is such a rich metaphor for loss, retreat from power, and vulnerability would not surprise youngsters. Children experiencing second dentition, firsthand, make it clear how upsetting the experience can be. At times, I've been told, losing a tooth can be worse than getting stitches, or worse than getting allergy shots. The loose tooth is aggravating and "bothers you." It hurts when you eat or brush your teeth. The bleeding is "icky" and "disgusting"—sending some tooth losers into a near panic. Especially for the first tooth, one is apt to be scared: The required courage is itself enough to make you into a "big girl," a girl named Sarah told me. And the concern that one might remain toothless, as Jimmy described, is a serious matter to some children. After all, one uses teeth to chew and eat and thereby survive. Kids losing their first tooth can worry that they "won't have no teeth," in the words of one first-grade girl, and "won't be able to eat."

If there is enchantment in the Tooth Fairy ritual, it partly comes from its power to allay these concerns through the transformative meaning of expressive symbolism, turning second dentition into a positive, valued experience. Consider the story told by Peter, age seven, whose father took it upon himself to yank out the child's tooth personally (as it is not atypical for control-minded fathers to do).

> When we were at our grandmas for a sleepover, [my dad] said, "Come here," and he yanked it out. It hurted pretty much. . . . I didn't know what he was gonna do. Finally, he just reaches into my mouth and yanks it out, and I'm [shrieking noise]. I'm screaming and I go, "OOOOOWWWWWW." And I said, "Did you do it to me?" and he goes. "Yeah." And he shows me that [tooth]. And I didn't feel the pain' cause I started jumping up and down and saying, "Yeah! I'm gonna get the money!"

Jennifer (age eight), explaining why she thought the existence of the Tooth Fairy is a "good idea," also testified to an attitudinal shift provoked by the ritual.

> Sometimes when you're a little kid, I know when I was five, when I heard I was gonna lose my teeth, I said, "Well, am I ever gonna get it back? What's gonna happen to me? Will I be toothless for the rest of my life?" And so I sort of got a little scared. And I think that it was a good idea because when you lose it, then you get something in return. And you'll get a new one that's better.

The Tooth Fairy is largely a Western custom, having evolved in the cultural melting pot of the United States, most likely during the nineteenth century.[2] But all over the world, shed-tooth rituals of varied forms have eased this process for children. Anthropologists and dental folklorists report a remarkable array of such customs, whereby the lost deciduous tooth is discarded in some meaningful way.[3] For example, the tooth might be buried with an ancestor (New Guinea), in the hearth or fire (Sheffield, England, ca. 1895), or at the entrance to the lodge (Teton); left for a squirrel (Bohemia) or beaver (Cherokee) or some other straight-toothed animal; blackened with charcoal (Chippewa); or tossed into a mouse's hole (Mexico) or into the sea for a many-toothed dolphin (Patagonia). Often, some kind of incantation is spoken aloud when the tooth is placed. In Vietnamese society, children toss the tooth over the roof of the house (if an upper tooth) or onto the ground (if a lower tooth), calling out to the rats: "Oh rats! Oh rats! Since your teeth are both long and pointed, you must work in such a way that mine shall grow as quickly as they fall out." A Cherokee child recites, "Beaver, put a new tooth into my jaw." . . .

A particularly exotic form of shed-tooth ritual occurs among the Wendish population of Spreewald: The parents are supposed to swallow their child's tooth—mother swallowing a son's, father swallowing a daughter's (parental control indeed!).

With striking regularity, the developmental process is aided by external powers (such as ancestors or potent animals), who are called upon to give good, straight teeth. Often this involves what anthropologists term "sympathetic magic"—calling upon an object with the necessary qualities (say a rodent with strong, prominent teeth) to impart these qualities to the needy party. (Presumably, dentistry, with its X-ray magic, reduces the worry about good, straight replacement teeth in our culture, since dentistry itself explains the process, to adults at least.)

Yet even with modern medicine, a child's body image needs to accommodate the loss of a body part, be it tonsils removed through surgery, hair cut off by the barber, or natural loss of teeth.[4] To come to terms with losing "a part of you," it is therapeutic—even cathartic—that the baby tooth be purposefully put to rest, rather than tossed off at random. The analogy to a funeral runs deep, in that the tooth is entrusted to a higher, supernatural domain (the realm of the Tooth Fairy) as a kind of final resting place.

The grief involved in coping with loss, whether loss of a loved one or of a body part, needs to be expressed. Ritual provides a way to work through the separation and to discharge fear and apprehension about a new status.[5] Even children sense the analogy to a funeral: When thinking about offering a tooth to the Tooth Fairy, Lisa was reminded of her backyard burial of a dead goldfish (buried ceremonially—and perhaps too appropriately—in the empty matchbox from a seafood restaurant).

Just as a corpse is placed in a casket prior to burial, a tooth is commonly placed in a special receptacle, a Tooth Fairy pouch, to wait for the Tooth Fairy's exchange. Such Tooth Fairy pouches are a fairly recent innovation, thought to be invented by Elizabeth Bryant of Winter Park, Florida, in 1974,[6] but since then widely copied. A Tooth Fairy pouch is usually a hand-crafted item, either crocheted, embroidered, or hand sewn. (My son has a wooden box bought at a church crafts fair, shaped and hand painted to look like a tooth.) Tooth pillows or pouches are commonly made for the child by a relative or perhaps purchased from the individual women who make them at crafts fairs. Often, a relative or friend gives a Tooth Fairy pouch to a child as a gift, before the child loses any baby teeth. Such a gift has the social effect of endorsing the Tooth Fairy custom and encouraging that the healing ritual be observed.

FEMININITY AND FAIRIES

Jimmy imagined the Tooth Fairy to be a miniature female, and this was a common perception in the imaginal experience of children. When asked to draw the Tooth Fairy, children drew pastel-colored female figures, often with wings or wands.

Cultural symbols tend to have systematic, interrelated meaning. Pastels are colors we associate with being female (or a baby). Fairies are female, not male: Who has ever heard of a fairy godfather? Intriguingly, the popular use of the word *fairy* to refer to a male homosexual has been used to satirize the Tooth Fairy in cartoons in dental journals, as if to underscore that she is actually female. By taking on a feminine gender, the Tooth Fairy identifies herself as belonging to the realm of home, domesticity, mothers, and early childhood (as opposed to the more mature, literate male world outside the home).

In her therapeutic, healing role, the Tooth Fairy deals with tooth-shedding children in a mode more feminine than masculine. There are ancient precedents for differing approaches to healing among female as opposed to male healers. Dental hygienists, typically female, take their name and their approach to health from the goddess Hygeia, who represented health as an ongoing, natural process of living wisely. . . . These female beings represented nurturance, warmth, concern, intuitive understanding, and relatedness, the very qualities children ascribe to the Tooth Fairy.

A RITE OF PASSAGE

As a part of the body, the baby tooth is symbolic not only of lost power and vulnerability, but of early childhood itself. For children, giving up their first teeth is symbolic of relinquishing early childhood and getting "big teeth" (so that, as one girl said, "no one can call you a baby"). How fitting, then, that Peter Pan—the mythical boy who never grew up—never gave up his baby teeth (and thereby avoided growing older).

Mothers are well aware that losing one's baby teeth constitutes a rite of passage, a milestone along the course of growing up. In interviews mothers drew comparisons between second dentition and other life transitions important in contemporary America: learning to walk or to ride a two-wheel bike, kindergarten, . . . Roman Catholic First Communion, . . . and so on. Explaining what the Tooth Fairy custom represents to her, Mrs. Smith replied:

> A rite of passage [laughter]. I don't know what better words to say to you. I don't know whatever words would fit it, except every kid loses their teeth in order to get their new teeth to grow up. So, it's a rite of passage.

Time and again, mothers said that tooth loss is a public, tangible sign that their child was "growing up," "getting older," and entering a stage of greater independence ("he's leaving us," "getting independent"). The change in a child's physical appearance during second dentition makes it hard for a mother to ignore her child's increasing maturity. As Mrs. Brown put it:

> If you look at someone and they're missing a tooth, [they] look really different. Or say a child who loses two at once in the front, and they start lisping. It just changes their way of talking, their looks. And when their baby teeth go and their adult teeth come in, it changes their whole look. . . . I used to try to picture my kids with adult teeth, with secondary teeth. [I'd think,] This kid is so cute right now. How in the world can he be any cuter with secondary teeth? Isn't that a weird thing to think? But I did. I used to look at their pictures from kindergarten and think, oh, I wish they could stay like this. I wish their little teeth could stay. . . . You don't have a choice in losing teeth. It happens. No one can get around it.

Second dentition, in American society, occurs simultaneously with the child's transition from home to formal education, associated with a host of other changes, such as learning to read and write, that indeed serve to make a boy or girl more independent of home and more socially and cognitively skilled within the public domain outside the home. Getting grown-up teeth signals that a child is ready for this major shift in arenas. Kindergarten and first-grade teachers often keep charts in their classrooms that mark the occasion when children lose teeth, treated as a cause for celebration. One educational researcher has gone so far as to suggest that second dentition should be used to judge school readiness, since it correlates well with other measures of readiness.[7]

Tooth loss, then, is a natural symbol of shedding one developmental stage and entering another. This is not unique to American society. Across cultures, it is common for children in the five-to-seven-year age range to shift social status and expectations with second dentition. The Ngoni of Malawi, in central Africa, believe that "children who [have] lost their first teeth, and acquired their second, [have] reached a new stage in their development." When Ngoni children complete second dentition, they are held accountable for discourtesy, they are recognized as "ready for a different kind of life," and boys change places of residency.[8] . . .

The loss of a deciduous tooth naturally *separates* the child from babyhood (just as ceremonies of mutilation accompany the separation phase of many initiation rites). Second, the child enters a naturally produced period of *ambiguity*—toothlessness—that embodies (quite literally) the "invisible" qualities often associated with the transition phase. (Jokes and humorous teasing are common at this ambiguous stage—called by dentists and some mothers the "ugly duckling" phase.) Third, the natural eruption of the secondary tooth quite literally *incorporates* in the child grown-up qualities. The three-part rite of passage is literally carried out as a bodily code in second dentition. . . .

. . . In the American Tooth Fairy custom: (1) The child *leaves* their tooth under the pillow to be *taken away* by a fairy (a Tinker Bell–like symbol of early childhood); (2) The child then goes to sleep amid dreamlike darkness (which gives effective invisibility and ambiguity); (3) The child awakens to find a gift of money (a symbol of the worldly, adult domain of grown-up people).

Because the Tooth Fairy visits repeatedly as successive teeth are lost, the actual sequence is not definitive and closed in its impact. (In this respect, the Tooth Fairy custom may differ from shed-tooth rituals in other cultures, where it is common to ritually discard only the *first* lost tooth.) Children lose teeth, one by one, over a period of years—in effect, an extended period of being betwixt and between, what dentists call "mixed dentition."

The child's belief in the Tooth Fairy also goes through a period of being betwixt and between, as children begin to doubt the Tooth Fairy as a separate figure and perhaps try to stay awake at night to catch the real fairy in the act. At this stage children are apt to vacillate between rational certainty and hopeful belief. One boy who completely discounted the Tooth Fairy's reality regained his faith entirely when he had to have two teeth pulled. The developmental process is fraught with paradox, reversal, and gradual change.

But eventually the child stops believing in the Tooth Fairy, once and for all. The emergence of disbelief is itself said by mothers to be a rite of passage. As Mrs. Martin expressed it:

> Anytime you have a kid that still believes in something magical. It still makes you feel that they're still little. Because as soon as they stop believing in all that stuff, and they're not involved in all the fun stuff that you do when you're little kid, and then you finally realize that, OK, they figured it out, they're smart enough now, it's another stepping stone.

Once children become disenchanted with the Tooth Fairy, they have, in effect, embraced adult-defined reality. The quintessential accusation of adult naïveté is the oft-heard comment "If you believe that, I bet you still believe in the Tooth Fairy." The Tooth Fairy metaphorically provides a kind of reality check, a check to see if one is living in a "childish, fairy-tale" world, or in a "rational, mature" world.

Typically, American mothers are not eager to break the bonds of their child's tender dependency. The maternal hope, rather, is to slow the rate of separation from their child, to make sure that he/she "doesn't grow up too fast." One mother, whose son had started kindergarten the week of my interview with her, became tearful when discussing her son's lost babyhood. Mothers certainly want their children to feel "special" when they lose a tooth. But they are not anxious for their children to stop believing in the Tooth Fairy, signaling the end of childhood in a fuller sense than losing a tooth. During interviews, mothers nervously double-checked that young believers were out of earshot before explaining, in whispered tones, their deceptive role in acting out the ritual. Mrs. Adams spoke of her warning to older siblings—to "break your neck then and there"—if they told their younger brother there was no Tooth Fairy.

According to mothers' reasoning, the harsh reality of (adult) society is held at bay as long as the childish world of make-believe (Santa Claus, the Easter Bunny, and the Tooth Fairy) is maintained. Mrs. O'Connor, explaining why she wished *she* could still be a child, said that, as a child, "I wouldn't have to worry about anything [because] as a kid, it always seems like it's such a make-believe world. Then you grow up and there's reality." This sentiment was echoed in Mrs. Green's comment.

> I would love him to believe in Santa for long. I want him to believe in everything. I want Danny to believe the whole world's fine, everything's wonderful, and all these great things happen to little kids. . . . I think it's very important that they just let their imagination go and go and go. Because eventually they're going to get older and they're going to realize, and that'll be it.

Maintaining a child's belief gives the mother some force toward extending childhood: Having a role as the Tooth Fairy vividly ensures that the child is "underneath my wings" (to quote the words of Mrs. White):

> I'm still known as Tooth Fairy. . . . it's kind of, I've kept them children—even though they do go and get on their bicycles and they ride down the block and see a friend. This is the one thing that keeps them underneath my wings, and I still have them in protection. . . . Even though they think, "i'm old, and my two-wheel bike, and I can cross the alley," . . . yet there's part, they are kids yet. 'Cause they still believe that. I think I might, the day I have to explain about Santa and the Tooth Fairy, I think I'll be a little crushed. Because it's almost like a magic spell I've broken a part of, another sign of growing up when this [ends,] the fairy tale, the imagination. 'Cause you want to cushion your kids. And you'd love to think you can cushion them all their life.

Out of thirty-two mothers interviewed about the Tooth Fairy, twenty-two kept their child's shed primary tooth/teeth after collecting them. The tooth was said to serve as a memento or reminder of the child's babyhood. Often, these dental keepsakes were put in a location signifying special value, such as the mother's jewelry box, a baby book, or, as with Jimmy's note, a wallet. Like bronzed baby shoes, a child's christening dress, or trimmings from a child's first haircut (or even, as true for one mother, a saved pacifier), the retained teeth were valued tokens of their child's first life stage. As best illustrated by their own comments, mothers hesitate to relinquish that first life stage completely.

> They just change so quickly, you can't hold on to it. But you can hold on to their teeth or a lock of their hair or something like that.
> Sometimes I stop and look at them [the teeth in my jewelry box] and sort of, I'll notice them, and I'll stop. And it's always amazing to me that they're so tiny. I suppose that's what I notice about them if I stop to notice them. Because, you know, adult teeth are really quite large. And these things are just teeny-weeny, teeny-weeny little teeth. Of course, they were teeny-weenier people, too. My older one is almost thirteen, so she thinks she's grown up.

In essence, the Tooth Fairy ritual provides the American mother with symbolic "reverse gears" that decelerate the process of recognizing their son's or daughter's new age status. By saving the child's primary teeth until feeling ready to discard them and by steadfastly protecting her child's belief in the Tooth Fairy (so much so that telling a child the truth is taboo), the mother makes the child seem, in maternal perception, less grown up.

But what about the child's perspective on the ritual? It is the *growth-enhancing* meaning brought by the Tooth Fairy that motivates children to gladly undergo the discomforts of tooth loss. Children feel that their teeth are put to rest by the Tooth Fairy in a suitably reverent manner: deposited in her ethereal home, which, like heaven, is "up there," in the sky, far away. Many youngsters imagine that the Fairy uses the teeth to make something valuable—jewelry, flowers, even stars. One child thought that she gives the tooth to a new baby, recycling it.

And children feel that the Tooth Fairy gives them fair compensation, in the form of money, for their shed teeth. Money is a grown-up, empowering entity. In American society, money is a symbolic means to obtain power and independence. No doubt money is made all the more culturally attractive by its early association with the awe-inspiring, supernatural Tooth Fairy: Several young informants felt that the monetary gift was manufactured by the Tooth Fairy with the aid of her magic wand.

Children perceive having money as a way to "buy whatever I want," to have buying power that is not dependent on parental benefactors. Six-year-old Carson said that, after the Tooth Fairy's visit, "I feel like I am a new person. . . . I feel like I'm seven"—partly due to the fact that "I lost lots of teeth," but also because "When you get older you get money." Eight-year-old Jan told the story of saving her Tooth Fairy money in order to treat her mother and sister to a snack at McDonald's—a gesture that led her to observe, "I like carrying around my own money. I feel more grown up and special." When their supply of Tooth Fairy money was kept at home, children were prone to run and fetch their stash of cash and to finger through it, Scrooge-like, while showing it to me. Several children had bank accounts in which to "save for college"—the ultimate training ground for adulthood. Clearly, the possession of money makes children feel independent (since independently wealthy) and empowered. The money received from the Tooth Fairy is a valued treasure connoting a degree of autonomy, escalating the child's sense that they are older, more grown up. The icons of maturity within the Tooth Fairy ritual are plural: The child gets adult teeth, but also gets money as a symbol of being grown up.

Writing encodes another form of maturity: literacy. Written correspondence between the child and the Tooth Fairy is a common occurrence. Letter writing typically begins out of necessity, such as when the child misplaces the lost tooth (as with Jimmy) or wants to ask the Tooth Fairy if they can keep the tooth. Occasionally, the correspondence starts at the mother's/Tooth Fairy's initiative ("Congratulations on losing your first tooth," or "Keep brushing your teeth"). A few young informants had decided to carry on extensive exchange of notes with the Tooth Fairy, so as to question her about certain facts ("Do you look like the picture in the book we have about you? [ ] Yes [ ] No"). In two families, this note writing became so extensive that the Tooth Fairy impersonator developed her own signature and handwriting (in very tiny letters) to use in replies. Ironically, as mothers used correspondence to encourage their daughter's or son's belief, all the while children were getting practice in the grown-up skills of reading and writing.

Here, then, is the paradoxical dynamic of the Tooth Fairy ritual, which makes it an apt (yet subtly complex) family rite. Some symbolic elements within this rite of passage, the money, the acquired secondary tooth, and—where applicable—the note writing, serve as accelerators that make a child feel older. Other symbolic elements, such as the belief in fairies and the primary tooth, are counterbalanced decelerators, used by a mother to slow down the growing-up process. Mother and child subconsciously pull and push, respectively, as they jointly determine the degree of social maturity to be attributed to the tooth-losing child. The outcome is gradual, flexible, interactive, and dynamic. The flight toward maturity is not, by any means, straightforward, unidirectional, or mechanical. . . . There are symbolic and human forces of both drag and lift alike.

Considering the experience of children leads to the realization that the Tooth Fairy ritual holds much complexity of meaning. The custom helps the child to undergo unavoidable physical transformation involving some discomfort. At the same time, it helps the family to work through the child's new status as an older, more independent person. It is a remarkable paradox that the Fairy's delivery of money, the symbolic means that helps a child feel older, simultaneously helps the mother to perceive the child as still young, since still believing. . . .

Children naturally concoct rituals to make themselves feel comfortable at bedtime (stories, stuffed animals, special pillowcases, and so on), and parents willingly participate.[9] Often, imaginal experience is part and parcel of such rituals sleeping with a special teddy bear friend, saying nighttime prayers, or expecting that the superheros depicted on the pillowcase will give protection. Understanding how such rituals work to ease the experience of all the individuals involved may well reveal dynamics as complex as those in the Tooth Fairy ritual. . . .

Far from trivial, the Tooth Fairy is a being who arrives on the scene during an important juncture in contemporary children's lives and delivers gifts (both tangible and spiritual) that are healing and enabling.

Discussion Questions

1. What purposes does the Tooth Fairy serve for children? For adults?

2. Discuss the role that consumption plays in the tooth fairy ritual.

3. What other rituals offer similar benefits to both children and their parents?

4. Did the Tooth Fairy "visit" you as a child? How did you feel when you learned that this ritual was make–believe?

Notes

1. Theodore Ziolkowski, "The Telltale Teeth: Psychodontia to Sociodontia," *PMLA* 91 (1976): 9–22.
2. William Carter, Bernard Butterworth, and Joseph Carter, *Ethnodentistry and Dental Folklore* (Kansas City, KS: Dental Folklore Books of Kansas City, 1987), 77. "Attitude toward and Special Treatment of Developmental Events." Human Relations Area Files, Topical Classification no. 856. Regenstein Library, University of Chicago.
3. "Attitude toward and Special Treatment of Developmental Events." Human Relations Area Files, Topical Classification no. 856.
4. Joyce Robertson, "A Mother's Observations of the Tonsillectomy of Her Four Year Old Daughter (with Commentary by Anna Freud)." *Psychoanalytic Study of the Child* 11 (1956): 410–33.
5. T. J. Scheff, *Catharsis in Healing, Ritual, and Drama* (Berkeley and Los Angeles: University of California Press, 1979).
6. Rosemary Wells, "The Tooth Fairy, Part II." *Cal Magazine,* February 1980, 18–24.
7. John Silvestro, "Second Dentition and School Readiness," *New York State Dental Journal* 43, no. 3 (1977): 155–58.
8. Barbara Rogoff et al., "Age of Assignment of Roles and Responsibilities in Children: A Cross-Cultural Survey," *Human Development* 18, no. 5 (1975): 354.
9. Stuart Albert et al., "Children's Bedtime Rituals as a Prototype Rite of Safe Passage," *Journal of Psychological Anthropology* 2, no. 1 (1979): 85–105.

Kids and Commerce

VIVIANA ZELIZER

INTRODUCTION

Rarely has anyone outside of market research studied how children spend their money. Traditional approaches view children as gullible and uninformed consumers. In Zelizer's examination of children's economic activities in the United States and abroad, she finds that the organization, consequences, and meanings that children create vary. Children not only engage in economic activity while shopping, but with family members and one another.

Here are four vignettes of children's economic activities:

1. Studying children's vital labor contributions to their parents' Chinese take-away family businesses in Britain, Miri Song reports how children carefully differentiated 'helping out' from formal employment. Parents' payments, for instance, were seldom treated as ordinary wages. As Anna, one of Song's respondents, recalled:

> We never asked for more, 'Cause it was seen as a bonus, 'cause we worked anyway. And it was just like a little token gesture to buy yourself a record or something nice to read. (Song, 1999: 85)

2. Elizabeth Chin's ethnographic account of 10-year-old, poor and working-class black children's consumption practices in Newhallville, New Haven, documents, among other patterns, children's contrasting relationships to shopkeepers in local neighborhood stores and downtown shops. Asia, one of Chin's young informants, tells her about her experience at Claire's, a popular jewelry shop in the downtown mall:

> 'Last time I was in there the lady was laughing because I didn't have enough money. The other day I went in, and I bought all this stuff and the lady said, 'that will be forty dollars.' I pulled out a fifty-dollar bill and said, "Here".' Asia demonstrated how she slapped the bill down on the counter, and the look on her face was both self-satisfied and challenging. 'I swear I was about to say "keep the change" until my grandmother came up.' (Chin, 2001: 103)

3. Observing children's birthday party practices among Parisian middle-class families, Régine Sirota found very young kids actively participating in gift selection. Until he was 3, for instance, Adrien's mother chose his friends' birthday gifts, but then the pattern shifted:

> She [now] always shops with him, accepting his choices. These are often the result of earlier negotiations among peers during recess: thus Tom (7 years old) arranged with his school pals to get what he wants: a stuffed Marsupilami, Batmans, a book about Knights of the Roundtable that one of them already owns. (Sirota, 1998: 458)

4. Bill Berkeley has been analyzing African political conflicts and covering them in major American media for two decades. He reports on a return to Liberia, where he earlier had been banned for his critical reporting. Here is one of the things he saw:

> On a Saturday morning in June 1992, the Liberian port of Buchanan sweltered in the dense tropical humidity of West Africa's rainy season. Four small boys ambled up a muddy and pothole-ridden sidewalk and entered a tea stall on the city's main street. They looked to be scarcely older than ten. Dressed in baggy jeans and grimy T-shirts, not much taller than the loaded Soviet-era Kalashnikov assault rifles they cradled in their arms, the boys shuffled heavily in big brown military boots that on them resembled the outsized paws on a puppy. 'How the day?' one of them muttered.
>
> A shudder ran down my spine. The bullets were bigger than his fingers. The boy brushed by the stool where I was sitting and approached the woman who owned the stall. He lifted his fingers to his mouth. The owner dutifully fetched some bananas and buttered some rolls. The boys shuffled out onto the street—no word of thanks, no suggestion of payment—savoring their breakfast as they walked. (Berkeley, 2001: 21)

These vignettes open up the largely uncharted economic worlds of children. Masked by persistent assumptions of children's remoteness from processes of production, consumption and distribution, children's economic practices have remained closeted, camouflaged by the supposedly exclusive dominance of play and learning over market activity. The image of an impenetrable (and desirable) barrier between children and the economy has so taken hold that it has produced a stock character in recent American humor: the child who dresses up in adult economic garments. Remember how deftly Charles Schultz (1999), whose *Peanuts* portrayed a perfectly separate world of childhood, lampooned Lucy's setting herself up in business as a 5-cent psychiatrist on the model of a child entrepreneur and a lemonade stand.

On the other side, the looming image of child labor as a corrupting force has also inhibited careful examination of children's economic activity. Long before Bill Berkeley's hardened child soldiers and anti-sweatshop campaigners' regimented child garment workers, the photographs of Jacob Riis warned Americans that premature economic involvement would make children old—and evil—before their time.

. . . To be sure, people have long since studied some features of childhood economic activity. Investigations of early socialization, for instance, extensively document children's cognitive understandings of work and money. Other scholars have concerned themselves with the moral or developmental impact of economic activity on children's welfare: does paid labor help or hinder children's schooling? Will an allowance turn the child into a better consumer? Does consumption tarnish kids' moral worlds? Does poverty encourage consumerist youngsters to steal and to take up dangerous occupations so they can acquire media-hyped goods? Most of these queries are framed by an adult point of view, asking how children understand the adult economy, how they learn it, how they fit in and how it affects them. . . .

My book *Pricing the Priceless Child* (Zelizer, 1985) emphasized adults' changing orientations to children in the US between the 1870s and 1930s. That emphasis proved fruitful; it brought out adults' increasing valuation of children not for their economic contributions but for their distinctive personal characteristics. It did not reach very far, however, into children's own experiences of economic change. This article reverses the perspective by considering children as active economic agents, and adults as simply one category of persons with whom children carry on economic activities.

Despite demands such as Deborah Levison's (2000) for consideration of children as authentic economic agents, the recent upsurge of work on children in the economy has also generally incorporated an adult perspective. . . .

Nevertheless, an increasing minority of specialists in childhood have been calling for a deliberate shift of perspective from adults' observations or reactions to children's own economic lives. The vignettes with which we began represent an important revision in perspective.

Marketing specialists actually got there first, identifying children as savvy, active economic agents. As the authoritative researcher James U. McNeal (1999) reports, over the past two decades, marketing for children has gone from a laughing stock to a major industry. In fact, in some respects, academic scholars have not yet caught up with market researchers: there are vast stores of information on children still untapped in the files and publications of marketing experts. McNeal extensively documents the multiple business potential of a growing 'kids market', as primary markets (spending their own money), influence markets (shaping their parents' expenditures) and future markets.

American children between the ages of 4 and 12, reports McNeal, with an annual income of over $27 billion, spend $23 billion, and save what is left. Over $7 billion a year of children's own money goes for snacks and a similar amount for play items. They influence about $188 billion of their parent's spending each year (McNeal, 1999: 29). Children's consumer power is not only an American phenomenon. In China's newly marketized economy, for instance, McNeal and his collaborators at China's Beijing University found that urban children control $6 billion per year in purchases, as well as influencing around 68 percent of their parents' consumption expenditures (McNeal, 1999: 250, 259). That consumption notably includes western-style snack food; in Asia, McDonalds and Kentucky Fried Chicken draw their principal customers from among children (Lozada, 2000; Watson, 1997).

Children, however, engage in a far wider range of economic activity than shopping (in this [chapter] 'children' means 14 years of age or younger). Despite the illusion of a historic shift of children from production to consumption, children have long engaged simultaneously in production, consumption and distribution as well. What has changed is the character of their engagement in these three spheres. To see these changes clearly, we must examine children themselves at work.

Recent research provides new ideas and information about children's place in economic production, consumption and distribution. It also helps identify three somewhat different sets of economic relations in which children regularly engage: with members (including adult members) of their own households, with children outside their households and with agents of other organizations such as outside households, schools, stores, firms, churches and voluntary associations. Contrary to cherished images of children as economic innocents, we discover children actively engaged in production, consumption and distribution. We also discover that their economic activity varies significantly from one category of social relations to another. . . .

I argue that:

- Once we examine social lives from children's own vantage points, we discover an extensive range of economic activity significantly differentiated by setting and social relation.
- On the whole, ethnographers have been more successful than other investigators in documenting that activity because they less often adopt adults' definitions of serious economic activity, rely less on individuals' conventionalized retrospective reports of activities, and more often observe negotiated social interaction as it occurs.
- Children develop extensive connections with adult-dominated spheres of production, consumption and distribution, but generally experience those encounters as unequal exercises of power.
- Despite adult efforts to contain them, they also establish segregated, partly autonomous spheres of production, consumption and distribution on their own.
- It is therefore useful to adopt rough distinctions among three sets of social relations: with other household members, especially adults; with agents of organizations outside children's own households; with other children.
- In all these social relations, children negotiate understandings and practices with other participants, however unequally they do so. . . .

In keeping with the common assumption of the child as consumer rather than as producer or distributor, researchers have so far given much more attention to consumption practices. This article again reverses the perspective by stressing production and distribution before turning to a briefer sketch of consumption. In each of these three sectors we find differentiation of children's economic activities depending on their predominant social relations. We focus here on three types of relations: with other household members; with agents of organizations outside the household; with other children.

CHILDREN AS PRODUCERS

. . . Production here means any effort that creates value (see Tilly and Tilly, 1998). Such a definition obviously includes far more than the conventional paid employment and production for the market. In this framework, Miri Song's (1999) respondents are exceptionally active producers, fully collaborating in their parents' take-away shops. With some variation from family to family as well as by age and gender, she shows us children—often as young as 7 or 8—in the evenings, after school, or during weekends, cooking, cleaning and taking customers' orders. At times, children were also involved in caring labor, translating and mediating for their non-English-speaking parents (see also Orellana, 2001; Valenzuela, 1999).

These child workers carefully differentiated what they saw as their 'helping out' from formal employment. As we heard earlier from Anna, bargaining with an employer-parent created distinct economic practices, turning compensation, for instance, into a perk or a bonus, rather than a standard wage. In fact, some children refused any payment at all. Laura, another of Song's respondents' explained:

> It's because being a family business, it's part of our lives, and you don't think, it
> doesn't feel like real work, you know? It felt awkward, the idea of receiving a
> wage. (Song, 1999: 86)

In some cases, children, while uneasy about taking money for their labor, felt obliged to accept their parents' payments, more as filial recognition of parental provider status, than as
payment for work. Others, meanwhile, welcomed the money as tangible recognition of their
household contributions. Paul told Song:

> Paying us was a nice way to do it; it meant that we weren't just putting out a hand
> and taking money from our parents. We were actually helping out as well. I felt
> sort of quite justified having taken it. (Song, 1999: 86)

On the other hand, some children resented parents' payments as unwelcome bribes, forcing
them into work they disliked. In all these cases, instead of passively accepting their parents'
handouts or a standard wage, the children were bargaining out a distinctive set of meanings
corresponding to their relationships with their parent-employer.

Similar bargaining occurs in households that do not run their own businesses. In an . . .
analysis of 7-year-olds' economic behavior in Nottingham, John and Elizabeth Newson (1976)
document a wide range of household work for compensation among both middle-class and
working-class families. Children, their mothers report, brought in the coal, dusted, helped in
the garden, cleaned the car, washed pots, polished brass, cared for younger siblings, ran errands, vacuumed, fetched clothing, cleaned shoes and even tickled their father's feet. Once
again, parents and children bargained out compensation systems; a fireman's wife explains:

> Sometimes he'll go and help his Dad with the garden, but not a set rule; although
> I do sort of say that their pocket money—they are given it in return for running er-
> rands and washing pots and helping with the little ones. I mean, Saturday they
> have it, and they do two or three errands before they get their money—they get
> them done very quickly! (Newson and Newson, 1976: 227; for other British cases
> and a New Zealand parallel see Morrow, 1994; Fleming, 1997)

In the US as well, children participate in a variety of productive domestic tasks, such as cleaning up their rooms, cooking, dusting, doing laundry, washing dishes, vacuuming, setting or
clearing the table, cleaning the bathroom, sweeping floors, carrying out garbage, mowing the
lawn, cleaning the yard or caring for younger siblings and pets. A 9-year-old girl that Victoria
Chapman (1994) classified as one of her 'Chore Hounds' reported a very wide range of household tasks. Among other things, she helped her mother with grocery shopping:

> I push the carriage. I hold coupons that she uses, and usually the coupons that she
> does not use I hold and sometimes she'll tell me to go get something and I'll go
> get it. (Chapman, 1994: 167)

Recent studies report that American children are spending increasing amounts of their time in
such household chores (see, for example, Lee et al., 2000). Children's marketing specialist
McNeal (1999: 71) estimates that children in the US perform 11 percent of total household
work.

Likewise, Anne Solberg's (1994: 84) study of 11- and 12-year-old Norwegian children's household work speculates that children, especially girls, may be more significant assistants to mothers than their fathers are (this sort of substitution raises interesting questions

about parallels between child/parent, and spousal bargaining over household work; see, for example, Brines, 1994; Gerson, 1993; Greenstein, 2000; Hochschild, 1989; Hochschild and Machung, 1989; Lundberg and Pollak, 1996).

In most cases, children expect some kind of domestic payment. Parents agree. McNeal (1999; 69, 71) itemizes five different sources of children's cash income. In the late 1990s, 16 percent of kids' income came from gifts from parents, 8 percent from others' gifts, 45 percent from allowances, 10 percent from work outside the home and 21 percent from household work. Significantly, McNeal notes that children's compensation from household work rose to 21 percent from 15 percent in the mid-1980s. However, since parents are not standard employers, negotiating suitable payment systems turns into a delicate and highly contested issue. At issue is not merely a wage bargain but a definition of proper relations between parents and their offspring.

Indeed, the nature of children's allowances has excited debate for over a century, with some experts and parents strongly advocating compensation for children's household work, and others insisting on a separation between work effort and allowances. In the latter cases, allowances qualify not as compensation but as a parent's discretionary gift or the child's entitlement. Nevertheless, whether compensation, gift, or entitlement, allowances are subject to continual bargaining between parents and children.

Negotiations occur over both allowances and other monetary transfers. Parents, for their own part, often impose a set of terms, deciding which chores to compensate with money or overseeing, and in some cases closely supervising, children's expenditure. In these transactions, however, children do not simply echo parents' preferences for household payments, but work out their own moral views and strategies. *The Kids' Allowance Book* (Nathan, 1998), based on interviews with 166 children between the ages of 9 and 14 from 11 schools around the US, reports a variety of such rationales and strategies. Children, for instance, repeatedly praise regular allowances as welcome sources of discretionary income. Before getting an allowance, Katie explains: 'If I wanted a pair of special sneakers, [my parents] might say it's too expensive and not a necessity. Now that I get an allowance, if they don't want to pay, I can pay for it myself' (Nathan, 1998: 6).

Children divide, however, over whether or not allowances should compensate for their domestic chores, some children insisting that helping out is an expected, fair, and therefore free, household contribution. Others forcefully defend their often elaborate monetized exchanges. Listen, for instance, to Amanda:

> On top of all the cleaning and garbage toting Amanda B has to do for her allowance, she regularly does freebies like folding the clothes or setting the table. 'If I'm sitting around and my mom asks me to do something, I'll say sure and won't ask to get paid,' she says, 'I do it to help out.' But if she is saving up for something special, she'll hunt for a big job that needs doing, such as basement cleaning. Ugh! She'll ask if her mom will pay extra for it. That's when the freebies pay off. 'Since I'm not always working just for money, when I ask if she'll pay me to do something extra, she usually does.' (Nathan, 1998: 15)

Children report numerous, often intricate, negotiating tips, ranging from how to choose chores (pick your own, 'if your mom chooses, she might give you a chore you can't even bear the *thought* of doing'); getting a fair wage (find out what other kids earn); how to make sure parents pay on time ('I remind my dad on the day *before,* to make sure he has the right change for my allowance the next day'); how to get a raise ('no-nos' include whining, begging, asking for way too much, or not doing chores on time; among the 'dos': 'do lots of stuff to help out and be nice to your brother or sister [if you have one]', and 'ask for a slightly *bigger* raise than you want so you can give in a little and still come out okay') (Nathan, 1998: 55, 52, 20, 46).[1]

To understand this unexplored household economy fully, we need much more systematic information about actual bargaining between parents and children. . . . We know even less about children's production involving their peers, or with agents of organizations, including other households. When it comes to children working with peers, we draw on little more than sentimentalized visions of future self-made capitalists learning their skills on lemonade stands or sharing newspaper routes. Take *Rich Dad Poor Dad,* the runaway 1997 best-seller guide to financial success: its key inspirational anecdote shows us two 9-year-olds cashing in from their partnership renting comic books to other kids. They learned early 'to have money work for us. . . . By starting our own business, the comic-book library, we were in control of our own finances, not dependent on an employer' (Kiyosaki and Lechter, 1997: 52).

In such parables, we see only the above surface of what is surely a huge undersea continent. Only infrequently do researchers provide glimpses of what lies underneath. Consider, for instance, Elizabeth Chin's observations of how Tionna and Tiffany—two of her 10-year-old Newhallville informants—managed their cucumber stand, selling cucumbers one of them had grown in her backyard. Pricing their goods, Chin reports, settled into a delicate social bargain. They asked 40 cents for the larger cucumbers, a quarter for smaller ones. Unsure of how much to ask for a larger cucumber:

> Tionna suggested sixty cents. Tiffany wondered if it should be seventy-five. Then, with authority, Tionna announced the price should be fifty cents because then they could split it easier and wouldn't have to wait for some change. . . . Tiffany's grandmother came by and bought a large cucumber, putting fifty, rather than forty, cents into the pot. The kids would occasionally count the money and divide it into two equal piles, since they were planning to split the money equally. They ended up with each having about a dollar seventy-five. (Chin, 2001: 72–3) . . .

What about production for outside organizations, including other households? McNeal (1999: 72) reports that children's income from work outside the home, unlike their increasing pay for household work, has remained fairly stable at around 10–13 percent for children under 12. Children earn by baby-sitting, raking leaves, mowing lawns, watering plants, shoveling snow, cleaning garages, selling cookies, candies or lottery tickets to raise funds for school activities or charities, washing cars, taking care of pets, as runners or lookouts for drug dealers, watching cars, or as baggers at supermarkets. More recently, some 11- and 12-year-olds have been making money with investments and savings (McNeal, 1999: 72; see also Lewis, 2001). Once we shift our attention outside households, it becomes clear how many of children's activities involve production, including volunteer work, and as Jens Qvortrup (1995) has forcefully argued, school work.

Production outside households draws children into a new set of economic relationships with other adults/employers. Consider the case of the Norwegian *passepike* or baby-walker, 9- to 15-year-old girls who for a fee take care of children up to the age of 3 for a couple of hours in the afternoon. Studying *passepike* in Bergen, Marianne Gullestad (1992) gives an account of their economic arrangements with employers. The fee, for instance, is established in relation to what the girls' friends get and what other mothers pay. Far more goes into this relationship, Gullestad observes, than purchasing the carer's time: mothers of smaller children often give *passepike* holiday gifts, birthday presents and clothing. For their part the girl carers offer gifts to their charges and regularly do more than their contract requires: 'She comes in earlier or gladly changes and feeds the child before they go out. Or in addition . . . she may be a baby-sitter in the evening, may do the dishes, wash the floors, etc.' (Gullestad, 1992: 121). Close personal ties to the mother, suggests Gullestad, become part of the *passepike*'s reward system (for related American practices; see Formanek-Brunell, 1998) . . .

Over most or the world, relatively young children not only engage in the intermittent production relationships reviewed here, but also take up full-time paid employment in agriculture, manufacturing, services, or even the military. The point should already be clear: like that of their elders, children's production takes place within negotiated sets of social relations, and varies significantly as a function of those social relations' content and meaning.

CHILDREN AS DISTRIBUTORS

As with production, a quick survey of distribution shows children at work negotiating various ties within their households, with peers, and in relation to outside households and organizations. . . . From very early in their lives—perhaps later than when they begin consuming, but earlier than when we can meaningfully think of them as regular producers—children engage in economically significant transfers. Those transfers generally begin within children's own households, usually next turn to peers, but involve outside households and organizations from quite young ages.

Since distribution within households and with organizations is more obvious, let us concentrate on peers. Régine Sirota's (1998) observations of Parisian children's birthday parties show even very young kids actively engaged in their gift economy, starting with peer collusion in gift selection. Children negotiate not only with their parents, but also with each other over the quality, value and character of their gifts . . . In their negotiations, children are working simultaneously to hammer out appropriate terms with their peers and with their parents who (at least for younger gift-givers) subsidize purchases. The problem for children is that parents may not be willing to pay for the gift the child regards as most appropriate. For instance, Sirota reports one strong maternal gift rule, adjusting the gift's price to the strength of friendship ties: 'For great buddies, great gifts, for lesser friends, lesser gifts' (Sirota, 1998: 459).

As for the matching of gifts to children's networks, Sirota observed regular correspondence between the intensity of friendship ties and the personalization of gifts: closer friends are expected to pay careful attention to the other's taste. Sirota's respondents praise successful gift-givers: 'He pays real attention to what he offers' or, 'She always gives me something really pretty.' Personalization turns even less popular objects, such as books, into prized gifts. Julien bought Barbara partly with his own pocket money the book Joffo's *Agate et calots,* because 'he had adored *Un sac de billes,* which he had just read, he was sure she would like it' (Sirota, 1998: 461).

Children's gift transfers do not simply translate parental values or social position into material objects. On the contrary, children's own relations and understandings play a significant part in organizing the birthday gift economy. What is more, these are economically serious matters. Sirota calculates that the average household involved spends the French equivalent of $150 a year per child on birthday gift exchanges (the cost includes counter-gifts offered by the birthday celebrant to party guests). As they grow older, children themselves increasingly spend their own pocket money on such gifts, thereby acquiring greater control over the entire process. With appropriate adjustment for class and national culture, similar arrangements seem to be very widespread in western countries.

Birthday gift transfers represent only one of children's multiple distribution systems, along with other holiday gifts, sales, trades, barter, treats, gambling and sharing. Beyond their households, in schools, stores, summer camps and other sites, children regularly engage in these sorts of economic transfers. Using a variety of monetary media, including cash, but also food, marbles, comic books and Pokemon cards they maintain a thriving distribution economy.

Schools provide a privileged location for observation of these processes. Notice what often goes on at lunch time. During the half-hour allotted to Newhallville children, Elizabeth Chin saw them 'trading portions of school lunch, homemade lunches, or cadging money to buy cookies' at a 'fevered pitch that often rivals that found on the trading floor of the New York Stock Exchange' (Chin, 2001: 77). As with birthday gift-giving among Parisian children, New Haven's youngsters enacted their social networks in food trades, sales and donations. Turning down a deal, therefore, implied social rejection. Chin reports how this worked:

> Kids very often refused to eat all or part of the lunch served; if they were willing to eat part of it (for instance the peanut butter and jelly on graham crackers) they would barter vigorously to get someone else's portion of that item and 'Are you going to eat that?' was a phrase often repeated throughout lunchtime, in concert with 'Can I have your milk?' or 'Do you want your pizza?' The negotiation of relationships between children lay clear on the face of these interactions and I have seen children pointedly dump uneaten portions of their lunches—coveted by others at their table—into the garbage. As a gesture of rejection, such an action could hardly be more decisive. (Chin, 2001: 78)

Studying first-grade African-American girls' friendships, Kim Scott identifies racial patterns in such distribution systems. For instance, in the racially mixed American elementary school that Kim Scott (1999) calls Rose Mount, she repeatedly found white girls, distributing gifts of candy, cookies, or quarters, while black girls (who in this school generally came from lower income families) were typically recipients, not distributors. In other regards, however, distribution patterns strikingly resembled what Chin found in New Haven: girls offered food and money gifts first of all to their best friends, and then to less intimate or favored classmates. Scott (1999: 130) notes that girls 'she does not like' are given an excuse, such as, 'I don't have that much . . . or a quick shake of the head no'. (For a linguistic analysis of 6-year-old children's food trades, see Mishler, 1979.)

But not all transfers of food are gifts. During her observations of African-American 11- and 12-year-old boys in an impoverished urban school, Ann Ferguson registered their 'thriving informal economy'. Surprised to notice Jamar distributing apples, oranges and bananas to kids outside his circle of friends, she discovered his apparent 'sharing' was in fact a sale when his teacher threatened to report Jamar's unauthorized business to the principal (Ferguson, 2000: 103).

Kids' commerce also takes place in the schoolroom. William Corsaro's comparison of American and Italian nursery schools shows us very young children defying school rules by bringing toys and other small objects—such as toy animals, matchbox cars, candy, or gum—to school, often concealed in their pockets. Children, reports Corsaro, 'often would show his or her "stashed loot" to a playmate and carefully share the forbidden object without catching the teachers' attention' (Corsaro, 1997: 42). Barrie Thorne's 1993 classic study of elementary school children introduces the gendering of such clandestine distribution flows. She found kids stashing and trading small objects such as '"pencil pals" (rubbery creatures designed to stick on the end of pencils), rabbit feet, special erasers and silver paper' as well as more gendered goods, toy cars or trucks by boys, lip gloss, nail polish or doll furniture by girls. These 'secret exchanges', Thorne discovered, followed rigid gender lines, marking 'circles of friendship that almost never included both girls and boys' (Thorne, 1993: 21; see also Feiring and Lewis, 1989).

Thus, in lunchrooms, schoolrooms and playgrounds, children fashion elaborate systems of distribution covering a wide variety of objects and representing both peer solidarities and their divisions. We could make the same demonstration for a variety of other encounters in which children interact. Researchers, for instance, have documented comic book trades in summer camps, bargaining by US and Canadian kids over sports 'chase' cards, Pokemon cards and Beanie Babies, English children's marble swapping and ritualized sharing among Israeli kids (see Cook, 2001; Katriel, 1987: Paris, 2000; Webley, 1996. . . .

Once we shake off adult prejudices, we discover extensively organized and differentiated children's distributional economies.

CHILDREN AS CONSUMERS

Because the consuming child has attracted greater media attention than the producer or distributor, we have more extensive documentation of children's consumption. Yet even that documentation misses the centrality of negotiated and differentiated social relations to youthful consumption activity. Marketers, for their part, mainly treat kids as a special category of individual purchasers. The growing social scientific literature, in contrast, has stressed political and moral concerns: to what extent does consumption standardize, commodify, or repress children's experiences? Are children tools of capitalist interests? Does desire for expensive goods lead children into dangerous behavior?. . .

Here, however, we follow the trail of children's social relations through consumption. Let us adopt the conventional understanding of consumption as acquisition of goods and services. . .

Earlier we saw Asia, one of Elizabeth Chin's New Haven informants, report her uneasy relationship to store clerks. . .

To understand Newhallville's children's practices better, Chin supplemented her 2-year participant observation in homes, schools and neighborhoods with shopping trips. She gave 23 children $20 each to spend entirely at their discretion (some of the children brought along other children—siblings, relatives, or classmates). Here's what 10-year-old Shaquita bought with her money: two pairs of shoes at Payless: $6.99 denim mules for herself, and $9.99 for a pair of golden slip-ons as a birthday gift for her mother. She spent the remainder at Rite-Aid: $0.99 for a bag of bubble gum to share with her older sister and $2.09 for foam hair rollers to give her grandmother (Chin, 2001: 126).

As with most of the other children, Shaquita's shopping spree did not turn into a wild, self-indulgent experience. Instead, Chin identified two notable features of child shoppers' purchases: practicality and generosity. They bought useful items for themselves, such as shoes, socks, underwear, or school notebooks, and picked gift goods for family members. Both types of purchases cemented children's position in the household. They also established or confirmed their social ties with family members.

Lest these New Haven children appear to be impossibly reasonable and altruistic, Chin reminds us the mixture of meanings that flowed from their purchases: obligation to share with other members of poor families, acting out of responsibility within the household, as well as the pleasure of giving. Chin sums this up:

> The deep sense of mutual obligation, and even debt, between family members played a central role. [For kids] these obligations and debts were often not only sustaining and joyful but also painful, onerous, and highly charged. I sometimes suspected that the lesson imparted to children and imparted by them was at times a coercive generosity: share or else. (Chin, 2001: 128)

Not all household relations of consumption, in any case, generate harmony and collaboration. In his study of Philadelphia's inner-city poor African-American children—which also includes teenagers—Carl Nightingale (1993) reports acute rancor and conflict between parents and children in their negotiations over consumption. Parents exasperated by their kids' unreasonable and persistent demands for spending money are pitted against children disappointed by their parents' inability to provide them with material goods. Contest over how to spend limited family monies, including income tax refunds or welfare checks, Nightingale observes, severely strains household relations:

> All the kids whose families I knew well lived through similar incidents: yelling matches between Fahim and his mother on how she spent her welfare check, Theresa's disgust when she found out she was not going to get a dress because her mom's boyfriend had demanded some of the family's monthly money for crack, and Omar's decision to leave his mother's house altogether because 'I hate her. She always be asking y'all [the Kids' Club] for money. That's going to get around, and people'll be talking.' Also he felt that she never had enough money for his school clothes. (Nightingale, 1993: 159)

In the course of his fieldwork, Philippe Bourgois (1995) heard similar stories coming from 'El Barrio', New York City's crack-ridden East Harlem. Ten-year-old Angel complained about his mother's boyfriend:

> . . .[He] had broken open his piggy bank and taken the twenty dollars' worth of tips he had saved from working as a delivery boy at the supermarket on our block. He blamed his mother for having provoked her boyfriend into beating her and robbing the apartment when she invited another man to visit her in her bedroom. 'I keep telling my mother to only have one boyfriend at a time, but she won't listen to me.' (Bourgois, 1995: 264)

Children's consumption within households takes place in a context of incessant negotiation, sometimes cooperative, other times full of conflict.

Among peers, consumption raises a different set of relational issues. We find unexpected evidence, for example, from recent studies of Chinese children. The success of China's one-child policy means that large numbers of the country's 90 million children under age 15 have no siblings; in urban areas, single children are a majority. These 'little emperors' as observers call them, have gained remarkable economic leverage within their households: young shoppers start spending money by age 4. The social investment of Chinese parents in their children's futures increases that leverage (see Chee, 2000; Davis and Sensenbrenner, 2000).

Among other influences, the newly empowered child consumers have turned 'trendy food' snacks, especially western style, into highly desirable goods. Interviewing 8- to 10-year-old only children in Beijing, Bernadine Chee (2000) found the *xiaochi* or snacks marking children's network position. Thus, the affluent Shen Li, one of Chee's interviewees, despite the dishonor of having his father in prison, achieved peer inclusion with his food purchases. As Chee describes it:

> Shen Li often bought different foods to eat. . . . He would taste it, and if he did not like it, he would give it to his classmates. 'Because I often give them something do eat,' Shen Li explained, 'they will also give something to me when they have it.' (Chee, 2000: 55)

Not that children democratically included every child in these distribution systems. In fact, Chee found they systematically excluded apparently rural children, who ate alone while others were sharing. However, as we learn from Gao Tianjun's experience, inclusion mattered greatly to individual children. Gao's father recalled one of their outings, when Gao unexpectedly asked him to buy the expensive Wall's ice cream. Considering their meager household income, the father was at first reluctant but, seeing his child's eagerness, he relented. He later discovered the reasons for Gao's insistence:

> His son explained that once when he was at school, his classmates had asked him: 'Gao Tianjun, have you tried Wall's?' He had told the classmates that he had tried it. The classmates then asked him: 'How did it taste?' He had replied that it tasted very good. Gao Tianjun's father remarked: 'Actually, the child had never tried it before.' (Chee, 2000: 54)

Chee's observations show us children not simply enacting their parents' social position and category but creating networks of their own.

As with production and distribution, consumption . . . reveals children as active, inventive, knowledgeable consumers. More importantly, it shows us dynamic, differentiated, social relations in action.

THE PRICELESS CHILD REVISITED

Does all this discovery of children's economic activities mean that the economically useless, emotionally priceless child was just a historical mirage? Far from it. To be sure, other parts of the world, with rampant paid and informal child labor, never had the luxury of establishing a priceless child. In the US, however, household economies were indeed transformed between the 1870s and the 1930s in ways that revolutionized children's economic practices. Just as middle-class women withdrew from paid employment, children were put out of wage work. Increased attention and concern with the emotional value of children's lives led to a growing uneasiness with their practical contributions. Children's worlds, it seemed to most observers, were to exist outside market concerns, in classrooms, playrooms, playgrounds, or summer camps. Indeed, child labor laws pushed most children out of market employment while new principles of domestic economy redefined their household contributions as worthy lessons, not real work.

Pricing the Priceless Child (Zelizer, 1985) traced this transformation by focusing on adults' changing evaluations of children and childhood. But there is more to the story that we can only capture by shifting our attention to children's experiences. When we do so, we discover that the creation of an ostensibly useless child never segregated children from economic life in general. Under changed symbolic and practical conditions, the priceless child remained a consumer, producer and distributor. What's more, as we have seen repeatedly throughout this article, children engaged actively in bargaining, contesting and transforming their own relations with the economy.

Rereading the book today suggests further questions. For instance, has the era of the priceless child ended? Focusing on the US alone, if we consider the growing inequality of national income, the extent of child poverty, as well as the largely undocumented child labor of immigrant and migrant workers, we could argue that the priceless child is being wiped out among the poor and near poor. The evidence is mixed. Despite strong evidence of child labor among some immigrant populations, observers of contemporary life, such as Carl Nightingale (1993) and Kathy Edin, and Laura Lein (1997), emphasize how even very poor parents make an effort to provide consumption goods to their children in order to match those of their peers.

In our middle and upper classes, meanwhile, the expensive priceless child still reigns. Certainly the cost of raising a child continues to escalate, starting with increasingly high tuition for nursery schools and tutoring for entrance exams to private elementary schools. Parents also subsidize the growing consumer clout of their young children. For 60 percent of American children, McNeal (1999: 69) reports, the no-strings-attached allowance constitutes the largest single source of income. Working parents, as Arlie Hochschild (1997: 216) found, engage in 'time-deficit "paybacks"', by buying their children gifts. It continues to be true, furthermore, that middle- and upper-class parents justify children's paid work not on the grounds of economic utility but its contribution to their moral upbringing.

What about my predictions of a contemporary useful 'housechild'? Here, as we saw earlier, studies suggest that as a majority of their mothers work, children are in fact starting to participate more actively in household economic activities. However, whether they are participating more in production, consumption, or distribution remains unclear. An important study of American 3- to 12-year-olds' time use in 1981 and 1997 indicates that among children of single parents household work increased from 42 minutes to 2 hours and 42 minutes (almost a fourfold rise) and shopping time from 1 hour 11 minutes to 1 hour and 57 minutes (a 65 percent rise). But in two-parent households average household work dropped from 4 hours and 11 minutes (far greater than the single-parent households) to 2 hours and 52 minutes (a bit more than the single-parent households). In those same two-parent households, meanwhile, shopping rose from 1 hour and 57 minutes to 3 hours and 8 minutes (Hofferth and Sandberg, 2001: Table 4). Judging from participation in shopping, American children's involvement in consumption is increasing not only in terms of dollar volume, but also in terms of time expended.

Evidence . . . suggests that . . . a significant share of the 26 hours 48 minutes American children spent at school in 1997, of the 12 hours 12 minutes spent at play and of the additional 8 hours 53 minutes devoted to church, youth groups, sports, outdoors, hobbies and art activities will turn out to consist of economically consequential production, consumption or distribution. Adults may consider children priceless and economically useless, but they cannot deny children's substantial economic activity.

Thus, a new agenda for research on children's economic experiences emerges from the old.

CHILDREN, NEGOTIATION AND ECONOMIC EXPERIENCE

Let us examine some possibilities for that new agenda. Here are some sample questions that follow from the literature that we have reviewed.

- How do children negotiate the amount, timing and compensation for household tasks with their parents and with siblings?

- What sorts of issues become matters of dispute, and how is conflict settled?
- What changes in bargaining should we expect if the reported increase in children's domestic work continues?
- Do children in ethnic businesses have more leverage in their bargaining than children in other households?
- How does the bargaining change in households where children earn more than their parents, e.g. child models, actors, singers, or athletes?
- How do changes in these respects affect children's relations with other children and with outside organizations?
- How do children's earmarking practices vary: do children spend money from different sources (allowance, gift, wage, found money) for different kinds of goods?
- How do sources and uses of children's money vary internationally?
- Which other kids do children consult about their purchases: best friends, close friends, or acquaintances?
- How does their consultation vary by type of purchase (toys, computers, food, clothing) and by site of purchase (shopping mall, neighborhood store, Internet, catalogue)?
- When are children likely to engage in theft, such as shoplifting? With whom and where? In supermarkets, shopping malls, neighborhood stores, school stores?
- How is trust established in children's school distribution networks? When and why do children give or accept loans of money or food?
- How, and when, do adult third parties—parents, teachers, clerks, shopping mall security guards, janitors, playground monitors and employers—intervene in children's economic practices?
- How, and why, do all of these vary by age, class, gender, race, nationality, religion and by household structure?
- What part do children's production, distribution and consumption play in the national economies and how does that part vary from one country to another?

Remember the terrible fourth vignette, the Liberian child soldiers and their gunpoint breakfast? It should remind us that the great bulk of recent research on children's economic lives concerns relatively protected capitalist enclaves. The full agenda for research on children's economic relations must reach outside those enclaves in three directions: toward the variable and unequal experiences of children within high-income capitalist countries; toward the enormous variety of children's circumstances in the lower-income regions where most of the world's kids actually live; toward the historical changes that are transforming children's economic relations in rich and poor countries alike.

Discussion Questions

1. What common assumptions do many people make about children's relationship with consumption?

2. How are children not just consumers, but producers too?

3. What does the author mean when she describes children as "distributors"?

4. Thinking back to your own childhood experiences, what was your relationship to money like?

Note

1. For other kids' strategies, see also *Consumer Reports for Kids*, at: www.zillions.org (accessed 25 July 2001) and *Kid's Money* website, at: kidsmoney.org (accessed 25 July 2001).

References

Berkely, Bill (2001) *The Graves Are Not Yet Full: Race, Tribe and Power in the Heart of Africa.* New York: Basic Books.

Bourgois, Philippe (1995) *In Search of Respect.* New York: Cambridge University Press.

Brines, Julie (1994) 'Economic Dependency, Gender, and the Division of Labor at Home', *American Journal of Sociology* 100: 652–88.

Chapman, Victoria (1994) 'Working Hard or Hardly Working? An Examination of Children's Household Contributions in the 1990s', unpublished doctoral dissertation, Princeton University.

Chee, Bernadine W. L. (2000) 'Eating Snacks and Biting Pressure: Only Children in Beijing', in Jun Jing (ed.) *Feeding China's Little Emperors,* pp. 48–70. Stanford, CA: Stanford University Press.

Chin, Elizabeth (2001) *Purchasing Power: Black Kids and American Consumer Culture.* Mineapolis: University of Minnesota Press.

Cook, Daniel (2001) 'Exchange Value as Pedagogy in Children's Leisure: Moral Panics in Children's Culture at Century's End', *Leisure Sciences* 23: 81–98.

Corsaro, William A. (1997) *The Sociology of Childhood.* Thousand Oaks. CA: Pine Forge.

Davis, Deborah S. and Julia S. Sensenbrenner (2000) 'Commercializing Childhood: Parental Purchases for Shanghai's Only Child', in Deborah S. Davis (ed.) *The Consumer Revolution in Urban China,* pp. 54–79. Berkeley: University of California Press.

Edin, Kathryn and Laura Lein (1997) *Making Ends Meet: How Single Mothers Survive Welfare and Low-Wage Work.* New York: Russell Sage Foundation.

Feiring, Candice and Michael Lewis (1989) 'The Social Networks of Girls and Boys from Early Through Middle Childhood', in Deborah Belle (ed.) *Children's Social Networks and Social Supports,* pp. 119–50. New York: Wiley.

Ferguson, Ann (2000) *Bad Boys: Public Schools in the Making of Black Masculinity.* Ann Arbor: University of Michigan Press.

Fleming, Robin (1997) *The Common Purse: Income Sharing in New Zealand Families.* Auckland: Auckland University Press.

Formanek-Brunell, Miriam (1998) 'Truculent and Tractable: The Gendering of Babysitting in Postwar America', in Sherrie A. Inness (ed.) *Delinquents and Debutantes: Twentieth-Century American Girls' Cultures,* pp. 61–82. New York: New York University Press.

Gerson, Kathleen (1993) *No Man's Land: Men's Changing Commitments to Family and Work.* New York: Basic Books.

Greenstein, Theodore N. (2000) 'Economic Dependence, Gender, and the Division of Labor at Home: A Replication and Extension', *Journal of Marriage and the Family* 62: 322–35.

Gullestad, Marianne (1992) *The Art of Social Relations: Essays on Culture, Social Action and Everyday Life in Modern Norway.* Oslo: Scandinavian University Press.

Hochschild, Arlie Russell (1989) 'The Economy of Gratitude', in Thomas Hood (ed.) *The Sociology of Emotions: Original Essays and Research Papers,* pp. 95–111. Greenwich, CT: JAI Press.

Hochschild, Arlie Russell (1997) *The Time Bind.* New York: Metropolitan Books.

Hochschild, Arlie Russell and Ann Machung (1989) *The Second Shift.* New York: Avon.

Hofferth, Sandra L. and Jack Sandberg (2001) 'Changes in American Children's Time, 1981–1997', in Timothy Owens and Sandra L. Hofferth (eds) *Children at the Millennium: Where Have We Come From, Where Are We Going?* New York: Elsevier Science.

Katriel, Tamar (1987) ' "Bexiúdim!" Ritualized Sharing among Israeli Children', *Language in Society* 16: 305–20.

Kiyosaki, Robert T. and Sharon L. Lechter (1997) *Rich Dad Poor Dad.* Scottsdale, AZ: Tech-Press.

Lee, Yun-Suk, Barbara Schneider and Linda J. Waite (2000) 'Determinants and Social and Educational Consequences of Children's Housework',

Working Paper No. 19, Alfred P. Sloan Center on Parents, Children, and Work. Chicago, IL: University of Chicago Press.

Levison, Deborah (2000) 'Children as Economic Agents', *Feminist Economics* 6: 125–34.

Lewis, Michael (2001) 'Jonathan Lebed's Extracurricular Activities', *The New York Times Magazine* 25 February: 26.

Lozada, Eriberto P., Jr (2000) 'Globalized Childhood? Kentucky Fried Chicken in Beijing', in Jun Jing (ed.) *Feeding China's Little Emperors*, pp. 114–340. Stanford, CA: Stanford University Press.

Luudberg, Shelley J. and Robert A. Pollak (1996) 'Bargaining and Distribution in Marriage', *Journal of Economic Perspectives* 10: 139–58.

McNeal, James U. (1999) *The Kids Market*. Ithaca, NY: Paramount.

Mishler, Elliot G. (1979) 'Wou' You Trade Cookies with the Popcorn? Talk of Trades Among Six Year Olds', in Olga K. Garnica and Martha L. King (eds) *Language, Children and Society*, pp. 221–36. New York: Pergamon Press.

Morrow, Virginia (1994) 'Responsible Children? Aspects of Children's Work and Employment Outside School in Contemporary UK', in Berry Mayall (ed.) *Children's Childhoods: Observed and Experienced,* pp. 128–43. London: Falmer Press.

Nathan, Amy (1998) *The Kids' Allowance Book.* New York: Walker.

Newson, John and Elizabeth Newson (1976) *Seven Years old in the Home Environment.* New York: Wiley.

Nightingale, Carl H. (1993) *On the Edge.* New York: Basic Books.

Orellana, Marjorie Faulstich (2001) 'The Work Kids Do: Mexican and Central American Immigrant Children's Contributions to Households and Schools in California', *Harvard Educational Review* 71: 366–89.

Paris, Leslie M. (2000) 'Children's Nature: Summer Camps in New York State, 1919–1941', unpublished doctoral dissertation, University of Michigan.

Qvortrup, Jens (1995) 'From Useful to Useful: The Historical Continuity of Children's Constructive Participation', *Sociological Studies of Children* 7: 49–76.

Schultz, Charles M. (1999) *Peanuts: A Golden Celebration,* ed. David Larkin. New York: HarperCollins.

Scott, Kim (1999) 'First-Grade African-American Girls' Play Patterns', unpublished doctoral dissertation, Rutgers University.

Sirota, Régine (1998) 'Les Copains d'abord: les anniversaires de I'enfance, donner et recevoir', *Ethnologie Française* XXVIII (October–December): 457–71.

Solberg, Anne (1994) *Negotiating Childhood.* Stockholm: Nordplan.

Song, Miri (1999) *Helping Out: Children's Labor in Ethnic Businesses.* Philadelphia: Temple University Press.

Sonuga-Barke, Edmund and Paul Webley (1992) *Children's Saving: A Study in the Development of Economic Behavior.* Hove and Hillsdale, NJ: Lawrence Erlbaum.

Thorne, Barrie (1993) *Gender Play.* New Brunswick, NJ: Rutgers University Press.

Tilly, Chris and Charles Tilly (1998) *Work Under Capitalism.* Boulder, CO: Westview Press.

Valenzuela, Abel, Jr (1999) 'Gender Roles and Settlement Activities Among Children and Their Immigrant Families', *American Behavioral Scientist* 42: 720–42.

Watson, James L. (ed.) (1997) *Golden Arches East: McDonald's in East Asia.* Stanford, CA: Stanford University Press.

Webley, Paul (1996) 'Playing the Market: The Autonomous Economic World of Children', in Peter Lunt and Adrian Furnham (eds) *Economic Socialization,* pp. 149–61. Cheltenham: Elgar.

Zelizer, Viviana A. (1985) *Pricing the Priceless Child: The Changing Social Value of Children.* New York: Basic Books.

Kids in Toyland

CHRISTINE L. WILLIAMS

INTRODUCTION

Toy shopping is an exciting activity for most children. But how do they actively negotiate purchases with their parents? In this selection, author Christine L. Williams discusses how adults try to shape children's toy-shopping experiences, and the cultural norms within toy stores. She conducted research while working as an employee in three different toy stores in distinct socioeconomic settings. Through her direct participation in the shopping experience, she observed parents attempting to teach kids to shop, while children maintain their role as experts in the process.

Everyone knows that children cost a lot of money. They also spend a lot of money. Those under thirteen spent over $40 billion of their own money in 2002, compared to just over $17 billion in 1994 (Center for a New American Dream 2003; McNeal 1990). They influence adult purchases as well. James McNeal, a children's marketing expert, estimates that kids twelve and under influence around $500 billion worth of adults' spending. Perhaps it is not surprising, then, that shopping is the number one leisure-time activity for most American children (Kline 1993, 176).

Experts are divided over the question of whether all of this shopping and spending is good for children (Zelizer 2002). They grapple over whether children should be protected from the marketplace and hence from capitalist exploitation in order to preserve their "innocence" or socialized into market relationships to make them savvy customers empowered to mate their own choices and influence the kinds of commodities available for their consumption. Postmodernist theorists favor the latter type of inquiry; not surprisingly, so do marketing researchers. As Dan Cook (2000, 503) observes: "The view of the child as a willful, knowledgeable, and desiring agent who is making her/his own decisions and exercising self-expression through the medium of the commodity form is, of course, favored by those who work in and profit from children's industries."

Zelizer and Cook are leading the way to a new type of inquiry that transcends this either-or debate. They are interested in exploring how children actually relate to the marketplace through ethnographic studies. Here the question isn't whether children should be engaged in market activity. Rather, it is how social relationships shape children's economic activities and how children respond to efforts to control them.

In this chapter, I focus on adults' efforts to shape children's toy-shopping experience. Children must be taught how to shop; this isn't a behavior that comes naturally. I argue that the lessons learned in the toy store have repercussions throughout society. How we shop is shaped by and contributes to social inequality. Obviously this happens in the economic sense: rich people can buy more things than poor people can. They also have more choices of where to shop. In recent years, inner-city neighborhoods have experienced a decline in retail tenants, constricting the shopping options of many poor people. As retail centers have shifted to suburban locations, they have become inaccessible (often by design) to those who lack private means of transportation (Cohen 2003).

My goal in this chapter, however, is to discuss, not the economic inequalities that are reflected and reproduced in shopping, but rather the cultural norms and practices that legitimize inequality. To make this argument, I draw on Pierre Bourdieu's theory of culture.[1] Bourdieu sought to understand how stratified social systems persist and reproduce themselves without powerful resistance and often without the conscious recognition of their members. He argues that *culture* is the key to understanding inequality: cultural resources, processes, and institutions hold individuals and groups in competitive hierarchies of domination. All cultural forms—including styles of dress, eating habits, religion, science, philosophy, and even toys—embody interests and function to enhance social distinctions, and thus social inequality (Swartz 1997). . . .

In toy shopping, this kind of status distinction is reflected in the decisions of both where to shop and what to buy. Diamond Toys, with its reputation for selling refined toys to sophisticated and discriminating adult consumers, conveyed high status to shoppers. Buying at Diamond Toys offered proof of one's cultural refinement. (Many shoppers requested extra shopping bags displaying the company logo.) Shopping at the Toy Warehouse, in contrast, conveyed no such superior status. Bourdieu would argue that this status distinction both obscures and legitimizes economic inequality. It obscures inequality by making it seem that shoppers at Diamond Toys simply have better "taste" than shoppers at the Toy Warehouse, when really they have more privilege (due to class and race inequality). It furthermore legitimizes the belief that those with highly cultivated tastes ought to be rewarded with superior service and merchandise. In this way, wealth disparity in our society is transformed into a matter of "choice" and "taste," not domination and inequality.

Just as some groups seem to know the "right" places to shop, other groups always seem to make the "wrong" shopping choices.

Ann Norton (1993, 56) argues that women, African Americans, and immigrants are often criticized for their shopping practices. They are seen as especially "prone to extravagance . . . , full of desires, easily lured by the pretty and the prestigious, seduced by advertising, and given to consumption and display." Their choices are taken as evidence of their low social and moral worth, which then justifies their economic marginality.

Norton (1993) doesn't include children in her analysis, but they certainly fit. Children are among those groups "on the periphery [who] are commonly excluded, by law, custom, or the lack of resources, from full participation in American economic structures" (56). Consequently, their consumer choices typically are considered unrefined and mark them as undeserving and in need of control.

Elizabeth Chin (2001) takes up this point in her study of black urban youth. This group is often criticized for "spending money they haven't earned on things they shouldn't have" (43), such as high-priced sneakers and flashy jewelry. Minority youth in particular are seen as destructive, greedy, and out-of-control consumers, highly susceptible to commodity fetishism, willing to compromise their health and well-being to acquire expensive yet tacky commodities. Ironically, the "outrageous" and unrefined consumer practices of marginal groups can become mainstream and "acceptable" once corporations appropriate them, repackage them, and sell them to the middle-class consumer. But before this happens, the consumer practices of minority groups are taken as emblematic of their inferior moral qualities.

In contrast, the extravagant tastes of the rich are not typically seen as reflecting character or group flaws. This is because their "choices" set the standards of high culture and define what does and what does not constitute cultural sophistication. These are the standards and values emulated by the middle class, who tend to look down on the "street" values attributed to minority youth and up to the "refined" lifestyles of the rich and famous. Chin (2001, 12) writes that many middle-class people assume that "if only those [poor] people would . . . want the right things, dress appropriately, buy the right foods, they too could be middle class." Their economic condition is thus explained as a consequence of their unrefined consumer choices. . . .

The struggle to define what is valuable is played out every day in the toy store. Adults and children are often locked in battle over the norms and values of shopping—evident in the number of temper tantrums I witnessed at the checkout line. Adults try to teach children a set of ideal norms regarding consumerism, while children struggle to satisfy their own sense of what is good and valuable. Toys are an obvious battleground, since they constitute a "lingua franca" of childhood (Seiter 1993), the means through which children forge their peer group alliances and stake out their independence from their parents. Children learn, resist, appeal, and negotiate the lessons of toy shopping, often to their parents' dismay. In very public disputes, they highlight the norms, making them more accessible to the sociologist's eye.

Adults also experience conflicts over shopping and consumerism, but they are more likely to be played out in private, or else internally. . . . Because in a consumer society we acquire things to express who we are and who we want to be, the experience of shopping can bring out deep ambivalence about our self-worth and our relationships. . . .

Yet somehow we are more disturbed when these characteristics are expressed openly in children. As Stephen Kline (1993) observes, when children feel the need to wear a designer label, or when they fight over a coveted object, adults feel that something is awry. Kline writes, "[I]t is easiest to recognize the deeper paradoxes of our consumer culture when it is refracted back to us through the mirror of childhood" (12). Adults' attempts to control children in the toy store and to teach them how to be good consumers can, in this sense, serve as a window into the cultural norms and psychological ambivalence that affect us all.

SHOPPING 101

Teaching children how to shop at the most basic level involves lessons in accounting and money management. The kids I observed in the Toy Warehouse often had their own money and were expected to pay for their own toys. This was the case even with very young children. Here is an excerpt from my field notes:

> A pregnant African American woman in her thirties came to my register with her two children. They were clearly middle to upper middle class. The children checked out first: the boy, probably seven, bought his toys (trucks and machines) and paid with a $20 bill. Kids are funny when they pay, they aren't sure how to do

it (the younger ones at least). They give the money right away; I have to tell them to wait until I tell them how much they owe. Mom was standing watch and making sure it went right. He got about $7 back, and I counted out his change to make it seem like a math lesson. Next the eight-year-old daughter bought her toys and also paid with a $20 bill. I made a comment to Mom about them spending their special birthday money or special gift, and she told me, no, they always paid with their own money. The daughter knew how to do a transaction. She bought a baby doll stroller and other baby doll toys that came out to about $19.50, so she had only a little bit of change compared to her brother, and she clearly felt accomplished about doing that. Next it was the mom's turn to buy her things, and she bought (real) baby things, like bibs and formula. A white woman behind her in line informed her that there was a $1 off coupon for two bibs in the sales circular, and they rushed to find it. I said, "Take your time, don't worry," and we eventually found it and rang up the sale. The women clearly bonded over this moment.

The overt lesson in shopping in this example involved learning how to conduct a transaction and audit the cashier. This part of shopping is highly routinized, and many adults consider it important that children learn how to do it at an early age. Kline (1993) points out that whereas an earlier generation of parents emphasized the importance of saving, today's parents expect their children to learn how to spend money in order to learn responsibility and consumer skills.[2] According to marketing researchers, children are shopping alone at very young ages: one study finds most children have shopped alone by age five, and by the age of eight, the average U.S. child is in a shop alone three times per week (Kline 1993, 182). This helps to explain why learning to audit the cashier is a top priority for many parents. . . .

At the Toy Warehouse, middle-class parents were often appalled by the kitschy toys that their children coveted and tried to interest them in other things. Children retained their authority as the ultimate decision makers in these instances. Most children seemed willing to accept more toys but never to relinquish their first choice. I say "most" instead of all because on rare occasions I witnessed children who were completely uninterested, in toys despite the urging of their parents. However, this was something I only observed at Diamond Toys. Here is an example:

A family came in [to Diamond Toys] to buy a push-type fire truck. These are little vehicles made out of molded plastic that young kids (around two to three) can sit on and push with their feet and steer with little steering wheels. Mom and Dad were there with two little kids in tow, one about three, getting the fire truck, and a baby in arms, younger than one. The mom couldn't decide which truck to buy, the red one or the blue one. She asked the kid, "Which one do you want?" The kid seemed completely bored and listless. They put him on one of the display models, where he sat, not smiling, not playing, apparently unimpressed. The mom kept trying to get him to decide, showing him the features of each one (bells, dials, horns, etc.). Eventually she decided that since he was sitting on the blue one he should get that. So we found it in the box and I went to ring her up. She kept trying to get the kid interested in the thing: "Here's your new truck!" "This is for you!" But the kid stayed expressionless. The mom told me that the kid was totally spoiled and that it was his grandparents' fault. He got whatever he wanted, she said, so I jokingly asked, did she want to buy more, then? . . . She also bought him a little backpack that was in the shape of a stuffed animal. The purchase came to over $60. The parents sighed and walked out with their silent kids. . . .

BARGAINING FOR TOYS

While for the most part younger children were profligate, I observed that older middle-class children were often reluctant to spend their own money even when they had it. I was often amazed at the older children's negotiating skills with their parents. They bargained over what to buy and whose money was going to pay for it. Here is one example:

> A white woman in her forties was shopping with her twelve-year-old daughter. They were looking for "My Generation Barbie," and they came to my register saying they couldn't find it; maybe we were sold out? I told them I thought we had it and left my register to help them look for it. We couldn't find it on the Barbie wall, but we did find "Jewel Barbie" and the girl said that her friend (this was a present for a friend) had specified that she wanted either Jewel Barbie or My Generation Barbie, so they would just purchase this one. But Mom insisted that we find My Generation, and I offered to find someone who could tell us about it. I looked for my coworker who was in charge of the section (eighteen-year-old Karelin), but, not surprisingly, she was nowhere to be found, and I came back and said no luck. The little girl was insisting that Jewel Barbie was just fine, but the mom wasn't so sure. So I said I would go to the front and we could search the inventory. The mom said great, and they followed me, but then, lo and behold, we ran right into the display of My Generation Girl (not Barbie after all), and they were very happy about this, especially the mom. (It is a really cool doll, with lots of tiny plastic accessories, like a skateboard and Walkman for the doll.) I went back to the register, and a couple of minutes later they were there purchasing the doll (plus some candy that the daughter had picked up—the mom tried to talk her out of that but it was too late—"You don't need candy"—"Yes I do," and besides, this was a cool, special kind of candy, a hollow chocolate ball the size of a racquetball filled with M&Ms). It was interesting to me how they paid: the girl got out a wad of cash and pulled out a ten, and the mom paid the rest (it cost about $25 total). So the deal was that the girl had to pay $10 of her "own" money for the doll for her friend (she didn't have to pay for the candy, though).

This arrangement was very curious to me, but over time I noticed that several middle-class children engaged in elaborate accounting methods with their parents. Some parents matched children's contributions toward a purchase dollar for dollar. These techniques enabled parents to exert control over their children's consumer choices while at the same time increasing the children's purchasing power.

In this case it was striking that the child appeared to be a more mature shopper than the mother. She was ready to settle on the first appropriate gift they found, while the mother seemed a little bit crazed to me. But the mother was teaching another lesson about consumerism to her daughter: the most important aspect of shopping was the comparison. We express ourselves and our personal feelings about the people we care about through the gifts we give them. The gift isn't meaningful if we don't choose it because then it wouldn't be a reflection of the individual giver. Of course, in this case, it was just the illusion of "choice," since the recipient of the gift was very specific about what she wanted. So the only way to "personalize" a gift was to compare it with the other items on the wish list. A quasi-choice was better than no choice at all. . . .

At the Toy Warehouse, . . . children paid at the register perhaps a third of the time. This was an extremely rare occurrence at Diamond Toys. Although there were always plenty of children in the store, I never witnessed one paying for his or her own toy. Parents seemed to be reserving the expensive toy store for themselves, tightly controlling any purchases for children.

It was not uncommon at the Toy Warehouse to witness children engaging in elaborate negotiations with their parents, something I rarely witnessed at Diamond Toys. Here is one example:

An African American father in his mid-thirties was shopping with his ten-year-old daughter and six-year-old son. He was buying toys for each of them. The boy was getting a couple of trucks, and the girl got a single Barbie (the $6 kind) plus a Mary-Kate and Ashley set of dolls with a playscape included. I rang up his purchases and it came to about $60, and he said, "Whoa, what happened there?" I looked at the tape and told him that the expensive part of the purchase was the Mary-Kate and Ashley doll set, which cost about $35. He looked at his daughter and said, "What's this? Bait and switch? That isn't what you had picked earlier. This is too much." She said that she really wanted this instead. The dad said no, she could have the other thing that he had already approved, but that other thing was long gone. She ran back out into the store and brought back another doll, this one a black Barbie in a laundry setting (Barbies were sold in every room of the house). Clever, because this was holding up the line and that put the parents on the spot having to make the decisions in front of a crowd. He asked how much it was, and it was $25, so he was unsure, but he said, "Well, OK, if you take out the other $6 Barbie you can have this one." So that is what happened. The girl managed to negotiate from what was originally a $15 total purchase up to a $25 purchase. She did this by sneaking in a $35 purchase, which she knew she had a very slim chance of getting, but because of that initial sticker shock, her dad was prepared for the toy that was somewhat less expensive (but more than he wanted to pay). I thought about how skilled a negotiator this girl was going to be. In retrospect, I recalled that she had tried to distract me and her dad during the transaction so that we wouldn't notice the expensive Mary-Kate and Ashley; as soon as I checked the tape she acted as if she had been busted and was disappointed in that.

Children in the Toy Warehouse would often try to increase the number of purchases or to upgrade the value of their purchase. One way they did this was to sneak an item onto the register counter at checkout. The Toy Warehouse catered to this practice by placing toys and trinkets right next to the counter at the child's eye level.

Although many children complained that their parents didn't buy them enough, I was constantly amazed at the amount of money parents were willing to spend on toys—although some experienced sticker shock, as in this example:

An Asian American mom was buying Game Boy video games for her four-year-old son and eight-year-old son, who was with a friend. The younger child picked one that cost $50 and two others that cost $20 each. The mother said, "You can't have all of them." The kid wasn't going to budge, he wanted them all. Mom insisted, "You can either have the expensive one or the other two," and the kid chose the expensive one. At that time the older boys came up to the counter and made fun of the kid for choosing one instead of two, but the little kid put his foot down and that was what he got. The mother said to me, "These games are really expensive," and I agreed. She said the problem was that the kids wouldn't share the games so she had to buy multiple copies of the same game. In fact, she told me, the older son already owned a copy of the game the younger son was purchasing and the two older children had bought copies of the same game. She was clearly disappointed in them for not sharing. . . .

Although gift giving forges bonds with others and in that sense is a highly social activity, giving a gift is also highly individual, in that gifts are intended for specific individuals to express something about their unique relationship with the giver. Suggesting that children share runs counter to the individualism that is so powerfully hegemonic in our culture. . . .

The Toy Warehouse encouraged the view that children should be showered with presents on their birthdays. An entire section of the store was devoted to birthday party decorations and accessories, such as piñatas and "party bags" (colorful paper bags that cost $2 for a pack of three) that were supposed to be filled with special "party favor" toys for the birthday guests. On a child's birthday, the store provided free helium-filled balloons, and the staff gathered around, sang "Happy Birthday," and posed for a Polaroid picture around the child.

In my experience, only middle-class children (and the children of the employees) took advantage of these services. The store was much less hospitable to the children from poor families. This was because poor people were assumed to be thieves, not paying consumers. They came under greater surveillance than middle-class people while in the store. Not surprisingly, they were caught stealing more often. In some cases, children were unwitting accomplices in this, as when one woman was caught stuffing merchandise under her child in the stroller. . . .

Poor kids often hung out in and around the Toy Warehouse without adult supervision. Sometimes children came in groups, just wanting to hang out, and I would feel sorry for them because they probably had no place else to go. The norm of service did not apply in their case. They got shooed out if they were not buying.

The neighborhoods surrounding the Toy Warehouse were impoverished and lacked park space. This mall of big box stores was one of the only destinations for the kids in the neighborhood, but it was not a friendly place for them. The land was private property, not public space, so the freedom to pass through and loiter was restricted. There were no park benches or patches of grass to sit on, no meandering sidewalks, no trees to climb, no street life (aside from one hot dog stand set up in the middle of the parking lot). Kids were drawn inside the store where pleasures abounded, but without their paying parents they were not welcomed.

Most of the children I saw on their own were boys, although occasionally groups of girls would wander into the store. I recorded this instance in my field notes:

> A group of three African American girls around age nine to eleven came up to my register to ask how much some candy cost (which they couldn't afford so they didn't buy). I offered them stickers, little promotional badges with the company logo, which they really liked. It was a slow day, hardly any customers at the registers. One of the girls asked me if I had a rubber band. She had been braiding another one's hair and needed to tie it off. I managed to scrounge one up and they were just delighted. So they were kind of hanging out in front of my register, sitting on the counter, not being obnoxious, just talking and laughing. Then a customer came up and I had to say, I have a customer now. They looked a little anxious and scampered out of the store.

Although I felt bad about sending them away, I reinforced the lesson that receiving positive attention from adults is contingent on being able to buy. . . .

Middle-class parents and their children would rarely linger and loiter in the Toy Warehouse, despite the efforts of the store to make it welcoming to them. Kids from the neighborhood apparently made middle-class parents very nervous. Once, while I was in my car on break, I saw two African American boys on bicycles (about fifteen and ten). They were riding around the cars and asking shoppers (mostly the children) what they had gotten and trying to engage them in conversation. I saw them ask a nine-year-old white boy what kind of Game Boy he had gotten as his mom shuffled him into their minivan. Within minutes, two police cars arrived. The officers talked to the boys on bikes, who then went away. The plainclothes security guard came out of the store afterwards and talked to the officers; he later told me that he had called them to complain about the boys. The store wanted to make itself more welcoming to middle-class shoppers; getting rid of neighborhood kids was part of this strategy.

Diamond Toys, on the other hand, extended a welcoming aura to middle-class families. It was a tourist destination that many middle-class adults treated like a hands-on children's museum. They would typically take their children through the store section by section, encouraging them to inspect and admire the toys, pointing out those they remembered from their youth. I never observed this in the Toy Warehouse, which seemed much more child dominated. . . .

Dorothy, my manager at Diamond Toys, instructed me to keep a close watch on any unaccompanied children in the store, but I rarely encountered any. Once a large group of twelve-to thirteen-year-olds entered my section; I later found out that they were on a school field trip into the city and that their teachers were letting them stop in for a bit of shopping before a Tennessee Williams play they were scheduled to see. Dorothy made me get rid of them.

Rarely did I encounter any minority youth in the store who were unaccompanied by adults. I didn't realize this until one day when Chandrika, the eighteen-year-old African American gift wrapper, told me that she thought she saw one of her friends in the store. We weren't allowed to leave our section, so she asked the plainclothes security guard to look around and see if there was a black guy in the store. I asked her about this. Was it really so uncommon for an African American teenager to be in the store that one black person would be so readily apparent? She assured me that a young black man would definitely stand out at Diamond Toys. . . .

CONCLUSION

Although we are not "born to shop," most American children learn how to do it at a very early age. Adults teach children consumer skills, including accounting, money management, and comparison shopping. They also teach children that we honor our loved ones by buying them things that reflect our feelings for them. What we buy is determined sometimes by the giver, sometimes by the receiver. The Toy Warehouse catered to the receiving child. Adults often rewarded children for their specialness by letting them select from the cornucopia of riches, but then they were disappointed when the child was too greedy. Diamond Toys catered instead to the giving adult. Many adults were keenly sensitive to the impact of their gifts on children, believing that they were shaping children through their purchases, so they selected toys with purported educational value, nostalgia toys, or toys that reflected idealized qualities they wished to see in the children's identity. Toy shopping was thus part of the child-rearing strategy of concerted cultivation favored by middle-class adults.

There are covert and unintended lessons in the shopping curriculum too, many involving the reproduction of social inequality. Rewarding good behavior with presents bolsters the view that only the "worthy" get rewarded, adding legitimacy to the system of class inequality. The fact that buying toys is mostly women's work that they do out of love (or their own emotional needs for love) reproduces gender differentiation and inequality. And reserving the expensive toy store for adults sends children the message that they cannot be trusted to buy expensive toys because they are not yet capable of making the "right" choices.

Other groups were also excluded from Diamond Toys, most notably minority youth, suggesting that they, too, could not be trusted to make the "right" choices. Unlike the Toy Warehouse, which was an amazing mix of social classes and racial/ethnic groups, Diamond Toys was virtually all white and middle to upper class. Although Diamond Toys cultivated its image as the seller of "exclusive" toys, in fact its exclusivity resided more in the clientele it served (and the staff it employed). This equation of "high-quality" merchandise with a predominantly white and wealthy shopping environment formed part of the hidden curriculum of shopping. It justified economic and racial inequality along the lines suggested by Bourdieu by confirming the view that only rich white people had cultivated tastes and hence that only they had the right to shop there. . . .

Learning to shop is necessary for living in a consumer society. Through our purchases, we acquire the means to survival, express who we are, and establish and maintain social relationships. Thus we have to teach children how to do it. Protecting them from shopping would disadvantage them later in life, denying them access to an important means of public participation. Some may fantasize about a halcyon past when people made things instead of buying them, but that is an extremely idealistic and unreasonable option for most people today. Consumerism is here to stay. But how we practice and organize consumption is a social negotiable. . . .

Discussion Questions

1. How did children try to maximize their gains at toy stores?
2. What do adults gain from the toy shopping experience and from purchasing items for children more generally?
3. What is the importance of socioeconomic status in children's shopping experiences?
4. Williams describes "the receiving child" in the chapter's conclusion. What does "the receiving child" imply about the social construction of childhood in the United States today?

Notes

1. Bourdieu's major relevant work on this topic is *Distinction* (1984). My discussion also relies on David Swartz's excellent introduction, *Culture and Power: The Sociology of Pierre Bourdieu* (1997) and Bourdieu and Wacquant (1992).
2. According to Viviana Zelizer (1985), this shift in emphasis from saving to spending occurred even earlier in the child-rearing advice literature. In the 1930s, experts urged parents to give children a regular allowance in order to train them to be efficient shoppers. The rise of a consumer society, she shows, demanded a child "who spends wisely, saves wisely and gives wisely" (106).

References

Bourdieu, Pierre. 1984. *Distinction: A Social Critique of the Judgement of Taste.* Cambridge, MA: Harvard University Press.

Center for a New American Dream. 2003. "Facts about Marketing to Children." Retrieved May 29, 2003, from www.newdream.org/kids/facts.php.

Chin, Elizabeth. 2001. *Purchasing Power: Black Kids and American Consumer Culture.* Minneapolis: University of Minnesota Press.

Cohen, Lizabeth. 2003. *A Consumers' Republic: The Politics of Mass Consumption in Postwar America.* New York: Knopf.

Cook, Daniel Thomas 2000. "The Other Child Study: Figuring Children as Consumers in Market Research, 1910s–1990s." *Sociological Quarterly* 41(3): 487–507.

Kline, Stephen. 1993. *Out of the Garden: Toys, TV, and Children's Culture in the Age of Marketing.* New York: Verso.

McNeal, James. 1999. *The Kids' Market Myths and Realities.* Ithaca, NY: Paramount Market Publishing.

Norton, Ann. 1993. *Republic of Signs: Liberal Theory and American Popular Culture.* Chicago: University of Chicago Press.

Seiter, Ellen. 1993. *Sold Separately: Children and Parents in Consumer Culture.* New Brunswick, NJ: Rutgers University Press.

Swartz, David. 1997. *Culture and Power: The Sociology of Pierre Bourdieu.* Chicago: University of Chicago Press.

Zelizer, Viviana. 2002. "Kids and Commerce," *Childhood* 9 (November): 375–96.

"We Pledge Allegiance to Kids": Nickelodeon and Citizenship

SARAH BANET-WEISER

INTRODUCTION

In this selection, communications scholar Sarah Banet-Weiser looks critically at how we define citizenship in the United States and how this definition often excludes children. She considers how the Nickelodeon network addresses its young audience both as consumers and as citizens; these issues are not contradictions, she says, but are constant tensions. Her study challenges the notion that kids neither know nor care about politics.

Within two weeks of the September 11, 2001, terrorist attacks on the World Trade Center and the Pentagon, Nickelodeon released a special episode of its children's news program, *Nick News.* "Kids, Terrorism, and the American Spirit" featured host Linda Ellerbee discussing the attacks with a group of children of various ages, genders, nationalities, and religions. The greater part of this *Nick News* episode was dedicated to defining the "American Spirit" for its audience through a mélange of patriotic images, liberal platitudes, and messages of "hope for the future." Then, in October 2001, Nickelodeon featured another special episode of another popular program. This program, the animated series, *Rugrats,* was aired in honor of Columbus Day, and was entitled "Rugrats Discover America." Unlike the *Nick News* special, *Rugrats* represented "America" through a variety of popular cultural and commercial references: Hollywood films, rock-and-roll music, and tourist souvenirs. These cultural artifacts were situated as "symbols" of America that were purchased on a cross-country vacation.

Both these programs contribute to a general discourse regarding children and citizenship, and both address, albeit in very different registers, questions about what it means to be an American. What I find particularly interesting about these two programs is that they are very good examples of Nickelodeon programming that attend to the tensions about citizenship within their narratives. The *Nick News* special attends to the various ways in which Americans unified around traditional liberal terms after September 11: individual displays of heroism, community mourning rituals, candlelight vigils for the victims, and melodramatic sequences of the flag and other national symbols. *Rugrats,* while also focusing on issues of patriotism, interprets the sentiment within a slightly different frame of reference: patriotism is defined through a collection of consumer items or *products* that symbolize national identity, commitment, and community. In both these programs, political empowerment is referenced as a key component of citizenship, represented on one end of a continuum as a commitment to liberal ideals of individual agency and on the other end, as a kind of "market patriotism" or consumer freedom.

Despite their seemingly obvious differences, these definitions of citizenship are not binary opposites. Rather, they work in conjunction with each other, demonstrating a different emphasis depending on the context. Within the Nickelodeon universe, these two definitions of citizenship intermix and represent a broader tension in recent debates framing discussions of children, media, and citizenship. In the following pages, I examine the way Nickelodeon balances these seemingly contradictory ideals of citizenship through its use of audience empowerment rhetoric and its cross-generational address that insists that "Nick Is for Kids!"

CHILDREN, MEDIA, AND POLITICAL EMPOWERMENT

During the last several decades in the United States the question of whether, and how, children are politically empowered has developed into an increasingly complicated public, mass-mediated debate. More specifically, a public focus on children and empowerment frequently includes a discussion of technology and the potential "effects" (either positive or negative) of technologies such as television, the movies, and most recently the Internet on the political empowerment of children. The perceived connection between technology and empowerment is certainly not a novel discovery; as many scholars have noted, public opinion about new developments in technologies throughout the twentieth century has been both optimistic and pessimistic about the influence of technology on individual agency.[1] And when the discourse involves children and their relation with technology, the stakes become even higher and the debate that much more hotly contested.

Although mass-mediated debates around the question of technology's influence on children have heightened in recent years as school shootings in Colorado, Kentucky, and Arkansas have been "connected" to violent television, video games, music, and the Internet, the relation between children and technology has historically been fraught with conflict and contradiction. For example, as Lynn Spigel has astutely documented, in post-war American culture television was popularly understood as being both an important factor in "family togetherness" and the primary culprit in the creation of the "juvenile delinquent."[2] Later in the twentieth century, television advertising and the apparent excessive influence it had on children generated other debates over the problems of the "commercialization of childhood," while at the same time child development specialists were advocating the purchase of *particular* products to aid in the intellectual development of children.[3] And most recently, while new technologies and the Internet have been widely recognized by corporate culture and politicians as offering an enormous potential in terms of democracy, tolerance, and most importantly, commerce, the "dark side" of technologies such as the Internet are often understood in terms of the influence and control they seemingly have over children.

Part of the reason the debate over children and technology is so fraught with tension is because the definition of the child is characterized by different emphases depending on the context. Is the child an innocent victim of the corporate giants of mass media, or is the child an active citizen, involved in the negotiation and struggle over meaning in a productive, identity-making manner? Or, as I hope to demonstrate in this essay, are these two positions *not* oppositional, but rather in constant tension and conversation with each other in the construction of citizenship?. . .

Although popular debate on the issue of children and the media has been largely formulated around these two oppositional extremes, it would be misleading to characterize scholarly debates around this issue as a simple binary opposition.[4] The "child as innocent victim" camp primarily understands the relationship between children and the media as one that needs to be continually supervised and protected (because of increasing violence, sexual activity among young adults, and so on). The "child as active player" camp challenges this cultural construction of the "innocence" of children and rather situates the child as a citizen who actively uses the media as a means to gain empowerment. Both sides, however, stipulate that the relationship between children and media is a complicated and contradictory set of historical arrangements, one that resists either a simple definition or a simple solution.

Thus, in order to theorize the complex relationship between children, empowerment, and media, we need to more sharply imagine the sense of contradiction that characterizes this relationship. By focusing on the instabilities and competing interests that permeate discussions of children and media, we witness how the category of "child" or, more broadly, "youth," operates as not only a social and political category but also as an important agenda for public debate about the broader concern of citizenship and empowerment. . . . " 'Youth' becomes a metaphor for perceived social change and its projected consequences, and as such it is an enduring locus for displaced social anxieties."[5] These anxieties reflect the tensions within the paradoxical constructions of young people, tensions that "highlight the bifurcated social identity of youth as a vicious, threatening sign of social decay and our best hope for the future."[6] Perhaps one of the most dynamic cultural sites for both the representation of and the struggle over these tensions is within entertainment and commercial culture.

Thus, I would like to shift the question of political empowerment to a commercial media audience of children. What, really, does it mean to invoke the idea of the "empowerment" of children? Can we, or how do we, take seriously the notion that a young media audience is "active" politically in the current political and commercial climate? Does conceptualizing children as "citizens" allow us to think of how and in what ways children are empowered politically? Children *are* in fact outside political life in the way that adults understand politics—they are not rights-bearing citizens of a nation in the way that adults are, they cannot vote, they do not have "free choice" as this is legally defined. However, to say that children are outside political life is not to say that they are outside relations of power. Indeed, the development of identity is *already* to be situated in relations of power, and children are developing their identities in part through their relationship to commercial media culture. . . .

NICK'S FOR KIDS! NICKELODEON'S MISSION

The early history of Nickelodeon is largely one of failure in the television market. The early programming itself is identified by Nickelodeon as "green vegetable" television, primarily understood as beneficial for children by parents, but not by the children themselves. Regardless of parental desire, however, from 1979 to 1984, Nickelodeon's subscription rates were too low for the network to sustain itself financially. In 1984, Geraldine Laybourne became general manager and transformed the network in two crucial and interrelated ways: the network began accepting commercial sponsorship, and thus advertising became a key element in its programming, and it adopted a new mission statement and overall philosophy that has since become its unique signature and contribution to children's television, a promise that Nickelodeon is a "kids first" or a "kids only" network.[7]

The result of these changes was the creation of a network that self-consciously and aggressively identifies as a "safe" place for children, a place that understands children *as* children, and somehow understands them differently than the rest of the world. As Laybourne puts it: "For kids, it is 'us versus them' in the grown-up world: you're either for kids or against them. Either you think kids should be quiet and behave or you believe kids should stand up for themselves and be free to play around, explore, and be who they really are. We were on the kids' side and we wanted them to know it."[8] Despite both the hyperbole and the arrogance of this statement, Nickelodeon has been unusually successful with its claim that it just "lets kids be kids," as well as with its apparent dedication to empowering children. The network self-consciously constructs itself as a "haven" for children in an otherwise confusing and scary world.

Nickelodeon consistently attributes its unusual success in an oversaturated children's market to its emphasis on the cultural divide between children and adults, and to its privileging of children as a separate, unique audience. Aside from commercial success, the use of a generational address is also an interesting challenge to dominant definitions of childhood as specifically adult-generated. In other words, many scholars have examined the ways in which the cultural construction of childhood as clearly separate from adulthood functions as a kind of strategy that supports the affirmation of adult identity. As Spigel puts it: "Childhood is the difference against which adults define themselves. It is a time of innocence, a time that refers back to a fantasy world where the painful realities and social constraints of adult culture no longer exist. Childhood has less to do with what children experience (since they too are subject to the evils of our social world) than with what adults want to believe."[9] Nickelodeon's challenge to this position is evident in the myriad pledges to children from the network, including: "Nickelodeon is what kids want, not just what adults think kids want," and "Nickelodeon is always there, from breakfast to bedtime, everyday, whenever kids want to watch. Nick is their home base, a place kids can count on and trust."[10] Clearly, Nickelodeon's claim that it allows children to explore their own self-agency, a specific identity construction that stands in contrast to childhood innocence that has served adults so well in the twentieth century, is one that we need to take seriously as an important element in the construction of citizenship. In line with this, Laybourne uses a kind of "liberal citizen" rhetoric profusely in describing Nickelodeon's mission:

> We are here to accept kids, to help them feel good about themselves. It's a philosophy that impacts everything we do. It impacts casting: we don't look for gorgeous kids, we cast kids who are fat and who are skinny, kids of all colors and nationalities, every kind of kid. We don't give out the message, this is what a cool kid should look or be like. The philosophy impacts our marketing: we don't market based on gender, because that implies exclusion, which is not what we are about. If we want to make kids feel good, we have to embrace them all.[11]

The notion of inclusion, and the implied claim of equal opportunity, that permeates Laybourne's vocabulary is part of the overall political address that hails Nickelodeon kids as particular kinds of citizens. Indeed, the construction of childhood as a discrete realm, not only separate from adults but situated oppositionally, has allowed Nickelodeon to claim that it escapes the dynamic that Spigel discusses, where childhood is both defined and supported as a specific means to affirm *adult* identity. Insisting upon childhood as an identity construction that is created *by* kids *for* kids is an important part of the way in which Nickelodeon constructs citizenship. This has resulted in the active self-construction of Nickelodeon as a champion and defender of kids' "rights": "The company's battle cry became that Nickelodeon stood with kids against anyone who found them 'unbearably loathsome' or sought to condescend to or undermine them. This voice gave the network a means to develop a style of comedy built on opposition to pompous or mean authority figures—bus drivers who yell at kids, anyone who treats them unfairly. In this regard, Nickelodeon's distinctive voice has not been uncontroversial, for some critics have viewed it as undermining the respect children should show adults."[12] The very element that has been seen as "controversial" is the one that allows Nickelodeon to set itself apart from other children's networks. And, although clearly Nickelodeon does construct children as citizens in relation to adults, the oppositional nature of this dynamic has permitted Nickelodeon to claim that it recognizes children as autonomous political subjects.

Part of the way in which Nickelodeon makes this claim about citizenship is through its original programming itself. Nickelodeon cartoons, game shows, and news programs challenge conventional understandings of what is "good" television for children by insisting not only that adults understand children's media on its own terms (not through an adult lens or viewpoint of what constitutes good or bad media), but also that *children themselves* understand that they are being addressed as an important group outside adult culture. Indeed, Nickelodeon has occupied an interesting position in the children's media market precisely because it has challenged the traditional adult-produced dichotomies that constitute the debate about "good" and "bad" TV, a debate that, as cultural theorist David Buckingham has argued, "rests on a series of binary oppositions that are routinely taken for granted: British is good, American is bad; public service is good, commercial is bad; live action is good, animation is bad; education is good, entertainment is bad; and so on. In the process, certain genres—game shows, action-adventure, teenage romance—are deemed to be simply incompatible with quality."[13] In resisting these kinds of conventional oppositions, Nickelodeon deliberately uses a generational divide to challenge the assumptions that structure the children and media debate, and in so doing, also challenges key cultural assumptions about childhood in general. Specifically, Nickelodeon challenges the assumption that children are not capable of making informed choices about not only what they like to watch on television, but also about the larger world in general. Through an examination of Nickelodeon's news program, *Nick News,* we can see at least one way in which the commercial network constructs its audience in these kinds of terms, as a group of political or civil citizens.

KIDS' EMPOWERMENT: POLITICAL CITIZENSHIP

Despite an increasingly negative public opinion in the United States about the corruption of "official" politics and growing frustrations with the intimate workings of the democratic process, the notion that citizenship is formed *via* the democratic process continues to have both social and political currency. . . .

News journalism, then, often has been situated as an essential part of democracy, and as the key to an informed citizenry. Buckingham theorizes the significance of news journalism for a young audience, attempting to determine what role the media plays in "extending and developing young people's sense of their own political agency."[14] Conventional wisdom (frequently supported by academic studies) increasingly maintains that modern children and youth are remarkably uninterested in reading and watching the news. This lack of interest is often attributed to either a postmodern citizenry comprised of a disaffected and cynical generation, or to a general understanding that children are politically "innocent" and thus incompetent to make informed decisions. Suggesting that both these positions are a kind of cop-out, Buckingham argues that "children will only be likely to become 'active citizens,' capable of exercising, thoughtful choice in political matters, if they are presumed to be capable of doing so."[15] Within these terms, news programs for children are recognized as an important means through which young audiences can construct themselves as citizens. News programs for children (the few that are produced) offer factual information about current events and politics, and are considered "educational" television by the Children's Television Act of 1990. Nickelodeon produces perhaps the most successful U.S. children's news program, *Nick News*.[16] The program airs once a week, and is hosted by former network newscaster Linda Ellerbee (and is produced by her production company, Lucky Duck Productions). While most *Nick News* programs typically include four or five segments, Ellerbee also produces "news specials" which are entire programs dedicated to a particular cultural event, such as the aforementioned special on the terrorist attacks of September 11, "Kids, Terrorism, and the American Spirit."

In this episode, Ellerbee begins by addressing the audience, asking children to make sure their parents believe it to be appropriate for them to watch a television program about terrorism. Aesthetically, the setup of the news program, unlike most news shows, is quite casual: Ellerbee wears jeans and tennis shoes and addresses a diverse group of children from a cross-legged position on the floor. She begins the discussion by saying to the kids in the studio and the national audience: "We will not lie to you, and so we begin with the facts." The "facts" include not only a description of the September 11 attacks on the World Trade Center and the Pentagon but also a definition of terrorism itself. The episode is interspersed with video segments portraying displays of mourning and patriotism: candlelight vigils, flags, firefighters, and so on. Together with a child psychiatrist, Ellerbee questions the children in the studio, two of whom are wearing traditional Muslim clothing and headdress. She asks the children if they had watched television since the attacks, querying: "Do you think that kids should have been forbidden to watch television?" The children unanimously answered "No" to that question, with one child claiming, "We have a right to know." Ellerbee also asks the children what the response of the United States should be to the terrorist attacks, and asks specifically if "we" should bomb "them." The kids' answers to this question consisted primarily of proactive suggestions, for example, that children write letters, give blood, or help other kids. One of the children suggested that the United States rebuild the Twin Towers, but even higher than they were originally, "to prove that it's not going to let us down."

An important part of this special *Nick News* is a segment called "American Spirit." In this segment, Ellerbee narrates a mélange of images showing people helping victims of the attacks, giving blood, firefighters volunteering, people embracing around national images such as flags, candles, and other icons. These jingoistic displays of patriotism represented, for *Nick News,* the "American Spirit." Ellerbee says, "What we were seeing was the American spirit, and more important than anything else, it is that spirit that defines us as a nation, and no act of terrorism can take that from us." She also informs the audience that there is a message board on the Nickelodeon website that includes discussions about patriotism and the uniting of America during this crisis. From the moment Ellerbee began the program by informing the audience that she would "not lie" to them, it was clear that Ellerbee was taking her audience seriously as citizens.

Children's culture is fraught with conflict, contradiction, and power dynamics, despite the efforts of politicians, educators, academics, and parents to insist on childhood as a place that is innocent of the politics and power struggles that characterize adult culture. Occasionally, events within children's culture challenge both the construction of childhood "innocence" as a moralizing strategy that functions to obscure a more overt political agenda, and the notion that children themselves are outside the political world. Cultural scholar Henry Jenkins sees Ellerbee's *Nick News* as one of these events. As he argues, Ellerbee confronts the assumption that children are outside power dynamics "when she creates television programs that encourage children's awareness of real-world problems, such as the Los Angeles riots, and enable children to find their own critical voice to speak back against the adult world. She trusts children to confront realities from which other adults might shield them, offering them the facts needed to form their own opinions and the air time to discuss issues."[17] Aside from the episode on September 11, *Nick News* has also had special shows on the Clinton-Lewinsky scandal (the program won a Peabody award for that episode), as well as a special episode on the fate of children in Afghanistan since the United States declared war on that country, "Faces of Hope: The Kids of Afghanistan."

However, like all media productions, *Nick News* is situated within the children's television market in ways marked by tension. In other words, *Nick News* is not immune from the pressures to be more entertaining and sensational that often inhibit "adult" news programs from function-ing as a public sphere.[18] On Nickelodeon's message board, which Ellerbee encourages children to visit, users exchange e-mails discussing programming. On the link for *Nick News*, there are many messages that claim the show is boring and unnecessary. For example, in one message ti-tled "Nick News is sooooo lame," the child writes: "Nick News is so lame because of the way the peoples [*sic*] set it up. Instead of talking about news that adults care about in kid form, they should talk about things that matter to us (a.k.a. bands, the singer from TLC dying).[19] This kind of sentiment reflects the way in which "traditional" news formats such as *Nick News* can also work to alienate viewers by refusing to "talk about things that matter to us."

But the website itself is an interesting example of political debate. For example, although the majority of the messages seem to claim that *Nick News* is boring, others challenged this po-sition. One child responded to the previous e-mail message in the following way:

> So you don't care that Saddam Hussein [*sic*] has nukes and could blow us up? Or that he is giving 25 grand to families that send their kids out to blow up other kids? Or that women in Afghanistan get beaten because their clothes slipped down? Or because they laughed in public? Or what about 911? Did you care about that? Or should Nick News talk about "Holy Fishpaste, News Flash! The guy from some boy band broke up with britney Spears!" This is whats goin on in the world today, people, and theres no denying it. As sad as it is that a singer is dying, there's mil-lions of other people that live lives that are worse than being dead. Nick news tells us whats goin on without the graphic images of reality thats on NBC.[20]

The message boards on the Nickelodeon website seem to confront the conventional wisdom that children are "innocent" and outside the political world by insisting that at least *some* kids are invested in traditional politics; as another website visitor argued: "I like Nick News because it shows a lot of interesting things I never knew before. I also watch CNN too. Kids should watch the new[s] so they know what is going on around the world.[21]

But the message board also reveals another contradiction within Nickelodeon's rhetori-cal address: when *Nick News* is situated within the context of the network's claim that "kids should just be kids," the national news becomes, for some kids, part of that boring world of adults, and current events and political issues are understood as "things that adults care about." While this could be read as mere political disaffection on the part of children, it could also be seen as a challenge to conceive of citizenship in a realm outside that of "official" politics. The child who complained about the way *Nick News* was "set up" argued that within the commercial and entertainment realm (bands, popular musicians) events occur that kids *do* care about. There are tensions involved, then, in maintaining the "kids only zone" as more than mere rhetoric. Constructing an active audience which is treated not as beings in constant need of protection from the "adult" world, but rather as agents in this world, requires more than simply an acknowledgment that children can think for themselves. Constructing this audience also requires providing children with the active *means to* think for themselves. *Nick News* seems to provide these means for some children by encouraging them to be informed about the world, or to take an active role in their communities. However, providing the means to think for oneself not only involves this kind of political action, but also engages the balancing of the tension between insisting that children are *citizens* and addressing them as *consumers*.

KIDS EMPOWERMENT CONSUMERS AS CITIZENS

"[The] notion that young people are not apathetic but rather disenfranchised continues to privilege a particular view of politics as official and real . . ., and romanticizes the news media as the best source for the construction of this kind of political identity.[22] It seems clear that in order to understand the complexities of citizenship, we need to broaden this framework to include other, more contemporary processes and practices of political agency. Forms of popular culture and, more specifically, commercial entertainment, are not outside the realm of "official" politics; on the contrary, it is often within these realms that our understanding, resistance, and acquiescence to "official" politics are constituted.[23]

For example, the generational address of Nickelodeon is not only dedicated to recognizing children's *political* agency as it has been traditionally defined. It also recognizes the politics involved in recognizing children as a powerful consumer market in their own right, separate from adults. As Laybourne argues, "Nick empowers kids by saying to them, 'You're important—important enough to have a network of your own.'"[24] Indeed, it is clear that in the current cultural climate, visibility (whether on television, music, or other media outlets) does equal power—especially for children. In other words, being recognized as a "demographic" indicates a certain kind of power, and Nickelodeon certainly picks up on this dynamic. The unproblematic collapse that Laybourne makes between the realization of children as an important consumer group and perceived political power—"you're important enough to have a network of your own"—is certainly not a new phenomenon with adults, but the steadily increasing purchasing power of children ages four to eleven (American companies spend more than twenty times what they spent ten years ago on advertising for children, approximately $2 billion each year) should be a reason to pause and consider how these issues of citizenship, perceived political power, and consumer power are crucially intertwined.[25] Consumption habits code individuals as members of particular communities, and grant individuals a kind of power that accompanies such membership. Thus, citizenship is increasingly defined within consumer culture—indeed, as a *process* of consumption itself. Nickelodeon's self-conscious address about kids "as kids" is as much about the *purchasing* power of kids as it is about the *political* power of kids; in fact, these two discourses inform and constitute each other.

It seems, then, that the grandiose claim made by Nickelodeon that they "pledge allegiance to kids" is about both these discourses simultaneously. Simply claiming that children are separate from adults, and have their own agendas, needs, and desires is not quite enough to make a claim of political agency, because political agency is not necessarily defined within terms such as autonomy, independence, and "rights-bearing" citizens any longer (if it ever truly was). But we *do* define citizenship (and thus political agency) in terms of our consumption habits, and we *are* recognized as meaningful citizens depending on both an economic and a cultural recognition of our purchasing power (hence the political power of boycotts). The ability to consume, and thus constitute a "market," has everything to do with one's perceived political power. Nickelodeon's claim to be a network "just for kids" is one of the ways in which it acknowledges the connection between political subjectivity and consumer identity: it is not simply a place defined exclusively for kids; it also capitalizes on the enormous commercial potential of its child audience. . . .

As I've discussed, an important element of Nickelodeon's self-construction is its insistence that kids are an active audience in their own right, separate from the world of adults. Indeed, as much of Nickelodeon's programming demonstrates, "adults just don't get it." Part of what adults "just don't get" are the consumption habits of youth, which are important markers of identity and ways of distinguishing one social group from another.[26] The boundary between the worlds of children and adults that is implied by the idea that adults "don't get" the world of children is important to the self-construction of children as particular kinds of citizens. Indeed, Allison James has argued that the deliberate mystification of children's culture by children is crucial for the self-conscious construction of the child as an individual: "The true nature of the culture of childhood frequently remains hidden from adults, for the semantic cues which permit social recognition have been manipulated and disguised by children in terms of their alternative society. . . . By confusing the adult order children create for themselves considerable room for movement with the limits imposed upon them by adult society."[27] A successful way of manipulating adult authority as a means to create a separate children's culture has been to select consumer goods that are distinctly outside the adult world, whether these choices be situated in popular music, fashion, or television programming. However, this strategy does not simply establish "an alternative system of meanings which adults cannot perceive"; it also constructs children as a very important demographic.[28] In fact, according to marketing specialist James McNeal, "tweens," children between the ages of eight and twelve have "become the 'powerhouse' of the kids' market, spending close to $14 billion a year" and thus becoming a "retailer's dream.[29] The children's media market is especially attractive because of its multidimensional appeal: children have money of their own (and more and more each year), they have influence over the purchasing power of their parents, and they are considered a market for the future.[30] The relatively newfound (or at least, newly energized) recognition of children as a lucrative market has resulted in their increased visibility in the mass media—after all, part of targeting the tween market means that corporate culture needs to provide a kind of representation that is both appealing and inclusive.

Nickelodeon's claim of being a "kids only zone," then, is not simply about acknowledging youth as an audience in their own right, but also about the specific recognition of this audience as an important group of consumers. However, the construction of children as consumers has historically been formulated as a relationship characterized by *dependence* and manipulation rather than *independence* and individual agency. For example, media scholar Marsha Kinder argues that Nickelodeon's persistence in claiming that the network is a place just for kids relies upon an overt strategy of dividing children from adults as two very different consumer groups. In fact, she reads Nickelodeon's emphasis on generational conflict as a strategy that actually functions commercially as *transgenerational*.[31] The issue of media inclusion—a "network of your own"—is thus inseparable from other corporate and commercial interests and points to Nickelodeon's transgenerational address as a slippery strategy to target the kid market, rather than a means to empower kids as citizens.

. . . It is not merely the advertising that supports Nickelodeon that constructs its audience as consumer-citizens. This address is also present in the tensions and ironies of much of the programming. For example, consider "Rugrats Discover America." Ostensibly in honor of Columbus Day (although neither the historical figure nor the federal holiday is mentioned in the special), the program was aired about a month after the World Trade Center and Pentagon attacks, and took a different tack at representing American citizenship from the *Nick News* special discussed earlier. The program is a widely popular animated series that features four babies who constantly get into trouble and a group of parents who are generally clueless about what their children are "really" up to, a direct reference to Nickelodeon's rhetoric of generational conflict. "Rugrats Discover America" opens with the grandparents of some of the characters distributing souvenirs to the children from their recent trip across America. The souvenirs include a Native American artifact and a toy Statue of Liberty. These souvenirs prompt a fantasy by the main characters involving a vacation across America in a tour bus, with stops at particular places of interest. These include the Grand Canyon, the American West, and New York City. A side story features two older child characters taking a motorcycle trip across the same terrain, complete with Easy Rider outfits and a version of "Born to Be Wild" playing on the soundtrack (a visual trope that assumes a transgenerational audience).

The *Rugrats* special offers a pointed and specific version of citizenship; focusing on popular culture and tourism, this program defines citizenship in terms of the consumer who acquires "national" knowledge at different tourist stops around the country that are then represented in souvenirs. This definition of citizenship, as an American consumer spirit represented in popular film references and commercial souvenirs (a kind of "cultural capital" that seems to be a specific prerequisite for citizenship), is offered alongside the broader, idealist American "spirit" represented in more jingoistic displays of patriotism such as the *Nick News* special. The two definitions of citizenship inform and constitute each other, and in so doing, help to form the social construction of the child-citizen for Nickelodeon's audience. This then combines with the recent marketing campaign for the network that celebrates the "Nickelodeon Nation," as well as the promises to "pledge allegiance to kids," the encouragement of its young audience to "exercise those choice muscles," and the insistence that "You have more power than you think!" As Heather Hendershot has pointed out, Nickelodeon's emphasis on the "rights" of kids places in bold relief the connection *and* the tension between rights and modern citizenship, where rights for kids who watch Nickelodeon are most crucially the "right" to make purchases, and the "choices" that are exercised are consumer choices.[32]

Finally, then, it is this *tension*, between political and consumer rights, that most profoundly characterizes a modern sense of citizenship for both adults and children. For children, who are culturally situated outside formal, legal political rights, consumption habits take on perhaps even added significance in the construction of citizenship. In other words, while it is certainly true that political rights remain an important democratic freedom in the construction of citizenship, it is also the case that these older forms of understanding oneself as a citizen have been reformulated in the context of modern consumer culture. Rather, it is the *intermingling* of political rights and consumption habits that most profoundly characterizes citizenship. . . .

Yet, as Ellen Seiter has argued, to be "just a kid" means in part to establish an imagined community with other children based on goods and commercial items. Seiter points out that

"Toys, commercials, and animated programs are the lingua franca of young children at babysitters' and grandmothers' houses, day-care centers, and preschools across the United States."[33] Seiter argues that commercial goods provide children with "a shared repository of images," and this in turn allows for processes of identification based on race, class, and citizenship. Nickelodeon's vast empire of programming, toys, clothing, and other commercial goods clearly establishes a "shared repository of images" for its audience, which in turn organizes an imagined community based on a sense of belonging and membership.

In fact, according to Geraldine Laybourne, Nickelodeon's licensing agreement with the toy company Mattel is based on creating "the ideal citizen" through the particular marketing of toys. According to Laybourne, Nickelodeon was faced with a dilemma when it began working with Mattel because of Mattel's obvious gender-specific marketing. Since Nickelodeon was committed to banning gender-specific programming from its lineup (in an effort to be more inclusive of girls, a severely neglected demographic in children's programming), and since Mattel designs most of its products specifically for boys or girls, Nickelodeon worked with Mattel to design toys with empowerment in mind: "We hold to a philosophy of quality, of variety, of self-discovery for kids. We believe that boys and girls should be treated as equals. We expect the unexpected. And we seek to build a bridge for kids with the past, with what their parents did, that connects them to the whole history of American childhood."[34] Laybourne also argues that Nickelodeon's use of focus groups in its toy design is about recognizing the agency of children: "Surveys and research are the first steps in empowering kids—Nickelodeon's central mission. As part of the Nickelodeon Experience, when kids are given self-esteem and a voice, they are encouraged to make choices."[35] Again, the "choices" that Nickelodeon's audience are encouraged to make are consumer choices, and the network's "central mission" of empowerment is as much about authorizing kids as consumers as it is about empowering them in a more traditional political sense.

CONCLUSION: CHILDREN AS CITIZENS

I really like nick news sometimes they have good topics sometimes and yes sometimes it makes me wanna go out and help others

Nick News Message Board
RE: nick news rocks
Date: 06/18/02

Kids need to hear about what's going on in the world now, so they'll be better prepared to face and deal with it when they step out of their homes, and into the real world. Yes, it might be boring at times, but it is a necessary evil—and one which we must acknowledge . . .

Nick News Message Board
RE: No kids care about this stuff? oh really!?!
Date: 06/26/02

This is a club for everyone!!!!!!!! As long as you like rugrats you can gone [join] my club!!!!!! All you have to do is tell me why you like the rugrats and then you can join!!!!!! bye

Rugrats Message Board
RE: a rugrats club
Date: 04/16/02. . .

Certainly children have been addressed historically as citizens-in-the-making or as potential citizens. Many patriotic rituals—the Pledge of Allegiance, the school textbook, or student government—are about the education of young children to be citizens. Much of children's television has also approached children through this education angle. But to be considered "in-process" is to deny a particular power dynamic involved in identity making. In other words, it is difficult to exercise empowered and informed choices when always considered in a state of becoming. Nickelodeon seems to challenge this by addressing children as *citizens already*, and attending to their needs accordingly. If citizenship is both something that is ideologically "imposed" upon a member of society, and something that one creates and produces through activity, interaction, and identity construction, then Nickelodeon's strategy of addressing kids "as kids" is to consider its audience as citizens. The commercial structure of the network allows for even more coherence to this community, and allows children to politically connect with their own needs and desires rather than those defined by adults.

But . . . consumption habits need to be combined with political action to elevate the status of consumers to that of citizens. Among other things, this means requiring "democratic participation by the principal sectors of civil society in material, symbolic, juridical, and political decisions that organize consumption.[36] It is unclear whether Nickelodeon truly fosters this kind of intermixing of democratic participation and consumption. For the one child who wrote to the website claiming that watching *Nick News* made him "wanna go out and help others," there are even more children who demonstrate a much more cynical and disaffected view toward reflexive political action. Nickelodeon, like citizenship itself, is characterized by tension. The empowerment rhetoric of the network is at times connected to a more traditional material politics, such as the *Nick News* specials and other social outreach programs developed by Nickelodeon. At the same time, this empowerment rhetoric must be read through the lens of consumer culture. Thus, Nickelodeon's insistence that kids "exercise their choice muscles" often indicates a kind of empowerment that emerges through the recognition that children are a lucrative market. Either way, children are constructed as citizens. Whether citizenship is formulated in a meaningful way *within* consumer culture, a way that allows for the production of the social and political life of youth as a specific *function* of consumption, remains to be seen.

Discussion Questions

1. Do you think *Nickelodeon* program *Nick News* helps its viewers become active, aware citizens?

2. How does the conception of children as "innocent victims" contrast with the "active players" perspective?

3. Nickelodeon boasts that its programs are on "for kids." Do you agree with this? Why or why not?

4. What do you think would best promote active citizenship amongst children, particularly since they are not eligible to vote?

Notes

1. See Carolyn Marvin, *When Old Technologies Were New: Thinking about Electric Communication in the Late Nineteenth Century* (London: Oxford University Press, 1990); Lynn Spigel, *Make Room for TV: Television and the Family Ideal in Postwar* America (Chicago: University of Chicago Press, 1992), Michele Hilmes, *Radio Voices: American Broadcasting, 1922–1952* (Minneapolis: University of Minnesota Press, 1997); and George Lipsitz, *Time Passages: Collective Memory and American*

Popular Culture (Minneapolis: University of Minnesota Press, 1990), among others.

2. Spigel, *Make Room for TV*, 53–55.

3. Ellen Seiter, *Sold Separately: Children and Parents in Consumer Culture* (New Brunswick: Rutgers University Press, 1993); and Stephen Kline, "The Making of Children's Culture," in Henry Jenkins, ed., *The Children's Culture Reader* (New York: NYU Press, 1998).

4. Henry Jenkins, "Introduction," in Jenkins, ed., *Children's Culture Reader;* and Marsha Kinder, "Kids' Media Culture: An introduction," in Marsha Kinder, ed., *Kids' Media Culture* (Durham: Duke University Press, 1999).

5. Joe Austin and Michael Nevin Willard, "Introduction: Angels of History, Demons of Culture," in Joe Austin and Michael Nevin, eds., *Generations of Youth: Youth Cultures and History in Twentieth-Century America* (New York: NYU Press, 1998), 1.

6. Ibid., 2.

7. Geraldine Laybourne, "The Nickelodeon Experience," in G. L. Berry and J. K. Asamen, eds., *Children and Television* (London: Sage, 1993). See also Sally Helgesen, *The Web of Inclusion* (New York: Doubleday), 1995.

8. Laybourne, "Nickelodeon Experience," 304.

9. Lynn Spigel, "Seducing the Innocent: Childhood and Television in Post-War America," in Jenkins, ed., *Children's Culture Reader*, 110.

10. Laybourne, "Nickelodeon Experience," 305.

11. Laybourne, cited in Helgesen, *Web of Inclusion*, 222.

12. Helgesen, *Web of Inclusion*, 222.

13. David Buckingham, *After the Death of Childhood: Growing Up in the Age of Electronic Media* (Cambridge: Polity Press, 2000), 163.

14. Buckingham, *After the Death of Childhood*, 168.

15. Ibid., 169.

16. Another U.S. children's news program, *Channel One News*, is arguably the least successful news program currently aired, at least in terms of the interests of its child audience. *Channel One News* is transmitted to U.S. schools, with the ostensible purpose of using the show as a kind of tutorial. According to David Buckingham, schools receive around $50,000 in equipment when they subscribe to the show, but part of the deal is to broadcast the programming to 90 percent of the students, including the two minutes of advertising that accompanies every ten-minute segment. Because of this, it has been extremely controversial in the United States, and as Buckingham points out, there is little evidence that the news show is actively used by either teachers or students. Buckingham, *Making of Citizens,* and David

Buckingham, "News and Advertising in the Classroom: Some Lessons from the Channel One Controversy," *International Journal of Media and Communication Studies* (1997, vol. 1).

17. Jenkins, "Introduction," 32.

18. Dana Polan, "The Public's Fear; or, Media as Monster in Habermas, Negt, and Kluge," in Robbins, *Phantom Public Sphere.*

19. Nickelodeon website, Message Board, *Nick News.* http://www.nick.com. Accessed June 2002.

20. Ibid.

21. Ibid.

22. Ibid., 175–182.

23. For more on this, see Robbins, *Phantom Public Sphere.*

24. Laybourne, "Nickelodeon Experience," 304.

25. Edward Cohn, "Marketwatch: Consuming Kids," *The American Prospect* 11:6 (June 28, 2002).

26. For more on this, see, for example, Dick Hebdige, *Subculture: The Meaning of Style* (London: Methuen, 1979); John Fiske, *Reading the Popular* (London: Unwyn Hyman, 1989); and Angela McRobbie, *Feminism and Youth Culture* (New York: Routledge, 1991).

27. Allison James, "Confections, Concoctions, and Conceptions," in Jenkins, ed., *Children's Culture Reader,* 394–395.

28. Ibid., 404.

29. Barbara Kantrowitz and Pat Wingert, "Tweens," *Newsweek* (October 18, 1999).

30. This point was made by Ellen Seiter in talk given to the Annenberg School for Communication, University of Southern California, April 2001.

31. Marsha Kinder, "Home Alone in the 90s: Generational War and Transgenerational Address in American Movies, Television, and Presidential Politics" in Cary Bazalgette and David Buckingham, eds., *In Front of the Children: Screen Entertainment and Young Audiences* (London: British Film Institute, 1995), 75–91.

32. Heather Hendershot, *Saturday Morning Censors: Television Regulation Before the V-Chip* (Durham: Duke University Press, 1998), 217–118.

33. Ellen Seiter, "Children's Desires/mothers' Dilemmas: The Social Contexts of Consumption," in Jenkins, ed., *Children's Culture Redder,* 297.

34. Laybourne, cited in Helgesen, *Web of Inclusion,* 230–231. Of course, this desire to "build a bridge for kids with the past," thus connecting kids with their parents, reveals a contradiction in Laybourne's idealist philosophy, for surely the parents of the current generation played with gender-specific toys.

35. Ibid., 228.

36. Canclini, *Consumers and Citizens,* 46.

Talking Dirty: Children, Sexual Knowledge, and Television

PETER KELLY, DAVID BUCKINGHAM, AND HANNAH DAVIES

INTRODUCTION

Television is often blamed for making sexual knowledge available to children, and thereby for promoting 'inappropriate' attitudes and behavior. [Peter Kelley, David Buckingham, and Hannah Davies gathered data] as part of a larger research project about the changing nature of the child television audience. [The research project] considers how children (aged 6–7 and 10–11) interpret and respond to the representations of sexual behavior they encounter on television, for example in genres such as soap operas and dating game shows; and how they define what is appropriate both for themselves and for children in general. Using discourse analysis, the [chapter] examines how children's discussions of these issues serve as a form of 'identity work', through which they define what it means to be a child.

Recent sociological studies have questioned many of the distinctions that are typically drawn between childhood and adulthood. Childhood, they argue, is a social construction that is defined in different ways in different cultures and in different historical periods. As such, the boundaries between childhood and adulthood are inevitably problematic: they are subject to an ongoing negotiation, and they have to be continually monitored and policed (James et al., 1998).

One of the most obvious ways in which this is manifested is in relation to sexual knowledge. Information about sexual behavior is typically deemed to be appropriate only for adolescents and adults. It is seen to be part of the essential condition of childhood that children should remain fundamentally 'innocent' (or ignorant) of such matters. In her book *Childhood and Sexuality*, Stevi Jackson argues that although the latter half of the 20th century (saw) the blurring of some of the boundaries between adulthood and childhood, the subject of children and sexuality remains extremely taboo: 'If we regard children as a special category of people and sexuality as a special area of life, then any meeting between the two is likely to be explosive' (Jackson, 1982: 2).

The issue of children and sexual knowledge thus provokes some of the fiercest arguments about the apparent erosion of traditional notions of childhood. As in many other areas, the notion of childhood comes to be used here as the vehicle for much broader concerns about the social order. Conservatives hold sexual permissiveness partly responsible for what they perceive as social decline; while liberals argue that sexual repression leads to a whole range of social ills. These views overlap in complex ways with different perspectives on childhood. Thus, on the one hand, children's awareness of sexuality can be seen as a healthy, natural phenomenon, which is distinguished from some of the more distorted or corrupted conceptions of adults. On the other hand, it can also be viewed as precocious or unnatural (see Hey, 1997: Ch. 6); and the acquisition of sexual knowledge can be seen to weaken the boundaries between childhood and adulthood, which are apparently designed to protect children. For conservatives, access to sexual knowledge is often regarded as part of a more general permissiveness, equated with a rise in violence, drug use and criminal activity among children. From this perspective, sexual knowledge places children *in danger,* but it also makes them potentially *dangerous.*

Like many other countries, Britain has seen a succession of 'moral panics' over the past decade around children and sex, ranging from issues such as the sexual abuse of children and pedophilia, to the . . . rates of teenage pregnancy. Many of these debates have hinged on the question of children's allegedly 'premature' access to sexual knowledge. Battles have repeatedly been fought in the media . . . about sex education, the availability of advice on contraception, education about HIV and AIDS and the supposed 'promotion' of non-monogamous or non-heterosexual 'lifestyles' in schools (Corteen and Scraton, 1997; Pilcher, 1996). There is now widespread confusion, both among professionals and among young people themselves, about the kinds of information that can legally be provided to children. As Jane Pilcher (1996) has argued, these debates raise much broader questions about children's competence as social actors, and their rights of citizenship. Typically, however, these eruptions of anxiety focus on the rights of *parents* to control their children's access to sexual knowledge, in the face of what is seen as 'interference' from others—not least from the media.

Childhood has been increasingly understood by adults in terms of risk (Hood et al., 1996); and sexual risks are high on the public agenda of potential threats to children and childhood. As Mary Douglas (1992) has pointed out, where there is risk, there is blame. Arguably, much of the blame for the supposed loosening of sexual boundaries and the subsequent 'loss' of children's innocence has been placed on television. . . . Neil Postman (1983), for example, claims that the creation of modern childhood was only made possible by the emergence of print literacy; and that the demise of print literacy and of rise of electronic media will lead to the disappearance of childhood as we know it. Postman describes television as a 'total disclosure medium': it makes the 'secrets' of the adult world—including sexual knowledge—available to children, and hence destroys the 'shame' that should surround them. Likewise, Joshua Meyrowitz (1985) argues that children's relatively open access to television allows them to share rituals and experiences previously confined to adults: undermining the separation between children and adults in this way will, he predicts, inevitably lead to a reduction in the power and authority of adults.

The evidence in support of these arguments is somewhat dubious, however. Most obviously, there is the danger of looking back to an imaginary 'age of innocence' before the advent of television—a notion that is largely rejected by most childhood historians.[1] Furthermore, holding television responsible reflects a kind of technological determinism.

While there clearly are connections between media such as print or television and broader developments in society, those connections are much more complex, and much less unidirectional than these authors would suggest. Nevertheless, even those who dissent from Postman's view recognize that television has played an important role in reflecting new conceptions of childhood and in shaping children's lives.

The concerns voiced by Postman, Meyrowitz and others apply primarily to children's access to adult television: the problem is precisely that both groups are watching the same things, or that children's and adults' programs are becoming indistinguishable (Davies, 1995: 30). In Britain, measures . . . for family viewing were specifically designed to separate adult and child audiences; and regulatory bodies have specific guidelines for monitoring standards of 'taste and decency' during periods when children are more likely to be viewing. However, concerns have also been raised in relation to representations of sexuality in *children's* television over the years. . . . Some children's broadcasters have hit back at these criticisms, arguing that while they may be disturbing to adults, such programs try to deal with the reality of the lives of older children in ways that are both entertaining and informative (Home, 1993: 14).

The debate about children's exposure to representations of sexuality on television is thus polarized. On one side, there are those who continue to argue that sex and sexuality should be kept secret from children, and consequently call for greater censorship and control. On the other side are those who claim that children have a right to watch programs which may deal with their emotional needs and concerns, including those relating to sexuality. Ultimately, however, even the most traditional moralists must recognize that children do not exist in a vacuum from the rest of society, and that they will inevitably acquire sexual knowledge in all sorts of ways—not only from television.

DEFINING THE CHILD AUDIENCE

If we look beyond the debate about censorship, however, some rather different questions emerge. The issue is not so much about what children should or should not know, but about what they do with what they actually *do* know, In other words, how do children interpret and respond to the various representations of sexual behavior that they encounter through television? What kinds of knowledge do *they* feel are 'appropriate' or 'suitable', both for themselves and for children in general? And how do their discussions of these issues help them to define what it means to be a 'child' or an 'adult'?

The data presented here are drawn from a larger study of changing views of the child audience for television.[2] . . . We wanted to understand how children perceived *themselves* as an audience (see Buckingham, 1994). To this end, we conducted a series of open-ended interviews and more structured activities with groups of children . . . age 6–7 and . . . age 10–11 in one socially and ethnically mixed inner London primary school.[3] Though our research was not intended to be ethnographic, we also spent several days with each class prior to the interviews, observing or helping out with classroom activities and talking with the children. On other occasions, such as before or after lessons, we also talked to the children more informally, for instance being given snippets of 'gossip' about classroom or staffroom romances (see Epstein and Johnson, 1997).

Our position in this context was profoundly ambiguous. In our interviews the children were away from their teacher, and were being asked their opinions about television—a subject still rarely considered to be a legitimate focus for discussion in classrooms. This in itself afforded us a considerable degree of access to children's out-of-school cultures. Nevertheless, talking about television in an interview setting obviously differs from doing so in the playground or at home (Buckingham, 1993a: Ch. 3); and as adults in the context of a school, we inevitably shared in a certain 'teacherly' authority. We were effectively inviting 'playground talk' of a kind that was generally frowned upon in the classroom,[4] and introducing issues such as sex or violence therefore served as a means for the children to 'test' the degree to which we might choose to exercise our authority. . . .

We began with a series of relatively open-ended discussions about the children's likes and dislikes in television.[5] These were followed by two more focused activities. The first was a scheduling exercise, in which the children were invited to construct 'ideal' viewing schedules for themselves (and in the case of the 10- to 11-year-olds, also for 6- to 7-year-olds) from a broad range of program titles provided. In terms of their original scheduling, some of these programs were aimed at an adult audience (that is, shown after 9 p.m.); some at family audiences (early evening); and some at children (morning/late afternoon). This activity therefore attempted to tap into children's understanding of how childhood and adulthood are constructed within television schedules, and how far they challenged these definitions of space and time. The second activity was a sorting exercise, in which children were invited to categorize a similarly broad assortment of program titles in terms of whether they were 'for children' or 'for adults'. In practice, of course, many groups chose to have more than two categories, including a pile for programs that were 'for everyone', or for 'teenagers' or 'babies'.

Throughout each of these activities, the children were invited to comment and reflect on their choices and decisions. They were also permitted to make changes as the discussion progressed. The activities were intended to facilitate discussion, rather than to accurately reflect children's viewing tastes or habits; and it is these discussions that we primarily focus on here. However, the 'results' of these two exercises (that is, the children's final choices) are of some interest, even if in many respects they were fairly predictable. The schedules devised by the 10- to 11-year-olds, for example, displayed a general preference for comedy and drama, though there was a mix between 'lighter' material such as the sitcoms *Friends* and *Sabrina the Teenage Witch* or the dating game show *Blind Date* and the more serious 'adult' dramas, such as *Casualty* and *The X-Files,* which were often scheduled later in the evening. The 6- to 7-year-olds tended to select children's programs such as *Rugrats, Goosebumps* and *Art Attack,* as well as light entertainment or 'family' programs, such as *Gladiators* and *You've Been Framed.* Animation such as *The Simpsons* and 'action' dramas such as *The New Adventures of Superman* were also popular; while most children avoided non-fiction programs, with the exception of the animal documentary *Vets in Practice*—a particularly popular choice for girls in both year groups.

Program choices made by 10- to 11-year-olds frequently centered around genres that explore the 'personal'. Soap-style dramas featured prominently in all or the older children's selections, among boys as well as girls. . . . Dating game shows such as *Blind Date* and talk shows such as *Rikki Lake* were also popular. Conversely, 6- to 7-yesr-olds were less likely to choose either soaps or 'romantic' dating games as preferred viewing; and boys especially dismissed the parts of programs that featured elements of romance, such as that between Superman and Lois Lane. In both instances, these children agreed that programs that dealt with personal/sexual matters were more for 'teenagers' or 'adults' than for children. Thus, while few of the 6- to 7-year-olds yet aspired to join this teen audience, most of the 10- to 11-year-olds positively identified with it.

In both activities, the children used many criteria in distinguishing 'children's' and 'adults'' programs;[6] and, predictably, the presence of 'sex' or 'rude words' was one of these.

Likewise, although we did not explicitly seek to introduce the topic, the children would commonly raise issues to do with sex and sexuality in more open-ended group discussions about television. As we indicate later, these discussions served particular and complex functions for the children, both in negotiating gender- and age-specific identities and relationships, and more broadly in making sense of their own experiences both at home and at school.

The kind of material referred to in these terms was quite diverse. In the following sections of this chapter we focus primarily on three distinct areas or genres of television: 'adult' films and dramas; dating game shows; . . . and situation comedies. In each case, sexual activity is clearly represented in quite different ways—for example, with greater or lesser 'explicitness', or with different degrees of humor or seriousness. Sex occasionally features in the context of marital relationships or alternatively outside them; as something associated with violence, and as something associated with pleasure; as something illicit or forbidden, or as something everyday and even banal. These differences clearly exert constraints on the kinds of positions the children are able to adopt in discussion.

CROSSING BOUNDARIES

For some children at least, sex in 'adult' programs has the appeal of 'forbidden fruit'. In our more open-ended discussions about television likes and dislikes, children from both . . . groups were fully aware that certain adult programs were supposedly 'off limits' because they contained sex, violence or bad language. Certain films or programs achieved a kind of mythic status in exchanges within the groups: children would frequently ask each other whether they had seen particular horror films, or those that contained notorious scenes of violence, rather than sex, such as Quentin Tarantino's *Pulp Fiction*.[7] The children's knowledge of these films sometimes appeared limited, and it wasn't always clear whether or not they had actually seen them, or were simply pretending that they had.[8] Nonetheless, they appeared to take great pleasure in recounting specific scenes from 'forbidden' films, not least because they knew they were 'not supposed' to watch them. In the following extract, three 10-year-old boys discuss the film *Trainspotting,* which two of them (and the male interviewer) had seen the previous evening.[9] Significantly, the boys refer to two scenes in the film: one in which an addict retrieves drugs from a filthy toilet, and another involving the same character's theft of a pornographic video belonging to (and featuring) his friend and girlfriend:

B1: [to 1] Did you watch *Trainspotting* last night?

I: I did, yes.

B2: I watched it, it was all about junkies.

B1: And he [character] went down the toilet.

I: Oh, that was horrible, that bit.

B3: I don't watch things like that.

B2: Disgusting!

I: So did you watch the whole of *Trainspotting,* or just some of it?

B1: All of it. He got dumped because he couldn't find the video.

Through their selective description of the film, the first two boys clearly set out to define themselves in a particular way. While they were friends, they appeared to be socially and academically marginalized in relation to the other children in the class.[10] Their discussion of the film is used to further cultivate and celebrate their 'bad boy' image in front of the two male interviewers, and in contrast to the third boy who comments (with implicit disapproval) that he doesn't watch 'things like that'. It is significant in this respect that the topic of *Trainspotting* is introduced by one of the boys, in an almost casual enquiry that seems to position the interviewer on a similar level to himself. Both boys are keen to illustrate the apparent lack of adult constraint on their viewing late into the night. In response to the interviewer's somewhat disbelieving question, the first boy is adamant that he saw the whole film, despite the fact that it began at 10 p.m. on a Sunday night, and describes an additional scene from it in order to back up his claim. The boy's selective reference to these two specific scenes is evidently intended to shock the interviewer, whom he knows has seen the film, and hence raise his status among the group for having seen some 'forbidden' material.[11] There is a kind of relish about the second boy's 'disgusting!' which distances him from the interviewer's professed squeamishness. These boys' defiance towards what they believe are adult conceptions of 'good' children is thus a kind of self-conscious celebration of the moralists' worst nightmare—children staying up late, in the company of adults, watching explicit 'adult' material.

An equally common—albeit more subtle—tactic here was for the children to use humor, often by ironically expressing shock at explicit sex scenes from a film. In doing so, the children were to some extent parodying adult conceptions of children as sexual 'innocents' by inferring their awareness of the sexual. In the following extract, for instance, one girl (in a group of three girls) describes a highly explicit scene at the beginning of the film *Rita, Sue and Bob Too*.[12] Without spelling out precisely what happens, her innuendo implies a certain sexual 'knowingness', and provokes much laughter from the others. At the same time she voices 'surprise' that such material was being shown when she was still viewing:

> G: I watched a film—*Rita, Sue, and Bob Too*. I only watched the beginning of it—[breaking into laughter]—and it was about this man, yeah, and he just started—[more laughing in the group]—and then this other man was lying on the floor and he was sick—it was on at 9 o'clock and it was *really early.*

The girl here self-consciously plays the role of the 'precocious' child. Clearly, the pleasure and status gained in revealing (or even implying) one's sexual knowledge to adults and other children derives from the fact that one is seen to be crossing into adult territory. The laughter here could be seen to reflect a recognition of this, and of the inappropriateness (and even subversiveness) of drawing attention to it in this context. Yet, as with the previous example, the girl's revelations are also predicated on the understanding that, as a child, she should not really know or speak about sex: the film has been shown '*really* early', thereby running the risk that it will be seen by children who (she implies) should be protected from such material. She thus mocks adult conventions around childhood and sexuality, while simultaneously reinforcing them: she herself knows about these things, but 'children' should nevertheless be protected from them.

The two excerpts above suggest that the appeal of such 'forbidden' programs is as much to do with the fact of gaining access to them as it is to do with their actual content. Programs notorious for featuring scenes of sex (or for the younger children, action and horror genres) were for many children symbolic of entry into adult time and space. Viewing adult television meant staying up late (whether by permission or not), and watching the same programs as older siblings, parents or other grown-ups.

Although they claimed to be crossing these boundaries, most of the children were still subject to differing levels of parental constraint placed on viewing. Unsurprisingly, the younger children's access to television appeared to be governed far more strictly. Many of the 6- to 7-year-olds were unfamiliar with popular adult programs shown later in the evening, and a number said that they were not allowed to watch television beyond a certain time. Older children claimed that access to late evening programs often involved negotiation with parents—although their accounts of these negotiations usually resulted in the child coming out 'on top'. In the context of group interviews, it was not surprising that they tended to play down the extent to which they were censored or constrained by bedtimes (see Buckingham, 1993a: Ch. 5). Children discussed a whole rang of strategies they employed in order to view these forbidden programs. For instance, those who had televisions in their bedrooms described how they would watch programs after their 'official' bedtimes without their parents finding out, or when other adults were watching in the living room. Other children talked about negotiating *between* parents about access to programs playing one off against the other.

Children's position within the family was another important factor here. Children who had older siblings or younger parents were more likely to mention co-viewing adult programs with them. For instance, a number of the 10- to 11-year-old girls talked about watching soaps and dramas with older sisters or mothers. Conversely, children with younger siblings had to negotiate more carefully with parents, since they were effectively testing new limits of parental regulation. In the following extract, another 10-year-old boy, who was the eldest child in a large family, describes how he has resolved the difficulties of having to fit in his preferred viewing with his younger siblings' bedtime patterns, with the collusion of his mother:

> B: What I do is I get my mum to tape everything that I really want to see, like
> *Friends, Frasier, You've Been Framed* and so on—and on Saturday mornings
> I just go upstairs, sit under the covers and watch television for about 3 hours.

DATING GAMES

Although adults continue to attempt to shield children from sexual knowledge, it is considered more acceptable for children to witness expressions of intimacy between adults that take the form of heterosexual 'romance'.[13] Thus, a number of groups selected and discussed the television game show *Blind Date*. . . .

In her study of children in US schools, Barrie Thorne (1993) observed that for boys and girls, discourse around 'going with' (that is, dating) members of the opposite sex took increasing precedence by this age. Dating, along with a growing interest in fashion and pop music, were positively linked to participating in teen cultures, and were part of what Thorne calls the 'rituals which shape the transition into adolescence' (Thorne, 1993: 140–1). Clearly, certain television genres form part of this culture. Debbie Epstein (1997), for instance, found that older primary schoolchildren borrowed elements of these dating shows and incorporated them into games and rituals that took place between girls and boys in the playground or classroom. Likewise, it became evident in our study that some of the children had participated in similar 'dating games', and one group discussed having staged a version of *Blind Date* with classmates the previous year.

At this age, the 'dating' appeared largely to be a form of role rehearsal, rather than leading to actual relationships. To an extent, 'playing' at dating, with all its emotional triumphs and cruelties, mirrored the playing out of romance on the television game shows; and this lack of seriousness was acknowledged as such by the children. In the following extract, (a) group of girls discusses whether or not children should watch *Blind Date*. One of the girls has reservations about 'children' watching (by which she means younger children), inferring that they should be shielded from such material:

G1: I don't think they [children] should watch it.

G2: I think it's for all ages really.

I: Do you think *Blind Date's* rude at all?

All: No, no!

G2: 'Cause they—they ask some silly questions, you go away with this guy you pick [then] come back [and say] 'Oh we didn't get on. . .'

When pressed by the (female) interviewer, the girls conclude that the program isn't really sexually 'rude'. They understand that the formula of *Blind Date* is ultimately about pretence and performance.

By contrast, while the 6- to 7-year-olds were familiar with *Blind Date,* they were generally dismissive of it. However, their rejection of the program was not on the grounds of its moral inappropriateness, as this might be understood by adults or indeed by the girl just quoted. On the contrary, these children claimed that they were simply not interested in the show's romantic content. They professed to know about romance or 'kissing', but equated this with the more 'boring' aspects of 'adult' television. At least in respect of this kind of material, the identity of the adult or teen viewer was not aspired to, but on the contrary rejected.

As this implies, such responses reflected the children's attempts to position themselves in relation to dominant, publicly available conceptions of age differences. Predictably, gender also played a role here. Thus, children sometimes expressed very strong views about what they regarded as programs 'for girls' and those 'for boys'. Younger boys in particular defined their 'maleness' principally through avoidance of anything associated with the 'feminine' or 'girlish' (Buckingham, 1993b). As Thorne (1993) found, young boys commonly saw girls as polluting, and 'kissing' or other expressions of romance as a kind of invasion. Boys' expressions of aversion to programs like *Blind Date* thus became a way of policing gender boundaries. In the next extract, for example, a group of 6- to 7-year-old boys being interviewed by a male and female interviewer are asked why they have put *Blind Date* into a category 'for teenagers':

I: Why do you think it's [*Blind Date*] for teenagers?

B1: 'Cause there's this old woman—

B2: [interrupting] No—because children don't like people smooching and things.

B1: 'Cause there's always a woman and stuff—

B2: Yeah, and they're always smooching when they win.

I: And you don't thing that's for children?

All: [shouting] No!!

I2: When do you think people start liking smooching?

B2: Well, about—[shrieks of laughter] well, because teenagers start to smooch—my brother—it was his birthday and he was 14 and he invited—I'd never seen her before and I didn't even know he had a girl friend [all laughing and screaming].

The boys strive to distance themselves from romance and sexuality, both on the grounds of gender and on the grounds of age. *Blind Date* and the 'smooching' it contains are identified with 'women' and with older children: yet this appears to invest it not with a 'forbidden' appeal, but merely to give grounds for expressions of disgust and rejection.

Nevertheless, such dating programs may have a rather different kind of 'child appeal', as our earlier extracts suggest. While authors such as Postman (1983) have castigated television for making children more like adults, the pleasure of dating shows appears to reflect a delight in seeing adults behaving 'childishly', which some critics appear to regard as equally subversive.[14] Dating shows were often defined by the children here as 'game shows', like other light entertainment or quiz shows. . . . In this respect, it may be its 'infantilization' of adults, as much as its sexual or romantic content, that accounts for the popularity of *Blind Date* and similar programs with children. . . .

SEX AND SITCOMS

Compulsory heterosexuality—or at least the *performance* of it—appeared equally rigid for boys of this age as for girls. However, many of the boys were not quite so comfortable with discussing these overtly sexual representation. As Buckingham (1993b: 103–5) notes, boys were more inclined to focus on programs and characters that allowed them to explore gender and sexuality from a 'safe' distance, particularly in the form of comedy. Situation comedies such as *Friends, Frasier* and *Men Behaving Badly* were especially popular with boys. Their discussions of these programs tended to focus on the male protagonists' adeptness or ineptitude with women, rather than on which of the female characters they 'fancied'. By describing comic situations, boys were able to [center] attention on the character and away from themselves, thus avoiding the possibility of being teased by others in the group. In the following extract, for instance, a boy discusses a scene from the US sitcom *Friends*:

B: The last time I watched it, it was funny . . . when they were going on about him [the character Ross] liking the bit in *Star Wars* where Princess Leia is wearing her bikini thing and then he makes Jennifer Aniston [another character] get dressed up in a bikini thing like her . . . and then he's looking at her, and then he goes 'you're my life'. . .

Undoubtedly, this boy wants us to know that he identifies with the heterosexual male gaze; but through his description of Ross projecting his comic sexual fantasies onto Jennifer Aniston, he maintains both involvement with and disengagement from this position. As Liesbeth de Block (1998) notes in her study of children and comedies, *Friends* and *Men Behaving Badly* seem to be popular with children partly because of their focus on personal relationships within non-family settings. While their portrayals of relationships between male and female characters are fairly hackneyed (and intentionally exaggerated to provide much of the comedy), their portrayal of adulthood is less stereotypical. On the one hand, the characters appear to have some of the desirable trappings of grown-ups—such as independence, money and control over their own space and time. Yet, unlike characters in more serious adult soaps or dramas for instance, the male characters in these comedies are not portrayed (or indeed perceived by children) as particularly mature. As de Block suggests, their appeal rests largely on the fact that they are men behaving like boys.

SUITABILITY AND CENSORSHIP

These extracts highlight the considerable 'cross-over' appeal of . . . sitcoms. In our sorting exercises, many of the older children were therefore uncertain about whether these should be categorized as adults' or children's programs. Most concluded that they were suitable for both children and adults—but then went on to discriminate between older and younger age groups. Notably, the 10- to 11-year-olds likened themselves to teenagers, with different tastes from those of younger children. . . .

While some of the older children used their knowledge of sex on television to demonstrate their 'adultness', others presented us with a different version of maturity, by adopting a more censorious attitude towards storylines that dealt with personal/sexual relationships. A number of children also drew on adult discourses concerned with the supposed 'effects' of television, and the need to shield 'children' from images of sex or bad language—particularly in children's programs and those adult programs that were considered to have cross-over appeal.

However, as Buckingham (1993a, 1996) has shown, children will commonly claim that media 'effects' only pose a danger to children *younger* than themselves—in rather the same way that adults claim that children are at greater risk. For instance, when we asked them to select an evening's viewing for younger children, some 10- to 11-year-olds claimed that certain shows were not suitable. As in the second quotation on *Blind Date* cited earlier, younger children were seen as more likely to be negatively influenced by television. In the next extract, a girl talks about the effect viewing *East Enders* has on her younger brother:

> G: Well it's [EastEnders] really scary—parts of it—some of it, not all of it. My brother, he's 4 now, but he swears sometimes, and he's always talking about sex. . .

Like many adult moralists, this girl slips easily between three of the most contentious concerns—violence, bad language and sex—implicitly accusing the program of introducing her brother to adult 'secrets' at too early an age. By contrast, while the younger children could also show a censorious attitude, they were less able to draw on the kinds of moralistic discourses familiar to the older children. For example, in the following extract, three 6- to 7-year-old girls debate whether *Blind Date* is a children's or adults' program:

> I: What about this one—*Blind Date*?
> G1: No—that's kind of for grown-ups, 'cause everybody's kissing and stuff.
> G2: I watch it.
> G3: So do I.
> I: So you think it's more for grown-ups because there's lots of kissing but you still watch it?
> All: Yes.
> G2: And everybody's going to places with each other, and they don't know each other really.

G1: And they get married.

I: So why is all that stuff just for grown-ups then?

G2: Because kids—

G1: I'm not really allowed to watch kissing and stuff 'cause it's—

G2: It's bad for—

I: Right, so it might make them want to do kissing when they grow up?

All: Yes.

I: Is that a bad thing?

G1: Not when they're at school. . .

G2: Sometimes people play kiss chase—

G1: —and kiss them on the lips.

I: And you don't think that's a very good thing?

G1: No.

Despite the fact that two of the girls here watch the program, all agree that *Blind Date* is 'adult'; and this is confirmed by the fact that one of the girls is forbidden from watching it. This adult status is explained by the presence of 'kissing', and there is perhaps a sense of moral disapproval in the suggestion that the participants 'don't know each other really'. Somewhat uncertainly, the girls suggest that such material might be 'bad for kids'; and when the interviewer asks about the consequences of viewing, they suggest that it might lead to inappropriate or 'bad' behavior, not so much when they 'grow up' but in the school playground. Yet again, however, the individuals affected remain in the third person—they are very definitely *other* 'people'.

Even among the older groups of children, however, there was some disagreement about what was suitable for *children's* television—whether or not the children actually watched these programs themselves. . . .

CONCLUSION

In this article, we have attempted to move on from the debate about what children should or should not know about sexual relationships. Children will inevitably find out about such matters, whether they do so from television or from elsewhere. The key question, we would suggest, is how they interpret the information and the representations they do encounter. More specifically, our emphasis here has been on the ways in which interpretation is *performed* in the context of group discussion; and on the functions that such talk might serve in terms of the ongoing formation of children's identities. As we have implied, this is very much a matter of interaction between the texts of television and their readers, in which neither holds anything approaching absolute power. Television obviously makes available particular representations and identities, and excludes others; but in defining and debating the meanings of television, readers also claim and construct identities of their own. In this chapter, we have focused particularly on how children's talk about sex on television serves as a means of defining identities in terms of *age* and *gender*. . . .

Clearly, there are limitations as to how far one can generalize from a qualitative study of this kind. . . . Peer group talk, gathered in the context of a school and at the invitation of an adult interviewer, does not necessarily tell us anything about what really goes on in these children's heads—or indeed in their everyday lives. But it is not our aim to uncover children's 'true' identities. On the contrary, we aim merely to provide an indication of some of the ways in which identities are . . . defined and negotiated by these particular children in the course of these particular social interactions.

Our analysis suggests that the functions and consequences of such talk are often profoundly ambiguous. On one level, witnessing and discussing representations of sexual behavior serves as a kind of index of maturity—and the fact that such representations are typically forbidden, or at least categorized, on the grounds of age only serves to reinforce this fact. Yet whether that 'maturity' is seen as desirable or not depends upon the position from which it is viewed. For some of the older children, claiming that one has seen such material (or pretending to have done so) represents a kind of *aspirational* claim, for an essentially desirable form of maturity—not only in terms of the behavior that is shown, but also in terms of the freedom from adult constraint that being able to view it is seen to represent. On the other hand, some of the younger children clearly did not aspire to partake in such behavior, even if they might have wished for the freedom to be allowed to watch it: 'kissing' was, if not positively disgusting (as it appeared to be for some of the boys), then at least 'boring', like so many other aspects of adult life.

Meanwhile, children of both age groups—but particularly the older ones—were also inclined to adopt a censorious stance, albeit on the understanding that this was only to be applied to *other* people. As in adult debates about the effects of television, this 'otherness' itself was also defined primarily in terms of age. In employing these arguments, the children were attempting to position themselves as mature, and hence as immune from the negative moral influences that applied to those younger than themselves. Yet this argument also reproduces a kind of logic which ultimately works to the benefit of adults: it seeks to determine access to knowledge (and hence to the power that it may confer) simply on the grounds of biological age.

These kinds of identity claims, defined primarily in terms of age, are crossed and inflected by those defined in terms of gender. As we have indicated, 'talking dirty' is one of the strategies that children employ in reproducing and policing gender identities, and in enforcing a form of compulsory heterosexuality. . . .

We . . . refuse any definition of television as simply a monolithic machine for imposing 'stereotypes' or 'gender roles'—or indeed for merely 'constructing' childhood identities. Nor (do) we accept that readers simply 'identify with' and hence take on the identities that are offered. On the contrary, we need to develop a more nuanced understanding of the *range* of identities that television makes available to children. As well as considering what children do with television, we also need to consider what television does for children.

Discussion Questions

1. How does this study challenge conventional thinking about children's sexual knowledge? About childhood more generally?

2. How is sexual content discussed differently by age? By gender?

3. If you were to design a similar study, what kinds of questions would you ask your informants to avoid the appearance of impropriety?

4. What do the authors say about the assumption of childhood "innocence"?

Notes

1. For instance, Cunningham (1995). Hendrick (1997) and Humphries et al. (1988).

2. 'Children's Media Culture: Education, Entertainment and the Public Sphere', based at the Institute of Education, University of London, and funded by the Economic and Social Research Council UK (award no. L126251026). The project also looked at the changing institutional and economic context of children's television production and the formal characteristics of texts produced for children. Further material from these aspects of the research is presented in Buckingham et al. (in press) and Buckingham (forthcoming) respectively. Other aspects of the audience research are presented in Davies et al. (forthcoming a, b).

3. We conducted 18 open-ended interviews about the children's general tastes and preferences in television, followed by 36 more structured activities (described later). All interviews were with groups of three children: those with the older children lasted an average of 50 minutes, while those with the younger children lasted around 40 minutes. These interviews took place outside the classroom, generally in an empty office in the school.

4. For instance, we did not observe any instances of children swearing or using sexist put-downs' in the classroom, although there were instances of these occurring in interviews.

5. Space precludes a more detailed discussion of the research methodology. For accounts of similar studies, see Buckingham (1993a) and Robinson (1997).

6. For a broader analysis of this, sec Davies et al. (1999).

7. Films aimed at adults (rather than children) featured in these discussions too, since children were more aware of film classifications that supposedly restricted their viewing than they were of the 9 o'clock 'watershed'.

8. Some children in Year 2 seemed especially confused. For instance, one boy who claimed to have seen Tarantino's *Reservoir Dogs* told us that the film was literally 'about some dogs'.

9. *Trainspotting* is a British film based on the 'cult' novel by Irving Welsh, featuring the lives of a group of drug addicts. All the movies mentioned in this paragraph have an '18' certificate for cinema or video release in Britain.

10. In this instance, the two boys were from a white working-class background. Both needed extra help with schoolwork. The third boy was from a middle-class background, but also appeared more marginal to the class because he had a form of autism.

11. What was 'censored' obviously varied from child to child. Some children claimed that their parents prevented them from seeing many '18'-rated, films, while others asserted that watching films like *Trainspotting* was not particularly exceptional.

12. This is a 'realist' British film featuring the lives of two working-class young women in a northern town. It is fairly sexually explicit, and again attracted an '18' rating for cinema/video release.

13. Romance has traditionally been tolerable in girls' teen culture, since sex is rarely made explicit, or even discouraged (see McRobbie, 1991). However, there have been significant changes in this respect in recent years: questions have even been asked in the British parliament about the sexually explicit content of newer girls' magazines such at *Bliss* and *More*.

14. See for instance, Mike Presdee 'Consumption and Enjoyment of Crime as Popular Pleasure' *(Daily Telegraph,* 4 April 1997).

References

Buckingham, D. (1993a) *Children Talking Television: The Making of Television Literacy.* London: Falmer Press.

Buckingham, D. (1993b) 'Boys' Talk: Television and the Policing of Masculinity', in D. Buckingham (ed.) *Reading Audiences: Young People and the Media,* pp. 89–115. Manchester: Manchester University Press.

Buckingham, D. (1994) 'Television and the Definition of Childhood', in B. Mayall (ed.) *Children's Childhoods Observed and Experienced,* pp. 79–96. London: Falmer Press.

Buckingham, D. (1996) *Moving Images: Understanding Children's Emotional Responses to Television.* Manchester: Manchester University Press.

Buckingham, D. (ed.) (forthcoming) *Television for Children: Texts and Genres.* London: British Film Institute.

Buckingham, D., H. Davies, K. Jones and P. Kelley (1999) *Children's Television in Britain: History, Discourse and Policy.* London: British Film Institute.

Corteen, K. and P. Scraton (1997) 'Prolonging "Childhood", Manufacturing "Innocence" and Regulating Sexuality', in P. Scraton (ed.) *'Childhood' in 'Crisis'?,* pp. 76–100. London: University College of London Press.

Cunningham, H. (1995) *Children and Childhood in Western Society Since 1500.* London: Longman.

Davies, H., D. Buckingham and P. Kelley (1999) 'Kids' Time: Childhood, Television and the Regulation of Time', *Journal of Educational Media* 24 (1).

Davies, H., D. Buckingham and P. Kelley (forthcoming b) 'In the Worst Possible Taste: Children, Television and Cultural Value', MS submitted for publication.

Davies, M. M. (1995) 'Babes 'n' the Hood', in C. Bazalgette and D. Buckingham (eds) *In Front of the Children: Scream Entertainment and Young Audiences,* pp. 15–33. London: British Film Institute.

Douglas, M. (1992) *Risk and Blame: Essays in Cultural Theory.* London: Routledge.

Epstein, D, (1997) 'Cultures of Schooling/Cultures of Sexuality', *International Journal of Inclusive Education* 1(1): 37–53.

Epstein, D. and R. Johnson (1997) *Schooling Sexualities.* Milton Keynes: Open University Press.

Hendrick, H. (1997) *Children, Childhood and English Society 1880–1990.* Cambridge: Cambridge University Press.

Hey, V. (1997) *The Company She Keeps: An Ethnography of Girls' Friendship.* Milton Keynes: Open University Press.

Home, A. (1993) *Into the Box of Delights.* London: BBC Books.

Hood, S., P. Kelley, B. Mayall and A. Oakley (1996) *Children, Parents and Risk.* London: Social Science Research Unit, Institute of Education, University of London.

Humphries, S., J. Mack and R. Perks (1988) *A Century of Childhood.* London: Sidgwick and Jackson.

Jackson, S. (1982) *Childhood and Sexuality.* Oxford: Basil Blackwell.

James, A., C. Jenks and A. Prout (1998) *Theorizing Childhood.* Cambridge: Polity Press.

McRobbie, A. (1991) *Feminism and Youth Culture: From Jackie to Just Seventeen.* London: Macmillan.

Meyrowitz, J. (1985) *No Sense of Place: The Impact of Electronic Media on Social Behavior.* New York: Oxford University Press.

Pilcher, J. (1996) "Gillick and After: Children and Sex in the 1980s and 1990s', in J. Pilcher and S. Wagg (eds) *Thatcher's Children: Politics, Childhood and Society in the 1980s and 1990s,* pp. 77–93. London: Falmer Press.

Postman, N. (1983) *The Disappearance of Childhood.* London: W.H. Allen.

Robinson, M. (1997) *Children Reading Print and Television.* London: Falmer.

Thorne, B. (1993) *Gender Play: Boys and Girls in School.* Milton Keynes: Open University Press.

PART SEVEN

Social Problems and Inequality

Are Young People Really Prized in American Society?

You are probably very familiar with well-worn clichés about children: they are our future, our most treasured assets, and so forth. But beyond what we tell ourselves, we must also understand some of the realities of children that belie these well-meaning sentiments. By viewing children as only innocent, empty vessels, we deny their humanity and fail to understand the complexity—and the challenges—within their experiences.

One of the biggest challenges children face is their lack of social power. As Barrie Thorne discussed in her piece in Part II, this is a central facet of childhood, yet one that is difficult to remedy due to children's dependence on adults. At the very least we can identify and understand their experiences with disempowerment. This is one of author Jenny Kitzinger's central points in her selection, "Who Are You Kidding? Children, Power, and the Struggle Against Sexual Abuse." Kitzinger details how the construction of children as passive victims not only erases the actions they take to resist abuse, but ironically empowers abusers, who are attracted to children for this very reason. She argues that to best understand child sexual abuse, we need to recognize that it is built into the institution of childhood due to children's lack of power with adults.

In addition to children who are sexually abused, children with serious chronic illnesses are also regarded as victims worthy of our sympathy—and our donations to charities on their behalf. Yet Cindy Dell Clark, author of "Children Coping with Chronic Illness," observes that children cope best with illness when they feel powerful, not powerless. Through interviews and observations, she found that children create rituals to help them deal with painful treatments and hospital stays. Their play frequently involved superheroes with uncommon strength, and they imagined that certain toys or objects helped ease the pain of illness. Yet by viewing these children as helpless, health care professionals and others ultimately hinder the healing process.

Of course there are many children without access to quality health care on a regular basis, due in part to the high cost of health insurance and policy decisions that have shuttered many public hospitals. Similar policy decisions have created vastly unequal educational opportunities for American children. Some benefit from well-funded public schools, while others receive substandard educations that allow them to fall further behind economically.

Educational policies have clear, direct effects on children. Yet other policies have a more indirect impact on kids. The United States incarcerates its citizens at a higher rate than any other country on earth, in large part due to strict sentencing laws for drug-related offenses. A large proportion of prisoners are also parents, meaning that many children have parents who are unable to take care of them and in many cases cannot even maintain contact. Nell Bernstein, author of "Children of the Incarcerated" explores this issue from the perspective of children. While people who commit serious crimes clearly need to be removed from society, this has unintended consequences for kids. As states face budget cuts, programs to keep families in communication have less support, and in some cases prisoners are transferred to serve their sentences far from home, too far for their children to be able to visit with them on a regular basis. Prisoners who maintain relationships with their children are more likely to do better upon release, so the benefits to helping children maintain these ties are not just for kids, but for society as a whole.

Other policies have unintended consequences as well, such as the globalization of goods. While most forms of child labor have been outlawed in the United States for more than seventy years, it is likely that many products bought and sold in the United States were produced by children. Allison James, Chris Jenks, and Alan Prout write in "Working Children" that we need to understand the contexts of children's lives to better understand how they experience "child labor," as we seldom hear children's perspectives on this issue. In some cases, they can only afford education through work, thus the authors suggest that we focus more heavily on the problem of exploitation. By better understanding the real circumstances of children's lives we can do more to support them—and understand how we might unwittingly be contributing to their disempowerment.

Who Are You Kidding? Children, Power, and the Struggle Against Sexual Abuse

JENNY KITZINGER

INTRODUCTION

In this provocative article, author Jenny Kitzinger challenges the way that we typically think about childhood sexual abuse. She argues that the construction of childhood innocence ironically may perpetuate abuse. First, "innocence" is often what draws abusers to children. Second, children who have been abused are seen as no longer "innocent" and sometimes penalized for that. Finally, the construction of innocence often serves to disempower children and reinforce adult authority, which also can enable abuse to take place.

INTRODUCTION

The child sits limp and despairing—her face hidden in her hands; the young girl clutches her blanket—the figure of a man lurks in the shadows; an infant cowers in the corner of his play pen, a blank-eyed Victorian china doll lies cracked and discarded on the floor. These are the images which appear in the publicity about, and campaigns against, child sexual abuse. They are used by people who are outraged by the abuse of children and are seeking to prevent it. While the images of alluring Lolitas and lying little minxes used by the *apologists* for sexual abuse have been widely criticized, less attention has been paid to the type of images described earlier and it is these images, those emerging from the campaigns *against* sexual abuse, that are explored in this chapter.

The debates around child sexual abuse draw on multi-stranded discourses about sexuality, the family, gender, class and race (Parton and Parton, 1988; Campbell, 1988). In addition, these debates are embedded within, and draw upon, a variety of discourses about childhood, for child sexual abuse is presented as, above all, a crime against childhood. It is the victim's youth that lends this form of assault its poignancy and it is that youth which is emphasized in the accompanying publicity. Documentation of specific cases in the press dwell on child-specific attributes such as the victim's favorite plastic purse with the rainbow handles, her pony tail, Paddington Bear watch and sailor suit dress (*The Sun* 10.12.86; *Today* 2.6.87; *The Mirror* 9.12.86). . . . References are made to picnics . . . and visits to the sea-side while the background music used in television discussions of this issue draw on a 'childish' repertoire of clockwork musical boxes and songs such as 'The Teddy Bears' Picnic' (Cook, 1987; *Testimony of a Child Debate*, 1989).

All these visual, written, and aural cues accentuate the fact that the victim is a child — and, ultimately, that childhood itself is at issue. 'Kevin's 8, but for him childhood's over' reads the headline of the National Children's Home advertisement—'Kevin's been raped'. Childhood then is not defined by age but by some set of qualities or experiences which are incompatible with being assaulted. The images of unhappy and frightened children (usually white) represent, not individuals, but a concept. The image of the solitary black child would represent a different concept—racism means that while a white child can represent 'Childhood' the black child is only used to represent *black* childhood, or 'The Third World' or 'Foreign' or 'Starvation'.[1] The concern is, therefore, not just about the assault on an individual child but with the attack upon, and defense of, childhood itself (that institution and ideal which exists independently from, and sometimes in spite of, actual flesh and blood children). Indeed, the sexual abuse of a child is often referred to as the 'theft' or 'violation' of childhood (e.g., Barr, 1986; *The sun*, 13.12.86; Bradbury, 1986).

In this chapter I draw on media coverage, leaflets, education videos, books, academic articles and survivors' personal testimonies to explore how childhood is constructed and reconstructed within the contemporary 'pro-child' debates and how these constructions affect our understandings of child sexual abuse as 'a problem' and our visions of 'a solution'. The first part of the chapter documents, and challenges, the discourses of childhood innocence, passivity and innate vulnerability. The second part introduces and questions one of the main *alternative* set of discourses—the discourse of empowerment in which children are viewed as socialized into victimhood and capable of escaping it.[2] All these mainstream approaches to child sexual abuse are, I argue, full of tensions and contradictions resulting from their failure to question the social construction of childhood itself, or fundamentally, to challenge children's oppression. Finally, I suggest ways in which we could begin to develop a radical, social constructionist approach to the struggle against, and prevention of, sexual exploitation.

CHILDHOOD INNOCENCE

Implicit in the presentation of sexual abuse as the 'violation of childhood' is an assertion of what childhood 'really' is, or should be. The experience of abuse is contrasted with the 'authentic experience of childhood': a carefree time of play; an asexual and peaceful existence within the protective bosom of the family.[3] The quality of childhood that is most surely 'stolen' by abuse is 'innocence'. Books and articles about this topic have titles such as: 'Shattered Innocence' (Kohn, 1987), *The Betrayal of Innocence* (Forward and Buck, 1981) and *The Death of Innocence* (Janus, 1981). Child sexual abuse is 'prototypical innocence as a foil for grandiose corruption, and, simply—a battle between good and evil . . .' (Summit, 1986, xi). Indeed, 'robbing children of their innocence', has become a synonym (and euphemism) for sexual assault (*The Sun*, 13.12.86).

Asserting that abuse is never the child's fault, declaring her innocent, is a necessary challenge to the long tradition of victim-blaming, which views abused children as active participants or even 'aggressors' (Nelson, 1987: 38–45). The notion of 'lost innocence' also 'rings true' for many adult survivors who feel guilty and ashamed; 'reclaiming' that innocence can be a potent symbol of healing (Bass and Thornton, 1983: 201). However, what is happening now is not simply a challenging of guilt. It is a fetishistic glorification of the 'innate innocence' of childhood, and, indeed, a rhetoric which implies that sexual abuse stains that innocence.

Using this concept of innocence to incite public revulsion against sexual abuse is problematic for three main reasons. First, the notion of childhood innocence is itself a source of titillation for abusers. A glance at pornography leaves little doubt that innocence is a sexual commodity. 'Kiddie porn' magazines specifically set out to highlight the purity of their child models (Rush, 1980: 164). Advertising makes use of images of young girls made up to look like Marilyn Monroe with slogans such as 'Innocence is sexier than you think' (Rush, 1980: 125), and the fashion industry cashes in with baby-doll nightdresses for adult women and, for girls, T-shirts emblazoned with the words 'Forbidden Fruit'. If defiling the pure and deflowering the virgin is supposed to be erotic, then focusing on children's presumed innocence only reinforces their desirability as sexual objects. As one child abuser wrote: 'It was so exciting, she was so young, so pure and clean' (*The Star*, 4.12.86).

Second, innocence is a double-edged sword in the fight against sexual abuse because it stigmatizes the 'knowing' child. The romanticization of childhood innocence excludes those who do not conform to the ideal. Innocence is used to imply asexuality, 'pre-sexual personhood' (Hancock and Mains, 1987: 32), or a limited and discrete 'childlike' sensuality. This penalizes the child who sexually responds to the abuse or who appears flirtatious and sexually aware. If the violation of innocence is the criterion against which the act of sexual abuse is judged then violating a 'knowing' child becomes a lesser offense than violating an 'innocent' child. It is this notion which allows an abuser to defend himself on the grounds that his victim was 'no angel', citing as evidence, that the girl drinks, smokes and often fails to do her homework on time (*Daily Mail*, 14.12.85). Without her innocence the child has lost the magic cloak supposed to make her impervious to harm. Thus, as Sgroi (1982: 114) suggests, 'the sexually victimized child may be viewed neither as a child nor as an adult but rather as a piece of "damaged goods" lacking the attributes of both childhood and adult . . . sexually victimized children may become "walking invitations" '. Indeed, a child who is known to be a victim of sexual abuse is often the target of further exploitation: 'Publicly deflowered as she is, she is regarded as no longer deserving respect or protection' (Summit and Kryso, 1978: 244).

The third, and most fundamental, reason why it is counterproductive to use 'innocence' in the fight against child sexual abuse is that it is an ideology used to deny children access to knowledge and power and hence actually increases their vulnerability to abuse. The twin concepts of innocence and ignorance are vehicles for adult double-standards: a child is ignorant if she doesn't know what adults want her to know, but innocent if she doesn't know what adults don't want her to know. Those adults who champion 'childhood' use innocence as an excuse to exclude children from 'the adult world' and indeed, to isolate them from other children's experiences. In the name of innocence adults repress children's own expressions of sexuality, such as masturbation (Stainton-Rogers, 1989), deny children control over their own bodies (e.g., . . . to prevent girls [from] gaining access to contraception) and seek to protect them from 'corrupting influences' . . . Highlighting child sexual abuse is even, in itself, seen to debase childhood and destroy 'the age of innocence' (*News on Sunday*, 3.5.87). Indeed, it is the notion of innocence which prevents some people from telling children about incest (*Independent*, 28.4.87) because they do not want to 'corrupt the few years of innocence that should be every child's right' (Brown, 1986).

THE PASSIVE VICTIM

Complementing the image of the *innocent* victim is that of the *passive* victim. Instead of presenting the child as an active 'participant' in the 'relationship' (as described in the old 'anti-child' research on child abuse e.g., Bender and Blau, 1937) the bulk of the recent 'pro-child' publicity shows the child as a helpless victim of adult sexual demands. The abused child is represented by a despairing and pathetic figure mutely appealing to the adult viewer for help or, sometimes, simply by a limp rag doll. She is described as a 'silent sufferer of victimization' but rarely allowed to speak about her own actions as opposed to the acts committed against her. Child survivors remain faceless and inaudible; their struggles to resist and endure abuse remain largely uncharted and unheard.

Many abused children, like adults in similar situations, not surprisingly, become resigned and listless in the face of overwhelming odds. The dramatic imbalance in power and socially sanctioned routine subordination of children means that they are often malleable 'objects of victimization'. Many, however, at least at some stage, rebel against what is happening to them. Some try (and a few succeed in) physically defending themselves with their teeth and nails, knives and hammers (Gordon, 1988: 213; Russell, 1986: 126). However, rather than (or as well as) engaging in the unequal struggle of direct physical combat, children employ the strategies of the most oppressed, dispossessed and victimized: joking and gossip, passive resistance and underground rebellion. My own research involving interviews with adult survivors suggests that, although such tactics are rarely recognized by adults, children seek to evade abuse with all the resources they have of cunning, manipulativeness, energy, anger and fear.[4]

Survivors describe how, as children, they induced nose bleeds, held their breath until they fainted, or had various 'accidents' to ensure they could not be sent off on their . . . visit with daddy or be left alone with the abusive babysitter. They also tried barricading their bedrooms, fleeing and hiding. Kate ran away to London on five different occasions and Lorna started going to church to avoid being called to her father's bed on Sunday mornings; one girl encircled her bed with squeaky toys (to ensure the abuser could not creep up on her while she slept); another enlisted her own bodyguard by taking her dog to bed (the dog would growl and lunge at her father when he approached) (Armstrong, 1987: 169). Joanne found a different kind of 'minder' when, at 15, she started to go out with 'the local thug'. 'I chose him specifically as a way of keeping my dad off,' she told me, 'my dad was quite a pathetic man and I knew as soon as he met this boy, that he was scared of him. So I went out with him, as a way of keeping my dad at bay.'

Whether overtly, or covertly children often gain comfort, information, and assistance from each other rather than from adults. Lynda's sister always hugged and soothed her after their uncle's assaults; Vida's best friend gave her the courage to phone Childline; Diane and her sister sustained each other with 'jokes' about killing their father and Rowena's brother helped her to rig up a shotgun against their step-father designed to fire when he opened the bedroom door. It was Hilda's sister who warned her about their uncle and Hilda's friend who then slept with her, thus successfully preempting an assault.

Victimized children also plead and bargain with their abusers or try to repel them by making themselves 'unattractive'—strapping down developing breasts, cutting off their hair, or hiding inside an armor of bulky [clothes] in all weathers. Samantha refused to wash, deliberately making herself physically disgusting: 'I told myself that if I was dirty and smelly no one would want to have sex with me.' Another girl, identifying being female with being vulnerable, rejected all the paraphernalia of femininity. 'He said I was ugly and just like a boy, and why didn't I ever wear pretty dresses, and make-up like other girls, and he bought me perfume and I broke the bottle. I would wear . . . boots, and always wear trousers. I really hated him then and he knew it.'

If the abuse is unavoidable some children try to make it less invasive by segregating it from their day to day lives. 'I blanked it [the abuse] off when I was at school', says Lisa, whose abusive step-father worked away from home during the week: 'It just wasn't there, it was only sometimes that I would remember. But I didn't normally, I mean it [the abuse] was usually only on Fridays, when he came home, but all the other days of the week I don't think I ever let myself remember really'. Other children withhold any physical or mental participation. One 16 year-old describes, with some satisfaction, how she discovered the art of 'blanking out':

> One day, I was about eight, he was making me dress up in my mother's clothes—bra and everything. He was looking at me in these clothes. I was thinking about school. Then all of a sudden, I got this great slap around my face—he says 'are you listening to me?' That is when I realized that I could take my mind somewhere else and it was really good because I thought 'ooh, great, I don't have to be here.' [. . .] It felt kind of freeing because before I had been suffering [. . .] but now I could take my mind somewhere else and please him, give him what he wanted but just shut everything off and not be hurt.

Another woman, who at first sexually responded to her uncle's manipulation of her genitals, learned to hold herself rigid during assaults: 'When he touched me I used to be really stiff, obviously I'd let him do it, but that didn't mean I had to take any type of part in it. I just felt like a doll'. Passivity, being as lifeless as 'a doll', is here chosen as a form of resistance—refusing to be involved.

Alternatively, submission to sex may be used as a bargaining point by children seeking rewards of 'affection', 'the right to stay up late' or 'a bit more freedom than my brothers'. Such 'privileges' make children feel implicated in their own violation but, for some, these pay offs are 'better than nothing'. As Imogen comments:

> In some families I think kids are pretty desperate for the attention they need to grow and live and if they have to trade a bit of pain for it, or a bit of sex for it, then they will do that. And there is a bit of me that says good luck to them. I am *glad* that I was the one in my family who managed to get something. The fact that I was entitled to an awful lot more is neither here nor there because there was no more available.

Children also try to limit the degree of physical invasion—learning to fake pleasure or quickly stimulate their abusers to orgasm so as to curtail the abuse and, perhaps, avoid the soreness and pain of persistent rubbing or penetration. 'I satisfied him and allowed him to satisfy himself without totally surrendering my body to him' writes Charlotte Vale Allen, explaining how she consistently avoided vaginal intercourse with her father, 'No matter what happened I was determined never to let him do that to me. I clung to my virginity—technical scrap of membrane—with passionate tenacity' (Allen, 1980: 110).

Children are constantly acting to preempt, evade, or modify sexual violence. However, 'adult-centric' discourses ignore such strategies: children are not seen as agents in their own lives. They are only visible as they relate (literally or theoretically) to 'the adult world'.[5] Working with children is a relatively low status activity and researchers who listen to children and take them seriously as 'objects' of study *in their own right* have sometimes found their work ridiculed . . . by association with their 'childish' subjects. . . . Such refusal to accept children as fully human and such negation of their ideas and strategies not only ignores children's *individual* acts of resistance but obscures relations *between* children and thus the importance of young people's alliances with one another as a resource against adult violence. Children's successful defenses rarely come to public/adult attention—they do not appear in the statistics, a preempted potential assault is a 'non-event'. When they 'fail' however their struggles also go unrecognized. The survival strategies described earlier are, in the mainstream literature, labeled 'symptoms' of abuse or listed as a catalogue of sickness illustrating the terrible consequences of incest. Activities that could be recognized as attempts to resist, or cope with abuse are, instead, labeled 'post-traumatic stress syndrome' or cited as evidence of deep psychic scarring. Such disease terminology obscures the child actively negotiating her way through the dangers of childhood. She is recast as a submissive object of victimization even by the process of intervention and treatment.[6]

PROTECTING THE WEAK

The logical extension of the image of the innately passive child and the refusal to recognize children's resistance strategies is to rely totally on adult protection to prevent, or interrupt, abuse. We are told that *all* children are at risk—the victim of sexual exploitation 'could come from anywhere—even next door . . . it could be anybody's little girl or boy' (Cook, 1987). Significantly, this is not matched by a similar focus on the abuser—we are not warned that the abuser could come from anywhere, 'even next door to you . . . it could be anyone's father, husband or son'. Focusing on children's weakness and 'incapacity', the call is for increased surveillance, we are urged to guard 'our' children closely and avoid letting them out alone or at night.

Such siege mentality places a huge strain on parents, and particularly mothers. Just as the Health Education Authority advertisement showed a busy mother 'allowing' her child to run out under a car, it is women who bear the greatest burden of chaperoning duties. Those who are unable to buy into the individualistic option of childcare substitution are censured for not being available to their children twenty-four hours a day. During a series of child murders in Atlanta, the press demanded 'Where were these children's mothers?' (Cooper, 1986: 40) and when a child was abducted while on her way to a bus stop her mother was blamed for not accompanying her: 'At times, the anger seemed more directed against her than at the murderer' (*Elliott, M.*, 1988: 25). Indeed, helpful hints on how to combat child sexual abuse include the suggestion that mothers of pre-school children should not go out to work at all (Kelly, R., 1988) and mothers of incest survivors are blamed for being unavailable to their children through illness, death, or because they were out at Bingo, doing the shopping or had 'abdicated' child care responsibilities to their husbands. As one lawyer defending an alleged child abuser pointed out—the mother must take some responsibility because: 'This woman repeatedly went out to the grocery store leaving this child alone with her father'! (quoted in MacFarlane, 1988).

The fate of women and children are intimately intertwined—not only because women (and men) spend many years *being* children but because women take primary responsibility for all types of childcare. We cannot construct and reconstruct childhood without constructing and reconstructing what it means to be a mother (or a teacher, or a health visitor and all the other, predominantly female, child care 'vocations').

In addition to the burdens it places on women, the protectionist approach encourages children to live in fear. At its most extreme it reflects a 'lock up your daughters' philosophy which, ironically (given that much abuse takes place within the home), increases children's isolation within the family by encouraging them to keep all other adults (literally) at arms' length; it also implies the need for increased parental control (Barrett and Coward. 1985: 23).

Protection, then, is neither a long term, nor even a short term, 'solution' to the exploitation of children. Such paternalistic approaches can, in fact, act *against* children's interests. Reforms which impose restrictions on children—'for their own good' are routinely turned against the very people they are meant to protect (Takanishi, 1978). The focus on children's innate vulnerability (as a biological fact unmediated by the world they live in) is an ideology of control which diverts attention away from the socially constructed oppression of young people. Children in western society are kept dependent for much longer than is considered necessary in other societies (Jackson, 1982). Currently . . . this dependence is being lengthened and intensified by . . . government policies in . . . health care . . . and education which increase parental responsibility for, and rights over, their daughters and sons. It is now harder for a young person to leave home and exist independently from her or his family (Shelter, 1989) and parents' increasing control over, for instance, children's sex education is, potentially, in direct conflict with their protection from sexual exploitation (Dingwall, 1987).

Attributing sexual violence to a decline of traditional values, and, specifically, to 'The Decay of Childhood' (Seabrook, 1987), some protectionists call for the 'preservation' of childhood. In this way, childhood is treated rather like a rare animal threatened with extinction. Just as early attempts to preserve endangered species relied on locking up specimens in zoos (rather than intervening against the 'man-made' attacks on their environment) so this child protection approach attempts to 'preserve childhood' by confining children behind bars. However, it is precisely this kind of 'protection' which leaves many survivors feeling trapped and imprisoned. As children they desperately longed to escape the restrictions of childhood: 'I used to sit at the window watching people walk along the street and think—one day I'll be out there. When I'm grown up I can get my own place, I can close the door, go to bed when I want, get up when I want, do what I want and, of course, IT won't happen anymore'.

The conflict between survivors who identify the barriers surrounding childhood as *restrictive* and those who see them as *protective* is perhaps best illustrated by their contrasting use of the imagery of bars. Adult and child survivors use prison-like bars in their pictures: the child is caged or chained, houses are drawn without doors or windows (Bacon and Richardson, 1989). By contrast, the child protection literature uses play-pen bars to symbolize safety and security (*Times* 17.12.87, and 18.12.87). Under the protectionist philosophy, childhood is a sanctuary to be lovingly preserved; little consideration is given to the implications for the children (or women) whose lives are increasingly confined, still less attention is paid to challenging the forces which make those bars 'necessary'. Such unreflective images of childhood are, however, being challenged by more hopeful developments in the area of child sexual abuse 'prevention'. I shall now go on to look at these developments and, in particular, at the notion of empowerment.

ADULT AWARENESS AND CHILD ASSERTIVENESS

Traditionally, attempts to prevent abuse have been in the form of veiled warnings to children about not taking sweets from strangers or not walking home from school on their own. Today, while some warnings . . . still follow the old 'Say No to Strangers' line, more innovative and radical programs have also appeared. These programs (many of which developed out of grass roots feminists' initiatives) vary in imagination, in degree of sophistication and in specific political perspective, but broadly they are all trying to assist children to identify abuse and obtain help.

The images of childhood presented by these programs are in striking contrast to the images of the innocent and passive child in need of protection.[7] Indeed, many activists in this area start by problematizing such adult attitudes toward children. Adults are, they argue, too ready to dismiss what children say as lies or fantasies or to belittle children's resistance, anger and grief with a terminology reserved for 'child-like' behavior: 'tantrums', 'home sickness', 'day dreaming' or 'sulking'. The abused child is often simply labeled 'naughty', 'clingy' or 'delinquent'. Her attempts to defend herself against adult demands are 'impudent', 'sullen' or 'uppity'. Her protests reduced to mere sound—'whining'. 'We are too accustomed to regarding children as an irritation, a noisy, messy nuisance,' declares one NSPCC officer 'If we continue to believe children should be seen and not heard, their silence protects the molester' (quoted in Rantzen, 1986).

Books and leaflets aim to alert adults to the effect that our routine exercise of power may have on children's self-confidence. Demanding unquestioning obedience from children ('Do as you're told, it's for your own good.' 'Because I say so,') is seen to create vulnerability (*Adams* and Fay, 1981). They challenge us to re-assess our own use of authority as parents, strangers, friends, and teachers. 'You can't teach children they are responsible for certain areas of their life,' points out one headmistress (talking about the Kidscape child safety program) 'and then expect them to sit in a classroom and force-feed them with information they are not encouraged to discuss or query. The compliant, conforming child becomes one who is at risk' (quoted in Aziz, 1987).

Taking on board their own challenge to conventional attitudes toward children, these prevention programs employ child-centred and child-sensitive methods of teaching that emphasize involving, rather than lecturing, children. The workers try to use media familiar to young people—enlisting glove-puppets and coloring books (and TV characters . . .) to introduce the topic in an accessible and non-intimidating way. Rejecting the idea that 'childhood innocence' precludes giving children information, these programs build on children's existing knowledge about bullying and unfairness, 'nice surprises' and 'nasty secrets' and encourage children to trust their own instincts (Finkelhor, 1986: 228–229; Elliott, M., 1988: 25).

Through listening to children, and incorporating their feedback, these programs can also constantly evolve. For instance, some educators now reject the terms 'good' and 'bad' touch (with their suggestions, for the child, of being 'naughty' and being punished) in favor of 'Yes' and 'No' touch or the 'Uh Oh!' feeling (with their emphasis on the child's own reactions and possible actions). Most of these programs have, however, had a lot to learn about the different media, concepts and terminology relevant to the majority of children who are not white, Christian, and middle class. The notion of 'individual rights', for instance, is such a fundamental part of white Anglo-American rhetoric (and indeed is assumed to have universal relevance) that this abstract, complex, and highly ethnocentric concept forms the basis of many of the programs. However, as one team of educators discovered, the 'individual's right to be safe' makes little sense to some Latin or Asian children (cited in Finkelhor, 1986: 228).

Starting from the dominant race/class perspective most of the prevention programs have only belatedly (if at all) addressed issues relevant to children with less positive relationships with the state and multiple oppressions. As one North American activist asks: 'What about the children whose lives are not reflected in the skits, the images, the plays or the books? What of the Black child whose older brother was beaten by a policeman? Or the Chinese child who lives with her grandmother, an undocumented worker whose presence at home must be kept from the white authorities?' (Butler, 1986: 10). What, also, of the child being raised by lesbians who must keep her 'life-style' secret or risk being taken into 'custody' by her father or the state? Children do not necessarily experience teachers, social workers and police-officers as potential allies. One attempt to encourage children to seek help from trustworthy adults, such as policemen, for instance, received a decidedly skeptical response from at least one group of children—in a Welsh pit village soon after a year-long miners' strike (during which the police were seen to be violent agents of the state). Although claiming to speak to all children, many of these programs thus fail to address the concerns of 'minority' children and rely on racist, classist and heterosexist assumptions about the 'nature' of childhood.

Empowering the Powerless

The central tenet of these child safety programs is not, however, only to assist children to identify abuse and seek help but to 'empower' children to help themselves. Rejecting assumptions of childhood passivity and defenselessness they build on children's existing sense of self-protection and their ability to kick, yell and run. Rather than seeing all children as inherently vulnerable, these activists pay attention to extra 'risk factors' such as an individual child's low self-esteem and target them for 'ego-enhancing' action. Instead of presenting children as 'natural victims' this approach celebrates their spirited and determined resistance (Caignon and Groves, 1989: 6). Rejecting the imposition of restriction on children, restrictions which can undermine 'the sense of personal independence that is as important as caution' (Brown, *1986*), these programs try to help children to be 'streetwise' and confident. Books and videos with titles like 'Strong Kids—Safe Kids'; 'Speak Up, Say No'; 'You're in Charge' and 'Feeling Yes, Feeling No' urge children to be assertive, to express their own feelings and to develop a sense of control over their own bodies (Brassard, *et al.,* 1983).

This is the positive side of the action taken in response to the concept of vulnerability. Vulnerability, here, is seen not just in terms of the need for adult protection but as something that children themselves can change by modifying their behavior. Role play, games, stories and songs are designed to help children resist abuse; the message is, as one catchy song boldly declares:

> My body's nobody's body but mine
> You run your own body
> Let me run mine

> [From 'Kids can Say No' video]

Such programs represent a challenging departure from the traditional approach to children and child protection. Indeed, they provoke considerable unease among those concerned with maintaining the status quo. These programs are accused of undermining parental rights, encouraging self-centeredness and failing to distinguish between the 'normal' and 'abnormal' exercise of parental authority. Gilbert (1988), for instance, bemoans the fact that only one of the programs he reviewed instructed teachers 'to point out that a bad touch is different from a spanking and to suggest that children may deserve to be spanked by parents if they do something naughty or dangerous' (Gilbert, 1988: 8). Another writer also concerned about 'strident' prevention compaigns concludes: 'Children who have been systematically taught to fight dirty, lie and be rude and unhelpful to strangers, may well be tougher propositions when it comes to resisting sexual abuse—but at what cost for the rest of their dealings with society?' (Tucker, 1985: 98).

Faced with such hostility, many people are understandably eager to protest that these programs are 'not subversive' (Frost quoted in Aziz, 1987). However, what change can be made to children's position within society *without* subverting existing hierarchies, *without* challenging 'society as we know it? If these preventive programs are not subversive then what are they? Where do the activists in this area 'draw the line' and what contradictions and dilemmas do they face?

The Limits of Empowering

One of the dilemmas for activists seeking to 'empower' children is how to make them feel they *can* resist abuse without making them feel guilty if they don't or can't. Placing the primary emphasis on teaching children to 'say no' risks making them feel responsible for their own victimization. Indeed, after one prevention program, the children were found to have a *greater* tendency to believe that, if they were abused, it would be their own fault (cited in Hamilton, 1989). Some adult survivors too find that these programs reflect negatively on their own experiences: 'I thought I had said no. Maybe I didn't say no as though I *really* meant it.' Many survivors (including those whose ingenious strategies are described-earlier), are made to feel that their victimization is evidence either of their collusion or their weakness. 'I let him do it to me' said Vida; 'Was it because I was a weakling?' asked Sadie, while another woman, reflecting on the abuse inflicted on her at a child-care center, stated: 'Now I can see that I gave my power away' (Asherah, 1983: 179).

Seeing power in individualistic terms as something that can be 'claimed' or 'given away' by an 8-year-old is, for many people, reassuring. Even some survivors talk of 'wanting' to believe that they had some influence over events, if only to cling to some illusion of control. Louise Wisechild, for instance, describes her childhood powerlessness but also identifies a function in believing that her own badness caused the abuse: 'If it is my fault and I'm bad, then trying to be good offers hope. If we're not bad [. . .] then maybe we can't make anything happen, not even bad things'. (Wisechild, 1988: 132). To have had *some* power (even if it was the power to provoke maltreatment) is less humiliating and terrifying than to have been a total victim with no power at all.

The idea that children have the ability to stop abuse, or that 'vulnerable' children can have this vulnerability erased by judicially applied 'ego-enhancing' education, is also a way of 'selling' sexual abuse prevention programs. Commercially produced prevention packages are now a multi-million dollar industry in North America and it makes sense for anyone seeking permission for children to attend such programs to promote the idea that, as stated in one letter sent out to parents: 'When interviewing people who have sexually assaulted children, it has been determined that in 80 per cent of the cases, the abuser would have stopped if the child had said "No" ' (quoted in Trudell and Whatley, 1988: 105). Such a suggestion is an insult to the many women and children who try to resist but are still abused and who, when they confide in family or friends, face the question 'But why didn't you say no?' The emphasis on 'personal power' and 'the right to say no', by locating change within the individual, distracts attention from social structural issues.[8] It fragments common experiences of oppression and thus undermines our perception of the necessity for collective, political action.

When children are cowed and unresisting, such behavior should not be seen simply as a 'bad habit' that can be 'corrected' by a few hours 'intervention'. It is a reflection of their experience of powerlessness. One of the ironies of the prevention campaigns is that children who start off with lowest self-esteem in the first place appear to benefit *least* from such interventions (Gough, 1989: 14). In other words it is precisely the children who are most vulnerable, eager to please and easily-led who obstinately reject any idea that they have 'rights' and refuse to develop a 'sense' of their own power. Such unexpected conviction from the most vulnerable children is understandable if we accept that a 'sense' of powerlessness may in fact reflect their external 'reality'. Children are sometimes hopeless because there is no hope, helpless because there is no help and compliant because there is no alternative. Powerlessness is in the food they eat, the air they breathe and the beds they sleep in. As one 9-year-old, explaining her own abuse, said simply: 'He was big and I was little. I had to do what he said' (Gilgun and Gordon, 1985: 47). Abusers rarely have to display any great brutality to get their own way: the father-abuser's power runs like an undercurrent through the whole family. In sensationalizing perpetrators' grosser *abuses* of power we forget the routine use of power over children, 'That's what makes me angry now,' explains one survivor, 'when the media says that all kids are told to shut up and threatened—that is often the case, but you can threaten without any words at all'.

Changing children's sense of power or adults' use of such power cannot be achieved without reference to their actual state of powerlessness or control. Telling children that they 'have' certain rights is not enough—they need either some practical experience of those rights and/or some idea of the forces which deny them those rights and ways of fighting for them. As 'Liz' writes: 'A child's right to her own body, autonomy and privacy is still a radical concept *which would require the transformation of family power relations.* (Liz, 1982: 217, my emphasis.) The limits and contradictions of the campaigns to 'empower' children are, perhaps, most clearly illustrated by cases where children have 'over-generalized' or 'gone too far' in their understanding of their 'rights'. One child, for instance, generalized her right to say no to any request that she did not like or made her feel uncomfortable. Her parents were apparently 'forced' to endure 'much anguish and frustration' and 'had to punish her in order to convince her that she did not have the right to disobey them whenever she wanted to' (Conte cited in Haugard and Reppucci, 1988). Clearly then adult intentions to permit, and children's ability to claim that, 'My body's nobody's body but mine' is severely limited, intertwined as it is with notions of 'obedience' and parental obligations.

Helping children resist abuse depends on paying close attention to their existing strategies and exploring why these are often insufficient protection: insufficient because of a lack of alternatives, resources and power. Children's resistance strategies fail *in spite of the* child not simply because of her lack of confidence. We need to examine children's material reality and recognize that children are vulnerable because they *are* children—childhood is a state of oppression (an oppression compounded by discrimination based upon sex, race, class and disability). Powerlessness is not 'all in the mind.' . . .

Many of the activists concerned with empowering children would probably agree with this analysis of structural power. There is even a tradition of ending reviews or evaluations of prevention programs with a caveat that goes something like: 'Of course, education is not enough—we need to look at wider power imbalances within society as a whole'. However, this understanding of structural power is not applied to the design, evaluation or review of prevention programs themselves. While writers pay great attention to the difficulties concerning, for instance, talking to children about sex, the dilemmas faced in talking with children about power are not even part of the debate. The implicit assumption is *either* that it is dealt with during discussion of such topics as 'bullying' *or* that it is not appropriate to talk directly to children about power at all. (Dealing with power is a big, grown up thing that the adults should just get on and tackle by themselves). Indeed, there seems to be a tacit agreement that talking to children about structural power is a dubious activity because it may erode their sense of 'personal power'. Identifying the odds stacked against children might be 'disempowering', making them feel helpless and vulnerable: to name power is to create it; to identify power is to activate it; once acknowledged its force increases. In fact, children are systematically denied a language of power and their experiences of powerlessness are obscured. Faced with children who are the victims of institutionalized bullying or sexist, racist or heterosexist abuse we often feel unable to explain the issue in terms of politics and oppression. We may not have a language of power with which we are comfortable ourselves, we may feel that children cannot grasp such abstract concepts or we may simply wish to protect them from confronting injustice and discrimination. Thus, a black child is told that the white children call her names because 'they are jealous', the bullies are 'just silly', the spanking was 'deserved'—'because you were naughty' and the unjust teacher 'probably had a bad day' (Kitzinger and Kitzinger, 1989).

However, it is only by discussing power with children that we can explain why some children 'passively' comply with abusers and why some 'actively' resist but are still abused. It is only by discussing power that we can place responsibility with abusers rather than their victims. When adults do find ways of talking about power then even quite young children are capable of understanding and working with the concept—power is, after all, part of their everyday experience and is a useful tool to make sense of their world (Kitzinger and Kitzinger, 1989). (The agility with which these programs are able to discuss sexual abuse *without* directly addressing either sex or power is testimony to the years of expertise built up around avoiding these two taboo subjects!) Preventive programs aimed at children need to explore ways of talking about power in accessible and directly relevant ways and must address issues such as: how are prevention programs affected by the context within which they are introduced (e.g., with the hierarchical and compulsory institution of school)? How do we usually *explain away* injustice and oppression? If power is 'given' can it also be taken away? What are the implications for adult 'caretakers' if children start questioning power?

A radical, deconstructionist approach to preventive work with children would focus *not* on 'giving' children a 'sense' of power and telling them their 'rights' but, instead, on supporting them to recognize and name their own oppression. Rather than encouraging adults to be nicer to children by simply negotiating with them or 'involving' them in decision making, a radical approach would explore ways of openly discussing power with children and would encourage us to consider how we, as adults, manipulate children in order to obfuscate our own power. . . .

In recognizing the political oppression of children (on the basis of age and of gender, race, class and disability), a radical approach would also recognize children as resisters to those oppressions. This means refusing to collaborate in the censorship of children's contemporary and historical struggles against injustice throughout the world. It also means countering adult-centric and ethno-centric western perceptions of child activists as victims of the machinations of adults (e.g., children involved in anti-nuclear actions at Greeham Common were frequently portrayed as 'victims' of their uncaring, unmotherly mothers who were 'using' them as political footballs) (Kitzinger, J., 1985). Once we stop denying children a language of power and of resistance then we remove one of the barriers to the transformation of childhood from within. We also open up the possibility for a different relationship between adults and their own childhoods, as well as between adults and other people's childhoods. While any 'education' bestowed upon children by adults is problematic, (and should certainly not be seen as the only or primary 'site of intervention') at least a 'consciousness raising' approach such as that suggested earlier does not gloss over inequalities or actually *undermine* the struggle against structural change.

CONCLUSION

Debates about the sexual abuse of children are deeply embedded in discourses about childhood—what it is and what it should be. However, much of the 'pro-child' discussion, even many of the most radical 'child-centered' or 'empowerment' approaches, have succeeded in problematizing child sexual abuse without problematizing childhood as a structural position within society. Indeed, the very term 'child abuse' allows an evasion of the issue of power because is takes the nature of 'the child' for granted: 'child abuse' is premised on the notion of the child, rather than say young(er), small(er), or weak(er) persons. Child abuse may be posed as a problem, yet in doing so the ageism of dominant social constructions of the child/ren may remain, even be perpetuated (Hearn, 1988: 534).[9]

Rather than relying on notions of 'protection' or even 'empowerment', activists engaged in the struggle against child abuse need to consciously grapple with the deconstruction and reconstruction of childhood. This means acknowledging and reinforcing children's strategies and identifying and challenging their powerlessness. It means dealing openly with children about power and thinking in terms of 'oppression' rather than 'vulnerability', 'liberation' rather than 'protection'. The deconstruction and reconstruction of childhood is also not something that just goes on in our own heads—it involves struggling to increase children's practical options and to transform the social and political context within which children exist. Children's need for protection (by adults, from adults) or their need for assertive self-defense strategies would be substantially reduced if they had more access to social, economic and political resources.

Ultimately, it is childhood as an institution that makes children 'vulnerable'. Millions of children endure different types of abuse every day. Abuse cannot be blamed on either 'the decay' of childhood or the inherent 'nature' of childhood; it is not a question of mothers going out to work, nor of 'incompetent' social workers; nor is it a question of the individual psyches of the abused or the abuser; rather, the risk of abuse is built into childhood as an institution itself. 'There is so much abuse of young people, as violence, as threatened and potential violence, and routine ageism, that it is not a "something" that can be solved by professional interventions and professional intervenors. It is a problem of this, patriarchal, society' (Hearn, 1989: 79).

Child abuse is not an anomaly but part of the structural oppression of children. Assault and exploitation are risks inherent to 'childhood' as it is currently lived. It is not just the *abuse* of power over children that is the problem but the existence and maintenance of that power itself.

Discussion Questions

1. Why does the author argue that the notion of childhood innocence may actually perpetuate the sexual abuse of children?
2. What role does power play in understanding childhood sexual abuse?
3. What are the ironies of the way society defines childhood innocence?
4. What does the author suggest will best reduce the sexual abuse of children?

Notes

Part of this chapter first appeared in the special issue of *Feminist Review* on child sex abuse, 28, Spring 1988.

1. The few images I found of clearly non-white children subject to sexual exploitation were in stories about wholesale child sexual slavery—exotic peeks into other cultures, at best, linked to a market created by white tourists but often, by implication, a reflection of something rotten within the culture. This kind of cultural analysis is not, of course, applied to the widespread abuse of children within white mainstream culture. Although 'sub-cultural' explanations have been applied to incest among white people in isolated rural areas, among the over-crowded working classes or within the individual 'dysfunctional family', it has certainly not been brought to bear on the large child prostitution and pornography rings organized by middle class white, professional men in Britain.

2. These themes appear in different guises and combinations—I am not claiming to describe a watertight and coherent body of beliefs propounded by one particular group of people.

3. Glib statements about 'the nature' of childhood obscure the fact that most children do not live in 'safe havens' but face disease, starvation, homelessness and war (Allsebrook and Swift, 1989). As Goode points out: 'For the eight year old guerilla in Nicaragua "doing the world" as a child is at best an occasional affair if not an impossibility' (Goode, 1986).

4. Unless otherwise specified, quotations come from my own research involving interviews with 39 women survivors of childhood sexual abuse. Psuedonyms have been used throughout. In using personal accounts I am not suggesting that these give the one and only 'true' and static understanding of events. We all experience and talk about out lives within particular frameworks, we construct and reconstruct accounts drawing, for instance, on notions of what it means to be a victim or a survivor and the meaning of sexual abuse in childhood.

5. Adult-centrism is evident in the calls to help children because they are 'the parents of tomorrow' and 'our most valuable human resource'. Children are valued because of the adults they will become and their pain is evaluated in terms of its effect on adult functioning. It is almost as if, on one level, childhood suffering is discounted because it is only 'a passing phase', an oppression that you, literally, 'out grow'. As Finkelhor points out: '. . . researchers and theoreticians persistently focus on the question of long term effects [. . .] The bottom line is always how does this event affect adult adjustment, adult feelings, adult capacities and adult attitudes?' (Finkelhor, 1984: 198).

6. One influential essay that *does* look at children's survival strategies is Summit's classic 'The Child Sexual Abuse Accommodation Syndrome'. However, the discussion is, ironically, packaged in medical terminology which, as feminists (among others) have pointed out, serves to depoliticize experience and reinforce the control of 'the experts' (Kelly, 1989).

7. These programs do, however, have to negotiate acceptance by parents and schools and are thus constrained by demands to preserve childhood innocence, obedience, and trust in parental and school authority. Thus, for instance, few programs even identify sexual anatomy let alone include any discussion of sexuality (Miller-Perrin and Wurtele, 1988: 316). Keeping children in ignorance about sex perpetuates their vulnerability and may be actively exploited by abusers. Gillian's father, for instance, obliged her to submit to his sexual demands as legitimate punishment after he discovered her masturbating, while Barbara, who was sexually involved with a female friend, submitted to her uncle because she thought he had a right to teach her about 'normal sex'. Similarly, another girl was made to feel responsible for the abuse by her father who deliberately set out to stimulate her sexuality (Touch, 1987, 147). All three girls were made vulnerable by the stigma surrounding children's sexuality and felt implicated in their own violation.

8. In fact, the notion of 'empowering' children is explicitly part of some 'paedophilic' arguments. In *Paedophilia: The Radical Case*, for instance, O'Carroll (1979) argues that '. . . if we are going to make more than a pretence of taking children seriously, they must be enabled to say *yes* as well as *no*. Children have to have a *choice* and should not be bound to either an anti-sex approach (as usually taken by parents, religious leaders, etc.) or a pro-sex approach (usually confined to peers and paedophiles)'. Dichotomizing attitudes into the 'anti-sex' and 'pro-sex' type ignores issues around the social construction of 'consent', 'desire' and 'compulsory hetero sexuality' (c.f. Jeffreys (1985), Dworkin (1987) and Leeds Revolutionary Feminist Groups (1981)).

9. The category 'child sexual abuse' also separates out the abuse of women under 16 or 18 years old from the abuse of women over that age. This allows for the diminution of children's experiences—where adult women can now talk of being 'sexually harassed', deceptively cosy words are applied to children—'being interfered with', 'fondled' or 'petted'. It also creates a false division between the abuse women suffer at different periods of our lives and obscures the fact that many fathers continue to assault their daughters well into adulthood.

References

Adams, C. and Fay, J. (1981) *No More Secrets*, California, Impact.

Allen, C. (1980) *Daddy's Girl*, London, New English Library.

Allsebrook, A. and Swift, A. (1989) *Broken Promise*, Seven Oaks, Hodder and Stoughton.

Armstrong, L. (1987) *Kiss Daddy Goodnight*, New York, Pocket Books.

Asherah, K. (1983) 'Daddy Kanagy', in Bass, E. and Thornton, L. (Eds) *I Never Told Anyone: Writings by Women Survivors of Child Sexual Abuse*, London, Harper and Row, pp. 179–81.

Aziz, C. (1987) 'Teaching children to say no', in *The Guardian*, 6 January, p. 10.

Bacon, H. and Richardson, S. (1989) 'Reflections on the psychology of the abused child', talk given at *Child Sexual Abuse: The Way Forward*, Teesside Polytechnic, 18–19 July.

Barr, A. (1986) 'Child sex abuse: We need money not sentiment' in *The Observer*, 9 November.

Barrett, M. and Coward, R. (1985) 'Don't talk to strangers', *New Socialist*, November, pp. 21–3.

Bass, E. and Thornton, L. (Eds) (1983) *I Never Told Anyone: Writings by Women Survivors of Child Sexual Abuse*, London, Harper and Row.

Bender, L. and Blau, A. (1937) 'The reaction of children to sexual relations with adults', *American Journal of Orthopsychiatry,* 7, 4, pp. 500–18.

Bradbury, A. (1986) 'A model of treatment', *Community Care*, 4, September, pp. 24–5.

Brassard, M., Tyler, A. and Keble, T. (1983) 'School programs to prevent intrafamilial child sexual abuse', *Child Abuse and Neglect*, 7, pp. 241–5.

Brown, M. (1986) 'A parent's dilemma', in *The Sunday Times*, 19 October.

Butler, S. (1986) 'Thinking about prevention: A critical look' in Nelson, M. and Clark, K. (Eds) (1986) *The Educator's Guide to preventing Child Sexual Abuse*, Santa Cruz, Network Publications.

Caignon, D. and Groves, G. (Eds) (1989) *Her Wits About Her: Self-Defense Success Stories by Women*, London, Women's Press.

Cook, R. (1987) *The Cook Report*, ITV, 8.30pm, 29 July.

Cooper, S. (1986) 'Confronting a near and present danger: How to teach children to resist assault' in Haden, D. (Ed) *Out of Harm's Way: Readings on Child Sexual Abuse, its prevention and Treatment*, Phoenix, Oryx Press, pp. 36–40.

Dingwall, R. (1987) 'A parental prerogative?' *Nursing Times-Nursing Mirror*, 83, 17, pp. 47–50.

Dworkin, A. (1987) *Intercourse*, London, Secker and Warburg.

Elliott, K. (1982) 'Diary of a feminist teacher', in Rowe, M. (Ed) *Spare Rib Reader*, Harmondsworth, Penguin, pp. 250–5.

Elliott, M. (1988) 'Caring about safety', *Social Work Today*, 19, 31, pp. 25–6, 32.

Finkelhor, D. (1984) *Child Sexual Abuse: New Theory and Research*, London, Collier-McMillan.

Finkelhor, D. (1986) 'Prevention: A review of programs and research', in Finkelhor, D. and Associates (Eds) *A Source Book on Child Sexual Abuse*, London, Sage, pp. 224–57.

Forward, S. and Buck, C. (1981) *Betrayal of Innocence: Incest and Its Devastation*, London, Penguin.

Gilbert, N. (1988) 'Teaching children to prevent sexual abuse', *The Public Interest*, 93, pp. 3–15.

Gilgun, J. and Gordon, S. (1985) 'Sex education and the prevention of child sexual abuse', *Journal of sex Education and Therapy,* 11, 1, Spring/Summer, pp. 46–52.

Goode, D. (1986) 'Kids, culture and innocents', *Human Studies*, 9, 1, pp. 83–106.

Gordon, L. (1988) *Heroes of Their Own Lives: The Politics and History of* Family Violence—1880–1960, New York, Viking.

Gough, D. (1989) *Child Abuse Intervention: A Review of the Research Literature*, Research Report to DHSS. (Available from SPORU, 1 Lilybank Gardens, Glasgow University).

Hamilton, S. (1989) 'Prevention of Child Sexual Abuse: An Evaluation of a Programme', MSc in advanced social work, Edinburgh University.

Hancock, M. and Mains, K. (1987) *Child Sexual Abuse: A Hope for Healing,* Illinois, Harold Shaw Publishers.

Haugard, J. and Reppucci, N. (1988) *The Sexual Abuse of Children: A Comprehensive Guide to Current Knowledge and Intervention Strategies*, San Francisco, Jossey-Bass.

Hearn, J. (1988) 'Child abuse: Violences and sexualities towards young people', *Sociology,* 22, 4, pp. 531–44.

Hearn, J. (1989) 'Child abuse and men's violence', in The Violence Against Children Study Group, *Taking Child Abuse Seriously: Contemporary*

Issues in Child Protection Theory and Practice, London, Unwin Hyman pp. 63–85.

Janus, S. (1981) *The Death of Innocence*, New York, Morrow.

Jackson, S. (1982) *Childhood and Sensuality*, Oxford, Basil Blackwell.

Jeffreys, S. (1985) *The Spinster and her Enemies*, London, Pandora.

Kelly, L. (1989) 'Bitter Ironies', *Trouble and Strife*, 16, Summer pp. 14–21.

Kelly, R. (1988) 'Protect your child from sexual abuse!', *The Plain Truth*, September, pp. 10–11.

Kitzinger, J. (1985) ' "Take the toys from the boys": The social construction of gender and the women's peace movement', in *Bulletin of the British Psychological Society*, 38, May, p. 68.

Kitzinger, S. and Kitzinger, C. (1989) *Talking to Children About Things that Really Matter*, London, Pandora.

Kohn, A. (1987) 'Shattered Innocence', *Psychology Today*, 21, February, pp. 54–8.

Leeds Revolutionary Feminist Group (1981) *Love Your Enemy: The Debate Between Heterosexual Feminism and Political Lesbianism*, London, Onlywomen Press.

Liz (1982) 'Too afraid to speak', *The Leveller*, 2–15th April, pp. 18–21.

MacFarlane, K. (1988) 'Current issues in child sexual abuse', Talk given at *Intervening in Child Sexual Abuse*, Glasgow, 1988.

Miller-Perrin, C. and Wurtele, S. (1988) 'The child sexual abuse prevention movement—A critical analysis of primary and secondary approaches', *Clinical Psychology Review*, 8, 3, pp. 313–29.

Nelson, S. (1987) *Incest: Fact and Myth*, Edinburgh, Stramullion.

O'Carroll, T. (1979) Paedophilia: The Radical Case, London, Peterowen.

Parton, C. and Parton, N. (1988) 'Women, the family and child protection', *Critical Social Policy*, Winter 88/89, pp. 38–49.

Rantzen, E. (1986) 'Dear Esther', in *The Sunday Times*, 9, November, p. 25.

Rush, F. (1980) *The Best Kept Secret: Sexual Abuse of Children*, New York, McGraw-Hill.

Russell, D. (1986) *The Secret Trauma: Incest in the Lives of Girls and Women*, New York, Basic Books.

Seabrook, J. (1987) 'The decay of childhood', *New Statesman*, 10 July, pp. 14–15.

Sgroi, S. (Ed) (1982) *Handbook of Clinical Intervention in Child Sexual Abuse*, Massachusetts, Lexington Books.

Shelter, (1989) *One Day I'll Have My Own Place to Stay*, London, Shelter, Publications.

Stacey, C. (1989) 'How to get ahead', Options, November, pp. 26–7.

Stainton-Rogers, R. (1989) 'The social construction of childhood', in Stainton-Rogers, W., Hevey, D. and Ash, E. (1989) *Child Abuse and Neglect: Facing the Challenge*, London, Open University Press, pp. 23–9.

Summit, R. (1986) 'Foreword', in MacFarlane, K. and Waterman, J. (1986) *Sexual Abuse of Young Children*, London, Holt, Rinehart and Winston, pp. xi–xv.

Summit, R. and Kryso, J. (1978) 'Sexual abuse of children: A clinical spectrum', *American Journal of Orthopsychiatry*, 48, pp. 237–51.

Takanishi, R. (1978) 'Childhood as a social issue: Historical roots of contemporary child advocacy movements', *Journal of Social Issues*, 34, 2, pp. 8–28.

Testimony of a Child Debate (1989) BBC2, 5 July, 11.15pm.

Touch, P. (1987) 'Stories my body tells', in Portwood, P., Gorcey, M. and Sanders, P. (Eds) (1987) *Rebirth of Power*, Racine, Illinois, Mother Courage Press.

Trudell, B. and Whatley, M. (1988) 'School sexual abuse prevention—Unintended consequences and dilemmas', *Child Abuse*, 12, 1, pp. 103–13.

Tucker, N. (1985) 'A panic over child abuse', *New Society*, 18 Oct, pp. 96–8.

Wisechild, L. (1988) *Obsidian Mirror: An Adult Healing from incest*, Seattle, Seal Press.

In Sickness and in Play: Children Coping with Chronic Illness

CINDY DELL CLARK

INTRODUCTION

Children suffering from illness elicit a lot of sympathy and compassion. They are often used symbolically to raise awareness about diseases or funds for research. In this selection, Cindy Dell Clark examines how children deal with chronic illness. Through interviews and observations, she notes that children frequently use play to cope with their fears surrounding their illness. Too often adults and even medical professionals discount the role of play in helping children feel more powerful in the face of serious health challenges.

. . . In American society, we glorify the inventions of adults—computers, medicines, scientific theories—yet often trivialize the fanciful inventions of children. Imaginary companions have received bad reviews, for example, being decried as maladaptive or as indicative of psychological disturbance.[1] Adults also malign the tooth fairy, such as in the mocking expression, "If you believe that, you must also believe in the tooth fairy."[2] Wishing and other forms of magical thinking have been relatively neglected as modes of thought worthy of study.[3] Mere child's play is discounted, while rational adult pursuits are given greater weight.

An exceptional instance to the dismissal of fantasy lies in hospital-based child life programs. Hospitals increasingly have come to incorporate therapeutic play into children's treatment as part of child life services.[4] Child life specialists familiarize children with treatment, making regular use of play to aid the child psychologically. But not all hospitals have child life departments. Much of children's chronic illness experience takes place in the home, at school, around the neighborhood, or within the family, where play is not officially a tool of treatment.

At hospitals without programs sensitive to children's need for play and symbolic communication, problems can arise. Consider the experience of Grace, a seven-year-old diabetic, who told me about her hospitalization five years earlier as she drew an illustrative picture for me from memory. Prominent in Grace's picture was a very large tiger. The tiger was positioned next to Grace's "jail bed," as she referred to the hospital crib with bars. The tiger was in fact a stuffed toy, presented to her by her uncle when she was diagnosed with diabetes and hospitalized at age twenty-two months. The hospital scared Grace with its cagelike crib and hurtful procedures.

> GRACE: I hated lying in that bed . . . and I had a tiger. My uncle . . . got it. It's like a huge tiger. . . . The nurses used to take it away because they thought it would scare me. But it didn't.
>
> [Sobs for several minutes.] And I was only two years old.
>
> CDC: How did the tiger make you feel?
>
> GRACE: It made me feel safe.
>
> CDC: Really? How come?
>
> GRACE: It kept me company.

Although the nurses thought the toy tiger frightened Grace, in fact the toy had been her helpmate, making her feel protected. The hospital, not the tiger, scared Grace intensely. Through a tragic misunderstanding, Grace's coping was misinterpreted and impeded by those caring for her. They took away her toy tiger just when she most needed it to face the hospital experience. A lack of understanding led to unnecessary emotional trauma, perhaps not an isolated circumstance across health care settings.

Grace had courage in envisioning her own protection through the toy tiger, a kind of transitional object. Children routinely muster such courage, very often without any aid from therapists or other adults, in coping with the hardships related to asthma or diabetes. This chapter examines the remarkable capacity of children for imaginal coping—coping through the use of imagination—and how imaginal coping aids their fortitude. My purpose here is to establish the importance of imaginal coping for children with chronic illness. . . .

COPING

A child with asthma or diabetes faces exceptional circumstances due to coupled problems— the symptoms of disease and the vicissitudes of treatment. Medical intervention, although intended to restore normal functioning, has an adverse impact also, bringing restrictions, interruptions, and intrusions upon physical and social experience. Troubles arise apart from the symptoms treated, taking the shape of fear, distaste, pain (for example, the pain of injections), inconvenience, and boredom. Stresses that spring from the treatment as well as the disease become a part of the child's daily lifeworld.

Adding to the child's predicament are the distancing social reactions of others in response to the child's symptoms and treatment. Some playmates flinch upon witnessing diabetic blood tests. Coaches and gym teachers may bench a child using an inhaler to treat exercise-induced asthma. Squeamish relatives of children with diabetes are known to impulsively walk away during injections. Such acts of exclusion can " spoil identity," as Goffman so well explained.[5] As young as age seven or eight, some children in our study had already grown embarrassed to use an asthma inhaler in front of classmates.[6] In social interaction, children constructed a sense of self threaded with exceptionality—ironically, a stigma deriving partly from the very treatment procedures meant to restore life to as normal as possible a condition. Children must cope, then, with social and taboolike consequences to their sense of self, derived from treatment as well as from the physical events of illness. . . .

COPING AS A PROCESS

. . . Coping takes place through the routine as well as the extraordinary social experiences of ill children. Coping may involve tacit levels of meaning that children do not necessarily articulate directly. That is, the contexts of meaning making may be implicit rather than explicitly stated or conscious.[7] Without intending to, parents or caretakers may hinder coping by such acts as taking away a stuffed animal, or they may encourage coping by providing a prop for play, a suggestion for a ritual, and so on. A parent or playmate may serve to co-construct a meaningful act of coping with a child, perhaps by devising or editing an act of play. For example, a parent might purchase medical toys and encourage the child to choose a stuffed animal upon which to "play doctor." The child may then choose to be a doctor who treats snakes (a veterinarian) and give mock injections to a toy snake, dramatizing courage in the act. . . .

At other times, children may engage in play with delight and openness, rather than consciously or explicitly to address suffering. As play therapists know, play is remarkable because it is not necessarily explicitly goal-oriented, yet it accomplishes profound outcomes. At the beach, for instance, a chronically ill child may become gleefully involved in a game of being buried in the sand by parents—and while the game seems just for fun, nevertheless the game may help the child to engage pertinent issues of control and surrender. . . .

THE CASE OF ILLNESS CAMP

Camps organized for children with illness have an impressive clinical track record. Research has widely found illness camps to be effective in improving children's control over symptoms.[8] In one such investigation, camp improved childhood asthma so markedly that it led to savings in health care costs of $2,014 per camper, through reduced hospitalization and other health care expenses.[9] . . .

Three investigators carried out participant observation while working at two camps for diabetes and one camp for asthma.[10] They were able to observe how campers interacted within each community, as well as how individuals paid attention to and made sense of the camp experience. They saw firsthand the process by which children reacted to the biomedical education and other activities at camp.

Young campers ignored, missed, or resisted a considerable part of the camp's biomedical education. That is, despite the best adult efforts to instill campers with biomedical knowledge about their disease, children paid less than full attention to their attempts. After one lesson at a diabetes camp for seven- and eight-year-olds, for example, some campers became restless, asking repeatedly, "When can we go home?" At a session about the long-term risks of diabetes, conducted while boys ages eight to twelve sat or lay down on their bunks, some of the boys fell asleep before the educational session ended. Campers asked if they could play video games meant to be educational about diabetes next time, instead of hearing another lesson. But when the next day's lesson came, the boys' interest in the diabetes-related games did not last: they wanted to play indoor floor hockey instead, which the educator vetoed to moans and groans. Ignoring the veto, the boys played floor hockey anyway.

At the camp for children ages eight to twelve with asthma, the campers enjoyed some parts of the educational program, but their reception was not consistently positive. . . .

Our investigation did not confirm the idea that the improved functioning of children attending camp happened mainly through didactic, biomedical education. As Mechling's work foretold, camp also provided a social and symbolic experience in which children created a separate realm of knowing. In this respect, camp was a backdrop for a unique social experience transformative in its own right.

Camp provided an opportunity for children to be with other children experiencing the same illness, so that the illness was "woven into the fabric of everyday life."[11] Children at camp shared the same medical condition and common treatments, which led to interactions related to issues of illness. For once, the children were not stigmatized in this social setting: here, their illness *defined* the standing social norm. Teasing about illness was pointless, since, as one camper pointed out, "Everyone is in the same boat as you." Non-diabetic siblings who attended diabetes day camp, in fact, perceptibly took on minority status. Siblings with unrestricted diets became the odd persons out, the deviants; an excerpt from field notes at a diabetes day camp illustrates the inverted status of healthy siblings. . . .

In a social world where being chronically ill was the norm and eating a typical diet was marginalizing, social interactions took on changed potential. . . . Illness-related behaviors constituted signs of belonging and were part of normal discourse. Diabetic children compared blood-sugar readings, looked at one another's ID bracelets, and kept a check on each other's well-being. Asthmatic children compared versions of inhalers,[1] asked about each other's peak-flow readings, and kept track to see if someone seemed to be breathing too fast or wheezing. . . .

At diabetes camp, a favorite and happily remembered activity was creating visual art using syringes and paint, an activity that placed the medicinal syringe in the role of a fun, expressive medium. At asthma camp, an involving hands-on activity was using nebulizer machines[2] to inflate balloons, thus reframing a medical device into light-hearted entertainment. Among asthmatic peers, playful use of spacer devices (usually used with inhalers, with a sound signal to indicate improper use) spread widely; spacers took on shared uses as intentional noisemakers or quasi-musical instruments. . . .

An innovative trick that diffused fadlike through the asthma camp's cabins was "cheating" on peak-flow tests. By holding one's thumb over the rear opening of the peak-flow meter[3], as one camper told and showed the next, a child could get a very high score, better than any nonasthmatic person could obtain. This was a gleefully satisfying trick to campers, to be able to propel the peak-flow indicator high without the frustration and self-criticism brought on by their usual low peak-flow readings. Peer culture taught campers to undercut the usual, "correct" ways of using devices.

Campers received prizes for distinctions such as having the neatest cabin or for winning at games. They especially liked prizes that were novelty versions of pervasive medical apparatus, such as a pencil case shaped like an inhaler, or a cup decorated with floating confetti in inhaler shapes. These prizes poked fun at familiar medical instruments, a joke appreciated by campers.

During the closing ritual at the overnight diabetes camp, to honor campers' fund-raising efforts before camp opened, the "kiss a pig" ceremony was held. A live pig, to be kissed by a human, represented the source of the insulin on which diabetic children depend, pigs. The pig is an animal at once repulsive yet life sustaining—an apt symbol for how children feel about insulin injections. . . .

---

[1] A medical device that delivers medication to the lungs.
[2] A medical device used to administer liquid mist medicine into the lungs.
[3] Monitors the airflow to the lungs and measures the ability to exhale.

By kissing the lowly swine whose food-obsessed species is responsible for insulin, participants in the kiss-a-pig event both applauded and mocked the significance of insulin. This was similar in impact to other camp lore that made light of wearisome medical paraphernalia, such as peak-flow meters or syringes, through playful uses. Camp . . . produced transformative consequences upon meaning. Shared antics lightened the meaning of illness, poking fun at implements that caused suffering alongside relief. When ill children collectively made light of the medical implements that sustained their life, cathartic laughter prevailed. . . .

Camp included some planned activities ripe for interactive improvisation. On the last night of asthma camp, a climactic event was a performance of skits written jointly by campers from each cabin. This activity explicitly set up a context for campers to interactively prepare a performance. A cabin of girls devised a skit that parodied the "Three Little Pigs" story. A featured character in their skit was a wolf afflicted with asthma. The girls' version of the three pigs story (which Bettelheim has interpreted as a tale in which planning and hard labor could defeat the most ferocious enemy) reflected their own particular concern: inadequate breathing.[12] In the campers' version, the wolf visited the homes of three pigs but was unable to blow down any house (in contrast to the original story) due to asthmatic coughing. When the skit was performed for the entire camp, prolonged and loud laughter occurred at the following plot element: The wolf had, upon measurement, a peak flow of fifty, too low by mature human terms of sustain life. Happily, the wolf was hospitalized, received a lung transplant, and ended by feeling good enough to "huff and puff and blow any house down." The skit dramatized the defeat of a ferocious enemy, bodily threatening even to a wolf: asthma. The performance enjoyed hearty and lengthy applause, as the play provided comic relief over an issue of deep anxiety (a fatally low peak flow) and its fantastic resolution.[13] . . .

STORIES

. . . Our research among children with asthma or diabetes directs attention to a particular facet of how stories "work" to help children cope—through identification or involvement with a main character. The children owned many toys of featured characters in a TV story or movie. Via possession of the toy, this main character in a sense entered the everyday world with the child, serving (if the child so chose) as a force comprised of pretense against miseries or challenges faced by the child. Characters used in this way included superheroes from TV shows such as *Power Rangers* or *Teenage Mutant Ninja Turtles*, and sometimes other characters, such as Snoopy, the Pink Panther, Ren and Stimpy, Sylvester the Cat, or Taz the Tasmanian Devil. Such characters served as imaginary companions or as transitional objects—toys animated by a child's devotion and willing suspension of doubt.[14] Like the Nutcracker, the Velveteen Rabbit, or Winnie the Pooh, these were toys (usually with an extensive fictional biography provided by film or TV) that reached out from the frame of the toy-pretend world to engage the world of the child.[15]

Superhero representations, in particular, served as powerful companions to ill (often male) children in situations of felt vulnerability. A diabetic boy, Carl, took a toy version of the Power Rangers TV character White Ranger to the doctor's office for his checkup and lab test, privately imagining that the White Ranger also had diabetes. The toy was a form of moral support as a character known to be powerful; in Carl's words, "You can count on him." Having the White Ranger as a privately fantasized companion led to the worried boy's assumed protection, even when facing a physical exam. The paradox that seemingly underlies the character's value—that the White Ranger is powerful even though imagined to have diabetes—couples protection with illness. In Carl's imagination, illness and power were not mutually exclusive.

Peter, seven years old and a severe asthmatic since the age of three, also made use of superhero characters. I asked him to draw a picture of "the worst time you ever remember, with your asthma," and he set out to draw a picture of himself sick in bed. At first he drew his own face wearing a concerned frown. Then he added to his drawing the sheets on his bed, which happened to be decorated in TV characters, the Teenage Mutant Ninja Turtles. Upon drawing the Ninja Turtles on the sheets, Peter erased the frown and drew a smile upon his own face, instead. The Turtles on his sheets, as Peter visually recorded, brightened his mood. Peter had developed a fantasized relationship with the figures on his bed linen, much as other boys might love a teddy bear. (Peter's allergies precluded owning stuffed toys.)

Peter's imagined relationship with the Turtles was one he counted on when he felt sick or anxious. "I think about, like, they'd be real. And they, like, help me try to get rid of . . . stop being sick and everything. They come up and help me." How would they do this? "He would disguise himself and go to the doctor's office in a suit. He would go in a doctor's office and tell him what's the problem. And he'd say, 'I've got a real sick person at the house, and he needs your help because his mom doesn't know what to do, and we need your help.' "

Peter was anxious about becoming sick at night, alone in his room, unable to breathe and unable to get help. But he expected these superhero reptiles (mutant and physically anomalous) to be strong enough to protect and help him. "Nothing can harm 'em," Peter said of the Turtles, explaining that they would help someone with asthma but would never get asthma themselves.

The Teenage Mutant Ninja Turtle characters were treasured figures to several children. James, another boy with asthma, ritually wore clothing depicting the Ninja Turtles when he received his allergy shots at the physician's office. James preferred to get his shots while costumed in symbolic strength, as represented by a Ninja Turtle. The mother of another boy purchased a different Mutant Ninja Turtles toy character each week, when she went to the store to purchase diabetes supplies for her son. He liked to pretend that he gave a shot to each of these reptilian figures, an instance in which the boy reworked the meaning of injections: He was for once in control, and the reptilian heroes shared the status of getting injected. The Ninja Turtles were toys that accompanied children to the hospital, served as decorations on Band-Aids, and fulfilled a role as transitional objects that made children feel secure. The Turtles represented a fictional context that gave personal solace to a considerable number of children, especially boys. Children borrowed distinctively personal meaning from these and other pop-culture figures.

A five-year-old with diabetes, Brian, engaged in imagined play with another animated TV character, which he drew in picture form, the animated character Pink Panther. Enacting events in pretend play, Brian showed me how he would give the Pink Panther an insulin injection. He claimed that the Pink Panther "has diabetes in real life." This assumption was based on the character's presumed behavior on TV: "On the Pink Panther show, somebody offered him food and he said, 'No thanks, I have diabetes.' " When I interviewed Brian's mother, she explained that she had obtained a handbook for diabetes in which the Pink Panther had a featured role. In the book the Pink Panther showed "how to give shots" and illustrated other skills of diabetes care. The Pink Panther—knowledgeable about diabetes lore—had become a fantasy companion for Brian relevant to his world. . . .

PLAY AND ITS PLACE

Theorist and master play therapist Erik Erikson formulated play in broad terms: "[Play is] the infantile form of the human propensity to create model situations in which aspects of the past are re-lived, the present re-presented and renewed, and the future anticipated." In other words, play enables the remodeling of our perceptions of past, present, and future experience. . . .

The important role of play was apparent early in my research among diabetic and asthmatic children. Throughout the home visits and other observations, play permeated children's lives. Play was subtly present, at times even pervasive, in everyday activities.

Consider Tina, an eight-year-old with diabetes who, during our interview, drank her milk from a cup shaped like an ice cream cone with ersatz chocolate syrup decorating the plastic. Tina talked of a past event and drew it for me: Her mother was in the kitchen eating a chocolate chip cookie, while Tina looked on sadly. "I always feel bad because my mommy always does that [eats cookies]. I don't think it's fair." During our meeting, Tina was eating a lunch of permitted foods. But Tina imaginatively used her imagination and the cup's ice cream "disguise" to reconceive plain milk as a sweet confection. This was a simple form of playfully redressed experience that Tina enjoyed many times over.

Another instance of food-related play occurred among children who were part of a diabetic support group—a group of friends who liked to play the board game Candyland during parents' meetings. Normally, the local world of these diabetic players barred sweet indulgence, even at social gatherings. But children converted restriction into indulgence by moving through Candyland's indulgent fantasy world. Candyland is a rule-bound game, but while they played, the children appropriated the game board's candy-laden imagery for an imaginary free-for-all diet.

Some mothers of children with asthma adopted a Poppins-like strategy, allowing the child to have a wanted taste along with bad-tasting medicine (akin to the "spoonful of sugar that makes the medicine go down" from the P. L. Travers work *Mary Poppins*). A mother gave her daughter a sweet snack (a fruit roll-up) after each inhaler burst. A pill was served in sweet jelly, for another child. At work was a "play" of tastes in which one flavor dresses up in the disguise of the other. It is a simple form of play, within which both mother and child jointly reconstrue an unpleasant experience into a pleasing one.

Time and again, treatment was the privy to playful transformation. A hospital that gave its pediatric blood-testing machine the nickname "Herbie" and an endearing ability to "suck in your blood" won over one six-year-old boy. Herbie the machine, he asserted, had been the best part of his hospitalization. Giving the machine a name, the boy assessed, made it seem like the test hurt less.

A mother of an asthmatic boy insisted that this strategy should go further, that hospital procedures should be called upon to render each device playful and fun. She raised the example of the asthmatic child who is about to put on a mouth-enclosing oxygen mask yet is already anxious about blocked breathing. She suggested that the child not simply be masked, but be shown the mask and encouraged to imagine it in positive ways ("Does it look like it has eyes?") with an attitude that the mask "is going to be your friend." Had a [hospital-based] child life specialist been involved with administering oxygen, this might have been a feasible improvisation, turning the scary breath-blocking oxygen mask into a "friend.". . .

Randy Sikes had dealt with the stress of asthma for almost all of his five years. By now a veteran of chronic illness, Randy had been hospitalized for pneumonia in the first year of life, and eventually the ensuing "cold that wouldn't leave," as his mother described it, was diagnosed as asthma. Randy's parents moved from urban Chicago to a small town in Wisconsin while I was engaged in research with them. Randy's family was economically pressed. They moved to seek a lower cost of living and to improve chances for Mr. Sikes to find remunerative work. Randy's severe asthma persisted in both Illinois and Wisconsin, oblivious to the economic impact on a family without medical insurance. Randy used metered-dose inhalers and in Chicago went to his grandmother's house to borrow her plug-in nebulizer. (His maternal grandmother also had asthma.) He kept a duplicate inhaler at school in the nurse's office; Mrs. Sikes instructed Randy's teacher how to use the device if needed. . . .

Mrs. Sikes recounted that from an early age, "as soon as he was walking," Randy had a special involvement with toy cars. He played with toy cars when he was ill. When I sat down with Randy to interview him about having asthma, he chose to begin our time together by running out of the room to retrieve his toy race car to show me.

RANDY: I'll show you my [car], that I like to play with.

CDC: Oh, you love that. Now do you play with that when you're sick, that car?

RANDY: [Nodding] Mm hm. [Zooming car around] Vroom! Vroom!

CDC: Let's say you're sick and you're pretending with that. What would you pretend with that big race car?

RANDY: The ride in it!

CV: And ride where? Where would you ride to?

RANDY: Chicago!

CDC: To Chicago! Uh huh.

RANDY: Mm hm. And every time we needed gas.

Through his toy car, Randy mentally transported himself out of the present setting to elsewhere, although his gasoline was in short supply. His mother kept field notes for the study over a course of months, which recorded how Randy relied on his car as a means of coping in times of suffering or fear. She documented the following event during a bout of breathing difficulty for Randy:

DECEMBER 6, 1994

It is very cold and damp, and Randy's breathing is not good. He was very restless and breathing hard when he was sleeping. He is still very pale and not looking himself. . . . When his breathing problems come and he is having an asthma attack he sometimes looks up to me with his big blue eyes with the dark rings around them, and asks me for his green race car. And I get it for him. He hugs it closely and falls asleep.

Randy had several race cars, all special to him. During interviews, he imputed magical qualities to each car as an object that, he insisted, "worked wonders." He volunteered that his race car could make bad medicine taste better. He claimed not to even feel a shot when his race car was with him. Mrs. Sikes confirmed that when Randy was allowed to hold his race car at the hospital emergency room, it calmed him, acting as a "godsend." Mrs. Sikes kept a race car on hand at all times, sending one to school in Randy's backpack, and keeping one in her actual car. She was sensitive to, and grateful for, Randy's reliance on the race car so that he could find calmness when he needed it. "The cars have gone through it all with him," she observed, in a voice that showed her credence and approval about Randy's play. Mrs. Sikes expected Randy to continue to have a race car "tucked away in the closet" even when he was old enough to marry.

Mrs. Sikes recalled barriers to Randy's play, in particular within the medical system. Randy was not allowed to have his entirely plastic car (or his mother) with him during an X-ray, even though the car might have comforted him about a procedure that made him anxious. On one occasion, a nurse had looked at her strangely when Randy brought the car along to the hospital. "What kind of parent are you? Normal kids have blankets or pillows or stuffed animals. You bring this kid to the hospital with a car?" Randy's mother got angry at the implied criticism and defended the car as an allergen-free toy that "makes him feel safe." Despite maternal support for Randy's car play, then, not all medical personnel were equally supportive. . . .

Many children used a toy (and sometimes a pet) to cope with medical procedures, just as did Randy.[16] Teddy bears accompanied children to hospitals. Toy animals got hugged during blood tests or sat beside children during a shot. Children's imaginings about playthings were apt to vary widely, ranging from toy cars or airplanes to animals or superheroes, depending on the whims of the child. The individual child needed and took license, flexibly and freely incorporating cultural symbols. One diabetic child imagined the syringe to be a zebra; another saw it as a polar bear.

Biomedicine is largely construed as an objective, controlled science rather than as an art of interpretation. Like any claim that presumes understanding, this assumed objectivity has a narrowing impact on the constitution of knowledge by precluding or discounting other ways of knowing.[17] Toys, cartoons, or tales tend, in particular, to be disregarded.

Unintentionally, biomedicine can undermine imaginal coping, as when Randy's car was banished during X-ray, or when Grace's protective tiger was removed. Despite the meaning-mending powers of both placebos and play, like the placebo effect to which it is cousin, play exists on the margins of medical care.[18] To be sure, play is recognized and honored by play therapists or child life specialists. But children treated in many settings do not have such an advocate for their play.

Rick, a mature-looking eight-year-old who was an avid player of video games at the time I met him, recalled such an experience. Despite his savvy cool, Rick summoned to mind without probing the "yellow giraffe blanket," a blanket depicting yellow giraffes that he had used to comfort himself before his diagnosis with asthma at nine months. Under a physician's instructions, the blanket was declared a potential allergic trigger and removed. Rick proceeded to wake up at night with severe panic attacks, interpreted by the physician as "just airway obstruction," according to Rick's mother. Rick's mother eventually decided to return the blanket to the child, since his asthma symptoms had shown no improvement in its absence. Upon the return of the blanket, Rick's panic attacks subsided completely, an improvement his mother in retrospect attributed to the blanket's return.[19] At age eight, Rick still had asthma but no longer carried the blanket or slept with it. Still, he said, it gave him a good feeling to know the blanket was in the house.

Some children expressed appreciation to medical professionals who supported imaginal coping. For instance, Mike, age seven, recalled how a hospital nurse presented him with a teddy bear to take home, when he had been hospitalized upon diagnosis of diabetes four years earlier. Mike put the bear to use. Upon arriving home, Mike decided that the teddy bear had diabetes too and was in need to the same regimen of care as Mike. The bear obtained, with the help of Mike's mother, its own injection gear for pretend blood tests, performed by the child. Mike's mother explained that it had been up to Mike to decide whether the bear's blood-sugar reading was normal, high, or low. His mother felt that in this play, Mike had a chance to "be in control" of the bear's readings as an antidote to "being at the mercy" of his illness. . . .

By providing resources for children's play, caretakers can choose to actively scaffold and support imaginal coping. If, however, imaginal coping is disregarded or eliminated, the severing can have unforeseen detrimental effects even years later. Recall the instances of Grace losing her tiger and Rick being deprived of his blanket—in both cases, the children reported grief years later. Medical treatment can disrupt an ongoing source of coping by denying access to an established routine. Play can serve to mediate the trauma of treatment, but only when caretakers are sensitive and supportive about the child's practices.[20] . . .

ROLE-REVERSAL PLAY

The playful reversal by which the child dispenses care to a pet, toy, or playmate was among the most common types of medical play among diabetic and asthmatic children. Perhaps this is to be expected. Other research shows that terminally ill children often engage in role-reversal play as a means to enhance the child's sense of control over traumatic, invasive, painful, or disfiguring procedures.[21] Diabetic children in this study zealously took on the pretend role of doctor, parent, or veterinarian, dispensing shots through a toy syringe. The recipient might be a human playmate, a sibling, myself (as interviewer-playmate), or very often a toy animal or doll. Pantomimed blood tests were also administered to toys. When an empty inhaler included among the interviewer's toys was available for play, asthmatic children took the initiative to administer a "dose" to a doll or toy.

Role-reversal play allows children to rework present experience. The dramatized patient enacted by the doll, animal, or playmate takes over the role usually occupied by the child, allowing for company in misery, if only in pretense. Additionally, role-reversal play enables the child to take a controlling, rather than subordinate, fictive identity. The dialectic relationship of caregiver-receiver thus undergoes a dynamic reversal. . . .

The play by which ill children reverse roles and claim ascendancy over a play-patient implies a kind of fictive resistance by a usually subordinated child. Brian Sutton-Smith has asserted that children's play contains a "hidden rhetoric" about issues of power and identity.[22] Play helps children to vent and express their need to circumvent power by reversing positions.

This reversal of positions is a pattern also seen in other contexts of human behavior. For example, many festivals incorporate a pattern whereby the lowly ascend and the mighty descend. Halloween, in which children symbolically threaten to plunder a treat from adults ("trick or treat"), has the markings of such a reversal. . . .

By inverting the roles in treatment, then, children give expression to inequities and, by so doing, reconsider their identity and position in the social order. As Erikson observed, children "hallucinate" through play the very mastery and power they lack at a given point in time.[23] Although this play may be less necessary as children grow older and more capable of self-care, dependency and subordination in early life are equilibrated by the play. Role-reversal play destroys the social order by inversion yet sustains current and future social relatedness in doing so. If play is a way of vandalizing everyday social reality (as the patient "becomes" a doctor), it also supports convention through rebalancing. Paradoxically, when a child takes free rein to playfully impersonate a medical caretaker, this act shores up the child's acceptance of the more subordinate role, patient. . . .

In role-reversal play, children imitate the discourse and behavior of caretakers. In turn, play provides an interim means for the child to understand the caretaker-patient relationship; this is of course, a relationship fraught with social inequities and implied vulnerabilities. Role reversal equips the child to give substance to, and to transcend, the ambivalence. Note, then, that turnabout through "playing doctor" seems not to lead a child to rebel, but rather to better accept treatment. A child's playful opportunity to usurp the caretaker role shores up the child's consent to be a care-receiving patient.

RITUAL

Blood tests and insulin injections involve the regularity and familiarity of ritual, if only in the steps required to administer them. As mentioned earlier, diabetic children many times reserve a particular site on their body where they prefer to have (or not have) injections or other procedures. This, of course, exemplifies a goal of ordered familiarity.

Eight-year-old Janet Moore had never allowed her thumbs to be "poked" in four years of blood checks. She also considered her smallest fingers to be "safety fingers," drafted into service only if blood did not flow from the other fingers. Mrs. Moore thought that Janet's reserved fingers and thumbs represented a need for control and self-protection. Mrs. Moore therefore honored Janet's wishes about where to draw blood. With each blood test, Janet and her mother observed a shared ritual involving which body sites could not be touched, a way of evoking protection within a self-puncturing act.

Families practiced myriad rituals involving blood tests. A finger might be pressed until the bleeding stopped or might be dressed in a colorful plastic bandage. One child liked to be "pinched first" to establish a contrast with the level of pain from the puncture. One family used only colored lancets, inviting the child to choose which color would be used. Another family saved the tops that are removed from the lancets before each blood check and took a trip to a popular restaurant-arcade after accumulating a hundred tops; this provided a positive incentive and positive meaning for each test. One mother chose one week a year in which the child took a break from blood testing altogether. Some rituals involved the output, the numerical readings as to whether a child's blood sugar was high or low. If one boy had an overly high reading on a blood test, for instance, he could pronounce a preferred, fantasized rating number aloud, say, pronouncing that the number was an optimal 100, even though the actual number was double that. Another boy received a dollar if ever his numerical reading was 123 or 456.

Insulin injections included a variety of rituals, too. . . . A telling example involved singing the refrain "Alleluia" from Handel's *Messiah*, a ritual practiced by a five-year-old boy, Tommy Dale. In an interview Tommy's mother compared his "Alleluia" singing to the act of prayer, understandable to her as a distraction amidst the pain of injection. Her husband had suggested the practice to ameliorate the suffering during injections. "When I was a kid my sister told me at the dentist to pray to the Hail Mary." She laughed. "Kinda takes your mind off it. So Tom [Tommy's father] would say that to him about his shot. . . . I think my husband's nervousness about giving it to him is why . . . he wanted to settle him down.". . .

Distraction during childhood medical procedures has been demonstrated to ease distress during immunizations by watching cartoons;[24] to lower perceived pain during venipuncture by having a kaleidoscope to play with;[25] to decrease anxiety during genital examinations through the use of video eyeglasses;[26] to ameliorate pain and anxiety during IV insertion through distraction by a nurse;[27] and to lessen pain and distress during cancer-related procedures through film or story.[28] Studies have shown distraction to be a "well-established treatment" for procedure-related pain and distress.[29]

. . . When an asthmatic child asks her mother to clap to mark time when the child is using an inhaler, or cuddles under a special blanket during a nebulizer treatment, or keeps a favorite blue spacer nearby even after the doctor has switched prescriptions, this proclivity for ritual has a rationale, although it may not be a conscious one. Ritual evokes significance and can subtly draw out social recognition of meaning through its orderliness and drama. A child's needs are less dubitable, and potentially more collectively acknowledged, when they are given expression through ritual.

Within the family, ritual can clarify roles, thereby serving to establish and preserve a family's sense of itself, even under the pressures of a child's illness. Ritual is a bulwark of familiarity amidst the uncertainty of chronic illness. This enables the child to be more flexible in accepting difficult burdens. Ritual behavior serves the child and the child's family relationships amidst unrelenting, depleting obligations. Children bear unbearable affliction partly through the lift of ritual, sometimes hugging a teddy bear during treatment to do so.

HUMOR

. . . When humor touches children's understandings of their own illness experience, it can serve to reduce their stressful concerns. Consider, for example, an eight-year-old facing open-heart surgery who, by appreciating a joke, made light of his exposed predicament: "Eight-year-old Mark . . . was hospitalized for open heart surgery. [His ambition for adulthood was to be] a fireman, to 'put out fires.' The nurse's response that firemen are called to act quickly so that 'he might get caught with his pants down' elicited two minutes of laughter in the child who was so fearful of surgery."[30]

In American culture, professional clowns have a standing tradition of visiting hospitalized children. A clown, of course, is particularly qualified to poke fun at doctors, routines, and treatments that are fearful to a child, since clowns are culturally expected to function as jesters—as mockers of conventional authority. Clowns play the fool (sometimes the knowing fool), authorizing them to mock or shift meaning.[31] . . .

An eight-year-old girl with diabetes showed how humor was precipitated when she told of having a traumatic "low" [hypoglycemia or low blood sugar]: "I laid down and fell asleep because I was so low. And then my mom couldn't wake me up. And I'm like"—she sighed to imitate the sounds of exhaustion. "I had dark circles around my eyes and I was very pale. And [my mother] said, um, she gave me some Life Savers, and glucose tablets, and then I was fine for a couple of minutes. . . . My mom went to call the ambulance because I was really low, and then my dad was giving me red Life Savers and I was coughing, like spitting them up. And the [medical] guy with the walkie-talkie was coming along, and he said 'She's spitting up blood! She's spitting up blood!'" She laughed at the medic's mistaking red Life Savers in her saliva for blood. "He thought I was really spitting up blood!" She ended her story, still laughing heartily at the misperception. . . .

Humor enables suffering to take on a new arrangement and tone, as if reset to music not in minor key, but in a more upbeat major key. This was literally true at overnight camp for children with diabetes. Campers sang songs that merrily lampooned troubles, such as blood tests: "Don't take a prick at my finger, my finger. / Don't take a prick at my finger, my finger.

/ My finger *hurts*" [screamed loudly]. Another song mocked insulin reactions: "What a reaction, what a reaction, doodle lee do. / Some folks shake, and some get clammy, doodle lee do." Another song campers sang, part of a decades-old camp tradition, set tongue-in-cheek lyrics to the cheerful melody of Stephen Foster's "Oh, Susannah": "Oh I went to diabetic camp, / With my needle and my syringe. / They made me prick my finger, / Til I thought I would cringe." The song's chorus made a positive pronouncement on the campers themselves: "We came to diabetes camp, / And learned that we're the *best*!"

Children struck by illness, whose emergent selves face social and physical experiences that are isolating and threatening, need mechanisms to "put things up for grabs," to reframe and redefine—if only for the viability of their developing selves. Humor—along with play, story, and ritual—negotiates and vents some of the tension brought on by dissonant interpretations of personhood. Humor empowers children to deal with the paradox of being both vulnerable and courageous, both exceptional and ordinary, both young and burdened. At home, some children acted "goofy" or enjoyed humor when they felt affronted or at risk, such as when they were talking about restrictions or fears in their lives. Distress before or after a particular threatening incident could be fodder for humor. Humor ameliorated everyday tension over self-affronting treatment. During insulin injections, a father would tell jokes, or a brother might make funny faces, assisting in the humorous engagement. . . .

Because laughter remakes meaning, it represents a dynamic of sanctuary from worry and constraint. "If you feel scared, and you start to laugh, do you remember that you're scared?" I asked a six-year-old boy with asthma. "No," he replied at once with a tone of sincerity. If, as in the popular song, whistling a happy tune can banish fear, so can humor allay threatening feelings. Children with a healthy funny bone considered the troubles they faced and refused to let despair take itself too seriously.

WHAT COPING ENTAILS

Children have impressive capacities to interpret their social worlds, and they put these abilities to work in making and remaking sense of the thorny issues of illness. Experience, including past and present social interactions, influences this process. Scientific truths or medical authorities are not necessarily privileged over other sorts of messages or messengers. Nor does the child merely concentrate on negative outcomes and distress. Children, it seems, tap positive affect also as part of the alchemy of meaning, in the process infusing unhappy events with positive worth. This ability to reinterpret the unpleasant in a more positive light pervades how children use the tensile strength and flexibility of imaginal coping.[32] . . .

The capacity for adaptable meaning, is a prerequisite to coping with chronic illness. When illness interrupts the construed world of normal childhood, the child's selfhood no longer flows harmoniously amidst the norms in the world. The habitual hidden assumptions of social life break down. An aberration in the web of meaning, a violation of the child's world and identity calls for renegotiating the sense of things. It is as if the child needs to construct a renovated self and a refigured world from a fresh vantage point[33]. . . .

Given the importance of ongoing patient cooperation to the treatment of chronic illness and the clinical outcome, caretakers cannot afford to ignore children's imaginations in the course of treatment. The poetic impulse of story, ritual, play, and humor can be powerfully therapeutic and empowering to the child—an advantage with potential for improving care, in ways not yet imagined.

Discussion Questions

1. Discuss how the social aspect of camp helped children cope with their illnesses.
2. Why do you think that many children coping with illness gravitated toward superhero characters in popular culture?
3. What role do rituals play in helping children cope with their illnesses?
4. Why is it so important for caregivers of sick children to recognize the importance of play in the coping and healing process?

Notes

1. M. Taylor, *Imaginary Companions and the Children Who Create Them* (New York: Oxford University Press, 1999).
2. Cindy Dell Clark, *Flights of Fancy, Leaps of Faith: Children's Myths in Contemporary America* (Chicago: University of Chicago Press, 1995).
3. Exceptions to the general dearth of research on imaginal thought include J. Wooley, "Thinking About Fantasy: Are Children Fundamentally Different Thinkers and Believers From Adults?" *Child Development* 68 (1997): 208–216; J. Wooley, K. Phelps, D. Davis, and D. Mandell, "Where Theories of Mind Meet Magic: The Development of Children's Beliefs About Wishing," *Child Development* 70 (1999): 571–587.
4. E. Oremland, *Protecting the Emotional Development of the Ill Child: The Essence of the Child Life Profession* (Madison, Conn.: Psychosocial Press, 2000).
5. Erving Goffman, *Stigma* (New York: Touchstone Press, 1963).
6. Rich and Chalfen similarly found social embarrassment about asthma treatments in a study in which teens with asthma videotaped daily life; M. Rich and R. Chalfen, "Showing and Telling Asthma: Children Teaching Physicians With Visual Narratives," *Visual Sociology* 14 (1999): 51–71.
7. See Eiser's review of coping research as it relates to childhood chronic illness: C. Eiser, *Chronic Childhood Disease: An Introduction to Psychological Theory* (Cambridge: Cambridge University Press, 1990).
8. Studies supporting the value of camp include C. Kelly, S. Shield, M. Gowen, N. Jaganjac, C. Anderson, and G. Strope, "Outcome Analysis of a Summer Asthma Camp," *Journal of Asthma* 35 (1998): 165–171; A. Misuraca, M. Di Gennaro, M. Lioniello, M. Duval, and G. Aloi, "Summer Camps for Diabetic Children: An Experience in Campaniam, Italy," *Diabetes Research and Clinical Practice* 32 (1996): 91–96; A. Punnett and S. Thurber, "Evaluation of Asthma Camp Experience for Children," *Journal of Asthma* 30 (1993): 195–198; S. Fitzpatrick, S. Coughlin, J. Chamberlin, and Pediatric Lung Committee of the American Lung Association, "A Novel Camp Intervention for Childhood Asthma Among Urban Blacks," *Journal

of the National Medical Association* 84 (1992): 233–237; G. Mimura, "Summer Camp," *Diabetes Research and Clinical Practice* 24 (1994): S287–S290; L. Sorells, W. Chung, and J. Schlumpberger, "The Impact of a Summer Camp Experience on Asthma Education and Morbidity in Children," *Journal of Family Practice* 41 (1995): 465–468; W. Silvers, M. Holbreich, S. Go, M. Morrison, W. Dennis, T. Marostica, and J. Buckley, "Champ Camp: The Colorado Children's Asthma Camp Experience," *Journal of Asthma* 29 (1992): 121–135.
9. Kelly et al., "Outcome Analysis."
10. More detail on the camps, and the ages of the campers at each camp, is included in Appendix A.
11. See M. Bluebond-Langner, D. Perkel, T. Goertzel, K. Nelson, and J. McGeary, "Children's Knowledge of Cancer and Its Treatment: Impact of an Oncology Camp Experience," *Journal of Pediatrics* 116 (1990): 207–213.
12. See Bruno Bettelheim, *The Uses of Enchantment* (New York: Vintage Books, 1977).
13. A written version of the three pigs story for asthmatic children, A. Zevy's *Once Upon a Breath* (Downsview, Ont.: Tumbleweed Press, 1997), takes a more didactic tack than the campers' version; campers made no mention of this version. The story, financed by an educational grant from Glaxo Welcome, features a wolf with asthma who plays a saxophone, uses his "puffer" to relieve symptoms, and takes issue when the three pigs bring allergy-causing cats to his nightclub.
14. Taylor, *Imaginary Companions*; D.W. Winnicott, "Transitional Objects and Transitional Phenomena," *Collected Papers* (New York: Basic Books, 1958).
15. Examples of toys that come alive in fictional treatment are discussed in L. Kuznets, *When Toys Come Alive: Narratives of Animation, Metamorphosis, and Development* (New Haven: Yale University Press, 1994).
16. This finding is consistent with a survey of coping strategies used by eight- to thirteen-year-olds attending asthmar camp that found 48 percent self-reported "cuddling a pet or stuffed animal" when coping; N. Ryan-Wenger and M. Walsh, "Children's Perspectives on Coping With Asthma," *Pediatric Nursing* 20 (1994): 224–228.

17. Byron Good, *Medicine, Rationality, and Experience: An Anthropological Perspective* (Cambridge: Cambridge University Press, 1994); L. Hunt and C. Mattingly, "Diverse Rationalities and Multiple Realities in Illness and Healing," *Medical Anthropological Quarterly* 12 (1998): 267–272.

18. See R. Hausner, "Medication and Transitional Phenomena," *International Journal of Psychoanalytic Psychotherapy* 11 (1986): 375–398. Placebos place meaning and belief at the center of the therapeutic encounter, as positive belief confers on placebos their efficacy or acceptance. The role of belief is relatively disregarded in biomedicine. See D. Morris, "Placebo, Pain, and Belief: A Biocultural Model," in A. Harrington, ed., *The Placebo Effect: An Interdisciplinary Exploration* (Cambridge: Harvard University Press, 1997).

19. One study found that healthy children used a transitional object more when they experienced intense hassles, suggesting that Rick's use of a blanket in the face of worries may also occur with pressures other than illness; S. Lookabaugh and V. Fu, "Children's Use of Inanimate Transitional Objects in Coping With Hassles," *Journal of Genetic Psychology* 153 (1992): 37–45.

20. I. D'Antonio, "Therapeutic Use of Play in Hospitals," *Nursing Clinics of North America* 19 (1984): 351–359.

21. Barbara Sourkes, *Armfuls of Time: The Psychological Experience of the Child With Life-Threatening Illness* (Pittsburgh: University of Pittsburgh Press, 1995).

22. Brian Sutton-Smith, *The Ambiguity of Play* (Cambridge: Harvard University Press, 1997).

23. See Erikson, *Childhood.*

24. L. Cohen and G. Panopoulos, "Nurse Coaching and Cartoon Distraction: An Effective and Practical Intervention to Reduce Child, Parent, and Nurse Distress During Immunizations," *Journal of Pediatric Psychology* 22 (1997): 355–370.

25. J. A. Vessey, K. L. Carlson, and J. McGill, "Use of Distraction With Children During an Acute Pain Experience," *Nursing Research* 43 (1994): 369–372.

26. A. B. Berenson, C. M. Wiemann, and V. I. Rickert, "Use of Video Eyeglasses to Decrease Anxiety Among Children Undergoing Genital Examinations," *American Journal of Obstetrics and Gynecology* 178 (1998): 1341–1345.

27. D. Fanurik, J. L. Koh, and M. L. Schmitz, "Distraction Techniques Combined With EMLA: Effects of IV Insertion Pain and Distress in Children," *Children's Health Care* 29 (2000): 87–101.

28. C. Kleiber and D. Harper, "Effects of Distraction on Children's Pain and Distress During Medical Procedures: A Meta Analysis," *Nursing Research* 48 (1999): 44–49.

29. S. W. Powers, "Empirically Supported Treatments in Pediatric Psychology: Procedure-Related Pain," *Journal of Pediatric Psychology* 24 (1999): 131–145.

30. Irma D'Antonio, "The Use of Humor With Children in Hospital Settings," in P. McGhee, ed., *Humor and Children's Development* (New York: Haworth Press, 1989), 167.

31. Linda Miller Van Berkon, "Clown Doctors: Shamanic Healers of Western Medicine," *Medical Anthropology Quarterly* 9 (1995): 462–475.

32. Coping influenced by positive affect is central to the argument of S. Folkman and J. Moskowitz, "Positive Affect and the Other Side of Coping," *American Psychologist* 55 (2000): 647–654.

33. See B. Babcock, "Arrange Me Into Disorder: Fragments and Reflections on Ritual Clowning," in J. MacAloon, ed., *Rite, Drama, Festival, Spectacle: Rehearsals Towards a Theory of Cultural Performance* (Philadelphia: Institute for the Study of Human Issues, 1984).

Children of the Incarcerated

NELL BERNSTEIN

INTRODUCTION

In this selection, author Nell Bernstein discusses her interviews with children whose parents are in prison. She notes that we seldom pay attention to the impact that incarceration has on the children of prisoners, who are often poor and have few resources to maintain contact. This is especially the case when prisoners get transferred far from their home, or as increasingly the case, to another state. Bernstein explores how children of incarcerated parents cope.

S usana does not remember ever seeing her father free. She recalls touching him only once, an embrace from which police forcibly removed her. He has never been able to feed or shelter his daughter, nor to protect her from the lifetime's worth of hurts she has accrued in her fifteen years. Yet he remains the most important person in her life, the one person she knows loves her—the only real parent she has.

Susana's dad is at San Quentin State Prison, serving twenty-one years to life under California's "Three Strikes" sentencing law. Having been caught with stolen property, and not for the first time, he has been determined by the court to be of no further use to society. But he matters to Susana. From the scraps of contact she has been granted over the years—a drawerful of letters, a few dozen collect calls, and intermittent visits—she has built herself a father.

The first time I met Susana, she was locked up in juvenile hall in San Jose, California, right next door to the county jail where she had come to know her father during sporadic visits over the course of nearly a decade. She was a pretty, broad-faced girl with wide-set brown eyes, a chipped front tooth, and long reddish-brown hair that draped over her oversized county-issue sweatshirt. In a glassed-in interview room with white cinder-block walls and a concrete floor, Susana spoke at length about the dad who spent most of her childhood in the place she referred to only as "next door."

"My dad's *handsome*," she said, straightening in her chair. "I wish I had pictures of him. He has my face, with a mustache and thicker eyebrows, and then his hair is shaved in the back, shaved on the sides, and he slicks it back with gel."

Susana's father has told her stories about early days together, when he was free and she was small and he would pick her up and take her places; carry her in his arms. Susana can't recall a single image from that time. Her memories of her father start when she was five or six years old. Her grandmother would retrieve her from the foster home where she spent most of her childhood and take her downtown to see her dad.

"We had to wait in a waiting room for a really long time," Susana remembers, "and when we finally got in, he was behind glass and you had to talk on a phone." Susana's foster mother had discouraged her from mentioning or seeing her father or her mother—who was also in and out of jail—and so, with the natural narcissism of a small child, she assumed the conventions of the visiting room existed to obstruct her in particular: "I figured they were trying to keep us apart, and that's why there was glass and a telephone, and we couldn't touch each other."

Within a few years, Susana figured out where her father was, and why he was there. He, like her mother, was addicted to drugs—cocaine and later heroin—and stole in order to sustain his habit. As a result, he spent most of Susana's life in and out of jail ("mostly in"). Susana has moved from one place to another over the years, and her father has not always been able to reach her. When he does, he asks questions no one else does, such as "Have you done your homework?". . .

"His love for me helps me," Susana said, "and his support, the way he tells me, 'Don't end up like this, you shouldn't be in gangs, you should be going to school and getting an education.' That helps me in a lot of ways, but I ask myself sometimes, 'Why couldn't he do it for him?' "

When Susana was thirteen, her foster mother threw her out and she went to live with her grandmother. That was the year she saw her father for the first and last time without a wall of glass between them. His brother had died of cirrhosis of the liver, and he was permitted to attend the funeral. Susana and her boyfriend went out and bought him a suit for the funeral, new shoes, and a shaving kit. But he arrived at the funeral home shackled at the hands, feet, and waist, accompanied by guards and police. The gifts Susana had bought stayed in the bag, and her father stayed in his prison jumpsuit.

"When he came in the room, he didn't look at any of us," Susana recalled. "He just went straight to the coffin and he was praying there. Finally he looked at us, but he wouldn't look us in the eyes. One of my aunts asked, 'Can we hug him?' The police officer said, 'You know that's against procedure, but go ahead.' I got to hug him first, and I was hugging him for a while, and then he went on and hugged everyone else. Then he came to me and hugged me again, and that time I didn't want to let go. A police officer literally had to pull me off him. He actually restrained me, put my hands behind my back. After they took my dad, the police officer finally let go of me.

"I knew it was procedure and I should have gotten off of him when they told me to. But I just wanted to hold him, because I knew that would probably be the last time I'd ever hug him, kiss him, anything."

The first time Susana went to juvenile hall, she had been charged with auto theft and evading police after she borrowed a friend's car without permission, then crashed it into a pole trying to avoid the police. She was released to her aunt on house arrest, with an electronic monitoring bracelet around her ankle. Not long after, she said, she and her aunt got into an argument and her aunt locked her out, causing her to violate her house arrest. She'd been sent back to juvenile hall to await placement in a group home.

Susana is an athletic girl—loves swimming, boxing, lifting weights—with plans to finish high school, join the Navy, go to college, and become a professional bodybuilder, and her confinement was making her crazy with impatience and worry. She hated the idea of her father finding out where she was, but hated even more that she had no way of keeping in touch with him—incarcerated minors are not allowed to write to, or receive letters from, adult prisoners, even if those prisoners are their parents. That Father's Day was around the corner only made matters worse: Susana usually sends her father a card with a money order and handwritten verses from the Bible; he writes her back with his interpretation of the scriptures she's chosen. This year, their mutual incarceration would preclude this ritual.

Once she was released from juvenile hall, Susana would be transferred to a group home and would be permitted to correspond with her father, but the odds of someone taking her to see him were slim.

The last time Susana saw her father had been eight months earlier, the day after he was sentenced for his third strike. Susana went to visit him in the county jail, where he was awaiting transfer to state prison. "*Mija,*" he told her, "this might be the last time I'll see you in a while, but keep strong and don't let nothing get to you. Don't let this get to you, either.". . .

Susana doesn't have too many other adults who want to be "that person" in her life. Like many children of incarcerated parents, Susana has bounced from one caregiver to another and been separated from her siblings. Her aunt and her grandmother won't take her calls now that she is locked up; she has no interest in maintaining a relationship with her former foster parents and no idea where her mother is. The last time Susana saw her mother was a couple of years ago, when she ran into her on a bus. Her mother didn't recognize her.

"I'm your daughter," Susana called out.

"Which one?" her mother asked.

In the face of this vacuum, the man Susana cannot, for the moment, write to, speak with, or touch—the man who will be behind bars until she is in well into adulthood—is the sustaining figure in Susana's life. She has no idea when she will see him next.

Prison visits matter. Children and parents will tell you again and again how important it is that they see each other, and research backs them up. Consistent, ongoing contact reduces the strain of separation, lowers recidivism, and is the single most important factor in determining whether a family will reunify after a prison term. . . .

A much-cited 1972 study of California prisoners found that those who had regular visits were six times less likely to reenter prison during the first year out than those who had none. These findings, wrote researchers Norman Holt and Donald Miller, suggest that "it might be well to view the inmate's family as the prime treatment agent and family contacts as a major correctional technique." This report was commissioned by the California Department of Corrections, which recently responded to budget difficulties by cutting visiting days from three or four to two—driving some families to spend the night in their car outside prison gates to secure a place in line for scarce visiting slots.

Subsequent research has bolstered Holt and Miller's conclusions. In a 2000 review of the literature, Terry Kupers, M.D., found "little if any contrary argument and conflicting data to the general principle that the better the quality of visitation throughout a prisoner's incarceration, the better the effects on the prisoner, his or her post-release adjustment, the family of the prisoner and the community."

Nationwide, however, the trend has been to curtail rather than create opportunities for family contact. In 1978, according to a study by the National Council on Crime and Delinquency, 92 percent of incarcerated mothers received visits from their children. By 1999, fewer than half of parents in state prison had received even a single visit from their children. Another survey found that among those children who were able to visit their incarcerated parents, three-quarters did so less than once a month.

As increasing numbers of prison facilities are built in remote rural areas, more and more prisoners are held at prohibitive distances from their families. More than 60 percent of parents in prison are held more than one hundred miles from home. In California, more than 5,000 of the state's approximately 7,400 incarcerated mothers are held in two facilities in the remote rural town of Chowchilla, eight hours away from the urban centers of Northern and Southern California where the great majority of their children live. In New York state, the main institution for women lies about four hundred miles from New York City. For federal prisoners, who may be shipped anywhere in the country, distance is an even greater obstacle: nearly half the parents in federal institutions are held more than five hundred miles from home.

An early visit can reassure a child that his parent is not confined in the storybook dungeon of his imagination; that she is alive and has not abandoned him by choice. But new arrestees often must wait several days to be "processed" before they can receive visits in local jails.

These county jails generally allow only the kind of window visits Susana described. The deprivation and humiliation a wall of glass evokes is visited on those on either side of the glass, each of whom will likely experience herself as walled off, walled in—jailed. Children will bang their fists or even heads against the glass in an effort to break through.

Denise Johnston—the director of the Center for Children of Incarcerated Parents in Pasadena, California—recalled a seven-year-old who was so confused by seeing her jailed mother behind glass that when her mother called the day after a visit, the little girl asked her, "Are you dead?" Another service provider described a toddler who sobbed so desperately after seeing his mother behind glass, and for so long, that he wound up in the emergency room.

For babies and small children, window visits are more than unsatisfying; they are largely incomprehensible. "Touch is more than just a nice thing for your relationship," said Dr. Barbara Howard, associate professor of pediatrics at the Johns Hopkins School of Medicine and co-director of the Center for Promotion of Child Development through Primary Care. "It is basic to the nurturing process. If you're talking about children under a year of age, your main means of communication is touch. A baby looking through a plate of glass at his incarcerated mother would really be looking at his reflection in the window, not making a connection with the parent at all."

Once parents are released, Dr. Howard noted, "if they don't have a good relationship with the child, then their ability to take care of the child and have the child be responsive to them will be much diminished. If there were no bodily contact, I would expect no relationship at all with young children."

Melinda went three months without touching her children. Undoing the damage took longer. She was in the county jail for credit fraud at the time. The thought of her small boys sitting in plastic chairs, shoulder to shoulder with other visitors, gaping at her through the glass, was too much for her—and, she feared, for them—so she chose to forgo visits altogether. "Every time I want to hug you, I have to go to your picture," her six-year-old told her when she called home.

When Melinda was transferred to a special mother/child facility where she could be with her children, she couldn't wait to hold them. The reunion was not as she had imagined it.

"When they came the first time, it was so sad," she recalled. "They just looked, and they smiled, but they were afraid to come touch me. I grabbed them and held them for a long time, but they were stiff, like I was a stranger. "

Donna Willmott's daughter was four years old when Willmott went to prison for two years on conspiracy charges related to her involvement with the Puerto Rican independence movement. Now the family advocacy coordinator at Legal Services for Prisoners with Children in San Francisco, Willmott spent her first weeks behind bars in solitary confinement. During that time, she was permitted only window visits. Her husband came twice a week, but Willmott asked him not to bring their daughter.

"I was desperate to see her, but I didn't want to put her through that," Willmott said. "If you put a glass barrier between a child and a parent, it's crazy-making for the children. They feel they can't get to the person they love—there's this wall between them that they don't understand. It's almost like putting the parent in a box. The message children get is, 'Your mother is so bad you can't touch her. She's dangerous.' "

State and federal prisons generally offer contact visits, but those visits are rarely structured with a child's needs in mind. Visitors often wait outside in line for hours, sometimes without access to bathrooms. Children may undergo a pat search or even a "diaper peek." They and their guardians must adhere to dress codes that vary from institution to institution and include vague prohibitions such as nothing that is "emotionally enticing to the inmate." Visitors who violate a dress code, often unwittingly, can be turned away.

Visitors must be approved before they are allowed to enter a prison, a process that can take several weeks. Some states require an original copy of a child's birth certificate, and a certified copy of a court order establishing a guardian's authority, before that guardian can bring a child to visit. New caregivers are unlikely to have these documents on hand, and obtaining them means paying money and taking time off from work. Children who lack these documents get turned away at the gate—as do those who are wearing the wrong clothes, have not been approved, or lack acceptable identification.

In their grandmother's living room in San Jose, California, sisters Kimara, Keneshia, and Kenyatta squabbled and giggled together until their grandmother gently steered the conversation to the topic of their incarcerated mother. "We were able to visit our mom only one time," thirteen-year-old Kimara volunteered. "The next time we went, they told us you have to have a birth certificate. Not the copy but the original. And so we didn't get to see her. "

Kenyatta, nine, had been playing with the volume on her Walkman, retreating from the conversation. Now she took off her headphones. Being turned away, she said, "didn't feel good, because the first time we went to see her she was hugging us and kissing us and talking about how it felt in jail." Kenyatta made a choking sound, a tearless sob that quieted the room.

"You see?" said her grandmother. "Kids still hurt, for a long time." . . .

"The heart of locking somebody up is the deprivation of love and touch," Denise Johnston observed. "The way you disempower people is to strip away all human contact." Intended for prisoners, this aspect of punishment falls heavily on children. In many facilities, physical contact—a small child's primary source of comfort and reassurance—is jealously rationed. Some facilities place an age limit on sitting on a parent's lap, so that a birthday celebration includes breaking the news that dad's lap is now off-limits. In some, a "brief embrace and kiss" at the beginning and end of a visit may be all that is permitted. Parents are required to enforce this regulation—which is to say, to push their children away.

The ritual humiliations that comprise most children's visiting experiences are justified in the name of security—necessary to guard against drugs in the diaper, or razor blades in a child's shoes. In fact, there is evidence that consistent visitation *enhances* security by motivating prisoners to follow the rules. Conditions that discourage visiting, it follows, might well pose a security threat.

A report to the Florida state legislature—which commissioned a study of prison security—contained this illuminating finding: while nearly half of all corrections officers believed that most contraband came from visitors, only 2.5 percent of contraband incidents statewide were in fact attributable to visitors. . . .

If visiting a parent in prison is a difficult experience, young people will tell you, the alternative is worse. Will, eighteen, grew up in foster care while both of his parents were in and out of prison. He was granted a single visit with his incarcerated mother when he was ten years old, then did not see her again until he was a teenager.

"If there had been some time set up where I could talk to my mom consistently on a one-on-one basis, I think my life would be completely different," said Will, whose tendency to "blow up" took him through thirty foster homes and six group homes before he turned eighteen. "Just knowing I had a mother that cared. Even if it was fake, it would have helped to know that someone is there. You're livin' life solo, but there's a mother out there that you came from."

Phone contact could provide a partial answer to the challenges posed by prison visitation, but prison phone systems are structured in such a way as to make telephone contact prohibitively costly for families, and excruciatingly difficult for children.

Calls are typically limited to fifteen minutes, and several young people described the knot that formed in their stomachs as they tried to share a week's or month's worth of news with a parent while keeping one eye on the clock; the sense of loss and abandonment that was reawakened each time the phone cut off. Calling repeatedly is rarely an option, as families are charged a "connection charge" to initiate each fifteen-minute call.

Prisoners cannot take incoming calls and typically can place only collect calls. Recipients are charged exorbitant rates—as much as twenty times that of standard collect calls—under arrangements in which phone companies pay huge fees to prison systems in return for exclusive contracts. California nets more than $35 million each year in phone-company commissions—money that the state deposits in its general fund, creating what is essentially a special tax burden on the families of inmates. New York collects more than $20 million annually. These windfalls—as well as those the phone companies themselves stand to gain—are drawn directly from the pockets of prisoners' families. In Florida, the legislature found, families subsidized the Department of Corrections to the tune of nearly $50 million a year through collect calls, food purchased in the visiting room, and money sent to inmates' canteen funds.

Many families have their phones disconnected within the early months of an incarceration. Those who do manage to keep current with the phone bill must cut corners in already-tight budgets in order to do so. When, as is often the case, the person paying for a prisoner's collect calls is the same one who is caring for her children, the cost of these calls takes food from children's mouths.

Restrictions such as those on telephone calls are generally perceived, and justified, as simply part of the punishment incarceration comprises, part of the "price you pay" for breaking the law. But prisoners are for the most part *prevented* from paying this price themselves; it is family members who pick up the bill.

Elizabeth Gaynes, director of the New York prisoner support organization the Osborne Association, carries a telling souvenir: a key chain adorned with miniature handcuffs, given her by a telephone-company representative whom she encountered at an American Correctional Association convention.

"If you could make criminals pay for their own incarceration, wouldn't you want to do that?" the rep had asked, assuming Gaynes worked for a corrections department, and launching into his sales pitch. "Well, we have a collect-call system through which criminals support the cost of incarceration instead of taxpayers."

"A collect-call system?" Gaynes asked him. "Isn't that the families paying for the calls?"

"Families, criminals—it's the same thing," the vendor replied. . . .

In 2001, the federal government closed Washington, D.C.'s decrepit Lorton Correctional Complex and began exporting its inhabitants. Today, nearly six thousand D.C. residents are in federal and private prisons across the country—some as far away as California. Children who were once able to visit their parents several times a month now see them only rarely—or not at all. A fifteen-minute phone call to the Washington, D.C. area cost a dollar from Lorton; now it can cost as much as $30.

Carol Fennelly spent the 1980s and most of the 1990s advocating for the homeless in Washington, D.C., living in and running that city's fourteen-thousand-bed Federal City Shelter. When D.C. started moving its prisoners out of state, Fennelly went with them. Starting out in Youngstown—a depressed former mill town that had come to depend on a constellation of private prisons for jobs and tax revenue—Fennelly began looking for ways to keep D.C.'s prisoners connected with home and family.

"Once a dad gets in prison, he's generally no longer considered a part of his family," Fennelly observed. "Nothing in our society encourages this man to stay involved with his children.". . .

Fennelly does not see teleconferencing as a substitute for hands-on contact—she also facilitates offline visits and summer camps where D.C. children spend several days with their incarcerated parents. But for many exiled parents, virtual contact with their kids may be the only kind they get. . . .

With budgets tightening and prison populations ballooning, family connections increasingly fall victim to fiscal concerns. Hawai'i, for example, sends nearly half of its approximately 3,500 prisoners to private prisons on the mainland, where they are housed at roughly half what it would cost to keep them at home—and where visits are prohibitively expensive for family members. Arizona sends prisoners to Texas; Indiana to Kentucky; Wisconsin to Oklahoma. Once they are in the private prison system, inmates may be moved again and again if cheaper beds turn up in another state. Hawai'i transferred some of its mainland prisoners from Arizona to Mississippi—more than four thousand miles from home—in order to save nine dollars per inmate per day. After my visit to D.C., the Youngstown prison was closed, and Fennelly moved her teleconferencing program to a private prison in North Carolina, which holds about 1,400 men from D.C.

The cost to families of outsourcing prisoners is not factored into budget deliberations, but the bill comes due all the same. Hawai'i is finding that the recidivism rate is higher for prisoners who have been held thousands of miles from home than for those kept on the islands. Given the evidence that consistent visits prevent recidivism, it is likely the same holds true for other prisoners shipped out of state in the name of short-term savings. . . .

In 2003, the U.S. Supreme Court upheld a Michigan policy that placed strict limits on prison visits. "The very object of imprisonment is confinement," explained Justice Anthony M. Kennedy, writing for the majority. "Many of the liberties and privileges enjoyed by other citizens must be surrendered by the prisoner."

Long before the Supreme Court made it explicit, visitation policy was guided by the construction of family contact as a privilege that is granted or denied inmates, rather than a right that accrues to children. In fact, the two are inextricable: to assert that prisoners have no intrinsic right to visitation is also, necessarily, to assert that children have no right to contact with their parents.

Discouraging visitation also reduces the odds that a prison term will serve a useful function. Prison may be intended to isolate, but it is also, at least ostensibly, intended to rehabilitate—and there is tremendous evidence that it is connection that rehabilitates. Restricting access to family only ups the odds of failure once a parent gets out . . . .

Discussion Questions

1. What are some of the challenges that children having a parent in prison face?
2. Discuss the benefits of promoting visits between inmates and their children.
3. How does an incarceration create financial hardships for children and other family members?

4. What legal policies have made incarceration more difficult for children? What policies would you propose to support the best interests of children of prisoners?

Working Children

ALLISON JAMES, CHRIS JENKS, AND ALAN PROUT

INTRODUCTION

In contemporary Western countries, the idea of children working for wages is often morally abhorrent. Authors James, Jenks, and Prout look critically at how work is defined, and how this definition often makes children's work invisible. By closely considering the contexts in which children work globally, particularly in developing nations, they take the position that we need to reconsider the assumption that children's work is universally bad. Instead, they suggest that activists focus on exploitation rather than labor itself. Finally, they remind us that we need to consider what working children themselves think about their labor.

Whatever the place of children is thought, to be in industrialized societies, it is not usually regarded as 'at work'. What children are supposed to do is play and learn—but that is not generally recognized as work. If they are seen to be working (either in paid employment or in household domestic or caring work), the reflex is towards constituting this as an aberration or an outrage—a social problem premised on children's vulnerability and need for protection. But at the same time, precisely because children do not work, they are again rendered problematic. . . .

Thus in mainstream sociological writings about work children are virtually invisible (see, for example, Grint 1991). Though more noticeable in historical accounts of early industrialization, children here are represented as the victims of super-exploitation who were rescued from the predations of capitalism by the combined influences of social reformers and moralists and by certain economic transformations which shifted demand away from unskilled towards more skilled and educated "labor" (Cooter 1992). With this, children were relocated in 'childhood'—an idealized and romanticized state—and sheltered from the competitive sphere of market relations and the public domain (Zelizer 1985). Even the conspicuously competitive and public world of schooling, into which children were shifted as a part of their exclusion from paid employment, . . . children's activities in the schoolroom (are separate) from the adult 'world of work'. Schooling is thought of not as work but as a preparation. . . . What children do there is dealt with, therefore, as the sociology of education, not that of work.

This invisibility of children in the sociology of work is particularly surprising when we consider the sophistication achieved in discussions of what constitutes work. . . . If, for example, the definition work is confined to paid employment, then what of the myriad unpaid tasks (often performed in households and by women) which are essential to the production and reproduction of the conditions which make it possible for anyone to engage in employment (Morris 1990)? How do we account for the widespread self-provisioning indexed by do-it-yourself activities or gardening and which are arguably essential to at least some household economies (Pahl 1984)? How do we categorize exchanges in kind between households and individuals or account for the apparently successful informal economy which takes place outside of official reckoning for tax and other purposes of governance? And if work is to be defined by its subjective qualities, being experienced as a non-discretionary use of time or not enjoyable, then how do we understand occupations such as farming where life and work intermingle, or the position of those such as professional sportsmen and women who are paid for doing what others do as a discretionary leisure activity?

Such discussions, which expand rather than restrict what might be seen as work, would seem to open up possibilities for recuperating some children's activities as work. And yet it is only recently that social scientists have begun to take a more systematic interest in children's activities as forms of work. However, questions are now being asked about the extent to which children are engaged in paid employment; about the social and historical contexts of this work and its place within labor markets and household economies; about the conditions of children's work and its significance to children and others; about children's contribution to household and caring work; and, most radically of all, about the status of schooling as a form of work.

One notable exception to the more general trend of excluding children from discussions of work must be recorded at the outset. There is a longstanding acknowledgement of children's work in societies outside the industrialized [world], recognizing its wide variety and complex character; domestic work such as cleaning the house, preparing food and taking care of younger siblings; subsistence work in fields or workshops which provides goods that can be exchanged on the market; work as apprentices living and working in other households while learning a trade or craft; as slaves or bonded labor, sold to others and put to work for their benefit; as beggars working the streets on their own behalf or as part of a collectivity, be it a family, clan or gang; as laborers earning a wage in the fields, workshops or factories.

However, notwithstanding these observations, it is clear that . . . divisions are both crude and problematic. There is no absolute distinction between the developing and the developed world; developing countries are not all alike and the picture changes according to the principle by which nation-states are grouped (Sklair 1991). Furthermore, nations are socially divided and what is true for rich inhabitants is not true for the poor and the poorest. And in the developed world child labor has certainly not disappeared. But against this, children at work are much more visible in [developing nations] their participation in productive work is more commonplace and its significance is somewhat different from that in industrialized countries. Dogramaci (cited in Boyden 1991: 19) makes a telling observation of this everyday presence:

> Child workers are highly visible . . . not only at the market place but at almost every street corner; from shoe shine boys to newspaper hawkers, from cigarette vendors and all manner of peddlers to messenger boys, from waiters in virtually every restaurant and coffee house, to helpers in all sorts of shops and establishments. They

can be seen guarding parked cars, collecting garbage, transporting materials at construction sites, working at automobile repair shops or gas stations, sweeping floors in office buildings. Even more significantly, they work in many places less obvious to the public eye: in the myriad of small factories or industries tucked into back streets or alleys of the cities. . .

So unremarkable are these sights that in the 1980s the Egyptian tourist authorities used a picture of a child picking cotton as part of their promotional literature, even though statute law forbids the employment of children under twelve in the agricultural sector (Abdalia 1988: 31). According to census returns at the time, children between ten and fourteen represented 11 per cent of the total workforce.

Current estimates of the number of children working worldwide are difficult to make and unofficial figures can vary from official ones by a factor of ten or more. In India, for example, official records show 10 million child workers, but trade unions place the figure at 100 million. This lack of reliable information, due in part to official indifference and obstructionism, also indicates that agreed definitions of what counts as work and who counts as a child are lacking. Nevertheless, it seems reasonable to assume that the number of children working worldwide greatly exceeds 100 million (Fyfe 1989). And the vast majority of these are to be found in the economies of developing countries, with the greatest number working in the agricultural sector.

. . . Detailed local studies (Bequele and Boyder 1988; Boyden and Myers 1994) are essential to understanding the circumstances of these working children for, as immediately becomes clear, the content and meaning of children's work is highly dependent on its social, cultural and economic context. . . .

Rogers and Standing (1981), for example, include categories of work as part of a whole range of children's activities. They suggest ten areas: domestic work; non-domestic work; non-monetary work; tied or bonded labor; wage labor; marginal economic activities; schooling; idleness and unemployment; recreation and leisure; and reproductive activities. Although broad (and therefore able to capture something of the wide range of children's activities) these categories appear quite . . . arbitrary. Nor are they mutually exclusive. UNICEF, on the other hand, is perhaps too parsimonious . . . , distinguishing only three main types of children's work:

1. *Unpaid work within the family* This is further divided into domestic work, agricultural . . . tasks such as planting, harvesting and herding livestock, and handicrafts or cottage industries such as woodworking or leather work.
2. *Work within the family but outside the home* Included in this are agricultural . . . work (which may be full-time or seasonal, local or migrational); domestic service (when a child is taken into the family of relations but is expected to do household work); construction work and employed or self-employed work in the informal economy.
3. *Work outside the family* This may involve being employed by others, a situation that includes bonded and slave labor, apprenticeships, skilled trades, commerce, industrial and similar unskilled work in mines etc., and domestic work. It may include begging or prostitution and pornography. Children may also be self-employed in the informal sector in a variety of different tasks such as shoe shining and car washing.

As is immediately apparent, the key distinction employed here is whether or not the work takes place within a family context. The assumption seems to be that children working in a family will face less risk of harm than in other contexts, a point of view which is extremely contentious. It implies that household production tends to be associated with agrarian settings and non-waged labor. In fact neither of these need be true. . . . It is by no means clear in any case that children working for or with kin are at lower risk. . . .

Children's work activities are most commonly discussed in terms of child protection. Drawing on . . . discourses of childhood as a time to be protected from adult responsibilities, discussion is often underpinned by an individualized, biological and psychological developmental perspective. This assumes that work contradicts the very essence of childhood. . . .

Apparently simple solutions to the 'problem' of working children, such as legally enforced abolition, are thus found increasingly wanting. Forcing children out of the labor market can lead to much worse outcomes (such as displacing them into prostitution). Thus many campaigners, especially those closest to the lived reality of poor children's lives, now focus their attention on improving the conditions of their work and ensuring its proper regulation by, for example, arguing for health and safety provisions and the right to exercise collective bargaining (Bequele and Boyden 1988).

This perspective shades into a more radical one which takes as its starting point children's right not only to protection, but also to participation. This view sees children as being excluded from work by adults, the implication being that children's right to employment should be extended as a way of improving children's social and economic status. . . . As White (1995) has argued, campaigns such as the US Harkin Bill which seek to boycott the importation of products unless they are certified as 'child labor free' concentrate on child labor in the export sector, despite the fact that in these industries conditions are sometimes better than those generally prevailing elsewhere and that child workers see such employment as preferable to unpaid work in the household or on family farms. This protectionist framework thus attends to children's voices in a highly selective way. It counterposes, for example, children's right to education with their engagement in work but fails to acknowledge that for most of the world's children, it is work which makes schooling possible. More generally, it ignores the claim from children that, for a variety of reasons, working can make a great deal of sense.

CHILD WORK VERSUS CHILD LABOR?

. . . Organizations concerned to protect children from abuse and exploitation mobilize the child labor/child work difference in order to classify some of what some children do as harmful. The designation of these kinds of activities as 'labor' enables them to create priorities for intervention, as well as drawing a line beyond which certain forms of child work should be abolished and the abolition enforced.

In one sense this is very useful. The distinction captures a strong sense of children's particular vulnerability to certain forms of work, especially that which is intrinsically dangerous and where children suffer particularly high rates of ill-health or injury. . . It also focuses attention on forms of enslavement such as bonded labor, now illegal in India but still practiced (Whittaker 1985; Karp 1996). Here debts incurred by a family have to be paid off by labor in industrial enterprises, with the brick-making industry a widely quoted and persistent example. In practice, through low wage rates and deliberate fraud, debt repayment becomes an almost impossible task and the debt is transferred to children whose entire lives can be spent in endless toil and spiralling indebtedness. In such examples, labor might seem to be an appropriate term to use.

However, although most countries of the world place controls on the work children are legally allowed to do, in practice these labor laws are widely ignored. In part this is because children's work is simply too diffuse. Normalized by its ubiquity, child work is rendered invisible. Consequently, working children who do come to the attention of the state may be seen less from a humanitarian perspective than as a problem of social order: 'young street workers engaged in retailing or services are not recognized as workers but are instead brought before the magistrate as vagrants, abandoned or perpetrators of anti-social acts' (Boyden 1990: 204). On the other hand, a substantial proportion of working children are not likely to come under scrutiny: the majority of child workers are to be found in the rural sector, away from official regulation, and often working with other members of their family. Others are kept in conditions designed to minimize outside contact, such as the child laborers in Thailand who are virtually imprisoned and whose letters home are censored (Boyden 1991: 124). These children often work in small workshops doing work subcontracted from larger businesses who can, knowingly or not, deny that they employ child labor.

In part, controls are evaded because there are widespread social and economic interests in so doing. Officials can be bribed to turn a blind eye to illegal labor practices which may be highly profitable although it is also the case that for some industries, for example carpet-making in India (Kanbargi 1988) or leather tanning in Egypt (Abdalla 1988), the low pay that child workers receive ensures their survival in competitive world markets. At the same time parents may actively resist state regulation of their children's work. This was certainly the case in the United States and Europe as progressively tighter controls were introduced in the nineteenth and early twentieth century (Stadum 1995). From the perspective of the poor families in the contemporary world, the harm that child labor may do to an individual child has to be weighed against the survival of the household as a whole.

The humanitarian impulse to protect children has, as noted earlier, therefore to be tempered by the realization that in many circumstances it is unrealistic and even undesirable that children should be excluded from work which helps their household to survive. The more grounded policy developments in this field are attempting to combine the abolition of the worst abuse of children with broader policies for improvement at the level of the household economy and beyond. As is often the case non-governmental organizations have been at the forefront of new thinking in this respect (Boyden and Myers 1994). Rather than focusing on children's work in isolation, they have adopted a broader approach which focuses on issues of both structure and agency. Household income as a whole is addressed by generating securer employment for adult members; increasing the appeal of schooling to poor families by gearing the curriculum more to their practical needs and adding in school meal provision as a way of redistributing wealth as well as increasing enrollment and attendance; and organizing alternative employment for children in cooperatives which offer training as well as income and which can foster children's sense of participation and agency. As Boyden has pointed out, such an approach is crucial since 'under present economic conditions, greater access to education for children may mean an increase, rather than a reduction in children's work responsibilities: many children work in order to pay school costs' (1994: 38).

However, although the distinction between child labor and child work may be useful in determining priorities for social policy and practice, it is far less helpful as an analytical term. Indeed, here we have used these interchangeably—a somewhat unusual practice. The reason for this is not hard to see: what is claimed as an analytical distinction is primarily a moral one. It invites a judgment about the value of children's activities in terms of what promotes or undermines 'childhood', 'health' and 'development', assuming that these can be treated as though they were self-evident universals. . . In fact there is a wide diversity of views about what work children should do, the conditions under which they should do it and the balance

of its various costs and benefits to individuals, groups and societies. All condemn g
tions of children's well-being, but beyond that there is rarely agreement. . . .

For example, attention is not drawn to the crucial differences between children's
labor on the market and 'unfree' or forced labor, such as chattel slavery, serfdom and
bondage (Archer 1988).[1]. . .

Indeed it is arguable that inappropriate responses make the problems faced by children
worse rather than better. One such example is the disastrous consequences which followed the
dismissal of child workers from the Bangladesh garment in the early 1990s. . . . About a tenth
of the three-quarters of a million workers in clothing factories were children under the age of
fourteen, mostly girls doing tasks which were not very physically demanding such as cutting
loose threads from garments and distributing garment sections to machine operators. Their
dismissal was a response by employers to the threat of an international boycott of their products on the grounds that they were manufactured using child labor. The result, shown by a
follow-up study, was that the dismissed children continued to work—not one had restarted
school—but in far more risky conditions in the informal and street economy (including
prostitution). They had reduced earnings, worse nutrition and poorer health compared with
the minority who had retained employment in the garment industry. The children themselves
argued, some of them in a petition to the press, that light factory work combined with attending school for two to three hours a day was the best solution to their poverty. The result was a
new scheme in which employers linked re-employment with schooling and future employment prospects (Boyden and Myers 1994).

When we turn to industrialized societies the labor–work distinction also proves quite
unhelpful. . . .

It . . . relies on the problematic division between public and private spheres, strongly
critiqued in the literature on women's work, which has drawn attention not only to the 'double shift' that the combination of paid employment and domestic work creates for many
women but also to the contribution that 'private' household work makes to the 'public' economy. Though children are made invisible in this debate—the assumption being that they are
the objects of work, not contributors to its accomplishment—it is clear that children also
engage in such work (Goodnow 1988), although as Brannen (1995) and Song (1996) show for
the UK, there are important differences of gender and ethnicity. Contributions to general
household work may be a point of contest between parents and children but the gradual
accomplishment of 'self-care' by children also makes a significant contribution to the public
economy through releasing women from mothering tasks (Mayall 1996). More poignantly,
when a parent is sick or disabled, children take on major caring responsibilities which otherwise would have to be shouldered by the state (Aldridge and Becker 1993). . . .

The notion that children's paid employment no longer exists within the economies of the
industrialized world is an illusion. The turning point for children's participation in the UK
labor market was between 1900 and 1920. During this period the practice of children devoting
the majority of their daytime hours to schooling became established and fourteen years old was
encoded in law as the minimum age for employment in factories. The current legal position in
Britain is defined by the 1973 Employment of Children Act. Building on and clarifying the
confusion of local and national legislation inherited from the 1930s, it limits the hours during
which children are allowed to work (they cannot work before 7 a.m. or after 7 p.m., or before
the end of the school day, or for more than two hours on Sunday) and in general forbids the employment of children under thirteen. In addition, those in employment have to be registered
practice, however, the 1973 Act remains virtually unenforced and is widely broken. Ov

last decade a series of surveys in different localities have demonstrated a significant proportion of children—one-third or above—with paid employment. . . .

European data from Holland and Germany show a similar proportion (Hobbs et al. 1992). . . .

Much of this work is undertaken illegally. Sometimes this is because of the type of work or because hours worked are longer than those permitted by the 1973 Act, but most frequently because the children are not registered as required. . . . Some work raises health and safety concerns: children doing milk rounds were found to be getting up every day to start work at 4 a.m. and then going on to school. Because most of the work is illegal it tends not to have any official recognition and is therefore very loosely regulated. One result of this is that while there are regulations limiting the weight of the load an adult postal worker is allowed to carry, there are no such limits for children: newspaper delivery boys and girls have been found to be carrying much heavier loads. . . .

Although it is certainly the case that child labor is less central to the functioning of the economies of industrialized societies than in developing countries, and is less visible, a series of studies show that children's paid employment is far more widespread than is generally recognized. One might go so far as to say that the predominant pattern for teenage children is still to combine schooling with paid employment for at least some of their final years of school education.

INVISIBLE WORK AND THE DEMOGRAPHIC TRANSITION

It seems, then, that what appears at first sight as a stark divide disguises a number of continuities between children in . . . [industrial and developing nations]. Though there are, of course, important questions of life circumstances. . . which cannot and should not be denied, it is simply not the case that children in industrialized societies are excluded from work activities. However, their involvement is certainly less visible, they have greater discretion over that involvement and their work is less central to the economies of the households they live in, and still less to survival. How, therefore, might we understand these differences?

One suggestion is to argue that children's work is not inherently invisible but is rendered so. Morrow sees this invisibility as an effect of:

> the social construction of childhood as a period marked by dependency and an absence of responsibility [that] prevents us from knowing about those cases of children working and taking responsibility. An analysis of children's everyday lives outside school reveals that children have continued to work, but their labor has been made invisible behind a conception of the child as dependent, nonproductive and maintained within the family unit. (1995: 226–7)

This stereotypical sequestration of children within the family is intimately connected with the pattern of social changes which occurred (unevenly and at different paces) in Western Europe and North America during the nineteenth and twentieth centuries. This included changes in the economy, such as the shift from household and local to national and international scope, from predominantly agricultural production to industrial and service economies, and from manual to non-manual labor. Concurrent shifts in the family involved a move from complex agricultural households, through the predominance of the nuclear family (with a male breadwinner, a female homemaker and two or three children) to a contemporary pattern which is more fragmented but which includes a large group of dual income families, together with more diversity of forms (such as lone-parenting and reconstituted families).

. . . Although many of these changes have affected adults and children alike, there is one remarkable difference: 'while adult's work has not only retained but generally increased its economic value, children's activities have entirely lost it' (Wintersberger 1996: 1). This point is an important one, even if a little overstated. Children are no longer seen as productive and any work-like activities are rendered invisible: their employment for paid work is seen by adults as marginal, their contribution to domestic and household work largely denied, and schoolwork is discounted as work altogether. . .

THE MEANINGS OF WORK

So far, our discussion in this chapter has drawn far more on what we identified at the outset as structural approaches in the new social studies of childhood. In part this is because there is relatively little existing research on children's work which asks how they might have agency within its organization and accomplishment or about the meaning which such work might have. This in itself might be seen as part of the invisibilizing of children's work—or the making visible of it only as a problem. . . .

Just as up to the mid-1970s it was assumed that domestic work fell outside the purview of the sociology of work, so it is noticeable that much of this research is still dominated by the (adult?) assumption that what children do is not real work. Serious attention, for example, is not given to health and safety in children's legal paid employment in industrial economies because it is held that such activities are really more akin to leisure or harmless character-building endeavors. A similar assumption pervades the sociological literature on schooling. As Prout has pointed out (1992: 137), what children do at school conforms to almost any definition of work which extends beyond paid employment. Certainly it is not at all unusual for children themselves to see it as work. But the literature on schooling has been generally unwilling to recognize this: for example, Sharp and Green's (1975) account systematically distinguishes between work (what children will do in the future) and 'work' (what children do at school which looks just like work but cannot be given equivalence with it).

We have remarkably little research evidence on how children themselves understand the different activities in which they are involved: how they handle and use categories of work; which of their activities they understand as work and how this might shift between contexts; what their motivation for engaging in different types of work is; how involvement in work affects and is affected by their kin and other social relationships, and so on. The very act of posing questions in this way suggests that studies of children's work could pay rather more attention to how it is involved in the construction of children's lives as a whole. . . .

In one of the relatively few studies of this kind Solberg (1994) draws attention to the possible implications which children's work has for the negotiation of age and its meanings. Her observation of children's everyday involvement in the Norwegian fishing industry, where children work alongside adults in the casual work of baiting long fishing lines, she noticed that the status of 'child' was frequently overridden by their acquired but temporary position as a worker. This was not a question of children being forced to work—involvement was discretionary for everyone—but once in the work setting children's attempts to make their age relevant to the completion of the task were simply ignored. She suggests children in this situation socially 'grow', taking on competences and other psychological attributes sometimes denied them in other contexts. In contrast, Song's (1996) account of children's labor in Chinese families' take-away businesses in Britain reveals how their work is embedded within discourses of family and goodwill which oblige children to work under the guise of 'helping out'.

Morrow's (1994) account of why children work explores the meanings which work has for children more explicitly. Citing evidence that much child work in Britain is done by children from relatively affluent families she argues that children's work cannot simply be understood in relation to family poverty, although in some families in Western Europe and North America the contribution made by children to family income is undoubtedly as important as it is for many families in developing contexts (Nieuwenhuys 1994). However, as Morrow points out, children living in poor families may often have fewer, rather than more, opportunities to work: travel to and from places of employment may be difficult and the local area may offer few opportunities for children to undertake babysitting, car washing, newspaper deliveries and so on. The reasons why children work must be sought from children themselves, Morrow argues, and she suggests that participation in the new teenage consumer markets may be an overwhelming factor. Although some children saw work as offering them confidence and experience for future adult work, for most it was the opportunity to purchase luxuries not financed by parents which was their reward for working.

CONCLUSION

Such studies highlight the need for much broader enquiry into the ways in which work, among other factors, affects how children and adults negotiate and renegotiate their identities and relationships. Similarly, the effects of working need to be understood within a life course perspective. What, for example, do children themselves see as the costs and benefits arising from work? It is clear that children (as well as parents and other adults) sometimes see working as a means of developing skills which will help them in their later lives. In the instance given earlier, children opposing their mass dismissal from the Bangladesh textile industry saw the benefits in combining work with schooling partly in these terms. At the other end of the spectrum of privilege, Allatt (1993) has suggested that when middle-class English children take part-time work while they are at school it is seen by their parents and themselves as a means of accumulating social and cultural capital—of enmeshing themselves in social and economic networks, making contacts, learning skills of interaction, etc.—that can at a later point in their life be transformed into economic rewards. . . .

Much of the attempt to map and quantify children's work comes from agencies intent on its reduction, control or elimination. The politics of such an endeavor often turns on a process of moral shaming in which governments, employers, consumers, etc. are pressured to make themselves appear progressive in relation to others. This may be politically and morally worthy (though this is usually more ambiguously the case than its proponents often like to admit) but it does not help to generate well-grounded understanding of the phenomenon. . . .

Discussion Questions

1. What kinds of work do children do that might be ignored by the broader society?
2. Although many forms of child labor are illegal in the United States and other Western nations, what forms are legal? At what ages? What does this tell us about the meanings of childhood?

3. Why do the authors suggest that universal abolition of child labor might not be as beneficial to children as many might think?
4. The authors conclude by suggesting we consider working children's views on their labor. How would you suggest gathering this information?

Note

1. Chattel slavery is marked by the comprehensive rights of ownership of the slave by the slave master; debt bondage arises from the pledging of labor services by a debtor to a creditor by way of guarantee and where these do not go towards the liquidation of the debt or where the length and nature of these services is not specified; serfdom arises from tenure to land being conditional on the tenant living and laboring on that land, rendering services to the owner but not being able to move away or otherwise change status.

References

Abdalla, A. (1988) 'Child Labor in Egypt: Leather Tanning in Cairo'. In A. Bequele and J. Boyden (eds), *Combating Child Labour,* Geneva: International Labour Office.

Aldridge, J. and Becker, S. (1993) *Children Who Care: Inside the World of Young Carers,* Loughborough: Department of Social Sciences, Loughborough University.

Allatt, P. (1993) 'Becoming Privileged: The Role of Family Processes'. In I. Bates and G. Risborough (eds), *Youth and Inequality,* Milton Keynes: Open University Press.

Archer, L. J. (1988) *Slavery and Other Forms of Unfree Labor,* London: Routledge.

Bequele, A. and Boyden, J. (eds) (1988) *Combating Child Labor,* Geneva: International Labor Office.

Boyden, J. (1990) 'Childhood and the Policy Markers: A Comparative Perspective on the Globalization of Childhood'. In A. James and A. Prout (eds), *Constructing and Reconstructing Childhood,* Basingstoke: Falmer Press.

Boyden, J. (1991) *Children of the Cities,* London: Zed Books.

Boyden, J. (1994) *The Relationship between Education and Child Work,* Child Rights Series no. 9, Florence: Innocenti Occasional Papers.

Boyden, J. and Myers, W. (1994) *Exploring Alternative Approaches to Combating Child Labour: Case Studies from Developing Countries,* Child Rights Series no. 8, Florence: Innocenti Occasional Papers.

Brannen, J. (1995) 'Young People and their Contribution to Household Work', *Sociology* 29(2): 317–38.

Cooter, R. (ed.) (1992) *In the Name of the Child: Health and Welfare 1880–1940,* London: Routledge.

Fyfe, A. (1989) *Child Labour,* Cambridge: Polity Press.

Goodnow, J. (1988) 'Children's Household Work: Its Nature and Functions', *Psychological Bulletin* 103(1): 5–26.

Grint, K. (1991) *The Sociology of Work: An Introduction,* Cambridge: Polity Press.

Hobbs, S., Lavalette, M. and McKechnie, J. (1992) 'The Emerging Problem of Child Labor', *Critical Social Policy* 12(1): 93–105.

Kanbargi, R. (1988) 'Child Labor in India: The Carpet Industry of Varanasi'. In A. Bequele and J. Boyden (eds), *Combating Child Labour,* Geneva: International Labor Office.

Karp, J. (1996) 'Caste-Iron Certitude: Rehabilitation Scheme Takes Aim at Feudalism', *Far Eastern Economic Review* 159(10): 57–8.

Mayall, B. (1993) 'Keeping Healthy at Home and School: It's my Body So It's my Job', *Sociology of Health and Illness* 15(4): 464–87.

Morris, L. (1990) *The Workings of the Household,* Cambridge: Polity Press.

Morrow, V. (1994) 'Responsible Children? Aspects of Children's Work and Employment outside School in Contemporary UK'. In B. Mayall (ed.), *Children's Childhoods: Observed and Experienced,* London: Falmer.

Nieuwenhuys, O. (1994) *Children's Life Worlds: Gender, Welfare and Labor in the Developing World,* London: Routledge.

Paul, R. E. (1984) *Divisions of Labor,* Oxford: Blackwell.

Prout, A. (1992) 'Work, Time and Sickness in the Lives of Schoolchildren'. In R. Frankenberg (ed.), *Time, Health and Medicine,* London: Sage.

Rogers, G. and Standing, G. (eds) (1981) *Child Work, Poverty and Underdevelopment,* Geneva: International Labor Office.

Sharp, R. and Green, A. (1975) *Educational and Social Control: A Study of Progressive Primary Education,* London: Routledge and Kegan Paul.

Sklair, L. (1991) *The Sociology of the Global System,* Hemel Hempstead: Harvester Wheatsheaf.

Solberg, A. (1994) *Negotiating Childhood: Empirical Investigations and Textual Representations of Children's Work and Everyday Lives,* Stockholm: Nordic Institute for Studies in Urban and Regional Planning.

Song, M. (1996) ' "Helping Out": Children's Labor Participation in Chinese Take-Away Business in Britain'. In J. Brannen, J. and M. O'Brien (eds), *Children and Families: Research and Policy,* London: Falmer Press.

Stadum, B. (1995) 'The Dilemma in Saving Children from Child Labor: Reform and Casework at Odds with Families' Needs', *Child Welfare* 74: 33–55.

White, B. (1995) 'Globalization and the Child Labor Problem', mimeo, Institute of Social Studies, The Hague.

Whittaker, A. (1985) 'Bonded Labor–India's Slavery', *The Reporter* 13(2) (Anti-Slavery Society, London).

Wintersberger, H. (1996) 'Children: Costs and Benefits', paper to International Workshop on Monitoring and Measuring the State of the Children, Jerusalem. To be published in A. Ben-Arieh and H. Wintersberger (eds), *Monitoring and Measuring the State of Children–Beyond Survival,* Eurosocial Report 26, Vienna: European Centre for Social Welfare Policy and Research.

Zelizer, V. A. (1985) *Pricing the Priceless Child: The Changing Social Value of Children,* New York: Basic Books.

CREDITS

1. Adapted from *Pricing the Priceless Child: The Changing Social Value of Children,* by Viviana A. Zelizer, from "Child Labor to Child Work: Redefining the Economic World of Children," pp. 73–112. © 1985 by Basic Books. Reprinted by permission of Basic Books, a member of Perseus Books Group.

2. Adapted from Heins, Marjorie. *Not in Front of the Children: 'Indecency,' Censorship, and the Innocence of Youth,* Copyright © 2007 by Marjorie Heins. Reprinted by permission of Rutgers University Press.

3. Adapted from *Childhood in America,* edited by Paula Fass and Mary Ann Mason, pp. 1–7. © 2000 NYU Press. Reprinted by permission of NYU Press.

4. Adapted from *Anxious Parents: A History of Modern Childrearing in America* by Peter Stearns. © 2003 New York University. All rights reserved. Reprinted by permission of NYU Press.

5. Adapted from *After the Death of Childhood: Growing Up in the Age of Electronic Media* by David Buckingham, pp. 4–16. © 2000 Polity Press Ltd. Reprinted by permission of Polity Press Ltd.

6. Adapted from *Kids These Days: Facts and Fictions about Today's Youth,* by Karen Sternheimer, Rowman & Littlefield © 2006, pp. 15–29. Reprinted by permission of Rowman & Littlefield Publishing Group.

7. Adapted from Barrie Thorne, "Re-Visioning Women and Social Change: Where are the Children?" from *Gender & Society,* 1, pp. 85–109, © 1987 by Sage Publications, Inc. Reprinted by Permission of SAGE Publications, Inc.

8. Adapted with permission of Sage Publications Inc. Books, from William A. Corsaro, "The Structure of Childhood and Children's Interpretive Reproductions," from *The Sociology of Childhood,* Second edition. Thousand Oaks, Pine Forge Press © 2004; permission conveyed through Copyright Clearance Center, Inc.

9. Adapted from Sarah H. Matthews, "A Window on the 'New' Sociology of Childhood," from *Sociology Compass,* v1.i1, © 2007, pp. 322–334. Reprinted with permission of Blackwell Publishing.

10. Adapted from Alan Prout and Allison James, "A New Paradigm for the Sociology of Childhood?" from Alan James & Allison Prout (eds.) *Constructing and Reconstructing Childhood,* London: Falmer Press, pp. 7–33. © 1997 Alan James and Allison Prout. Reproduced with permission of Taylor & Francis Books UK.

11. Adapted from Michael Wyness, "Researching Children and Childhood," from *Childhood and Society: An Introduction to the Sociology of Childhood.* New York: Palgrave Macmillan, 2006. Reproduced with permission Palgrave Macmillan.

12. Adapted from *Knowing Children: Participant Observation with Minors (Paper)* by Fine and Sandstrom. Copyright © 1998 by Sage Publications Inc Books. Reproduced with permission of Sage Publications Inc Books in the format Textbook via Copyright Clearance Center.

13. Adapted from William Corsaro, "Yeah, You're Big Bill," from *We're Friends, Right? Inside Kids' Cultures,* Joseph Henry Press (NAS), pp. 7–17, 25–29, © 2003. Reprinted with permission by National Academy of Sciences.

14. Adapted from Adler, Patricia A., and Peter Adler. *Peer Power: Preadolescent Culture and Identity.* Copyright © 1998 by Patricia A. Adler and Peter Adler. Reprinted by permission of Rutgers University Press.

15. Adapted from *Freaks, Geeks, and Cool Kids: American Teenagers, Schools, and the Culture of Consumption* by Murray Milner, Jr. Copyright 2006 by Taylor and Francis Group LLC—Books. Reproduced with permission of Taylor & Francis Group LLC—Books in the format Textbook via Copyright Clearance Center.

16. Adapted from Abel Valenzuela, Jr., "Gender Roles and Settlement Activities Among Children and Their Immigrant Families" from *American Behavioral Scientist,* 42, pp. 720–742, © 1999 by Sage Publications, Inc. Reprinted by Permission of Sage Publications, Inc.

17. Adapted from Annette Lareau, *Unequal Childhoods: Class, Race, and Family Life.* © 2003 University of California Press. Reprinted by permission of University of California Press.

18. Adapted from Eder, Donna, Catherine Colleen Evans, and Stephen Parker. *School Talk: Gender and*

Adolescent Culture. Copyright © 1995 by Donna Eder, Catherine Colleen Evans, and Stephen Parker. Reprinted by permission of Rutgers University Press.

19. Adapted from Debra Van Ausdale and Joe R. Feagin, "Using Racial and Ethnic Concepts: The Critical Case of Very Young Children," from *American Sociological Review,* 61, 1996, pp. 779–793. Reprinted with permission of American Sociological Association and the authors.

20. Adapted from Valerie Ann Moore, "The Collaborative Emergence of Race in Children's Play: A Case Study of Two Summer Camps," *Social Problems,* Vol. 49, No. 1: 58–78. © 2003, The Society for the Study of Social Problems Inc. Used by permission. All rights reserved.

21. Adapted from Lewis, Amanda E. *Race in the Schoolyard: Negotiating the Color Line in Classrooms and Communities.* Copyright © 2003 by Amanda E. Lewis. Reprinted by permission of Rutgers University Press.

22. Adapted from Michael A. Messner, "Barbie Girls Versus Sea Monsters: Children Constructing Gender," from *Gender & Society,* 14, pp. 765–784, © 2000 by Sage Publications, Inc. Reprinted by Permission of SAGE Publications, Inc.

23. Adapted from Thorne, Barrie. *Gender Play: Girls and Boys in School.* Copyright © 1993 by Barrie Thorne. Reprinted by permission of Rutgers University Press.

24. Adapted from Julie Bettie, *Women Without Class: Girls, Race, and Identity.* © 2003 University of California Press. Reprinted by permission of University of California Press.

25. Adapted from Sarah Banet-Weiser, "We Pledge Allegiance to the Kids,": Nickelodeon and Citizenship. From *Nickelodeon Nation: The History, Politics, and Economics of America's Only TV Channel for Kids,* ed. by Heather Hendeshot, abridged from pp. 209–237, New York: NYU Press, 2004. Reprinted with permission of NYU Press.

26. Adapted from Cindy Dell Clark, "Flight toward Maturity: The Tooth Fairy," from *Flights of Fancy, Leaps of Faith: Children's Myths in Contemporary America.* Chicago: University of Chicago Press, 1995, adapted from pp. 5–21. Reprinted by permission of University of Chicago Press and the author.

27. Adapted version reproduced with permission from Viviana Zelizer, "Kids and Commerce," from *Childhood* 9, 2002: 375–396, © 2002 by permission of Sage Publications Ltd.

28. Adapted from Christine L. Williams, *Inside Toyland: Working, Shopping, and Social Inequality.* © 2006 University of California Press. Reprinted by permission of University of California Press.

29. Adapted version reproduced with permission from Peter Kelly, David Buckingham, and Hannah Davies, "Talking Dirty: Children, Sexual Knowledge, and Television," from *Childhood* 6, 1999: 221–242, © 1999 by permission of Sage Publications Ltd.

30. "Outside Class: A Historical Analysis of American Children's Competitive Activities," by Hilary Levey, Wallace Hall, Dept. of Sociology, Princeton University, Princeton, NJ 08544.

31. Adapted from Jenny Kitzinger, "Who Are You Kidding? Children, Power, and the Struggle Against Sexual Abuse," from A. James & A. Prout (eds.) *Constructing and Reconstructing Childhood,* London: Falmer Press, pp. 165–189. © 1997 A. James and A. Prout. Reproduced with permission of Taylor and Francis Books UK.

32. Adapted from Clark, Cindy Dell. *In Sickness and in Play: Children Coping with Chronic Illness.* Copyright (c) 2003 by Cindy Dell Clark. Reprinted by permission of Rutgers University Press.

33. Copyright © 2005 by Nell Bernstein. An expanded version of this essay, entitled "Visiting" by Nell Bernstein, originally appeared in *All Alone in the World: Children of the Incarcerated* by Nell Bernstein (The New Press, 2005). Abridged version reprinted by permission of the author and The New Press. www.thenewpress.com

34. Adapted from Theorizing Childhood by Allison James, Chris Jenks, and Alan Prout, pp. 101–123. © 1998 Polity Press Ltd. Reprinted by permission of Polity Press Ltd.